D0786680

THE LOEB CLASSICAL LIBRARY

FOUNDED BY JAMES LOEB, LL.D.

EDITED BY

† T. E. PAGE, C.H., LITT.D.

E. CAPPS, PH.D., LL.D.   † W. H. D. ROUSE, LITT.D.

. A. POST, L.H.D.   E. H. WARMINGTON, M.A., F.R.HIST.SOC.

DEMOSTHENES
IV

PRIVATE ORATIONS
XXVII–XL

DEMOSTHENES

IV ⟨Works⟩

PRIVATE ORATIONS
XXVII–XL

WITH AN ENGLISH TRANSLATION BY

A. T. MURRAY, Ph.D., LL.D.

EMERITUS PROFESSOR OF CLASSICAL LITERATURE
STANFORD UNIVERSITY, CALIFORNIA

CAMBRIDGE, MASSACHUSETTS
HARVARD UNIVERSITY PRESS
LONDON
WILLIAM HEINEMANN LTD
MCMLXV

First printed 1936
Reprinted 1946, 1958, 1965

Printed in Great Britain

CONTENTS

v

CONTENTS

vi

GENERAL INTRODUCTION

A SKETCH of the life of Demosthenes has already been presented in an earlier volume of this series, and adequate information has been given regarding his public activities and his work as statesman and orator. A few remarks will, however, be here in place regarding the speeches delivered in private law-suits, of which upwards of thirty have come down to us in the Demosthenic corpus.

These are of high interest not only to the student of ancient oratory, but to all who seek to know ancient Greek life. They deal, not with statecraft, nor with political affairs, but with business-contracts, bankers' loans, suits over inheritances, and other such matters ; and they throw a flood of light on the daily life of mercantile Athens in the fourth century B.C. Some of them are models of forensic pleading, clear and precise in their statements of fact and cogent in their reasoning ; and if they sometimes offend against modern canons of good taste by stooping to personal vituperation, this is explained by the circumstances attending their delivery. In ancient Athens the plaintiff appeared before the court to plead in person ; he was not represented by counsel, though he was permitted to have friends to assist him. Personal feeling therefore sometimes ran high, and naturally found ready expression. Moreover the court was made up of people like the speaker, drawn by lot from the ranks of his fellow-citizens. They, as well as he, loved a sharp retort, a pointed argument,—even what may at times seem to us to be subtle quibbling ; and they were not averse to hearing appeals to their own interests. That the juries were so large—501 was a usual number for the jurymen—was an element tending naturally in the same direction.

The brief introduction prefixed to each oration is intended to give the reader sufficient information regarding the matters leading up to the suit in which the speech was delivered to make it easy for him to follow the argument. It has seemed unwise to enter into a detailed discussion of the vexed problems of authenticity, as these must in the nature of the case depend for their solution upon matters with which only specialists can deal, and with which the general reader has little concern. It is enough to state that most at least of the speeches may safely be accepted as genuine in the sense that they were composed for delivery in a court of law, whether or not they can be proved to have been written by Demosthenes ; and of not a few it may be affirmed with certainty that they come to us from his hand. References to the discussions of this question in the standard works of Schaefer and Blass are given as an aid to those who wish to study it more closely.

The text given in this edition is that of Blass (Teubner) with only minor changes. These have been noted under the text, save that words bracketed by Blass have often been omitted entirely, or else the brackets have been removed to avoid disfigurement of the page.

Brief notes have been added in explanation of

INTRODUCTION

points regarding which the reader may desire more help than is afforded by the text ; but it has seemed wiser not to burden the volume with an elaborate discussion of Athenian legal procedure. The manuals in which adequate information regarding this is readily available are mentioned in the brief bibliography.

The translator desires to express his sense of indebtedness to the translations of Kennedy and Dareste, and to the edition of *Select Private Orations of Demosthenes* by Paley and Sandys.

PALO ALTO, CALIFORNIA,
September 1935

A. T. M.

BIBLIOGRAPHY

Arnold Schaefer, *Demosthenes und seine Zeit*, Leipzig 1858.

F. Blass, *Die attische Beredsamkeit*, ed. 2, Leipzig, 1893.

S. H. Butcher, *Demosthenes*, London, 1881.

C. R. Kennedy, *The Orations of Demosthenes*, translated with notes, etc., five vols. in Bohn's Classical Library.

R. Dareste, *Les Plaidoyers civils de Démosthène*, Paris, 1875.

W. H. Kirk, *Demosthenic Style in the Private Orations*, Baltimore, 1895.

S. Preuss, *Index Demosthenicus*, Leipzig, 1895.

———

A. Boeckh, *The Public Economy of Athens*, translated by Lewis, London, 1842 ; ed. 2, translated by Lamb, Boston, 1857.

K. F. Hermann, *Lehrbuch der griechischen Rechtsalter-thuemer*, ed. 3, revised by Thalheim, Freiburg, 1884.

G. F. Schoemann, *Antiquities of Greece*, translated by Hardy and Mann, London, 1890.

Gardner and Jevons, *Manual of Greek Antiquities*, New York, 1895.

L. Whibley, *Companion to Greek Studies*, Cambridge, 1905.

Meier und Schoemann, *Der attische Process*, revised by Lipsius, Berlin, 1883–1887.

THE ORATIONS OF DEMOSTHENES

The numbers of the Orations are those used in Blass's text and generally followed by editors.

THE ORATIONS OF DEMOSTHENES

THE ORATIONS OF DEMOSTHENES

TABLE OF ATHENIAN MONEY

1 Talent	= 60 Minae
1 Mina	= 100 Drachmae
1 Drachma	= 6 Obols
1 Obol	= 8 Chalkoi

(The Talent and the Mina represent values, not coins)

In bullion value the Talent may be regarded as worth something more than two hundred Pounds Sterling, but its purchasing power was very much greater.

Besides the regular Attic coins there is mention in this volume also of the Stater of Cyzicus, the value of which is given as twenty-eight Attic Drachmae, and that of Phocaea, a somewhat heavier coin. These were both of electrum, an alloy of gold and silver.

AGAINST APHOBUS

I

INTRODUCTION

DEMOSTHENES, the father of the orator, left at his death a considerable estate, which, as appears from this oration, included the following items :

	Talents	Minae
32 or 33 slaves engaged in sword-making, and 22 in making sofas (?)	3	50
Materials on hand in the two factories	2	30
A dwelling-house	...	30
Furniture, jewels, etc.	1	40
Money loaned at 12 per cent	1	...
Money loaned on bottomry contract	1	10
Money loaned without interest	1	...
Cash	1	20
Money in Pasion's bank	...	24
Money in Pylades' bank	...	6
Money in Demomeles' bank	...	16
	13	46

He left a widow and two children : a son (the orator) aged seven, and a daughter, aged five. By his will he appointed as guardians of his children and trustees of his estate Aphobus and Demophon, both nephews of his, and Therippides, an old friend. The terms of the will provided that Aphobus should marry the widow and receive with her eighty minae as her marriage-portion ; that Demophon should receive a bequest of two talents on condition that he should marry the daughter when she came to marriageable age ; and that Therippides was to receive the interest of seventy minae until the boy should come of age. The balance of the estate was to be invested, and both principal and accumulated profits were to become the property of the son, Demosthenes, when he should attain his majority.

We learn from this oration that the guardians showed the most reckless disregard of the instructions given them by the testator. They at once appropriated their own legacies—without, however, complying with the terms of the will,—and instead of investing the residue of the estate in the interest of the heir, they appropriated it to their own use, and squandered it, so that when Demosthenes completed his seventeenth year he found that the residue of the estate amounted to less than one-tenth of the amount left by his father, whereas by careful management it might have doubled or even trebled in value. The property actually turned over to him consisted merely of the house, fourteen slaves, and thirty minae in money, representing, as he puts it, a total value of only seventy minae.

Under these circumstances Demosthenes sought the aid of the courts, and as Athenian law required him to appear in person, it was necessary for him to prepare himself for a task which must have seemed formidable, if not almost hopeless. He was but a youth, unversed in the technicalities of Attic law, and without experience in pleading, while his adversaries were men of wealth and experience, unscrupulous enough, as their past actions had shown, to avail themselves of every possible trick and artifice to prevent their being forced to disgorge their ill-gotten gains. Demosthenes, therefore, sought the aid of the orator Isaeus, whose wide knowledge of law and wide experience in dealing with inheritance cases, made him perhaps the best qualified man in Athens to give him the help he needed. He spent two years in study under Isaeus, and then, feeling himself in a position to deal adequately with the complicated problem before him, instituted three separate suits against the three guardians. This was in 364 B.C. in the archonship of Timocrates. The suit against Aphobus was pressed immediately. Those against Demophon and Therippides were postponed to await the outcome of the first, and appear never to have been tried. They may well have been compromised after the judgement given against Aphobus.

It would appear that before the suit came to trial Aphobus agreed with Demosthenes to settle the matter by arbitration. The case was to be submitted to three private arbitrators; but, according to Demosthenes' statements, Aphobus, through fear that their decision would be against him, withdrew his consent.

When finally the case was brought before the archon it was referred to one of the official arbitrators, and his decision was given against Aphobus, who then appealed to a jury. Even after this he sought to quash the whole matter by a trick which the peculiar system of financing public projects in vogue at Athens made possible. He induced a certain friend of his, named Thrasylochus, to demand of Demosthenes that he assume the trierarchy or else exchange properties with him.[a] In the expectation that it

---

[a] This process, called ἀντίδοσις, was open to any Athenian citizen chosen by the tax-company (συμμορία) to perform one of the public services (trierarchy, choregia, etc.) imposed

4

would be impossible for Demosthenes to do anything but accept the exchange, he had prepared a release for the guardians from the impending actions. Demosthenes met this by raising sufficient funds (20 minae) and accepting the trierarchy (see the Oration against Meidias, §§ 78 ff.).

The trial was decided in Demosthenes' favour, and the damages were assessed at ten talents, the amount claimed by the plaintiff, which sum was one-third of the total loss suffered by him. For the other two-thirds Demophon and Therippides were regarded as responsible.

The two following orations against Aphobus and the two against Onetor tell us of further difficulties which Demosthenes had to meet in seeking to collect the sum awarded him. What amount he actually recovered is not known, but we learn from Plutarch that it was but a small part of the entire estate. (Plut. *Vit. Dem.* 6.)

The first two orations against Aphobus are discussed in Schaefer, i. pp. 261 ff., and Blass, iii. pp. 226 ff.

upon wealthy citizens. If the man in question claimed that another, regarded by him as more wealthy than himself, should with more justice be required to assume this burden, he had the right to demand of that other that he do so, or else exchange properties with him.

ΔΗΜΟΣΘΕΝΟΥΣ

XXVII

ΚΑΤ' ΑΦΟΒΟΥ ΕΠΙΤΡΟΠΗΣ

Α

[813] Εἰ μὲν ἐβούλετ' Ἄφοβος, ὦ ἄνδρες δικασταί, τὰ
δίκαια ποιεῖν, ἢ περὶ ὧν διαφερόμεθα τοῖς οἰκείοις
ἐπιτρέπειν, οὐδὲν ἂν ἔδει δικῶν οὐδὲ πραγμάτων·
ἀπέχρη γὰρ ἂν τοῖς ὑπ' ἐκείνων γνωσθεῖσιν ἐμμένειν, ὥστε μηδεμίαν ἡμῖν εἶναι πρὸς τοῦτον
διαφοράν. ἐπειδὴ δ' οὗτος τοὺς μὲν σαφῶς εἰδότας
τὰ ἡμέτερ' ἔφυγε μηδὲν διαγνῶναι περὶ αὐτῶν, εἰς
δ' ὑμᾶς τοὺς οὐδὲν τῶν ἡμετέρων ἀκριβῶς ἐπιστα-
μένους ἐλήλυθεν, ἀνάγκη ἐστὶν ἐν ὑμῖν παρ' αὐτοῦ
2 πειρᾶσθαι τῶν δικαίων τυγχάνειν. οἶδα μὲν οὖν,
ὦ ἄνδρες δικασταί, ὅτι πρὸς ἄνδρας καὶ λέγειν
ἱκανοὺς καὶ παρασκευάσασθαι δυναμένους χαλεπόν
ἐστιν εἰς ἀγῶνα καθίστασθαι περὶ τῶν ὄντων
ἁπάντων, ἄπειρον ὄντα παντάπασι πραγμάτων διὰ
τὴν ἡλικίαν· ὅμως δέ, καίπερ πολὺ τούτων κατα-
δεέστερος ὤν, πολλὰς ἐλπίδας ἔχω καὶ παρ' ὑμῖν
τεύξεσθαι τῶν δικαίων, καὶ μέχρι γε τοῦ τὰ γεγενημένα διεξελθεῖν καὶ αὐτὸς ἀρκούντως ἐρεῖν,
ὥσθ' ὑμᾶς μήτ' ἀπολειφθῆναι τῶν πραγμάτων μηδὲ
[814] καθ' ἕν, μήτ' ἀγνοῆσαι περὶ ὧν δεήσει τὴν ψῆφον

6

DEMOSTHENES

XXVII

AGAINST APHOBUS, IN REGARD TO
HIS GUARDIANSHIP

I

If Aphobus, men of the jury, had been willing to do
what is fair, or to submit the matters in dispute
between us to the arbitration of friends, there would
be no occasion for a troublesome lawsuit; for I should
have been satisfied to abide by their decision, and
we should have had no controversy with him. Since,
however, he has refused to let those well acquainted
with our affairs give a decision, and has come before
you, who have no accurate knowledge of them, it
must be in your court that I try to win from him what
is my due.   I know well, men of the jury, that it is 2
a hard task to enter into a contest in which all my
fortune is at stake with men who are able speakers
and clever in preparing their case, while I because of
my youth am wholly without experience in affairs.
Yet nevertheless, although they have every advantage
over me, I have strong hopes that I shall obtain justice
in your court, and that, as far at least as relating
the facts, I shall myself speak well enough to ensure
that not a single detail shall escape you, and that
you will not be in the dark regarding the matters
concerning which you are to cast your vote.   I beg 3

3 ἐνεγκεῖν. δέομαι δ' ὑμῶν, ὦ ἄνδρες δικασταί,
μετ' εὐνοίας τ' ἀκοῦσαί μου, κἂν ἠδικῆσθαι δοκῶ,
βοηθῆσαί μοι τὰ δίκαια. ποιήσομαι δ' ὡς ἂν
δύνωμαι διὰ βραχυτάτων τοὺς λόγους. ὅθεν οὖν
ῥᾷστα μαθήσεσθε περὶ αὐτῶν, ἐντεῦθεν ὑμᾶς καὶ
ἐγὼ πρῶτον πειράσομαι διδάσκειν.

4 Δημοσθένης γὰρ οὑμὸς πατήρ, ὦ ἄνδρες δικασταί,
κατέλιπεν οὐσίαν μὲν σχεδὸν τεττάρων καὶ δέκα
ταλάντων, ἐμὲ δ' ἔπτ' ἐτῶν ὄντα καὶ τὴν ἀδελφὴν
πέντε, ἔτι δὲ τὴν ἡμετέραν μητέρα πεντήκοντα
μνᾶς εἰς τὸν οἶκον εἰσενηνεγμένην. βουλευσάμενος
δὲ περὶ ἡμῶν, ὅτ' ἔμελλε τελευτᾶν, ἅπαντα ταῦτ'
ἐνεχείρισεν Ἀφόβῳ τε τουτῳὶ καὶ Δημοφῶντι τῷ
Δήμωνος υἱεῖ, τούτοιν μὲν ἀδελφιδοῖν ὄντοιν, τῷ
μὲν ἐξ ἀδελφοῦ, τῷ δ' ἐξ ἀδελφῆς γεγονότοιν, ἔτι
δὲ Θηριππίδῃ τῷ Παιανιεῖ, γένει μὲν οὐδὲν προσ-
5 ήκοντι, φίλῳ δ' ἐκ παιδὸς ὑπάρχοντι. κἀκείνῳ
μὲν ἔδωκεν ἐκ τῶν ἐμῶν ἑβδομήκοντα μνᾶς καρπώσασθαι τοσοῦτον χρόνον, ἕως ἐγὼ ἀνὴρ εἶναι δοκι-
μασθείην, ὅπως μὴ δι' ἐπιθυμίαν χρημάτων χεῖρόν
τι τῶν ἐμῶν διοικήσειε· Δημοφῶντι δὲ τὴν ἐμὴν
ἀδελφὴν καὶ δύο τάλαντ' εὐθὺς ἔδωκεν ἔχειν, αὐτῷ
δὲ τούτῳ τὴν μητέρα τὴν ἡμετέραν, καὶ προῖκά τ'
ὀγδοήκοντα μνᾶς, καὶ τὴν οἰκίαν οἰκεῖν καὶ σκεύεσι
χρῆσθαι τοῖς ἐμοῖς, ἡγούμενος, καὶ τούτους ἔτ'
οἰκειοτέρους εἴ μοι ποιήσειεν, οὐκ ἂν χεῖρόν μ'
ἐπιτροπευθῆναι ταύτης τῆς οἰκειότητος προσγενο-
6 μένης. λαβόντες δ' οὗτοι ταῦτα πρῶτον σφίσιν
αὐτοῖς ἐκ τῶν χρημάτων, καὶ τὴν ἄλλην οὐσίαν
[815] ἅπασαν διαχειρίσαντες, καὶ δέκ' ἔτη ἡμᾶς ἐπι-

8

of you, men of the jury, to give me a favourable
hearing, and, if you judge that I have been wronged,
to render me the aid which is my due. I shall make
my speech as brief as possible, and shall begin by
endeavouring to inform you of the facts from which
you will most readily understand the case.

Demosthenes, my father, men of the jury, left at 4
his death an estate of nearly fourteen talents, a son,
myself, aged seven, and my sister, aged five, and his
widow, our mother, who had brought him a fortune of
fifty minae. He had taken thought for our welfare,
and, when he was about to die, put all this property
in the hands of the defendant, Aphobus, and Demophon, son of Demo, nephews of his, one by his
brother, the other by his sister, and of Therippides
of Paeania,[a] who was not a relative, but had been
his friend from boyhood. To Therippides he gave 5
the interest on seventy minae of my property, to be
enjoyed by him until I should come of age,[b] in order
that avarice might not tempt him to mismanage my
affairs. To Demophon he gave my sister with a
dowry of two talents, to be paid at once, and to the
defendant himself he gave our mother with a dowry
of eighty minae, and the right to use my house and
furniture. His thought was that, if he should unite
these men to me by still closer ties, they would look
after my interests the better because of this added
bond of kinship. But these men, who took at once their 6
own legacies from the estate, and as my guardians
administered all the remainder for ten years, have

---

[a] Paeania was a deme of the tribe Pandionis.
[b] At Athens a youth, on reaching the age of eighteen, was,
after an official examination (δοκιμασία), duly entered on the
list of the members of his tribe, and assumed the status and
the duties of a citizen.

τροπεύσαντες, τὰ μὲν ἄλλα πάντ' ἀπεστερήκασι,
τὴν οἰκίαν δὲ καὶ ἀνδράποδα τέτταρα καὶ δέκα καὶ
ἀργυρίου μνᾶς τριάκοντα, μάλιστα σύμπαντα ταῦτ'
7 εἰς ἑβδομήκοντα μνᾶς παραδεδώκασιν. καὶ τὸ μὲν
κεφάλαιον τῶν ἀδικημάτων, ὡς ἂν συντομώτατ'
εἴποι τις, τοῦτ' ἔστιν, ὦ ἄνδρες δικασταί· τὸ δὲ
πλῆθος τῆς οὐσίας ὅτι τοῦτ' ἦν τὸ καταλειφθέν,
μέγιστοι μὲν αὐτοὶ μάρτυρές μοι γεγόνασιν· εἰς γὰρ
τὴν συμμορίαν ὑπὲρ ἐμοῦ συνετάξαντο κατὰ τὰς
πέντε καὶ εἴκοσι μνᾶς πεντακοσίας δραχμὰς εἰσφέρειν, ὅσονπερ Τιμόθεος ὁ Κόνωνος καὶ οἱ τὰ
μέγιστα κεκτημένοι τιμήματ' εἰσέφερον· δεῖ δὲ καὶ
καθ' ἕκαστον ὑμᾶς ἀκοῦσαι τά τ' ἐνεργὰ αὐτῶν καὶ
ὅσ' ἦν ἀργὰ καὶ ὅσου ἦν ἄξι' ἕκαστα. ταῦτα γὰρ
μαθόντες ἀκριβῶς εἴσεσθε, ὅτι τῶν πώποτ' ἐπι-
τροπευσάντων οὐδένες ἀναιδέστερον οὐδὲ περιφανέ-
8 στερον ἢ οὗτοι τὰ ἡμέτερα διηρπάκασιν. πρῶτον
μὲν οὖν ὡς συνετιμήσανθ' ὑπὲρ ἐμοῦ ταύτην τὴν
εἰσφορὰν εἰς τὴν συμμορίαν, παρέξομαι τούτων
μάρτυρας, ἔπειθ'[1] ὅτι οὐ πένητα κατέλιπέ μ' ὁ
πατὴρ οὐδ' ἑβδομήκοντα μνῶν οὐσίαν κεκτημένον,
ἀλλὰ τοσαύτην, ὅσην οὐδ' αὐτοὶ οὗτοι ἀποκρύψα-
σθαι διὰ τὸ μέγεθος πρὸς τὴν πόλιν ἐδυνήθησαν.

Καί μοι ἀναγίγνωσκε λαβὼν ταύτην τὴν μαρτυρίαν.

---

[1] ἔπειθ'] ἵν' εἰδῆθ' Blass.

---

[a] Each of the ten Athenian tribes selected one hundred and
twenty men as their richest members. These twelve hundred
men were divided into twenty groups of sixty each (called
συμμορίαι), and from them certain men were designated to
bear the burdens of public service (the trierarchy, choregia,
etc.) and of the special property-tax imposed in time of need.

robbed me of my entire fortune except the house, and fourteen slaves and thirty silver minae, which they have handed over to me—amounting in all to about seventy minae. This, men of the jury, to put it as 7 briefly as possible, is a summing up of the wrongs they have done me. But of the fact that the amount of property left by my father was as much as I have stated these men themselves have proved the most convincing witnesses, for in the tax-company *a* they agreed on my behalf to a tax of five hundred drachmae on every twenty-five minae *b*—a tax equal to that paid by Timotheüs, son of Conon,*c* and those possessing the largest fortunes. However, I had better inform you in detail what portions of the property were producing a profit and what were unproductive, and what were their respective values ; for when you have accurate information regarding these matters, you will know that of all who have ever acted as trustees none have so shamelessly and so openly plundered an estate as these men have plundered ours. I shall produce witnesses to prove, first, that in 8 the tax-company they agreed on my behalf to be taxed to the amount which I have stated, and, next, that my father did not leave me a poor man, nor one possessing an estate of merely seventy minae. On the contrary, my estate was so considerable that these men were themselves unable to hide its value from the state.

Take,*d* please, and read this deposition.

b This was a tax of 20 per cent of the man's entire property, and was the maximum.

c Timotheüs was one of the leading citizens of Athens. His father, Conon, was the famous general who in 395 had destroyed the Lacedemonian fleet at Cnidos.

d These words were addressed to the clerk of the court.

DEMOSTHENES

9 Δῆλον μὲν τοίνυν καὶ ἐκ τούτων ἐστὶ τὸ πλῆθος
[816] τῆς οὐσίας. πεντεκαίδεκα ταλάντων γὰρ τρία τάλαντα τίμημα· ταύτην ἠξίουν εἰσφέρειν τὴν εἰσ-
φοράν. ἔτι δ' ἀκριβέστερον εἴσεσθε τὴν οὐσίαν
αὐτὴν ἀκούσαντες. ὁ γὰρ πατήρ, ὦ ἄνδρες δικασταί,
κατέλιπε δύ' ἐργαστήρια τέχνης οὐ μικρᾶς ἑκάτερον, μαχαιροποιοὺς μὲν τριάκοντα καὶ δύ' ἢ τρεῖς,
ἀνὰ πέντε μνᾶς καὶ ἕξ, τοὺς δ' οὐκ ἐλάττονος ἢ
τριῶν μνῶν ἀξίους, ἀφ' ὧν τριάκοντα μνᾶς ἀτελεῖς
ἐλάμβανε τοῦ ἐνιαυτοῦ τὴν πρόσοδον, κλινοποιοὺς
δ' εἴκοσι τὸν ἀριθμόν, τετταράκοντα μνῶν ὑποκει-
μένους, οἳ δώδεκα μνᾶς ἀτελεῖς αὐτῷ προσέφερον,
ἀργυρίου δ' εἰς τάλαντον ἐπὶ δραχμῇ δεδανεισμένον,
οὗ τόκος ἐγίγνετο τοῦ ἐνιαυτοῦ ἑκάστου πλεῖν ἢ
10 ἑπτὰ μναῖ. καὶ ταῦτα μὲν ἐνεργὰ κατέλιπεν, ὡς
καὶ αὐτοὶ οὗτοι ὁμολογήσουσιν· ὧν γίγνεται τοῦ
μὲν ἀρχαίου κεφάλαιον τέτταρα τάλαντα καὶ πεν-
τακισχίλιαι, τὸ δ' ἔργον αὐτῶν πεντήκοντα μναῖ
τοῦ ἐνιαυτοῦ ἑκάστου. χωρὶς δὲ τούτων ἐλέφαντα
μὲν καὶ σίδηρον, ὃν κατειργάζοντο, καὶ ξύλα κλίνει·
εἰς ὀγδοήκοντα μνᾶς ἄξια, κηκῖδα δὲ καὶ χαλκὸν
ἑβδομήκοντα μνῶν ἐωνημένα, ἔτι δ' οἰκίαν τρισχιλίων, ἔπιπλα δὲ καὶ ἐκπώματα καὶ χρυσία καὶ
ἱμάτια, τὸν κόσμον τῆς μητρός, ἄξια σύμπαντα
ταῦτ' εἰς μυρίας δραχμάς, ἀργυρίου δ' ἔνδον ὀγ-
11 δοήκοντα μνᾶς. καὶ ταῦτα μὲν οἴκοι κατέλιπε
πάντα, ναυτικὰ δ' ἑβδομήκοντα μνᾶς, ἔκδοσιν παρὰ

ᵃ A drachma, that is, on each mina. This (12 per cent)
was the normal rate of interest on well-secured loans.

THE DEPOSITION

From this evidence it is clear what the value of the 9
property was. Three talents is the tax on an estate
of fifteen, and this tax they saw fit to pay. But you
will see this more clearly if you hear what the property
was. My father, men of the jury, left two factories,
both doing a large business. One was a sword-
manufactory, employing thirty-two or thirty-three
slaves, most of them worth five or six minae each and
none worth less than three minae. From these my
father received a clear income of thirty minae each
year. The other was a sofa-manufactory, employing
twenty slaves, given to my father as security for a
debt of forty minae. These brought him in a clear
income of twelve minae. In money he left as much
as a talent, loaned at the rate of a drachma a month,[a]
the interest of which amounted to more than seven
minae a year. This was the amount of productive 10
capital which my father left, as these men will themselves admit, the principal amounting to four talents
and five thousand drachmae,[b] and the proceeds to
fifty minae each year. Besides this, he left ivory and
iron, used in the factory, and wood for sofas, worth
about eighty minae ; and gall [c] and copper, which he
had bought for seventy minae ; furthermore, a house
worth three thousand drachmae, and furniture and
plate, and my mother's jewelry and apparel and orna-
ments, worth in all ten thousand drachmae, and
in the house eighty minae in silver. To these sums 11
left by him at home we must add seventy minae,

[b] In mercantile affairs the Greeks often preferred to reckon
in thousands of drachmae instead of tens of minae.

[c] This was obtained from the oak-apple and was used for
staining wood or ivory.

Ξούθῳ, τετρακοσίας δὲ καὶ δισχιλίας ἐπὶ τῇ τραπέζῃ τῇ Πασίωνος, ἑξακοσίας δ' ἐπὶ τῇ Πυλάδου,
[817] παρὰ Δημομέλει δὲ τῷ Δήμωνος υἱεῖ χιλίας καὶ
ἑξακοσίας, κατὰ διακοσίας δὲ καὶ τριακοσίας ὁμοῦ
τι τάλαντον διακεχρημένον. καὶ τούτων αὖ τῶν
χρημάτων τὸ κεφάλαιον πλέον ἢ ὀκτὼ τάλαντα καὶ
πεντήκοντα μναῖ γίγνονται. συμπάντων δ' εἰς τέτταρα καὶ δέκα τάλανθ' εὑρήσετε σκοποῦντες.

12 Καὶ τὸ μὲν πλῆθος τῆς οὐσίας τοῦτ' ἦν τὸ
καταλειφθέν, ὦ ἄνδρες δικασταί. ὅσα δ' αὐτῆς
διακέκλεπται καὶ ὅσ' ἰδίᾳ θ' ἕκαστος εἴληφε καὶ
ὁπόσα κοινῇ πάντες ἀποστεροῦσιν, οὐκ ἐνδέχεται
πρὸς ταὐτὸ ὕδωρ εἰπεῖν, ἀλλ' ἀνάγκη χωρὶς ἕκαστον
διελεῖν ἐστίν. ἃ μὲν οὖν Δημοφῶν ἢ Θηριππίδης
ἔχουσι τῶν ἐμῶν, τότ' ἐξαρκέσει περὶ αὐτῶν εἰπεῖν,
ὅταν κατ' αὐτῶν τὰς γραφὰς ἀπενέγκωμεν· ἃ δὲ
τοῦτον ἔχοντ' ἐξελέγχουσιν ἐκεῖνοι καὶ ἔγωγ' οἶδ'
αὐτὸν εἰληφότα, περὶ τούτων ἤδη ποιήσομαι τοὺς
λόγους πρὸς ὑμᾶς. πρῶτον μὲν οὖν ὡς ἔχει τὴν
προῖκα, τὰς ὀγδοήκοντα μνᾶς, τοῦθ' ὑμῖν ἐπιδείξω,
μετὰ δὲ ταῦτα καὶ περὶ τῶν ἄλλων, ὡς ἂν δύνωμαι
διὰ βραχυτάτων.

13 Οὗτος γὰρ εὐθὺς μετὰ τὸν τοῦ πατρὸς θάνατον
ᾤκει τὴν οἰκίαν εἰσελθὼν κατὰ τὴν ἐκείνου διαθήκην, καὶ λαμβάνει τά τε χρυσία τῆς μητρὸς καὶ
τὰ ἐκπώματα τὰ καταλειφθέντα. καὶ ταῦτα μὲν
ὡς εἰς πεντήκοντα μνᾶς εἶχεν, ἔτι δὲ τῶν ἀνδραπόδων τῶν πιπρασκομένων παρά τε Θηριππίδου
καὶ Δημοφῶντος τὰς τιμὰς ἐλάμβανεν, ἕως ἀν-

---

[a] Strictly, thirteen talents and forty-six minae ; see the
Introduction.

[b] A speaker's time was measured by a water-clock,

a maritime loan to Xuthus; twenty-four hundred drachmae in the bank of Pasion, six hundred in that of Pylades, sixteen hundred in the hands of Demomeles, son of Demon, and about a talent loaned without interest in sums of two hundred or three hundred drachmae. The total of these last sums amounts to more than eight talents and fifty minae, and the whole taken together you will find on examination to come to about fourteen talents.[a]

This, then, men of the jury, was the amount of 12 property left by my father. How much of it has been squandered, how much they have severally taken, and of how much they have jointly robbed me, it is impossible to tell in the time [b] allotted to one plea. I must discuss each one of these questions separately. I pass over the question as to what property of mine Demophon or Therippides are holding. It will be time enough to discuss this when I bring in my accusations against them. I shall speak to you now of the defendant and shall state what his colleagues prove that he has in his hands, and what I know he has taken. In the first place I shall show that he has the marriage-portion, the eighty minae, and after that shall take up the other matters and discuss them with the utmost brevity.

Immediately after my father's death the defendant 13 came and dwelt in the house according to the terms of the will, and took possession of my mother's jewels and the plate. In these he received the equivalent of about fifty minae. Furthermore, he received from Therippides and Demophon the proceeds of the sale of the slaves until he had made up the full amount of

klepsydra; one specimen has been found, *cf. Hesperia* viii. 274 ff.

15

14 ἐπληρώσατο τὴν προῖκα, τὰς ὀγδοήκοντα μνᾶς. καὶ
ἐπειδὴ εἶχεν, ἐκπλεῖν μέλλων εἰς Κέρκυραν τριήρ
αρχος, ἀπέγραψε ταῦτα πρὸς Θηριππίδην ἔχονθ᾽
[818] ἑαυτὸν καὶ ὡμολόγει κεκομίσθαι τὴν προῖκα. καὶ
πρῶτον μὲν τούτων Δημοφῶν καὶ Θηριππίδης, οἱ
τούτου συνεπίτροποι, μάρτυρές εἰσιν· ἔτι δὲ καὶ ὡς
αὐτὸς ὡμολόγει ταῦτ᾽ ἔχειν, Δημοχάρης θ᾽ ὁ Λευ
κονοεύς, ὁ τὴν τηθίδα τὴν ἐμὴν ἔχων, καὶ ἄλλοι
15 πολλοὶ μάρτυρες γεγόνασιν. οὐ γὰρ διδόντος τού
του σῖτον τῇ μητρί, τὴν δὲ προῖκ᾽ ἔχοντος, οὐδὲ τὸν
οἶκον μισθοῦν ἐθέλοντος, ἀλλὰ μετὰ τῶν ἄλλων
ἐπιτρόπων διαχειρίζειν ἀξιοῦντος, ἐποιήσατο λόγους
περὶ τούτων ὁ Δημοχάρης. οὗτος δ᾽ ἀκούσας οὔτ᾽
ἠμφεσβήτησε μὴ ἔχειν,[1] οὔτε χαλεπῶς ἤνεγκεν ὡς
οὐκ εἰληφώς, ἀλλ᾽ ὡμολόγει καί τι μικρὸν ἔφη πρὸς
τὴν ἐμὴν μητέρα περὶ χρυσιδίων ἀντιλέγεσθαι· τοῦτ᾽
οὖν διευκρινησάμενος, καὶ περὶ τῆς τροφῆς καὶ περὶ
τῶν ἄλλων ποιήσειν οὕτως ὥστ᾽ ἔχειν μοι πάντα
16 καλῶς. καίτοι εἰ φανήσεται πρός τε τὸν Δημοχάρη
ταῦθ᾽ ὡμολογηκὼς καὶ πρὸς τοὺς ἄλλους οἳ παρ
ῆσαν, παρά τε τοῦ Δημοφῶντος καὶ τοῦ Θηρ
ιππίδου τῶν ἀνδραπόδων εἰς τὴν προῖκα τὰς τιμὰς
εἰληφώς, αὐτός θ᾽ ἑαυτὸν ἔχειν τὴν προῖκ᾽ ἀπο
γράψας πρὸς τοὺς συνεπιτρόπους, οἰκῶν τε τὴν
οἰκίαν ἐπειδὴ τάχιστ᾽ ἐτελεύτησεν ὁ πατήρ, πῶς
οὐκ ἐκ πάντων ὁμολογουμένου τοῦ πράγματος
εὑρεθήσεται φανερῶς τὴν προῖκα, τὰς ὀγδοήκοντα

[1] ἔχειν] σχεῖν Blass.

---

[a] That is, in command of a trireme which he had himself
equipped for service.

16

the marriage-portion, eighty minae; and after getting 14
this, when he was about to set sail for Corcyra as
trierarch,[a] he sent Therippides a written acknowledgement that he had these sums in his possession, and
admitted that he had received the marriage-portion.
Of these matters Demophon and Therippides, his co-
trustees, are witnesses, and, besides this, his own
acknowledgement of having received these moneys is
attested by Demochares, of Leuconion,[b] who is the
husband of my aunt, and by many other witnesses.
For when it proved that Aphobus, though he had her 15
fortune, would not maintain my mother, and refused
to let the property, choosing rather to administer it
himself in conjunction with the other guardians,
Demochares remonstrated with him about the matter;
and Aphobus, when he had heard him, neither denied
that he had the money nor waxed indignant as one
who had received nothing, but admitted the fact, and
said that he was having a little dispute with my
mother about her jewels, and that, when he had
settled this matter, he would act regarding the maintenance and all else in such a way that I should have
no ground for complaint. Yet, if it be shown that 16
he made these admissions before Demochares and the
others who were present; that he received from
Demophon and Therippides the money accruing from
the sale of the slaves in part settlement of the
marriage portion; that he gave to his co-trustees a
written acknowledgement that he had received the
portion; and that he occupied the house immediately
after the death of my father; will it not be clear—
the matter being admitted by everybody—that he
has received the portion, the eighty minae, and that

[b] Leuconion, or Leuconoë, was a deme of the tribe Leontis.

μνᾶς, κεκομισμένος, καὶ λίαν ἀναιδῶς μὴ λαβεῖν
ἐξαρνούμενος;

17 Ἀλλὰ μὴν ὡς ἀληθῆ λέγω, λαβὲ τὰς μαρτυρίας
καὶ ἀνάγνωθι.

MAPTΥPIAI

Τὴν μὲν τοίνυν προῖκα τοῦτον τὸν τρόπον ἔχει
λαβών. μὴ γήμαντος δ' αὐτοῦ τὴν μητέρα τὴν
ἐμήν, ὁ μὲν νόμος κελεύει τὴν προῖκ' ὀφείλειν ἐπ'
ἐννέ' ὀβολοῖς, ἐγὼ δ' ἐπὶ δραχμῇ μόνον τίθημι.
[819] γίγνεται δ', ἐάν τις συντιθῇ τό τ' ἀρχαῖον καὶ τὸ
18 ἔργον τῶν δέκ' ἐτῶν, μάλιστα τρία τάλαντα. καὶ
ταῦτα μὲν οὕτως ὑμῖν ἐπιδείκνυμι λαβόντα καὶ
ἔχειν ὁμολογήσαντα μαρτύρων ἐναντίον τοσούτων·
ἄλλας τοίνυν ἔχει τριάκοντα μνᾶς, τοῦ ἐργαστηρίου
λαβὼν τὴν πρόσοδον, καὶ ἀναισχυντότατ' ἀνθρώπων
ἀποστερεῖν ἐπικεχείρηκεν. ἐμοὶ δ' ὁ πατὴρ κατέλιπε τριάκοντα μνᾶς ἀπ' αὐτῶν τὴν πρόσοδον· ἀπο-
δομένων δὲ τούτων τὰ ἡμίσεα τῶν ἀνδραπόδων,
πεντεκαίδεκά μοι μνᾶς γίγνεσθαι κατὰ λόγον προσ-
19 ῆκεν. Θηριππίδης μὲν οὖν ἑπτ' ἔτη τῶν ἀνδραπόδων ἐπιμεληθεὶς ἕνδεκα μνᾶς τοῦ ἐνιαυτοῦ
ἀπέφηνε, τέτταρσι μναῖς καθ' ἕκαστον ἐνιαυτὸν
ἔλαττον ἢ ὅσον προσῆκε λογιζόμενος. οὗτος δὲ
δύ' ἔτη τὰ πρῶτ' ἐπιμεληθεὶς οὐδ' ὁτιοῦν ἀπο-
δείκνυσιν, ἀλλ' ἐνίοτε μέν φησιν ἀργῆσαι τὸ ἐργαστήριον, ἐνίοτε δ' ὡς αὐτὸς μὲν οὐκ ἐπεμελήθη
τούτων, ὁ δ' ἐπίτροπος Μιλύας, ὁ ἀπελεύθερος ὁ
ἡμέτερος, διῴκησεν αὐτά, καὶ παρ' ἐκείνου μοι
προσήκει λόγον λαβεῖν. ἂν οὖν καὶ νῦν εἴπῃ τινὰ
τούτων τῶν λόγων, ῥᾳδίως ἐλεγχθήσεται ψευδό-
20 μενος. ἂν μὲν οὖν ἀργὸν φῇ γενέσθαι, λόγον αὐτὸς

ᵃ That is, at 18 per cent.

his denial of having received it is a piece of shameless impudence ?

To prove that what I say is true, take and read 17 the depositions.

THE DEPOSITIONS

The dowry, then, he got in this way, and kept. But in the event of his not marrying my mother the law declares that he owes me the amount of the dowry with interest at nine obols a month.[a] However, I set it down at a drachma a month only. This comes, if one adds the principle and the interest for ten years, to about three talents. This money I have thus shown 18 you that he received and that he confessed in the presence of a host of witnesses that he had it. Then he has also in his possession thirty minae besides, which he received as the revenue from the factory, and of which he has tried to defraud me in the most shameless manner possible. My father left me a revenue of thirty minae accruing from the factory ; and after the sale by these men of one-half of the slaves, I should receive the proportionate sum of fifteen minae. Therippides, however, who had charge of the slaves 19 for seven years, has submitted an account of eleven minae a year, four minae a year less than it should have been ; and the defendant who had charge of the business at the first for two years shows no profit whatever, but says sometimes that the factory was idle, and sometimes that he was not himself the manager, but that the foreman, Milyas, a freedman of ours, had charge of it, and that I should look for an accounting from him. If he persists even now in making any of these statements he will easily be convicted of falsehood. If he declares that the 20

ἀπενήνοχεν ἀναλωμάτων οὐκ εἰς σιτία τοῖς ἀνθρώποις, ἀλλ' εἰς ἔργα, τὸν εἰς τὴν τέχνην ἐλέφαντα εἰς
μαχαιρῶν λαβὰς καὶ ἄλλας ἐπισκευάς, ὡς ἐργαζομένων τῶν δημιουργῶν. ἔτι δὲ Θηριππίδη τριῶν
ἀνδραπόδων, ἃ ἦν αὐτῷ ἐν τῷ ἐμῷ ἐργαστηρίῳ,
μισθὸν ἀποδεδωκέναι λογίζεται. καίτοι μὴ γενο-
21 μένης ἐργασίας, οὔτ' ἐκείνῳ λαβεῖν μισθόν, οὔτ'
[820] ἐμοὶ τὰ ἀναλώματα ταῦτα λογισθῆναι προσῆκεν. εἰ
δ' αὖ γενέσθαι μὲν φήσει, τῶν δ' ἔργων ἀπρασίαν
εἶναι, δεῖ δήπου τά γ' ἔργ' αὐτὸν ἀποδεδωκότα μοι
φαίνεσθαι, καὶ ὧν ἐναντίον ἀπέδωκε παρασχέσθαι
μάρτυρας. εἰ δὲ μηδὲν τούτων πεποίηκε, πῶς οὐκ
ἔχει τὴν πρόσοδον δυοῖν ἐτοῖν τὴν ἐκ τοῦ ἐργαστηρίου τριάκοντα μνᾶς, φανερῶς οὕτως τῶν ἔργων
22 γεγενημένων; εἰ δ' αὖ τούτων μὲν μηδὲν ἐρεῖ,
Μιλύαν δ' αὐτὰ φήσει πάντα διῳκηκέναι, πῶς χρὴ
πιστεύειν, ὅταν φῇ τὰ μὲν ἀναλώματ' αὐτὸς ἀνηλωκέναι, πλέον ἢ πεντακοσίας δραχμάς, λῆμμα δ' εἴ
τι γέγονεν, ἐκεῖνον ἔχειν; ἐμοὶ μὲν γὰρ δοκεῖ
τοὐναντίον ἂν γενέσθαι τούτων, εἰ καὶ Μιλύας
αὐτῶν ἐπεμελεῖτο, τὰ μὲν ἀναλώματ' ἐκεῖνος ἀνα-
λῶσαι, τὰ δὲ λήμμαθ' οὗτος λαβεῖν, εἴ τι δεῖ
τεκμαίρεσθαι πρὸς τὸν ἄλλον τρόπον καὶ τὴν
ἀναίδειαν.

Λάβ' οὖν τὰς μαρτυρίας ταύτας, καὶ ἀνάγνωθ'
αὐτοῖς.

MΑΡΤΥΡΙΑΙ

23 Ταύτας τοίνυν ἔχει τριάκοντα μνᾶς ἀπὸ τοῦ
ἐργαστηρίου, καὶ τὸ ἔργον αὐτῶν ὀκτὼ ἐτῶν. ὃ ἂν

factory was idle, yet he has himself rendered an
account of money expended, not on provisions for the
men, but for their work—ivory for the trade, sword-
handles, and other supplies—indicating that the
workmen were busy. Furthermore, he charges me
with money which he has paid to Therippides for the
hire of three slaves of his who were in my factory.
Yet if no work was being done, Therippides should
have received no pay, nor should these expenditures
have been charged to me. Again, if he alleges that the 21
work was done, but that there was no market for goods
manufactured, he ought at any rate to show that he
has delivered to me these goods, and to produce
witnesses in whose presence he delivered them.
Seeing that he has done neither of these things, how
can you doubt that he is keeping thirty minae, the
two years' income from the factory, since the business
has so manifestly been carried on ? If, however, he 22
shall make none of these statements, but shall assert
that Milyas had charge of everything, how can you
believe him, when he alleges that he himself made the
disbursements amounting to more than five hundred
drachmae, but that any profits which accrued are in
the hands of Milyas ? For my part, I think it likely
that the very opposite is the case, supposing that
Milyas actually did have charge of the work,—that he
made the disbursements, and that Aphobus received
the profits, if we may draw any conclusion from the
general character and the shamelessness of the man.

Take now and read these depositions to the jury.

THE DEPOSITIONS

These thirty minae, then, he has received from the 23
factory, and the interest on them for eight years; and

ἐπὶ δραχμῇ τις τιθῇ μόνον, ἄλλας¹ τριάκοντα μνᾶς
εὑρήσει. καὶ ταῦτα μὲν ἰδίᾳ μόνος εἴληφεν· ἃ
συντεθέντα πρὸς τὴν προῖκα μάλιστα τέτταρα τάλαντα γίγνεται σὺν τοῖς ἀρχαίοις. ἃ δὲ μετὰ τῶν
ἄλλων ἐπιτρόπων κοινῇ διήρπακε, καὶ ὅσ' ἔνια μηδὲ
καταλειφθῆναι παντάπασιν ἠμφεσβήτηκε, ταῦθ' ὑμῖν
24 ἤδη ἐπιδείξω καθ' ἕκαστον. πρῶτον μὲν οὖν περὶ
τῶν κλινοποιῶν, οὓς κατέλιπε μὲν ὁ πατήρ, ἀφανί-
ζουσι δ' οὗτοι, τετταράκοντα μὲν μνῶν ὑποκει-
[821] μένους, εἴκοσι δ' ὄντας τὸν ἀριθμόν, ἐπιδείξω ὑμῖν
ὡς λίαν ἀναιδῶς καὶ φανερῶς μ' ἀποστεροῦσιν.
τούτους γὰρ καταλειφθῆναι μὲν οἴκοι παρ' ἡμῖν
πάντες ὁμολογοῦσι, καὶ τὰς δώδεκα μνᾶς ἑκάστου
τοῦ ἐνιαυτοῦ τῷ πατρὶ γίγνεσθαί φασιν· αὐτοὶ δὲ
λῆμμα μὲν παρ' αὑτῶν ἐν δέκ' ἔτεσιν οὐδὲν ἐμοὶ
γεγενημένον ἀποφαίνουσιν ἀλλ' οὐδὲ μικρόν, ἀναλώ-
ματος δὲ κεφάλαιον εἰς αὑτοὺς οὗτος ὀλίγου δεῖν
25 λογίζεται χιλίας· εἰς τοῦτ' ἀναιδείας ἐλήλυθεν. αὐτοὺς δὲ τοὺς ἀνθρώπους, εἰς οὓς ταῦτ' ἀνηλωκέναι
φησίν, οὐδαμοῦ μοι παραδεδώκασιν, ἀλλὰ πάντων
κενότατον λόγον λέγουσιν, ὡς ὁ ὑποθεὶς τῷ πατρὶ
τἀνδράποδα πονηρότατος ἀνθρώπων ἐστί, καὶ ἐρά-
νους τε λέλοιπε πλείστους καὶ ὑπέρχρεως γέγονε,
καὶ τούτων οὐκ ὀλίγους κεκλήκασι κατ' ἐκείνου
μάρτυρας. τὰ δ' ἀνδράποδ' ὅστις ἐστὶν ὁ λαβών, ἢ
πῶς ἐκ τῆς οἰκίας ἐξῆλθεν, ἢ τίς ἀφείλετο, ἢ πρὸς

¹ ἄλλας : ἄλλας ὁμοῦ Blass.

---

[a] That is, at 12 per cent, instead of 18 per cent, which was
normal in the case of marriage-portions.
[b] The ἔρανος, originally a meal to which each contributed

if one sets this down at the rate of a drachma only,[a] it will make thirty minae more. These sums he has himself embezzled, and, if they be added to the marriage-portion, the total is about four talents, principal and interest combined. Now I shall go on to show you what sums he has embezzled in conjunction with his co-trustees, and what sums he asserts were never left by my father at all. First, regarding 24 the twenty sofa-makers, given to my father as security for a debt of forty minae, whom my father certainly left behind him at his death, but of whom these men show not a trace—let me prove to you with what utter shamelessness and how openly they are seeking to cheat me of these. That these slaves were left by my father in the house they all admit, and that they brought him in an income of twelve minae every year. Yet these men report no receipts as having come in to my credit from them in ten years, and Aphobus reckons up a total expenditure on them of nearly a thousand drachmae. To such a pitch of effrontery has he come! And these slaves themselves, upon 25 whom he alleges that he has expended the money, they have never handed over to me. On the contrary, they tell the idlest tale imaginable, to the effect that the man who pledged the slaves to my father is the vilest sort of a fellow, who has left many friendly loans[b] unpaid, and who is overwhelmed with debt; and to prove this against him they have called a large number of witnesses. But as for the slaves—who got them; how they went out of the house; who took

his due portion, came not unnaturally to mean a " club " to which each member contributed, and from which he could claim help, if need arose. Then it was also used, as here, of the " contribution " or better, the " loan," made to such members.

τίνα δίκην ἥττηνται περὶ αὐτῶν, οὐκ ἔχουσιν εἰπεῖν.
26 καίτοι εἴ τι ἔλεγον ὑγιές, οὐκ ἂν κατὰ τῆς ἐκείνου
πονηρίας παρείχοντο μάρτυρας, ἧς οὐδέν μοι προσήκει φροντίζειν, ἀλλὰ τούτων ἂν ἀντελαμβάνοντο
καὶ τοὺς λαβόντας ἀπεδείκνυσαν καὶ οὐδὲν ἂν αὐτῶν
παρέλειπον. νῦν δ' ὠμότατ' ἀνθρώπων, ὁμολογοῦντες καταλειφθῆναι καὶ λαβόντες ὡς αὐτοὺς καὶ
καρπωσάμενοι δέκ' ἔτη τοὺς ἀνθρώπους, ἄρδην
ὅλον τὸ ἐργαστήριον ἀφανίζουσιν.

Καὶ ταῦθ' ὡς ἀληθῆ λέγω, λαβέ μοι τὰς
μαρτυρίας καὶ ἀναγίγνωσκε.

ΜΑΡΤΥΡΙΑΙ

27 Ὅτι τοίνυν οὐκ ἄπορος ἦν ὁ Μοιριάδης, οὐδ' ἦν
τῷ πατρὶ τοῦτο τὸ συμβόλαιον εἰς τἀνδράποδ'
ἠλιθίῳ συμβεβλημένον, μεγίστῳ τεκμηρίῳ γνώ-
σεσθε· λαβὼν γὰρ ὡς ἑαυτὸν Ἄφοβος τοῦτο τὸ
ἐργαστήριον, ὡς αὐτοὶ τῶν μαρτύρων ἠκούσατε,
καὶ δέον αὐτόν, εἰ καί τις ἄλλος ἐβούλετ' εἰς ταῦτα
συμβαλεῖν, τοῦτον κωλύειν ἐπίτροπόν γ' ὄντα, αὐτὸς
ἐπὶ τούτοις τοῖς ἀνδραπόδοις τῷ Μοιριάδη πεντακοσίας δραχμὰς ἐδάνεισεν, ἃς ὀρθῶς καὶ δικαίως
28 παρ' ἐκείνου κεκομίσθαι ὡμολόγηκεν. καίτοι πῶς
οὐ δεινόν, εἰ ἡμῖν μὲν πρὸς τῷ λήμμ' ἀπ' αὐτῶν
μηδὲν γεγονέναι καὶ αὐτὰ τὰ ὑποτεθέντ' ἀπόλωλεν,
οἳ πρότερον συνεβάλομεν, τῷ δ' εἰς τὰ ἡμέτερα
δανείσαντι καὶ τοσούτῳ χρόνῳ πράξαντι, καὶ οἱ
τόκοι καὶ τἀρχαῖ' ἐκ τῶν ἡμετέρων ἀποδέδοται
καὶ οὐδεμί' ἀπορία γέγονεν;

24

them away ; or in what suit they lost them by judgement, they are unable to say. Yet, if there were any 26 truth in what they allege they would not be bringing forward witnesses to prove this man's vile character (with which I have no concern), but would be holding on to the slaves, or would show who took them, and would have left not one of them out of sight. But as it is, though they admit that the slaves were left by my father, and though they took possession of them and enjoyed the profits from them for ten years, they have in the most ruthless manner possible done away with the whole factory.

To prove that I am speaking the truth in this, take, please, and read the depositions.

THE DEPOSITIONS

That, moreover, Moeriades was not without re- 27 sources and that my father did not act foolishly in making the contract with him about the slaves, I will show you by the clearest proof. For after Aphobus took into his own hands the factory as you have yourselves heard from the witnesses, when it was his duty as my guardian to prevent anyone else from advancing money on the same security, he himself loaned to Moeriades on the security of these same slaves the sum of five hundred drachmae, which he admits he has duly recovered from him in full. And yet is it 28 not outrageous that we who made the prior loan should, besides having received no profit from the slaves, have lost our security, while this fellow, who loaned money on security belonging to us, and whose loan was so long subsequent to ours, should from funds that were ours have recovered both principal and interest, and have suffered no loss whatever ?

DEMOSTHENES

Ἀλλὰ μὴν ὡς ἀληθῆ λέγω, λαβὲ τὴν μαρτυρίαν
καὶ ἀνάγνωθι.

ΜΑΡΤΥΡΙΑ

29 Σκέψασθε τοίνυν ὅσον ἀργύριον οὗτοι παρὰ τοὺς
κλινοποιοὺς κλέπτουσι, τετταράκοντα μὲν μνᾶς
αὐτὸ τὸ ἀρχαῖον, δέκα δ' ἐτῶν τὸ ἔργον αὐτῶν δύο
τάλαντα· δώδεκα γὰρ μνᾶς ἑκάστου τοῦ ἐνιαυτοῦ
τὴν πρόσοδον αὐτῶν ἐλάμβανον. ἆρα μικρόν τι
καὶ ἐξ ἀφανοῦς ποθὲν καὶ παραλογίσασθαι ῥάδιον,
ἀλλ' οὐ φανερῶς οὑτωσὶ μικροῦ δεῖν τρία τάλαντα
ταῦτ' ἀνηρπάκασιν; ὧν κοινῇ διαπεφορημένων τὸ
τρίτον δήπου μέρος παρὰ τούτου μοι προσήκει
κεκομίσθαι.

30 Καὶ μήν, ὦ ἄνδρες δικασταί, καὶ τὰ περὶ τοῦ
[823] ἐλέφαντος καὶ σιδήρου τοῦ καταλειφθέντος παρα-
πλήσιά πως τούτοις πεποιήκασιν· οὐδὲ γὰρ ταῦτ'
ἀποφαίνουσιν. καίτοι κεκτημένον μὲν τοσούτους
κλινοποιούς, κεκτημένον δὲ μαχαιροποιούς, οὐχ οἷόν
τε μὴ οὐχὶ καὶ σίδηρον καὶ ἐλέφαντα καταλιπεῖν,
ἀλλ' ἀνάγκη ταῦτά γ' ὑπάρχειν· τί γὰρ ἂν ἠργά-
31 ζοντο τούτων μὴ ὑπαρξάντων; τὸν τοίνυν πλεῖν ἢ
πεντήκοντ' ἀνδράποδα κεκτημένον καὶ δυοῖν τέχναιν
ἐπιμελούμενον, ὧν θάτερον ἐργαστήριον εἰς τὰς
κλίνας ῥᾳδίως δύο μνᾶς τοῦ μηνὸς ἀνήλισκεν
ἐλέφαντος, τὸ δὲ μαχαιροποιεῖον οὐκ ἔλαττον ἢ
τοσοῦτον ἕτερον, σὺν σιδήρῳ, τοῦτον οὔ φασι καταλιπεῖν οὐδὲν τούτων· εἰς τοῦτ' ἀναιδείας ἐληλύθασιν.
32 ὅτι μὲν οὖν οὐ πιστὰ λέγουσι, καὶ ἐκ τούτων αὐτῶν
ῥάδιόν ἐστι μαθεῖν· ὅτι δ' ἐκεῖνος κατέλιπε τοσοῦτον
τὸ πλῆθος, ὥστε μὴ μόνον ἱκανὸν εἶναι κατεργάζε-

26

To prove that what I say is true, take the deposition and read it.

The Deposition

Consider now of how large a sum they are defraud- **29** ing me in the matter of these sofa-makers : the principal alone, forty minae, and interest upon it for ten years, two talents ; for they obtained from the slaves a profit of twelve minae each year. Is this a trifling sum drawn from some obscure source, which might easily have been miscalculated, or have they not manifestly robbed me of nearly three talents [a] ? Of this sum which they have jointly scattered to the winds, it is surely right that I should recover a third from the defendant.

Furthermore, men of the jury, they have dealt in **30** much the same way with the ivory and iron which were left me. They do not produce them. Yet it is impossible that one who possessed so many sofa-makers and so many sword-makers should not also have left iron and ivory. These things must have been available, for what could the slaves have pro- duced without these materials ? Well then, though **31** my father possessed more than fifty slaves and con- ducted two factories, one of which easily consumed two minae worth of ivory per month for the sofas, while the sword-factory consumed as much more, and iron besides, these men declare that he left no ivory and no iron ; to such a pitch of shamelessness have they come ! From these facts alone it is easy to see **32** that no credence is to be given to their statements ; but that my father actually did leave such an amount of these materials as not only to suffice for his own

[a] Strictly, two talents and forty minae. See the table on p. xi.

σθαι τοῖς ἑαυτοῦ δημιουργοῖς, ἀλλὰ καὶ τῷ βουλο-
μένῳ πρὸς ὠνεῖσθαι τῶν ἄλλων, ἐκεῖθεν φανερόν,
ὅτι αὐτός τ' ἐπώλει ζῶν, καὶ Δημοφῶν καὶ οὗτος
τοῦ πατρὸς ἤδη τετελευτηκότος ἐκ τῆς οἰκίας τῆς
33 ἐμῆς ἀπεδίδοντο τοῖς βουλομένοις. καίτοι πόσον
τινὰ χρὴ τὸν καταλειφθέντα νομίζειν εἶναι, ὅταν
φαίνηται τηλικούτοις τ' ἐργαστηρίοις ἐξαρκῶν, καὶ
χωρὶς ὑπὸ τῶν ἐπιτρόπων πιπρασκόμενος; ἆρ'
ὀλίγον, ἀλλ' οὐ πολλῷ πλείω τῶν ἐγκεκλημένων;
    Λαβὲ τοίνυν τὰς μαρτυρίας ταυτασὶ καὶ ἀνάγνωθ'
αὐτοῖς.

ΜΑΡΤΥΡΙΑΙ

    Τούτου τοίνυν τοῦ ἐλέφαντός ἐστι πλέον ἢ τά-
λαντον, ὃν οὔτ' αὐτὸν οὔτε τὸ ἔργον ἀποφαίνουσιν,
ἀλλὰ καὶ τοῦτον ἄρδην ἀφανίζουσιν ὅλον.
34   Ἔτι τοίνυν, ὦ ἄνδρες δικασταί, παρὰ τὸν λόγον
ὃν ἀποφέρουσιν, ἐξ ὧν αὐτοὶ λαβεῖν ὁμολογοῦσιν,
ἐπιδείξω ὑμῖν τρεῖς μὲν ὄντας αὐτοὺς πλέον ἢ ὀκτὼ
τάλαντ' ἐκ τῶν ἐμῶν ἔχοντας, ἰδίᾳ δ' ἐκ τούτων
Ἄφοβον τρία τάλαντα καὶ χιλίας εἰληφότα, τά τ'
ἀνηλωμένα χωρὶς τούτων πλείω τιθεὶς καὶ ὅσ' ἐκ
τούτων ἀπέδοσαν ἀφαιρῶν, ἵν' εἰδῆθ' ὅτι οὐ μικρᾶς
35 ἀναιδείας τὰ ἐγχειρήματ' αὐτῶν ἐστιν. λαβεῖν γὰρ
ἐκ τῶν ἐμῶν ὁμολογοῦσιν οὗτος μὲν ὀκτὼ καὶ
ἑκατὸν μνᾶς, χωρὶς ὧν ἔχοντ' αὐτὸν ἐγὼ ἐπιδείξω
νῦν, Θηριππίδης δὲ δύο τάλαντα, Δημοφῶν δ' ἑπτὰ
καὶ ὀγδοήκοντα μνᾶς. τοῦτο δ' ἐστὶ πέντε τάλαντα
28

workmen to use in their trade, but also for sale to anyone else who wished to buy, is made clear by the fact that he himself during his lifetime used to sell these materials, and that after his death Demophon and the defendant continued to sell them from out my house to those wishing to buy. And yet how **33** large must one suppose the quantity left by my father to have been, when it is shown to have sufficed for such extensive factories, and to have been sold by the guardians besides? Was it a small amount, or not rather much more than I have charged?

Take now these depositions and read them to the jury.

THE DEPOSITIONS

Of this ivory, you see, there is more than a talent's worth of which they make no report—neither of the raw material nor of the finished product. No; this also they have utterly and absolutely made away with.

Furthermore, men of the jury, I shall prove to you **34** from the account which they render, and from the receipts admitted by themselves, that these three men have in their possession more than eight talents of my money, and that of this amount Aphobus has separately taken three talents and one thousand drachmae. I shall set down separately at a higher figure than they do themselves the moneys they have expended, and shall deduct all the sums they have paid me, that you may see the utter shamelessness of their attempts. They confess to have received from **35** my estate, Aphobus one hundred and eight minae (besides what I shall now show to be in his hands); Therippides two talents; and Demophon eighty-seven minae. This makes altogether five talents and

καὶ πεντεκαίδεκα μναῖ. τούτου τοίνυν ὃ μὲν οὐχ
ἄθρουν ἐλήφθη, σχεδόν εἰσιν ἑβδομήκοντα μναῖ καὶ
ἑπτά, ἡ πρόσοδος ἡ ἀπὸ τῶν ἀνδραπόδων, ὃ δ᾽
εὐθὺς ἔλαβον οὗτοι, μικροῦ δέοντα τέτταρα τά-
λαντα· οἷς τὸ ἔργον ἂν προσθῇτ᾽ ἐπὶ δραχμῇ μόνον
τῶν δέκ᾽ ἐτῶν, ὀκτὼ τάλανθ᾽ εὑρήσετε σὺν τοῖς
36 ἀρχαίοις καὶ χιλίας γιγνομένας. τὴν μὲν τοίνυν
τροφὴν ἀπὸ τῶν ἑβδομήκοντα μνῶν καὶ ἑπτὰ λο-
γιστέον τῶν ἀπὸ τοῦ ἐργαστηρίου γενομένων.
Θηριππίδης γὰρ ἑπτὰ μνᾶς ἐδίδου καθ᾽ ἕκαστον
τὸν ἐνιαυτὸν εἰς ταῦτα, καὶ ἡμεῖς τοῦτο λαβεῖν ὁμο-
λογοῦμεν. ὥσθ᾽ ἑβδομήκοντα μνῶν ἐν τοῖς δέκ᾽ ἔτεσι
[825] τροφὴν τούτων ἡμῖν ἀνηλωκότων, τὸ περιὸν τὰς
ἑπτακοσίας προστίθημ᾽ αὐτοῖς, καὶ τούτων πλεῖον᾽
εἰμὶ τεθηκώς. ὃ δ᾽ ἐμοὶ δοκιμασθέντι παρέδοσαν
καὶ ὅσον εἰς τὴν πόλιν εἰσενηνόχασι, τοῦτ᾽ ἀπὸ τῶν
ὀκτὼ ταλάντων καὶ τοῦ προσόντος ἀφαιρετέον
37 ἐστίν. ἀπέδοσαν μὲν τοίνυν οὗτος καὶ Θηριππίδης
μίαν καὶ τριάκοντα μνᾶς, εἰσφορὰς δ᾽ εἰσενηνοχέναι
λογίζονται δυοῖν δεούσας εἴκοσι μνᾶς. ἐγὼ δ᾽
ὑπερβαλὼν καὶ τοῦτο ποιήσω τριάκοντα μνᾶς, ἵνα
πρὸς ταῦτα μηδ᾽ ἀντειπεῖν ἔχωσιν. οὐκοῦν ἂν
ἀφέλητε τὸ τάλαντον ἀπὸ τῶν ὀκτὼ ταλάντων, ἑπτὰ
τὰ λειπόμεν᾽ ἐστί, καὶ ταῦτ᾽, ἐξ ὧν αὐτοὶ λαβεῖν
ὁμολογοῦσι, τούτους ἔχειν ἐστὶν ἀναγκαῖον. τοῦτο
τοίνυν, εἰ καὶ τἆλλα πάντ᾽ ἀποστεροῦσιν ἀρνούμενοι
μὴ ἔχειν, ἀποδοῦναι προσῆκεν, ὁμολογοῦντάς γε

ᵃ That is, at 12 per cent, as above. Demosthenes is liberal
indeed in his allowances. The entire sum of seventy-seven
minae is crossed off as balanced by expenditures; the interest
on four talents for ten years is set down as four talents forty
minae, instead of four talents forty-eight minae, so that the

fifteen minae. Of this sum there are nearly seventy-seven minae, the income from the slaves, which were not received all at once, and a little less than four talents of which they got possession immediately. Now, if you add to this last sum the interest for ten years, reckoned at a drachma only,[a] you will find that the whole, principal and interest, amounts to eight talents and four thousand drachmae. From the **36** seventy-seven minae, the profits of the factory, the cost of maintenance of the men must be deducted, for Therippides expended for this seven minae a year, and I admit having received thus much. Thus they expended on our behalf in the ten years seventy minae for maintenance; to this I add the balance, seven hundred drachmae, and thus credit them with a larger expenditure than they do themselves. There must also be deducted from the eight talents and more the sum they handed over to me when I came of age, and the taxes which they have paid to the state. The defendant and Therippides paid me **37** thirty-one minae, and they compute that they have paid eighteen minae in taxes. I will go beyond them and will make this sum thirty minae, that they may have not a word to say in protest. Well, then, if you take away one talent from the eight, seven are left, which, according to their own admissions of receipts, they must necessarily have in their possession. This sum, then, even if they rob me of everything else and deny that they have it, they ought at least to have paid me, seeing that they admit having

total amount becomes eight talents and forty minae. From this there are deducted the moneys paid to him (thirty-one minae) and those paid in taxes (set down as thirty minae, instead of eighteen) and the balance (roughly, eight talents less one talent), is reckoned as seven talents.

38 λαβεῖν ταῦτ᾽ ἐκ τῶν ἐμῶν. νῦν δὲ τί ποιοῦσιν;
ἔργον μὲν οὐδὲν ἀποφαίνουσι τοῖς χρήμασιν, αὐτὰ
δὲ τὰ ἀρχαῖα πάντ᾽ ἀνηλωκέναι φασὶ σὺν ταῖς ἑπτὰ
καὶ ἑβδομήκοντα μναῖς· Δημοφῶν δὲ καὶ πρὸς
ὀφείλοντας ἡμᾶς ἐνέγραψεν. ταῦτ᾽ οὐ μεγάλη καὶ
περιφανὴς ἀναισχυντία; ταῦτ᾽ οὐχ ὑπερβολὴ δεινῆς
αἰσχροκερδείας; τί οὖν ποτ᾽ ἐστὶ τὸ δεινόν, εἰ μὴ
39 ταῦτα δόξει τηλικαύτας ὑπερβολὰς ἔχοντα; οὗτος
τοίνυν τὸ καθ᾽ αὑτὸν ὀκτὼ καὶ ἑκατὸν μνᾶς λαβεῖν
ὁμολογῶν, ἔχει καὶ αὐτὰς καὶ τὸ ἔργον δέκ᾽ ἐτῶν,
μάλιστα τρία τάλαντα καὶ χιλίας.

Καὶ ταῦθ᾽ ὡς ἀληθῆ λέγω, καὶ ἐν τοῖς λόγοις
τοῖς τῆς ἐπιτροπῆς τὸ λῆμμ᾽ ἕκαστος τοῦθ᾽ ὁμο-
[826] λογῶν λαβεῖν ἅπαν ἀνηλωκέναι λογίζεται, λαβὲ
τὰς μαρτυρίας καὶ ἀνάγνωθι.

MΑΡΤΥΡΙΑΙ

40 Νομίζω τοίνυν, ὦ ἄνδρες δικασταί, περὶ τούτων
ἱκανῶς μὲν ὑμᾶς μεμαθηκέναι, καὶ ὅσα κλέπτουσι
καὶ κακουργοῦσιν ἕκαστος αὐτῶν· ἔτι δ᾽ ἀκριβέστερον ἔγνωτ᾽ ἄν, εἴ μοι τὰς διαθήκας, ἃς ὁ πατὴρ
κατέλιπεν, οὗτοι ἀποδοῦναι ἠθέλησαν. ἐν γὰρ ἐκεί-
ναις ἐγέγραπτο, ὥς φησιν ἡ μήτηρ, ἃ κατέλιπεν ὁ
πατὴρ πάντα, καὶ ἐξ ὧν ἔδει τούτους λαβεῖν τὰ
41 δοθέντα, καὶ τὸν οἶκον ὅπως μισθώσουσι. νῦν δ᾽
ἀπαιτοῦντος ἐμοῦ καταλειφθῆναι μὲν ὁμολογοῦσιν,
αὐτὰς δ᾽ οὐκ ἀποφαίνουσιν. ταῦτα δὲ ποιοῦσι τό
τε πλῆθος οὐ βουλόμενοι καταφανὲς ποιῆσαι τῆς

received it from my estate. But what is it that they 38 do? They report no return in interest for this money, and tell me that they have expended the entire principal together with the seventy-seven minae; and Demophon has, moreover, actually set me down as indebted to him. Is not this absolute and barefaced effrontery? Is it not the very excess of outrageous rapacity? What is the meaning of outrageous, if matters pushed to this extreme are not to be so called? The defendant, then, for his own 39 part, since he admits having received one hundred and eight minae, has in his possession these and the interest on them for ten years, in all about three talents and one thousand drachmae.

In proof that what I say is true—that each one of them in the account of his guardianship admits that he has received the money, but claims to have spent it all—take the depositions and read them.

THE DEPOSITIONS

I think, men of the jury, that you have now been 40 fully informed regarding the theft and wrongdoings of each of these men. You would, however, have had more exact knowledge of the matter, if they had been willing to give up to me the will which my father left; for it contained (so my mother tells me) a statement of all the property that my father left, along with instructions regarding the funds from which these men were to take what had been given them, and regarding the letting of the property. But as 41 it is, on my demanding it, they admit that there was a will, but they do not produce it; and they take this course because they do not want to make known

οὐσίας τὸ καταλειφθέν, ὃ διηρπάκασιν οὗτοι, τάς τε
δωρειὰς ἵνα μὴ δοκῶσιν ἔχειν, ὥσπερ οὐκ ἐξ αὐτοῦ
τοῦ πράγματος ἐξελεγχθησόμενοι ῥᾳδίως.

Λαβὲ δ' αὐτοῖς τὰς μαρτυρίας ὧν ἐναντίον ἀπεκρίναντο, καὶ ἀνάγνωθι.

MΑΡΤΥΡΙΑΙ

42 Οὗτος διαθήκην μὲν γενέσθαι φησί, καὶ τὰ δύο
τάλαντα Δημοφῶντι καὶ τὰς ὀγδοήκοντα μνᾶς
τούτῳ δοθῆναι μαρτυρεῖ· τὰς δ' ἑβδομήκοντα μνᾶς,
ἃς Θηριππίδης ἔλαβεν, οὐ προσγραφῆναί φησιν,
οὐδὲ τὸ πλῆθος τῆς οὐσίας τὸ καταλειφθέν, οὐδὲ
τὸν οἶκον ὅπως μισθώσουσιν· οὐ γὰρ αὐτῷ συμφέρει προσομολογῆσαι ταῦτα.

Λαβὲ δὴ τὴν τούτου ἀπόκρισιν.

[827]   MΑΡΤΥΡΙΑ

43 Οὗτος αὖ τὴν μὲν διαθήκην γενέσθαι φησί, καὶ
τὸ ἀργύριον ἐκ τοῦ χαλκοῦ καὶ τῆς κηκίδος ἀπο-
δοθῆναι τῷ Θηριππίδῃ, ὃ ἐκεῖνος οὔ φησι, καὶ τὰ
δύο τάλαντα τῷ Δημοφῶντι· περὶ δὲ τῶν αὑτῷ
δοθέντων γραφῆναι μέν φησιν, οὐχ ὁμολογῆσαι δ'
αὐτός, ἵνα μὴ δοκῇ λαβεῖν. τὸ δὲ πλῆθος τῆς
οὐσίας οὐδ' οὗτος ἀποφαίνει καθόλου,[1] οὐδὲ τὸ
μισθοῦν τὸν οἶκον· οὐδὲ γὰρ οὐδὲ τούτῳ συμφέρει
44 προσομολογῆσαι ταῦτα. δῆλον τοίνυν ἐστὶν οὐδὲν
ἧττον τὸ πλῆθος τῶν καταλειφθέντων, καίπερ
ἀφανιζόντων τούτων τὴν οὐσίαν, ἐκ τῶν διαθηκῶν,
ἐξ ὧν τοσαῦτα χρήματ' ἀλλήλοις φασὶ δοθῆναι.

---

[1] καθόλου] καθόλου τὸ καταλειφθέν Blass.

---

[a] "This man" appears to refer to Therippides.

34

the amount of the property which was left, and which they have embezzled, and to the end that they may not appear to have received their legacies—as though they would not easily be convicted by the facts themselves.

Take now, and read them the evidence of those in whose presence they made their answers.

THE DEPOSITIONS

This man*a* declares that a will was made and testifies 42 that in it the two talents were given to Demophon, and the eighty minae to Aphobus ; but he declares there was no additional clause regarding the seventy minae which Therippides received, or regarding the amount of the property bequeathed, or instructions as to the letting of it ; for it was not to his interest to make these further admissions.

Now take the answer of the defendant.

THE DEPOSITION

He also declares that the will was made, and that 43 the money accruing from the copper and the gall was duly paid to Therippides, which Therippides denies ; and that the two talents were paid to Demophon ; but in regard to the money given to himself, while he admits that the clause was written in the will, he declares that he did not assent to it, in order that he may not appear to have received it. But as to the amount of the estate he, too, reveals absolutely nothing, nor as to letting the property. For it was not to his interest either to make these further admissions. The amount of the property that was 44 left is, however, none the less clear (though these men seek to conceal it) from the terms of the will, in accordance with which they state that such large sums were given to them severally. When a man

35

ὅστις γὰρ ἐκ τεττάρων ταλάντων καὶ τρισχιλίων
τοῖς μὲν τρία τάλαντα καὶ δισχιλίας προῖκ' ἔδωκε,
τῷ δ' ἑβδομήκοντα μνᾶς καρποῦσθαι, φανερὸν
δήπου πᾶσιν ὅτι οὐκ ἀπὸ μικρᾶς οὐσίας, ἀλλὰ πλέον
45 ἢ διπλασίας ἧς ἐμοὶ κατέλειπε ταῦτ' ἀφεῖλεν. οὐ
γὰρ δήπου τὸν μὲν υἱὸν ἐμὲ πένητ' ἠβούλετο καταλιπεῖν, τούτους δὲ πλουσίους ὄντας ἔτι πλουσιωτέρους ποιῆσαι ἐπεθύμησεν, ἀλλ' ἕνεκα τοῦ πλήθους
τῶν ἐμοὶ καταλειπομένων Θηριππίδῃ τε τοσοῦτον
ἀργύριον καὶ Δημοφῶντι τὰ δύο τάλαντα, οὔπω
μέλλοντι τῇ ἀδελφῇ τῇ ἐμῇ συνοικήσειν, καρποῦσθαι ἔδωκεν, ἵνα δυοῖν θάτερον διαπράξαιτο, ἢ διὰ
τὰ διδόμενα βελτίους αὐτοὺς εἶναι τὰ περὶ τὴν ἐπι-
τροπὴν προτρέψειεν, ἢ εἰ κακοὶ γίγνοιντο, μηδεμιᾶς
[828] συγγνώμης παρ' ὑμῶν τυγχάνοιεν, εἰ τοσούτων
46 ἀξιωθέντες τοιαῦτ' εἰς ἡμᾶς ἐξαμαρτάνοιεν. οὗτος
τοίνυν καὶ αὐτὸς πρὸς τῇ προικὶ καὶ τὰς θεραπαίνας
λαβὼν καὶ τὴν οἰκίαν οἰκῶν, ἐπειδὴ δεῖ λόγον αὐτὸν
δοῦναι τούτων, τά θ' αὑτοῦ πράττειν φησί, καὶ εἰς
τοσοῦτον αἰσχροκερδείας ἦλθεν, ὥστε καὶ τοὺς δι-
δασκάλους τοὺς μισθοὺς ἀπεστέρηκε, καὶ τῶν εἰσ-
φορῶν ἔστιν ἃς οὐ κατέθηκεν, ἐμοὶ δὲ λογίζεται.

Λαβὲ δὴ καὶ ταύτας αὐτοῖς τὰς μαρτυρίας καὶ
ἀνάγνωθι.

MAPTYPIAI

47 Πῶς οὖν ἄν τις σαφέστερον ἐπιδείξειε πάντα
διηρπακότα καὶ μηδὲ τῶν μικρῶν ἀπεσχημένον, ἢ
τοῦτον τὸν τρόπον ἐπιδεικνὺς μετὰ τοσούτων μαρ-

36

out of four talents and three thousand drachmae
has given to two of these men three talents and two
thousand drachmae as marriage-portions, and to the
third the interest on seventy minae, it is clear, I
fancy, that he took these sums, not from a small
estate, but from one bequeathed to me of more than
double this amount. For, I take it, he would not 45
wish to leave me, his son, in poverty, and be eager
further to enrich these men, who were already
wealthy. No ; it was because of the size of the estate
left to me that he gave to Therippides the interest on
a sum so considerable, and to Demophon that on the
two talents—though he was not yet to marry my
sister—in order to accomplish one or the other of two
ends : either he would by his gifts encourage them to
act the more honourably in the guardianship, or, if
they should prove dishonest, they would meet with
no leniency at your hands, seeing that, after being so
liberally treated, they sinned so grievously against
us. Well now, the defendant, who in addition to my 46
mother's marriage-portion has taken the female
servants, and has lived in the house, when it becomes
necessary to render an account of these matters, says
he is busy with his own affairs ; and he has come to
such a pitch of rapaciousness, that he has even cheated
my instructors of their fees, and has left unpaid
some of the taxes, although he charges me with the
amounts.

Take these depositions too, and read them to the jury.

The Depositions

How could one show more clearly that he has made 47
havoc of the whole estate, sparing nothing, however
small, than by proving, as I have done by so many

τύρων καὶ τεκμηρίων; τὴν μὲν προῖκα λαβεῖν ὁμολογήσαντα καὶ ἔχειν αὐτὸν πρὸς τοὺς ἐπιτρόπους
ἀπογράψαντα, τὸ δ' ἐργαστήριον κεκαρπωμένον
48 αὐτὸν καὶ τὴν πρόσοδον οὐκ ἀποφαίνοντα, τῶν
δ' ἄλλων τὰ μὲν πεπρακότα καὶ τὰς τιμὰς οὐκ
ἀποδεδωκότα, τὰ δ' ὡς ἑαυτὸν λαβόντα καὶ ταῦτ'
ἠφανικότα, ἔτι δὲ παρὰ τὸν λόγον ὃν αὐτὸς ἀπέδωκε
τοσαῦτα κλέπτοντα, πρὸς δὲ τούτοις τὴν διαθήκην
ἠφανικότα, τὰ ἀνδράποδα πεπρακότα, τἆλλ' οὕτω
πάντα διῳκηκότα, ὡς οὐδ' ἂν οἱ ἔχθιστοι διοική-
σειαν· ἐγὼ μὲν οὐκ οἶδ' ὅπως ἄν τις σαφέστερον
ἐπιδείξειεν.

49 Ἐτόλμα τοίνυν πρὸς τῷ διαιτητῇ λέγειν, ὡς ἀπὸ
τῶν χρημάτων χρέα τε πάμπολλ' ἐκτέτεικεν ὑπὲρ
ἐμοῦ Δημοφῶντι καὶ Θηριππίδῃ τοῖς συνεπιτρόποις,
καὶ ὡς πολλὰ τῶν ἐμῶν λάβοιεν, οὐδέτερ' ἔχων
ἐπιδεικνύναι τούτων. οὔτε γὰρ ὡς ὀφείλοντά με
κατέλιπεν ὁ πατὴρ ἐν τοῖς γράμμασιν ἀπέφηνεν,
[829] οὐδ' οἷς ἀποδεδωκέναι ταῦτ' ἔφη παρέσχηται μάρτυρας, οὔτ' αὖ τὸν ἀριθμὸν τῶν χρημάτων εἰς τοὺς
συνεπιτρόπους ἐπανέφερεν ὅσον αὐτὸς φαίνεται
50 λαβών, ἀλλὰ πολλοῖς ἐλάττω χρήμασιν. ἐρωτηθεὶς
δ' ὑπὸ τοῦ διαιτητοῦ ταῦτά τε καθ' ἕκαστον, καὶ
τὴν οὐσίαν τὴν αὐτοῦ πότερον ἐκ τῶν ἐπικαρπιῶν
ἢ τἀρχαῖ' ἀναλίσκων διῴκηκε, καὶ πότερον ἐπι-
τροπευθεὶς ἀπεδέξατ' ἂν τοῦτον τὸν λόγον παρὰ
τῶν ἐπιτρόπων, ἢ τἀρχαῖ' ἂν ἀπολαβεῖν ἠξίου σὺν
τοῖς ἔργοις τοῖς γεγενημένοις, πρὸς μὲν ταῦτ' ἀπ-

ᵃ The public arbitrators at Athens were chosen from a
body of citizens of advanced age. To one or another of
these men (selected by lot) the magistrate would refer civil

witnesses and proofs, that he admitted having received the marriage-portion, and that he acknowledged in writing to the guardians that he had it ; that he enjoyed the profits of the factory, but makes report of none ; that of our other effects he has sold some **48** without paying to us the proceeds, while others he has taken to himself and hidden ; that according to the account which he has himself rendered, he has embezzled large sums ; that in addition to all this he has made away with the will, sold the slaves, and in all other respects has administered the estate as not even the bitterest enemies would have done ?   I do not see how anyone could prove the matter more clearly.

He had the audacity to say before the arbitrator [a] **49** that he had paid many debts for me out of the estate to Demophon and Therippides, his fellow-guardians, and that they received a large part of my property, yet neither of these facts was he able to prove. He did not show by the books that my father left me in debt, nor has he brought forward as witnesses the men whom he says he paid ; nor, again, is the amount of money which he charged against his fellow-guardians equal to the amount which he is shown to have received himself. On the contrary, it is much less. When the arbitrator questioned him about each of **50** these matters, and asked him whether he had managed his own estate from the interest or had spent the principal, and whether, if he had been under guardian-ship, he would have accepted an account of this sort from his guardians or would have demanded that the money be duly paid to him with the accrued interest,

cases before trial in hopes of bringing about a settlement of the points at issue out of court.   *Cf.* Aristotle, *Constitution of Athens* 53.

ἐκρίνατ᾽ οὐδέν, προὐκαλεῖτο δ᾽ ἐθέλειν ἐπιδεῖξαί μοι
τὴν οὐσίαν δέκα ταλάντων οὖσαν· εἰ δέ τι ἐλλείποι,
51 αὐτὸς ἔφη προσθήσειν. κελεύοντος δ᾽ ἐμοῦ πρὸς
τὸν διαιτητὴν ἐπιδεικνύναι ταῦτ᾽ οὐκ ἐπέδειξεν,
οὐδ᾽ ὡς οἱ συνεπίτροποι παρέδοσαν· (οὐ γὰρ ἂν
αὐτοῦ κατεδιῄτησε), μαρτυρίαν δ᾽ ἐνεβάλετο τοιαύτην, περὶ ἧς πειράσεταί τι λέγειν.

Ἂν μὲν οὖν καὶ νῦν ἔχειν με φῇ, τίνος παραδόντος ἐρωτᾶτ᾽ αὐτόν, καὶ καθ᾽ ἕκαστον παρα-
52 σχέσθαι μάρτυρας ἀξιοῦτε. ἐὰν δ᾽ εἶναί μοι φῇ
τοῦτον τὸν τρόπον, λογιζόμενος τὰ παρ᾽ ἑκατέρῳ
τῶν ἐπιτρόπων, διπλασίοις ἐλάττω φανήσεται
λέγων, ἔχοντα δ᾽ οὐδὲν μᾶλλον ἀποφαίνων. ἐγὼ
γὰρ ὥσπερ καὶ τοῦτον τοσαῦτ᾽ ἔχοντ᾽ ἐξήλεγξα,
οὕτως κἀκείνων ἑκάτερον οὐκ ἐλάττω τούτων
ἔχοντ᾽ ἐπιδείξω. ὥστ᾽ οὐ τοῦτ᾽ αὐτῷ λεκτέον,
ἀλλ᾽ ὡς ἢ αὐτὸς ἢ οἱ συνεπίτροποι παρέδοσαν.
εἰ δὲ μὴ τοῦτ᾽ ἐπιδείξει, πῶς χρὴ ταύτῃ τῇ
προκλήσει προσέχειν ὑμᾶς τὸν νοῦν; οὐδὲν γὰρ
[830] μᾶλλον ἔχοντά μ᾽ ἐπιδείκνυσιν.

53 Πολλὰ τοίνυν ἀπορηθεὶς πρὸς τῷ διαιτητῇ περὶ
πάντων τούτων, καὶ καθ᾽ ἕκαστον ἐξελεγχόμενος
ὥσπερ νυνὶ παρ᾽ ὑμῖν, ἐτόλμησε ψεύσασθαι πάντων
δεινότατον, ὡς τέτταρά μοι τάλανθ᾽ ὁ πατὴρ κατέλιπε κατορωρυγμένα, καὶ τούτων κυρίαν τὴν μητέρ᾽

---

[a] The challenge was often used in Athenian lawsuits.
Here Aphobus virtually offers Demosthenes a compromise,
fixing the value of the estate at ten talents instead of thirty.
Sometimes the challenger "dares" his opponent to give an
oath, or to offer a slave for torture.
[b] The speaker would have the jury think that the bit of
evidence in question is unworthy of further notice.

he made no answer to these questions, but tendered me a challenge [a] to the effect that he was ready to show that my property was worth ten talents, and said that, if it fell short of this amount, he would himself make up the difference. When I bade him prove 51 this to the arbitrator, he did not do so, nor did he show that his fellow-guardians had paid me (for if he had, the arbitrator would not have given judgement against him) ; but he put in a piece of evidence [b] of a sort regarding which he will try to find something to say.

If even now he still tries to assert that I am in possession of property, ask him who handed it over to me, and demand that he produce witnesses to prove each statement. If he declares that it is my 52 possession in this sense, that he reckons up what is in the hands of either of the trustees, it will be clear that he accounts for only a third part, and still does not prove that I have possession of it. For as I have convicted the defendant of having in his possession the large amount I have stated, I shall also prove that each of them has not less than he. This statement, therefore, will not help him. No ; he must show that either he or his fellow-trustees really handed the money over to me. If he fails to prove this, why should you pay any attention to his challenge ? He still does not prove that I have the money.

Being sorely at a loss to explain any of these 53 matters before the arbitrator, and being convicted on each point, just as he is now before you, he had the audacity to make an outrageously false statement, to the effect that my father left me four talents buried in the ground, and that he had put my mother in

ἐποίησεν. ταῦτα δ᾽ εἶπεν, ἵν᾽ εἰ μὲν καὶ νῦν προσ-
δοκήσαιμ᾽ αὐτὸν ἐρεῖν, ἀπολογούμενος περὶ αὐτῶν
διατρίβοιμι, δέον ἕτερά μ᾽ αὐτοῦ κατηγορεῖν πρὸς
ὑμᾶς· εἰ δ᾽ ὡς οὐ ῥηθησομένων παραλίποιμι, νῦν
αὐτὸς εἴποι, ἵνα δοκῶν εἶναι πλούσιος ἧττον ὑφ᾽
54 ὑμῶν ἐλεοίμην. καὶ μαρτυρίαν μὲν οὐδεμίαν ἐνεβάλετο τούτων ὁ ταῦτ᾽ εἰπεῖν ἀξιώσας, ψιλῷ δὲ
λόγῳ χρησάμενος, ὡς πιστευθησόμενος εἰκῇ. καὶ
ὅταν μὲν ἔρηταί τις αὐτόν, εἰς τί τῶν ἐμῶν τοσαῦτα
χρήματ᾽ ἀνήλωκε, χρέα φησὶν ὑπὲρ ἐμοῦ ἐκτετει-
κέναι καὶ πένητ᾽ ἐνταυθοῖ ζητεῖ ποιεῖν· ὅταν δὲ
βούληται, πλούσιον, ὡς ἔοικεν, εἴπερ γε καὶ τοσοῦτον ἐκεῖνος ἀργύριον οἴκοι κατέλιπεν. ὡς δ᾽ οὐκ
ἀληθῆ λέγειν οἷόν τ᾽ αὐτόν, ἀλλ᾽ ἀδύνατόν τι γενέ-
55 σθαι τούτων, ἐκ πολλῶν ῥᾴδιον μαθεῖν. εἰ μὲν γὰρ
ὁ πατὴρ ἠπίστει τούτοις, δῆλον ὅτι οὔτ᾽ ἂν τἆλλ᾽
ἐπέτρεπεν, οὔτ᾽ ἂν ταῦθ᾽ οὕτω καταλείπων αὐτοῖς
ἔφραζε· μανία γὰρ δεινὴ τὰ κεκρυμμέν᾽ εἰπεῖν, μηδὲ
τῶν φανερῶν μέλλοντ᾽ ἐπιτρόπους καταστήσειν. εἰ
δ᾽ ἐπίστευεν, οὐκ ἂν δήπου τὰ μὲν πλεῖστ᾽ αὐτοῖς
τῶν χρημάτων ἐνεχείρισε, τῶν δ᾽ οὐκ ἂν κυρίους
ἐποίησεν. οὐδ᾽ ἂν τῇ μὲν μητρί μου ταῦτα φυλάτ-
[831] τειν ἔδωκεν, αὐτὴν δ᾽ ἐκείνην ἑνὶ τῶν ἐπιτρόπων
τούτῳ γυναῖκ᾽ ἔδωκεν· οὐ γὰρ ἔχει λόγον, σῴζειν
μὲν τὰ χρήματα διὰ τῆς ἐμῆς μητρὸς ζητεῖν, ἕνα δὲ
τῶν ἀπιστουμένων καὶ αὐτῆς καὶ τῶν χρημάτων
56 κύριον ποιεῖν. ἔτι δέ, τούτων εἴ τι ἦν ἀληθές,
42

charge of them. He made this statement in order
that, if I should assume that he would repeat it here,
I might waste my time in refuting it, when I ought
to be preferring the rest of my charges against him ;
or if I should pass it over, not expecting him to repeat
it, then he himself might now bring it up, in the hope
that I, by seeming to be rich, might meet with less
compassion from you. Yet he who dared to make 54
such a statement put in no evidence to prove it, but
relied on his bare word, as though you would lightly
give him credence. When one asks him upon what he
has spent so much of my money, he says he has paid
debts for me, and so represents me as poor ; yet,
when it pleases him, he makes me rich, as it seems,
seeing that my father left such a sum of money in the
house. It is easy to see, however, from many considerations that he is lying, and that there is no basis of
fact in this story. For if my father had no confidence 55
in these men, it is plain that he would neither have
entrusted to them the rest of his property, nor, if he
had left this money in the way alleged, would he have
told them of it. It would have been the height of
madness to tell them of hidden treasure, when he was
not going to make them trustees even of his visible
property. But if he had confidence in them, he
would not, I take it, have given into their hands the
bulk of his property, and not have put them in control
of this. Nor would he have entrusted this remainder
to my mother to keep, and then have given her herself
in marriage to this man who was one of the guardians.
For it is not reasonable that he should seek to secure
the money through my mother, and yet to put one of
the men whom he distrusted in control both of her and
of it. Furthermore, if there were any truth in all this, 56

DEMOSTHENES

οἴεσθ᾽ οὐκ ἂν αὐτὴν λαβεῖν δοθεῖσαν ὑπὸ τοῦ
πατρός; ὃς τὴν μὲν προῖκ᾽ αὐτῆς ἤδη, τὰς ὀγδοήκοντα μνᾶς, ἔχων ὡς συνοικήσων αὐτῇ, τὴν
Φιλωνίδου τοῦ Μελιτέως θυγατέρ᾽ ἔγημε· τεττάρων δὲ ταλάντων ἔνδον ὄντων, καὶ ταῦτ᾽ ἐκείνης
ἐχούσης, ὡς οὗτός φησιν, οὐκ ἂν ἡγεῖσθ᾽ αὐτὸν
κἂν ἐπιδραμεῖν, ὥστε γενέσθαι μετ᾽ ἐκείνης
57 αὐτῶν κύριον; ἢ τὴν μὲν φανερὰν οὐσίαν, ἣν καὶ
ὑμῶν πολλοὶ συνῄδεσαν ὅτι κατελείφθη, μετὰ τῶν
συνεπιτρόπων οὕτως αἰσχρῶς διήρπασεν· ὧν δ᾽ οὐκ
ἠμέλλεθ᾽ ὑμεῖς ἔσεσθαι μάρτυρες, ἀπέσχετ᾽ ἂν ἐξὸν
αὐτῷ λαβεῖν; καὶ τίς ἂν πιστεύσειεν; οὐκ ἔστι
ταῦτ᾽, ὦ ἄνδρες δικασταί, οὐκ ἔστιν, ἀλλὰ τὰ μὲν
χρήμαθ᾽, ὅσα κατέλιπεν ὁ πατήρ, πάντα τούτοις
παρέδωκεν, οὗτος δ᾽, ἵν᾽ ἧττον ἐλεηθῶ παρ᾽ ὑμῖν,
τούτοις τοῖς λόγοις χρήσεται.
58 Πολλὰ μὲν οὖν ἔγωγ᾽ ἔχω καὶ ἄλλα τούτου κατ-
ηγορεῖν· ἓν δὲ περὶ πάντων κεφάλαιον εἰπών, πάσας
αὐτοῦ διαλύσω τὰς ἀπολογίας. τούτῳ γὰρ ἐξῆν
μηδὲν ἔχειν τούτων τῶν πραγμάτων, μισθώσαντι
τὸν οἶκον κατὰ τουτουσὶ τοὺς νόμους.

Λαβὲ τοὺς νόμους καὶ ἀνάγνωθι.

NOMOI

Κατὰ τούτους τοὺς νόμους Ἀντιδώρῳ μὲν ἐκ
[832] τριῶν ταλάντων καὶ τρισχιλίων ἐν ἓξ ἔτεσιν ἓξ
τάλαντα καὶ πλέον ἐκ τοῦ μισθωθῆναι παρεδόθη,
καὶ ταῦθ᾽ ὑμῶν τινες εἶδον· Θεογένης γὰρ ὁ Προ-
βαλίσιος, ὁ μισθωσάμενος αὐτοῦ τὸν οἶκον, ἐν τῇ

ᵃ Melitè was a deme of the tribe Cecropis.
ᵇ Probalinthus was a deme of the tribe Pandionis.

44

do you suppose Aphobus would not have taken my mother to wife, bequeathed to him as she was by my father ? He had already taken her marriage-portion —the eighty minae—as though he were going to marry her ; but he subsequently married the daughter of Philonides of Melitê.[a] But if there had been four talents in the house and in her custody, as he alleges, don't you imagine he would have raced to get possession both of her and of them ? Would he have joined 57 with his co-trustees in so shamefully plundering my visible property, which many of you knew had been left me, and have refrained, when he had the chance, from seizing a fund to the evidence of which you would not be able to testify ? Who can believe this ? It is impossible, men of the jury ; it is impossible. No ; my father entrusted to these men all the property which he left, and the defendant will tell this story, that I may meet with less compassion from you.

I have many other charges to make against him, 58 but summing them all up in one, I will break down every defence of his. He could have avoided all this trouble, had he let the estate in accordance with these laws.

Take the laws and read them.

THE LAWS

In the case of Antidorus, as a result of his property having been let in accordance with these laws, there was given over to him, at the end of six years, an estate of six talents and more from an original amount of three talents and three thousand drachmae ; and this some of you have seen with your own eyes ; for Theogenes of Probalinthus,[b] who leased the estate, counted out that sum

45

59 ἀγορᾷ ταῦτα τὰ χρήματ᾽ ἐξηρίθμησεν. ἐμοὶ δ᾽ ἐκ
τεττάρων καὶ δέκα ταλάντων ἐν δέκ᾽ ἔτεσι πρὸς τὸν
χρόνον τε καὶ τὴν ἐκείνου μίσθωσιν πλέον ἢ τρι-
πλάσια κατὰ τὸ εἰκὸς προσῆκον γενέσθαι, τοῦτο
διὰ τί οὐκ ἐποίησεν, ἐρωτᾶτ᾽ αὐτόν. εἰ μὲν γὰρ
βέλτιόν φησιν εἶναι μὴ μισθωθῆναι τὸν οἶκον, δει-
ξάτω μὴ διπλάσια μηδὲ τριπλάσιά μοι γενενημένα,
ἀλλ᾽ αὐτὰ τὰ ἀρχαῖά μοι πάντ᾽ ἀποδεδομένα. εἰ δ᾽
ἐκ τεττάρων καὶ δέκα ταλάντων ἐμοὶ[1] μὲν μηδ᾽
ἑβδομήκοντα μνᾶς παραδεδώκασιν, ὁ δὲ καὶ πρὸς
ὀφείλοντά μ᾽ αὑτῷ ἀπέγραψε, πῶς ἀποδέξασθαί τι
προσήκει τούτων λεγόντων; οὐδαμῶς δήπουθεν.

60 Τοσαύτης τοίνυν οὐσίας μοι καταλειφθείσης ὅσην
ἐξ ἀρχῆς ἠκούσατε, καὶ τοῦ τρίτου μέρους πρόσοδον αὐτῆς φερούσης πεντήκοντα μνᾶς, ἐξὸν τούτοις τοῖς ἀπληστοτάτοις χρημάτων, καὶ εἰ μὴ
μισθοῦν τὸν οἶκον ἐβούλοντο, ἀπὸ μὲν τούτων τῶν
προσιόντων, ἐῶντας ὥσπερ εἶχε κατὰ χώραν, ἡμᾶς
τε τρέφειν καὶ τὰ πρὸς τὴν πόλιν διοικεῖν, καὶ ὅσ᾽

61 ἐξ αὐτῶν περιεγίγνετο, ταῦτα προσπεριποιεῖν, τὴν
δ᾽ ἄλλην οὐσίαν ἐνεργὸν ποιήσασιν, οὖσαν ταύτης
διπλασίαν, αὐτοῖς τ᾽, εἰ χρημάτων ἐπεθύμουν, μέτρι᾽
ἐξ αὐτῶν λαβεῖν, ἐμοί τε σὺν τοῖς ἀρχαίοις τὸν
οἶκον ἐκ τῶν προσόδων μείζω ποιῆσαι, τούτων μὲν
οὐδὲν ἐποίησαν, ἀποδόμενοι δ᾽ ἀλλήλοις τὰ πλείστου
[833] ἄξια τῶν ἀνδραπόδων, τὰ δὲ παντάπασιν ἀφανί-
σαντες, ἐμοῦ μὲν ἀνεῖλον καὶ τὴν ὑπάρχουσαν
πρόσοδον, σφίσι δ᾽ αὐτοῖς οὐ μικρὰν ἐκ τῶν ἐμῶν

62 κατεσκευάσαντο. λαβόντες δὲ καὶ τἄλλ᾽ αἰσχρῶς
οὑτωσὶ πάντα, πλέον ἢ τὰ ἡμίσεα τῶν χρημάτων
μηδὲ καταλειφθῆναι κοινῇ πάντες ἀμφισβητοῦσιν,

[1] ἐμοί] οἱ Blass.

46

in the market-place. But in my case, fourteen 59
talents in ten years, when consideration is given to
the time and the terms of his lease, ought to have
been more than trebled. Ask him why he did not
do this. If he declares that it was better not to let
the estate, let him show, not that it has been doubled
or trebled, but that the mere principal has been paid
back to me in full. But if out of fourteen talents
they have handed over to me not even seventy minae,
and one of them has actually recorded me as in his
debt, how can it be right to accept any word they
say? It is surely impossible.

Seeing that the fortune left me was of so great 60
value, as you heard at the beginning, the third
part of it bringing in an income of fifty minae, these
men, albeit insatiate in their greed, even if they
refused to let the property, might out of this income
and leaving the principal untouched, have maintained
us, paid the taxes to the state, and saved the residue.
The rest of the estate—an amount twice as large— 61
they might have invested profitably, and, if greedy
for money, have taken a reasonable amount for
themselves, and have increased my estate from the
income, besides keeping the principal intact. Yet
they did nothing of the sort. Instead, by selling to
one another the most valuable of the slaves and by
absolutely doing away with the rest, they destroyed
the existing source of my income and secured a
considerable one for themselves at my cost. Having 62
taken all the rest thus shamefully, they unite in
maintaining that more than half of my property
was never left to me at all. They have rendered

ὡς πεντεταλάντου δὲ μόνον τῆς οὐσίας οὔσης ἐκ
τοσαύτης τοὺς λόγους ἀπενηνόχασιν, οὐ πρόσοδον
μὲν ἐξ αὐτῶν οὐκ ἀποφαίνοντες, τὰ δὲ κεφάλαια
φανέρ' ἀποδεικνύντες, ἀλλ' αὐτὰ τὰ ἀρχαῖ' οὕτως
ἀναιδῶς ἀνηλῶσθαι φάσκοντες. καὶ οὐδ' αἰσχύ-
63 νονται ταῦτα τολμῶντες. καίτοι τί ποτ' ἂν ἔπαθον
ὑπ' αὐτῶν, εἰ πλείω χρόνον ἐπετροπεύθην; οὐκ ἂν
ἔχοιεν εἰπεῖν. ὅπου γὰρ δέκ' ἐτῶν διαγενομένων
παρὰ μὲν τῶν οὕτω μικρὰ κεκόμισμαι, τῷ δὲ καὶ
προσοφείλων ἐγγέγραμμαι, πῶς οὐκ ἄξιον διαγανα-
κτεῖν; δῆλον δὴ παντάπασιν· εἰ κατελείφθην μὲν
ἐνιαύσιος, ἐξ ἔτη δὲ προσεπετροπεύθην ὑπ' αὐτῶν,
οὐδ' ἂν τὰ μικρὰ ταῦτα παρ' αὐτῶν ἀπέλαβον. εἰ
γὰρ ἐκεῖν' ἀνήλωται ὀρθῶς, οὐδὲν ἂν τῶν νῦν
παραδοθέντων ἐξήρκεσεν εἰς ἕκτον ἔτος, ἀλλ' ἢ
παρ' αὐτῶν ἄν μ' ἔτρεφον, ἢ τῷ λιμῷ περιεῖδον
64 ἀπολόμενον. καίτοι πῶς οὐ δεινόν, εἰ ἕτεροι μὲν
οἴκοι ταλαντιαῖοι καὶ διτάλαντοι καταλειφθέντες, ἐκ
τοῦ μισθωθῆναι διπλάσιοι καὶ τριπλάσιοι γεγόνασιν,
ὥστ' ἀξιοῦσθαι λητουργεῖν, ὁ δ' ἐμὸς τριηραρχεῖν
εἰθισμένος καὶ μεγάλας εἰσφορὰς εἰσφέρειν, μηδὲ
μικρὰς δυνήσεται διὰ τὰς τούτων ἀναισχυντίας;
τίνας δ' οὗτοι λελοίπασιν ὑπερβολὰς εἰπεῖν; οἳ καὶ
[834] τὴν διαθήκην ἠφανίκασιν ὡς λήσοντες, καὶ τὰς μὲν
σφετέρας αὐτῶν οὐσίας ἐκ τῶν ἐπικαρπιῶν διῳκή-
κασι, καὶ τἀρχαῖα τῶν ὑπαρχόντων ἐκ τῶν ἐμῶν
πολλῷ μείζω πεποιήκασι, τῆς δ' ἐμῆς οὐσίας,
ὥσπερ τὰ μέγισθ' ὑφ' ἡμῶν ἀδικηθέντες, ὅλον τὸ
65 κεφάλαιον ἀνηρήκασιν; καὶ ὑμεῖς μὲν οὐδὲ τῶν εἰς

ᵃ That is, they have been classed among the wealthy
citizens. See note a on p. 10, above.

48

an account as though the estate were one of five talents only ; they do not produce the principal, though reporting no income from it, but have the impudence to tell me that the capital itself has been expended. And for this audacity they feel no shame! What, pray, would have been my plight, if I had 63 continued longer as their ward ? They would have hard work to tell. For when, after the lapse of ten years, I have recovered so little from two of these men, and by the third am even set down as a debtor, have I not good ground for indignation ? Nay, it is wholly clear. If I had been left an orphan of a year old, and had been six years longer under their guardianship, I should never have recovered even the pitiful amounts I now have. For, if the expenditures they have made were justifiable, the sums they have handed over to me would not have lasted six years, but they would either have had to support me themselves or to have let me perish from hunger. Yet 64 is it not an outrage, if estates left to others of a value of one or two talents have as a result of letting been doubled or trebled, so that the owners have been called upon for state services,[a] while mine, which has been wont to equip triremes and to make large contributions in taxes, will be unable to contribute even small sums thanks to the shameless acts of these men ? What words are gross enough to describe their conduct ? They have done away with the will, thinking to avoid discovery, their own estates they have administered from the income, and have greatly increased their capital by drawing upon my funds, while, as for my own estate, they have destroyed my entire capital, as if in requital for some grievous wrong we had done them. You, on your part, do not 65

ὑμᾶς ἁμαρτανόντων ὅταν τινὸς καταψηφίσησθε, οὐ
πάντα τὰ ὄντ᾽ ἀφείλεσθε, ἀλλ᾽ ἢ γυναῖκας¹ ἢ παιδί᾽
αὐτῶν ἐλεήσαντες μέρος τι κἀκείνοις ὑπελίπετε·
οὗτοι δὲ τοσοῦτον διαφέρουσιν ὑμῶν, ὥστε καὶ
δωρεὰς παρ᾽ ἡμῶν προσλαβόντες, ἵνα δικαίως ἐπι-
τροπεύσωσι, τοιαῦτ᾽ εἰς ἡμᾶς ὑβρίκασι. καὶ οὐδ᾽
ᾐσχύνθησαν, εἰ μὴ ἠλέησαν τὴν ἐμὴν ἀδελφήν, εἰ
δυοῖν ταλάντοιν ὑπὸ τοῦ πατρὸς ἀξιωθεῖσα, μηδενὸς
τεύξεται τῶν προσηκόντων, ἀλλ᾽ ὥσπερ ἔχθιστοί
τινες, ἀλλ᾽ οὐ φίλοι καὶ συγγενεῖς καταλειφθέντες,
οὐδὲν τῆς οἰκειότητος ἐφρόντισαν.

66 ’Αλλ᾽ ἐγὼ μὲν ὁ πάντων ταλαιπωρότατος πρὸς
ἀμφότερ᾽ ἀπορῶ, ταύτην θ᾽ ὅπως ἐκδῶ καὶ τἆλλ᾽
ὁπόθεν διοικῶ. προσεπίκειται δ᾽ ἡ πόλις ἀξιοῦσ᾽ εἰσφέρειν, δικαίως· οὐσίαν γὰρ ἱκανὴν πρὸς ταῦτα κατέλιπέ μοι ὁ πατήρ. τὰ δὲ χρήματα τὰ καταλειφθένθ᾽
67 οὗτοι πάντ᾽ εἰλήφασι. καὶ νῦν κομίσασθαι τἀμαυτοῦ
ζητῶν εἰς κίνδυνον καθέστηκα τὸν μέγιστον. ἂν
γὰρ ἀποφύγῃ μ᾽ οὗτος, ὃ μὴ γένοιτο, τὴν ἐπωβελίαν
ὀφλήσω μνᾶς ἑκατόν. καὶ τούτῳ μέν, ἐὰν καταψηφίσησθε, τιμητόν, κοὐκ ἐκ τῶν ἑαυτοῦ χρημάτων,
ἀλλ᾽ ἐκ τῶν ἐμῶν ποιήσεται τὴν ἔκτεισιν· ἐμοὶ δ᾽
ἀτίμητον τοῦτ᾽ ἔστιν, ὥστ᾽ οὐ μόνον ἔσομαι τῶν
πατρῴων ἐστερημένος, ἀλλὰ καὶ πρὸς ἠτιμωμένος,
68 ἂν μὴ νῦν ἡμᾶς ὑμεῖς ἐλεήσητε. δέομαι οὖν ὑμῶν,

¹ γυναῖκας: γυναῖκ᾽ Blass.

ᵃ The plaintiff in a private suit who was so far from being
able to prove his case that he did not receive a fifth part of
the votes, was subject to a fine of one-sixth of the damages
claimed (an obol for each drachma). Failure to pay entailed

act thus even toward those who sin against you : when you give judgement against any of them, you do not take away all that they have, but in pity for their wives and children you leave something even to these. But these men are so different from you that, although they had received legacies from us to make them administer their trust faithfully, they have done us these outrageous wrongs. They felt no touch of shame for their ruthlessness toward my sister, who, though my father left two talents as the dowry due her, will now get no fitting portion. Nay, they have recked nothing of kinship, as though they had been left to us, not as friends and kinsfolk, but as bitterest enemies.

For myself, I am the most wretched of men. 66 I am helpless both to give my sister a portion and to maintain myself. Besides this, the state is pressing me hard, demanding taxes, and with right, for my father left me an estate large enough to pay them ; but these men have taken all the money left me. And now, in seeking to recover what is mine, 67 I have come into the greatest peril ; for if the defendant is acquitted (which heaven forbid !) I shall have to pay one-sixth of the damages,[a] one hundred minae. The defendant, if you give judgement against him, will be liable for a sum to be determined, and will make payment, not out of his own funds, but out of mine ; while in my case the sum is fixed, so that I shall not only have been robbed of my inheritance, but shall also lose my civic rights, unless you now take pity on me. I beg you, therefore, men of the 68

the loss of civic rights. Compare the next oration § 18, end. In the case of Aphobus, the amount for which he would be held liable, if he lost the suit, would be fixed by the court.

ὦ ἄνδρες δικασταί, καὶ ἱκετεύω καὶ ἀντιβολῶ,
μνησθέντας καὶ τῶν νόμων καὶ τῶν ὅρκων, οὓς
ὀμόσαντες δικάζετε, βοηθῆσαι ἡμῖν τὰ δίκαια, καὶ
μὴ περὶ πλείονος τὰς τούτου δεήσεις ἢ τὰς ἡμετέρας ποιήσασθαι. δίκαιοι δ᾽ ἔστ᾽ ἐλεεῖν οὐ τοὺς
ἀδίκους τῶν ἀνθρώπων, ἀλλὰ τοὺς παρὰ λόγον
δυστυχοῦντας, οὐδὲ τοὺς ὠμῶς οὕτως τἀλλότρι᾽
ἀποστεροῦντας, ἀλλ᾽ ἡμᾶς τοὺς πολὺν χρόνον ὧν ὁ
πατὴρ ἡμῖν κατέλιπε στερομένους καὶ πρὸς ὑπὸ
τούτων ὑβριζομένους καὶ νῦν περὶ ἀτιμίας κινδυ-
69 νεύοντας. μέγα δ᾽ ἂν οἶμαι στενάξαι τὸν πατέρ᾽
ἡμῶν, εἰ αἴσθοιτο τῶν προικῶν καὶ τῶν δωρειῶν,
ὧν αὐτὸς τούτοις ἔδωκεν, ὑπὲρ τούτων τῆς ἐπωβελίας τὸν αὑτοῦ υἱὸν ἐμὲ κινδυνεύοντα, καὶ ἄλλους
μέν τινας ἤδη τῶν πολιτῶν οὐ μόνον συγγενῶν,
ἀλλὰ καὶ φίλων ἀνδρῶν ἀπορούντων θυγατέρας
παρὰ σφῶν αὐτῶν ἐκδόντας, Ἄφοβον δὲ μηδ᾽ ἣν
ἔλαβε προῖκ᾽ ἐθέλοντ᾽ ἀποδοῦναι, καὶ ταῦτ᾽ ἔτει
δεκάτῳ.

jury, I entreat, I implore you, to remember the laws and the oaths which you took as jurors, to render me the aid that is my due, and not to count the pleas of this man of higher worth than mine. It is your duty to show pity, not toward the guilty, but toward those in unmerited misfortune ; not upon those who so cruelly rob another of his goods, but upon me, who have for so long a time been deprived of my inheritance and treated with outrage by these men, and who am now in danger of losing my civic rights. Loudly methinks, would my father groan, should he 69 learn that I, his son, am in danger of being forced to pay the sixth part of the marriage-portions and legacies given by himself to these men ; and that, while others of our countrymen out of their own funds have dowered the daughters of impoverished kinsfolk and even friends, Aphobus refuses to pay back even the marriage-portion which he took, and that too in the tenth year.

AGAINST APHOBUS
II

INTRODUCTION

THIS second speech against Aphobus was delivered in reply to one which the latter had made, in which he had charged that Gylon, the maternal grandfather of Demosthenes, had been a debtor to the state. For that reason, he alleged, the father of Demosthenes had sought to conceal his fortune and had urged his executors to keep his will from coming to light.

Demosthenes' reply is the natural one that the question was not whether his grandfather had been thus indebted to the state, but whether the obligation still existed. That this was not the case, but that the indebtedness had been paid in full before Gylon's death he makes clear, and easily refutes the charge that his father sought to hide the fact of his wealth.

Precisely what the indebtedness was, and how it was incurred, are matters about which we lack definite information.

Gylon, we are told by Aeschines (*Against Ctesiphon*, §§ 172 f.) in the closing years of the Peloponnesian war, had betrayed to the enemy the harbour of Nymphaeum in the Tauric Chersonesus, and for this crime had been impeached by the Athenians. Not daring to stand trial he had fled to the Bosporus, where, having received an estate as a reward for his treason, he had settled down. There he married a wealthy lady (Aeschines calls her a Scythian), who brought him a large dowry. By her he had two daughters, whom he subsequently sent with ample means to Athens. In Athens both of them found husbands. One wedded Demochares, and the other Demosthenes, the father of the orator, in defiance, Aeschines states, of the law whereby marriage with an alien entailed illegitimacy upon the children born of such a union. Aeschines therefore calls Demosthenes " a Scythian on his mother's side, a barbarian, Greek only in speech " (τὰ ἀπὸ τῆς μητρὸς Σκύθης, βάρβαρος ἑλληνίζων τῇ φωνῇ).

In weighing these statements we must remember the vicious habit of vilification so often indulged in by the Attic orators, and the glaring disregard of facts which often accompanied it. That Demosthenes was in truth an alien it is impossible to believe. Aeschines himself and the other enemies of the orator would surely have made capital out of such a charge, could it have been substantiated. It is easy to assume that Gylon wedded a Greek woman—the whole of the region about the Bosporus was studded with Greek settlements—or the orator's mother may have been born before 403 B.C., the date when the law to which Aeschines alludes was enacted.

The charge, too, that Gylon was condemned to death for treason may also be a distortion of the truth. As to it Plutarch (*Demos.* iv.) was as much in the dark as we. It seems clear that it would have in any case been impossible for Athens to maintain her control over outlying stations, such as Nymphaeum, and to surrender it, not to " the enemy " but to a friendly power before it was forcibly taken by the Peloponnesians, may have seemed a venial offence, if not a stroke of wise policy. For his act

Gylon may have been fined, or, if the harsher sentence was imposed, it may have been commuted. Otherwise Gylon would hardly have sent his daughters to reside in Athens. Aphobus makes no more serious charge than that Gylon was, or had been, a state-debtor ; which suggests a fine.

XXVIII

KAT' ΑΦΟΒΟΥ

B

Πολλὰ καὶ μεγάλ' ἐψευσμένου πρὸς ὑμᾶς 'Αφό-
βου, τοῦτ' αὐτὸν ἐλέγξαι πειράσομαι πρῶτον, ἐφ'
ᾧ μάλιστ' ἠγανάκτησα τῶν ῥηθέντων. εἶπε γὰρ
[836] ὡς ὁ πάππος ὤφειλε τῷ δημοσίῳ, καὶ διὰ ταῦθ' ὁ
πατὴρ οὐκ ἐβούλετο μισθωθῆναι τὸν οἶκον, ἵνα μὴ
κινδυνεύσῃ. καὶ τὴν μὲν πρόφασιν ποιεῖται ταύτην,
ὡς δ' ὀφείλων ἐτελεύτησεν ἐκεῖνος, οὐδεμίαν παρ-
έσχετο μαρτυρίαν· ἀλλ' ὡς μὲν ὦφλεν, ἐνεβάλετο
τηρήσας τὴν τελευταίαν ἡμέραν, ταύτην δ' εἰς τὸν
ὕστερον λόγον ὑπελίπετο, ὡς διαβαλεῖν τὸ πρᾶγμ'
2 ἐξ αὐτῆς δυνησόμενος. ἐὰν οὖν ἀναγνῷ, προσέχετ'
αὐτῇ τὸν νοῦν· εὑρήσετε γὰρ οὐχ ὡς ὀφείλει με-
μαρτυρημένον, ἀλλ' ὡς ὦφλεν. τοῦτ' οὖν ἐλέγξαι
πειράσομαι πρῶτον, ἐφ' ᾧ φρονεῖ μάλιστα· ὃ καὶ

---

^a The property would be let at a public hearing before
the Archon, and its value could not be concealed. If, therefore, the elder Demosthenes, as the heir of Gylon, was
indebted to the state, the property might be confiscated to
satisfy the debt.

^b All documents, citations of statutes, etc., pertaining to
the case had to be submitted in written form before the suit
was called. They were then sealed in a box (ἐχῖνος), which

XXVIII

AGAINST APHOBUS

II

Of the many outrageous lies which Aphobus uttered in his address to you, I shall try to refute, first, that one at which I felt greater indignation than at anything else he said. For he declared that my grandfather was a debtor to the state, and that for this reason my father would not have the property let, for fear of the risks he would run.[a] This is the pretence he uses ; but he brought forward no proof that my grandfather died indebted to the state. He did introduce evidence that he became a state-debtor, but he waited until the last day,[b] and kept this evidence for his second speech, thinking that by it he would be able to give a malicious turn to the matter. So, if he reads it, give close heed. For you **2** will find that the evidence adduced proves not that my grandfather is a state-debtor, but that he was one. I shall undertake first to refute this charge of which he thinks to make so much, and which we

might not be opened until the documents in question were wanted in the trial. By waiting until the last day to file this particular bit of evidence Aphobus prevented Demosthenes from filing any documents to combat it. The latter was therefore " ensnared by lack of time " (§ 2).

ἡμεῖς ἀμφισβητοῦμεν. εἰ μὲν οὖν τότ' ἐξεγένετο
καὶ μὴ τῷ χρόνῳ τοῦτ' ἐνηδρεύθημεν, παρεσχόμεθ'
ἂν μάρτυρας, ὡς ἐξετείσθη τὰ χρήματα καὶ πάντ'
αὐτῷ διελέλυτο τὰ πρὸς τὴν πόλιν· νῦν δὲ τεκμηρίοις μεγάλοις ἐπιδείξομεν, ὡς οὔτ' ὤφειλεν οὔτ'
ἦν κίνδυνος οὐδεὶς ἡμῖν φανερὰ κεκτημένοις τὰ
ὄντα.

3 Πρῶτον μὲν γὰρ Δημοχάρης, ἔχων ἀδελφὴν τῆς
ἐμῆς μητρός, θυγατέρα δὲ Γύλωνος, οὐκ ἀπο-
κέκρυπται τὴν οὐσίαν, ἀλλὰ χορηγεῖ καὶ τριηραρχεῖ
καὶ τὰς ἄλλας λῃτουργίας λῃτουργεῖ καὶ οὐδὲν τῶν
τοιούτων δέδοικεν. ἔπειτ' αὐτὸς ὁ πατὴρ τήν τ'
ἄλλην οὐσίαν καὶ τέτταρα τάλαντα καὶ τρισχιλίας
φανερὰς ἐποίησεν, ἃς οὗτοι γραφῆναί τ' ἐν ταῖς
διαθήκαις καὶ λαβεῖν σφᾶς αὐτοὺς κατ' ἀλλήλων
4 καταμαρτυροῦσιν. ἔτι δὲ καὶ αὐτὸς Ἄφοβος μετὰ
τῶν συνεπιτρόπων τῇ πόλει τὸ πλῆθος τῶν καταλειφθέντων χρημάτων ἐμφανὲς ἐποίησεν, ἡγεμόνα
με τῆς συμμορίας καταστήσας οὐκ ἐπὶ μικροῖς
[837] τιμήμασιν, ἀλλ' ἐπὶ τηλικούτοις, ὥστε κατὰ τὰς
πέντε καὶ εἴκοσι μνᾶς πεντακοσίας εἰσφέρειν. καίτοι
τούτων εἴ τι ἦν ἀληθές, οὐδὲν ἂν αὐτῶν ἐποίησεν,
ἀλλὰ πάντ' ἂν ηὐλαβήθη. νῦν δὲ καὶ Δημοχάρης
καὶ ὁ πατὴρ καὶ αὐτοὶ οὗτοι φαίνονται φανερὰ
ποιοῦντες, καὶ οὐδένα τοιοῦτον κίνδυνον δεδιότες.

5 Πάντων δ' ἀτοπώτατόν ἐστι, λέγοντας ὡς ὁ πατὴρ
οὐκ εἴα μισθοῦν τὸν οἶκον, τὴν μὲν διαθήκην μη-
δαμοῦ ταύτην ἀποφαίνειν, ἐξ ἧς ἦν εἰδέναι τἀκριβές,

---

^a See the preceding oration, § 7, with the notes.

declare to be false. If I had been able to do so, and had not been thus ensnared by lack of time, I should have brought forward witnesses to prove that the money was paid in full, and that everything was settled between my grandfather and the state; as it is, I shall show by strong proofs that he was not indebted at the time of his death, and that we incurred no risks in letting our wealth be known.

In the first place Demochares, who married my 3 mother's sister, a daughter of Gylon, has not concealed his property, but acts as choregus and as trierarch, and performs other public services, without any fear of such consequences. In the second place, my father voluntarily revealed the rest of his property, and in particular the four talents and three thousand drachmae, which these men by their accusations against one another admit to have been mentioned in the will, and to have been received by them. Furthermore, Aphobus himself in conjunction with 4 his co-trustees revealed to the state the amount of the property left me, when he appointed me leader of the tax-group and that at no low rating, but at one so high as to entail a payment of five hundred drachmae on each twenty-five minae.[a] And yet, if there were any truth in what he says, he would not have acted thus, but would have taken every precaution. But, as it is, Demochares, and my father, and these men themselves have manifestly let their wealth be known; they plainly feared no such risk as that of which he speaks.

Strangest of all is it that, though they allege that 5 my father would not permit them to let the property, they should never produce this will from which one could have learned the truth, and that having de-

τηλικαύτην δ' ἀνελόντας μαρτυρίαν οὕτως οἴεσθαι
δεῖν εἰκῇ πιστεύεσθαι παρ' ὑμῖν. ἀλλ' ἐχρῆν,
ἐπειδὴ τάχιστ' ἐτελεύτησεν ὁ πατήρ, εἰσκαλέσαντας
μάρτυρας πολλοὺς παρασημήνασθαι κελεῦσαι τὰς
διαθήκας, ἵν' εἴ τι ἐγίγνετ' ἀμφισβητήσιμον, ἦν εἰς
τὰ γράμματα ταῦτ' ἐπανελθεῖν καὶ τὴν ἀλήθειαν
6 πάντων εὑρεῖν. νῦν δ' ἕτερα μὲν παρασημήνασθαι ἠξίωσαν, ἐν οἷς πολλὰ τῶν καταλειπομένων
οὐκ ἐγέγραπτο, ὑπομνήματα δ' ἦν· αὐτὴν δὲ τὴν
διαθήκην, δι' ἧς καὶ τούτων ὧν ἐσημήναντο
γραμμάτων καὶ τῶν ἄλλων ἁπάντων χρημάτων
ἐγίγνοντο κύριοι, καὶ τοῦ μὴ μισθοῦν τὸν οἶκον
τῆς αἰτίας ἀπελέλυντο, ταύτην δ' οὐκ ἐσημήναντο.
οὐδ' αὐτὴν ἀπέδοσαν. ἄξιόν γε πιστεύειν αὐτοῖς
ὅ τι ἂν περὶ τούτων λέγωσιν.

7 Ἀλλ' ἔγωγ' οὐκ οἶδ' ὅ τι τοῦτ' ἔστιν. οὐκ εἴα
μισθοῦν τὸν οἶκον οὐδ' ἐμφανῆ τὰ χρήματα ποιεῖν
ὁ πατήρ. πότερον ἐμοί[1]; ἢ τῇ πόλει; φαίνεσθε
μὲν γὰρ τοὐναντίον ἐκείνῃ μὲν φανερὰ ποιήσαντες,
ἐμοὶ δὲ παντάπασιν ἀφανῆ πεποιηκότες, καὶ οὐδὲ
ταῦτ' ἀποφαίνοντες, ἐξ ὧν τιμησάμενοι τὰς εἰσ-
[838] φορὰς εἰσεφέρετε. δείξατε γὰρ ταύτην τὴν οὐσίαν,
8 τίς ἦν καὶ ποῦ παρέδοτέ μοι καὶ τίνος ἐναντίον. τὰ
μὲν γὰρ δύο τάλαντα καὶ τὰς ὀγδοήκοντα μνᾶς ἀπὸ
τῶν τεττάρων ταλάντων καὶ τρισχιλίων ἐλάβετε,
ὥστ' οὐδὲ ταύτας ὑπὲρ ἐμοῦ εἰς τὸ δημόσιον
ἐτιμήσασθε· ὑμέτεραι γὰρ ἦσαν ἐν ἐκείνοις τοῖς
χρόνοις. ἀλλὰ μὴν ἔκ γε τῆς οἰκίας καὶ τῶν
τεττάρων καὶ δέκ' ἀνδραπόδων καὶ τῶν τριάκοντα
μνῶν, ἅ μοι παρεδώκατε, τὴν εἰσφορὰν οὐχ οἷον

---

[1] ἐμοί] ἐμοὶ ταῦτ' Blass.

64

stroyed so important a piece of evidence, they should expect you to believe them on their mere word. It was their duty, on the contrary, as soon as my father died, to call in a number of witnesses and to bid them seal the will, so that, in case any dispute should arise, it would have been possible to refer to the writing itself, and so learn the whole truth. But, as 6 it is, they thought proper to have some other papers sealed, in which many items of the property left were not inscribed—papers which were mere memoranda ; but the will itself, which gave them possession of the papers to which they affixed their seals, and all the rest of the property, and which acquitted them of all responsibility for not letting the estate, they did not seal, nor yet produce. You ought presumably to believe them in anything they say about this matter !

I, for my part, cannot understand what it is they 7 mean. My father, they say, would not suffer them to let the estate, or to disclose the value of the property. To me, do you mean, or to the state ? Quite the contrary : you have plainly disclosed it to the state, but have hidden it absolutely from me. You have not even revealed the fund which was the basis for your assessment in the payment of the property-tax. Show me this fund. What was it ? Where did you deliver it over to me, and in whose presence ? Of the four talents and three thousand drachmae, 8 you received the two talents and eighty minae, so that you did not include even these in the return you made on my behalf to the public treasury ; for at that time they were your property. But the house and the fourteen slaves and the thirty minae which you gave over into my hands, could not have been

τε γενέσθαι τοσαύτην, ὅσην ὑμεῖς συνετάξασθε πρὸς
9 τὴν συμμορίαν. ἀλλ' ἀνάγκη μεγάλη τὰ καταλειφθέντα, πολλῷ πλεῖον' ὄντα τούτων, πάνθ' ὑμᾶς
ἔχειν ἐστίν, ἃ φανερῶς ὅτι διηρπάκατ' ἐξελεγχόμενοι τοιαῦτα πλάττεσθαι τολμᾶτε. καὶ τοτὲ μὲν
εἰς ἀλλήλους ἀναφέρετε, πάλιν δ' εἰληφέναι κατ'
ἀλλήλων μαρτυρεῖτε. φάσκοντες δ' οὐ πολλὰ
λαβεῖν, μεγάλων ἀναλωμάτων λόγους ἀπενηνόχατε.
10 πάντες δὲ κοινῇ μ' ἐπιτροπεύσαντες, ἰδίᾳ μετὰ
ταῦθ' ἕκαστοι μηχανᾶσθε. καὶ τὴν μὲν διαθήκην
ἠφανίκατε, ἐξ ἧς ἦν εἰδέναι περὶ πάντων τὴν ἀλήθειαν, φαίνεσθε δ' οὐδέποτε ταὐτὰ περὶ ἀλλήλων
λέγοντες.

Λαβὲ δὴ τὰς μαρτυρίας καὶ ἀνάγνωθ' αὐτοῖς
πάσας ἐφεξῆς, ἵνα μνησθέντες καὶ τῶν μεμαρτυρημένων καὶ τῶν εἰρημένων ἀκριβέστερον γιγνώ-
σκωσι περὶ αὐτῶν.

MAPTYPIAI

11   Ταῦθ' οὗτοι πρὸς πεντεκαιδεκαταλάντους οἴκους
συνετιμήσανθ' ὑπὲρ ἐμοῦ· μνῶν δ' οὐδ' ἑβδομήκοντ'
ἀξίαν μοι παραδεδώκασι τὴν οὐσίαν τρεῖς ὄντες.
Λέγε τὰς ἐφεξῆς.

MAPTYPIAI

Ταύτην τὴν προῖκα οἵ τ' ἐπίτροποι καταμαρτυροῦσιν αὐτὸν λαβεῖν, ἄλλοι τε πρὸς οὓς ἔχειν
ὡμολόγησε. ταύτην οὔτ' αὐτὴν οὔτε τὸν σῖτον
ἀποδέδωκεν.

Λάβ' ἄλλας καὶ ἀναγίγνωσκε.

66

assessed at any such sum as that which you agreed to pay to the tax-group. Nay ; it is absolutely certain 9 that the property left by my father was much more than this, and that it is all in your possession. It is because you are plainly proved to have made havoc of it that you have the audacity to make up such falsehoods. Sometimes you refer the responsibility to one another ; again you mutually accuse one another of having received funds ; you claim to have received but little, yet you have made reports of large expenditures. You have acted jointly as my 10 guardians, but thereafter you scheme each one for himself. The will from which we could have learned the truth about everything you have made to disappear ; and it appears that you are never in agreement when you speak of one another.

Take the depositions and read them all in turn to the jury, that they may bear in mind the testimony that has been brought and the statements that have been made, and so reach a more correct decision.

THE DEPOSITIONS

There you have the assessment to which these men 11 consented in my name, placing my estate in the class of those possessing fifteen talents, whereas the property which the three together have handed over to me is not worth seventy minae.

Read the next.

THE DEPOSITIONS

This dowry, his possession of which is proved by the testimony of the trustees and of others to whom he confessed that he had received it, he has never paid back, nor has he furnished maintenance.

Take the others and read them.

12 Δύ' ἔτη τὸ ἐργαστήριον διοικήσας, Θηριππίδῃ
μὲν ἀποδέδωκε τὴν μίσθωσιν· ἐμοὶ δέ, δυοῖν ἐτοῖν
λαβὼν τὴν πρόσοδον, τριάκοντα μνᾶς, οὔτ' αὐτὰς
οὔτε τὸ ἔργον ἀποδέδωκεν.

Λάβ' ἑτέραν καὶ ἀνάγνωθι.

Ταῦτα τἀνδράποδ' ὡς αὐτὸν λαβὼν οὗτος, καὶ
τἆλλα τὰ μετὰ τούτων ὑποτεθένθ' ἡμῖν, ἀνάλωμα
μὲν εἰς αὐτὰ τοσοῦτο λελόγισται, λῆμμα δ' ἀπ'
αὐτῶν οὐδ' ὁτιοῦν, καὶ αὐτοὺς δὲ τοὺς ἀνθρώπους
ἠφάνικεν, οἳ δώδεκα μνᾶς ἀτελεῖς ἑκάστου τοῦ
ἐνιαυτοῦ προσέφερον.

Λέγ' ἑτέραν.

13 Τοῦτον τὸν ἐλέφαντα καὶ τὸν σίδηρον πεπρακὼς
οὐδὲ καταλειφθῆναί φησιν, ἀλλὰ καὶ τούτων τὴν
τιμὴν ἀποστερεῖ με, μάλιστα τάλαντον.

Λέγε ταυτασί.

Ταῦθ' οὗτος τρία τάλαντα καὶ χιλίας ἔχει χωρὶς
τῶν ἄλλων. καὶ τοῦ μὲν ἀρχαίου πέντε τάλαντ'
εἴληφε· σὺν δὲ τοῖς ἔργοις, ἂν ἐπὶ δραχμῇ τις τιθῇ
μόνον, πλέον ἢ δέκα τάλαντ' ἔχει.

Λέγε τὰς ἐφεξῆς.

14 Ταῦθ' οὗτοι γραφῆναί τ' ἐν ταῖς διαθήκαις καὶ
λαβεῖν σφᾶς αὐτοὺς κατ' ἀλλήλων μαρτυροῦσιν.

THE DEPOSITIONS

For two years he conducted the business of the 12
factory and paid to Therippides the hire of the slaves,
but to me, though he took the profits for two years,
amounting to thirty minae, he has turned over neither
that sum nor the interest upon it.

Take and read the next.

THE DEPOSITION

These slaves the defendant took to himself, together with all the other things given to us as surety
with them. He has reckoned up so heavy an outlay
for their maintenance, but absolutely nothing as profit
from them ; and the men themselves he has made
to vanish, though they brought in a clear profit of
twelve minae each year.

Read the next.

THE DEPOSITION

After selling this ivory and iron, he declares that 13
none had been left me, but tries to defraud me of
the value of these articles also, about a talent.

Read these.

THE DEPOSITIONS

These three talents and one thousand drachmae he
has in his hands besides the rest—five talents of
capital of which he has taken possession. Adding
the interest, if one reckons it at a drachma a month
only, he holds more than ten talents.

Read the next ones.

THE DEPOSITIONS

That these items were written in the will, and 14
were received by them, is proved by their testimony

οὗτος δὲ καὶ μεταπεμφθῆναι φάσκων ὑπὸ τοῦ
[840] πατρός, καὶ ἐλθὼν εἰς τὴν οἰκίαν, εἰσελθεῖν μὲν οὔ
φησιν ὡς τὸν μεταπεμψάμενον, οὐδ᾽ ὁμολογῆσαι
περὶ τούτων οὐδέν, Δημοφῶντος δ᾽ ἀκοῦσαι γραμματεῖον ἀναγιγνώσκοντος καὶ Θηριππίδου λέγοντος
ὡς ἐκεῖνος ταῦτα διέθετο, καὶ προεισεληλυθὼς καὶ
ἅπαντα διωμολογημένος πρὸς τὸν πατέρα, ἅπερ
15 ἐκεῖνος γράψας κατέλιπεν. ὁ γὰρ πατήρ, ὦ ἄνδρες
δικασταί, ὡς ᾔσθετο τὴν νόσον οὐκ ἀποφευξόμενος,
συγκαλέσας τούτους τρεῖς ὄντας, καὶ συμπαρα-
καθισάμενος Δήμωνα τὸν ἀδελφόν, τὰ σώμαθ᾽
ἡμῶν εἰς τὰς χεῖρας ἐνέθηκε παρακαταθήκην ἐπ-
ονομάζων, τὴν μὲν ἀδελφὴν Δημοφῶντι καὶ δύο
τάλαντα προῖκα διδοὺς εὐθύς, καὶ γυναῖκ᾽ αὐτῷ
ταύτην ἐγγυῶν, ἐμὲ δὲ πᾶσι κοινῇ μετὰ τῶν χρημάτων παρακατατιθέμενος, καὶ ἐπισκήπτων μι-
σθῶσαί τε τὸν οἶκον καὶ διασῶσαί μοι τὴν οὐσίαν,
16 διδοὺς ἅμα Θηριππίδῃ τε τὰς ἑβδομήκοντα μνᾶς,
καὶ τούτῳ τήν τ᾽ ἐμὴν μητέρ᾽ ἐγγυῶν ἐπὶ ταῖς
ὀγδοήκοντα μναῖς, κἄμ᾽ εἰς τὰ τούτου γόνατα
τιθείς· ὧν οὗτος ὁ πάντων ἀνθρώπων ἀνοσιώτατος
οὐδένα[1] λόγον ἐποιήσατο, κύριος τῶν ἐμῶν γενόμενος ἐπὶ τούτοις, ἀλλὰ τὰ χρήματά με[2] πάντ᾽
ἀπεστερηκὼς μετὰ τῶν συνεπιτρόπων, ἐλεεῖσθαι
νῦν ὑφ᾽ ὑμῶν ἀξιώσει, μνῶν οὐδ᾽ ἑβδομήκοντ᾽ ἄξια
τρίτος αὐτὸς ἀποδεδωκώς, εἶτα καὶ τούτοις αὐτοῖς
17 πάλιν ἐπιβεβουλευκώς. ὡς γὰρ τὰς δίκας ταύτας
ἔμελλον εἰσιέναι κατ᾽ αὐτῶν, ἀντίδοσιν ἐπ᾽ ἐμὲ
παρεσκεύασαν, ἵν᾽ εἰ μὲν ἀντιδοίην, μὴ ἐξείη μοι

---

[1] οὐδένα] οὐδενὸς Blass. [2] με omitted by Blass.

ᵃ See note a on p. 4.

against one another. But Aphobus, though admitting that he was sent for by my father, and though he came to the house, declares that he did not come into the presence of my father, who had sent for him, nor enter into any agreement in regard to these matters, but merely heard Demophon read a document and Therippides say that my father made these arrangements; whereas in fact he was the first to go in and had agreed with my father to carry out in all respects precisely what he wrote in his will. For my father, men **15** of the jury, when he saw that he was not to recover from his sickness, called together these three men, and causing his brother Demon to sit with them by his side, placed our persons in their hands, calling us a sacred deposit. My sister he gave to Demophon with a dowry of two talents to be paid at once, and betrothed her to him in marriage; me, together with my property, he committed to the care of them all in common, charging them to let the property, and by their joint efforts to preserve the estate for me. At **16** the same time he gave to Therippides the seventy minae, and betrothed my mother to the defendant with her portion of eighty minae, and placed me on his knees. To all this Aphobus, the most impious of men, has paid no heed, although these were the terms upon which he became possessed of my estate. Nay, after joining with his co-trustees in robbing me of everything, he will now claim your compassion, although what he with the two others has paid back to me does not amount even to seventy minae, and even this he is plotting to get back again. For when I **17** was on the point of instituting this suit against them they attacked me by having an exchange of estates tendered me,[a] in order that, if I accepted it, I might

DEMOSTHENES

πρὸς αὐτοὺς ἀντιδικεῖν, ὡς καὶ τῶν δικῶν τούτων
[841] τοῦ ἀντιδόντος γιγνομένων, εἰ δὲ μηδὲν τούτων
ποιοίην, ἵν' ἐκ βραχείας οὐσίας λῃτουργῶν παντάπασιν ἀναιρεθείην. καὶ τοῦτ' αὐτοῖς ὑπηρέτησε
Θρασύλοχος ὁ Ἀναγυράσιος· ᾧ τούτων οὐδὲν ἐν-
θυμηθεὶς ἀντέδωκα μέν, ἀπέκλεισα δ' ὡς διαδικα-
σίας τευξόμενος· οὐ τυχὼν δὲ ταύτης, τῶν χρόνων
ὑπογύων ὄντων, ἵνα μὴ στερηθῶ τῶν δικῶν,
ἀπέτεισα τὴν λῃτουργίαν ὑποθεὶς τὴν οἰκίαν καὶ
τἀμαυτοῦ πάντα, βουλόμενος εἰς ὑμᾶς εἰσελθεῖν
τὰς πρὸς τουτουσὶ δίκας.

18 Ἆρ' οὐ μεγάλα μὲν ἐξ ἀρχῆς ἠδίκημαι, μεγάλα
δ', ὅτι δίκην ζητῶ λαβεῖν, νῦν ὑπ' αὐτῶν βλά-
πτομαι; τίς δ' οὐκ ἂν ὑμῶν τούτῳ μὲν φθονήσειε
δικαίως, ἡμᾶς δ' ἐλεήσειεν, ὁρῶν τῷ μὲν πρὸς τῇ
οὐσίᾳ τῇ παραδοθείσῃ πλεῖν ἢ δέκα ταλάντων τὴν
ἐμὴν τοσαύτην οὖσαν προσγεγενημένην, ἡμᾶς δὲ μὴ
μόνον τῶν πατρῴων διημαρτηκότας, ἀλλὰ καὶ τῶν
νῦν παραδοθέντων διὰ τὴν τούτων πονηρίαν ἀπ-
εστερημένους; ποῖ δ' ἂν τραποίμεθα, εἴ τι ἄλλο
ψηφίσαισθ' ὑμεῖς περὶ αὐτῶν; εἰς τὰ ὑποκείμενα
τοῖς δανείσασιν; ἀλλὰ τῶν ὑποθεμένων ἐστίν. ἀλλ'

ᵃ That is, they hoped that the exchange of properties, if
carried out, would transfer to Thrasylochus also the claims
of Demosthenes against them, and so debar the latter from
taking further action.

ᵇ Thrasylochus was the brother of the Meidias against
whom Demosthenes brought action for assault (see Oration
XXI.). Anagyrus was a deme of the tribe Erechtheïs.

ᶜ If the exchange of properties was accepted, either party
had the right to enter and search the house and land cf
the other. Demosthenes denies this right to Thrasylochus,
hoping that he might win a decision from the generals, before

72

not be allowed to pursue my action against them,[a] since (they thought) this suit would then belong to the one tendering the exchange ; and if I did not do so, I might undertake the service with slender means, and so be absolutely ruined. In this matter Thrasylochus of Anagyrus [b] was their tool. I, with no thought of the consequences, accepted the exchange with him, but excluded him from the premises hoping to win a court decision,[c] but, failing of this, and being hard pressed for time, rather than be forced to give up my suit, I mortgaged my house and all my property, and paid the cost of the service in question,[d] being eager to bring before you my suit against these men.

Is not the wrong I have suffered from the beginning **18** great indeed, and great the harm they are striving to do me now, because I seek to obtain redress ? Who of you would not rightly feel indignation against this man and pity for me, seeing that to the estate of more than ten talents which he inherited there has been added my own of such considerable size, while I have not only been defrauded of my inheritance, but am by the rascality of these men being robbed even of what they have now repaid me ? To what are we to turn, if you give an adverse decision regarding them ? To the goods mortgaged to our creditors ? But they belong to the holders of

whom such cases were heard, as to whether or not his claim against his guardians would pass to Thrasylochus together with his visible property. From the oration against Meidias we learn that Meidias and Thrasylochus came jointly to Demosthenes' house, and with great violence forced themselves even into the women's apartments before they were finally ejected.

[d] The service was the trierarchy, and the cost entailed amounted to twenty minae.

εἰς τὰ περιόντ' αὐτῶν· ἀλλὰ τούτου γίγνεται, τὴν
19 ἐπωβελίαν ἐὰν ὄφλωμεν. μηδαμῶς, ὦ ἄνδρες
δικασταί, γένησθ' ἡμῖν τοσούτων αἴτιοι κακῶν·
μηδὲ τὴν μητέρα κἀμὲ καὶ τὴν ἀδελφὴν ἀνάξια
παθόντας περιίδητε, οὓς ὁ πατὴρ οὐκ ἐπὶ ταύταις
ταῖς ἐλπίσι κατέλιπεν, ἀλλὰ τὴν μὲν ὡς Δημοφῶντι
συνοικήσουσαν ἐπὶ δυοῖν ταλάντοιν προικί, τὴν
[842] δ' ἐπ' ὀγδοήκοντα μναῖς τούτῳ τῷ σχετλιωτάτῳ
πάντων ἀνθρώπων, ἐμὲ δ' ὑμῖν διάδοχον ἀνθ' αὑτοῦ
20 τῶν λῃτουργιῶν ἐσόμενον. βοηθήσατ' οὖν ἡμῖν,
βοηθήσατε, καὶ τοῦ δικαίου καὶ ὑμῶν αὐτῶν ἕνεκα
καὶ ἡμῶν καὶ τοῦ πατρὸς τοῦ τετελευτηκότος.
σώσατ', ἐλεήσατε, ἐπειδή μ' οὗτοι συγγενεῖς ὄντες
οὐκ ἠλέησαν. εἰς ὑμᾶς καταπεφεύγαμεν. ἱκετεύω,
ἀντιβολῶ πρὸς παίδων, πρὸς γυναικῶν, πρὸς τῶν
ὄντων ἀγαθῶν ὑμῖν. οὕτως ὄναισθε τούτων, μὴ
περιίδητέ με, μηδὲ ποιήσητε τὴν μητέρα καὶ τῶν
ἐπιλοίπων ἐλπίδων εἰς τὸν βίον στερηθεῖσαν ἀνάξιον
21 αὑτῆς τι παθεῖν· ἢ νῦν μὲν οἴεται τυχόντα με τῶν
δικαίων παρ' ὑμῖν ὑποδέξεσθαι καὶ τὴν ἀδελφὴν
ἐκδώσειν· εἰ δ' ὑμεῖς ἄλλο τι γνώσεσθε, ὃ μὴ
γένοιτο, τίν' οἴεσθ' αὐτὴν ψυχὴν ἕξειν, ὅταν ἐμὲ μὲν
ἴδῃ μὴ μόνον τῶν πατρῴων ἀπεστερημένον, ἀλλὰ
καὶ πρὸς ἠτιμωμένον, περὶ δὲ τῆς ἀδελφῆς μηδ'
ἐλπίδ' ἔχουσαν ὡς τεύξεταί τινος τῶν προσηκόντων
22 διὰ τὴν ἐσομένην ἀπορίαν; οὐκ ἄξιος, ὦ ἄνδρες
δικασταί, οὔτ' ἐγὼ δίκης ἐν ὑμῖν μὴ τυχεῖν, οὔθ'
οὗτος τοσαῦτα χρήματ' ἀδίκως κατασχεῖν. ἐμοῦ

---

[a] See note a on the preceding oration, p. 50. The entire
property of the plaintiff would be exhausted in payment of
the damages imposed.

the mortgage. To what is left after the creditors are paid? But that becomes the property of the defendant, if you condemn me to pay an obol on each drachma.[a] Do not, men of the jury, be to us the 19 cause of such deep distress ; do not allow my mother, my sister and myself to suffer undeserved misfortunes. It was not to prospects such as these that my father left us. Nay, my sister was to be the wife of Demophon with a dowry of two talents, my mother the wife of this most ruthless of all men with a dowry of eighty minae, and I as my father's successor was to perform state services as he had done. Succour us, then, 20 succour us, for the sake of justice, for your own sakes, for ours, and for my dead father's sake. Save us ; have compassion on us ; since these, our relatives, have felt no compassion. It is to you that we have fled for protection. I beseech you, I implore you by your children, by your wives, by all the good things you possess. So may heaven give you joy of them, do not look upon me with indifference ; nor cause my mother, deprived of the hopes in life that are left her, to suffer a lot unworthy of her. She 21 now thinks that she is to welcome me home after I have won a just verdict from you, and that my sister will not be portionless. But, if you decide adversely (which may heaven forfend) what, think you, will be her anguish of soul when she sees me not only robbed of my patrimony, but disenfranchised as well, and has no hope that my sister will find an establishment that befits her station because of the poverty that will be ours? I have not deserved, men of the jury, to fail 22 of justice at your hands, nor has Aphobus deserved that he should retain all the money that he has wrongfully taken. Regarding myself, even though you have

μὲν γὰρ εἰ καὶ μήπω πεῖραν εἰλήφατε, ποῖός τις ἂν
εἰς ὑμᾶς εἴην, ἐλπίζειν προσήκει μὴ χείρω τοῦ
πατρὸς ἔσεσθαι. τούτου δὲ πεῖραν ἔχετε, καὶ
σαφῶς ἴσθ᾿ ὅτι πολλὴν οὐσίαν παραλαβών, οὐ μόνον
οὐδὲν πεφιλοτίμηται πρὸς ὑμᾶς, ἀλλὰ καὶ τἀλλότρι᾿
ἀποστερῶν ἀποδέδεικται.[1]

23 Ταῦτ᾿ οὖν σκοποῦντες καὶ τἄλλα μνησθέντες, ᾗ
δίκαιόν ἐστι, ταύτῃ ψηφίσασθε. πίστεις δ᾿ ἔχεθ᾿
[843] ἱκανὰς ἐκ μαρτύρων, ἐκ τεκμηρίων, ἐκ τῶν εἰκότων,
ἐξ ὧν οὗτοι λαβεῖν ὁμολογοῦντες ἀθρόα τἀμά, ταῦτ᾿
ἀνηλωκέναι φασὶν οὐκ ἀνηλωκότες, ἀλλ᾿ αὐτοὶ πάντ᾿
ἔχοντες.

24 Ὧν ἐνθυμουμένους χρὴ ποιήσασθαί τιν᾿ ἡμῶν
πρόνοιαν, εἰδότας ὅτι ἐγὼ μὲν τἀμαυτοῦ δι᾿ ὑμῶν
κομισάμενος, εἰκότως λῃτουργεῖν ἐθελήσω, χάριτας
ὀφείλων ὅτι μοι δικαίως ἀπέδοτε τὴν οὐσίαν, οὗτος δ᾿,
ἐὰν αὐτὸν ποιήσητε τῶν ἐμῶν κύριον, οὐδὲν ποιήσει
τοιοῦτον. μὴ γὰρ οἴεσθ᾿ αὐτόν, ὑπὲρ ὧν ἤρνηται
μὴ λαβεῖν, ὑπὲρ τούτων ὑμῖν λῃτουργεῖν ἐθελήσειν,
ἀλλ᾿ ἀποκρύψεσθαι μᾶλλον, ἵνα δικαίως ἀποπεφευ-
γέναι δοκῇ.

¹ ἀποδέδεικται] ἐπιδέδεικται Blass.

as yet had no experience to prove what manner of
man I am in my relations to you, yet it is fair to
expect that I shall not be worse than my father;
but of this man you have had experience, and you
know well that, though he inherited a large estate,
he has shown no generosity toward you, but has been
proven to be a defrauder of others.

Look, then, to this, and bear in mind the other facts ; 23
and then cast your vote on the side of justice.   You
have evidence that is adequate, evidence from witnesses, from depositions, from probabilities, from the
statements of these men themselves who acknowledge that they took possession of my entire estate.
They say they have spent it, but they have not spent
it ; they have it all in their own possession.

All these things should be in your minds, and you 24
should show some consideration for us, knowing that,
if I recover my property through your aid, I shall
naturally be ready to undertake public services, being
grateful to you for rightfully restoring to me my
estate ; while this fellow, if you make him master
of my goods, will do nothing of the kind.   Do not
imagine that he will be ready to undertake public
services for you on behalf of property which he denies
having received.   Nay ; he will conceal it rather,
that it may appear that he was justly acquitted.

AGAINST APHOBUS

III

INTRODUCTION

THIS oration was delivered in defence of a certain Phanus, whom Aphobus had charged with giving false testimony, hoping doubtless for a reversal of the adverse judgement given against himself.

The facts lying behind the charge are these :

Aphobus, before the suit was decided against him, had called upon Demosthenes to surrender Milyas, who had been foreman of the sword-factory (see Oration XXVII. § 19), to be examined by torture. This Demosthenes refused to do, stating that Milyas was no longer a slave, having been set free by the elder Demosthenes on his death-bed. Moreover he called upon Phanus, Philip, and Aesius, brother of Aphobus, to prove that, when questioned by the official arbitrator, Aphobus had admitted that Milyas was a freeman. Aphobus then brought suit against Phanus and Philip for giving this testimony, alleging that it was false.

Demosthenes naturally took up the defence of Phanus, for a judgement against him might have seemed to invalidate the decision of the court in his own suit against Aphobus, and have necessitated a new trial. He argues, therefore, that the testimony of Phanus was true, and claims that, even if it had been false, the fact should not prejudice his own case, for any testimony Milyas might have given would have had little bearing on the question of Aphobus's guilt or innocence.

On this speech see Schaefer, iii.[2] pp. 82 ff., and Blass, iii. pp. 232 ff. It is also discussed by Professor G. M. Calhoun in the *Transactions of the American Philological Association* for 1934, pp. 80 ff. This scholar shows how far from compelling are the arguments advanced against its authenticity.

XXIX

ΠΡΟΣ ΑΦΟΒΟΝ ΥΠΕΡ ΦΑΝΟΥ
ΨΕΥΔΟΜΑΡΤΥΡΙΩΝ

Γ

Εἰ μὴ πρότερόν μοι δίκης γενομένης πρὸς Ἄφοβον, ὦ ἄνδρες δικασταί, συνῄδειν πολλῷ τούτων
μείζω καὶ δεινότερ' αὐτοῦ ψευσαμένου ῥᾳδίως
ἐξελέγξας διὰ τὴν περιφάνειαν τῶν ἀδικημάτων,
θαυμασίως ἂν ὡς ηὐλαβούμην, μὴ καὶ νῦν οὐ
δυνηθῶ δεῖξαι, πῇ παρακρούεταί ποθ' ἕκασθ' ὑμᾶς
αὐτῶν. νῦν δέ, σὺν θεοῖς εἰπεῖν, ἄνπερ ἴσοι καὶ
κοινοὶ γένησθ' ἀκροαταί, πολλὰς ἐλπίδας ἔχω μηδὲν
ἧττον ὑμᾶς τὴν ἀναίδειαν τὴν τούτου γνώσεσθαι
τῶν πρότερον δικασάντων. καὶ ταῦτ' εἰ μὲν ἐδεῖτο
λόγου τινὸς ἢ ποικιλίας, ἔγωγε κατώκνουν ἂν τὴν
ἐμαυτοῦ καταμεμφόμενος ἡλικίαν· νῦν δ' ἁπλῶς
δεῖ διδάξαι καὶ διηγήσασθαι τὰ τούτῳ πεπραγμένα περὶ ἡμῶν· ἐκ δὲ τούτων οἶμαι πᾶσιν ὑμῖν
εὔγνωστον ἔσεσθαι, πότερός ποθ' ἡμῶν ἐσθ' ὁ
πονηρός.

2 Οἶδα μὲν οὖν ὅτι τὴν δίκην οὗτος εἴληχε ταύτην,
οὐχὶ τῷ τὰ ψευδῆ τιν' αὐτοῦ καταμεμαρτυρηκέναι
ἐξελέγξειν πιστεύων, ἀλλ' ἡγούμενος διὰ τὸ μέ-
[845] γεθος τοῦ τιμήματος τῆς δίκης, ἣν ὦφλεν, ἐμοὶ μὲν

82

XXIX

AGAINST APHOBUS IN DEFENCE OF PHANUS CHARGED WITH GIVING FALSE TESTIMONY

III

If I were not conscious, men of the jury, that in a former suit against Aphobus I had readily (so absolutely manifest were his wrongdoings) convicted him of lies greater and more outrageous than these which he now utters, I should have grave doubts of my ability to show how he seeks to lead you astray in regard to each one of them. As it is, however (be it said with the favour of heaven), if you prove fair and impartial hearers, I have strong hopes that you will become as fully aware of the shamelessness of this man as were the jurors in the former trial. If the case required eloquence or cleverness I should shrink through distrust of my youth ; but, as matters are, I need merely point out and rehearse to you what the plaintiff's conduct toward us has been. From this it will be easy, I think, for all of you to determine which of us is the villain.

I know that the plaintiff has instituted this suit, 2 not because he believes he can convict anyone of having borne false witness against him, but because he thinks that the large amount of damages which he was condemned to pay will give rise to a feeling

ἂν γενέσθαι τινὰ φθόνον, αὑτῷ δ' ἔλεον. καὶ διὰ
ταῦτα περὶ τῆς γεγενημένης δίκης νῦν ἀπολογεῖται,
περὶ ἧς τότ' οὐδὲν ἔσχε δίκαιον εἰπεῖν. ἐγὼ δ', ὦ
ἄνδρες δικασταί, εἰ μὲν ἐπεπράγμην τοῦτον τὴν
δίκην ἢ μηδὲν ἤθελον μέτριον συγχωρεῖν, ἠδίκουν
μὲν οὐδ' ἂν οὕτως, τὰ παρ' ὑμῖν γνωσθέντα πραττό-
μενος αὐτόν, ὅμως δ' ἂν εἶχέ τις εἰπεῖν, ὡς λίαν
ὠμῶς καὶ πικρῶς ὄντα συγγενῆ τοῦτον ἐκ τῆς
3 οὐσίας ἁπάσης¹ ἐκβέβληκα. νῦν δὲ τοὐναντίον
ἐστίν· οὗτος ἐμὲ τῶν πατρῴων ἁπάντων μετὰ τῶν
συνεπιτρόπων ἀπεστέρηκε, καὶ οὐδ' ἐν ὑμῖν φανερῶς ἐξελεγχθεὶς οἴεται δεῖν οὐδὲν τῶν μετρίων
ποιεῖν, ἀλλὰ διασκευασάμενος τὴν οὐσίαν, καὶ
παραδοὺς τὴν μὲν συνοικίαν Αἰσίῳ, τὸν δ' ἀγρὸν
Ὀνήτορι, πρὸς μὲν ἐκείνους δίκην καὶ πράγματ'
ἔχειν ἐμὲ πεποίηκεν, ἐκ δὲ τῆς οἰκίας αὐτὸς τὰ
σκεύη λαβὼν καὶ τἀνδράποδ' ἐξαγαγὼν καὶ τὸν
λάκκον συντρίψας καὶ τὰ θυρώματ' ἀποσπάσας καὶ
μόνον οὐκ αὐτὴν τὴν οἰκίαν ἐμπρήσας, Μέγαράδ'
ἐξῴκηκε κἀκεῖ μετοίκιον τέθηκεν. ὥστε πολὺ ἂν
δικαιότερον διὰ ταῦτα τὰ ἔργα τοῦτον μισήσαιτε,
ἢ ἐμοῦ τιν' ἀνεπιείκειαν καταγνοίητε.

4 Περὶ μὲν οὖν τῆς αἰσχροκερδείας τῆς τούτου
καὶ μιαρίας ὕστερόν μοι δοκεῖ διεξελθεῖν πρὸς ὑμᾶς·
καὶ νῦν δ' ὡς ἐν κεφαλαίοις ἀκηκόατε· περὶ δὲ
τῶν μεμαρτυρημένων, ὡς ἔστιν ἀληθῆ, περὶ ὧνπερ
οἴσετε τὴν ψῆφον, ἤδη πειράσομαι διδάσκειν ὑμᾶς.

---

¹ ἁπάσης omitted by Blass.

of prejudice against me, and of compassion toward himself. For this reason he is now seeking to defend himself against charges made in a suit that has already been decided, regarding which he had at the time no reasonable defence to make. I, for my part, men of the jury, if I had proceeded to execute the judgement against him and had been unwilling to make any reasonable concession, should even so have done no wrong in exacting the damages awarded by your decision ; but for all that it might have been said that I had shown undue ruthlessness and enmity toward a man who is a relative in depriving him of all his property. But, as it is, the precise contrary **3** is the truth. This man with his co-trustees has robbed me of my entire patrimony, and, even after being clearly convicted in your court, he does not consider himself obliged to do anything reasonable. On the contrary he has dispersed his property, giving his farm-buildings to Aesius and his farm to Onetor, against whom he has forced me to engage in a troublesome lawsuit. He himself stripped the house of its furniture, took away the slaves, destroyed the wine-vat, tore off the doors, and all but set fire to the house itself ; then he made off to Megara, where he has settled and paid the alien's tax. You would, therefore, with better ground loathe this man for deeds like these, than judge me guilty of undue severity.

Regarding the rapacity and vile character of the **4** plaintiff I purpose to speak at length before you later on, though what you have even now heard gives you a fair idea of it. But I shall now undertake to show you, that the testimony which has been given, about which you are going to cast your votes, is true. But

DEMOSTHENES

δέομαι δ' ὑμῶν, ὦ ἄνδρες δικασταί, δικαίαν δέησιν,
[846] ἐξ ἴσου ἡμῶν ἀμφοτέρων ἀκοῦσαι. τοῦτο δ' ἐστὶ
καὶ ὑπὲρ ὑμῶν ὁμοίως· ὅσῳ γὰρ ἂν ἀκριβέστερον τὰ
πεπραγμένα μάθητε, τοσούτῳ δικαιοτέραν καὶ εὐ-
5 ορκοτέραν θήσεσθε τὴν ψῆφον περὶ αὐτῶν. ἐπιδείξω δὲ τοῦτον οὐ μόνον ὡμολογηκότ' εἶναι τὸν
Μιλύαν ἐλεύθερον, ἀλλὰ καὶ φανερὸν τοῦτ' ἔργῳ
πεποιηκότα, καὶ πρὸς τούτοις ἐκ βασάνου περὶ
αὐτῶν πεφευγότα τοῦτον τοὺς ἀκριβεστάτους ἐλέγχους, καὶ οὐκ ἐθελήσαντ' ἐκ τούτων ἐπιδεῖξαι τὴν
ἀλήθειαν, ἀλλὰ πανουργοῦντα καὶ μάρτυρας ψευδεῖς
παρεχόμενον καὶ διακλέπτοντα τοῖς ἑαυτοῦ λόγοις
τὴν ἀλήθειαν τῶν πεπραγμένων, οὕτω μεγάλοις καὶ
φανεροῖς ἐλέγχοις, ὥσθ' ὑμᾶς πάντας εἴσεσθαι
σαφῶς, ὅτι ἡμεῖς μὲν ἀληθῆ λέγομεν, οὗτος δ'
οὐδὲν ὑγιὲς εἴρηκεν. ἄρξομαι δ' ἐντεῦθεν, ὅθεν καὶ
ὑμεῖς ῥᾷστ' ἂν μάθοιτε κἀγὼ τάχιστ' ἂν διδάξαιμι.
6 Ἐγὼ γάρ, ὦ ἄνδρες δικασταί, Δημοφῶντι καὶ
Θηριππίδῃ καὶ τούτῳ δίκας ἔλαχον ἐπιτροπῆς ἀπο-
στερηθεὶς ἁπάντων τῶν ὄντων. γενομένης δέ μοι
τῆς δίκης πρὸς τοῦτον πρῶτον, ἐπέδειξα σαφῶς
τοῖς δικάζουσιν, ὥσπερ ὑμῖν ἐπιδείξω, πάνθ' ὅσ'
ἡμῖν κατελείφθη χρήματ' ἀπεστερηκότα τοῦτον μετ'
7 ἐκείνων, οὐ καταψευδομαρτυρησάμενος. τεκμήριον
δὲ μέγιστον· μαρτυριῶν γὰρ πλέον ἢ πάνυ πολλῶν
τῶν ἁπασῶν ἀναγνωσθεισῶν ἐπὶ τῇ δίκῃ, καὶ τούτων τῶν μὲν ὡς ἔδοσάν τι τούτῳ τῶν ἐμῶν κατα-
μαρτυρουσῶν, τῶν δ' ὡς παρῆσαν κομιζομένῳ, τῶν

---

[a] On the high value attributed by the Greeks to evidence
secured from a slave under threat of torture *cf.* Aristotle,
Rhet. i. 15 and Dem. XXX. § 37.

one request I make of you, men of the jury, and it is a reasonable one—that you will give us both a fair hearing. This is as much in your interest as in mine, for the more accurate your knowledge of the facts, the more just and in harmony with your oaths will be the vote you will cast regarding them. I shall show 5 that Aphobus has not only acknowledged Milyas to be a freeman, but has even proved it by his actions ; that, furthermore, about this matter he has declined the absolutely sure test by torture,[a] and does not wish to have the truth brought to light; that on the contrary he has recourse to trickery, brings forward false witnesses, and by his own words distorts the truth regarding what has taken place. So strong and so plain is the evidence by which I shall prove these statements that you will all see clearly that it is I who am speaking the truth, and that he has uttered not a word worthy of credence. I shall begin at a point which will make it easiest for you to learn the facts, and for me to instruct you regarding them in the briefest time.

I instituted suit, men of the jury, against Demo- 6 phon, Therippides and the plaintiff for breach of trust in their guardianship, for I had been defrauded by them of all my inheritance. When my suit against Aphobus in the first instance came up for trial, I proved clearly to the jury, as I shall prove to you, that he, in conjunction with the others, had robbed me of all the property that had been left me ; and I relied upon no false testimony. Here is a clear 7 proof of this. A host of depositions was read at the trial, some of the deponents declaring that they had given to the plaintiff property of mine, others that he had received such property in their presence, still

δ' ὡς πριάμενοι παρὰ τούτου τούτῳ τὰς τιμὰς
διέλυσαν, οὐδ' ᾗ τινι τούτων[1] τῶν ψευδομαρτυριῶν
ἐπεσκήψατο, οὐδὲ τετόλμηκε διώκειν ἀλλ' ἢ ταύτην
[847] μίαν οὖσαν, ἐν ᾗ δραχμὴν οὐκ ἂν ἔχοι δεῖξαι μεμαρ-
τυρημένην. καίτοι τό γε τίμημα τῶν χρημάτων,
8 ὧν ἀπεστερήμην, οὐκ ἐκ ταύτης συντιθεὶς ἐλο-
γιζόμην τοσοῦτον (οὐ γὰρ ἔνεστ' ἀργύριον), ἀλλ'
ἐξ ἐκείνων καθ' ἕκαστα τιθείς, αἷς οὗτος οὐκ ἐπεσκήψατο. ὅθεν οἱ τότ' ἀκούσαντες οὐ μόνον
αὐτοῦ κατέγνωσαν, ἀλλὰ καὶ τῶν ἐπιγεγραμμένων
ἐτίμησαν. τίνος οὖν εἵνεκ' ἐκείνας μὲν εἴασε,
τῇδε δ' ἐπεσκήψατο; ἐγὼ καὶ τοῦτο διδάξω. τῶν
9 μαρτυριῶν ὅσαι μὲν αὐτοῦ χρήματ' ἔχειν κατεμαρτύρουν, ᾔδει σαφῶς ὅτι τοσούτῳ μᾶλλον
ἐλεγχθήσεται ταῦτ' ἔχων, ὅσῳ πλείων λόγος
δοθήσεται καθ' ἓν περὶ ἑκάστου. τοῦτο δ' ἔμελλεν
ἐν τῇ τῶν ψευδομαρτυριῶν ἔσεσθαι κρίσει· ὃ γὰρ
τότ' ἐν μικρῷ μέρει τινὶ τοῦ παντὸς ὕδατος μετὰ
τῶν ἄλλων κατηγορήσαμεν, νῦν πρὸς ἅπαν τὸ ὕδωρ
αὐτὸ καθ' αὑτὸ διδάξειν ἐμέλλομεν. ἀποκρίσει δ'
10 ἐπισκηψάμενος ἐνόμιζεν, ὥσπερ τόθ' ὡμολόγησεν,
οὕτω πάλιν ἔξαρνος γενέσθαι ταῦτ' ἐφ' ἑαυτῷ
γενήσεσθαι. διὰ ταῦτα τήνδε διώκει. βούλομαι
δὴ ταύτην, ὡς ἔστιν ἀληθής, ἐπιδεῖξαι σαφῶς πᾶσιν
ὑμῖν, οὐκ ἐξ εἰκότων οὐδὲ λόγων πρὸς τὸ παρὸν
μεμηχανημένων, ἀλλ' ἐκ τοῦ παρὰ πᾶσιν ὑμῖν
δόξοντος, ὡς ἐγὼ νομίζω, δικαίου. σκοπεῖτε δ'
ἀκούσαντες.

---

[1] τούτων omitted by Blass.

---

[a] That is, in attacking the testimony of the deponent he
would deny his own previous admissions.

others that they had purchased goods from him, and
paid him the price ; yet he has charged not a single
one of these with bearing false testimony. He has
dared to attack this one piece of testimony, and it
alone, although in it he cannot show that there was
mention even of one single drachma. And yet for 8
the computation of the sums of which I had been
robbed, I relied not so much on this man's testimony, for there was no mention of money in it, but
on the several statements of the others, against whom
the plaintiff has made no charges. Therefore the
jurymen who at that time heard my plea, not only
found him guilty, but fixed the damages at the full
amount stated in my complaint. Why was it, then,
that he passed over the other witnesses and sued the
defendant alone ? I will tell you. In regard to all 9
the witnesses who testified that he had received
the money, he knew that the more discussion there
should be over each separate point, the more convincingly would he be convicted of possessing it, and
this was bound to be the case in a trial for false
witness ; for the accusations which I then made
along with all the others in a small part of the time
allotted me, I should now discuss severally and in
detail in the time of an entire speech ; whereas, if 10
he attacked an answer given, he thought that as he
had made an admission before, so now it would be
in his power to make a denial.[a] That is the reason
why he attacks the testimony of this witness, the
truth of whose testimony I mean to prove conclusively to you all, not on the basis of probabilities,
or of arguments made up to fit the occasion, but by
reasoning which, I am sure, will approve itself to you
all as just and fair. Listen, and judge.

11 Ἐγὼ γάρ, ὦ ἄνδρες δικασταί, περὶ τῆς μαρτυρίας
τῆς ἐν τῷ γραμματείῳ γεγραμμένης εἰδὼς ὄντα
μοι τὸν ἀγῶνα, καὶ περὶ τούτου τὴν ψῆφον ὑμᾶς
οἴσοντας ἐπιστάμενος, ᾠήθην δεῖν μηδὲν ἄλλο τούτου πρότερον ἢ τοῦτον προκαλούμενος ἐλέγξαι.
[848] καὶ τί ποιῶ; παραδοῦναι παῖδ᾽ ἤθελον αὐτῷ
γράμματ᾽ ἐπιστάμενον βασανίζειν, ὃς παρῆν ὅθ᾽
ὡμολόγει ταῦθ᾽ οὗτος, καὶ τὴν μαρτυρίαν ἔγραφεν,
οὐδὲν ὑφ᾽ ἡμῶν κελευσθεὶς κακοτεχνεῖν, οὐδὲ τὸ
μὲν γράφειν, τὸ δ᾽ ἀφαιρεῖν ὧν οὗτος εἰρήκει περὶ
τούτων, ἀλλ᾽ ἁπλῶς ὑπὲρ τοῦ πάντα τἀληθῆ καὶ
12 τὰ τούτῳ ῥηθέντα γράψαι. καίτοι τί κάλλιον ἦν
τοῦ τὸν παῖδα στρεβλοῦντ᾽ ἐλέγξαι ψευδομένους
ἡμᾶς; ἀλλὰ συνῄδει πάντων μάλιστ᾽ ἀνθρώπων
ὅτι τἀληθῆ μεμαρτύρηται· διόπερ ἔφυγε τὴν βάσανον. ἀλλὰ μὴν οὐχ εἷς οὐδὲ δύο ταῦτ᾽ ἴσασιν,
οὐδ᾽ ὑπὸ μάλης ἡ πρόκλησις γέγονεν, ἀλλ᾽ ἐν τῇ
ἀγορᾷ μέσῃ πολλῶν παρόντων.

Καί μοι κάλει τούτων τοὺς μάρτυρας.

MAΡΤΥΡΕΣ

13 Οὕτω τοίνυν οὗτός ἐστι σοφιστὴς καὶ σφόδρ᾽
ἑκὼν τὰ δίκαι᾽ ἀγνοεῖν προσποιούμενος, ὥστε ψευδομαρτυριῶν διώκων, καὶ περὶ τούτου τὴν ψῆφον
ὑμῶν μελλόντων οἴσειν καὶ ὀμωμοκότων, περὶ τῆς
μαρτυρίας μὲν ἔφυγε τὴν βάσανον, περὶ οὗ μάλιστα
προσῆκεν αὐτῷ τὸν λόγον ποιεῖσθαι, περὶ δ᾽ ἄλλων

I knew, men of the jury, that I should find the 11
whole contest centring about the deposition inserted
in the record, and that it would be regarding the
truth or falsehood of this that you would cast your
votes, and I therefore determined that the first step
for me to take was to offer Aphobus a challenge.
What, then, did I do ? I offered to surrender to him
for examination by torture a slave who knew how
to read and write, and who had been present when
Aphobus made the admission in question, and who
wrote down the statement of the witness. This man
had been ordered by me not to use any fraud or
trickery, nor to write down some and suppress others
of the statements made by the plaintiff regarding the
matters at issue, but simply to write the absolute
truth, and what Aphobus actually said. What better 12
opportunity could he have had of convicting us of
falsehood than by putting my slave to torture ? But
Aphobus knew better than anyone else that the slave
had borne true testimony, and therefore he declined
the test. And in truth it is not one or two only who
know these facts ; the challenge was not made in secret,
but in the midst of the agora where many were present.

Call, please, the witnesses to these facts.

THE WITNESSES

The fellow is so cunning, and so ready to pretend 13
ignorance of what is right, that, although he is pressing a suit for false witness, and although you are to
cast your votes regarding this, and have sworn so
to do, he refused the proffered examination by torture
in regard to the testimony (the point to which he
should have devoted his argument), and declares that
he requires the slave to be given up for testing in

14 φησὶν ἐξαιτεῖν, ψευδόμενος. καίτοι πῶς οὐχ ὑπερ-
φυές, αὐτὸν μὲν δεινὰ πεπονθέναι φάσκειν, εἰ τὸν
ἐλεύθερον ἐξαιτῶν, ὡς ἐγὼ σαφῶς ὑμῖν ἐπιδείξω,
μὴ παρέλαβε, τοὺς δὲ μάρτυρας οὐ δεινὰ πάσχειν
νομίζειν, τὸν ὁμολογουμένως δοῦλον περὶ ὧν ἐμαρτύρησαν ἐκδιδόντος, οὐκ ἐθέλοντος τούτου παραλαβεῖν; οὐ γὰρ δὴ τοῦτό γ᾽ ἔνεστιν εἰπεῖν, ὡς περὶ
μὲν τινῶν ὧν αὐτὸς βούλεται σαφὴς ἡ βάσανος,
περὶ δ᾽ αὖ τινῶν οὐ σαφής.

15
[849]
"Ετι τοίνυν, ὦ ἄνδρες δικασταί, ταύτην τὴν μαρτυρίαν ἐμαρτύρησεν ἀδελφὸς ὁ τούτου πρῶτος
Αἴσιος, ὃς νῦν μὲν ἔξαρνός ἐστι τούτῳ συναγωνιζό-
μενος, τότε δ᾽ ἐμαρτύρησε ταῦτα μετὰ τῶν ἄλλων,
οὔτ᾽ ἐπιορκεῖν οὔτ᾽ εὐθὺς παραχρῆμα δίκην ὀφλισκάνειν βουλόμενος. ὃν οὐκ ἂν δήπου, ψευδῆ
μαρτυρίαν εἰ παρεσκευαζόμην, ἐνέγραψα ἂν εἰς τοὺς
μάρτυρας, ὁρῶν μὲν Ἀφόβῳ χρώμενον μάλιστ᾽
ἀνθρώπων ἁπάντων, εἰδὼς δὲ συνεροῦντ᾽ αὐτῷ τὴν
δίκην, ἔτι δ᾽ ἐμαυτοῦ ὄντ᾽ ἀντίδικον· οὐ γὰρ ἔχει
λόγον τὸν ἑαυτοῦ διάφορον μὴ ἀληθινῆς μαρτυρίας
16 ἐγγράψαι μάρτυρα. τούτων τοίνυν εἰσὶ μὲν πολλοὶ
μάρτυρες, ἔτι δ᾽ οὐκ ἐλάττω τεκμήρια τῶν μαρτύρων. πρῶτον μὲν γάρ, εἴπερ ὡς ἀληθῶς ταῦτα
μὴ ἐμαρτύρησεν, οὐκ ἂν νῦν ἔξαρνος ἦν, ἀλλὰ τότ᾽
εὐθὺς ἐπὶ τοῦ δικαστηρίου τῆς μαρτυρίας ἀναγιγνωσκομένης, ἡνίκα μᾶλλον ἂν αὐτὸν ἢ νῦν ὠφέλει.
92

regard to other matters. In this he is lying. Is it **14** not indeed monstrous that he should claim that he is being outrageously treated by my refusal of his demand to have delivered to him for torture a freeman (for such I shall conclusively prove Milyas to be), and should not consider that my witnesses are being outrageously treated, when I offer him one who is admittedly a slave, to be tested by torture regarding their testimony, and he refuses? For he surely cannot maintain this, that for some matters, which he himself desires, torture is a certain test, and for others not.

Furthermore, men of the jury, the first witness to **15** give this testimony was Aesius, the brother of the plaintiff. He now denies it, because he has allied himself in the suit with Aphobus ; but at that time he gave this testimony along with the other witnesses, for he had no desire to perjure himself, or to suffer the penalty which would straightway follow. Surely now, if I had been getting up false testimony, I should not have put this man in my list of witnesses, seeing that he was more intimate with Aphobus than with anyone else in the world, and knowing that he was going to plead for him in the suit, and that he was an adversary of my own. It is not reasonable that one should call as witness to a false statement one who is an opponent of his own, and a brother of his adversary. I have many witnesses to these facts, **16** and circumstantial proofs no fewer in number than the witnesses. In the first place, if he did not in very truth give this testimony, he would not be denying it now, but would have done so at once in the court-room, when the deposition was read, for it would have answered his purpose better then than now. In the

δεύτερον δ' οὐκ ἂν ἡσυχίαν ἦγεν, ἀλλὰ δίκην ἄν
μοι βλάβης ἔλαχεν, εἰ ψευδομαρτυριῶν ὑπόδικον
αὐτὸν ἐποίουν κατὰ τἀδελφοῦ οὐ προσῆκον, ἐν ᾗ
καὶ περὶ χρημάτων καὶ περὶ ἀτιμίας ἄνθρωποι
17 κινδυνεύουσιν. ἔτι δὲ τὸ πρᾶγμ' ἂν ἐξελέγξαι
ζητῶν, ἐξήτησεν ἄν με τὸν παῖδα τὸν γράφοντα τὰς
μαρτυρίας, ἵν' εἰ μὴ παρεδίδουν, μηδὲν δίκαιον
λέγειν ἐδόκουν. νῦν δὲ τοσούτου ποιῆσαί τι τούτων
ἐδέησεν, ὥστ' οὐδ' ἐμοῦ παραδιδόντος, ἐπειδὴ ταῦτ'
ἔξαρνος ἐγένεθ' οὗτος, παραλαβεῖν ἠθέλησεν, ἀλλ'
ὁμοίως φαίνονται καὶ περὶ τούτων φεύγοντες τὰς
βασάνους.

18
[850] Καὶ ταῦθ' ὡς ἀληθῆ λέγω, καὶ ἔν τε τοῖς μάρτυσιν μεμαρτυρηκὼς Αἴσιος οὐκ ἠρνήθη ταῦτ' ἐπὶ
τοῦ δικαστηρίου τούτῳ παρεστηκὼς τῆς μαρτυρίας
ἀναγιγνωσκομένης, ἐμοῦ τ' ἐκδιδόντος τὸν παῖδα
περὶ ἁπάντων τούτων βασανίζειν αὐτοῖς οὐκ
ἠθέλησαν παραλαβεῖν, καθ' ἕκαστον ὑμῖν παρέξομαι
τοὺς μάρτυρας. καί μοι κάλει δεῦρ' αὐτούς.

ΜΑΡΤΥΡΕΣ

19 Ὁ τοίνυν, ὦ ἄνδρες δικασταί, πάντων τῶν εἰρημένων οἶμαι μέγιστον ὑμῖν ἐρεῖν σημεῖον τοῦ ταῦτ'
ἀποκρίνασθαι τοῦτον, βούλομαι διελθεῖν. ἐπειδὴ
γὰρ ἐξήτει με τὸν ἄνθρωπον ταῦθ' ὡμολογηκὼς ἃ
μεμαρτύρηται, βουλόμενος καὶ τότ' αὐτὸν ἐξελέγξαι

94

second place Aesius would not have kept quiet, but would have sued me for damages, if without cause I had made him liable to a charge of bearing false witness against his brother, a charge on which men run the risk both of damages in money and the loss of citizenship. Again, in seeking to bring the truth 17 of the matter to light, he would have demanded of me the slave who wrote the depositions, in order that, if I refused to give him up, I might seem to have no just ground for my statements. But, as it is, so far from doing anything of the sort, he refused to accept the slave for torture, when I, on his denial that he had given the evidence, offered him. So plain is it that regarding this matter too both he and Aphobus as well were alike unwilling to have recourse to torture.

To prove that my words are true, that after Aesius 18 had given his testimony with the other witnesses, he made no denial of the fact, when, standing by the plaintiff's side in the court-room, he heard the deposition read, and that, when I offered the slave to them to be questioned by torture regarding all these matters, he refused to accept the offer—regarding each of these points severally I shall produce witnesses. Please call them here.

THE WITNESSES

I wish now to set forth to you, men of the jury, 19 what I consider a stronger proof than all those that have been mentioned, to show that the plaintiff did give this answer. When, despite the admissions which he is proved to have made, he demanded of me Milyas for torture, I was so eager to show on the spot that this, too, was a subterfuge on his part, that what do you

20 τεχνάζοντα τί ποιῶ; προσκαλοῦμαι[1] κατὰ Δήμωνος εἰς μαρτυρίαν, ὄντος αὐτῷ θείου καὶ κοινωνοῦ
τῶν ἀδικημάτων, καὶ συγγράψας ταῦτ' ἐκέλευον
μαρτυρεῖν, ἃ νῦν διώκει τῶν ψευδομαρτυριῶν.
οὗτος δὲ τὸ μὲν πρῶτον ἀπηναισχύντει, τοῦ
δὲ διαιτητοῦ κελεύοντος μαρτυρεῖν ἢ ἐξομνύειν,
ἐμαρτύρησε πάνυ μόγις. καίτοι εἴ γ' ἦν δοῦλος
ἄνθρωπος καὶ μὴ προωμολόγητο πρὸς τοῦδ'
ἐλεύθερος εἶναι, τί μαθὼν ἐμαρτύρησεν, ἀλλ' οὐκ
21 ἐξομόσας ἀπηλλάγη τοῦ πράγματος; ἀλλὰ μὴν
καὶ περὶ τούτων ἤθελον παραδοῦναι τὸν παῖδα τὸν
γράφοντα τὴν μαρτυρίαν, ὃς τά τε γράμματ' ἔμελλε
γνώσεσθαι τὰ ἑαυτοῦ καὶ τοῦτον ἐμνημόνευεν
ἀκριβῶς μαρτυρήσαντα ταῦτα. καὶ ταῦτ' ἤθελον
οὐχὶ μαρτύρων ἀπορῶν οἳ παρῆσαν· ἦσαν γάρ· ἀλλ'
ἵνα μὴ τούτους αἰτιῷτο τὰ ψευδῆ μαρτυρεῖν, ἀλλὰ
[851] τὸ πιστὸν ἐκ τῆς βασάνου τούτοις ὑπάρχοι. καίτοι
πῶς ἄξιόν ἐστι καταγνῶναι τῶν μαρτύρων διὰ
τοῦτον, οἳ μόνοι τῶν πώποτ' ἠγωνισμένων δίκην ἐν
ὑμῖν τὸν διώκοντ' αὐτὸν αὐτοῖς μάρτυρα τούτων
ἐπιδεικνύουσιν γεγενημένον;

Ἀλλὰ μὴν ὡς ἀληθῆ λέγω, λαβὲ τὴν πρόκλησιν
καὶ τὴν μαρτυρίαν.

ΠΡΟΚΛΗΣΙΣ. ΜΑΡΤΥΡΙΑ

22 Τηλικαῦτα τοίνυν δίκαια φυγὼν οὗτος, καὶ ἐκ
τοσούτων τεκμηρίων ἐπιδεικνύμενος ὅτι συκοφαντεῖ τοῖς μὲν αὐτοῦ μάρτυσιν ἀξιοῖ πιστεύειν

---

[1] προσκαλοῦμαι] προκαλοῦμαι Blass.

think I did ? I summoned Aphobus to give evidence 20
against Demo, his uncle and a partner in his crimes.
I wrote out the testimony which he now attacks as
false and ordered him to make a deposition to it.
At first he brazenly refused, but when the arbitrator
bade him depose, or deny the fact under oath, he
deposed, sorely against his will. And yet if the man
was a slave, and had not been already admitted by
Aphobus here to be free, what in the world induced
him to make this deposition ? Why did he not deny it
on oath, and so get free of the affair ? Pray note that 21
in regard to this matter also I was ready to give over
to him for torture the slave who had written the deposition, who would know his own handwriting, and
who clearly remembered that Aphobus had made the
deposition. I was ready to do this, not for want of
witnesses who were present, for there were some ;
but in order that he might not accuse these men of
giving false testimony, and that the result of the
torture might support them. Yet it is not fair to
condemn the witnesses on his account. They alone
of men who have as yet stood trial before you can
show that the plaintiff himself has borne witness to
their testimony as to these matters.

To prove that I am speaking the truth, take the
challenge and the deposition.

THE CHALLENGE. THE DEPOSITION

Such are the legal tests which he has refused, and 22
so numerous the proofs by which he is shown to be
acting with malice and insincerity ; yet he demands
that you put credence in his own witnesses, and he

ὑμᾶς, τοὺς δ' ἐμοὺς διαβάλλει καί φησιν οὐ τἀληθῆ
μαρτυρεῖν.

Βούλομαι δὴ καὶ ἐκ τῶν εἰκότων περὶ αὐτῶν
εἰπεῖν. οἶδ' οὖν ὅτι πάντες ἂν ὁμολογήσαιτε τοὺς
τὰ ψευδῆ μαρτυροῦντας ἢ κέρδεσι δι' ἀπορίαν
ἐπαιρομένους ἢ δι' ἑταιρίαν ἢ καὶ δι' ἔχθραν τῶν
23 ἀντιδίκων ἐθέλειν ἄν τι τοιοῦτον ποιῆσαι. τούτων
τοίνυν οὐδὲ δι' ἓν ἂν εἶεν ἐμοὶ μεμαρτυρηκότες.
οὔτε γὰρ ἑταιρίᾳ· πῶς γάρ, οἵ γε μήτ' ἐν ταῖς
αὐταῖς διατριβαῖς μήτε καθ' ἡλικίαν, μὴ ὅτι ἐμοί
τινες αὐτῶν, ἀλλ' οὐδὲ σφίσιν αὐτοῖς εἰσίν; οὔτ'
ἔχθρᾳ τούτου· φανερὸν γὰρ καὶ τοῦτ' ἔστιν· ὁ μὲν
γὰρ ἀδελφὸς καὶ σύνδικος, Φᾶνος δ' ἐπιτήδειος καὶ
φυλέτης, Φίλιππος δ' οὔτε φίλος οὔτ' ἐχθρός, ὥστ'
οὐδὲ ταύτην ἄν τις ἐπενέγκοι δικαίως τὴν αἰτίαν.
24 καὶ μὴν οὐδὲ δι' ἀπορίαν ἄν τις φήσειε· πάντες γὰρ
κέκτηνται τοσαύτην οὐσίαν, ὥστε καὶ λῃτουργεῖν
ὑμῖν προθύμως καὶ τὰ προστάττόμενα ποιεῖν.
χωρὶς δὲ τούτων οὔτ' ἀγνῶτες ὑμῖν οὔτ' ἐπὶ τὰ
χείρω γιγνωσκόμενοι, μέτριοι δ' ὄντες ἄνθρωποι.
καίτοι εἰ μήτ' ἄποροι μήτ' ἐχθροὶ τούτου μήτ' ἐμοὶ
[852] φίλοι, πῶς χρὴ κατὰ τούτων λαβεῖν τιν' ὑποψίαν ὡς
τὰ ψευδῆ μαρτυροῦσιν; ἐγὼ μὲν γὰρ οὐκ οἶδα.
25 Ταῦτα τοίνυν οὗτος εἰδώς, καὶ πάντων μάλιστ'
ἐπιστάμενος τἀληθῆ μεμαρτυρηκότας αὐτούς, ὅμως
συκοφαντεῖ καί φησιν οὐ μόνον οὐκ εἰπεῖν ταῦτα,
ἃ πῶς τις ἂν μᾶλλον ἐξελέγξειεν εἰρηκότα; ἀλλὰ
καὶ δοῦλον εἶναι τὸν ἄνθρωπον τῷ ὄντι. βούλομαι
δὴ διὰ βραχέων εἰπὼν πρὸς ὑμᾶς ἐξελέγξαι καὶ

slanders mine, and declares that their testimony is false.

I wish now to speak of the matter on the basis of probabilities. I am certain that you would all agree that those who give false testimony are led to do so by bribes through stress of poverty, or by friendship, or else by enmity toward the opposite party in the suit. Now no one of these reasons would have led the 23 men to testify in my favour. Not friendship; how could that be, seeing that they are not engaged in the same pursuits, nor are they of like age, I will not say with me, but with one another? Not enmity against my adversary, that is plain; for one of them is his brother and pleads on his side; Phanus is a close friend and a member of the same tribe; and Philip is neither friend nor enemy, so that this motive, too, cannot be justly charged against them. Further- 24 more, no one could say that poverty was the ground, for they all possess means so ample that they willingly assume the expense of public services, and discharge whatever duties are laid upon them. Besides all this, they are well known to you, and you know nothing to their discredit; for they are worthy citizens. Yet, if they are not poor, nor enemies of the plaintiff, nor friends of mine, how can it be right to suspect them of bearing false witness? I certainly do not know.

My opponent was aware of all this, and knew better 25 than anybody else that their testimony was true, but none the less he brings forward a malicious charge against them, and not only declares that he did not make the statement which I have proved in the most conclusive manner that he did make, but even asserts that the man, Milyas, is in fact a slave. I wish in a very few words to prove that in this, too, he is lying.

ταῦτ' αὐτὸν ψευδόμενον. ἐγὼ γάρ, ὦ ἄνδρες δικασταί, καὶ περὶ τούτων ἠθέλησα τούτῳ παραδοῦναι
βασανίζειν τὰς θεραπαίνας, αἳ τελευτῶντος τοῦ
πατρὸς μνημονεύουσ' ἀφεθέντα τοῦτον ἐλεύθερον
26 εἶναι τότε. καὶ πρὸς τούτοις ἡ μήτηρ κατ' ἐμοῦ
καὶ τῆς ἀδελφῆς, οἳ μόνοι παῖδές ἐσμεν αὐτῇ, δι'
οὓς κατεχήρευσε τὸν βίον, πίστιν ἠθέλησ' ἐπιθεῖναι
παραστησαμένη, τὸν ἄνθρωπον τοῦτον ἀφεῖναι τὸν
πατέρ' ἡνίκ' ἐτελεύτα, καὶ νομίζεσθαι παρ' ἡμῖν
τοῦτον ἐλεύθερον· ἣν μηδεὶς ὑμῶν νομιζέτω καθ'
ἡμῶν ποτ' ἂν ὀμνύναι ταῦτ' ἐθέλειν, εἰ μὴ σαφῶς
ᾔδει τὰ εὔορκ' ὀμουμένη.

Ἀλλὰ μὴν ὡς ἀληθῆ λέγω καὶ ταῦτ' ἦμεν ἕτοιμοι
ποιεῖν, κάλει τούτων τοὺς μάρτυρας.

MΑΡΤΥΡΕΣ

27 Τοσαῦτα τοίνυν δίκαια λέγειν ἐχόντων ἡμῶν, καὶ
καταφεύγειν εἰς τοὺς μεγίστους ἐλέγχους ἐθελόντων
περὶ τῶν μεμαρτυρημένων, πάντα ταῦτα φυγὼν
οὗτος οἴεται, περὶ τῆς γεγενημένης δίκης δια-
βάλλων καὶ κατηγορῶν ἐμοῦ, τοῦ μάρτυρος ὑμᾶς
πείσειν καταψηφίσασθαι, πάντων οἶμαι πρᾶγμα
κατασκευάσας ἀδικώτατον καὶ πλεονεκτικώτατον.
28 αὐτὸς μὲν γὰρ μάρτυρας ψευδεῖς παρεσκεύασται
[853] περὶ τούτων, συγχορηγὸν ἔχων Ὀνήτορα τὸν κηδεστὴν καὶ Τιμοκράτην· ἡμεῖς δ' οὐχὶ προειδότες,
ἀλλ' ὑπὲρ αὐτῆς τῆς μαρτυρίας ἡγούμενοι τὸν ἀγῶν'
ἔσεσθαι, τοὺς περὶ τῶν ἐκ τῆς ἐπιτροπῆς χρημάτων
μάρτυρας οὐ παρεσκευάσμεθα νῦν. ὅμως δὲ καίπερ

ᵃ Timocrates : possibly the same as the Timocrates against
whom Demosthenes delivered Oration XXIV.

I was ready, men of the jury, regarding this point also to give over to him to be tested by torture my female slaves, who remember that my father on his death-bed set this man free. Besides this, my mother 26 was ready to call to her side my sister and myself, and swear, with imprecations on our heads if she spoke falsely—we were her only children, and it was for our sakes that she gave herself up to a life of widowhood—that my father when he was about to die had set this man free, and that Milyas was regarded by us as free thereafter. Let no one of you assume that she would have been willing to make this oath with imprecations on our heads if she had not known well that what she was to swear to was true.

Come now, to prove that I am speaking the truth and that we were ready to do these things, call the witnesses thereto.

THE WITNESSES

So many were the just arguments we had to urge, 27 and so ready were we to have recourse to the most infallible tests regarding the testimony given ; and yet the plaintiff evades all these, and fancies that by slandering me regarding the trial which has already taken place, and bringing accusations against me, he can induce you to convict the witness,—a piece of trickery the most unfair and the most rapacious imaginable. For he has himself suborned men 28 to bear false witness about these matters, having as co-workers his brother-in-law Onetor, and Timocrates [a] ; we had no forewarning of this, and supposed that the contest would be regarding the deposition alone, and therefore have not come prepared with witnesses regarding the guardianship accounts.

οὕτω τούτου σεσοφισμένου, τὰ πράγματ' αὐτὰ δι-
εξιὼν οἶμαι ῥᾳδίως ὑμῖν ἐπιδείξειν, δικαιόταт'
29 ἀνθρώπων τοῦτον ὠφληκότα τὴν δίκην, οὐχ ὅτι τὸν
Μιλύαν ἐκώλυον βασανίζειν, οὐδ' ὅτι τοῦτον ἐλεύθερον ὡμολόγησεν, οἱ δὲ μάρτυρες οἶδ' ἐμαρτύρησαν, ἀλλ' ὅτι πολλὰ τῶν ἐμῶν ἐξηλέγχθη λαβών,
καὶ τὸν οἶκον οὐκ ἐμίσθωσε τῶν νόμων κελευόντων
καὶ τοῦ πατρὸς ἐν τῇ διαθήκῃ γράψαντος, ὡς ἐγὼ
σαφῶς ὑμῖν ἐπιδείξω· ταῦτα μὲν γὰρ ἦν πᾶσιν
ἰδεῖν, οἱ νόμοι καὶ τὸ πλῆθος ὧν οὗτοι διηρπάκεσαν
χρημάτων· τὸν Μιλύαν δ' οὐδ' ὅστις ἔστιν οὐδεὶς
ᾔδει. γνώσεσθε δ' ἐκ τῶν ἐγκεκλημένων ὅτι ταῦθ'
οὕτως ἔχοντ' ἐστίν.
30   Ἐγὼ γάρ, ὦ ἄνδρες δικασταί, τὴν δίκην ἔλαχον
τούτῳ τῆς ἐπιτροπῆς οὐχ ἓν τίμημα συνθείς, ὥσπερ
ἄν τις συκοφαντεῖν ἐπιχειρῶν, ἀλλ' ἕκαστον ἐγγράψας καὶ πόθεν λαβὼν καὶ πόσον τὸ πλῆθος καὶ
παρὰ τοῦ, καὶ οὐδαμοῦ τὸν Μιλύαν παρέγραψα ὡς
31 εἰδότα τι τούτων. ἔστιν οὖν τοῦ μὲν ἐγκλήματος
ἀρχὴ " τάδ' ἐγκαλεῖ Δημοσθένης Ἀφόβῳ· ἔχει μου
χρήματ' Ἄφοβος ἀπ' ἐπιτροπῆς ἐχόμενα, ὀγδοήκοντα μὲν μνᾶς, ἣν ἔλαβε προῖκα τῆς μητρὸς κατὰ
τὴν διαθήκην τοῦ πατρός." τοῦτο πρῶτόν ἐστι
τῶν χρημάτων, ὧν ἀπεστερῆσθαί φημι. τοῖς δὲ
μάρτυσιν τί μεμαρτύρηται; " μαρτυροῦσι παρα-
[854] γενέσθαι πρὸς τῷ διαιτητῇ Νοθάρχῳ, ὅτ' Ἄφοβος

102

Nevertheless, despite the fellow's trickery, I think that, simply by reciting the facts, I shall easily convince you that no man was ever more justly convicted than he. It was not because I refused to allow Milyas 29 to be put to the torture, nor because he himself admitted the man to be a freeman, nor yet because these witnesses gave their testimony ; but because he was proved to have taken possession of large sums belonging to me, and because he did not let the estate, though the laws so ordered and my father had so directed in his will, as I shall plainly show you. For these were things that anyone could see, the laws, namely, and the amount of my property which these men had taken as plunder ; but as for Milyas, nobody knew even who he was. You will see from the charges brought against Aphobus that these things are so.

For, men of the jury, when I instituted my suit 30 against him concerning his guardianship, I did not fix the damages at a lump sum, as one bringing forward a baseless charge out of malice would have done, but specified each item, stating the source of each, the precise amount, and the person from whom it had been received. In no case did I add mention of Milyas as having knowledge of any of these matters. Hence 31 this is the beginning of the complaint : " Demosthenes makes the following charges against Aphobus. Aphobus has in his possession moneys of mine, received by him in his capacity as guardian, as follows : eighty minae, which he received as the marriage-portion of my mother in accordance with the terms of my father's will." This is the first of the sums of which I claim to have been defrauded. Now what was the declaration of the witnesses ? " That they were present before the arbitrator, Notharchus, when

103

ὡμολόγει Μιλύαν ἐλεύθερον εἶναι, ἀφεθέντα ὑπὸ
32 τοῦ Δημοσθένους πατρός." σκοπεῖτε τοίνυν παρ'
ὑμῖν αὐτοῖς, εἴ τις ἂν ὑμῖν ἢ ῥήτωρ ἢ σοφιστὴς ἢ
γόης οὕτω θαυμάσιος δοκεῖ γενέσθαι καὶ λέγειν
δεινός, ὥστ' ἐκ ταύτης τῆς μαρτυρίας διδάξαι τιν'
ἀνθρώπων, ὡς ἔχει τὴν προῖκ' Ἄφοβος τῆς μητρὸς
τῆς ἑαυτοῦ. καὶ τί λέγων, ὦ πρὸς Διός; "ὡμολόγησεν εἶναι Μιλύαν ἐλεύθερον." καὶ τί μᾶλλον
ἔχων τὴν προῖκα; οὐδὲν ἂν δήπου διὰ τοῦτό γε
33 δόξειεν. ἀλλὰ πόθεν τοῦτ' ἐδείχθη; πρῶτον μὲν
Θηριππίδης ὢν αὐτῷ συνεπίτροπος κατεμαρτύρησε
δοῦναι· δεύτερον δὲ Δήμων θεῖος ὢν καὶ τῶν ἄλλων
οἱ παρόντες ἐμαρτύρησαν, σῖτον τῇ μητρὶ δώσειν
ὁμολογεῖν τοῦτον ὡς ἔχοντα τὴν προῖκα. καὶ τούτοις οὐκ ἐπεσκήψατο, δηλονότι τἀληθῆ μεμαρτυρηκότας εἰδώς. ἔτι τοίνυν ἡ μήτηρ πίστιν ἠθέλησ'
ἐπιθεῖναι κατ' ἐμοῦ καὶ τῆς ἀδελφῆς παραστησαμένη, λαβεῖν τὴν προῖκα τοῦτον τὴν ἑαυτῆς κατὰ
34 τὴν τοῦ πατρὸς διαθήκην. ταύτας τὰς ὀγδοήκοντα
μνᾶς πότερ' αὐτὸν ἔχειν φῶμεν ἢ μή; καὶ πότερον
διὰ τούσδ' ὀφλεῖν τοὺς μάρτυρας ἢ διὰ τούσδε; ἐγὼ
μὲν γὰρ οἶμαι διὰ τὴν ἀλήθειαν. ταύτας τοίνυν δέκ'
ἔτη κεκαρπωμένος, καὶ οὐδὲ δίκην ὀφλὼν ἀποδοῦναι
τετολμηκώς, δεινὰ πεπονθέναι φησὶ καὶ διὰ τούσδε
τοὺς μάρτυρας ὠφληκέναι. καίτοι τούτων γ' οὐδεὶς αὐτὸν ἔχειν ταύτην ἐμαρτύρησεν.

Aphobus admitted that Milyas was a freeman, having been emancipated by the father of Demosthenes." Consider now for yourselves whether in your judge- 32 ment there could be an orator, or sophist or magician so wondrously clever in speaking as by means of this testimony to convince any man on earth that Aphobus is in possession of the marriage-portion of the speaker's mother. What in heaven's name would he say? " Aphobus has admitted that Milyas is a freeman." And why on that account is he any the more in pos- session of the marriage-portion? The statement would surely not seem to prove it. But how was it proved? 33 In the first place, Therippides, his co-trustee, testified that he had given him the money. Secondly, Demo, his uncle, and the rest of the witnesses who were present, testified that he agreed to supply my mother with maintenance, as being in possession of her por- tion. Against these men he has lodged no charges, plainly because he knew that their testimony was true. Besides this, my mother was ready to call to her side my sister and myself, and swear with imprecations on our heads, if she spoke falsely, that Aphobus had received her marriage-portion according to the terms of my father's will. Shall we, then, say, or shall we 34 not, that he has possession of these eighty minae? And was it on the evidence of these witnesses here or of those that he was convicted? I think it was on the evidence of truth. He has enjoyed the interest on this sum for ten years, and even though judgement has been given against him, cannot bring himself to pay it back. Despite this, he declares that he has been outrageously treated and that he lost the suit by reason of these witnesses. Yet not one of them testified that he had received the marriage-portion.

35 Περὶ τοίνυν τῆς ἐκδόσεως καὶ τῶν κλινοποιῶν
καὶ τοῦ καταλειφθέντος ἡμῖν ἐλέφαντος καὶ τοῦ
σιδήρου καὶ τῆς προικὸς τῆς ἀδελφῆς, ἣν οὗτος
καθυφεῖκεν ὑπὲρ τοῦ καὶ αὐτὸς ἔχειν ὅσα βούλοιτο
[855] τῶν ἐμῶν, ἀκούσατε, καὶ σκοπεῖθ' ὡς δικαίως τ'
ὤφληκε, καὶ οὐδὲν ἦν Μιλύαν περὶ τούτων βασα-
νιστέον.

36 Περὶ μὲν γὰρ ὧν καθυφεῖκας, νόμος ἔστι, διαρρήδην ὃς κελεύει σ' ὁμοίως ὀφλισκάνειν, ὥσπερ
ἂν αὐτὸς ἔχῃς· ὥστε τί τῷ νόμῳ καὶ τῇ βασάνῳ;
περὶ δ' αὖ τῆς ἐκδόσεως, ἐπικοινωνήσαντες τῷ
Ξούθῳ καὶ διανειμάμενοι τὰ χρήματα καὶ τὰς συγγραφὰς ἀνελόντες, καὶ πάνθ' ὃν τρόπον ἠβούλεσθε
κατασκευάσαντες, καὶ διαφθείραντες τὰ γράμμαθ',
ὡς ὑμῶν ὁ Δῆμων κατεμαρτύρει, φενακίζετε καὶ
37 τουτουσὶ παρακρούσασθαι ζητεῖτε. περὶ τοίνυν
τῶν κλινοποιῶν, εἰ σὺ λαβὼν ἀργύριον[1] καὶ πόλλ'
ἰδίᾳ κερδάνας ἐπὶ τοῖς ἐμοῖς δανείζων, ὃν καὶ τοὺς
ἄλλους προσῆκε κωλύειν, εἶτ' ἀφανεῖς πεποίηκας,
τί σοι ποιήσωσιν οἱ μάρτυρες; οὐ γὰρ οὗτοί γε
μεμαρτυρήκασιν, ὡς ὡμολόγεις ἐπὶ τοῖς ἐμοῖς
δανείζειν καὶ λαβεῖν τἀνδράποδ' ὡς σαυτόν, ἀλλ' ἐν
τῷ λόγῳ τοῦτ' ἔγραψας σύ, κατεμαρτύρησαν[2] δ' οἱ
μάρτυρες.

38 Ἀλλὰ μὴν περὶ τοῦ γ' ἐλέφαντος καὶ τοῦ
σιδήρου, πάντας ἐγώ φημι τοὺς οἰκέτας εἰδέναι

---

[1] ἀργύριον ὡς σαυτὸν Blass, comparing XXVII. § 27.
[2] σύ, κατεμαρτύρησαν συγκατεμαρτύρησαν Blass.

---

[a] With reference to these items see Oration XXVII. § 9.
[b] In the inventory of the estate of the father of Demosthenes, given in Oration XXVII. § 11, there is mention of a
bottomry loan to Xuthus, amounting to seventy minae.

With regard to the maritime loan,[a] the sofa-makers, 35
and the iron and the ivory that were left me, and my
sister's marriage-portion, at the purloining of which
Aphobus connived in order to secure for himself the
right to take whatever he pleased of my goods, listen,
and see how just was the verdict given against him,
and how absurd it would have been to examine
Milyas by torture regarding any of these matters.

For as regards the purloining of funds at which you 36
connived there is a law which expressly declares that
you are responsible for them exactly as if you had
them in your own possession. So what has the law to
do with the testing of a slave by torture ? But in the
matter of the maritime loan you made common cause
with Xuthus,[b] divided the money with him, and destroyed the contract, and now that you have arranged
everything to suit your wish, and have done away with
the documentary evidence (as Demo testified against
you), you have recourse to trickery, and endeavour
to mislead these gentlemen. Regarding the sofa- 37
makers, if you took money, and made large profits
for yourself by making loans on security that was
mine—you, who should rather have prevented others
from doing so—and finally made away with the
slaves altogether, what, pray, can the witnesses do
in your behalf ? These men at any rate have not
testified that you admitted lending money on the
security of my slaves, and that you appropriated the
slaves to yourself. On the contrary, it was you who
acknowledged this in your account, and the witnesses
testified to the fact against you.

Now look you, as to the ivory and iron, I have this 38
to say : all the slaves of the household know that the

τοῦτον πωλοῦντα, καὶ παραδοῦναι καὶ τότε καὶ νῦν
ἤθελον αὐτῷ τούτων ὅντινα βούλοιτο λαβὼν βασανίζειν. εἰ τοίνυν φήσει με, τὸν εἰδότ᾽ οὐκ ἐθέλοντ᾽
ἐκδοῦναι, τοὺς οὐκ εἰδότας ἐκδιδόναι, πολὺ δὴ
μᾶλλον αὐτῷ παραλαβεῖν φανήσεται προσῆκον· εἰ
γάρ, οὓς ὡς εἰδότας ἐξεδίδουν ἐγώ, μηδὲν ἔχειν
ἔφασαν τούτων αὐτόν, ἀπήλλακτο δήπουθεν ἂν τῆς
39 αἰτίας. ἀλλ᾽ οὐχὶ τοιοῦτόν ἐστιν, ἀλλὰ σαφῶς ἂν
ἐξηλέγχθη πωλῶν καὶ τὴν τιμὴν κεκομισμένος.
[856] διόπερ τοὺς ὁμολογουμένως δούλους παραβὰς τὸν
ἐλεύθερον ἠξίου βασανίζειν, ὃν οὐδ᾽ ὅσιον παραδοῦναι, τὸ πρᾶγμ᾽ οὐκ ἀγαγεῖν εἰς ἔλεγχον ζητῶν,
ἀλλὰ μὴ παραλαμβάνων βουλόμενός τι δοκεῖν λέγειν.

Περὶ τοίνυν πάντων τούτων, πρῶτον μὲν περὶ
τῆς προικός, εἶθ᾽ ὑπὲρ ὧν καθυφεῖκεν, εἶθ᾽ ὑπὲρ
τῶν ἄλλων, ἀναγνώσεται τούς τε νόμους καὶ τὰς
μαρτυρίας ἵν᾽ εἰδῆτε.

NOMOI. ΜΑΡΤΥΡΙΑΙ

40 Οὐ τοίνυν μόνον ἐκ τούτων ἂν γνοίητε, ὅτι δεινὸν
οὐδ᾽ ὁτιοῦν πέπονθε τὸν ἄνθρωπον οὐκ ἐκδόντος
ἐμοῦ βασανίζειν, ἀλλὰ καὶ τὸ πρᾶγμ᾽ αὔτ᾽ εἰ σκέ-
ψαισθε. θῶμεν γὰρ δὴ τὸν Μιλύαν ἐπὶ τοῦ τροχοῦ
στρεβλοῦσθαι, καὶ τί μάλιστ᾽ ἂν αὐτὸν εὔξαιτο
λέγειν σκοπῶμεν. οὐχ ὅτι τῶν χρημάτων οὐδ᾽
ὁτιοῦν οἶδε τοῦτον ἔχοντα; καὶ δὴ λέγει. διὰ

108

plaintiff used to sell these articles. I am ready now, as I was then, to give over to him any one of these slaves whom he may choose to be examined by torture. If, then, he alleges that I refuse to surrender the man who has knowledge of the facts, and offer him others who have no such knowledge, he will but show that he ought all the more to have accepted my offer. For if those whom I offered to him as having knowledge of the facts, declared that he had none of these articles in his possession, he would of course have been acquitted of the charge. But nothing of the 39 sort is the truth. It would have been proved past all question that he had sold the goods, and appropriated the profits. Therefore, he passed over those who were admittedly slaves, and demanded that a freeman be examined by torture, whom it would have been a crime for me to surrender ; for it was not his purpose that he should sift out the matter, but that he might make a specious argument out of the fact that his demand was refused.

Regarding, therefore, all these facts, first the marriage-portion, then his connivance with fraud, then all the rest, there shall be read to you the laws and the depositions, that you may have full knowledge.

THE LAWS. THE DEPOSITIONS

Not only from the facts already adduced can you 40 see that Aphobus was not in any respect whatever prejudiced by my refusal to give the man up for torture, but also from a consideration of the matter itself. Let us suppose that Milyas is being racked upon the wheel, and consider what Aphobus would most wish him to say. Would it not be that he was not aware that the plaintiff had any of the property in his possession ? Well, suppose he says so. Does

τοῦτ' ἄρ' οὐκ ἔχει; πολλοῦ γε καὶ δεῖ· τοὺς γὰρ
εἰδότας καὶ δόντας καὶ παρόντας μάρτυρας παρεσχόμην ἐγώ. τεκμήριον δὲ καὶ πίστις ἐστίν, οὐκ εἴ
τίς τι μὴ οἶδε τοῦτον ἔχοντα (πολλοὶ γὰρ ἂν εἶεν),

41 ἀλλ' εἴ τις οἶδεν. καταμαρτυρησάντων τοίνυν
τοσούτων σου μαρτύρων, τίνι τῶν ψευδομαρτυριῶν
ἐπεσκήψω; δεῖξον. ἀλλ' οὐκ ἂν ἔχοις δεῖξαι.
καίτοι πῶς οὐ σαφῶς σὺ σαυτὸν ἐξελέγχεις, ὅτι
ψεύδει δεινὰ πεπονθέναι φάσκων καὶ τὴν δίκην
ἀδίκως ὠφληκέναι τὸν ἄνθρωπον οὐ παραλαβών, ὃς
τοὺς ταῦτα μαρτυρήσαντας ἔχειν σε καὶ λαβεῖν,
περὶ ὧν ὡς οὐ καταλειφθέντων σὺ τὸν Μιλύαν
ἐξῄτεις, ἀφῆκας τῶν ψευδομαρτυριῶν; οὓς πολὺ
κάλλιον ἦν, εἴπερ ἠδίκησο, διώκειν. ἀλλ' οὐκ
ἠδικημένος συκοφαντεῖς.

42
[857]   Πολλαχόθεν μὲν οὖν ἄν τις ἴδοι τὴν σὴν πονηρίαν,
μάλιστα δ' εἰ περὶ τῆς διαθήκης ἀκούσειεν. τοῦ
γὰρ πατρός, ὦ ἄνδρες δικασταί, τὰ καταλειφθέντα
πάντ' ἐν τῇ διαθήκῃ γράψαντος, καὶ τὸν οἶκον ὅπως
μισθώσουσι, ταύτην μὲν οὐκ ἀπέδωκεν, ἵνα μὴ
τὸ πλῆθος εὕροιμ' ἐγὼ τῶν χρημάτων ἐξ αὐτῆς,
ὡμολόγει δὲ κεκτῆσθαι ταῦτα, ἃ μάλιστ' οὐχ οἷόν

43 τ' ἦν ἐξάρνῳ γενέσθαι διὰ τὴν περιφάνειαν. ἦν δὲ
ταῦθ' ἃ γεγράφθαι φησὶν ἐν τῇ διαθήκῃ, δύο μὲν
τάλαντα Δημοφῶντα λαβεῖν εὐθύς, τὴν δ' ἀδελφὴν
ὅταν ἡλικίαν ἔχῃ (τοῦτο δ' ἔμελλεν εἰς ἔτος δέκατον
γενήσεσθαι), τοῦτον δ' ὀγδοήκοντα μνᾶς καὶ τὴν

110

that prove that the plaintiff has none ? Far from it ;
for I produced men who knew, men who paid him
the money, men who were present in person, as witnesses. It is convincing proof, not if one is ignorant
that a man has something in his possession (for there
might be many such), but if one knows that he has it.
But of the many witnesses who testified against you, 41
what one have you sued for false testimony ? Tell
us. But you cannot. Yet you plainly convict yourself, and prove that you lie when you declare that
you have been outrageously treated, and that you
lost the suit unjustly because this man was not given
up to you—you who made no charge of giving false
testimony against the witnesses who testified that
you received and had in your possession the property,
concerning which you demanded Milyas for torture
to prove that it was never left us. If you had really
been wronged, it would have been more fitting to
proceed against them. But you were not wronged,
and are bringing a baseless suit out of malice.

There are many points from which one may see 42
your rascality, but most of all if one hears how you
acted regarding the will. For although my father,
men of the jury, wrote a will containing an inventory
of all that he left, with instructions for letting the
property, this will Aphobus never gave up to me,
lest I should learn from it the value of the estate, and
admitted possessing only those items which were so
well known that he could not deny that he had them.
The will, according to his statement, contained these 43
provisions : that Demophon should at once receive
two talents, and should marry my sister when she
should come of age (this would be in ten years); that
Aphobus himself should have eighty minae with my

μητέρα τὴν ἐμὴν καὶ τὴν οἰκίαν οἰκεῖν, Θηριππίδην
δ᾽ ἑβδομήκοντα μνᾶς λαβόντα καρπώσασθαι, τέως
ἀνὴρ γενοίμην. τὰ δ᾽ ἄλλ᾽ ὅσ᾽ ἐμοὶ χωρὶς τούτων
κατελείφθη, καὶ τὸ μισθοῦν τὸν οἶκον ἠφάνιζεν ἐκ
τῆς διαθήκης, οὐ συμφέρον αὐτῷ νομίζων ταῦτ᾽
44 ἐπιδειχθῆναι παρ᾽ ὑμῖν. ἐπειδὴ τοίνυν ὡμολόγηθ᾽
ὑπ᾽ αὐτοῦ τούτου,[1] τὸν πατέρ᾽ ἡμῶν τελευτῶντα
τοσοῦτον ἀργύριον τούτων ἑκάστῳ δοῦναι, τεκμήριον οἱ δικάζοντες τότε τὰς ὁμολογίας ἐποιήσαντο
ταύτας τοῦ πλήθους τῶν χρημάτων· ὅστις γὰρ ἀπὸ
τῶν ὄντων τέτταρα τάλαντα καὶ τρισχιλίας προῖκα
καὶ δωρειὰν ἔδωκε, φανερὸν ἦν ὅτι οὐκ ἀπὸ μικρᾶς
οὐσίας, ἀλλὰ πλέον ἢ διπλασίας ἧς ἐμοὶ κατέλειπε
45 ταῦτ᾽ ἀφεῖλεν. οὐ γὰρ ἂν ἐδόκει τὸν μὲν υἱὸν
ἐμὲ πένητα βούλεσθαι καταστῆσαι, τούτους δὲ
πλουσίους ὄντας ἔτι πλουσιωτέρους ποιῆσαι ἐπι-
θυμεῖν, ἀλλ᾽ ἕνεκα τοῦ πλήθους τῶν ἐμοὶ καταλειπομένων Θηριππίδῃ τε τὰς ἑβδομήκοντα μνᾶς
[858] καὶ Δημοφῶντι τὰ δύο τάλαντα, οὔπω μέλλοντι τῇ
ἀδελφῇ τῇ ἐμῇ συνοικήσειν, καρποῦσθαι δοῦναι.
ταῦτα δὴ τὰ χρήματ᾽ οὐδαμοῦ παραδοὺς ἐφαίνετο,
οὐδ᾽ ἐλάττω μικροῖς· ἀλλὰ τὰ μὲν ἀνηλωκέναι, τὰ δ᾽
οὐ λαβεῖν ἔφη, τὰ δ᾽ οὐκ εἰδέναι, τὰ δὲ τὸν δεῖν᾽
ἔχειν, τὰ δ᾽ ἔνδον εἶναι, τὰ δὲ πάντα μᾶλλον ἢ ὅπου
παρέδωκεν εἶχε λέγειν.
46 Περὶ δὲ τοῦ καταλειφθῆναι[2] τὰ χρήματ᾽ ἔνδον,
βούλομαι σαφῶς ὑμῖν ἐπιδεῖξαι ψευδόμενον. τοῦτον γὰρ τὸν λόγον καθεῖκεν, ἐπειδὴ τὰ χρήματα μὲν

---

[1] αὐτοῦ τούτου] αὐτῶν τούτων Blass.
[2] καταλειφθῆναι] μὴ καταλειφθῆναι Blass.

ᵃ The following passage up to the middle of the section
is repeated almost verbatim from Oration XXVII. § 45.

mother, and the house to live in; and that Therippides should enjoy the interest on seventy minae until I should reach manhood. All the rest of the property left to me apart from these items, and the clause regarding the letting of the estate, he suppressed from the will, not thinking that it was to his interest that these matters should be made known in your court. However, since it was admitted by 44 Aphobus himself that my father on his death-bed gave to each of these men such large sums of money, the jurymen at the former trial considered these admissions to be a proof of the size of the estate. For when a man gave out of his estate four talents and three thousand drachmae by way of marriage-portion and legacy, it was plain that he took these sums, not from a small estate, but from one (bequeathed to me) of more than double this amount. ᵃFor it cannot be supposed that he would wish to 45 leave me, his son, in poverty, and be eager further to enrich these men, who were already wealthy. No; it was because of the size of the estate left to me that he gave to Therippides the interest on seventy minae, and to Demophon that on the two talents—though he was not yet to marry my sister. These moneys it has been proved that Aphobus never gave over to me, nor even an amount slightly less. Part of it he said he had spent, part he had never received, part he knew nothing about, part was in the hands of so-and-so, part was in the house, and of part he could say anything except when and where he had paid it over.

As to his story of money left in the house I shall 46 clearly prove to you that he is lying. This argument he speciously introduced, when it had become clear

πολλὰ πέφηνεν ὄντα, οὐκ ἔχει δ' ἐπιδεῖξαι ταῦθ' ὡς
ἀποδέδωκεν, ἵν' ἐξ εἰκότος οὐδὲν προσῆκον ἡμῖν
47 φανῇ κομίζεσθαι τά γ' ὄντα παρ' ἡμῖν. εἰ μὲν
τοίνυν ὁ πατὴρ ἠπίστει τούτοις, δῆλον ὅτι οὔτ'
ἂν τἄλλ' ἐπέτρεπεν, οὔτ' ἂν ἐκεῖν' οὕτω καταλείπων αὐτοῖς ἔφραζεν· ὥστε πόθεν ἴσασιν; εἰ δ'
ἐπίστευεν, οὐκ ἂν δήπου τὰ μὲν πλεῖστ' αὐτοῖς τῶν
χρημάτων ἐνεχείρισε, τῶν δ' οὐκ ἂν κυρίους ἐποίησεν, οὐδ' ἂν τῇ μὲν μητρί μου ταῦτα φυλάττειν
παρέδωκεν, αὐτὴν δὲ ταύτην ἑνὶ τῶν ἐπιτρόπων
τούτῳ γυναῖκ' ἠγγύησεν· οὐ γὰρ ἔχει λόγον, σῶσαι
μὲν τὰ χρήματα δι' ἐκείνης ζητεῖν, ἕνα δὲ τῶν
ἀπιστουμένων καὶ αὐτῆς κἀκείνων κύριον ποιεῖν.
48 ἔτι δέ, τούτων εἴ τι ἀληθὲς ἦν, οἴεσθ' οὐκ ἂν αὐτὴν
λαβεῖν δοθεῖσαν ὑπὸ τοῦ πατρός; ὃς τὴν μὲν προῖκ'
αὐτῆς ἤδη, τὰς ὀγδοήκοντα μνᾶς, ἔχων ὡς αὐτῇ
συνοικήσων, τὴν Φιλωνίδου τοῦ Μελιτέως θυγατέρ'
ἔγημε δι' αἰσχροκέρδειαν, ἵνα πρὸς αἷς εἶχε παρ'
ἡμῶν, ἑτέρας ὀγδοήκοντα μνᾶς λάβοι παρ' ἐκείνου·
τεττάρων δὲ ταλάντων ἔνδον ὄντων, καὶ ταῦτ'
[859] ἐκείνης ἐχούσης, ὡς οὗτός φησιν, οὐκ ἂν ἡγεῖσθ'
αὐτὸν κἂν ἐπιδραμεῖν, ὥστε γενέσθαι μετ' ἐκείνης
49 αὐτῶν κύριον; ἢ τὴν μὲν φανερὰν οὐσίαν, ἣν καὶ
ὑμῶν πολλοὶ συνῄδεσαν ὅτι κατελείφθη, μετὰ τῶν
συνεπιτρόπων οὕτως αἰσχρῶς διήρπασεν· ὧν δ' οὐκ

---

[a] This passage repeats very closely the language of
Oration XXVII. §§ 55-57.

114

that the property was large and was unable to show
that he had paid it back, in order that it might appear
a reasonable inference that I was wrongfully seeking
to recover what was already in my possession. ^aIf my 47
father had no confidence in these men it is plain
that he would neither have entrusted them with the
rest of his property, nor, if he had left this money
in the way alleged, would he have told them of it.
How, then, do they know about it? But, if he had
confidence in them, he would not, I take it, have
given into their hands the bulk of his property, and
not have put them in charge of the rest. Nor would
he have entrusted this remainder to my mother to
keep and then have pledged her herself in marriage
to this man, who was one of the guardians. For
it is not reasonable that he should seek to make
the money secure through her, and yet put one of
the men whom he distrusted in control both of her
and of it. Furthermore, if there were any truth 48
in all this, do you suppose that Aphobus would
not have taken my mother to wife, bequeathed to
him as she was by my father? He had already
taken her marriage-portion—the eighty minae—
as though he were going to marry her; but he
subsequently married the daughter of Philonides
of Melitê, from motives of avarice, in order that,
in addition to what he had received from us, he might
get from him other eighty minae. But, if there had
been four talents in the house, and in her custody,
as he alleges, don't you imagine he would have raced
to get possession both of her and of them? Would 49
he have joined with his co-trustees in so shamefully
plundering my visible property, which many of you
knew had been left me, and have refrained, when he

ἐμέλλεθ' ὑμεῖς ἔσεσθαι μάρτυρες, ἀπέσχετ' ἂν ἐξὸν
αὐτῷ λαβεῖν; καὶ τίς ἂν πιστεύσειεν; οὐκ ἔστι
ταῦτ', ὦ ἄνδρες δικασταί, οὐκ ἔστιν· ἀλλὰ τὰ μὲν
χρήμαθ', ὅσα κατέλιπεν ὁ πατήρ, ἐκείνῃ τῇ ἡμέρᾳ
κατωρύττετο, ὅτ' εἰς τὰς τούτων χεῖρας ἦλθεν,
οὗτος δ' οὐκ ἔχων ἂν εἰπεῖν ὅπου τι τούτων ἀπέδωκεν, ἵν' εὔπορος εἶναι δοκῶν μηδενὸς τύχω
παρ' ὑμῶν ἐλέου, τούτοις χρῆται τοῖς λόγοις.

50   Πολλὰ μὲν οὖν ἔγωγ' ἔχω καὶ ἄλλα τούτου κατη-
γορεῖν· οὐκ ἐνδέχεται δέ μοι, τῷ μάρτυρι τοῦ
κινδύνου περὶ τῆς ἐπιτιμίας ὄντος, περὶ ὧν αὐτὸς
ἠδίκημαι λέγειν. ἀλλὰ βούλομαι πρόκλησιν ὑμῖν
ἀναγνῶναι· γνώσεσθε γὰρ ἐξ αὐτῆς ἀκούσαντες, τὰ
μεμαρτυρημέν' ὡς ἔστιν ἀληθῆ, καὶ τὸν Μιλύαν ὅτι
νῦν μὲν περὶ πάντων φησὶν ἐξαιτεῖν, τὸ δὲ πρῶτον
ὑπὲρ τριάκοντα μόνον μνῶν ἐξῄτει, καὶ προσέτι
51 ζημιοῦται κατὰ τὴν μαρτυρίαν οὐδέν. ἐγὼ γὰρ
πανταχῇ τοῦτον ἐλέγξαι βουλόμενος, καὶ τὰς τέχνας
αὐτοῦ καὶ τὰς πανουργίας ἐμφανεῖς ὑμῖν καταστῆσαι πειρώμενος, ἠρόμην αὐτὸν πόσ' εἴη τὰ
χρήματα τὸ πλῆθος, καθ' ἃ τὸν Μιλύαν ὡς εἰδότ'
ἐξῄτησεν· οὗτος δὲ ψευσάμενος περὶ πάντων ἔφησεν.
" περὶ μὲν τοίνυν," ἔφην ἐγώ, " τούτου παραδώσω
σοι τὸν ἔχοντα τἀντίγραφα ὧν σύ με προὐκαλέσω.
52   προομόσαντος δέ μου τὸν ἄνθρωπον ὡς ὡμολόγησας
[860] ἐλεύθερον εἶναι καὶ κατὰ Δήμωνος ἐμαρτύρησας, ἂν
ἀπομόσῃς τἀναντία τούτων κατὰ τῆς θυγατρός,
ἀφίημί σοι πάνθ' ὑπὲρ ὧν ἂν ἐξαιτήσας φανῇς τὸ
116

had the chance, from seizing a fund to the existence
of which you would not be able to testify? Who can
believe this? It is impossible, men of the jury; it is
impossible. No; all the money which my father left
was indeed buried on the day on which it came into
the hands of these men; and the defendant, not being
able to tell when and where he paid back any of it,
makes use of these arguments, hoping that I may
seem to be a rich man, and so meet with no compassion from you.

I have many other charges to make against him, 50
but I have not the right to speak of the injuries I
myself have suffered, when the witness is in danger
of losing his civic rights. Still I wish to read to you
a challenge, for you will know, when you have heard
it, that the testimony was true, and that Aphobus,
who now declares that he demands Milyas to be examined about all the matters involved in the suit,
at first demanded him only in regard to a question
of thirty minae; and, furthermore, that he has been
put to no disadvantage because of the testimony.
For I, in my desire to refute him in every particular, 51
and in my attempt to make clear to you his tricks and
his villainies, asked him how large the sum was regarding which he demanded to examine Milyas, as
one who had knowledge of the facts. To this he
replied falsely, that it was in regard to the whole
amount. "Well then," said I, " as to this I will give
up to you for examination by torture the slave who
has the copy of your challenge to me. If, when I have 52
given oath that you acknowledged the man to be free,
and that you so testified against Demo, you will swear
to the contrary with imprecations upon your daughter,
I release to you the entire sum, for which you shall

DEMOSTHENES

πρῶτον βασανιζομένου τοῦ παιδός, καὶ τοσούτῳ
σοι γενέσθω τὸ τίμημ' ἔλαττον ὧν ὦφλες, καθ' ὃ
τὸν Μιλύαν ἐξῄτησας, ἵνα μηδὲν ζημιωθῇς παρὰ
53 τοὺς μάρτυρας." ταῦτ' ἐμοῦ προκαλεσαμένου πολλῶν παρόντων, οὐκ ἂν ἔφη ποιῆσαι. καίτοι ὅστις
αὐτὸς αὑτῷ ταῦτ' ἔφυγεν δικάσαι, πῶς ὑμᾶς χρὴ
τοὺς ὀμωμοκότας τούτῳ πιθομένους καταγνῶναι
τῶν μαρτύρων, ἀλλ' οὐ τοῦτον ἀναισχυντότατον
πάντων ἀνθρώπων εἶναι νομίζειν;

Ἀλλὰ μὴν ὡς ἀληθῆ λέγω, κάλει τούτων τοὺς
μάρτυρας.

ΜΑΡΤΥΡΕΣ

54 Οὐ τοίνυν ἐγὼ μὲν ταῦθ' ἕτοιμος ἦν, οἱ δὲ
μάρτυρες οὐ τὴν αὐτήν μοι γνώμην εἶχον, ἀλλὰ
κἀκεῖνοι παραστησάμενοι τοὺς παῖδας, ὑπὲρ ὧν
ἐμαρτύρησαν, πίστιν ἐπιθεῖναι ἠθέλησαν κατ'
ἐκείνων. ὁ δ' οὔτ' ἐκείνοις οὔτ' ἐμοὶ δοῦναι τὸν
ὅρκον ἠξίωσεν, ἀλλ' ἐπὶ λόγοις μεμηχανημένοις καὶ
μάρτυσιν οὐ τἀληθῆ μαρτυρεῖν εἰθισμένοις τὸ
πρᾶγμα καταστήσας, ἐλπίζει ῥᾳδίως ὑμᾶς ἐξαπατήσειν.

Λάβ' οὖν αὐτοῖς καὶ ταύτην τὴν μαρτυρίαν.

ΜΑΡΤΥΡΙΑ

55 Πῶς οὖν ἄν τις σαφέστερον ἐξελέγξειε συκοφαν-
τουμένους ἡμᾶς καὶ καταμεμαρτυρημένον τἀληθῆ
καὶ τὴν δίκην δικαίως ὠφλημένην, ἢ τοῦτον τὸν

118

be shown by the examination of the slave to have at the first demanded Milyas ; and the damages which you were condemned to pay shall be lessened by thus much—that is, by the amount in regard to which you demanded Milyas, to the end that you may be found to have been put to no disadvantage by the witnesses." This challenge I made to him 53 in the presence of many witnesses ; but he said he could not accept it. Yet, if a man refused to give this judgement in his own favour, how can it be right for you, who are upon your oaths, to give credence to his words and convict the witnesses, and not rather to regard this man as the most shameless of human-kind ?

To prove that my words are true, call the witnesses to these facts.

THE WITNESSES

Do not suppose that while I was ready to take this 54 course, the witnesses did not hold the same opinion. No ; they too were ready to place their children by their side, and in confirmation of the testimony they had given, to take an oath with imprecations upon them, if they swore falsely. But Aphobus did not see fit to allow an oath to be given either to them or to me. Instead, he rests his case on arguments subtly planned and on witnesses accustomed to per-jury, and thinks thereby easily to mislead you.

So take and read to the jury this deposition also.

THE DEPOSITION

How could one prove more clearly than I have 55 proved that we are the object of a malicious charge ; that the evidence brought forward against my opponent is true ; and that his condemnation was

τρόπον ἐπιδεικνύς; οἰκέτην τὸν τὴν μαρτυρίαν
[861] γράφοντ' οὐκ ἐθελήσαντα τοῦτον βασανίζειν περὶ
αὑτῶν τῶν μεμαρτυρημένων· Αἴσιον τὸν ἀδελφὸν
αὐτοῦ ταῦτα μεμαρτυρηκότα, ἅ φησιν εἶναι ψευδῆ·
56 τοῦτον αὐτὸν ταὐτὰ τοῖς μάρτυσιν οὓς διώκει μεμαρτυρηκότα μοι κατὰ Δήμωνος, ὄντος αὐτῷ θείου
καὶ συνεπιτρόπου· τὰς θεραπαίνας οὐκ ἐθελήσανθ'
ὑπὲρ τοῦ τὸν ἄνθρωπον ἐλεύθερον εἶναι βασανίζειν·
τὴν μητέρα τὴν ἐμαυτοῦ πίστιν περὶ τούτων ἐπιθεῖναι καθ' ἡμῶν ἐθέλουσαν· τῶν ἄλλων οἰκετῶν
οὐκ ἐθελήσαντα τοῦτον παραλαμβάνειν οὐδένα, τῶν
πάντ' εἰδότων μᾶλλον ἢ Μιλύας· τῶν μαρτύρων οἳ
κατεμαρτύρουν χρήματ' ἔχειν αὐτόν, οὐδενὶ τῶν
57 ψευδομαρτυριῶν ἐπεσκημμένον· τὴν διαθήκην οὐκ
ἀποδόντα, οὐδὲ τὸν οἶκον μισθώσαντα τῶν νόμων
κελευόντων· πίστιν ἐπιθεῖναι προομνύντος ἐμοῦ καὶ
τῶν μαρτύρων, ὥστ' ἀφεῖσθαι τοῦτον τῶν χρημάτων καθ' ἃ τὸν Μιλύαν ἐξήτησεν, οὐκ οἰηθέντα
δεῖν; μὰ τοὺς θεούς, ἐγὼ μὲν οὐκ ἂν ἔχοιμ'
ἐπιδεῖξαι ταῦτ' ἀκριβέστερον ἢ τοῦτον τὸν τρόπον.
οὕτω τοίνυν φανερῶς τῶν τε μαρτύρων καταψευδό-
μενος, καὶ ἐκ τῶν πραγμάτων οὐδὲν ζημιούμενος,
καὶ τὴν δίκην δικαίως ὠφληκώς, ὅμως ἀναισχυντεῖ·
58 καὶ εἰ μὲν μὴ καὶ παρὰ τοῖς αὑτοῦ φίλοις καὶ παρὰ
τῷ διαιτητῇ προεγνωσμένος ἀδικεῖν τούτους ἐποιεῖτο τοὺς λόγους, ἧττον ἂν ἦν ἄξιον θαυμάζειν· νῦν

---

[a] Demo was not actually a trustee, but in Oration XXVIII.
§ 15 it is stated that the elder Demosthenes had called him to
be present, when, on his death-bed, he had entrusted his
affairs and the guardianship of his children to the three
named as trustees. He was the father of Demophon, and had
very possibly taken part in the management of the trust.
120

just ? I have shown that he refused to examine by
torture the slave who wrote the testimony regarding
the very things to which he had testified ; that his
brother, Aesius, has attested the facts which he on
his part declares to be false ; that Aphobus himself **56**
has, at my summons, given against Demo,^{a} his uncle
and co-trustee, the same testimony as the witnesses
whom he is suing ; that he refused to examine my
women-servants as to the fact of Milyas being a freeman ; that my own mother was ready to give an
oath regarding these matters with imprecations upon
us ; that he refused to accept for examination any
one of my other slaves who knew all the circumstances
better than Milyas did ; that he has not brought a
charge of false witness against any one of those who
testified that he had the money ; that he did not **57**
give over the will, nor let the house, although the laws
so bade ; and finally that he did not see fit to give
an oath, after the witnesses and I myself had
sworn, whereby he could have secured release to the
amount of the sums regarding which he had demanded Milyas for torture. By heaven, I certainly
could think of no better way than this to establish
these facts. Yet, plain as it is that he falsely attacks
the witnesses ; that he suffers no damage from the
facts adduced ; that he was justly condemned ; he
still tries to brazen it out. If it were not that he **58**
uses his present language after having at the outset
been judged to be in the wrong by his own friends and
by the arbitrator, there would be less reason to wonder

Another alternative suggestion is that Demosthenes may
have instituted suit against Demo on quite other grounds
of which we have no knowledge. This complicated problem
is ably discussed by Calhoun, *l.c.* pp. 88 ff.

δ᾽ ἐπιτρέψαι με πείσας Ἀρχένεῳ καὶ Δρακοντίδῃ καὶ Φάνῳ τούτῳ τῷ νῦν ὑπ᾽ αὐτοῦ φεύγοντι τῶν ψευδομαρτυριῶν, τούτους μὲν ἀφῆκεν ἀκούσας [862] αὐτῶν ὅτι, εἰ μεθ᾽ ὅρκου ταῦτα διαιτήσουσι, καταγνώσονται τὴν ἐπιτροπήν, ἐπὶ τὸν κληρωτὸν δὲ διαιτητὴν ἐλθὼν καὶ οὐδὲν ἔχων ἀπολύσασθαι τῶν 59 ἐγκεκλημένων, ὦφλε τὴν δίαιταν. οἱ δικασταὶ δ᾽ ἀκούσαντες, εἰς οὓς ἐφῆκε, ταὐτὰ καὶ τοῖς τούτου φίλοις καὶ τῷ διαιτητῇ περὶ αὐτῶν ἔγνωσαν καὶ δέκα ταλάντων ἐτίμησαν, οὐ μὰ Δι᾽ οὐχ ὅτι τὸν Μιλύαν ὡμολόγησεν εἶναι ἐλεύθερον (τοῦτο μὲν γὰρ οὐδὲν ἦν), ἀλλ᾽ ὅτι πεντεκαίδεκα ταλάντων οὐσίας μοι καταλειφθείσης, τὸν μὲν οἶκον οὐκ ἐμίσθωσε, δέκα δ᾽ ἔτη μετὰ τῶν συνεπιτρόπων διαχειρίσας, πρὸς μὲν τὴν συμμορίαν ὑπὲρ παιδὸς ὄντος ἐμοῦ 60 πέντε μνᾶς συνετάξατ᾽ εἰσφέρειν, ὅσονπερ Τιμόθεος ὁ Κόνωνος καὶ οἱ τὰ μέγιστα κεκτημένοι τιμήματ᾽ εἰσέφερον, χρόνον δὲ τοσοῦτον τὰ χρήματα ταῦτ᾽ ἐπιτροπεύσας, ὑπὲρ ὧν τηλικαύτην αὐτὸς εἰσφορὰν ἠξίωσεν εἰσφέρειν, ἐμοὶ τὸ μὲν καθ᾽ αὑτὸν οὐδ᾽ εἴκοσι μνῶν ἄξια παρέδωκε, μετὰ δ᾽ ἐκείνων ὅλα τὰ κεφάλαια καὶ τὰς ἐπικαρπίας ἀπεστέρησεν. θέντες οὖν οἱ δικασταὶ τοῖς πᾶσι χρήμασιν οὐκ ἐφ᾽ ὅσῳ μισθοῦσι τοὺς οἴκους τόκον, ἀλλ᾽ ὃς ἦν ἐλάχιστος, εὗρον τὸ σύμπαν πλέον ἢ τριάκοντα τάλαντ᾽ αὐτοὺς ἀποστεροῦντας· διὸ τούτῳ τῶν δέκα ταλάντων ἐτίμησαν.

---

a See notes b and c on Oration XXVII. p. 11.

at all this. But the fact is, that after persuading
me to refer the matter to Archeneüs and Dracontides
and Phanus (the last of whom he is now suing on a
charge of giving false witness), he rejected them
(having heard them say that, if they decided on oath,
they would condemn his conduct as guardian), and
appeared before the official arbitrator, who, since
Aphobus was unable to clear himself from the charges
which I brought, gave judgement against him. The 59
jury, to whom he then appealed, having heard the
case, gave the same decision that his own friends and
the arbitrator had given, and fixed the damages at
ten talents. This was not, heaven knows, because
he had admitted Milyas to be a freeman (for this
was nothing to the point), but because, a fortune of
fifteen talents having been left me, he had not let
the property ; because further, he with his co-trustees
had the management of the estate for ten years,
and agreed on behalf of me, a child, to pay a property-
tax at the rate of five minae,[a] the same rate at which 60
Timotheüs, son of Conon, and those possessing the
largest fortunes were assessed ; and because, after
administering for so long an estate, on which he
voluntarily chose to pay so high a tax, he turned
over to me, as the amount due from him, property
not even of the value of twenty minae, having together with those others robbed me of my whole
estate, principal as well as interest. The jurymen,
therefore, although they allowed interest on the
whole property at the lowest rate, and not that at
which estates are ordinarily let, found that these men
had robbed me of more than thirty talents, and
accordingly fixed the damages against Aphobus at
ten talents.

AGAINST ONETOR

I

INTRODUCTION

WE are told in the preceding speech (§ 3) that Aphobus, after being condemned to pay Demosthenes damages in the amount of ten talents, proceeded to make it as difficult as possible for Demosthenes to collect that sum, or, indeed, anything at all. He disposed of his visible property, and himself took up residence at Megara. He had a farm, valued at a talent, of which Demosthenes sought to take possession, only to find that Onetor, the brother-in-law of Aphobus, was occupying it, claiming that it had been mortgaged to him as security for the amount of his sister's dowry. This dowry, alleged to have been paid to Aphobus at the time of the marriage, had become repayable, inasmuch as Aphobus had divorced his wife. On attempting to take possession of the land, as he had to do for himself, there being in Athens no officer corresponding to our sheriff, Demosthenes was driven off by Onetor; hence the present suit—technically a δίκη ἐξούλης, a suit for ejectment. The speaker's contention is that the marriage-portion had never been really paid, that the divorce was a fiction, and that the alleged mortgage was but a scheme devised by Aphobus and Onetor to prevent him (Demosthenes) from securing the property.

The speeches against Onetor are discussed in Schaefer, i. pp. 267 ff., and in Blass, iii. pp. 238 ff.

XXX

ΠΡΟΣ ΟΝΗΤΟΡΑ ΕΞΟΥΛΗΣ

Α

[864] Περὶ πολλοῦ ποιούμενος, ὦ ἄνδρες δικασταί, μήτε πρὸς Ἄφοβόν μοι συμβῆναι τὴν γενομένην διαφοράν, μήτε τὴν νῦν οὖσαν πρὸς Ὀνήτορα τουτονί, κηδεστὴν ὄντ᾽ αὐτοῦ, πολλὰ καὶ δίκαια προκαλεσάμενος ἀμφοτέρους, οὐδενὸς ἐδυνήθην τυχεῖν τῶν μετρίων, ἀλλ᾽ εὕρηκα πολὺ τοῦτον ἐκείνου δυσκολώτερον καὶ μᾶλλον ἄξιον ὄντα δοῦναι δίκην.

2 τὸν μὲν γὰρ οἰόμενος δεῖν ἐν τοῖς φίλοις διαδικάσασθαι τὰ πρὸς ἐμέ, καὶ μὴ λαβεῖν ὑμῶν πεῖραν, οὐχ οἷός τ᾽ ἐγενόμην πεῖσαι· τοῦτον δ᾽ αὐτὸν αὐτῷ κελεύων γενέσθαι δικαστήν, ἵνα μὴ παρ᾽ ὑμῖν κινδυνεύσῃ, τοσοῦτον κατεφρονήθην, ὥστ᾽ οὐχὶ μόνον λόγου τυχεῖν οὐκ ἠξιώθην, ἀλλὰ καὶ ἐκ τῆς γῆς ἧς Ἄφοβος ἐκέκτητο, ὅτ᾽ ὠφλίσκανέ μοι τὴν δίκην, 3 ὑβριστικῶς ὑπ᾽ αὐτοῦ πάνυ ἐξεβλήθην. ἐπειδὴ οὖν συναποστερεῖ τέ με τῶν ὄντων τῷ ἑαυτοῦ κηδεστῇ, πιστεύων τ᾽ εἰς ὑμᾶς εἰσελήλυθε ταῖς αὐτοῦ παρασκευαῖς, ὑπόλοιπόν ἐστιν ἐν ὑμῖν πειρᾶσθαι παρ᾽ αὐτοῦ τῶν δικαίων τυγχάνειν. οἶδα μὲν οὖν, ὦ ἄνδρες δικασταί, ὅτι μοι πρὸς παρασκευὰς λόγων

128

XXX
AGAINST ONETOR, AN EJECTMENT SUIT

I

I SHOULD have been most glad, men of the jury, had the difference which I have had with Aphobus, and also that in which I am now involved with this man Onetor, his brother-in-law, not come about. Accordingly, I made to them both many fair offers, but I have been unable to secure any reasonable action from either of them. On the contrary, I have found this man far harder to deal with, and more worthy of punishment than the other. In the case of Aphobus, I held 2 that his controversy with me should be settled among our friends, and not come to trial before you, but I could not persuade him. But this man, when I bade him act as judge in his own case, that he might not risk a trial before you, treated me with such contempt, that not only did he not think fit to give me a hearing, but I was even in the most outrageous manner driven off the land, which belonged to Aphobus, when he lost his suit to me. Since, therefore, he joins with 3 his brother-in-law in seeking to deprive me of what is mine, and has come before you, trusting in the measures he has concocted, there is no other course open to me than to try in your court to get justice from him. I know well, men of the jury, that I have to con-

καὶ μάρτυρας οὐ τἀληθῆ μαρτυρήσοντας ὁ ἀγών
ἐστιν· ὅμως μέντοι τοσοῦτον οἶμαι διοίσειν τῷ
4 δικαιότερα τούτου λέγειν, ὥστ᾽ εἰ καί τις ὑμῶν
πρότερον τοῦτον ἡγεῖτ᾽ εἶναι μὴ πονηρόν, ἔκ γε τῶν
[865] πρὸς ἐμὲ πεπραγμένων γνώσεσθαι, ὅτι καὶ τὸν
ἄλλον χρόνον ἐλάνθανεν αὐτὸν κάκιστος ὢν καὶ
ἀδικώτατος ἁπάντων. ἀποδείξω γὰρ αὐτὸν οὐ
μόνον τὴν προῖκ᾽ οὐ δεδωκότα, ἧς φησι νῦν ἀποτετιμῆσθαι τὸ χωρίον, ἀλλὰ καὶ ἐξ ἀρχῆς τοῖς ἐμοῖς
ἐπιβουλεύσαντα, καὶ πρὸς τούτοις τὴν μὲν γυναῖκ᾽
οὐκ ἀπολελοιπυῖαν, ὑπὲρ ἧς ἐξήγαγέ μ᾽ ἐκ ταύτης
5 τῆς γῆς, προϊστάμενον δ᾽ ἐπ᾽ ἀποστερήσει τῶν
ἐμῶν Ἀφόβου καὶ τούτους ὑπομένοντα τοὺς ἀγῶ-
νας, οὕτω μεγάλοις τεκμηρίοις καὶ φανεροῖς ἐλέγχοις, ὥσθ᾽ ὑμᾶς ἅπαντας εἴσεσθαι σαφῶς, ὅτι
δικαίως καὶ προσηκόντως οὗτος φεύγει ταύτην ὑπ᾽
ἐμοῦ τὴν δίκην. ὅθεν δὲ ῥᾷστα μαθήσεσθε περὶ
αὐτῶν, ἐντεῦθεν ὑμᾶς καὶ ἐγὼ πρῶτον πειράσομαι
διδάσκειν.

6 Ἐγὼ γάρ, ὦ ἄνδρες δικασταί, πολλούς τ᾽ ἄλλους
Ἀθηναίων καὶ τοῦτον οὐκ ἐλάνθανον κακῶς ἐπιτρο-
πευόμενος, ἀλλ᾽ ἦν καταφανὴς εὐθὺς ἀδικούμενος·
τοσαῦται πραγματεῖαι καὶ λόγοι καὶ παρὰ τῷ
ἄρχοντι καὶ παρὰ τοῖς ἄλλοις ἐγίγνονθ᾽ ὑπὲρ τῶν
ἐμῶν. τό τε γὰρ πλῆθος τῶν καταλειφθέντων ἦν
φανερόν, ὅτι τ᾽ ἀμίσθωτον τὸν οἶκον ἐποίουν οἱ
ἰαχε ιρίζοντες, ἵν᾽ αὐτοὶ τὰ χρήματα καρποῖντο,
οὐκ ἄδηλον ἦν. ὥστ᾽ ἐκ τῶν γιγνομένων οὐκ ἔσθ᾽
ὅστις οὐχ ἡγεῖτο τῶν εἰδότων δίκην με λήψεσθαι

tend against arguments craftily prepared, and against witnesses who are going to give false testimony; nevertheless I think that I shall have such an advantage over him because of the justice of my cause, that, even if any one of you heretofore thought him 4 an honest man, he will learn from the defendant's acts toward me that even in time past he has been, without your knowing it, the basest and most unrighteous of men. I shall show, namely, that he has not only never paid the marriage-portion, to secure which he alleges that the land has been mortgaged, but from the very start has schemed to defraud me of my rights; that, further, the lady, on whose behalf he drove me from the land in question, has not been divorced at all; and that he is now screening 5 Aphobus, and standing this trial with the purpose of depriving me of what is mine. This I shall show by such strong and manifest proofs, that you will see how just and proper it is that I have instituted this action against him. I shall commence with matters which will best enable you to grasp the facts of the case.

In common with many others of the Athenians, 6 men of the jury, this man was well aware that my guardians were proving false to their trust. Indeed, it became clear very early that I was being wronged, so many were the discussions and arguments regarding my affairs held before the archon and before other officials. For the value of the property left me was well known, and it was pretty clear that the administrators were leaving it unlet in order that they might have the use of the money themselves. There was not a single one, therefore, among those who realized what was going on, who did not expect that I should obtain a judgement for damages from these men, as

παρ' αὐτῶν, ἐπειδὴ τάχιστ' ἀνὴρ εἶναι δοκιμα-
7 σθείην. ἐν οἷς καὶ Τιμοκράτης καὶ Ὀνήτωρ ταύτην
ἔχοντες διετέλεσαν τὴν διάνοιαν. τεκμήριον δὲ
πάντων μέγιστον· οὗτος γὰρ ἐβουλήθη μὲν Ἀφόβῳ
δοῦναι τὴν ἀδελφήν, ὁρῶν τῆς θ' αὐτοῦ πατρῴας
οὐσίας καὶ τῆς ἐμῆς οὐκ ὀλίγης αὐτὸν κύριον
[866] γεγενημένον, προέσθαι δὲ τὴν προῖκ' οὐκ ἐπίστευσεν, ὥσπερ εἰ τὰ τῶν ἐπιτροπευόντων χρήματ'
ἀποτίμημα τοῖς ἐπιτροπευομένοις καθεστάναι νομίζων. ἀλλὰ τὴν μὲν ἀδελφὴν ἔδωκε, τὴν δὲ προῖκ'
αὐτῷ Τιμοκράτης ἐπὶ πέντ' ὀβολοῖς ὀφειλήσειν
ὡμολόγησεν, ᾧ πρότερον ἡ γυνὴ συνοικοῦσ' ἐτύγ-
8 χανεν. ὀφλόντος δέ μοι τὴν δίκην Ἀφόβου τῆς
ἐπιτροπῆς, καὶ οὐδὲν δίκαιον ποιεῖν ἐθέλοντος,
διαλύειν μὲν ἡμᾶς Ὀνήτωρ οὐδ' ἐπεχείρησεν, οὐκ
ἀποδεδωκὼς δὲ τὴν προῖκα, ἀλλ' αὐτὸς κύριος ὤν,
ὡς ἀπολελοιπυίας τῆς ἀδελφῆς καὶ δούς, κομίσασθαι δ' οὐ δυνάμενος, ἀποτιμήσασθαι φάσκων τὴν
γῆν ἐξάγειν μ' ἐξ αὐτῆς ἐτόλμησε· τοσοῦτον καὶ
ἐμοῦ καὶ ὑμῶν καὶ τῶν κειμένων νόμων κατ-
9 εφρόνησεν. καὶ τὰ μὲν γενόμενα, καὶ δι' ἃ φεύγει
τὴν δίκην καὶ περὶ ὧν οἴσετε τὴν ψῆφον, ταῦτ'
ἐστίν, ὦ ἄνδρες δικασταί· παρέξομαι δὲ μάρτυρας
πρῶτον μὲν αὐτὸν Τιμοκράτην, ὡς ὡμολόγησεν
ὀφειλήσειν τὴν προῖκα, καὶ τὸν τόκον ἀπεδίδου τῆς
προικὸς Ἀφόβῳ κατὰ τὰς ὁμολογίας, ἔπειθ' ὡς

---

[a] The remark is sarcastic. Demosthenes represents Onetor
as fearing lest the suit of Demosthenes against Aphobus

soon as I should attain my majority. Among those 7
who from first to last held this opinion were Timocrates and Onetor. Of this I can give you the
strongest of proofs. For the defendant wished to
give his sister in marriage to Aphobus, seeing that
he had got into his hands his own patrimony and mine
(which was not inconsiderable) as well ; but he had
not confidence enough in him to abandon her marriage-
portion. It was as if he felt, forsooth, that the property
of guardians was a security for their wards.[a] He did,
however, give him his sister, but the portion, Timocrates, who had been her former husband, agreed to
keep as a loan with interest at the rate of five obols.[b]
When I had won my suit against Aphobus in the 8
matter of the guardianship and he still refused to
make any just settlement, Onetor did not even try
to settle our dispute, but, alleging that his sister
had been divorced, and that he was unable to get
back her marriage-portion, which he had paid (although he had not paid it, and it was even then in his
possession), declared that he had taken a mortgage
on the land, and had the effrontery to expel me from
it ; such was his contempt for me, and for you,
and for the laws which were in force. These, men 9
of the jury, are the facts because of which he is
defendant in the present suit, and regarding which
you are to cast your vote. I shall bring forward witnesses, and in the first instance Timocrates himself,
who will testify that he agreed to hold the dowry
as a loan, and that he continued to pay interest on it
to Aphobus according to the agreement ; also that

might make it questionable whether the latter would be in
a position to repay the marriage-portion, if called upon to
do so.

[b] That is, at 10 per cent, instead of the ordinary 18 per cent.

αὐτὸς Ἄφοβος ὡμολόγει κομίζεσθαι τὸν τόκον
παρὰ Τιμοκράτους.

Καί μοι λαβὲ τὰς μαρτυρίας.

10   Ἐξ ἀρχῆς μὲν τοίνυν ὁμολογεῖται μὴ δοθῆναι τὴν
προῖκα μηδὲ γενέσθαι κύριον αὐτῆς Ἄφοβον. δῆλον
δὲ καὶ ἐκ τῶν εἰκότων, ὅτι τούτων ἕνεχ' ὧν εἴρηκα
ὀφείλειν εἴλοντο μᾶλλον, ἢ καταμεῖξαι τὴν προῖκ'
εἰς τὴν οὐσίαν τὴν Ἀφόβου τὴν οὕτω κινδυνευθή-
σεσθαι μέλλουσαν. οὔτε γὰρ δι' ἀπορίαν οἷόν τ'
εἰπεῖν ὡς οὐκ εὐθὺς ἀπέδοσαν· Τιμοκράτει τε γὰρ
ἐστιν οὐσία πλέον ἢ δέκα ταλάντων, Ὀνήτορί τε
[867] πλέον ἢ τριάκοντα, ὥστ' οὐκ ἂν διὰ τοῦτό γ' εἶεν
11   οὐκ εὐθὺς δεδωκότες· οὔτε κτήματα μὲν ἦν αὐτοῖς,
ἀργύριον δ' οὐκ ἔτυχε παρόν, ἡ γυνὴ δ' ἐχήρευε,
διὸ πρᾶξαι ταῦτ' ἠπείχθησαν οὐχ ἅμα τὴν προῖκα
διδόντες· ἀργύριόν τε γὰρ οὗτοι δανείζουσιν ἄλλοις
οὐκ ὀλίγον, συνοικοῦσάν τε ταύτην, ἀλλ' οὐ χη-
ρεύουσαν παρὰ Τιμοκράτους ἐξέδοσαν, ὥστ' οὐδ' ἂν
ταύτην τὴν σκῆψιν εἰκότως αὐτῶν τις ἀποδέξαιτο.
12   καὶ μὲν δή, ὦ ἄνδρες δικασταί, κἀκεῖνο ἂν πάντες
ὁμολογήσαιτε, ὅτι τοιοῦτο πρᾶγμα συναλλάττων
ὁστισοῦν ἕλοιτ' ἂν ἑτέρῳ μᾶλλον ὀφείλειν, ἢ
κηδεστῇ τὴν προῖκα μὴ ἀποδοῦναι. μὴ διαλυσά-
μενος μὲν γὰρ γίγνεται[1] χρήστης ἄδηλος εἴτ' ἀπο-
δώσει δικαίως εἴτε μή, μετὰ δὲ τῆς γυναικὸς

---

¹ γίγνεται] [ἔσται] Blass.

Aphobus himself acknowledged that he received the interest from Timocrates.

Take the depositions.

THE DEPOSITIONS

From the very first, you see, it is admitted that the 10 dowry was not paid to Aphobus, and that he did not get it under his control. And it seems very probable that on account of the facts which I have mentioned, they chose to continue as debtors for the dowry, rather than to have it involved in the estate of Aphobus which was sure to be so seriously endangered. For it is impossible for them to claim that poverty prevented their paying it over at once, since Timocrates has an estate of more than ten talents, and Onetor one of more than thirty ; so this cannot have been the reason why they have not made an immediate payment. Nor can they claim that they had property 11 indeed, but no ready money, or that the lady was a widow, and that they therefore hastened to conclude matters without at once paying her portion. For these men are in the habit of lending considerable sums to others, and moreover, the lady was not a widow, but when they gave her in marriage, it was from the house of Timocrates, where she was living with him as his wife ; so that there is no reasonable ground why one should accept this excuse either. Further, men of the jury, I think you would all agree 12 to this, that, in arranging a matter of this sort, anyone would choose to borrow money of another, rather than fail to pay the dowry to his sister's husband. For if a man does not settle this matter he becomes a debtor, regarding whom it is uncertain whether he will meet his just obligations or not ; but if together with the lady he gives also what is hers, he becomes a

13 τἀκείνης ἀποδοὺς οἰκεῖος καὶ κηδεστής· ἐν οὐδεμιᾷ
γάρ ἐστιν ὑποψίᾳ τὰ δίκαια πάντα ποιήσας. ὥσθ᾽
οὕτως τοῦ πράγματος ἔχοντος, καὶ τούτων οὐδὲ
καθ᾽ ἓν ὧν εἶπον ὀφείλειν ἀναγκασθέντων, οὐδὲ
βουληθέντων ἄν, οὐκ ἔστ᾽ εἰπεῖν ἄλλην πρόφασιν δι᾽
ἣν οὐκ ἀπέδοσαν, ἀλλ᾽ ἀνάγκη ταύτην εἶναι τὴν
αἰτίαν, δι᾽ ἣν δοῦναι τὴν προῖκ᾽ οὐκ ἐπίστευσαν.

14 Ἐγὼ τοίνυν ὁμολογουμένως οὕτω ταῦτ᾽ ἐλέγχων,
ὡς οὐδ᾽ ὕστερον ἀπέδοσαν, οἶμαι ῥᾳδίως ἐπιδείξειν
ἐξ αὐτῶν τῶν πεπραγμένων, ὥσθ᾽ ὑμῖν γενέσθαι
φανερόν, ὅτι κἂν εἰ μὴ ἐπὶ τούτοις, ἀλλ᾽ ἐπὶ τῷ διὰ
ταχέων ἀποδοῦναι τἀργύριον εἶχον, οὐκ ἄν ποτ᾽
ἀπέδοσαν οὐδ᾽ ἂν προεῖντο· τοιαύτας ἀνάγκας εἶχεν

15 αὐτοῖς τὸ πρᾶγμα. δύο μὲν γάρ ἐστιν ἔτη τὰ
μεταξὺ τοῦ συνοικῆσαί τε τὴν γυναῖκα καὶ φῆσαι
[868] τούτους πεποιῆσθαι τὴν ἀπόλειψιν· ἐγήματο μὲν
γὰρ ἐπὶ Πολυζήλου ἄρχοντος σκιροφοριῶνος μηνός,
ἡ δ᾽ ἀπόλειψις ἐγράφη ποσιδεῶνος μηνὸς ἐπὶ
Τιμοκράτους· ἐγὼ δ᾽ εὐθέως μετὰ τοὺς γάμους

---

^a To understand the argument of the speech the reader
should bear in mind certain facts regarding the Athenian
laws concerning marriage and divorce.

To make a marriage legal at Athens it was necessary that
both bride and bridegroom be of pure Athenian stock, and
that the bride be given away by her father, or, if she had no
father living, by her nearest male relative (her guardian or
κύριος). The marriage-contract was between the bridegroom
and this guardian, and the marriage-portion was paid by the
guardian to the bridegroom. In the case of Onetor's sister
Demosthenes asserts that the portion was not paid outright
to Aphobus, but was retained by her former husband,
Timocrates, who was to pay interest on it at 10 per cent.

The husband might divorce his wife, but he was required
to send her back to her guardian with her personal effects
and her portion, or to pay interest on the portion, normally

kinsman and a brother-in law, for he is not under any **13**
suspicion, since he has done all that justice demanded.
Seeing that the matter stands thus, and that they
were not forced by a single one of the causes which
I have mentioned to let this debt stand, and could
not have desired to do so, it is not possible to suggest
any other excuse for non-payment. It must be for
the reason which I have mentioned—that they did
not trust Aphobus enough to pay him the dowry.[a]

I have established this point, then, in this way **14**
beyond all controversy ; and I think I shall easily demonstrate from the facts themselves that they did not
pay the portion subsequently either ; so that it will
be clear to you that even if they withheld the money,
not for the reasons I have mentioned, but with the
intention of speedy payment, they would never
actually have paid it, or let it slip out of their hands ;
with such urgency did the case press upon them.
There was an interval of two years between the **15**
marriage of the woman and their declaration that
the divorce had taken place. She was married in the
archonship of Polyzelus, in the month of Sciropho-
rion,[b] and the divorce was registered in the month
of Posideon,[c] in the archonship of Timocrates.
I, on my part, was admitted to citizenship[d] immedi-

at 18 per cent until it was paid. His action in sending away
his wife was technically called ἀπόπεμψις.

On the other hand the wife might leave her husband with
his consent, or for cause. If the husband's consent could
not be obtained, the woman presented herself before the
archon and stated her case. The act, taken on her initiative,
was termed ἀπόλειψις, and in this case, too, her portion went
with her.

[b] That is, in June 366.   [c] That is, in December 364.
[d] See note *b*, on p. 9, and Aristotle, *Constitution of
Athens*, 42. 2.

δοκιμασθεὶς ἐνεκάλουν καὶ λόγον ἀπῄτουν, καὶ
πάντων ἀποστερούμενος τὰς δίκας ἐλάγχανον ἐπὶ
16 τοῦ αὐτοῦ ἄρχοντος. ὁ δὴ χρόνος οὗτος ὀφειλῆσαι
μὲν ἐνδέχεται κατὰ τὰς ὁμολογίας, ἀποδοῦναι δ'
οὐκ ἔχει πίστιν. ὃς γὰρ διὰ ταῦτ' ἐξ ἀρχῆς ὀφείλειν εἵλετο καὶ τόκον φέρειν, ἵνα μὴ κινδυνεύοι ἡ
προὶξ μετὰ τῆς ἄλλης οὐσίας, πῶς οὗτος ἂν ἀπέδωκεν ἤδη τὴν δίκην φεύγοντος, ὃς εἰ καὶ τότ'
ἐπίστευσε, τηνικαῦτ' ἂν ἀπολαβεῖν ἐζήτησεν; οὐκ
ἔνεστι δήπουθεν, ὦ ἄνδρες δικασταί.

17 Ἀλλὰ μὴν ὡς ἐγήματο μὲν ἡ γυνὴ καθ' ὃν ἐγὼ
λέγω χρόνον, ἀντίδικοι δ' ἡμεῖς ἤδη πρὸς ἀλλήλους
ἐν τῷ μεταξὺ χρόνῳ κατέστημεν, ὕστερον δ' ἢ
ἐγὼ τὴν δίκην ἔλαχον τὴν ἀπόλειψιν οὗτοι πρὸς
τὸν ἄρχοντ' ἀπεγράψαντο, λαβέ μοι καθ' ἕκαστον
ταύτας τὰς μαρτυρίας.

ΜΑΡΤΥΡΙΑ

Μετὰ τοίνυν τοῦτον τὸν ἄρχοντα Κηφισόδωρος,
Χίων. ἐπὶ τούτων ἐνεκάλουν δοκιμασθείς, ἔλαχον
δὲ τὴν δίκην ἐπὶ Τιμοκράτους.
Λαβέ ταύτην τὴν μαρτυρίαν.

ΜΑΡΤΥΡΙΑ

18 Ἀνάγνωθι δὲ καὶ ταύτην τὴν μαρτυρίαν.

ΜΑΡΤΥΡΙΑ

Δῆλον μὲν τοίνυν καὶ ἐκ τῶν μεμαρτυρημένων,
ὅτι τὴν προῖκ' οὐ δόντες, ἀλλ' ἐπὶ τῷ διασῴζειν
138

ately after the marriage, laid my charges, and demanded an accounting; and, finding that I was being robbed of all my property, instituted my suit under the last-mentioned archon. The shortness of **16** the time makes the continuance of the debt in accordance with the agreement not unlikely, but it is incredible that it should have been paid. For do you suppose that the defendant here, a man who at the first chose to owe the money and to pay interest on it, in order that his sister's dowry might not be jeopardized along with the rest of her husband's property, would have paid it when suit had already been instituted against that husband? Why, even if he had at the first trusted him with the money, he would then at once have sought to recover it. No, men of the jury; the supposition is, I presume, impossible.

To prove that the woman married at the time I **17** mention; that in the interim Aphobus and I had already gone to law; and that those men did not register the divorce with the archon until after I had instituted my suit, take, please, these depositions regarding each point.

THE DEPOSITIONS

After this archon came Cephisodorus and then Chion. During their term of office, having been admitted to citizenship, I continued to press my charges, and in the archonship of Timocrates I began my suit.

Take this deposition, please.

THE DEPOSITION

Read also this deposition. **18**

THE DEPOSITION

It is clear, then, from the evidence adduced that it is not because they have paid the dowry, but because

Ἀφόβῳ τὴν οὐσίαν ταῦτα τολμῶσι πράττειν. οἱ
γὰρ ἐν τοσούτῳ χρόνῳ καὶ ὀφειλῆσαι καὶ ἀποδοῦναι καὶ τὴν γυναῖκ᾽ ἀπολιπεῖν καὶ οὐ κομίσα-
[869] σθαι καὶ τὸ χωρίον ἀποτιμήσασθαί φασι, πῶς οὐ
φανερὸν ὅτι προστάντες τοῦ πράγματος τὰ γνω-
19 σθένθ᾽ ὑφ᾽ ὑμῶν ἀποστερῆσαί με ζητοῦσιν; ὡς δὲ
καὶ ἐξ ὧν αὐτὸς οὗτος καὶ Τιμοκράτης καὶ Ἄφοβος
ἀπεκρίναντο, οὐχ οἷόν τ᾽ ἀποδεδόσθαι τὴν προῖκα,
ταῦτ᾽ ἤδη πειράσομαι διδάσκειν ὑμᾶς. ἐγὼ γάρ,
ὦ ἄνδρες δικασταί, τούτων ἕκαστον ἠρόμην πολλῶν
ἐναντίον μαρτύρων, Ὀνήτορα μὲν καὶ Τιμοκράτην,
εἴ τινες εἶεν μάρτυρες ὧν ἐναντίον τὴν προῖκ᾽ ἀπέδοσαν, αὐτὸν δ᾽ Ἄφοβον, εἴ τινες παρῆσαν ὅτ᾽
20 ἀπελάμβανεν. καί μοι πάντες ἀπεκρίναντο καθ᾽
ἕκαστον, ὅτι οὐδεὶς μάρτυς παρείη, κομίζοιτο δὲ
λαμβάνων καθ᾽ ὁποσονοῦν δέοιτ᾽ Ἄφοβος παρ᾽
αὐτῶν. καίτοι τῷ τοῦθ᾽ ὑμῶν πιστόν, ὡς ταλάντου
τῆς προικὸς οὔσης ἄνευ μαρτύρων Ὀνήτωρ καὶ
Τιμοκράτης Ἀφόβῳ τοσοῦτον ἀργύριον ἐνεχεί-
ρισαν; ᾧ μὴ ὅτι τοῦτον τὸν τρόπον, ἀλλ᾽ οὐδὲ
μετὰ πολλῶν μαρτύρων ἀποδιδοὺς εἰκῇ τις ἂν
ἐπίστευσεν, ἵν᾽ εἴ τις γίγνοιτο διαφορά, κομίσασθαι
21 ῥᾳδίως παρ᾽ ὑμῖν δύνηται. μὴ γὰρ ὅτι πρὸς τοῦτον
τοιοῦτον ὄντα, ἀλλ᾽ οὐδὲ πρὸς ἄλλον, οὐδ᾽ ἂν εἰς
οὐδὲ ἕνα τοιοῦτον συνάλλαγμα ποιούμενος ἀμαρ-
τύρως ἂν ἔπραξεν· ἀλλὰ τῶν τοιούτων ἕνεκα καὶ
γάμους ποιοῦμεν καὶ τοὺς ἀναγκαιοτάτους παρα-
καλοῦμεν, ὅτι οὐ πάρεργον, ἀλλ᾽ ἀδελφῶν καὶ

ᵃ More literally, "one would have been rash to have
trusted him."
140

they wish to save his property for Aphobus, that they
have had the audacity to act as they have done. For
when in so short a time they allege that they owed
the money ; that they paid it; that the woman was
divorced and could not recover the dowry ; and that
they took a mortgage on the land ; how can it be
other than clear that they are acting in collusion in
their attempt to defraud me of the damages awarded
me by you ? I shall now endeavour to prove to you 19
from the answers given by the defendant himself, and
by Timocrates, and Aphobus, that it is impossible that
the dowry should have been paid. For, men of the
jury, I questioned each of these men in the presence
of many witnesses. I asked Onetor and Timocrates
whether any witnesses were present when they paid
the dowry, and Aphobus himself whether any were
present when he received it ; and they all answered 20
severally that no witness was present, but that
Aphobus got it from them by instalments, in such
sums as he needed from time to time. And yet can
any one of you believe this, that, when the dowry
was a talent, Onetor and Timocrates put so large a
sum into the hands of Aphobus without witnesses ?
Why, in paying him money, I will not say in this
manner, but even in the presence of many witnesses,
one would have taken every possible precaution *a* in
order, if a dispute should arise, to be able readily to
recover in your court what was due. No man, in con- 21
cluding a transaction of such importance, I will not say
with such a man as Aphobus, but with anybody whatever, would have acted without a witness. This is the
reason why we celebrate marriage-feasts and call
together our closest friends and relations, because
we are dealing with no light affair, but are entrusting

θυγατέρων βίους ἐγχειρίζομεν, ὑπὲρ ὧν τὰς ἀσφα-
22 λείας μάλιστα σκοποῦμεν. εἰκὸς τοίνυν καὶ τοῦτον,
ὧνπερ ἐναντίον ὀφείλειν ὡμολόγησε καὶ τὸν τόκον
οἴσειν, τῶν αὐτῶν τούτων παρόντων διαλύσασθαι
[870] πρὸς Ἄφοβον, εἴπερ ὡς ἀληθῶς ἀπεδίδου τὴν
προῖκ' αὐτῷ. τοῦτον μὲν γὰρ τὸν τρόπον πράξας,
ὅλου τοῦ πράγματος ἀπηλλάττετο, μόνος μόνῳ
δ' ἀποδιδούς, τοὺς ἐπὶ ταῖς ὁμολογίαις παραγενο-
μένους ὡς κατ' ὀφείλοντος ἂν αὐτοῦ μάρτυρας
23 ὑπελείπετο. νῦν τοίνυν τοὺς μὲν ὄντας οἰκείους καὶ
βελτίους αὐτῶν οὐκ ἐδύναντο πεῖσαι τὴν προῖκ'
ἀποδεδωκέναι σφᾶς μαρτυρεῖν, ἑτέρους δ' εἰ παρ-
έχοιντο μάρτυρας μηδὲν γένει προσήκοντας, οὐκ ἂν
ἡγοῦνθ' ὑμᾶς αὐτοῖς πιστεύειν. ἔτι δ' ἀθρόαν μὲν
φάσκοντες δεδωκέναι τὴν προῖκα, ᾔδεσαν ὅτι τοὺς
ἀπενεγκόντας οἰκέτας ἐξαιτήσομεν, οὓς μὴ γεγενημένης τῆς δόσεως παραδοῦναι μὴ θέλοντες ἠλέγ-
χοντ' ἄν· εἰ δ' αὐτοὶ μόνοι μόνῳ τοῦτον τὸν τρόπον
δεδωκέναι λέγοιεν, ἐνόμιζον οὐκ ἐλεγχθήσεσθαι.
24 διὰ τοῦτο τοῦτον εἵλοντ' ἐξ ἀνάγκης ψεύδεσθαι τὸν
τρόπον. τοιαύταις τέχναις καὶ πανουργίαις, ὡς
ἁπλοῖ τινες εἶναι δόξοντες, ἡγοῦνται ῥᾳδίως ὑμᾶς
ἐξαπατήσειν, ἁπλῶς οὐδ' ἂν μικρὸν ὑπὲρ τῶν
διαφερόντων, ἀλλ' ὡς οἷόν τ' ἀκριβέστατα πρά-
ξαντες.

Λαβὲ τὰς μαρτυρίας αὐτοῖς ὧν ἐναντίον ἀπεκρίναντο, καὶ ἀνάγνωθι.

142

to the care of others the lives of our sisters and
daughters, for whom we seek the greatest possible
security. The presumption is, then, that the de- 22
fendant made the settlement in the presence of the
same witnesses before whom he had admitted the
indebtedness and promised to pay the interest, if he
really did pay the dowry to Aphobus. For, if he had
acted in this way, he would have cleared himself of the
whole matter ; but by paying him when they were
alone, he would have left those in whose presence he
had made the agreement as witnesses that he was
still a debtor. As it was, they could not induce their 23
friends, who were more honest men than themselves,
to bear witness to the payment of the money, and
they thought that, if they produced other witnesses,
not related to them, you would not believe them.
Again, if they said the payment had been made all at
once, they knew that we should demand for examination by torture the slaves who had brought the money.
These, if the payment had not been made, they
would have refused to give up, and so they would
have been convicted of fraud. But if they maintained
that they had paid the money without witnesses in
the manner alleged, they thought to escape detec-
tion. For this reason they were driven through stress 24
of necessity to make up this false story. By such
tricks and pieces of villainy, while hoping themselves
to pass for simple folk, they think they will easily
deceive you ; whereas in the slightest matter affect-
ing their interest they would act, not with simplicity,
but with every possible precaution.

Take now the depositions of the persons in whose
presence they gave their answers, and read them to
the jury.

ΜΑΡΤΥΡΙΑΙ

25 Φέρε δή, ὦ ἄνδρες δικασταί, καὶ τὴν γυναῖχ'
ὑμῖν ἐπιδείξω λόγῳ μὲν ἀπολελοιπυῖαν, ἔργῳ δὲ
συνοικοῦσαν Ἀφόβῳ· νομίζω γάρ, ἂν τοῦτ' ἀκριβῶς μάθητε, μᾶλλον ὑμᾶς τούτοις μὲν ἀπιστήσειν,
ἐμοὶ δ' ἀδικουμένῳ τὰ δίκαια βοηθήσειν. μάρτυρας
δὲ τῶν μὲν ὑμῖν παρέξομαι, τῶν δ' ἐπιδείξω μεγάλα
26
[871] τεκμήρια καὶ πίστεις ἱκανάς. ἐγὼ γάρ, ὦ ἄνδρες
δικασταί, μετὰ τὸ γεγράφθαι παρὰ τῷ ἄρχοντι
ταύτην τὴν γυναῖκ' ἀπολελοιπυῖαν, καὶ τὸ φάσκειν
Ὀνήτορ' ἀντὶ τῆς προικὸς ἀποτετιμῆσθαι τὸ
χωρίον, ὁρῶν Ἄφοβον ὁμοίως ἔχοντα καὶ γεωργοῦντα τὴν γῆν καὶ τῇ γυναικὶ συνοικοῦντα, σαφῶς
ᾔδειν ὅτι λόγος ταῦτα καὶ παραγωγὴ τοῦ πράγ-
27 ματός ἐστι. βουλόμενος δ' ἐμφανῆ ποιῆσαι ταῦτα
πᾶσιν ὑμῖν, ἐλέγχειν αὐτὸν ἠξίουν ἐναντίον μαρτύρων, εἰ μὴ φάσκοι ταῦθ' οὕτως ἔχειν, καὶ παρεδίδουν οἰκέτην εἰς βάσανον, ὃς συνῄδει πάντ'
ἀκριβῶς· ὃν ἔλαβον κατὰ τὴν ὑπερημερίαν ἐκ τῶν
Ἀφόβου. οὗτος δ' ἐμοῦ ταῦτ' ἀξιώσαντος, περὶ
μὲν τοῦ συνοικεῖν Ἀφόβῳ τὴν ἀδελφὴν ἔφυγε τὴν
βάσανον· ὡς δ' οὐκ ἐκεῖνος ἐγεώργει τὴν γῆν,
οὐκ ἐδύνατ' ἀρνηθῆναι διὰ τὴν περιφάνειαν, ἀλλὰ
28 προσωμολόγησεν. οὐ μόνον δ' ἐκ τούτων ἦν
ῥᾴδιον[1] γνῶναι, ὅτι καὶ συνῴκει τῇ γυναικὶ καὶ τὸ
χωρίον ἐκέκτητ' ἔτι πρὶν γενέσθαι τὴν δίκην, ἀλλὰ
καὶ ἐξ ὧν ὀφλὼν διεπράξατο περὶ αὐτῶν. ὡς γὰρ
οὐκ ἀποτετιμηκώς, ἀλλ' ἐμῶν ἐσομένων κατὰ τὴν

---

[1] ῥᾴδιον] omitted by Blass.

THE DEPOSITIONS

Now, men of the jury, I shall prove to you that the 25
woman made a merely nominal divorce, but was in
reality living with Aphobus as his wife. I think that,
if you are thoroughly convinced of this, you will be
more inclined to distrust these men, and to give me
the aid that is my due. Of some of the facts I shall
produce witnesses : others I shall establish by strong
presumptions and by adequate proofs. When I saw, 26
men of the jury, that after the woman's divorce had
been registered with the archon, and after the defendant's declaration that he had taken a mortgage
on the farm to secure her marriage-portion, Aphobus
continued to hold and till the land just as before,
and to dwell with his wife, I knew well that all this
was fiction and a pretence to cover up the facts.
And wishing to make this clear to you all, I deemed 27
it right to convict him in the presence of witnesses,
in case he should deny that matters are as I have
stated ; and I offered to him for torture a slave who
knew well all the facts—one whom I had taken from
among those of Aphobus, since he had not paid the
damages within the time fixed by law. When I made
this demand, Onetor declined to put the slave to
torture as to the question of his sister's living with
Aphobus ; and, as to Aphobus's tilling the land, the
fact was too plain to be denied, so he confessed it.
Nor are these the only proofs which make it easy to 28
see that Aphobus continued to live with his wife and
to possess the land up to the time when the suit was
begun ; it is plain also from the way in which he
dealt with the land after judgement was given against
him. For, as though the property had not been
mortgaged, but was to belong to me according to

145

δίκην, ἃ μὲν οἷόν τ᾽ ἦν ἐξενεγκεῖν, ᾤχετο λαβών,
τοὺς καρποὺς καὶ τὰ σκεύη τὰ γεωργικὰ πάντα
πλὴν τῶν πιθακνῶν· ὃ δ᾽ οὐχ οἷόν τ᾽ ἦν ἀνελεῖν, ἐξ
ἀνάγκης ὑπέλιπεν, ὥστ᾽ ἐγγενέσθαι τούτῳ νῦν
29 αὐτῆς τῆς γῆς ἀμφισβητεῖν. καίτοι δεινὸν τὸν μὲν
λέγειν ὡς ἀπετιμήσατο τὸ χωρίον, τὸν δ᾽ ἀποτετι-
μηκότα φαίνεσθαι γεωργοῦντα, καὶ φάσκειν μὲν
ἀπολελοιπέναι τὴν ἀδελφήν, ὑπὲρ αὐτῶν δὲ τούτων
φανερὸν εἶναι φεύγοντα τοὺς ἐλέγχους, καὶ τὸν μὲν
[872] οὐ συνοικοῦνθ᾽, ὡς οὗτός φησι, καὶ τοὺς καρποὺς
καὶ τὰ ἐκ τῆς γεωργίας ἅπαντ᾽ ἐξενεγκεῖν, τὸν δ᾽
ὑπὲρ τῆς ἀπολελοιπυίας πράττοντα, ὑπὲρ ἧς ἀπο-
τετιμῆσθαί φησι τὸ χωρίον, φαίνεσθαι μηδ᾽ ὑπὲρ
ἑνὸς τούτων ἀγανακτοῦντα, ἀλλ᾽ ἡσυχίαν ἔχοντα.
30 ταῦτ᾽ οὐ πολλὴ περιφάνει᾽ ἐστί; ταῦτ᾽ οὐχ ὁμο-
λογουμένη προστασία; φήσειέ γ᾽ ἄν τις, εἰ δια-
λογίζοιτ᾽ ὀρθῶς ἕκαστ᾽ αὐτῶν.

Ὡς τοίνυν ὡμολόγει μὲν ἐκεῖνον γεωργεῖν πρὶν
γενέσθαι τὴν δίκην ἐμοὶ πρὸς αὐτόν, ὑπὲρ δὲ τοῦ
μὴ συνοικεῖν τὴν ἀδελφὴν οὐκ ἠθέλησε ποιήσασθαι
τὴν βάσανον, ἡ γεωργία δ᾽ ἐξεσκευάσθη μετὰ τὴν
δίκην πλὴν τῶν ἐγγείων, λαβὲ τὰς μαρτυρίας καὶ
ἀνάγνωθι.

ΜΑΡΤΥΡΙΑΙ

31 Ἐμοὶ τοίνυν τοσούτων ὑπαρχόντων τεκμηρίων,
οὐχ ἥκιστ᾽ αὐτὸς ἔδειξεν Ὀνήτωρ, ὅτι οὐκ ἀληθινὴν ἐποιήσατο τὴν ἀπόλειψιν. ᾧ γὰρ προσῆκε

―――――――

ᵃ These were underground, as appears from the phrase
πλὴν τῶν ἐγγείων in § 30.

the court's decision, he made off with everything that
could be carried away—the produce, and all the farm
implements, except the storage-tanks.[a] What he
could not take away he necessarily left behind, so that
Onetor was now at liberty to lay claim merely to the
bare land. It is an outrage, though, that one of them 29
should say that the land was mortgaged to him, while
the mortgagor is to be seen cultivating it ; that he
should claim that his sister has left her husband, when
he is shown to have refused to accept the test by torture
regarding this very point ; and that the one who is
not living with his wife (as Onetor claims) should
carry off all the produce and implements from the
farm, while the man acting as guardian for the
divorced woman, to secure whose portion he claims
to have taken a mortgage on the land, plainly shows
no anger at a single one of these acts, but takes
everything quietly. Is the whole thing not abso- 30
lutely clear ? Is it not confessedly a scheme to protect Aphobus ? One certainly would so declare, if he
duly considered each one of the facts.

Now, to prove that the defendant acknowledged
that Aphobus farmed the land up to the time of the
commencement of my action against him ; that he
refused the inquiry by torture as to his sister's con-
tinuing to live with Aphobus ; and that the farm was
stripped after the court's decision of everything save
what was attached to the soil ; take these depositions, and read them.

THE DEPOSITIONS

Although I have so many proofs ready to hand it is 31
Onetor himself who most convincingly showed that
the divorce was not a genuine one. He, who should

χαλεπῶς φέρειν, εἰ τὴν προῖκα δούς, ὥς φησιν, ἀντ᾽
ἀργυρίου χωρίον ἀμφισβητούμενον ἀπελάμβανεν,
οὗτος οὐχ ὡς διάφορος οὐδ᾽ ὡς ἀδικούμενος, ἀλλ᾽
ὡς οἰκειότατος πάντων τὴν πρὸς ἐμὲ δίκην αὐτῷ
συνηγωνίζετο. κἀμὲ μὲν συναποστερῆσαι μετ᾽
ἐκείνου τῶν πατρῴων ἐπεχείρησε, καθ᾽ ὅσον αὐτὸς
οἷός τ᾽ ἦν, ὑφ᾽ οὗ κακὸν οὐδ᾽ ὁτιοῦν ἦν πεπονθώς·
Ἀφόβῳ δ᾽, ὃν ἀλλότριον εἶναι προσῆκε νομίζειν, εἴ
τι τούτων ἀληθὲς ἦν ὧν νῦν λέγουσι, καὶ τἀμὰ πρὸς
32 τοῖς ἐκείνου περιποιεῖν ἐζήτησεν. καὶ οὐ μόνον
ἐνταῦθα τοῦτ᾽ ἐποίησεν, ἀλλὰ καὶ κατεγνωσμένης
ἤδη τῆς δίκης, ἀναβὰς ἐπὶ τὸ δικαστήριον ἐδεῖθ᾽
ἱκετεύων ὑπὲρ αὐτοῦ καὶ ἀντιβολῶν καὶ δάκρυσι
[873] κλάων ταλάντου τιμῆσαι, καὶ τούτων αὐτὸς ἐγίγνετ᾽
ἐγγυητής. καὶ ταῦθ᾽ ὁμολογούμενα μέν ἐστι πολ-
λαχόθεν· οἵ τε γὰρ ἐν τῷ δικαστηρίῳ τότε δικάζοντες καὶ τῶν ἔξωθεν παρόντων πολλοὶ συνίσασιν·
ὅμως δὲ καὶ μάρτυρας ὑμῖν παρέξομαι.
Καί μοι λαβὲ ταύτην τὴν μαρτυρίαν.

ΜΑΡΤΥΡΙΑ

33 Ἔτι τοίνυν, ὦ ἄνδρες δικασταί, καὶ τεκμηρίῳ
μεγάλῳ γνῶναι ῥᾴδιον, ὅτι τῇ ἀληθείᾳ συνῴκει καὶ
οὐδέπω καὶ τήμερον ἀπολέλοιπεν. αὕτη γὰρ ἡ
γυνή, πρὶν μὲν ὡς Ἄφοβον ἐλθεῖν, μίαν ἡμέραν οὐκ
ἐχήρευσεν, ἀλλὰ παρὰ ζῶντος Τιμοκράτους ἐκείνῳ
148

have felt outraged, when, after paying the dowry, as he claims, he got back, not the money, but a farm whose title was under dispute —this very man, as though he had had no quarrel, and were in no way being wronged, but as though he were on the most intimate terms possible with Aphobus, pleaded for the latter in the suit which I brought against him ! As for myself, though I had done him no conceivable injury, he leagued with Aphobus, and sought by every means in his power to join in robbing me of my patrimony, while for Aphobus, whom he should have regarded as a stranger, if there is any truth in their present story, he sought to acquire possession of my property in addition to what he already had. Nor 32 was it only at the trial that he acted thus, but after judgement had been rendered against Aphobus, he got up before the court and begged the jurymen, beseeching and imploring them on behalf of Aphobus with tears in his eyes, to fix the damages at a talent, and offered himself as surety for this amount. These facts are admitted on all hands. Those who were then serving on the jury in the court-room and many of the bystanders know them well. Nevertheless I will produce witnesses.

Take, and read this deposition.

THE DEPOSITION

Besides all this, men of the jury, there is strong 33 evidence from which it is easy to see that the woman in reality continued to live with Aphobus and even up to the present day has not separated from him. In fact, this woman, before she came to Aphobus, was not unwedded for one single day, but left her living husband, Timocrates, to come and live with

149

συνῴκησε, νῦν δ' ἐν τρισὶν ἔτεσιν ἄλλῳ συνοικοῦσ'
οὐδενὶ φαίνεται. καίτοι τῷ πιστόν, ὡς τότε μέν,
ἵνα μὴ χηρεύσειε, παρ' ἀνδρὸς ὡς ἄνδρ' ἐβάδιζε,
νῦν δ', εἴπερ ὡς ἀληθῶς ἀπολέλοιπε,[1] τοσοῦτον
ἂν χρόνον χηρεύουσ' ἠνείχετ' ἐξὸν ἄλλῳ συνοικεῖν,
τοῦ τ' ἀδελφοῦ κεκτημένου τοσαύτην οὐσίαν, αὐτή
34 τε ταύτην ἔχουσα τὴν ἡλικίαν; οὐκ ἔχει ταῦτ'
ἀλήθειαν, ὦ ἄνδρες δικασταί, πιθανήν, ἀλλὰ
λόγοι ταῦτ' εἰσί, συνοικεῖ δ' ἡ γυνὴ φανερῶς καὶ
οὐδ' ἐπικρύπτεται τὸ πρᾶγμα. παρέξομαι δ' ὑμῖν
Πασιφῶντος μαρτυρίαν, ὃς ἀρρωστοῦσαν αὐτὴν
θεραπεύων ἑώρα παρακαθήμενον Ἄφοβον ἐπὶ τούτου τοῦ ἄρχοντος, ἤδη τούτῳ ταυτησὶ τῆς δίκης
εἰλημμένης.

Καί μοι λαβὲ τὴν Πασιφῶντος μαρτυρίαν.

ΜΑΡΤΥΡΙΑ

35 Ἐγὼ τοίνυν εἰδώς, ὦ ἄνδρες δικασταί, καὶ μετὰ
τὴν δίκην τοῦτον εὐθὺς ἀποδεδεγμένον τὰ ἐκ τῆς
οἰκίας τῆς Ἀφόβου χρήματα, καὶ κύριον τῶν τ'
[874] ἐκείνου καὶ τῶν ἐμῶν ἁπάντων γεγενημένον, καὶ
συνοικοῦσαν αὐτῷ τὴν γυναῖκα σαφῶς ἐπιστάμενος, τρεῖς θεραπαίνας ἐξῄτησ' αὐτόν, αἳ συνοικοῦσάν τε τὴν γυναῖκ' ᾔδεσαν καὶ τὰ χρήμαθ'
ὅτι παρὰ τούτοις ἦν, ἵνα μὴ λόγοι μόνον, ἀλλὰ
36 καὶ βάσανοι περὶ αὐτῶν γίγνοιντο. οὗτος δ' ἐμοῦ
προκαλεσαμένου ταῦτα, καὶ πάντων τῶν παρόντων
δίκαια λέγειν μ' ἀποφηναμένων, οὐκ ἠθέλησεν εἰς
τοῦτο τἀκριβὲς καταφυγεῖν, ἀλλ' ὥσπερ ἑτέρων
τινῶν ὄντων περὶ τῶν τοιούτων σαφεστέρων ἐλέγ-

---

[1] ἀπολέλοιπε] ἀπελελοίπει Blass.

Aphobus ; and now during the space of three years she has manifestly married no one else. Can anyone believe that she then went directly from husband to husband, in order to avoid living as a widow, but that now, supposing she has really left her husband, she would have endured to remain a widow for so long when she might have married someone else, seeing that her brother possessed so large a fortune, and she herself was so young ? There is no truth in it, 34 men of the jury ; you cannot believe it. It is a pure fiction. No ; the woman is living openly with Aphobus, and makes no secret of the matter. I shall bring before you the evidence of Pasiphon, who cared for her when she was ill, and who saw Aphobus sitting by her side in this very year, when my suit against the defendant had already been instituted.

Take Pasiphon's deposition.

THE DEPOSITION

I knew, men of the jury, that the defendant, im- 35 mediately on the conclusion of the suit, had received the goods from the house of Aphobus, and had come into control of his property and all my estate as well, and I knew, further, that beyond all doubt the woman was living with Aphobus. I therefore demanded of Onetor three female slaves, who knew that the woman was living with Aphobus and that the effects were in the hands of these men, in order that we might not have mere statements but that the matters might be established by proof from the torture. But 36 Onetor, when I made this challenge to him, and all those present declared that my proposal was just, refused to have recourse to this certain test, but, as though there were other and surer proofs regarding

151

χων ἢ βασάνων καὶ μαρτυριῶν, οὔτε μάρτυρας
παρεχόμενος τὴν προῖχ' ὡς ἀποδέδωκεν, οὔτ' εἰς
βάσανον ἐκδιδοὺς τὰς συνειδυίας περὶ τοῦ μὴ
συνοικεῖν τὴν ἀδελφήν, ὅτι ταῦτ' ἠξίουν, ὑβριστικῶς πάνυ καὶ προπηλακιστικῶς οὐκ εἴα μ' αὐτῷ
διαλέγεσθαι. τούτου γένοιτ' ἄν τις σχετλιώτερος
ἄνθρωπος, ἢ μᾶλλον ἑκὼν τὰ δίκαι' ἀγνοεῖν προσποιούμενος; λαβὲ δ' αὐτὴν τὴν πρόκλησιν καὶ
ἀνάγνωθι.

ΠΡΟΚΛΗΣΙΣ

37 Ὑμεῖς μὲν τοίνυν καὶ ἰδίᾳ καὶ δημοσίᾳ βάσανον
ἀκριβεστάτην πασῶν πίστεων νομίζετε, καὶ ὁπόταν
δοῦλοι καὶ ἐλεύθεροι παραγένωνται, δέῃ δ' εὑρεθῆναι τὸ ζητούμενον, οὐ χρῆσθε ταῖς τῶν ἐλευθέρων
μαρτυρίαις, ἀλλὰ τοὺς δούλους βασανίζοντες, οὕτω
ζητεῖτε τὴν ἀλήθειαν εὑρεῖν. εἰκότως, ὦ ἄνδρες
δικασταί· τῶν μὲν γὰρ μαρτυρησάντων ἤδη τινὲς οὐ
τἀληθῆ μαρτυρῆσαι ἔδοξαν· τῶν δὲ βασανισθέντων
οὐδένες πώποτ' ἐξηλέγχθησαν, ὡς οὐκ ἀληθῆ τὰ ἐκ
38 τῶν βασάνων εἶπον. οὗτος δὲ τηλικαῦτα δίκαια
[875] φυγών, καὶ σαφεῖς οὕτω καὶ μεγάλους ἐλέγχους
παραλιπών, Ἄφοβον παρεχόμενος μάρτυρα καὶ
Τιμοκράτην, τὸν μὲν ὡς ἀποδέδωκε τὴν προῖκα,
τὸν δ' ὡς ἀπείληφεν, ἀξιώσει πιστεύεσθαι παρ'
ὑμῖν, ἀμάρτυρον τὴν πρὸς τούτους πρᾶξιν γεγενῆσθαι προσποιούμενος· τοσαύτην ὑμῶν εὐήθειαν
39 κατέγνωκεν. ὅτι μὲν τοίνυν οὔτ' ἀληθῆ οὔτ'
ἀληθείαις ἐοικότα λέξουσι, καὶ ἐκ τοῦ ἐξ ἀρχῆς
αὐτοὺς ὁμολογεῖν τὴν προῖκα μὴ δοῦναι, καὶ ἐκ

152

such matters than torture and testimony, he produced
no witnesses to prove that he had paid the dowry,
nor would he give up for torture the female slaves
who knew the fact, to prove that his sister was not
living with Aphobus ; and, because I made this demand of him, he in an outrageous and insulting
manner refused to let me talk to him. Could there
be a man more impossible to deal with than he, or
more ready to pretend ignorance of what is right ?
Take the challenge itself and read it.

THE CHALLENGE

You on your part hold that in both private and 37
public matters the torture is the most certain of all
methods of proof, and when slaves and freemen are
both available, and the truth of a matter is to be
sought out, you make no use of the testimony of
the freemen, but seek to ascertain the truth by torturing the slaves ; and very properly, men of the
jury. For of witnesses who have given testimony
there have been some ere now who have been thought
not to tell the truth ; but of slaves put to the torture
no one has ever been convicted of giving false testimony. Yet Onetor, after refusing a test so fair, and 38
rejecting proofs so clear and so convincing, will produce Aphobus and Timocrates as witnesses, the one
that he has paid the dowry, and the other that he has
received it, and will demand that you believe him,
when he pretends that his transactions with them
were without witnesses. For such simpletons does
he take you. But that their words are neither true 39
nor like the truth I think I have—by the fact that at
the first they confessed that they had not paid the

τοῦ πάλιν ἄνευ μαρτύρων ἀποδεδωκέναι φάσκειν,
καὶ ἐκ τοῦ τὸν χρόνον μὴ ἐγχωρεῖν ἀμφισβη-
τουμένης ἤδη τῆς οὐσίας ἀποδοῦναι τἀργύριον,
καὶ ἐκ τῶν ἄλλων ἁπάντων ἱκανῶς ἀποδεδεῖχθαι
νομίζω.

dowry, that again they pretended to have paid it without witnesses, that the dates do not admit of their having paid the money, seeing that the property was already in litigation, and finally by all the other evidences adduced, I have, as I think, conclusively proved.

AGAINST ONETOR
II

INTRODUCTION

THIS second speech is in reply to one delivered by
Onetor in the case brought against him by Demosthenes. It reasserts the plaintiff's contention that
the marriage-portion had not been paid, and that the
alleged mortgage is merely a scheme to protect the
property for Aphobus.

XXXI

ΠΡΟΣ ΟΝΗΤΟΡΑ ΕΞΟΥΛΗΣ

B

[876] Ὃ παρέλιπον ἐν τῷ προτέρῳ λόγῳ τεκμήριον,
οὐδενὸς τῶν εἰρημένων ἔλαττον, τοῦ μὴ δεδωκέναι
τὴν προῖκα τούτους Ἀφόβῳ, τοῦτο πρῶτον εἰπών,
μετὰ τοῦτο καὶ περὶ ὧν οὗτος ἔψευσται πρὸς ὑμᾶς
ἐξελέγχειν αὐτὸν πειράσομαι. οὗτος γάρ, ὦ ἄνδρες
δικασταί, τὸ πρῶτον ὅτε τῶν Ἀφόβου διενοεῖτ᾽
ἀμφισβητεῖν, οὐχὶ τάλαντον ἔφη τὴν προῖχ᾽, ὥσπερ
νῦν, ἀλλ᾽ ὀγδοήκοντα μνᾶς δεδωκέναι, καὶ τίθησιν
ὅρους ἐπὶ μὲν τὴν οἰκίαν δισχιλίων, ἐπὶ δὲ τὸ
χωρίον ταλάντου, βουλόμενος μὴ μόνον τοῦτο,
2 ἀλλὰ κἀκείνην διασῴζειν αὐτῷ. γενομένης δέ μοι
τῆς δίκης πρὸς αὐτόν, ἰδὼν ὡς διάκεισθ᾽ ὑμεῖς πρὸς
τοὺς λίαν ἀναιδῶς ἀδικοῦντας, ἔννους γίγνεται, καὶ
δεινὰ πάσχειν ἡγήσατο δόξειν ἐμὲ τοσούτων χρημάτων ἀπεστερημένον, εἰ μηδ᾽ ὁτιοῦν ἔξοιμι τῶν
Ἀφόβου λαβεῖν τοῦ τἄμ᾽ ἔχοντος, ἀλλ᾽ ὑπὸ τούτου
3 κωλυόμενος φανερὸς γενήσομαι. καὶ τί ποιεῖ;

---

[a] To signify that the property was mortgaged.

XXXI

AGAINST ONETOR, AN EJECTMENT SUIT

II

THERE is one proof which I omitted in my former speech, quite as important as any of those which were brought forward, to prove that these men did not pay the marriage-portion to Aphobus. This I shall speak of first, and shall then undertake to refute the falsehoods which the defendant has uttered before you. For the fellow, men of the jury, when he first determined to lay claim to the property of Aphobus, declared that he had paid as the marriage-portion, not a talent, as he now alleges, but eighty minae; and he set up pillars *a* on the house for two thousand drachmae, and on the land for a talent, wishing to preserve both the one and the other for Aphobus. When, however, the trial against him had been de- 2 cided, and he saw what your attitude was toward those who were too brazen in their wrongdoings, he came to his senses, and concluded that I should appear to be suffering outrageous treatment, if, after being robbed of such large sums, I should be unable to recover anything whatever from Aphobus, who had my property in his possession, but it should become clear that I was prevented by the defendant from recovering anything. What, then, does he do? 3

τοὺς ὅρους ἀπὸ τῆς οἰκίας ἀφαιρεῖ, καὶ τάλαντον
μόνον εἶναι τὴν προῖκά φησιν, ἐν ᾧ τὸ χωρίον ἀποτετιμῆσθαι. καίτοι δῆλον ὅτι τοὺς ἐπὶ τῆς οἰκίας
ὅρους εἰ δικαίως ἔθηκε καὶ ὄντως ἀληθεῖς, δικαίως
καὶ τοὺς ἐπὶ τοῦ χωρίου τέθηκεν· εἰ δ' εὐθὺς ἀδικεῖν
βουλόμενος ψευδεῖς ἔθηκεν ἐκείνους, εἰκὸς καὶ τού-
4 τους οὐκ ἀληθεῖς ὑπάρχειν. τοῦτο τοίνυν οὐκ ἐξ
[877] ὧν ἐγὼ δεδήλωκα λόγων δεῖ σκοπεῖν, ἀλλ' ἐξ ὧν
αὐτὸς οὗτος διεπράξατο· οὐδ' ὑφ' ἑνὸς γὰρ ἀναγκασθεὶς ἀνθρώπων αὐτὸς ἀνεῖλε τοὺς ὅρους, ἔργῳ
φανερὸν ποιήσας ὅτι ψεύδεται. καὶ ταῦθ' ὡς ἀληθῆ
λέγω, τὸ μὲν χωρίον καὶ νῦν οὗτός φησιν ἀποτετιμῆσθαι ταλάντου, τὴν δ' οἰκίαν ὡς προσωρίσατο
δισχιλίων, καὶ πάλιν τοὺς ὅρους ἀνεῖλε γενομένης
τῆς δίκης, τοὺς εἰδότας ὑμῖν μάρτυρας παρέξομαι.
Καί μοι λαβὲ τὴν μαρτυρίαν.

ΜΑΡΤΥΡΙΑ

5 Δῆλον τοίνυν ὅτι δισχιλίων μὲν ὡρισμένος τὴν
οἰκίαν, ταλάντου δὲ τὸ χωρίον, ὡς ὀγδοήκοντα μνᾶς
δεδωκὼς ἔμελλεν ἀμφισβητήσειν. μεῖζον οὖν ἄν τι
γένοιτο τεκμήριον ὑμῖν τοῦ μηδὲν ἀληθὲς νῦν λέγειν
τοῦτον, ἢ εἰ φανείη μὴ ταῦτα λέγων τοῖς ἐξ ἀρχῆς
περὶ τῶν αὐτῶν; ἐμοὶ μὲν γὰρ οὐδὲν ἂν δοκεῖ
τούτου μεῖζον εὑρεθῆναι.

6 Σκέψασθε τοίνυν τὴν ἀναίδειαν, ὅς γ' ἐν ὑμῖν ἐτόλμησεν εἰπεῖν, ὡς οὐκ ἀποστερεῖ μ' ὅσῳ πλείονος
ἄξιόν ἐστι ταλάντου, καὶ ταῦτ' αὐτὸς τιμήσας οὐκ

He removes the pillars from the house, and declares that the marriage-portion was a talent only, which sum was guaranteed by a mortgage on the land. Yet, if the inscription on the house was set up by him in fairness and sincerity, it is plain that the one on the land was also. But if he set up a false inscription in the former case with the intent to commit fraud, it is probable that the latter one was false also. This matter you should consider, not in the 4 light of the proofs which I have advanced, but from the conduct of Onetor himself. No man on earth compelled him; he took down the pillars himself; and thus by his own act he makes clear that he is a liar. To prove that these statements of mine are true, that he even now declares that the land is mortgaged for a talent, but that he laid claim to two thousand drachmae more on the house, and took the pillars down after the suit was decided, I shall bring forward witnesses who know the facts.

Now take the deposition.

The Deposition

It is plain, then, that Onetor having put up pillars 5 on the house for two thousand drachmae, and on the land for a talent, intended to push his claim as though he had paid eighty minae. Could you have stronger proof that there is not a word of truth in what he now says, than the fact that his present story is different from the one he told at first about the same matters? To me it seems that no stronger proof than this could be found.

Now note the shamelessness of the man. He had 6 the audacity to say before you that he is not depriving me of what the land is worth beyond a talent, and that, too, when he has himself fixed its value

ἄξιον εἶναι πλείονος. τί γὰρ βουλόμενος δισχιλίων
προσωρίσω τὴν οἰκίαν, ὅτε τὰς ὀγδοήκοντα μνᾶς
ἐνεκάλεις, εἴ γε τὸ χωρίον ἄξιον ἦν πλείονος, ἀλλ᾽

7 οὐκ ἐπὶ τούτῳ καὶ τὰς δισχιλίας ἐτίθεις; ἢ ὅταν
μέν σοι δοκῇ πάντα τὰ Ἀφόβου διασῴζειν, τό τε
χωρίον ἔσται ταλάντου μόνον ἄξιον, καὶ τὴν οἰκίαν
ἐν δισχιλίαις προσέξεις, ἥ τε προὶξ ὀγδοήκοντα μναῖ
γενήσονται, καὶ ἀξιώσεις ἔχειν ἀμφότερα· ὅταν δέ
σοι μὴ συμφέρῃ, τἀναντία πάλιν ἡ μὲν οἰκία ταλάν-

[878] του, διότι νῦν ἐγὼ ταύτην ἔχω, τοῦ δὲ χωρίου τὸ
περιὸν οὐκ ἐλάττονος ἢ δυοῖν ἄξιον, ἵν᾽ ἐγὼ δοκῶ

8 βλάπτειν τοῦτον, οὐκ ἀποστερεῖσθαι; ὁρᾷς ὡς
ὑποκρίνῃ μὲν δεδωκέναι τὴν προῖκα, φαίνῃ δὲ κατ᾽
οὐδ᾽ ὀντινοῦν τρόπον δεδωκώς; τὰ γὰρ ἀληθῆ καὶ
μὴ κακουργούμενα τῶν πραγμάτων ἁπλῶς, οἷ᾽ ἂν
ἐξ ἀρχῆς πραχθῇ, τοιαῦτ᾽ ἐστί· σὺ δὲ τοὐναντίον
ἐξελέγχῃ πράξας εἰς τὴν καθ᾽ ἡμῶν ὑπηρεσίαν.

9 Ἄξιον τοίνυν καὶ τὸν ὅρκον, ὁποῖόν τιν᾽ ἂν
ὤμοσεν, εἴ τις ἔδωκεν, ἐκ τούτων ἰδεῖν. ὃς γὰρ
ὀγδοήκοντα μνᾶς ἔφη τὴν προῖκ᾽ εἶναι, εἰ τότ᾽ αὐτῷ
τις ἔδωκεν, ὀμόσαντι ταῦτ᾽ ἀληθῆ λέγειν, κομίσασθαι, τί ἐποίησεν ἄν; ἢ δῆλον ὅτι ὤμοσε· τί γὰρ
καὶ λέγων οὐ φήσει τότ᾽ ἂν ὀμόσαι, νῦν γε τοῦτ᾽

as nothing more. With what end in view, Onetor,
did you fix your pillars on the house for the two
thousand extra drachmae, when you were demanding eighty minae, if the land was really worth more,
instead of securing the two thousand drachmae
also by a mortgage on the land ? Or, when it suits 7
your purpose to save all of the property of
Aphobus, is the land to be worth a talent only, and
are you to hold the house on a mortgage of two
thousand drachmae more ; and the marriage-portion
being eighty minae, will you claim the right to hold
both the land and the house ; or again, when this
is not to your interest, is all to be different : the
house is to be worth a talent, because now it is I that
hold it, and what is left of the farm is to be worth
not less than two talents, in order that it may seem
that I am wronging Aphobus, not myself being
robbed ? Do you see that, while you pretend to have 8
paid the dowry, you are shown not to have paid it
in any way whatsoever ? For that line of conduct is
sincere and free from guile, which remains throughout
such as it was at the first, but you are proven to
have followed the contrary course, so as to fulfil
your service as an underling to my detriment.

It is worth while to consider in the light of these 9
facts what sort of an oath he would have sworn, if an
oath had been tendered him. For, when he declared
that the dowry was eighty minae, if one had granted
that he should recover that sum on condition of his
swearing that this statement of his was true, what
would he have done ? Is it not plain that he would
have taken the oath ? What can he say to deny that
he would have sworn it under those circumstances,
when he demands the right to do so now ? Well

ἀξιῶν; οὐκοῦν ὅτι γ' ἐπιώρκησεν ἄν, ἑαυτὸν
ἐξελέγχει· νῦν γὰρ οὐκ ὀγδοήκοντα μνᾶς, ἀλλὰ
τάλαντον δεδωκέναι φησίν. τί μᾶλλον ἂν οὖν
εἰκότως τις αὐτὸν ἐκεῖνα ἐπιορκεῖν ἢ τάδ' ἡγοῖτο;
ἢ τίνα τις δικαίως ἂν ἔχοι περὶ τούτου διάνοιαν, τοῦ
ῥᾳδίως οὕτως αὐτὸν ἐξελέγχοντος ὄντ' ἐπίορκον;

10 Ἀλλὰ νὴ Δί' ἴσως οὐχὶ πάντ' αὐτῷ τοιαῦτα
πέπρακται, οὐδὲ πανταχόθεν δῆλός ἐστι τεχνάζων.
ἀλλὰ καὶ τιμώμενος φανερὸς γέγονεν ὑπὲρ Ἀφόβου
ταλάντου, καὶ τοῦτ' αὐτὸς ἡμῖν ἀποδώσειν ἐγγυώ-
μενος. καίτοι σκέψασθ' ὅτι τοῦτ' ἔστι τεκμήριον
οὐ μόνον τοῦ τὴν γυναῖκα συνοικεῖν Ἀφόβῳ καὶ
τοῦτον οἰκείως ἔχειν, ἀλλὰ καὶ τοῦ μὴ δεδωκέναι
11 τὴν προῖκα. τίς γὰρ ἀνθρώπων ἠλίθιός ἐστιν
οὕτως, ὥστ' ἀργύριον μὲν δοὺς τοσοῦτον, ἔπειθ' ἐν
λαβὼν χωρίον ἀμφισβητούμενον εἰς ἀποτίμησιν,
[879] σὺν οἷς πρότερον ἐζημίωτο, τὸν ἀδικήσανθ' ὡς
δίκαιόν τι ποιήσοντα καὶ τοῦ τῆς δίκης ὀφλήματος
προσεγγυήσασθαι; ἐγὼ μὲν οὐδέν' οἶμαι. καὶ γὰρ
οὐδὲ λόγον τὸ πρᾶγμ' ἔχον ἐστί, τὸν αὐτὸν αὑτῷ
μὴ δυνάμενον κομίσασθαι τάλαντον, τοῦτον ἄλλῳ
τινὶ φάσκειν ἀποτείσειν καὶ ταῦτ' ἐγγυᾶσθαι. ἀλλὰ
καὶ ἀπ' αὐτῶν τούτων ἐστὶ δῆλον, ὅτι τὴν μὲν
προῖκ' οὐ δέδωκεν, ἀντὶ δὲ πολλῶν χρημάτων τῶν
ἐμῶν οἰκεῖος ὢν Ἀφόβῳ ταῦτ' ἀπετιμᾶτο, κληρονόμον τὴν ἀδελφὴν τῶν ἐμῶν μετ' ἐκείνου κατα-
12 στῆσαι βουλόμενος. εἶτα νῦν παρακρούσασθαι
ζητεῖ καὶ φενακίζει, λέγων ὡς πρότερον τοὺς ὅρους
ἔστησεν, ἢ ἐκεῖνον τὴν δίκην ὀφλεῖν. οὐ πρότερόν

then, his own words prove that he would have perjured himself; for he now claims that he paid, not eighty minae, but. a talent. What reason is there why one should believe that he is forswearing himself in one statement rather than in the other? Or what opinion should one rightly hold of a man who thus lightly convicts himself of perjury?

But perhaps not all of his acts have been of this 10 nature, nor is he proven in every instance to be a trickster. Yet it has been shown that he sought in Aphobus's interest to have the damages fixed at a talent, and himself offered to act as bail for the payment to me of that sum. Yet observe that this is a proof not only that his wife was living with Aphobus and that Onetor was on intimate terms with him, but also that he had not paid the dowry. For what man 11 would be so foolish as, first, to pay out so large a sum, then to take as security a single piece of property, the title to which was under dispute, and finally, not satisfied with his previous losses and assuming that the one who had wronged him was now going to act justly, to become his bail for the damages assessed by the court? Nobody would, to my thinking. The assumption is not even rational, that a man unable to recover a talent for himself, should promise to pay that sum to another, and further to give bail for it. No; from these facts alone it is clear that he has never paid the dowry, but as a close friend of Aphobus he took this mortgage in return for my large property, wishing to make his sister jointly with Aphobus an inheritor of my estate. Then he seeks now to deceive 12 and beguile you by claiming that he set up the pillars before judgement was given against Aphobus. Aye, Onetor; but not before it was given by you, if what

γ' ἢ παρὰ σοί, νῦν εἰ ἀληθῆ λέγεις. δῆλον γὰρ ὅτι
καταγνοὺς ἀδικίαν αὐτοῦ ταῦτ' ἐποίεις. εἶτα καὶ
γελοῖον τοῦτο λέγειν, ὥσπερ οὐκ εἰδότων ὑμῶν,
ὅτι πάντες οἱ τὰ τοιαῦτ' ἀδικοῦντες σκοποῦσι τί
λέξουσιν, καὶ οὐδεὶς πώποτ' ὦφλε σιωπῶν οὐδ'
ἀδικεῖν ὁμολογῶν· ἀλλ' ἐπειδὰν οἶμαι μηδὲν ἀληθὲς
λέγων ἐξελεγχθῇ, τότε γιγνώσκεται ὁποῖός ἐστιν.
13 ὅπερ καὶ οὗτος ἔμοιγε δοκεῖ πάσχειν. ἐπεί, φέρε,
πῶς ἐστι δίκαιον, ἐὰν μὲν ὀγδοήκοντα μνῶν θῆς
ὅρους, ὀγδοήκοντα μνᾶς εἶναι τὴν προῖκα, ἐὰν δὲ
πλείονος πλέον, ἐὰν δ' ἐλάττονος ἔλαττον; ἢ πῶς
ἐστι δίκαιον, τῆς ἀδελφῆς τῆς σῆς μηδέπω καὶ
τήμερον ἄλλῳ συνοικούσης μηδ' ἀπηλλαγμένης
Ἀφόβου, μηδὲ τὴν προῖκα δεδωκότος σοῦ, μηδ'
ὑπὲρ τούτων εἰς βάσανον μηδ' εἰς ἄλλο δίκαιον
μηδὲν καταφεύγειν ἐθέλοντος, ὅτι σὺ στῆσαι φὴς
ὅρους, σὸν εἶναι τὸ χωρίον; ἐγὼ μὲν οὐδαμῶς
[880] οἶμαι· τὴν γὰρ ἀλήθειαν σκεπτέον, οὐχ ἅ τις αὑτῷ
παρεσκεύασεν ἐξεπίτηδες εἰς τὸ λέγειν τι δοκεῖν,
14 ὥσπερ ὑμεῖς. ἔπειτα τὸ δεινότατον· εἰ καὶ δε-
δωκότες ἦθ' ὡς μάλιστα τὴν προῖκα, ἣν οὐ δεδώ-
κατε, τίς ὁ τούτων αἴτιος; οὐχ ὑμεῖς, ἐπεὶ ταῦτ'
ἐπὶ τἄμ' ἔδοτε; οὐχ ὅλοις ἔτεσιν πρότερον δέκα
τἀμὰ λαβὼν εἶχεν ἐκεῖνος ὧν ὦφλεν τὴν δίκην, ἢ
κηδεστήν σοι γενέσθαι; ἢ σὲ μὲν δεῖ κομίσασθαι
πάντα, τὸν δὲ καὶ καταδικασάμενον καὶ δι' ὀρφανίαν
ἠδικημένον καὶ προικὸς ἀληθινῆς ἀπεστερημένον,
168

you now say is true. For it is clear that you acted
as you did because you were convinced of his guilt.
Again, this language of yours is absurd, as though
you, men of the jury, did not know that all those who
commit frauds of this sort determine what they are
going to say, and that no one ever lost a suit through
keeping quiet, or admitting that he was in the wrong ;
but it is, I think, when he has been convicted of making a false statement, that men know what manner of
man he is.   And this is what appears to me to be 13
exactly the plight of Onetor.   For tell me, how can it
be just, if you set up pillars for eighty minae, that the
dowry should be eighty minae ; and, if for more, more ;
and, if for less, less ?   Or how is it just, when your
sister up to this present day has never lived with any
other man, or been separated from Aphobus, when
you have neither paid the dowry, nor been willing to
have recourse to the torture, or to any other fair means
of determining the matters at issue, that because you
claim to have set up pillars, the farm shall belong
to you ?   I certainly do not see how it can be.   It is 14
the truth to which we must look, not to arguments
which a man has contrived (as you are doing) in order
to seem to speak with some plausibility.   Then—the
most outrageous thing of all—suppose you had in
reality paid the marriage-portion (which you have
not paid), whose fault was it ?   Was it not yours ?
For you paid it on the security of my property.   Was
it not ten full years before he became your brother-
in-law that Aphobus took possession of my estate for
which judgement has been rendered against him ?
And was it right for you to recover the whole amount,
while I, who had been awarded damages against him,
I, an orphan who had been wronged and robbed of a

ὃν μόνον ἀνθρώπων οὐδὲ τῆς ἐπωβελίας ἄξιον ἦν
κινδυνεύειν, ἠναγκάσθαι τοιαῦτα παθεῖν, κεκομι-
σμένον μηδ' ὁτιοῦν, καὶ ταῦτ' ἐθέλοντα ποιεῖν ἐφ'
ὑμῖν αὐτοῖς, εἴ τι τῶν δεόντων ἐβούλεσθε πράττειν;

---

^a See note a on p. 50.
^b The pronoun is in the plural and refers to Onetor and
Aphobus.

marriage-portion that was genuine, I who with better right than any other man should have been exempted from the risk of having to pay costs,[a] should be forced to suffer thus, and should have recovered nothing whatever, though ready to meet any of your [b] proposals, had you been willing to do anything that justice required ?

AGAINST ZENOTHEMIS

INTRODUCTION

THIS speech was written by Demosthenes for his uncle Demo (the father of Demophon, who was one of the writer's faithless guardians ; see Oration XXVII. § 4), who had been sued by a certain Zeno-themis regarding a cargo of grain. Demo had entered a special plea ($\pi\alpha\rho\alpha\gamma\rho\alpha\phi\eta$) that the action was not admissible, and this speech is in reply to one by the plaintiff, of the contents of which we have no knowledge, save in so far as they can be inferred from this reply. This speech, however, gives us much information in regard to the circumstances leading up to the suit. These were in brief as follows :

Demo had lent a sum of money to a certain Protus, a grain-merchant, who was to purchase a cargo of grain in Sicily and bring it to Athens. Such ventures were frequent on the Athenian exchange, and, while the risks were great (for in the event of the loss of the ship the lender had no redress), the rate of interest on the loan was high. Similar transactions form the subjects of Orations XXXIV. and XXXV. Protus, having obtained the money, set out for Sicily in a ship belonging to a man named Hegestratus, Zenothemis also being one of the passengers on board. On reaching Syracuse, Protus purchased a quantity of grain and had it put on board the vessel. Mean-while Hegestratus and Zenothemis borrowed funds, each vouching for the other's financial standing, and telling of a rich cargo already on board. In this way they secured a considerable amount of money, which they promptly shipped to Massalia (Marseille), of which city both were natives.

As the repayment of the loans secured was conditional upon the safe return of the vessel to Syracuse, the two rascals laid a nefarious scheme to sink the ship, planning themselves to escape in the ship's boat, and thus be free from any obligation to their creditors.

When the vessel, therefore, was three days out of Syracuse, Hegestratus went down into the hold in the night, and began cutting a hole in the ship's bottom. Caught in the act by the passengers, who had heard the noise, he barely escaped suffering violence at their hands by leaping overboard. In the dark he missed the boat and was drowned. Zenothemis then sought to induce the crew to abandon the ship, declaring that she must presently sink, but Protus persuaded them by the offer of large rewards to seek to repair the damage and continue their voyage. This was done, and they succeeded in reaching Cephallenia,[a] where repairs were made. Zenothemis then wanted them to make for Massalia, but, when the matter was submitted to the authorities, it was determined that the vessel should continue her voyage to Athens.

When the ship reached the harbour of Peiraeus, Protus announced to Demo and his associates that the grain was safely in port, and they came at once to take possession of it, in order to satisfy their claim

---

[a] A large island opposite the west entrance to the Corinthian Gulf.

as lenders of the purchase money. They found, however, that Zenothemis, alleging that the grain had been bought by Hegestratus with money advanced by himself, had laid claim to the cargo, and was about to unload it. He was forcibly prevented from doing this by Protus and Demo, and then proceeded to seek redress by bringing separate suits against them. In this speech Demo claims that the action of Zenothemis is not maintainable, as there had been no contract whatever between them, but he deals at greatest length with the enormity of the plaintiff's conduct.

The difficulty of arriving at a just conclusion regarding the merits of the case is necessarily great, as we have the presentation of one side only ; and it is further enhanced by the fact that Protus (who would naturally, as purchaser of the grain, have been Demo's chief witness) appears to have come to some sort of an agreement with Zenothemis. He not only allowed judgement to be given against him by default in Zenothemis's suit against him, but left Athens in order not to have to testify in the present suit.

The speech is mutilated at the end, and our text breaks off in the middle of a sentence. This speech is discussed in Schaefer, iii.² pp. 292 ff., and in Blass, iii. pp. 492 ff.

XXXII

ΠΡΟΣ ΖΗΝΟΘΕΜΙΝ ΠΑΡΑΓΡΑΦΗ

Ἄνδρες δικασταί, βούλομαι παραγεγραμμένος μὴ
εἰσαγώγιμον εἶναι τὴν δίκην, περὶ τῶν νόμων
πρῶτον εἰπεῖν, καθ' οὓς παρεγραψάμην. οἱ νόμοι
κελεύουσιν, ὦ ἄνδρες δικασταί, τὰς δίκας εἶναι
τοῖς ναυκλήροις καὶ τοῖς ἐμπόροις τῶν Ἀθήναζε
καὶ τῶν Ἀθήνηθεν συμβολαίων, καὶ περὶ ὧν ἂν
ὦσι συγγραφαί· ἐὰν δέ τις παρὰ ταῦτα δικάζηται,
2 μὴ εἰσαγώγιμον εἶναι τὴν δίκην. τουτωὶ τοίνυν
Ζηνοθέμιδι πρὸς μὲν ἔμ' ὅτι οὐδὲν ἦν συμβόλαιον
οὐδὲ συγγραφή, καὐτὸς ὁμολογεῖ ἐν τῷ ἐγκλήματι·
δανεῖσαι δέ φησιν Ἡγεστράτῳ ναυκλήρῳ, τούτου
δ' ἀπολομένου ἐν τῷ πελάγει, ἡμᾶς τὸ ναῦλον
σφετερίσασθαι· τουτὶ τὸ ἔγκλημ' ἐστίν. ἐκ δὴ τοῦ
αὐτοῦ λόγου τήν τε δίκην οὐκ εἰσαγώγιμον οὖσαν
μαθήσεσθε, καὶ τὴν ὅλην ἐπιβουλὴν καὶ πονηρίαν
3 τουτουὶ τοῦ ἀνθρώπου ὄψεσθε. δέομαι δ' ὑμῶν
πάντων, ὦ ἄνδρες δικασταί, εἴπερ ἄλλῳ τινὶ πώποτε
πράγματι τὸν νοῦν προσέσχετε, καὶ τούτῳ προσ-
σχεῖν· ἀκούσεσθε γὰρ ἀνθρώπου τόλμαν καὶ πονη-
[883] ρίαν οὐ τὴν τυχοῦσαν, ἄνπερ ἐγὼ τὰ πεπραγμέν'
αὐτῷ πρὸς ὑμᾶς πολλάκις εἰπεῖν δυνηθῶ, οἶμαι δέ.
4 Ζηνόθεμις γὰρ οὑτοσί, ὢν ὑπηρέτης Ἡγεστράτου τοῦ ναυκλήρου, ὃν καὐτὸς ἔγραψεν ἐν
178

XXXII

PLEA OF DEMO AGAINST ZENOTHEMIS, A SPECIAL PLEA

Men of the jury, having entered a plea that the action is not admissible, I wish first to speak concerning the laws in accordance with which the plea was entered. The laws, men of the jury, ordain that actions for shipowners and merchants shall be upon loans for shipments to or from Athens, concerning which there shall be written agreements; and if anyone brings suit in violation of this provision, the action shall not be maintainable. Now between this man 2 Zenothemis and myself there has been no contract or agreement in writing, as he himself acknowledges in his complaint. He states that he made a loan to Hegestratus, a shipowner, and that after the latter was lost at sea, we appropriated the cargo. This is his charge in the complaint. The same speech will suffice to prove to you that his action is not maintainable, and to make you see the whole of his plot and his rascality. I beg of you all, men of the jury, if you ever attended 3 closely to any matter, to attend to this. You will hear of a man's audacity and villainy that go beyond all bounds, provided I am able, as I hope to be, to tell you the whole tale of what he has done.

Zenothemis, who is here before you, being an 4 underling of Hegestratus, the shipowner, who he

τῷ ἐγκλήματι, ὡς ἐν τῷ πελάγει ἀπώλετο (πῶς δ᾽,
οὐ προσέγραψεν, ἀλλ᾽ ἐγὼ φράσω), ἀδίκημα τοιου-
τονὶ μετ᾽ ἐκείνου συνεσκευάσατο. χρήματ᾽ ἐν ταῖς
Συρακούσαις ἐδανείζεθ᾽ οὗτος κἀκεῖνος. ὡμολόγει
δ᾽ ἐκεῖνος μὲν πρὸς τοὺς τούτῳ δανείζοντας, εἴ τις
ἔροιτο, ἐνεῖναι σῖτον ἐν τῇ νηὶ τούτῳ πολύν, οὗτος
δὲ πρὸς τοὺς ἐκείνῳ, τὸν γόμον οἰκεῖον ἔχειν αὑτὸν
τῆς νεώς· ὢν δ᾽ ὁ μὲν ναύκληρος, ὁ δ᾽ ἐπιβάτης,
5 ἐπιστεύοντ᾽ εἰκότως ἃ περὶ ἀλλήλων ἔλεγον. λαμ-
βάνοντες δὲ τὰ χρήματα, οἴκαδ᾽ ἀπέστελλον εἰς
τὴν Μασσαλίαν, καὶ οὐδὲν εἰς τὴν ναῦν εἰσέφερον.
οὐσῶν δὲ τῶν συγγραφῶν, ὥσπερ εἰώθασιν ἅπασαι,
σωθείσης τῆς νεὼς ἀποδοῦναι τὰ χρήματα, ἵν᾽ ἀπο-
στερήσαιεν τοὺς δανείσαντας, τὴν ναῦν καταδῦσαι
ἐβουλεύσαντο. ὁ μὲν οὖν Ἡγέστρατος, ὡς ἀπὸ τῆς
γῆς ἀπῆραν δυοῖν ἢ τριῶν ἡμερῶν πλοῦν, καταβὰς
τῆς νυκτὸς εἰς κοίλην ναῦν, διέκοπτε τοῦ πλοίου
τοὔδαφος. οὑτοσὶ δ᾽, ὡς οὐδὲν εἰδώς, ἄνω μετὰ
τῶν ἄλλων ἐπιβατῶν διέτριβεν. ψόφου δὲ γενο-
μένου, αἰσθάνονται οἱ ἐν τῷ πλοίῳ, ὅτι κακόν τι ἐν
6 κοίλῃ νηὶ γίγνεται, καὶ βοηθοῦσι κάτω. ὡς δ᾽ ἡλί-
σκεθ᾽ ὁ Ἡγέστρατος καὶ δίκην δώσειν ὑπελάμβανε,
φεύγει καὶ ἐκδιωκόμενος ῥίπτει αὑτὸν εἰς τὴν
θάλατταν, διαμαρτὼν δὲ τοῦ λέμβου διὰ τὸ νύκτ᾽
[884] εἶναι, ἀπεπνίγη. ἐκεῖνος μὲν οὖν οὕτως, ὥσπερ
ἄξιος ἦν, κακὸς κακῶς ἀπώλετο, ἃ τοὺς ἄλλους
7 ἐπεβούλευσε ποιῆσαι, ταῦτα παθὼν αὐτός. οὑτοσὶ
δ᾽ ὁ κοινωνὸς αὑτοῦ καὶ συνεργός, τὸ μὲν πρῶτον
εὐθὺς ἐν τῷ πλοίῳ παρὰ τἀδικήματα, ὡς οὐδὲν

himself in his complaint states to have been lost at sea (how, he does not add, but I will tell you), concocted with him the following fraud. Both of them borrowed money in Syracuse. Hegestratus admitted to those lending money to Zenothemis, if inquiries were made, that there was on board the ship a large amount of grain belonging to the latter ; and the plaintiff admitted to those lending money to Hegestratus that the cargo of the ship was his. As one was the shipowner and the other a passenger, they were naturally believed in what they said of one another. But immediately on getting the money, **5** they sent it home to Massalia, and put nothing on board the ship. The agreement being, as is usual in all such cases, that the money was to be paid back if the ship reached port safely, they laid a plot to sink the ship, that so they might defraud their creditors. Hegestratus, accordingly, when they were two or three days' voyage from land, went down by night into the hold of the vessel, and began to cut a hole in the ship's bottom, while Zenothemis, as though knowing nothing about it, remained on deck with the rest of the passengers. When the noise was heard, those on the vessel saw that something wrong was going on in the hold, and rushed down to bear aid. Hegestratus, being caught in the act, and ex- **6** pecting to pay the penalty, took to flight, and, hotly pursued by the others, flung himself into the sea. It was dark, and he missed the ship's boat, and so was drowned. Thus, miserable as he was, he met a miserable end as he deserved, suffering the fate which he purposed to bring about for others. As for this **7** fellow, his associate and accomplice, at first being on board the ship immediately after the attempted

εἰδώς, ἀλλ' ἐκπεπληγμένος καὶ αὐτός, ἔπειθε τὸν
πρῳρέα καὶ τοὺς ναύτας εἰς τὸν λέμβον ἐκβαίνειν
καὶ ἐκλείπειν τὴν ναῦν τὴν ταχίστην, ὡς ἀνελπίστου
τῆς σωτηρίας οὔσης καὶ καταδυσομένης τῆς νεὼς
αὐτίκα μάλα, ἵν', ὅπερ διενοήθησαν, τοῦτ' ἐπιτελε-
σθείη καὶ ἡ ναῦς ἀπόλοιτο καὶ τὰ συμβόλαι' ἀπο-
8 στερήσαιεν. ἀποτυχὼν δὲ τούτου, καὶ τοῦ παρ'
ἡμῶν ἐμπλέοντος ἐναντιωθέντος, καὶ τοῖς ναύταις
μισθούς, εἰ διασώσαιεν τὴν ναῦν, μεγάλους ἐπ-
αγγειλαμένου, σωθείσης εἰς Κεφαλληνίαν τῆς νεὼς
διὰ τοὺς θεοὺς μάλιστά γε, εἶτα καὶ διὰ τὴν τῶν
ναυτῶν ἀρετήν, πάλιν μετὰ τῶν Μασσαλιωτῶν τῶν
τοῦ Ἡγεστράτου πολιτῶν μὴ καταπλεῖν Ἀθήναζε τὸ
πλοῖον ἔπραττε, λέγων ὡς αὐτός τε καὶ τὰ χρήματ'
ἐκεῖθέν ἐστι, καὶ ὁ ναύκληρος εἴη καὶ οἱ δεδανει-
9 κότες Μασσαλιῶται. ἀποτυχὼν δὲ καὶ τούτου, καὶ
τῶν ἀρχόντων τῶν ἐν τῇ Κεφαλληνίᾳ γνόντων
Ἀθήναζε τὴν ναῦν καταπλεῖν, ὅθενπερ ἀνήχθη, ὃν
οὐδ' ἂν εἷς ἐλθεῖν ᾤετο δεῦρο τολμῆσαι τοιαῦτά γ'
ἐσκευωρημένον καὶ πεποιηκότα, οὗτος, ὦ ἄνδρες
Ἀθηναῖοι, τοσοῦτον ὑπερβέβληκεν ἀναιδείᾳ καὶ
τόλμῃ, ὥστ' οὐκ ἐλήλυθεν μόνον, ἀλλὰ καὶ τοῦ
σίτου τοῦ ἡμετέρου ἀμφισβητήσας ἡμῖν δίκην
προσείληχεν.

10 Τί οὖν ποτ' ἐστὶ τὸ αἴτιον, καὶ τῷ ποτ' ἐπηρμένος
οὗτος καὶ ἐλήλυθε καὶ τὴν δίκην εἴληχεν; ἐγὼ ὑμῖν
ἐρῶ, ἄνδρες δικασταί, ἀχθόμενος μὲν νὴ τὸν Δία
[885] καὶ θεούς, ἀναγκαζόμενος δέ. ἔστιν ἐργαστήριον
182

crime, just as though he knew nothing of it but was himself in utter consternation, he sought to induce the sailing-master and the seamen to embark in the boat and abandon the vessel with all speed, declaring that there was no hope of safety and that the ship would presently sink ; thinking that thus their design might be accomplished, the ship be lost, and the creditors thus be robbed of their money. In this he 8 failed, for our agent,[a] who was on board, opposed the plan, and promised the sailors large rewards if they should bring the ship safe into port. The ship was safely brought to Cephallenia, thanks chiefly to the gods, and after them to the bravery of the seamen. Again after this he schemed together with the Massaliotes, the fellow-countrymen of Hegestratus, to prevent the vessel from completing her voyage to Athens, saying that he himself was from Massalia ; that the money came from thence ; and that the shipowner and the lenders were Massaliotes. In this, too, he 9 failed ; for the magistrates in Cephallenia decided that the vessel should return to Athens, from which port she had set sail. Then the man, whom no one would have thought audacious enough to come here, after having plotted and wrought such deeds—this man, Athenians, has so surpassed all in shamelessness and audacity, that he has not only come, but has actually laid claim to my grain, and has brought suit against me !

What, then, is the reason for this ? and what can 10 have induced the fellow to come here and commence this suit ? I will tell you, men of the jury, though Heaven knows it gives me pain to do so ; but I must.

---

[a] Presumably Protus, who seems to have sailed as supercargo.

μοχθηρῶν ἀνθρώπων συνεστηκότων ἐν τῷ Πειραιεῖ·
11 οὓς οὐδ' ὑμεῖς ἀγνοήσαιτ' ἂν ἰδόντες. ἐκ τούτων
ἔν', ἡνίχ' οὗτος ἔπραττεν ὅπως ἡ ναῦς μὴ κατα-
πλεύσεται δεῦρο, πρεσβευτὴν ἐκ βουλῆς τινα λαμ-
βάνομεν γνώριμον οὑτωσί, ὅ τι δ' ἦν οὐκ εἰδότες,
ἀτύχημ' οὐδὲν ἔλαττον, εἰ οἷόν τ' εἰπεῖν, ἀτυχή-
σαντες, ἢ τὸ ἐξ ἀρχῆς πονηροῖς ἀνθρώποις συμ-
μεῖξαι. οὗτος ὁ πεμφθεὶς ὑφ' ἡμῶν, 'Αριστοφῶν
ὄνομ' αὐτῷ, ὃς καὶ τὰ τοῦ Μικκαλίωνος πράγματ'
ἐσκευώρηται (ταῦτα γὰρ νῦν ἀκούομεν), ἡργο-
λάβηκεν αὐτὸς καὶ κατεπήγγελται τουτῳί, καὶ
ὅλως ἐστὶν ὁ πάντα πράττων οὗτος· ὁδὶ δ' ἄσμενος
12 δέδεκται ταῦτα. ὡς γὰρ διήμαρτε τοῦ διαφθαρῆναι
τὸ πλοῖον, οὐκ ἔχων ἀποδοῦναι τὰ χρήματα τοῖς
δανείσασι (πῶς γὰρ, ἅ γ' ἐξ ἀρχῆς μὴ ἐνέθετο;)
ἀντιποιεῖται τῶν ἡμετέρων, καί φησι τῷ 'Ηγε-
στράτῳ ἐπὶ τούτῳ τῷ σίτῳ δεδανεικέναι, ὃν ὁ παρ'
ἡμῶν ἐπιπλέων ἐπρίατο. οἱ δὲ δανεισταὶ τὸ ἐξ
ἀρχῆς ἠπατημένοι, ὁρῶντες ἑαυτοῖς ἀντὶ τῶν
χρημάτων ἄνθρωπον πονηρὸν χρήστην, ἄλλο δ'
οὐδέν, ἐλπίδ' ἔχοντες ὑπὸ τούτου παρακρουσθέντων
ὑμῶν ἐκ τῶν ἡμετέρων ἀπολήψεσθαι τὰ ἑαυτῶν,
ὃν ἴσασι ψευδόμενον ταῦτα καθ' ἡμῶν, τούτῳ
συνδικεῖν ἀναγκάζονται τοῦ συμφέροντος εἵνεκα τοῦ
ἑαυτῶν.
13 Τὸ μὲν οὖν πρᾶγμ', ὑπὲρ οὗ τὴν ψῆφον οἴσετε,
ὡς εἰπεῖν ἐν κεφαλαίῳ, τοιοῦτόν ἐστι. βούλομαι δὲ

ᵃ For the Greek phrase compare Orations XXXVII. § 39,
XXXIX. § 2, and XL. § 9.
ᵇ The precise meaning of the phrase ἐκ βουλῆς is disputed.
Others take it as meaning that the man in question was a
member of the Athenian βουλή, or Senate.

There exists in the Peiraeus a gang of scoundrels ᵃ
closely leagued with one another. You would know **11**
them at once, should you see them. When this man
Zenothemis was scheming to prevent the vessel from
completing her voyage to Athens we chose one of
these men after consulting with one another ᵇ as our
representative. He was known to us after a fashion,
but we had no idea of his real character. This was
in fact a piece of misfortune for us as great, if so much
may be said, as our having to deal with rascals at the
start. This man who was sent out by us—his name
was Aristophon, and he is the same one, as we now
hear, who managed the business of Miccalion—has
entered into an agreement with the plaintiff, and has
sold him his services. In a word he is the one who is
managing the whole affair, and Zenothemis has been
glad to accept this help. For when he failed in his **12**
scheme to destroy the vessel, not being able to pay
back their money to his creditors—how could he pay,
when at the start he had put nothing on board ?—he
lays claim to my goods, and declares that he has lent
money to Hegestratus on the security of the grain
which our agent sailing with him had purchased. The
creditors, who had been deceived in the first instance,
seeing that instead of receiving their money, they
have a scoundrel as their debtor and nothing more,
and hoping that, if you are imposed upon by Zenothemis, they may recover their own out of my property, are forced to make common cause with him
in order to protect their own interests, although
they know him to be making these false charges
against me.

Such, to speak briefly, is the matter on which you **13**
are to cast your votes. But I wish first to bring before

τοὺς μάρτυρας ὧν λέγω πρῶτον ὑμῖν παρασχόμενος, μετὰ ταῦτ' ἤδη καὶ τἄλλα διδάσκειν.

Καί μοι λέγε τὰς μαρτυρίας.

ΜΑΡΤΥΡΙΑΙ

14 Ἐπειδὴ τοίνυν ἀφίκετο δεῦρο τὸ πλοῖον, γνόντων τῶν Κεφαλλήνων ἀντιπράττοντος τούτου, ὅθεν ἐξέπλευσε τὸ πλοῖον, ἐνταῦθα καὶ καταπλεῖν αὐτό, τὴν μὲν ναῦν οἱ ἐπὶ τῇ νηὶ δεδανεικότες ἐνθένδ' εὐθέως εἶχον, τὸν δὲ σῖτον ὁ ἠγορακὼς εἶχεν· ἦν δ' οὗτος ὁ ἡμῖν τὰ χρήματ' ὀφείλων. μετὰ ταῦθ' ἧκεν οὗτος ἔχων τὸν παρ' ἡμῶν πεμφθέντα πρεσβευτήν, τὸν Ἀριστοφῶντα, καὶ ἠμφεσβήτει τοῦ σίτου, φάσκων 15 Ἡγεστράτῳ δεδανεικέναι. '' τί λέγεις, ἄνθρωπε; '' εὐθέως ὁ Πρῶτος (τοῦτο γὰρ ἦν τοὔνομα τῷ τὸν σῖτον εἰσαγαγόντι, τῷ τὰ χρήμαθ' ἡμῖν ὀφείλοντι) '' σὺ χρήματα δέδωκας Ἡγεστράτῳ, μεθ' οὗ τοὺς ἄλλους ἐξηπάτηκας, ὅπως δανείσηται; καὶ σοὶ πολλάκις λέγοντος, ὅτι τοῖς προϊεμένοις ἀπολεῖται τὰ χρήματα, σὺ οὖν ταῦτ' ἀκούων αὐτὸς ἂν προήκω; '' ἔφη, καὶ ἀναιδὴς ἦν. '' οὐκοῦν εἰ τὰ μάλιστ' ἀληθῆ λέγεις,'' τῶν παρόντων τις ὑπέλαβεν, '' ὁ σὸς κοινωνὸς καὶ πολίτης, ὁ Ἡγέστρατος, ὡς ἔοικεν, ἐξηπάτηκέ σε, καὶ ὑπὲρ τούτων 16 αὐτὸς αὑτῷ θανάτου τιμήσας ἀπόλωλεν.'' '' καὶ ὅτι γ','' ἔφη τις τῶν παρόντων, '' ἁπάντων ἐστὶ συνεργὸς οὗτος ἐκείνῳ, σημεῖον ὑμῖν ἐρῶ· πρὸ γὰρ τοῦ διακόπτειν ἐπιχειρῆσαι τὴν ναῦν, τίθενται πρός τινα τῶν συμπλεόντων οὗτος καὶ ὁ Ἡγέστρατος

you the witnesses to what I am saying, and then to instruct you regarding other aspects of the case.

Please read the depositions.

THE DEPOSITIONS

When the vessel arrived here—for the Cephallen- **14** ians ordered, despite the plaintiff's machinations, that it should put into the port from which it first sailed—those who had lent money on the ship immediately took possession of her, and the man who had bought the grain took possession of it ; he was the one who had borrowed the money of us. After this the plaintiff came, having with him Aristophon, the man sent out as our representative, and laid claim to the grain, saying that he had lent money to Hegestratus. "What are you saying, fellow?" **15** exclaimed Protus immediately. (This was the name of the man who imported the grain, and who owed us the money.) Is it you who have given money to Hegestratus, you who aided him to deceive the others, that he might borrow of them? Would you who often heard him say that those who ventured their money would lose it, would you, I say, hearing this, have ventured yours?" "Yes," said he impudently. "Well, then," interrupted one of those present, "if what you say is never so true, your partner and fellow-countryman, Hegestratus, has taken you in, it appears, and for that has passed sentence of death upon himself, and is dead." "Yes," **16** said another of the bystanders, "and that this fellow has co-operated with Hegestratus in the whole matter, I will give you a proof. For before the attempt was made to cut through the ship's bottom, this man and Hegestratus deposited with one of the ship's com-

187

συγγραφήν. καίτοι εἰ μὲν εἰς πίστιν ἔδωκας, τί
πρὸ τοῦ κακουργήματος ἂν τὰ βέβαι' ἐποιοῦ; εἰ
δ' ἀπιστῶν ἐτύγχανες, τί οὐχ, ὥσπερ οἱ ἄλλοι, τὰ
17 δίκαι' ἐλάμβανες ἐν τῇ γῇ;" τί ἂν τὰ πολλὰ
λέγοι τις; ἦν γὰρ οὐδ' ὁτιοῦν πλέον ἡμῖν ταῦτα
[887] λέγουσιν, ἀλλ' εἴχετο τοῦ σίτου. ἐξῆγεν αὐτὸν ὁ
Πρῶτος καὶ ὁ κοινωνὸς τοῦ Πρώτου, Φέρτατος·
οὑτοσὶ δ' οὐκ ἐξήγετο, οὐδ' ἂν ἔφη διαρρήδην ὑπ'
18 οὐδενὸς ἐξαχθῆναι, εἰ μὴ αὐτὸν ἐγὼ ἐξάξω. μετὰ
ταῦτα προὐκαλεῖθ' ὁ Πρῶτος αὐτὸν καὶ ἡμεῖς ἐπὶ
τὴν ἀρχὴν τὴν τῶν Συρακοσίων, κἂν μὲν ἐωνημένος
τὸν σῖτον ἐκεῖνος φαίνηται καὶ τὰ τέλη κείμεν'
ἐκείνῳ καὶ τὰς τιμὰς ὁ διαλύων ἐκεῖνος, τοῦτον
πονηρὸν ὄντ' ἠξιοῦμεν ζημιοῦσθαι, εἰ δὲ μή, καὶ
τὰ διάφορ' ἀπολαβεῖν καὶ τάλαντον προσλαβεῖν, καὶ
τοῦ σίτου ἀφιστάμεθα. ταῦτ' ἐκείνου προκαλου-
μένου καὶ λέγοντος καὶ ἡμῶν οὐδὲν ἦν πλέον, ἀλλ'
ἦν αἵρεσις ἢ τοῦτον ἐξάγειν, ἢ ἀπολωλεκέναι
19 σωθέντα καὶ παρόντα τὰ ἡμέτερ' αὐτῶν. ὁ γὰρ αὖ
Πρῶτος διεμαρτύρετ' ἐξάγειν, βεβαιῶν ἀναπλεῖν
ἐθέλειν εἰς τὴν Σικελίαν· εἰ δὲ ταῦτ' ἐθέλοντος
αὐτοῦ προησόμεθ' ἡμεῖς τούτῳ τὸν σῖτον, οὐδὲν
αὐτῷ μέλειν. καὶ ὅτι ταῦτ' ἀληθῆ λέγω, καὶ οὔτ'
ἂν ἐξαχθῆναι ἔφη, εἰ μὴ ὑπ' ἐμοῦ, οὔθ' ἃ προὐκαλεῖτο περὶ τοῦ ἀναπλεῖν ἐδέχετο, ἔν τε τῷ πλῷ
τὴν συγγραφὴν ἔθετο, λέγε τὰς μαρτυρίας.

---

^a The meaning appears to be that Zenothemis considered
Demo, rather than Protus, a person from whom he might
hope to win damages for ejectment.

pany a written agreement. Yet, if you had confidence in him when you gave the money, why should you have sought some security for yourself before the crime ? But if you distrusted him, why did you not, like the others, get a legal acknowledgement before sailing ? " But why relate all that was said ? We 17 made no progress by all this talking ; he held on to the grain. Protus tried to put him out, and so did Phertatus, Protus's partner ; but he wouldn't budge, declaring point-blank that he would not be put out of possession by anyone, unless I myself should put him out.[a] After this Protus and I challenged him to go 18 before the Syracusan authorities, and, if it should be shown that Protus had bought the grain, that the customs duties were recorded in his name, and that it was he who had paid the price, we demanded that Zenothemis be punished as a rascal ; if this were not proved, we agreed that he should receive back all he had expended and a talent in addition and that we would relinquish our claim to the grain. Despite this challenge and all that Protus and I could say, we made no progress, but I had to choose either to put Zenothemis out, or to lose my property which had been brought safe to port and was there before my eyes. Protus on his part adjured us by the gods to 19 put him out, declaring himself ready to sail back to Sicily ; but if, despite this willingness of his, I should give up the grain to Zenothemis, he said it made no difference to him. To prove that I am telling the truth in this—that the plaintiff refused to be put out of possession except by me, that he refused the challenge to sail back to Sicily, and that he deposited the agreement in the course of the voyage—read the depositions.

ΜΑΡΤΥΡΙΑΙ

20 Ἐπειδὴ τοίνυν οὔτ' ἐξάγεσθαι ἤθελεν ὑπὸ τοῦ
Πρώτου, οὔτ' εἰς τὴν Σικελίαν ἀναπλεῖν ἐπὶ τὰ
δίκαια, προειδώς θ' ἅπαντ' ἐφαίνετο, ἃ ὁ Ἡγέστρατος ἐκακούργει, λοιπὸν ἦν ἡμῖν τοῖς ἐνθένδε
μὲν πεποιημένοις τὸ συμβόλαιον, παρειληφόσιν δὲ
τὸν σῖτον παρὰ τοῦ δικαίως ἐκεῖ πριαμένου, ἐξάγειν
21 τοῦτον. τί γὰρ ἂν καὶ ἄλλ' ἐποιοῦμεν; οὔπω γὰρ
τοῦτό γ' οὐδεὶς ἡμῶν τῶν κοινωνῶν ὑπελάμβανεν,
[888] ὡς ὑμεῖς γνώσεσθέ ποτ' εἶναι τούτου τὸν σῖτον, ὃν
καταλιπεῖν οὗτος ἔπειθε τοὺς ναύτας, ὅπως ἀπόλοιτο τοῦ πλοίου καταδύντος. ὃ καὶ μέγιστόν ἐστι
σημεῖον τοῦ μηδὲν προσήκειν αὐτῷ. τίς γὰρ ἂν
τὸν ἑαυτοῦ σῖτον ἔπειθε προέσθαι τοὺς σῴζειν
βουλομένους; ἢ τίς οὐκ ἂν ἔπλει δεξάμενος τὴν
πρόκλησιν εἰς τὴν Σικελίαν, οὗ ταῦτ' ἦν ἐλέγξαι
22 καθαρῶς; καὶ μὴν οὐδὲ τοῦτ' ἐμέλλομεν ὑμῶν
καταγνώσεσθαι, ὡς εἰσαγώγιμον ψηφιεῖσθε τούτῳ
τὴν δίκην περὶ τούτων τῶν χρημάτων, ἃ κατὰ πολλοὺς τρόπους οὗτος ἔπραττεν ὅπως μὴ εἰσαγώγιμα
δεῦρ' ἔσται, πρῶτον μὲν ὅτ' αὐτὰ καταλιπεῖν τοὺς
ναύτας ἔπειθεν, εἶθ' ὅτ' ἐν Κεφαλληνίᾳ μὴ δεῦρο
23 πλεῖν τὴν ναῦν ἔπραττεν. πῶς γὰρ οὐκ αἰσχρὸν
καὶ δεινὸν ἂν γένοιτο, εἰ Κεφαλλῆνες μέν, ὅπως
τοῖς Ἀθηναίοις σωθῇ τὰ χρήματα, δεῦρο πλεῖν
τὴν ναῦν ἔκριναν, ὑμεῖς δ' ὄντες Ἀθηναῖοι τὰ
τῶν πολιτῶν τοῖς καταποντίσαι βουληθεῖσι δοῦναι
γνοίητε, καὶ ἃ μὴ καταπλεῖν ὅλως οὗτος δεῦρ'

THE DEPOSITIONS

When, therefore, he refused to be put out of 20
possession by Protus, or to sail back to Sicily for an
equitable settlement, and when it was proved that he
was an accomplice in all the villainy of Hegestratus,
the only course left for us, who had lent our
money here at Athens and had taken over the grain
from the man who had honestly purchased it there
in Sicily, was to dispossess the plaintiff. What else 21
could we have done? Not one of us partners had
as yet any idea that you would ever declare the
grain to be this man's property—grain which he
tried to induce the sailors to abandon, that it might
be lost by the sinking of the ship. This fact is the
strongest proof that none of it belonged to him;
for who would have tried to induce those who were
attempting to save it to abandon grain which
belonged to himself? Or who would not have accepted the challenge and have sailed to Sicily, where
these matters might have been clearly proved? And 22
surely I was not going to have so poor an opinion
of you as to imagine that you would vote to allow
this man to enter a suit regarding these goods, whose
entry into your port he had sought by every means
to prevent,—first when he tried to induce the sailors
to abandon them, and again when in Cephallenia he
strove to prevent the ship from sailing here. Would 23
it not be a shameful and outrageous thing, if Cephal-
lenians, in order to save property for Athenians,
ordered the ship to be brought here, but you, who
are Athenians, should order the property of your
citizens to be given up to those who wished to throw
it into the sea, and should allow this fellow to enter

ἔπραττε, ταῦτ᾽ εἰσαγώγιμα τούτῳ ψηφίσαισθε;
μὴ δῆτ᾽, ὦ Ζεῦ καὶ θεοί. λέγε δή μοι τί παρα-
γέγραμμαι.

ΠΑΡΑΓΡΑΦΗ

Λέγε δή μοι τὸν νόμον.

ΝΟΜΟΣ

24 Ὅτι μὲν τοίνυν ἐκ τῶν νόμων παρεγραψάμην μὴ
εἰσαγώγιμον εἶναι τὴν δίκην, ἱκανῶς οἶμαι δεδεῖ-
χθαι· τέχνην δ᾽ ἀκούσεσθε τοῦ σοφοῦ τοῦ ταῦτα
πάντα συντεθηκότος, τοῦ Ἀριστοφῶντος. ὡς γὰρ
ἐκ τῶν πραγμάτων ἁπλῶς οὐδὲν ἑώρων δίκαιον
[889] ἑαυτοῖς ἐνόν, ἐπικηρυκεύονται τῷ Πρώτῳ καὶ
πείθουσι τὸν ἄνθρωπον ἐνδοῦναι τὰ πράγμαθ᾽ ἑαυτοῖς, πράττοντες μὲν ὡς ἔοικε καὶ ἐξ ἀρχῆς τοῦτο,
ὡς ἡμῖν νῦν φανερὸν γέγονεν, οὐ δυνάμενοι δὲ
25 πεῖσαι. ὁ γὰρ Πρῶτος, ἕως μὲν ᾤετο τὸν σῖτον
κέρδος ἐλθόντα ποιήσειν, ἀντείχετο τούτου, καὶ
μᾶλλον ᾑρεῖθ᾽ αὐτός τε κερδᾶναι καὶ ἡμῖν τὰ δίκαι᾽
ἀποδοῦναι, ἢ κατακοινωνήσας τούτοις, τῆς μὲν
ὠφελείας τούτους ποιῆσαι μερίτας, ἡμᾶς δ᾽ ἀδι-
κῆσαι· ὡς δὲ δεῦρ᾽ ἥκοντος αὐτοῦ καὶ περὶ ταῦτα
πραγματευομένου, ἐπανῆκεν ὁ σῖτος, ἄλλην εὐθέως
26 ἔλαβε γνώμην. καὶ ἅμ᾽ (εἰρήσεται γάρ, ἄνδρες
Ἀθηναῖοι, πᾶσα πρὸς ὑμᾶς ἡ ἀλήθεια) καὶ ἡμεῖς οἱ
δεδανεικότες προσεκρούομεν αὐτῷ καὶ πικρῶς
εἴχομεν, τῆς τε ζημίας ἐφ᾽ ἡμᾶς ἰούσης τῆς περὶ
τὸν σῖτον, καὶ συκοφάντην ἀντὶ χρημάτων αἰτιώ-

an action for goods which he schemed to prevent from being brought here at all ? Do not do that, I implore you by Zeus and the Gods. Now read, please, the special plea which I entered.

THE PLEA

Now please read the law.

THE LAW

That my plea that the action is not admissible 24 is in harmony with the laws, has, I think, been sufficiently proved ; but you must hear the trick of this clever fellow Aristophon, who has concocted the whole scheme. When they saw that, in the light of the facts, they had absolutely no basis of right, they made overtures to Protus, and induced him to leave the matter wholly in their hands. From the first, as has now become plain to us, they had been working to this end, but had been unable to carry their point. For 25 Protus, so long as he thought to get a profit for himself from the grain by going, clung to it, and chose rather to make his profit, and to render to us what was our due, than to make common cause with these men, sharing with them the advantage gained and doing us an injury. But when, after he had come back here and was negotiating about these matters, grain fell in price, he straightway changed his mind. At the same time (for, men of 26 Athens, the whole truth shall be told you), we on our part, who had made the loan, came to a quarrel and felt bitter against him (for the loss on the grain was falling on us), and charged that he had secured for us this pettifogging scoundrel instead of our

μενοι τοῦτον ἡμῖν κεκομικέναι. ἐκ τούτων, οὐδὲ
φύσει χρηστὸς ὢν ἄνθρωπος δηλονότι, ἐπὶ τούτους
ἀποκλίνει, καὶ συγχωρεῖ τὴν δίκην ἔρημον ὀφλεῖν,
ἣν οὗτος αὐτῷ λαγχάνει τότε, ὅτ᾽ οὔπω ταῦτ᾽

27 ἐφρόνουν. εἰ μὲν γὰρ ἀφῆκε τὸν Πρῶτον, ἐξ-
ελήλεγκτ᾽ ἂν εὐθέως ἡμᾶς συκοφαντῶν· ὀφλεῖν δὲ
παρὼν ἐκεῖνος οὐ συνεχώρει, ἵν᾽ ἐὰν μὲν αὐτῷ
ποιῶσιν ἃ ὡμολογήκασιν—, εἰ δὲ μή, τὴν ἔρημον
ἀντιλάχῃ. ἀλλὰ τί ταῦτα; εἰ μὲν γὰρ ἃ γέγραφεν
οὗτος εἰς τὸ ἔγκλημ᾽ ἐποίει, οὐκ ὀφλεῖν ἂν δίκην
δικαίως, ἀλλ᾽ ἀποθανεῖν ὁ Πρῶτος ἔμοιγε δοκεῖ.
εἰ γὰρ ἐν κακοῖς καὶ χειμῶνι τοσοῦτον οἶνον ἔπινεν,
ὥσθ᾽ ὅμοιον εἶναι μανίᾳ, τί οὐκ ἄξιός ἐστι παθεῖν;

28 ἢ εἰ γράμματ᾽ ἔκλεπτεν; ἢ εἰ ὑπανέῳγεν; ἀλλὰ
ταῦτα μὲν αὐτοὶ πρὸς ἑαυτοὺς ὑμεῖς ὅπως ποτ᾽ ἔχει

[890] διακρινεῖσθε· τῇ δ᾽ ἐμῇ δίκῃ μηδὲν ἐκείνης πρόσαγε.
εἴ τί σ᾽ ἠδίκηκεν ὁ Πρῶτος ἢ λέγων ἢ ποιῶν,
ἔχεις ὡς ἔοικε δίκην· οὐδεὶς ἡμῶν ἐκώλυεν, οὐδὲ
νῦν παραιτεῖται. εἰ σεσυκοφάντηκας, οὐ περιεργα-
ζόμεθα. νὴ Δί᾽, ἀλλ᾽ ἐκποδών ἐστιν ἄνθρωπος.

29 διά γ᾽ ὑμᾶς, ἵνα τάς τε μαρτυρίας τὰς ἡμετέρας
λίπῃ, καὶ νῦν ὑμεῖς ὅ τι ἂν βούλησθε λέγητε κατ᾽
αὐτοῦ. εἰ γὰρ μὴ δι᾽ ὑμῶν ἔρημος ἐγίγνεθ᾽ ἡ δίκη,
ἅμ᾽ ἂν αὐτὸν προσεκαλοῦ καὶ κατηγγύας πρὸς τὸν
πολέμαρχον, καὶ εἰ μὲν κατέστησέ σοι τοὺς ἐγ-

money. After this, being manifestly none too honest by nature, he went over to their side, and agreed to let judgement go by default in the suit which Zenothemis had brought against him before they had come to an agreement with one another. For, if he 27 had dropped his suit against Protus, it would have been made clear at once that his action against us was a malicious one, and Protus would not consent to have judgement given against him while he was here present, in order that, if they should do for him what they had agreed—well and good ; but, if not, he might have the judgement by default set aside. But why speak of all this ? If Protus really did what Zenothemis here has written in his complaint, he justly deserves, as it seems to me at least, not merely to have judgement given against him, but to be put to death. For if in danger and tempest he drank so much wine as to be like a madman, what punishment does he not deserve to suffer ? Or, if he 28 stole documents, or secretly broke the seals ? However, the facts regarding all these things you will determine in your own minds ; but, Zenothemis, do not mix up that action with mine. If Protus has wronged you in word or deed, you have, it seems, had satisfaction. No one of us sought to hinder you, or now begs for leniency for him. If you have brought a baseless charge against him, that is no affair of ours. Ah, but the fellow has disappeared. Yes ; thanks to 29 you, who wished to deprive us of his testimony, and to be able yourselves to say against him whatever you please. For if the judgement by default had not been of your own contriving, you would at the same time have called him before the Polemarch, and have had him put under bail ; and, if he had appointed sureties,

γυητάς, μένειν ἠναγκάζετ' ἄν, ἢ σὺ παρ' ὧν λήψει
δίκην ἑτοίμους εἶχες, εἰ δὲ μὴ κατέστησεν, εἰς τὸ
30 οἴκημ' ἂν ᾔει. νῦν δὲ κοινωσάμενοι τὸ πρᾶγμα, ὁ
μὲν διὰ σοῦ τὴν γεγονυῖαν ἔκδειαν οὐκ ἀποδώσειν
ἡμῖν οἴεται, σὺ δ' ἐκείνου κατηγορῶν τῶν ἡμετέρων
κύριος γενήσεσθαι. τεκμήριον δέ· ἐγὼ μὲν γὰρ
αὐτὸν κλητεύσω, σὺ δ' οὔτε κατηγγύησας οὔτε νῦν
κλητεύσεις.

31 Ἔτι τοίνυν ἑτέρα τις ἐστὶν ἐλπὶς αὐτοῖς τοῦ
παρακρούσεσθαι καὶ φενακιεῖν ὑμᾶς. αἰτιάσονται
Δημοσθένην, καὶ ἐκείνῳ με πιστεύοντα φήσουσιν
ἐξάγειν τουτονί, ὑπολαμβάνοντες τῷ ῥήτορα καὶ
γνώριμον εἶναι ἐκεῖνον πιθανὴν ἔχειν τὴν αἰτίαν.
ἐμοὶ δ' ἐστὶ μέν, ὦ ἄνδρες Ἀθηναῖοι, Δημοσθένης
οἰκεῖος γένει (καὶ πάντας ὑμῖν ὄμνυμι τοὺς θεοὺς
32 ἦ μὴν ἐρεῖν τἀληθῆ), προσελθόντος δ' αὐτῷ μου
καὶ παρεῖναι καὶ βοηθεῖν ἀξιοῦντος εἴ τι ἔχοι,
" Δήμων," ἔφη, " ἐγὼ ποιήσω μὲν ὡς ἂν σὺ
κελεύῃς· καὶ γὰρ ἂν δεινὸν εἴη. δεῖ μέντοι καὶ τὸ
[891] σαυτοῦ καὶ τοὐμὸν λογίσασθαι. ἐμοὶ συμβέβηκεν,
ἀφ' οὗ περὶ τῶν κοινῶν λέγειν ἠρξάμην, μηδὲ
πρὸς ἓν πρᾶγμ' ἴδιον προσεληλυθέναι· ἀλλὰ καὶ τῆς
πολιτείας αὐτῆς τὰ τοιαῦτ' ἐξέστηκα. * * *

(Desunt quaedam.)

ª The word οἴκημα, " lodging," is used as a euphemism for
δεσμωτήριον, " prison." *Cf.* Oration LVI. § 4.

he would have been forced to remain, or you would have had persons from whom you could recover damages ; if he had not given bail, he would have gone to prison.[a] But, as it is, you have made common **30** cause ; he thinks that through your help he will escape paying us the deficiency that has come about ; and you, through accusing him, hope to get control of my property. Here is a proof of this. I shall summon him as a witness ; you, Zenothemis, did not have him put under bail, nor do you now summon him.

There is yet another way in which they hope to **31** deceive and trick you. They will accuse Demosthenes, and will say that I relied upon his help when I put Zenothemis out of possession of the grain, assuming that this charge will be credited because he is an orator and a well-known personage. Demosthenes, men of Athens, is indeed my blood-relation (I swear to you by all the gods that I shall speak the truth), but when I approached **32** him, and entreated him to be present and to aid me in any way he could, he said to me, " Demo, I will do as you bid me ; it would be cruel to refuse you. You must, however, consider both your own circumstances and mine. My own position is this : from the time when I first began to speak on public affairs I have not come forward to plead in a single private case, but . . ."[b]

[b] The speech is mutilated at the end, and the concluding words yield no satisfactory sense.

AGAINST APATURIUS

INTRODUCTION

THE defendant in this suit, whose name is not mentioned, was sued for twenty minae by Apaturius. Again, as in the preceding case, a special plea is made that the suit is not maintainable, and again the speech deals largely with the circumstances leading up to the suit. These were substantially as follows.

Apaturius, a merchant of Byzantium, found himself unable to meet a debt of forty minae, secured by his vessel, which lay in the harbour of Peiraeus. The period for which the loan had been made had expired, and his creditors were pressing him. He therefore approached an exiled compatriot of his, a certain Parmeno, who promised him ten minae, giving him three at the time. They then jointly approached the defendant in this suit, who on his own security induced a banker, Heracleides, to advance the thirty minae needed. He took this sum in addition to the ten minae secured from Parmeno, paid off the creditors, and protected himself by taking a mortgage of forty minae on the ship of Apaturius and its crew of slaves.

At this juncture the bank of Heracleides failed, and demand was made upon the defendant for the forty minae, the liability for which he had assumed. At the same time Apaturius tried to remove the slaves and get his ship secretly out of the harbour. The defendant at once transferred his mortgage to the creditors of the bank, who in turn gave him a release from his obligation, and he filed a lien on the ship for ten minae to protect Parmeno. The vessel was then sold for forty minae, all claims were settled, and mutual releases were given in the presence of witnesses by those involved in the transaction.

After this suits were instituted against one another by Apaturius and Parmeno on account of violence used when the latter had prevented Apaturius from taking his ship out of the harbour. It was agreed that the matter should be settled by arbitration, but the articles of agreement disappeared (that they were purposely made away with is claimed by the writer of this speech), and it was a matter of dispute whether the reference was to a single arbitrator or to a board of three. Meanwhile Parmeno was obliged to leave Athens. An earthquake occurred in the Chersonese, where he was making his home on account of his exile from Byzantium, and in the disaster his house was destroyed and his wife and children perished. In his absence judgement was given against him by default, and the damages were assessed at twenty minae.

Apaturius then filed suit against the unnamed defendant, alleging that he was surety for Parmeno. This the defendant denies, and he charges further that the award was a fraudulent one.

On this speech see Schaefer, iii.² pp. 297 ff., and Blass, iii. pp. 572 ff.

201

XXXIII

ΠΡΟΣ ΑΠΑΤΟΥΡΙΟΝ ΠΑΡΑΓΡΑΦΗ

Τοῖς μὲν ἐμπόροις, ὦ ἄνδρες δικασταί, καὶ τοῖς
ναυκλήροις κελεύει ὁ νόμος εἶναι τὰς δίκας πρὸς τοὺς
θεσμοθέτας, ἐάν τι ἀδικῶνται ἐν τῷ ἐμπορίῳ ἢ
ἐνθένδε ποι πλέοντες ἢ ἑτέρωθεν δεῦρο, καὶ τοῖς
ἀδικοῦσι δεσμὸν ἔταξε τοὐπιτίμιον, ἕως ἂν ἐκτεί-
σωσιν ὅ τι ἂν αὐτῶν καταγνωσθῇ, ἵνα μηδεὶς ἀδικῇ
2 μηδένα τῶν ἐμπόρων εἰκῇ. τοῖς δὲ περὶ τῶν μὴ
γενομένων συμβολαίων εἰς κρίσιν καθισταμένοις ἐπὶ
[893] τὴν παραγραφὴν καταφεύγειν ἔδωκεν ὁ νόμος, ἵνα
μηδεὶς συκοφαντῆται, ἀλλ᾽ αὐτοῖς τοῖς τῇ ἀληθείᾳ
ἀδικουμένοις τῶν ἐμπόρων καὶ τῶν ναυκλήρων αἱ
δίκαι ὦσιν. καὶ πολλοὶ ἤδη τῶν φευγόντων ἐν ταῖς
ἐμπορικαῖς, παραγραψάμενοι κατὰ τὸν νόμον τουτονὶ καὶ εἰσελθόντες εἰς ὑμᾶς, ἐξήλεγξαν τοὺς δικα-
ζομένους ἀδίκως ἐγκαλοῦντας, καὶ ἐπὶ τῇ προφάσει
3 τοῦ ἐμπορεύεσθαι συκοφαντοῦντας. ὁ μὲν οὖν μετὰ
τούτου μοι ἐπιβεβουλευκὼς καὶ τὸν ἀγῶνα τουτονὶ
κατεσκευακώς, προϊόντος τοῦ λόγου καταφανὴς

ᵃ The Thesmothetae were the six archons (other than the
Eponymus, the Basileus, and the Polemarch), and were
empowered to administer justice in cases not specifically
within the province of any other magistrate.

XXXIII

AN UNKNOWN PLEADER AGAINST APATURIUS, A SPECIAL PLEA

THE law, men of Athens, ordains that actions for merchants and shipowners shall be before the Thesmothetae [a] if they have been in any way wronged in the market either in connexion with a voyage from Athens to any point, or from some other port to Athens ; and it fixes imprisonment as the penalty for wrongdoers until such time as they shall have paid the amount adjudged against them, so that no one may lightly do wrong to any merchant. To those, 2 however, who are brought into court in cases where no contract has been made, the law gives the right to have recourse to a special plea, that no one may bring a baseless or malicious suit, but that actions may be confined to those among the merchants and shipowners who are really wronged. Many defendants in mercantile suits have before now entered special pleas in accordance with this law, and have come before you and proved that their adversaries were making unjust charges and bringing baseless suits under pretence of being engaged in commerce. Who it is that has conspired with this fellow against 3 me and who has concocted this suit, will become clear to you as my speech goes on. Since, however,

ὑμῖν ἔσται· ἐγκαλοῦντος δέ μοι Ἀπατουρίου τὰ
ψευδῆ καὶ παρὰ τοὺς νόμους δικαζομένου, καὶ ὅσα
μὲν ἐμοὶ καὶ τούτῳ ἐγένετο συμβόλαια, πάντων
ἀπαλλαγῆς καὶ ἀφέσεως γενομένης, ἄλλου δὲ συμβολαίου οὐκ ὄντος ἐμοὶ πρὸς τοῦτον, οὔτε ναυτικοῦ
οὔτ' ἐγγείου, παρεγραψάμην τὴν δίκην μὴ εἰσαγώγιμον εἶναι κατὰ τοὺς νόμους τουτουσί.

NOMOI

4 Ὡς τοίνυν παρὰ τοὺς νόμους τούτους εἴληχέ μοι
τὴν δίκην Ἀπατούριος καὶ τὰ ψευδῆ ἐγκέκληκεν, ἐκ
πολλῶν ὑμῖν τοῦτ' ἐπιδείξω. ἐγὼ γάρ, ὦ ἄνδρες
δικασταί, πολὺν ἤδη χρόνον ἐπὶ τῆς ἐργασίας ὢν
τῆς κατὰ θάλατταν, μέχρι μέν τινος αὐτὸς ἐκιν-
δύνευον, οὔπω δ' ἔτη ἐστὶν ἑπτά, ἀφ' οὗ τὸ μὲν
πλεῖν καταλέλυκα, μέτρια δ' ἔχων τούτοις πειρῶμαι
5 ναυτικοῖς ἐργάζεσθαι. διὰ δὲ τὸ ἀφῖχθαι πολ-
λαχόσε καὶ διὰ τὸ εἶναί μοι τὰς διατριβὰς περὶ τὸ
ἐμπόριον, γνωρίμως ἔχω τοῖς πλείστοις τῶν πλεόντων τὴν θάλατταν, τούτοις δὲ τοῖς ἐκ Βυζαντίου καὶ
πάνυ οἰκείως χρῶμαι διὰ τὸ ἐνδιατρῖψαι αὐτόθι.
[894] ἔχοντος δέ μου οὕτως ὡς λέγω, κατέπλευσαν δεῦρο
τρίτον ἔτος οὗτός τε καὶ πολίτης αὐτοῦ Παρμένων,
6 Βυζάντιος μὲν τὸ γένος, φυγὰς δ' ἐκεῖθεν. προσ-
ελθόντες δέ μοι ἐν τῷ ἐμπορίῳ οὗτος καὶ ὁ Παρμένων, ἐμνήσθησαν περὶ ἀργυρίου. ἔτυχε δὲ οὑτοσὶ
ὀφείλων ἐπὶ τῇ νηὶ τῇ ἑαυτοῦ τετταράκοντα μνᾶς,
καὶ οἱ χρῆσται κατήπειγον αὐτὸν ἀπαιτοῦντες καὶ
ἐνεβάτευον εἰς τὴν ναῦν, εἰληφότες τῇ ὑπερημερίᾳ.
ἀπορουμένῳ δ' αὐτῷ, μνᾶς μὲν δέκα ὁ Παρμένων
ὡμολόγησε δώσειν, τριάκοντα δὲ μνᾶς ἐδεῖτό μου

Apaturius has made a false charge against me, and is suing me contrary to law, seeing that there had been a release and discharge from all contracts made between him and me, and there exists no other contract made with him by me whether for business by sea or on land, I have entered the special plea that the action is not maintainable, according to the following laws.

THE LAWS

That Apaturius, then, has instituted suit against 4 me contrary to these laws and that his charges are false, I shall show you by many proofs. I, men of the jury, have by now been for a long time engaged in foreign trade, and up to a certain time risked the sea in my own person; it is not quite seven years since I gave up voyaging, and, having a moderate capital, I try to put it to work by making loans on adventures overseas. As I have visited many places 5 and spend my time in your exchange, I know most of those who are seafarers, and with these men from Byzantium I am on intimate terms through having myself spent much time there. My position, then, was such as I have described, when this fellow put into our port with a fellow-countryman of his, named Parmeno, a Byzantine by birth, who was an exile from his country. The plaintiff and Parmeno came up to me 6 on the exchange and spoke about money. It happened that the plaintiff owed forty minae on his ship, and his creditors were pressing him hard with demands for their money, and were about to board the ship and take possession of it, as his note was overdue. While he was in this embarrassment, Parmeno agreed to give him ten minae, and the plaintiff asked me to

οὗτος συνευπορῆσαι, αἰτιώμενος τοὺς χρήστας ἐπι-
θυμοῦντας τῆς νεὼς διαβεβληκέναι αὐτὸν ἐν τῷ
ἐμπορίῳ, ἵνα κατάσχωσι τὴν ναῦν εἰς ἀπορίαν κατα-
7 στήσαντες τοῦ ἀποδοῦναι τὰ χρήματα. ἐμοὶ μὲν
οὖν οὐκ ἔτυχε παρὸν ἀργύριον, χρώμενος δ' Ἡρα-
κλείδῃ τῷ τραπεζίτῃ, ἔπεισα αὐτὸν δανεῖσαι τὰ
χρήματα λαβόντα ἐμὲ ἐγγυητήν. ἤδη δὲ τῶν τριάκοντα μνῶν πεπορισμένων, ἔτυχε προσκεκρουκὼς
τι τούτῳ ὁ Παρμένων· ὡμολογηκὼς δ' εὐπορή-
σειν αὐτῷ δέκα μνᾶς, καὶ τούτων δεδωκὼς τὰς
τρεῖς, διὰ τὸ προειμένον ἀργύριον ἠναγκάζετο
8 καὶ τὸ λοιπὸν διδόναι. αὐτὸς μὲν οὖν διὰ τοῦτ' οὐκ
ἐβούλετο ποιήσασθαι τὸ συμβόλαιον, ἐμὲ δ' ἐκέλευε
πρᾶξαι ὅπως αὐτῷ ὡς ἀσφαλέστατα ἕξει. λαβὼν
δ' ἐγὼ τὰς ἑπτὰ μνᾶς παρὰ τοῦ Παρμένοντος, καὶ
τὰς τρεῖς, ἃς προειλήφει οὗτος παρ' ἐκείνου, ἀν-
ομολογησάμενος πρὸς τοῦτον, ὠνὴν ποιοῦμαι τῆς
νεὼς καὶ τῶν παίδων, ἕως ἀποδοίη τάς τε δέκα
μνᾶς, ἃς δι' ἐμοῦ ἔλαβε, καὶ τὰς τριάκοντα, ὧν
[895] κατέστησεν ἐμὲ ἐγγυητὴν τῷ τραπεζίτῃ. καὶ ὡς
ἀληθῆ λέγω, ἀκούσατε τῶν μαρτυριῶν.

MΑΡΤΥΡΙΑΙ

9 Τὸν μὲν τρόπον τοῦτον ἀπήλλαξε τοὺς χρήστας
Ἀπατούριος οὑτοσί. οὐ πολλῷ δὲ χρόνῳ μετὰ
ταῦτα τῆς τραπέζης ἀνασκευασθείσης, καὶ τοῦ
Ἡρακλείδου κατ' ἀρχὰς κεκρυμμένου, ἐπιβουλεύει
οὑτοσὶ τούς τε παῖδας ἐκπέμψαι Ἀθήνηθεν καὶ τὴν
ναῦν ἐξορμίσαι ἐκ τοῦ λιμένος. ὅθεν ἐμοὶ πρὸς
τοῦτον ἡ πρώτη διαφορὰ ἐγένετο. αἰσθόμενος γὰρ
ὁ Παρμένων, ἐξαγομένων τῶν παίδων ἐπιλαμβά-
206

contribute thirty minae, charging that the creditors in their eagerness to secure the ship had slandered him on the exchange, that they might seize the ship by putting him in a position where he could not pay. I **7** happened to have no ready money in hand, but being acquainted with Heracleides, the banker, I persuaded him to lend the money, and to take me as surety. But when now the thirty minae had been procured, Parmeno happened to fall out with the plaintiff. However, seeing that he had agreed to furnish him with ten minae and had already given him three of them, he was compelled on account of the money he had given to pay the remainder as well. Not wishing, **8** however, for the reason given, to make the loan in his own name, he bade me to arrange it so that things should be as safe as possible for him. So I took over the seven minae from Parmeno, and having had transferred to myself the obligation for the three, which the plaintiff had already received from him, caused a bill of sale to be executed on the ship and the slaves until such time as he should repay me the ten minae, which he had received through me, and also the thirty for which he had made me his surety with the banker. In proof that my words are true, hear the depositions.

THE DEPOSITIONS

In this way, then, Apaturius here got rid of his **9** creditors. Not long after this, the bank having failed, and Heracleides for a time having gone into hiding, the plaintiff schemed to send the slaves from Athens, and to remove the ship from the harbour. This was the cause of my first quarrel with him. For Parmeno, learning of the fact, laid hands on the slaves as they

νεται καὶ τὴν ναῦν κατεκώλυσεν αὐτὸν ἐξορμίζειν,
10 καὶ μεταπεμψάμενος ἐμὲ λέγει τὸ πρᾶγμα. ὡς δ᾽
ἤκουσα, τοῦτον μὲν ἀνοσιώτατον ἡγησάμην εἶναι
τῷ ἐπιχειρήματι, ἐσκοπούμην δὲ ὅπως αὐτός τε
ἀπολυθήσομαι τῆς ἐγγύης τῆς ἐπὶ τὴν τράπεζαν,
καὶ ὁ ξένος μὴ ἀπολεῖ ἃ δι᾽ ἐμοῦ τούτῳ ἐδάνεισεν.
καταστήσας δὲ φύλακας τῆς νεώς, διηγησάμην τοῖς
ἐγγυηταῖς τῆς τραπέζης τὴν πρᾶξιν, καὶ παρέδωκα
τὸ ἐνέχυρον, εἰπὼν αὐτοῖς ὅτι δέκα μναῖ ἐνείησαν
τῷ ξένῳ ἐν τῇ νηί. ταῦτα δὲ πράξας κατηγγύησα
τοὺς παῖδας, ἵν᾽ εἴ τις ἔκδεια γίγνοιτο, τὰ ἐλλεί-
11 ποντα ἐκ τῶν παίδων εἴη. καὶ ἐγὼ μὲν ἐπειδὴ
ἔλαβον τοῦτον ἀδικοῦντα, διωρθωσάμην ὑπὲρ ἐμαυτοῦ καὶ τοῦ ξένου· ὁ δ᾽ ὥσπερ ἀδικούμενος, ἀλλ᾽
οὐκ ἀδικῶν ἐμέμφετό μοι, καὶ ἠρώτα εἰ οὐχ ἱκανόν
μοι εἴη αὐτῷ ἀπολυθῆναι τῆς ἐγγύης τῆς πρὸς τὴν
τράπεζαν, ἀλλὰ καὶ ὑπὲρ τοῦ ἀργυρίου τοῦ Παρμένοντος τὴν ναῦν κατεγγυῶ καὶ τοὺς παῖδας, καὶ
12 ὑπὲρ ἀνθρώπου φυγάδος ἀπεχθανοίμην αὐτῷ. ἐγὼ
[896] δὲ τὸν πιστεύσαντα ἐμαυτῷ τοσούτῳ ἔφην ἧττον ἂν
περιιδεῖν, ὅσῳ φυγὰς ὢν καὶ ἀτυχῶν ἠδικεῖτο ὑπὸ
τούτου. πάντα δὲ ποιήσας καὶ εἰς πᾶσαν ἀπέχθειαν
τούτῳ ἐλθών, μόλις εἰσέπραξα τὸ ἀργύριον, πρα-
θείσης τῆς νεὼς τετταράκοντα μνῶν, ὅσουπερ ἡ
θέσις ἦν. ἀποδοθεισῶν δὲ τῶν τριάκοντα μνῶν
ἐπὶ τὴν τράπεζαν καὶ τῶν δέκα τῷ Παρμένοντι,
ἐναντίον πολλῶν μαρτύρων τάς τε συγγραφὰς
ἀνειλόμεθα, καθ᾽ ἃς ἐδανείσθη τὰ χρήματα, καὶ

ᵃ The foreigner is, of course, Parmeno.

were being taken away, and prevented the sailing
of the ship; then he sent for me, and told me of the
affair. When I heard him, thinking this fellow a most 10
impious wretch because of his attempt, I set about
considering how I might myself get free from my
guaranty to the bank, and how the foreigner[a] might
avoid the loss of the money he had lent this fellow
through me. After stationing men to guard the ship
I told the whole story to the sureties of the bank and
turned the security over to them, telling them that the
foreigner had a lien of ten minae on the ship. Having
arranged this, I attached the slaves, in order that, if
any shortage occurred, the deficiency might be made
up by the proceeds of their sale. In this way, when 11
I found that Apaturius was a rascal, I set matters
right in my own interest and in the interest of the
foreigner. But Apaturius, as though the wrong was
on my side, and not on his, made complaint to me,
and asked if it were not enough for me to be released
from my guaranty to the bank, without also attaching
the ship and the slaves to secure his money for
Parmeno, and thus making an enemy of himself in
the interest of one who was an exile. I replied that, 12
when a man had put his trust in me, I was all the less
inclined to leave him in the lurch, because, while he
was an exile and in misfortune, he was being wronged
by the plaintiff; and after I had done everything possible, and had incurred the utmost enmity on the part
of this fellow, I with difficulty secured the money, the
ship being sold for forty minae, the precise amount
for which she was mortgaged. The thirty minae then
having been paid back to the bank, and the ten minae
to Parmeno, in the presence of many witnesses, we
cancelled the bond in accordance with which the

τῶν συναλλαγμάτων ἀφεῖμεν καὶ ἀπηλλάξαμεν
ἀλλήλους, ὥστε μήτε τούτῳ πρὸς ἐμὲ μήτ' ἐμοὶ
πρὸς τοῦτον πρᾶγμ' εἶναι μηδέν. καὶ ὡς ἀληθῆ
λέγω, ἀκούσατε τῶν μαρτυριῶν.

ΜΑΡΤΥΡΙΑΙ

13 Μετὰ ταῦτα τοίνυν ἐμοὶ μὲν οὔτε μεῖζον οὔτ'
ἔλαττον πρὸς αὐτὸν συμβόλαιον γέγονεν· ὁ δὲ
Παρμένων ἐδικάζετο τούτῳ τῶν τε πληγῶν ὧν
ἔλαβεν ὑπὸ τούτου, ὅτε τῶν παίδων ἐξαγομένων
ἐπελάβετο, καὶ ὅτι τοῦ εἰς Σικελίαν πλοῦ διὰ τοῦτον
κατεκωλύθη. ἐνεστηκυίας δὲ τῆς δίκης, δίδωσιν ὁ
Παρμένων ὅρκον τούτῳ περί τινων ἐγκλημάτων,
καὶ οὗτος ἐδέξατο, ἐπιδιαθέμενος ἀργύριον, ἐὰν μὴ
ὀμόσῃ τὸν ὅρκον.
Καὶ ὅτι ἀληθῆ λέγω, λαβέ μοι τὴν μαρτυρίαν.

ΜΑΡΤΥΡΙΑ

14 Δεξάμενος τοίνυν τὸν ὅρκον, εἰδὼς ὅτι πολλοὶ
αὐτῷ συνείσονται ἐπιορκήσαντι, ἐπὶ μὲν τὸ ὀμόσαι
οὐκ ἀπῆντα, ὡς δὲ δίκῃ λύσων τὸν ὅρκον προσκαλεῖται τὸν Παρμένοντα. ἐνεστηκυιῶν δ' αὐτοῖς
[897] τῶν δικῶν, πεισθέντες ὑπὸ τῶν παρόντων εἰς ἐπι-
τροπὴν ἔρχονται, καὶ γράψαντες συνθήκας ἐπιτρέ-
πουσιν ἑνὶ μὲν διαιτητῇ κοινῷ Φωκρίτῳ πολίτῃ
αὐτῶν, ἕνα δ' ἑκάτερος παρεκαθίσατο, οὗτος μὲν
15 Ἀριστοκλέα Ὀῆθεν,[a] ὁ δὲ Παρμένων ἐμέ. καὶ
συνέθεντο ἐν ταῖς συνθήκαις, εἰ μὲν τρεῖς ὄντες
ὁμογνώμονες γενοίμεθα, ταῦτα κύρια εἶναι αὐτοῖς,

---

[a] A deme of the tribe Oeneïs

money had been lent, and mutually released and discharged one another from our engagements ; so that the plaintiff had nothing more to do with me, nor I with him. In proof that my words are true, hear the depositions.

THE DEPOSITIONS

Since then I have had no business transaction with 13 the fellow, whether great or small, but Parmeno sued him for damages for the blows which he received from him when he laid hands on the slaves as they were being carried off, and because he had been prevented by him from making the voyage to Sicily. When the action had been instituted, Parmeno tendered an oath to Apaturius regarding some of his charges, and he accepted it, and furthermore made a deposit to be forfeited if he did not swear the oath.

In proof that my words are true, take the deposition.

THE DEPOSITION

Having accepted the oath, since he was aware that 14 many would know that he had perjured himself, he did not present himself for the swearing, but, as though he could get free of the oath by an action, he summoned Parmeno into court. When both actions had been instituted, on the advice of persons present they proceeded to an arbitration, and after drawing up an agreement they submitted the matter to one common arbitrator, Phocritus, a fellow-countryman of theirs ; and each one appointed one man to sit with Phocritus, Apaturius choosing Aristocles of Oea,[a] and Parmeno choosing me. They agreed in 15 the articles that, if we three were of one mind, our decision should be binding on them, but, if not,

εἰ δὲ μή, οἷς οἱ δύο γνοίησαν, τούτοις ἐπάναγκες
εἶναι ἐμμένειν. συνθέμενοι δὲ ταῦτα, ἐγγυητὰς
τούτων ἀλλήλοις κατέστησαν, οὗτος μὲν ἐκείνῳ τὸν
Ἀριστοκλέα, ὁ δὲ Παρμένων τούτῳ Ἄρχιππον
Μυρρινούσιον. καὶ τὸ μὲν πρῶτον ἐτίθεντο τὰς
συνθήκας παρὰ τῷ Φωκρίτῳ, εἶτα κελεύσαντος τοῦ
Φωκρίτου παρ' ἄλλῳ τινὶ θέσθαι, τίθενται παρὰ τῷ
Ἀριστοκλεῖ.

Καὶ ὡς ἀληθῆ λέγω, ἀκούσατε τῶν μαρτυριῶν.

16 Ὅτι μὲν ἐτέθησαν αἱ συνθῆκαι παρ' Ἀριστοκλεῖ
καὶ ἡ ἐπιτροπὴ ἐγένετο Φωκρίτῳ καὶ Ἀριστοκλεῖ
καὶ ἐμοί, οἱ εἰδότες ταῦτα μεμαρτυρήκασιν ὑμῖν.
δέομαι δέ, ὦ ἄνδρες δικασταί, τὰ μετὰ ταῦτα
πραχθέντ' ἀκοῦσαί μου· ἐντεῦθεν γὰρ ἔσται φανερὸν
ὑμῖν, ὅτι συκοφαντοῦμαι ὑπὸ τουτουὶ Ἀπατουρίου.
ἐπειδὴ γὰρ ᾔσθετο ὁμογνώμονας ὄντας ἐμὲ καὶ τὸν
Φώκριτον, καὶ ἔγνω καταδιαιτήσοντας ἡμᾶς ἑαυτοῦ,
λῦσαι βουλόμενος τὴν ἐπιτροπήν, διαφθεῖραι τὰς
17 συνθήκας ἐπεχείρησε μετὰ τοῦ ἔχοντος αὐτάς. καὶ
ἦλθεν ἐπὶ τὸ ἀμφισβητεῖν, ὡς αὑτῷ διαιτητὴς εἴη
ὁ Ἀριστοκλῆς, τὸν δὲ Φώκριτον καὶ ἐμὲ οὐδενὸς
κυρίους ἔφησεν εἶναι ἀλλ' ἢ τοῦ διαλῦσαι. ἀγα-
νακτήσας δὲ τῷ λόγῳ ὁ Παρμένων, ἠξίου τὸν
[898] Ἀριστοκλέα ἐκφέρειν τὰς συνθήκας, οὐ πόρρω
φάσκων εἶναι τὸν ἔλεγχον, εἴ τι κακουργοῖτο περὶ
τὰ γράμματα· γεγραφέναι γὰρ αὐτὰ οἰκέτην ἑαυτοῦ.
18 ὁμολογήσας δ' ἐξοίσειν τὰς συνθήκας ὁ Ἀριστοκλῆς, ἐμφανεῖς μὲν οὐδέπω καὶ τήμερον ἐνήνοχεν,

---

ᵃ A deme of the tribe Pandionis.

then they should be bound to abide by what the two should determine. Having made this agreement, they appointed sureties for one another to guarantee its fulfilment. Apaturius appointed Aristocles, and Parmeno Archippus of Myrrhinus.[a] At the outset they deposited their agreement with Phocritus, but upon his bidding them to deposit it with someone else, they deposited it with Aristocles.

In proof that my words are true, hear the depositions.

THE DEPOSITIONS

That the agreements were deposited with **16** Aristocles, and that the arbitration was left with Phocritus, Aristocles and myself, has been testified to you by witnesses who know the facts. And now, men of the jury, I beg of you to hear from me what happened after this ; for from this it will be clear to you that this man Apaturius is making a claim upon me which is baseless and malicious. For when he saw that Phocritus and I were of one mind, and realized that we should give judgement against him, wishing to break down the arbitration, he sought, in collusion with the man who held them, to destroy the articles of agreement, and he proceeded to con- **17** tend that Aristocles was his arbitrator, and declared that Phocritus and I were empowered to do nothing else than seek to bring about a reconciliation. Angered at this statement, Parmeno demanded of Aristocles that he produce the agreement, adding that if there had been any criminal meddling with the papers, proof of the fact would not be far to seek, for his own slave had written them. Aristocles **18** promised that he would produce the articles, but up to this day has not brought them to light. He did

DEMOSTHENES

εἰς δὲ τὴν ἡμέραν τὴν συγκειμένην ἀπαντήσας εἰς τὸ Ἡφαιστεῖον, προὐφασίζετο ὡς ὁ παῖς περιμένων αὐτὸν ἀπολωλεκὼς εἴη τὸ γραμματεῖον καθεύδων. ὁ δὲ ταῦτα κατασκευάζων ἦν Ἐρυξίας ὁ ἰατρὸς ὁ ἐκ Πειραιῶς, οἰκείως ἔχων τῷ Ἀριστοκλεῖ· ὅσπερ καὶ ἐμοὶ τοῦ ἀγῶνος αἴτιός ἐστι, διαφόρως ἔχων.

Καὶ ὡς ἐσκήψατο ἀπολωλέναι ὁ Ἀριστοκλῆς, ἀκούσατε τῶν μαρτυριῶν.

ΜΑΡΤΥΡΙΑΙ

19 Ἐντεῦθεν τοίνυν τὸ μὲν τῆς ἐπιτροπῆς ἐλέλυτο, ἠφανισμένων τῶν συνθηκῶν καὶ τῶν διαιτητῶν ἀντιλεγομένων· ἐπιχειροῦντες δὲ γράφειν ἑτέρας συνθήκας περὶ τούτων διηνέχθησαν, οὗτος μὲν ἀξιῶν τὸν Ἀριστοκλέα, ὁ δὲ Παρμένων τοὺς τρεῖς, οἷσπερ τὸ ἐξ ἀρχῆς ἡ ἐπιτροπὴ ἐγένετο. οὐ γραφεισῶν δ᾽ ἑτέρων συνθηκῶν, τῶν δ᾽ ἐξ ἀρχῆς ἀφανισθεισῶν, εἰς τοῦτ᾽ ἦλθεν ἀναιδείας ὁ ἠφανικὼς τὰς συνθήκας, ὥστε εἷς ὢν ἀποφανεῖσθαι ἔφη τὴν δίαιταν. παρακαλέσας δ᾽ ὁ Παρμένων μάρτυρας, ἀπεῖπε τῷ Ἀριστοκλεῖ μὴ ἀποφαίνεσθαι παρὰ τὰς συνθήκας καθ᾽ αὑτοῦ ἄνευ τῶν συνδιαιτητῶν.

Καὶ ὧν ἐναντίον ἀπεῖπεν, ἀκούσατε τῆς μαρτυρίας.

ΜΑΡΤΥΡΙΑ

20 Μετὰ ταῦτα τοίνυν τῷ Παρμένοντι συνέβη συμ-
[899] φορὰ δεινή, ὦ ἄνδρες δικασταί. οἰκοῦντος γὰρ αὐτοῦ ἐν Ὀφρυνείῳ διὰ τὴν οἴκοθεν φυγήν, ὅτε ὁ

---

[a] Probably the structure commonly called the Theseum. *Cf.* Dinsmoor, *Hesperia*, Supplement v.
[b] A city in the Troad.

214

meet us on the appointed day at the Hephaesteum,[a] but made the excuse that his slave while waiting for him had fallen asleep and lost the document. The man who concocted this plot was Eryxias, the physician from Peiraeus, an intimate friend of Aristocles, the same man who out of enmity toward me has also got up this action against me.

Now in proof that Aristocles pretended that he had lost the document, hear the depositions.

THE DEPOSITIONS

After this the arbitration was done away with, the **19** articles of agreement having disappeared and the authority of the arbitrators being questioned. They did endeavour to draw up new articles about these matters, but could come to no agreement, as the plaintiff insisted on having Aristocles, and Parmeno the three to whom in the first instance the arbitration had been referred. Nevertheless, although no new articles had been drawn, and those originally drawn had been made away with, the man who had made away with them came to such a pitch of shamelessness that he declared he would in his own single person pronounce the award. Parmeno called witnesses to be present, and forbade Aristocles to pronounce an award against him, without his co-arbitrators, in defiance of the articles of agreement.

Hear the deposition of those in whose presence he thus forbade him.

THE DEPOSITION

After this there befell Parmeno, men of the jury, a **20** dire misfortune. He was dwelling in Ophrynium[b] because of his being an exile from home, when the

215

σεισμὸς ἐγένετο ὁ περὶ Χερρόνησον, συμπεσούσης
αὐτῷ τῆς οἰκίας ἀπώλοντο ἡ γυνὴ καὶ οἱ παῖδες.
καὶ ὁ μὲν πυθόμενος τὴν συμφορὰν ᾤχετο ἐνθένδε
ἀποπλέων· ὁ δ' Ἀριστοκλῆς, διαμαρτυραμένου τοῦ
ἀνθρώπου ἐναντίον μαρτύρων, μὴ ἀποφαίνεσθαι
καθ' αὑτοῦ ἄνευ τῶν συνδιαιτητῶν, ἀποδημήσαντος
τοῦ ἀνθρώπου διὰ τὴν συμφορὰν ἐρήμην κατ' αὐτοῦ
21 ἀπεφήνατο τὴν δίαιταν. καὶ ἐγὼ μὲν καὶ ὁ Φώ-
κριτος ἐν ταῖς αὐταῖς συνθήκαις γεγραμμένοι, ὅτι
ἠμφεσβήτησεν οὗτος μὴ εἶναι ἡμᾶς διαιτητὰς αὐτῷ,
ἐφύγομεν τὸ διαιτῆσαι· ὁ δ' οὐ μόνον ἀμφισβητη-
θείς, ἀλλὰ καὶ ἀπορρηθὲν αὐτῷ, οὐδὲν ἧττον τὴν
ἀπόφασιν ἐποιήσατο. ὃ οὔθ' ὑμῶν οὔτε τῶν ἄλλων
Ἀθηναίων ὑπομεῖναι ἂν ποιῆσαι οὐδείς.

22 Ἃ μὲν οὖν περὶ τὴν ἀφάνισιν τῶν συνθηκῶν καὶ
περὶ τὴν γνῶσιν τῆς διαίτης Ἀπατουρίῳ καὶ τῷ
διαιτητῇ πέπρακται, ἐάν ποτε σωθῇ ὁ ἠδικημένος,
δίκην παρ' αὐτῶν λήψεται· ἐπειδὴ δ' εἰς τοῦτο
ἐλήλυθεν Ἀπατούριος ἀναιδείας, ὥστε κἀμοὶ δικάζεται, ἐπιφέρων αἰτίαν ὡς ἀνεδεξάμην ἐκτείσειν,
εἴ τι καταγνωσθείη τοῦ Παρμένοντος, καί φησιν
ἐγγραφῆναι εἰς τὰς συνθήκας ἐμὲ ἐγγυητήν, ὥσπερ
προσήκει τοιαύτην αἰτίαν ἀπολύσασθαι, πρῶτον μὲν
ὑμῖν μάρτυρας παρασχήσομαι, ὡς οὐκ ἠγγυησάμην
ἐγὼ τὸν Παρμένοντα, ἀλλ' Ἄρχιππος Μυρρινού-
σιος, ἔπειτα πειράσομαι καὶ ἐκ τεκμηρίων τὴν
ἀπολογίαν ποιήσασθαι, ὦ ἄνδρες δικασταί.

23 Πρῶτον μὲν οὖν τὸν χρόνον ἐμαυτῷ ἡγοῦμαι
[900] μάρτυρα εἶναι τοῦ μὴ ἀληθὲς τὸ ἔγκλημα εἶναι. ἡ
μὲν γὰρ ἐπιτροπὴ τούτῳ πρὸς τὸν Παρμένοντα

216

earthquake in the Chersonese occurred ; and in the collapse of his house his wife and children perished. Immediately on hearing of the disaster he departed by ship from Athens. Aristocles, although the man had adjured him in the presence of witnesses not to pronounce judgement against him without his co-arbitrators, when Parmeno had left the country because of the disaster, pronounced an award against him by default. Phocritus and I, who were named 21 in the same articles, refused to participate in the award, because the plaintiff denied that in his view we were arbitrators ; but Aristocles, whose authority was not only disputed, but who had expressly been forbidden to act, nevertheless made the declaration— a thing which not one of you and not one of all the other Athenians could have been induced to do.

For all that Apaturius and the arbitrator did in 22 connexion with the disappearance of the articles and the pronouncing of the award, the man wronged, if ever he comes safely back to Athens, will obtain satisfaction from them. But since Apaturius has come to such a pitch of shamelessness as to bring suit against me also, charging that I undertook to pay any sum that might be awarded against Parmeno, and since he declares that my name was entered in the articles as surety, I shall free myself from such a charge in the proper way ; I shall first bring forward witnesses to prove that it was not I who became surety for Parmeno, but Archippus of Myrrhinus ; and I shall then undertake, men of the jury, to make my defence by circumstantial proofs.

In the first place, I hold that the time is a witness 23 for me to prove that the charge is groundless. For the agreement to arbitrate made by this fellow and

τρίτον ἔτος γέγονε καὶ ἡ γνῶσις τοῦ Ἀριστοκλέους·
αἱ δὲ λήξεις τοῖς ἐμπόροις τῶν δικῶν ἔμμηνοί εἰσιν
ἀπὸ τοῦ βοηδρομιῶνος μέχρι τοῦ μουνιχιῶνος, ἵνα
παραχρῆμα τῶν δικαίων τυχόντες ἀνάγωνται. εἰ
δὴ τῇ ἀληθείᾳ ἐγγυητὴς ἦν τοῦ Παρμένοντος, διὰ
τί πρῶτον μὲν οὐκ εὐθὺς τῆς γνώσεως γενομένης
24 ἐπράττετο τὴν ἐγγύην; οὐ γὰρ δὴ τοῦτό γ' αὐτῷ
ἔνι εἰπεῖν, ὡς διὰ τὴν πρὸς ἐμὲ φιλίαν ὤκνει μοι
ἀπεχθέσθαι. αὐτὸς γὰρ εἰσεπέπρακτο ὑπ' ἐμοῦ
πρὸς ἔχθραν τὰς χιλίας δραχμὰς τὰς τοῦ Παρμένοντος, καὶ ὅτ' ἐξώρμιζε τὴν ναῦν ἐπιβουλεύων
ἀποδρᾶναι καὶ ἀποστερῆσαι τὸ ἐπὶ τὴν τράπεζαν
χρέως, ἐκωλύθη ὑπ' ἐμοῦ. ὥστε εἰ ἦν ἠγγυημένος
ἐγὼ τὸν Παρμένοντα, οὐκ ἂν τρίτῳ ἔτει ὕστερον,
ἀλλ' εὐθὺς τότε εἰσέπραττεν ἄν με τὴν ἐγγύην.

25 Ἀλλὰ νὴ Δία εὐπόρως διέκειτο, ὥστ' ἐνεδέχετο
αὐτῷ καὶ ὕστερον ἐπ' ἐμὲ ἐλθεῖν, τότε δ' ἀσχόλως
εἶχε περὶ ἀναγωγὴν ὤν. ἀλλὰ δι' ἀπορίαν ἐξειστή-
κει τῶν ἑαυτοῦ καὶ τὴν ναῦν ἐπεπράκει. εἰ δ' ἄρ'
ἐμποδών τι αὐτῷ ἐγένετο τοῦ μὴ εὐθὺς τότε δικάσασθαι, διὰ τί πέρυσιν ἐπιδημῶν, μὴ ὅτι δικάσασθαι, ἀλλ' οὐδ' ἐγκαλέσαι μοι ἐτόλμησεν; καίτοι
προσῆκεν, εἰ ὁ μὲν Παρμένων ὠφλήκει αὐτῷ τὴν
δίκην, ἐγὼ δ' ἐγγυητὴς ἦν, προσελθεῖν αὐτόν μοι
ἔχοντα μάρτυρας καὶ ἀπαιτῆσαι τὴν ἐγγύην, εἰ μὴ
πρωπέρυσιν, ἐν τῷ ἐξελθόντι ἐνιαυτῷ· καὶ εἰ μὲν
αὐτῷ ἀπεδίδουν, κομίσασθαι, εἰ δὲ μή, δικάζεσθαι.

---

[a] Roughly, from September to April, the period when the
seas were closed, and the ships laid up in port.

218

Parmeno and the award of Aristocles took place two years ago ; but merchants may bring action every month from Boëdromion to Munichion,[a] in order that they may obtain their rights without delay and put to sea. So, if I was in truth a surety for Parmeno, why did not Apaturius immediately after the award proceed to collect the sum guaranteed ? It is not open to him to say that because of his friendship for me he was loth to incur my enmity, for he had himself in utter unfriendliness been forced by me to pay the one thousand drachmae due to Parmeno ; and when he was trying to get his ship out of the port in his plot to sneak away and to defraud the bank of what was due, it was I who prevented him. So, if I had become a surety for Parmeno, he would not have waited until two years afterward to exact the sum guaranteed, but would have proceeded to do so at once.

Ah, but he was well provided with funds, so that it was open to him to proceed against me later on, and at the moment he had no time, as he was about to put to sea ! On the contrary, he was in such straits that he had lost all his effects, and had sold his ship. And, if there really had been anything to prevent his immediately bringing suit against me, why, when he was in town last year, did he not dare, I will not say to bring suit, but even to make a demand ? It was surely the proper course for him, if judgement had been given against Parmeno in his favour, and if I was the latter's surety, to come to me himself accompanied by witnesses, and to demand the amount guaranteed, if not the year before last, at any rate in the year just past ; and then, if I proffered payment, to take his money, and, if I did not, to bring suit. For

219

26
[901] τῶν γὰρ τοιούτων ἐγκλημάτων πρότερον τὰς ἀπαι-
τήσεις ποιοῦνται ἅπαντες ἢ δικάζονται. οὐκ ἔστι
τοίνυν ὅστις μαρτυρήσει παραγενέσθαι, ὅπου οὗτος
ἢ πέρυσιν ἢ πρωπέρυσιν ἐδικάσατο ἢ λόγον ὁντινοῦν
ἐποιήσατο πρὸς ἐμὲ περὶ ὧν νυνί μοι δικάζεται.

"Ὅτι δ' ἐπεδήμει πέρυσιν, ὅτε αἱ δίκαι ἦσαν, λαβέ
μοι τὴν μαρτυρίαν.

ΜΑΡΤΥΡΙΑ

27 Λαβὲ δή μοι καὶ τὸν νόμον, ὃς κελεύει τὰς
ἐγγύας ἐπετείους εἶναι. καὶ οὐκ ἰσχυρίζομαι τῷ
νόμῳ, ὡς οὐ δεῖ με δίκην δοῦναι εἰ ἠγγυησάμην,
ἀλλὰ μάρτυρά μοί φημι τὸν νόμον εἶναι τοῦ μὴ
ἐγγυήσασθαι καὶ αὐτὸν τοῦτον· ἐδεδίκαστο γὰρ
ἄν μοι τῆς ἐγγύης ἐν τῷ χρόνῳ τῷ ἐν τῷ νόμῳ
γεγραμμένῳ.

ΝΟΜΟΣ

28 Γενέσθω τοίνυν καὶ τοῦτο ὑμῖν τεκμήριον τοῦ
ψεύδεσθαι Ἀπατούριον· εἰ γὰρ ἠγγυησάμην ἐγὼ
τούτῳ τὸν Παρμένοντα, οὐκ ἔστιν ὅπως τούτῳ μὲν
ὑπὲρ ἐκείνου ἀπηχθανόμην, πρόνοιαν ποιούμενος
ὅπως μὴ ἀπολεῖ ἃ δι' ἐμοῦ τούτῳ συνέβαλεν, αὐτὸς
δ' ἐμαυτὸν περιεῖδον ἂν ὑπ' ἐκείνου πρὸς τοῦτον
ἐν ἐγγύῃ καταλειπόμενον. τίνα γὰρ ἐλπίδα ἔσχον
τοῦτον ἀποσχήσεσθαί μου, ὃν αὐτὸς ἠναγκάκειν
ἐκείνῳ τὰ δίκαια ποιῆσαι; καὶ τὴν ἐγγύην αὐτὸν
εἰσπράξας τὴν εἰς τὴν τράπεζαν πρὸς ἀπέχθειαν, τί
προσεδόκων ὑπὸ τούτου αὐτὸς πείσεσθαι;

---

^a That is, they become invalid, if not renewed at the end
of a year.

220

in claims of this sort everyone makes demand before he brings suit. Well, there isn't a person living who will testify that he was present either last year or the year before, when this man either instituted proceedings against me or made any mention to me whatever of the claims for which he is now suing me.

To prove that he was in town last year when the courts were open, please take the deposition.

THE DEPOSITION

Now, please take the law which declares that 27 guaranties shall be for a year only.[a] I do not lay stress on the law to show that I should not pay what is due, if I actually became a surety, but I declare that the law is a witness that I did not become one, and so is the fellow himself; for otherwise he would have brought suit against me within the time specified by the law.

THE LAW

Let this, then, be another proof to you that 28 Apaturius is lying. If I had become surety to him for Parmeno, it is inconceivable that I should have made the plaintiff my enemy for Parmeno's sake, taking every care that the latter should not lose what he had lent the plaintiff through me, and yet have allowed myself to be left in the lurch by him as his surety to the plaintiff. For what ground had I to hope that leniency would be shown me by the man whom I had compelled to do justice to Parmeno? And when I had made him my enemy by exacting from him what was guaranteed to the bank, what treatment could I myself have expected to receive at his hands?

29 Ἄξιον τοίνυν καὶ τοῦτ' ἐνθυμηθῆναι, ὦ ἄνδρες
δικασταί, ὅτι οὐκ ἄν ποτε ἔξαρνος ἐγενόμην, εἰ
ἠγγυήμην· πολὺ γὰρ ὁ λόγος ἦν μοι ἰσχυρότερος,
ὁμολογοῦντι τὴν ἐγγύην ἐπὶ τὰς συνθήκας ἰέναι,
καθ' ἃς ἡ ἐπιτροπὴ ἐγένετο. ὅτι μὲν γὰρ τρισὶν
ἐπετράπη διαιτηταῖς, μεμαρτύρηται ὑμῖν· ὁπότε
[902] δὲ μὴ ἔγνωσται ὑπὸ τῶν τριῶν, τί βουλόμενος
ἠρνούμην ἂν τὴν ἐγγύην; μὴ γὰρ γενομένης
τῆς γνώσεως κατὰ τὰς συνθήκας, οὐδ' ἂν ἐγὼ τῆς
ἐγγύης ὑπόδικος ἦν. ὥστε οὐκ ἄν ποτε, ὦ ἄνδρες
δικασταί, παραλιπὼν τὴν οὖσάν μοι ἀπολογίαν, εἰ
ἠγγυησάμην, ἐπὶ τὸ ἀρνεῖσθαι ἦλθον.

30 Ἀλλὰ μὴν καὶ τοῦτο μεμαρτύρηται ὑμῖν, ὅτι
ἐπειδὴ ἠφανίσθησαν αἱ συνθῆκαι ὑπὸ τούτων,
ἐζήτουν ἑτέρας γράφεσθαι οὗτος καὶ ὁ Παρμένων,
ὡς ἀκύρων ὄντων αὐτοῖς τῶν πρότερον ὡμολογη-
μένων. καίτοι ὁπότε περὶ τῆς μελλούσης γνώσεως
γενήσεσθαι ἑτέρας ἐνεχείρουν συνθήκας γράφεσθαι,
ἐπειδὴ αἱ ὑπάρχουσαι ἀπώλοντο, πῶς ἐνῆν μὴ
γραφεισῶν συνθηκῶν ἑτέρων ἢ δίαιταν γενέσθαι ἢ
ἐγγύην; περὶ αὐτοῦ γὰρ τούτου διενεχθέντες οὐκ
ἔγραψαν ἕτερα γράμματα, ὁ μὲν ἀξιῶν ἕνα διαιτητὴν αὐτῷ εἶναι, ὁ δὲ τρεῖς. ὁπότε δ' αἱ μὲν
ἐξ ἀρχῆς συνθῆκαι ἠφανίσθησαν, καθ' ἃς ἐμέ φησι
γενέσθαι ἐγγυητήν, ἕτεραι δὲ μὴ ἐγράφησαν, πῶς
ὀρθῶς ἂν ἐμοὶ δικάζοιτο, καθ' οὗ μὴ ἔχει παρασχέσθαι συνθήκας;

It is worth while also for you to bear this in mind, 29
men of the jury, that, if I had been surety, I should
never have denied it. For my argument was much
stronger, if I admitted the guaranty and appealed
to the agreement in accordance with which the arbitration was to be held. That the matter was referred
to three arbitrators has been shown by testimony.
When, then, there had been no decision by the three,
why in the world should I have denied the guaranty ?
For, if judgement had not been given in accordance
with the agreement, neither should I have been open
to action for my guaranty. Therefore, men of the
jury, if I had really become a surety, I should not
have given up a defence which was at hand, and have
proceeded to deny the fact.

Again, the following fact has been testified to you 30
by witnesses, that, after the articles of agreement
had been made away with by these men, the plaintiff
and Parmeno sought to have new articles drawn up,
thus admitting that their former agreement was without force. Yet, when they sought to have other
articles drawn in regard to the judgement that was
to be given, since the existing ones had been lost,
how was it possible that, if other articles were not
drawn, there could be either arbitration or guaranty ?
It was the fact that they disagreed upon this very
point that prevented their writing new articles,
Apaturius demanding that there should be one arbitrator, and Parmeno that there should be three.
But, since the original articles were made away with,
in accordance with which he alleges that I became a
surety, and other articles were not written, what
right has he to bring suit against me, against whom
he is able to produce no agreement ?

31 Ἀλλὰ μὴν καὶ ὡς ἀπηγόρευεν ὁ Παρμένων τῷ
Ἀριστοκλεῖ καθ᾽ αὑτοῦ μὴ γιγνώσκειν ἄνευ τῶν
συνδιαιτητῶν, μεμαρτύρηται ὑμῖν. ὅταν δὴ ὁ
αὐτὸς ἠφανικὼς φαίνηται τὰ γράμματα, καθ᾽ ἃ
ἔδει τὴν δίαιταν γενέσθαι, καὶ ἄνευ τῶν συνδιαιτητῶν παρὰ τὴν ἀπόρρησιν φῇ δεδιῃτηκέναι, πῶς ἂν
τούτῳ τῷ ἀνθρώπῳ πιστεύσαντες δικαίως ἐμὲ ἀπ-
32 ολέσαιτε; σκέψασθε γὰρ τοῦτ᾽, ὦ ἄνδρες δικασταί·
εἰ μὴ ἐμὲ νυνί, ἀλλὰ τὸν Παρμένοντα ἐδίωκεν
Ἀπατούριος οὑτοσί, εἰσπράττων τὰς εἴκοσι μνᾶς,
[903] ἰσχυριζόμενος τῇ Ἀριστοκλέους γνώσει, ὁ δὲ
Παρμένων παρὼν ἀπελογεῖτο ὑμῖν καὶ μάρτυρας
παρείχετο, τοῦτο μὲν ὅτι οὐ μόνῳ τῷ Ἀριστοκλεῖ,
33 ἀλλὰ τρίτῳ ἐπέτρεψεν, εἶθ᾽ ὅτι ἀπεῖπεν αὐτῷ ἄνευ
τῶν συνδιαιτητῶν καθ᾽ αὑτοῦ μὴ ἀποφαίνεσθαι, καὶ
ὅτι ἀπολομένης αὐτῷ τῆς γυναικὸς καὶ τῶν παίδων
ὑπὸ τοῦ σεισμοῦ, καὶ ἐπὶ τηλικαύτην συμφορὰν
ἀπάραντος οἴκαδε, ὁ τὰς συνθήκας ἠφανικὼς ἐρήμην
αὐτοῦ ἐν τῇ ἀποδημίᾳ κατέγνω τὴν δίαιταν, ἔστιν
ὅστις ἂν ὑμῶν ταῦτα τοῦ Παρμένοντος ἀπολογου-
μένου, τὴν οὕτω παρανόμως γνωσθεῖσαν δίαιταν
34 κυρίαν ἔγνω εἶναι; μὴ γὰρ ὅτι ἀμφισβητουμένων
ἁπάντων, ἀλλ᾽ εἰ ἦσαν μὲν αἱ συνθῆκαι, ὡμολογεῖτο
δ᾽ εἷς εἶναι ὁ διαιτητὴς Ἀριστοκλῆς, μὴ ἀπεῖπε δὲ
ὁ Παρμένων αὐτῷ καθ᾽ αὑτοῦ μὴ διαιτᾶν, ἀλλὰ
συνέβη πρὶν τὴν ἀπόφασιν γενέσθαι τῆς διαίτης

Further, it has been testified to you by witnesses 31
that Parmeno forbade Aristocles to give judgement
against him without the concurrence of his co-arbitrators. When, therefore, it is shown that the same
person has made away with the document in accordance with the terms of which the arbitration was to
be made, and declares that he has made the decision
without his co-arbitrators, and in defiance of the
notice forbidding him to do so, how can you with
any fairness credit the fellow and condemn me?
Consider this, men of the jury: suppose it was not 32
against me, but against Parmeno, that this man
Apaturius were now taking action, seeking to recover
the twenty minae in reliance upon the judgement of
Aristocles; and that Parmeno was present and making his defence, calling witnesses to prove that he
had turned the matter over to Aristocles, not as a
single arbitrator, but as one of three; that he had 33
forbidden him to announce a decision against him
without his co-arbitrators; and that, after his wife
and children had perished in the earthquake, and he
in the face of a disaster so appalling had sailed for
home, the man who had made away with the articles
of agreement announced a judgement against him by
default in his absence, is there a single one of you
who, when Parmeno had brought out these facts
in his defence, would have considered an award so
unjustly made to be valid? More than this; sup- 34
pose that not every point was under dispute; that
there were in existence articles of agreement; that
Aristocles was admittedly an arbitrator having sole
authority; that Parmeno had not forbidden him to
make the award; but that the calamity had befallen
the man before the announcement of the award;

ἢ συμφορὰ τῷ ἀνθρώπῳ, τίς οὕτως ὠμός ἐστιν
ἀντίδικος ἢ διαιτητής, ὃς οὐκ ἂν ἀνεβάλετο εἰς τὸ
ἐπιδημῆσαι τὸν ἄνθρωπον; εἰ δ' ὁ Παρμένων εἰς
λόγον καταστὰς πανταχοῦ δικαιότερ' ἂν φαίνοιτο
λέγων τούτου, πῶς ἂν ὀρθῶς ἐμοῦ καταγιγνώ-
σκοιτε, ᾧ τὸ παράπαν πρὸς τὸν ἄνθρωπον τοῦτον
μηδὲν συμβόλαιόν ἐστιν;

35 Ὅτι μὲν οὖν ἐγὼ μὲν ὀρθῶς τὴν παραγραφὴν
πεποίημαι, Ἀπατούριος δὲ τὰ ψευδῆ ἐγκέκληκε
καὶ παρὰ τοὺς νόμους τὴν λῆξιν πεποίηται, ἐκ
πολλῶν οἶμαι ἐπιδεδεῖχθαι τοῦτο ὑμῖν, ὦ ἄνδρες
δικασταί· τὸ δὲ κεφάλαιον, πρὸς ἐμὲ οὐδ' ἐπιχειρήσει λέγειν Ἀπατούριος ὡς συνθῆκαί τινες
[904] αὐτῷ εἰσίν. ὅταν δὲ λέγῃ ψευδόμενος, ὡς ἐν ταῖς
πρὸς τὸν Παρμένοντα συνθήκαις ἐνεγράφην ἐγ-
36 γυητής, ἀπαιτεῖτε αὐτὸν τὰς συνθήκας. καὶ
ἐνταῦθ' αὐτῷ ἀπαντᾶτε, ὅτι πάντες ἄνθρωποι, ὅταν
πρὸς ἀλλήλους ποιῶνται συγγραφάς, τούτου ἕνεκα
σημηνάμενοι τίθενται παρ' οἷς ἂν πιστεύσωσιν,
ἵν', ἐάν τι ἀντιλέγωσιν, ᾖ αὐτοῖς ἐπανελθοῦσιν ἐπὶ
τὰ γράμματα, ἐντεῦθεν τὸν ἔλεγχον ποιήσασθαι περὶ
τοῦ ἀμφισβητουμένου. ὅταν δ' ἀφανίσας τις
τἀκριβές, λόγῳ ἐξαπατᾶν πειρᾶται, πῶς ἂν δικαίως
37 πιστεύοιτο; ἀλλὰ νὴ Δία (τὸ ῥᾷστον τοῖς ἀδικεῖν
καὶ συκοφαντεῖν προῃρημένοις) μαρτυρήσει τις
αὐτῷ κατ' ἐμοῦ. ἐὰν οὖν ἐπισκήψωμαι αὐτῷ,
πόθεν τὴν ἀπόδειξιν ποιήσεται τοῦ ἀληθῆ μαρτυρεῖν; ἐκ τῶν συνθηκῶν; τοῦτο τοίνυν μὴ
ἀναβαλλέσθω, ἀλλ' ἤδη φερέτω ὁ ἔχων τὰς συνθήκας. εἰ δ' ἀπολωλέναι φησί, πόθεν λάβω ἐγὼ

what adversary or what arbitrator would have been
so cruel as not to postpone the case until the man
returned to the country ? Then, if Parmeno, coming
to plead before you, should be judged in every point
to speak with more justice than the plaintiff, how can
you justly give judgement against me, who have
absolutely no contract with this man ?

That I, on my part, have made my special plea 35
with good right, and that Apaturius has lodged
against me a claim that is baseless, and instituted a
suit contrary to law, has, I think, been shown to you,
men of the jury, by many proofs. The main point is
this : Apaturius will not even attempt to say that he
has any articles showing an agreement between us.
When he falsely states that my name was written in
as surety in the agreement made with Parmeno, demand of him the articles. Meet him on this ground : 36
that all men, when they make agreements with one
another, seal the articles and deposit them with
persons whom they can trust, for this very purpose,
that, if a dispute arises between them, they may refer
to the document and so settle the point at issue.
But when a man, after doing away with the source
of accurate knowledge, undertakes to deceive you
with words, how can you with justice put any confidence in him ? But perhaps some witness (for this 37
is the easiest course for those who have chosen to do
wrong and to bring baseless charges) will testify for
him against me. If, then, I take action against the
witness, how will he prove that his testimony is true ?
By the articles of agreement ? Well, then, let there
be no delay about this ; let the one who has them
bring forward the articles at once. But if he says
they have been lost, how, then, shall I find means of

τὸν ἔλεγχον καταψευδομαρτυρηθείς; εἰ μὲν γὰρ
παρ' ἐμοὶ ἐτέθη τὸ γραμματεῖον, ἐνῆν ἂν αἰτιάσασθαι 'Απατουρίῳ, ὡς ἐγὼ διὰ τὴν ἐγγύην ἠφάνικα
38 τὰς συνθήκας· εἰ δὲ παρὰ τῷ 'Αριστοκλεῖ, διὰ τί,
εἴπερ ἄνευ τῆς τούτου γνώμης ἀπολώλασιν αἱ
συνθῆκαι, τῷ μὲν λαβόντι αὐτὰς καὶ οὐ παρέχοντι
οὐ δικάζεται, ἐμοὶ δ' ἐγκαλεῖ, μάρτυρα παρεχόμενος κατ' ἐμοῦ τὸν ἠφανικότα τὰς συνθήκας,
ᾧ προσῆκεν αὐτὸν ὀργίζεσθαι, εἴπερ μὴ κοινῇ μετὰ
τούτου ἐκακοτέχνει;

Εἴρηταί μοι τὰ δίκαια, ὅσα ἐδυνάμην. ὑμεῖς οὖν
κατὰ τοὺς νόμους γιγνώσκετε τὰ δίκαια.

refuting the false testimony brought against me?
If the document had been deposited with me, it
would have been open to Apaturius to charge that I
had made away with it because of my guaranty; but, 38
if it was deposited with Aristocles, why is it, if the
agreement has been lost without the plaintiff's knowledge, that instead of bringing suit against the man
who received the agreement but does not produce it,
he makes charges against me, bringing forward as
a witness against me the man who made away with
the agreement, against whom he ought to feel resentment, if it were not that they are leagued together
in their evil scheming?

I have made a just plea to the best of my ability.
Do you now give a just decision in accordance with
the laws.

AGAINST PHORMIO

contract.

INTRODUCTION

THE circumstances giving rise to the suit in which
this oration was delivered were as follows. Chrysippus, apparently an alien residing at Athens, had
lent to Phormio, a merchant-trader, the sum of
twenty minae on what is called a bottomry contract.
The terms were that Phormio should convey a ship-
load of goods to Bosporus, in the Crimea, and, after
disposing of his cargo there, should bring back a return cargo to Athens. From the profits of the venture
he was to repay the loan with interest at 30 per
cent. In the event of his failing to ship a return
cargo he was to pay a fine of fifty minae; though it
would seem that he had the option of paying the
twenty-six minae (the amount of the loan and interest) to the shipowner, Lampis, in which case he
was to be freed from the obligation to ship a return
cargo. The rate of interest in such cases was always
high, because in case of the loss of the vessel the
lender could recover nothing; yet on account of the
large importations of grain such contracts were very
common on the Athenian exchange. (Compare
Orations XXXII., XXXV., and LVI.)

It proved, however, that Phormio on his arrival at
Bosporus found it impossible to dispose of his cargo,
and he ordered Lampis to return to Athens without
him, stating that he would himself follow shortly.

Lampis set out, but the vessel was wrecked; and Phormio after his own return to Athens claimed that this relieved him of all responsibility. Subsequently, however, he shifted his ground and claimed that he had paid to Lampis, before the latter left Pontus, the full amount due under the contract.

Lampis plays a sorry part in the whole affair. On his return to Athens he had told his story of the shipwreck, and had denied receiving the money from Phormio; but later on, when he appeared as a witness before the arbitrator, he had reversed his story and claimed that he must have been out of his mind when he made his previous statements, asserting now that Phormio had indeed paid him the money in Pontus, and that it had been lost with the wrecked ship.

Chrysippus, then, and his partner brought suit against Phormio to recover the amount due, and Phormio countered by entering a special plea (παραγραφή), asserting the action was not admissible, inasmuch as he (Phormio) had in no way violated the terms of the contract.

This matter was brought before the court. Phormio made his argument, and the present oration is a reply, delivered by the two plaintiffs, speaking in turn. Their contention is that the special plea in bar of action is inadmissible in this case, since the law expressly stated that all disputes regarding contracts made in connexion with shipments to or from Athens should be settled in the Athenian courts. They hold that Phormio's claim that the loss of the vessel freed him from his liability is invalid, since he had shipped no return cargo; and that his subsequent claim that he had paid the money to Lampis in Bosporus is to be ruled out as wholly unworthy of credence.

This speech is discussed in Schaefer, iii.[2] pp. 300 ff., and in Blass, iii. pp. 576 ff.

XXXIV

ΠΡΟΣ ΦΟΡΜΙΩΝΑ ΠΕΡΙ ΔΑΝΕΙΟΥ

[907]   Δίκαια ὑμῶν δεησόμεθ', ὦ ἄνδρες δικασταί,
ἀκοῦσαι ἡμῶν μετ' εὐνοίας ἐν τῷ μέρει λεγόντων,
γνόντας ὅτι ἰδιῶται παντελῶς ἐσμεν, καὶ πολὺν
χρόνον εἰς τὸ ὑμέτερον ἐμπόριον εἰσαφικνούμενοι καὶ
συμβόλαια πολλοῖς συμβάλλοντες, οὐδεμίαν πώποτε
δίκην πρὸς ὑμᾶς εἰσήλθομεν, οὔτ' ἐγκαλοῦντες οὔτ'
2 ἐγκαλούμενοι ὑφ' ἑτέρων. οὐδ' ἂν νῦν, ἀκριβῶς
ἴστε, ὦ ἄνδρες Ἀθηναῖοι, εἰ ὑπελαμβάνομεν ἀπολωλέναι τὰ χρήματα ἐπὶ τῆς νεὼς τῆς δια-
φθαρείσης, ἃ ἐδανείσαμεν Φορμίωνι, οὐκ ἄν ποτ'
ἐλάχομεν τὴν δίκην αὐτῷ· οὐχ οὕτως ἡμεῖς ἀναί-
σχυντοί ἐσμεν οὐδ' ἄπειροι τοῦ ζημιοῦσθαι. πολλῶν
δ' ἡμᾶς κακιζόντων, καὶ μάλιστα τῶν ἐν Βοσπόρῳ
ἐπιδημησάντων ἅμα Φορμίωνι, οἵπερ τοῦτον ᾔδεσαν
οὐ συναπολέσαντα τὰ χρήματα ἐν τῇ νηί, δεινὸν
ἡγούμεθ' εἶναι τὸ μὴ βοηθῆσαι ἡμῖν αὐτοῖς ἀδικουμένοις ὑπὸ τούτου.

3   Περὶ μὲν οὖν τῆς παραγραφῆς βραχύς ἐστιν ὁ
λόγος· καὶ γὰρ οὗτοι οὐ τὸ παράπαν συμβόλαιον

---

^a Others, less probably, render, " as we take our turns
in addressing you."

236

XXXIV

THE PLEA OF CHRYSIPPUS AND HIS PARTNER AGAINST PHORMIO IN THE MATTER OF A LOAN

THE request that I shall make of you, men of the jury, is a fair one, that you should hear us with good-will as we speak in our turn,[a] knowing well that we are wholly without experience in the art of speaking; and long as we have been frequenting your mart, and many as are the merchants to whom we have made loans, we have never until now appeared in any suit before you either as plaintiffs or as defendants. And 2 you may be sure, men of Athens, that we should not even now have brought this action against Phormio, if we believed that the money which we lent him had been lost on the ship that was wrecked; we are not so shameless nor so unaccustomed to losses. But as many have kept taunting us, and especially those who were in Bosporus with Phormio, who knew that he had not lost the money together with the ship, we thought it a dreadful thing not to seek redress after being wronged as we had been by this man.

With reference to the special plea my argument is 3 a brief one. For even the defendants do not ab-

237

ἐξαρνοῦνται μὴ γενέσθαι ἐν τῷ ἐμπορίῳ τῷ ὑμε
τέρῳ, ἀλλ' οὐκέτι εἶναί φασι πρὸς ἑαυτοὺς οὐδὲν
[908] συμβόλαιον, πεποιηκέναι γὰρ οὐδὲν ἔξω τῶν ἐν τῇ
4 συγγραφῇ γεγραμμένων. οἱ μέντοι νόμοι, καθ' οὓς
ὑμεῖς δικασταὶ κάθησθε, οὐχ οὕτω λέγουσιν, ἀλλ'
ὑπὲρ μὲν τῶν μὴ γενομένων ὅλως συμβολαίων
Ἀθήνησι μηδ' εἰς τὸ Ἀθηναίων ἐμπόριον παρα
γράφεσθαι δεδώκασιν, ἐὰν δέ τις γενέσθαι μὲν
ὁμολογῇ, ἀμφισβητῇ δὲ ὡς πάντα πεποίηκε τὰ
συγκείμενα, ἀπολογεῖσθαι κελεύουσιν εὐθυδικίαν
εἰσιόντα, οὐ κατηγορεῖν τοῦ διώκοντος. οὐ μὴν
ἀλλ' ἔγωγε ἐλπίζω καὶ ἐξ αὐτοῦ τοῦ πράγματος
5 δείξειν εἰσαγώγιμον τὴν δίκην οὖσαν. σκέψασθε δ',
ὦ ἄνδρες Ἀθηναῖοι, τί ὁμολογεῖται παρ' αὐτῶν
τούτων καὶ τί ἀντιλέγεται· οὕτω γὰρ ἂν ἄριστα
ἐξετάσαιτε. οὐκοῦν δανείσασθαι μὲν ὁμολογοῦσι
καὶ συνθήκας ποιήσασθαι τοῦ δανείσματος, φασὶ
δ' ἀποδεδωκέναι τὸ χρυσίον Λάμπιδι τῷ Δίωνος
οἰκέτῃ ἐν Βοσπόρῳ. ἡμεῖς τοίνυν οὐ μόνον τοῦτο
δείξομεν, ὡς οὐκ ἀπέδωκεν, ἀλλ' ὡς οὐδ' ἦν αὐτῷ
ἀποδοῦναι. ἀναγκαῖον δ' ἐστὶ βραχέα τῶν ἐξ ἀρχῆς
διηγήσασθαι ὑμῖν.

6 Ἐγὼ γάρ, ὦ ἄνδρες Ἀθηναῖοι, ἐδάνεισα Φορ
μίωνι τουτωὶ εἴκοσι μνᾶς ἀμφοτερόπλουν εἰς τὸν
Πόντον ἐπὶ ἑτέρα ὑποθήκῃ, καὶ συγγραφὴν ἐθέμην
παρὰ Κίττῳ τῷ τραπεζίτῃ. κελευούσης δὲ τῆς
συγγραφῆς ἐνθέσθαι εἰς τὴν ναῦν τετρακισχιλίων
φορτία ἄξια, πρᾶγμα ποιεῖ πάντων δεινότατον·

---

[a] The word rendered " exchange " or " market," may well
designate merely the Peiraeus, which was in a very real sense
the ἐμπόριον of Athens.

[b] As happened, of course, when a plea in bar of action
was introduced.

238

solutely deny that a contract was made on your exchange[a]; but they claim that there exists no longer any obligation on their part due to the contract, for they have done nothing that contravenes the terms of the agreement. The laws, however, in accordance **4** with which you sit as jurors, do not use this language. They do indeed allow the production of a special plea when there has been no contract at all at Athens or for the Athenian market; but if a man admits that a contract was made, yet contends that he has done everything that the contract requires, they bid him to make a defence on the merits of the case, and not to make the plaintiff a defendant.[b] Not but that I hope to prove from the facts of the case itself that this suit of mine is admissible. And I beg you, men of **5** Athens, to consider what is admitted by these men, and what is disputed; for in this way you will best sift the question. They admit that they borrowed the money, and that they had contracts made to secure the loan; but they claim that they have paid the money to Lampis, the servant of Dio, in Bosporus. We, on our part, shall prove, not only that Phormio did not pay it, but that it was actually impossible for him to pay it. But I must recount to you a few of the things that happened at the outset.

I, men of Athens, lent to this man, Phormio, twenty **6** minae for the double voyage to Pontus and back, on the security of goods of twice that value,[c] and deposited a contract with Cittus the banker. But, although the contract required him to put on board the ship goods to the value of four thousand drachmae, he did the most outrageous thing possible. For while still

[c] Such seems the most probable meaning of the disputed phrase ἐπὶ ἑτέρᾳ ὑποθήκῃ.

εὐθὺς γὰρ ἐν τῷ Πειραιεῖ ἐπιδανείζεται λάθρᾳ ἡμῶν παρὰ μὲν Θεοδώρου τοῦ Φοίνικος τετρακισχιλίας πεντακοσίας δραχμάς, παρὰ δὲ τοῦ ναυκλήρου

7 Λάμπιδος χιλίας. δέον δ' αὐτὸν καταγοράσαι

[909] φορτία Ἀθήνηθεν μνῶν ἑκατὸν δέκα πέντε,[1] εἰ ἔμελλε τοῖς δανεισταῖς πᾶσι ποιήσειν τὰ ἐν ταῖς συγγραφαῖς γεγραμμένα, οὐ κατηγόρασεν ἀλλ' ἢ πεντακισχιλίων καὶ πεντακοσίων δραχμῶν, σὺν τῷ ἐπισιτισμῷ· ὀφείλει δ' ἑβδομήκοντα μνᾶς καὶ πέντε. ἀρχὴ μὲν οὖν αὕτη ἐγένετο τοῦ ἀδικήματος, ὦ ἄνδρες Ἀθηναῖοι· οὔτε γὰρ τὴν ὑποθήκην παρέσχεν οὔτε τὰ χρήματ' ἐνέθετ' εἰς τὴν ναῦν, κελευούσης τῆς συγγραφῆς ἐπάναγκες ἐντίθεσθαι.

Καί μοι λαβὲ τὴν συγγραφήν.

ΣΥΓΓΡΑΦΗ

Λαβὲ δὴ καὶ τὴν τῶν πεντηκοστολόγων ἀπογραφὴν καὶ τὰς μαρτυρίας.

ΑΠΟΓΡΑΦΗ. ΜΑΡΤΥΡΙΑΙ

8 Ἐλθὼν τοίνυν εἰς τὸν Βόσπορον, ἔχων ἐπιστολὰς παρ' ἐμοῦ, ἃς ἔδωκ' αὐτῷ ἀπενεγκεῖν τῷ παιδὶ τῷ ἐμῷ παραχειμάζοντι ἐκεῖ καὶ κοινωνῷ τινί, γράψας ἐν τῇ ἐπιστολῇ τό τε ἀργύριον ὃ ἐδεδανείκειν καὶ τὴν ὑποθήκην, καὶ προστάξας, ἐπειδὰν τάχιστ' ἐξαιρεθῇ τὰ χρήματα, ἐξετάζειν καὶ παρακολουθεῖν, τὰς μὲν ἐπιστολὰς οὐκ ἀποδίδωσιν οὗτος[2] ἃς ἔλαβε

---

[1] δέκα πέντε] πεντήκοντα Blass.
[2] οὗτος] αὐτοῖς Blass.

---

[a] If the loans were all made on the same basis (*i.e.* on the security of goods of a value twice as great as the loan) we should have to read one hundred and fifty instead of one hundred and fifteen, as the combined loans amounted to

240

in the Peiraeus he, without our knowledge, secured an additional loan of four thousand five hundred drachmae from Theodorus the Phoenician, and one of one thousand drachmae from Lampis the ship-owner. And, whereas he was bound to purchase at 7 Athens a cargo worth one hundred and fifteen minae,[a] if he was to perform for all his creditors what was written in their agreements, he purchased only a cargo worth five thousand five hundred drachmae, including the provisions; while his debts were seventy-five minae. This was the beginning of his fraud, men of Athens; he neither furnished security, nor put the goods on board the ship, although the agreement absolutely bade him do so.

Take the agreement, please.

THE AGREEMENT

Now take also the entry made by the customs-officers and the depositions.

THE ENTRY OF THE CUSTOMS. THE DEPOSITIONS

When he came, then, to Bosporus, having letters 8 from me, which I had given him to deliver to my slave, who was spending the winter there, and to a partner of mine,—in which letter I had stated the sum which I had lent and the security, and bade them, as soon as the goods should be unshipped, to inspect them and keep an eye on them,—the fellow did not deliver to them the letters which he had

seventy-five minae. It is possible, however, that Theodorus and Lampis, whose loans were for the outward voyage only, and who sailed with Phormio, accepted a lower rate than that demanded by Chrysippus and his partner, who remained in Athens.

παρ' ἐμοῦ, ἵνα μηδὲν εἰδείησαν ὧν ἔπραττεν οὗτος, καταλαβὼν δ' ἐν τῷ Βοσπόρῳ μοχθηρὰ τὰ πράγματα διὰ τὸν συμβάντα πόλεμον τῷ Παιρισάδῃ πρὸς τὸν Σκύθην καὶ τῶν φορτίων ὧν ἦγε πολλὴν ἀπρασίαν, ἐν πάσῃ ἀπορίᾳ ἦν· καὶ γὰρ οἱ δανεισταὶ 9 εἴχοντο αὐτοῦ οἱ τὰ ἑτερόπλοα δανείσαντες. ὥστε τοῦ ναυκλήρου κελεύοντος αὐτὸν κατὰ τὴν συγγραφὴν ἐντίθεσθαι τὰ ἀγοράσματα τῶν ἐμῶν χρημάτων, εἶπεν οὗτος ὁ νῦν φάσκων ἀποδεδωκέναι τὸ χρυσίον, ὅτι οὐκ ἂν δύναιτο ἐνθέσθαι εἰς τὴν [910] ναῦν τὰ χρήματα· ἄπρατον γὰρ εἶναι τὸν ῥῶπον. κἀκεῖνον μὲν ἐκέλευεν ἀνάγεσθαι, αὐτὸς δ', ἐπειδὰν διαθῆται τὰ φορτία, ἐφ' ἑτέρας νεὼς ἔφη ἐκπλεύσεσθαι.

Καί μοι λαβὲ ταύτην τὴν μαρτυρίαν.

MAPTYPIA

10 Μετὰ ταῦτα τοίνυν, ὦ ἄνδρες Ἀθηναῖοι, οὗτος μὲν ἐν τῷ Βοσπόρῳ κατελέλειπτο, ὁ δὲ Λάμπις ἀναχθεὶς ἐναυάγησεν οὐ μακρὰν ἀπὸ τοῦ ἐμπορίου· γεγεμισμένης γὰρ ἤδη τῆς νεώς, ὡς ἀκούομεν, μᾶλλον τοῦ δέοντος, προσανέλαβεν ἐπὶ τὸ κατάστρωμα χιλίας βύρσας, ὅθεν καὶ ἡ διαφθορὰ τῇ νηὶ συνέβη. καὶ αὐτὸς μὲν ἀπεσώθη ἐν τῷ λέμβῳ μετὰ τῶν ἄλλων παίδων τῶν Δίωνος, ἀπώλεσε δὲ πλέον ἢ τριάκοντα σώματα ἐλεύθερα χωρὶς τῶν ἄλλων. πολλοῦ δὲ πένθους ἐν τῷ Βοσπόρῳ ὄντος, ὡς ἐπύθοντο τὴν διαφθορὰν τῆς νεώς, ηὐδαιμόνιζον

---

[a] The King of Pontus.
[b] The MS. reading is τριακόσια (300), but it is most unlikely

received from me, in order that they might know nothing of what he was doing; and, finding that business in Bosporus was bad owing to the war which had broken out between Paerisades [a] and the Scythian, and that there was no market for the goods which he had brought, he was in great perplexity; for his creditors, who had lent him money for the outward voyage, were pressing him for payment. When, therefore, the shipowner bade him put on 9 board according to the agreement the goods bought with my money, this fellow, who now alleges that he has paid the debt in full, said that he could not ship the goods because his trash was unsalable; and he bade him put to sea, saying that he himself would sail in another ship as soon as he should dispose of the cargo.

Please take this deposition.

THE DEPOSITION

After this, men of Athens, the defendant was left 10 in Bosporus, while Lampis put to sea, and was ship-wrecked not far from the port; for although his ship was already overloaded, as we learn, he took on an additional deck-load of one thousand hides, which proved the cause of the loss of the vessel. He himself made his escape in the boat with the rest of Dio's servants, but he lost more than thirty [b] lives besides the cargo. There was much mourning in Bosporus when they learned of the loss of the ship, and everybody deemed this Phormio lucky in that

that there were so many persons on board, unless this was a slave ship. Such an assumption, however, seems improbable, and does not accord well with the statement that there was much mourning in Bosporus over the disaster.

Φορμίωνα πάντες τουτονί, ὅτι οὔτε συνανήχθη οὔτ᾽ ἐνέθετο εἰς τὴν ναῦν οὐδέν. συνέβαινε δὲ παρά τε τῶν ἄλλων καὶ παρὰ τούτου ὁ αὐτὸς λόγος.

Καί μοι ἀνάγνωθι ταύτας τὰς μαρτυρίας.

ΜΑΡΤΥΡΙΑΙ

11 Αὐτὸς τοίνυν ὁ Λάμπις, ᾧ φησιν ἀποδεδωκέναι τὸ χρυσίον (τούτῳ γὰρ προσέχετε τὸν νοῦν), προσελθόντος αὐτῷ ἐμοῦ, ἐπειδὴ τάχιστα κατέπλευσεν ἐκ τῆς ναυαγίας Ἀθήναζε, καὶ ἐρωτῶντος ὑπὲρ τούτων, ἔλεγεν ὅτι οὔτε τὰ χρήματα ἔνθοιτο εἰς τὴν ναῦν οὗτος κατὰ τὴν συγγραφήν, οὔτε τὸ χρυσίον εἰληφὼς εἴη παρ᾽ αὐτοῦ ἐν Βοσπόρῳ τότε.[1]

Καί μοι ἀνάγνωθι τὴν μαρτυρίαν τῶν παραγενομένων.

ΜΑΡΤΥΡΙΑ

12 Ἐπειδὴ τοίνυν, ὦ ἄνδρες Ἀθηναῖοι, ἐπεδήμησε Φορμίων οὑτοσὶ σεσωσμένος ἐφ᾽ ἑτέρας νεώς, προσῄειν αὐτῷ ἀπαιτῶν τὸ δάνειον. καὶ οὗτος κατὰ μὲν ἀρχὰς οὐδεπώποτ᾽, ὦ ἄνδρες Ἀθηναῖοι, εἶπε τὸν λόγον τοῦτον ὃν νυνὶ λέγει, ἀλλ᾽ ἀεὶ ὡμολόγει ἀποδώσειν· ἐπειδὴ δ᾽ ἀνεκοινώσατο τοῖς νῦν παροῦσιν αὐτῷ καὶ συνδικοῦσιν, ἕτερος ἤδη ἦν καὶ οὐχ 13 ὁ αὐτός. ὡς δ᾽ ᾐσθόμην αὐτὸν διακρουόμενόν με, προσέρχομαι τῷ Λάμπιδι, λέγων ὅτι οὐδὲν ποιεῖ τῶν δικαίων Φορμίων οὐδ᾽ ἀποδίδωσι τὸ δάνειον, καὶ ἅμα ἠρόμην αὐτὸν εἰ εἰδείη ὅπου ἐστίν, ἵνα προσκαλεσαίμην αὐτόν. ὁ δ᾽ ἀκολουθεῖν μ᾽ ἐκέλευεν ἑαυτῷ, καὶ καταλαμβάνομεν πρὸς τοῖς μυροπωλίοις

---

[1] τότε omitted by Blass.

he had not sailed with the others, nor put any goods on board the ship. The same story was told by the others and by Phormio himself.

Read me, please, these depositions.

THE DEPOSITIONS

Lampis himself, to whom Phormio declares he 11 had paid the gold (pray note this carefully), when I approached him as soon as he had returned to Athens after the shipwreck and asked him about these matters, said that Phormio did not put the goods on board the ship according to our agreement, nor had he himself received the gold from him at that time in Bosporus.

Read, please, the deposition of those who were present.

THE DEPOSITION

Now, men of Athens, when this man Phormio 12 reached Athens, after completing his voyage in safety on another ship, I approached him and demanded payment of the loan. And at the first, men of Athens, he did not in any instance make the statement which he now makes, but always agreed that he would pay ; but after he had entered into an agreement with those who are now at his side and are advocates with him, he was then and there different and not at all the same man. When I saw 13 that he was trying to cheat me, I went to Lampis and told him that Phormio was not doing what was right nor paying back the loan ; and at the same time I asked him if he knew where Phormio was, in order that I might summon him. He bade me follow him, and we found the fellow at the perfumery shops;

DEMOSTHENES

τουτονί· κἀγὼ κλητῆρας ἔχων προσεκαλεσάμην
14 αὐτόν. καὶ ὁ Λάμπις, ὦ ἄνδρες Ἀθηναῖοι, παρὼν
προσκαλουμένῳ μοι οὐδαμοῦ ἐτόλμησεν εἰπεῖν ὡς
ἀπείληφε παρὰ τούτου τὸ χρυσίον, οὐδ' ὃ εἰκὸς ἦν
εἰπεῖν " Χρύσιππε, μαίνει· τί τοῦτον προσκαλεῖ;
ἐμοὶ γὰρ ἀποδέδωκε τὸ χρυσίον." ἀλλὰ μὴ ὅτι
ὁ Λάμπις ἐφθέγξατο, ἀλλ' οὐδ' αὐτὸς οὗτος οὐδὲν
ἠξίωσεν εἰπεῖν, παρεστηκότος τοῦ Λάμπιδος, ᾧ
15 νυνὶ φησιν ἀποδεδωκέναι τὸ χρυσίον. καίτοι εἰκός
γ' ἦν αὐτὸν εἰπεῖν, ὦ ἄνδρες Ἀθηναῖοι, " τί με
προσκαλεῖ, ἄνθρωπε; ἀποδέδωκα γὰρ τούτῳ τῷ
παρεστηκότι τὸ χρυσίον," καὶ ἅμα ὁμολογοῦντα
παρέχειν τὸν Λάμπιν· νῦν δ' οὐδέτερος αὐτῶν οὐδ'
ὁτιοῦν εἶπεν ἐν τοιούτῳ καιρῷ.

Καὶ ὅτι ἀληθῆ λέγω, λαβέ μοι τὴν μαρτυρίαν
τῶν κλητήρων.

ΜΑΡΤΥΡΙΑ

16 Λαβὲ δή μοι καὶ τὸ ἔγκλημα ὃ ἔλαχον αὐτῷ
πέρυσιν· ὅ ἐστιν οὐδενὸς ἔλαττον τεκμήριον, ὅτι
οὐδέπω τότ' ἔφησε Φορμίων ἀποδεδωκέναι τὸ
χρυσίον Λάμπιδι.

                    ΕΓΚΛΗΜΑ

Τοῦτο τὸ ἔγκλημα ἔγραφον ἐγώ, ὦ ἄνδρες Ἀθηναῖοι, οὐδαμόθεν ἄλλοθεν σκοπῶν, ἀλλ' ἢ ἐκ τῆς
ἀπαγγελίας τῆς Λάμπιδος, ὃς οὐκ ἔφασκεν οὔτε τὰ
χρήματα ἐντεθεῖσθαι τοῦτον οὔτε τὸ χρυσίον ἀπ-
ειληφέναι· μὴ γὰρ οἴεσθέ με οὕτως ἀπόπληκτον εἶναι
καὶ παντελῶς μαινόμενον, ὥστε τοιοῦτο γράφειν
246

and I, having witnesses with me, served the summons. Lampis, men of Athens, was close at hand when I did 14 this, yet he never ventured to say that he had received the money from Phormio, nor did he say, as he naturally would have done supposing his story to be true, "Chrysippus, you are mad. Why do you summon this man? He has paid me the money." And not only did Lampis not say a word, but neither did Phormio himself venture to say anything, although Lampis was standing by his side, to whom he now declares he had paid the money. Yet, men 15 of Athens, it would surely have been natural for him to say, "Why do you summon me, fellow? I have paid the money to this man who is standing here" —and at the same time to call upon Lampis to corroborate his words. As it was, however, neither of them uttered a syllable on an occasion so opportune.

In proof that my words are true, take, please, the deposition of those who witnessed the summons.

THE DEPOSITION

Now take the complaint in the action which I 16 commenced against him last year, for this is the strongest possible proof that up to that time Phormio had never stated that he had paid the money to Lampis.

THE COMPLAINT

This action I commenced, men of Athens, basing my complaint upon nothing else than the report of Lampis, who denied that Phormio had put the goods on board the ship or that he himself had received the money. Do not imagine that I am so senseless, so absolutely crazy, as to have drawn up a complaint

DEMOSTHENES

ἔγκλημα ὁμολογοῦντος τοῦ Λάμπιδος ἀπειληφέναι
τὸ χρυσίον ὑφ' οὗ ἔμελλον ἐξελεγχθήσεσθαι.

17 Ἔτι δ', ὦ ἄνδρες Ἀθηναῖοι, κἀκεῖνο σκέψασθε·
αὐτοὶ γὰρ οὗτοι παραγραφὴν διδόντες πέρυσιν,
οὐκ ἐτόλμησαν ἐν τῇ παραγραφῇ γράψαι ὡς ἀπο-
δεδώκασι Λάμπιδι τὸ χρυσίον.
Καί μοι λαβὲ αὐτὴν τὴν παραγραφήν.

ΠΑΡΑΓΡΑΦΗ

Ἀκούετε, ὦ ἄνδρες Ἀθηναῖοι, ὅτι οὐδαμοῦ γέγραπται ἐν τῇ παραγραφῇ ὡς ἀποδέδωκε τὸ χρυσίον
Φορμίων Λάμπιδι, καὶ ταῦτ' ἐμοῦ διαρρήδην
γράψαντος εἰς τὸ ἔγκλημα ὃ ἠκούσατ' ἀρτίως, ὅτι
οὔτε τὰ χρήματ' ἔνθοιτο εἰς τὴν ναῦν οὔτ' ἀπέδωκε
τὸ χρυσίον. τίνα οὖν ἄλλον χρὴ περιμένειν ὑμᾶς
μάρτυρα, ὅταν τηλικαύτην μαρτυρίαν παρ' αὐτῶν
τούτων ἔχητε;

18 Μελλούσης δὲ τῆς δίκης εἰσιέναι εἰς τὸ δικαστήριον ἐδέοντο ἡμῶν ἐπιτρέψαι τινί· καὶ ἡμεῖς ἐπετρέψαμεν Θεοδότῳ ἰσοτελεῖ κατὰ συνθήκας. καὶ
ὁ Λάμπις μετὰ ταῦτα νομίσας αὐτῷ ἀσφαλὲς ἤδη
[913] εἶναι πρὸς διαιτητῇ μαρτυρεῖν ὅ τι βούλοιτο, μερι-
σάμενος τὸ ἐμὸν χρυσίον μετὰ Φορμίωνος τουτουί,

19 ἐμαρτύρει τἀναντία οἷς πρότερον εἰρήκει. οὐ γὰρ
ὅμοιόν ἐστιν, ὦ ἄνδρες Ἀθηναῖοι, εἰς τὰ ὑμέτερα
πρόσωπα ἐμβλέποντα τὰ ψευδῆ μαρτυρεῖν καὶ πρὸς
διαιτητῇ· παρ' ὑμῖν μὲν γὰρ ὀργὴ μεγάλη καὶ
τιμωρία ὑπόκειται τοῖς τὰ ψευδῆ μαρτυροῦσι, πρὸς
δὲ τῷ διαιτητῇ ἀκινδύνως καὶ ἀναισχύντως μαρτυροῦσιν ὅ τι ἂν βούλωνται. ἀγανακτοῦντος δέ μου

---

[a] The word is used of one who, though an alien, paid only

248

like this, if Lampis (whose words would prove my contention false) admitted that he had received the money.

More than this, men of Athens, note another fact. **17** These very men entered a special plea last year, but dared not assert in their plea that they had paid the money to Lampis.

Now, pray take the plea itself.

THE SPECIAL PLEA

You hear, men of Athens. Nowhere in the plea is it stated that Phormio had paid the money to Lampis, though I had expressly written in the complaint, which you heard a moment ago, that Phormio had not put the goods on board the ship nor paid the money. For what other witness, then, should you wait, when you have so significant a piece of evidence from these men themselves ?

When the suit was about to come into court, they **18** begged us to refer it to an arbitrator ; and we referred it by agreement to Theodotus, a privileged alien.[a] Lampis after that, thinking that it would now, before an arbitrator, be safe for him to testify just as he pleased, divided my money with this fellow Phormio, and then gave testimony the very opposite of what he had stated before. For it is not the same **19** thing, men of Athens, to give false testimony while face to face with you and to do so before an arbitrator. With you heavy indignation and severe penalty await those who bear false witness ; but before an arbitrator they give what testimony they please without risk and without shame. When I expostulated and

the taxes paid by citizens without the addition of the special tax on aliens.

καὶ σχετλιάζοντος, ὦ ἄνδρες Ἀθηναῖοι, ἐπὶ τῇ
20 τόλμῃ τοῦ Λάμπιδος, καὶ παρεχομένου πρὸς τὸν
διαιτητὴν τὴν αὐτὴν μαρτυρίαν ἥνπερ καὶ νῦν πρὸς
ὑμᾶς παρέχομαι, τῶν ἐξ ἀρχῆς προσελθόντων αὐτῷ
μεθ᾽ ἡμῶν, ὅτε οὔτε τὸ χρυσίον ἔφη ἀπειληφέναι
παρὰ τούτου οὔτε τὰ χρήματ᾽ αὐτὸν ἐνθέσθαι εἰς
τὴν ναῦν, οὕτως ὁ Λάμπις κατὰ κράτος ἐξελεγχόμενος τὰ ψευδῆ μαρτυρῶν καὶ πονηρὸς ὤν,
ὡμολόγει μὲν εἰρηκέναι ταῦτα πρὸς τοῦτον, οὐ
μέντοι ἐντός γε ὢν εἰπεῖν αὐτοῦ.
Καί μοι ἀνάγνωθι ταύτην τὴν μαρτυρίαν.

21 Ἀκούσας τοίνυν ἡμῶν, ὦ ἄνδρες Ἀθηναῖοι, ὁ
Θεόδοτος πολλάκις, καὶ νομίσας τὸν Λάμπιν ψευδῆ
μαρτυρεῖν, οὐκ ἀπέγνω τῆς δίκης, ἀλλ᾽ ἀφῆκεν
ἡμᾶς εἰς τὸ δικαστήριον· καταγνῶναι μὲν γὰρ οὐκ
ἐβουλήθη διὰ τὸ οἰκείως ἔχειν Φορμίωνι τουτῳί,
ὡς ἡμεῖς ὕστερον ἐπυθόμεθα, ἀπογνῶναι δὲ τῆς
δίκης ὤκνει, ἵνα μὴ ἐπιορκήσειεν.
22 Ἐξ αὐτοῦ δὴ τοῦ πράγματος λογίσασθε, ὦ ἄνδρες
δικασταί, παρ᾽ ὑμῖν αὐτοῖς, ὁπόθεν ἔμελλεν οὗτος
ἀποδώσειν τὸ χρυσίον. ἐνθένδε μὲν γὰρ ἐξέπλει οὐκ
[914] ἐνθέμενος εἰς τὴν ναῦν τὰ χρήματα καὶ ὑποθήκην
οὐκ ἔχων, ἀλλ᾽ ἐπὶ τοῖς ἐμοῖς χρήμασιν ἐπιδανεισά-
μενος· ἐν Βοσπόρῳ δ᾽ ἀπρασίαν τῶν φορτίων κατ-
έλαβε, καὶ τοὺς τὰ ἑτερόπλοα δανείσαντας μόλις

---

[a] I take the phrase πρὸς τοῦτον with εἰρηκέναι, assuming
that the reference is to the partner of Chrysippus, who
apparently takes the latter's place as speaker at the beginning
of the next paragraph.

[b] It is commonly assumed that the second speaker begins

expressed strong indignation, men of Athens, at the effrontery of Lampis, and produced before the arbi- 20 trator the same testimony as I now produce before you—that, namely, of the persons who at the first went to him with me, when he stated that he had not received the money from Phormio, and that Phormio had not put the goods on board the ship— Lampis, being so plainly convicted of bearing false witness and of playing the rogue, admitted that he had made the statement to my partner here,[a] but declared that he was out of his mind when he made it.

Now read me this deposition.

THE DEPOSITION

[The partner of Chrysippus now speaks.]

[b] Theodotus, men of Athens, after hearing us several 21 times, and being convinced that Lampis was giving false testimony, did not dismiss the suit, but referred us to the court. He was loth to give an adverse decision because he was a friend of this man Phormio, as we afterwards learned, yet he hesitated to dismiss the suit lest he should himself commit perjury.

Now, in the light of the facts themselves, consider 22 in your own minds, men of the jury, what means the man was likely to have for discharging the debt. He sailed from this port without having put the goods on board the ship, and having no adequate security ; on the contrary, he had made additional loans on the credit of the money lent by me. In Bosporus he found no market for his wares, and had difficulty in getting rid of those who had lent money for the outward

with this paragraph. In § 23 Chrysippus is referred to as οὗτος, so the fact of a change of speakers is patent.

23 ἀπήλλαξεν. καὶ οὗτος μὲν ἐδάνεισεν αὐτῷ δισχιλίας
δραχμὰς ἀμφοτερόπλουν, ὥστ' ἀπολαβεῖν Ἀθήνησι
δισχιλίας ἑξακοσίας δραχμάς· Φορμίων δέ φησιν
ἀποδοῦναι Λάμπιδι ἐν Βοσπόρῳ ἑκατὸν καὶ εἴκοσι
στατῆρας Κυζικηνούς (τούτῳ γὰρ προσέχετε τὸν
νοῦν) δανεισάμενος ἐγγείων τόκων. ἦσαν δὲ ἔφεκτοι
οἱ ἔγγειοι τόκοι, ὁ δὲ Κυζικηνὸς ἐδύνατο ἐκεῖ εἴκοσι
24 καὶ ὀκτὼ δραχμὰς Ἀττικάς. δεῖ δὴ μαθεῖν ὑμᾶς
ὅσα φησὶ χρήματ' ἀποδεδωκέναι. τῶν μὲν γὰρ
ἑκατὸν εἴκοσι στατήρων γίγνονται τρισχίλιαι τρια-
κόσιαι ἑξήκοντα, ὁ δὲ τόκος ὁ ἔγγειος ὁ ἔφεκτος
τῶν τριάκοντα μνῶν καὶ τριῶν καὶ ἑξήκοντα
πεντακόσιαι δραχμαὶ καὶ ἑξήκοντα· τὸ δὲ σύμπαν
25 κεφάλαιον γίγνεται τόσον καὶ τόσον. ἔστιν οὖν, ὦ
ἄνδρες δικασταί, οὗτος ὁ ἄνθρωπος ἢ γενήσεταί
ποτε, ὃς ἀντὶ δισχιλίων ἑξακοσίων δραχμῶν τριάκοντα μνᾶς καὶ τριακοσίας καὶ ἑξήκοντα ἀποτίνειν
προείλετ' ἄν, καὶ τόκον πεντακοσίας δραχμὰς καὶ
ἑξήκοντα δανεισάμενος, ἃς φησιν ἀποδεδωκέναι
Φορμίων Λάμπιδι, τρισχιλίας ἐνακοσίας εἴκοσιν;
ἐξὸν δ' αὐτῷ ἀμφοτερόπλουν Ἀθήνησιν ἀποδοῦναι
τὸ ἀργύριον, ἐν Βοσπόρῳ ἀπέδωκε, τρισὶ καὶ δέκα
26 μναῖς πλέον; καὶ τοῖς μὲν τὰ ἑτερόπλοα δανείσασι

ᵃ The stater of Cyzicus (a town on the south shore of the
Propontis, or sea of Marmora) was a coin made of electrum,
an alloy of approximately three-quarters gold and one-
quarter silver. It was nearly twice as heavy as the ordinary
gold stater, which was worth twenty drachmae, and had a
value (as stated in the text) of twenty-eight drachmae. The
addition of the word " there " indicates that the value
differed in different places according to the rate of exchange.
ᵇ That is, of course, the sum of the two items, or three
thousand nine hundred and twenty drachmae. The total is

voyage. My partner here had lent him two thousand **23**
drachmae for the double voyage on terms that he
should receive at Athens two thousand six hundred
drachmae ; but Phormio declares that he paid Lampis
in Bosporus one hundred and twenty Cyzicene staters[a]
(note this carefully) which he borrowed at the interest
paid on loans secured by real property. Now interest on real security was sixteen and two-thirds
per cent, and the Cyzicene stater was worth there
twenty-eight Attic drachmae. It is necessary that **24**
you should understand how large a sum he claims to
have paid. A hundred and twenty staters amount
to three thousand three hundred and sixty drachmae,
and the interest at the land rate of sixteen and
two-thirds per cent on thirty-three minae and sixty
drachmae is five hundred and sixty drachmae,
and the total amount comes to so much.[b] Now, **25**
men of the jury, is there a man, or will the man
ever be born, who, instead of twenty-six hundred
drachmae would prefer to pay thirty minae and three
hundred and sixty drachmae, and as interest five
hundred and sixty drachmae by virtue of his loan,
both which sums Phormio says he has paid Lampis,
in all three thousand nine hundred and twenty drachmae ? And when he might have paid the money
in Athens, seeing that it had been lent for the
double voyage, has he paid it in Bosporus, and too
much by thirteen minae ? And to the creditors who **26**
lent money for the outward voyage you had difficulty

not mentioned here, as it is given in the lines immediately
following. Note that the speaker inexactly speaks as if the
whole sum (including the interest) had been paid to Lampis
(according to Phormio's claim). The argument is, however,
valid, as the sum represents the cost to Phormio of paying
off the loan.

μόλις τἀρχαῖα ἀποδέδωκας, οἳ συνέπλευσάν σοι καὶ
προσήδρευον· τούτῳ δὲ τῷ μὴ παρόντι οὐ μόνον
[915] τἀρχαῖα καὶ τοὺς τόκους ἀπεδίδους, ἀλλὰ καὶ τὰ
ἐπιτίμια τὰ ἐκ τῆς συγγραφῆς ἀπέτινες, οὐδεμιᾶς
27 σοι ἀνάγκης οὔσης; κἀκείνους μὲν οὐκ ἐδεδίεις,
οἷς αἱ συγγραφαὶ ἐν Βοσπόρῳ τὴν πρᾶξιν ἐδίδοσαν·
τούτου δὲ φῂς φροντίζειν, ὃν ἐξ ἀρχῆς εὐθὺς ἠδίκεις
οὐκ ἐνθέμενος τὰ χρήματ᾽ εἰς τὴν ναῦν κατὰ τὴν
συγγραφὴν Ἀθήνηθεν; καὶ νῦν μὲν εἰς τὸ ἐμπόριον
ἥκων, οὗ τὸ συμβόλαιον ἐγένετο, οὐκ ὀκνεῖς ἀποστερεῖν τὸν δανείσαντα· ἐν Βοσπόρῳ δὲ πλείω τῶν
δικαίων φῂς ποιεῖν, οὗ δίκην οὐκ ἔμελλες δώσειν·
28 καὶ οἱ μὲν ἄλλοι πάντες οἱ τὰ ἀμφοτερόπλοα δα-
νειζόμενοι, ὅταν ἀποστέλλωνται ἐκ τῶν ἐμπορίων,
πολλοὺς παρίστανται, ἐπιμαρτυρόμενοι ὅτι τὰ χρήματα ἤδη κινδυνεύεται τῷ δανείσαντι· σὺ δ᾽ ἑνὶ
σκήπτει μάρτυρι αὐτῷ τῷ συναδικοῦντι, καὶ οὔτε
τὸν παῖδα τὸν ἡμέτερον παρέλαβες ἐν Βοσπόρῳ
ὄντα οὔτε τὸν κοινωνόν, οὐδὲ τὰς ἐπιστολὰς ἀπ-
έδωκας αὐτοῖς, ἃς ἡμεῖς ἐπεθήκαμεν, ἐν αἷς ἐγέ-
29 γραπτο παρακολουθεῖν σοι οἷς ἂν πράττῃς; καίτοι,
ὦ ἄνδρες δικασταί, τί οὐκ ἂν πράξειεν ὁ τοιοῦτος,
ὅστις γράμματα λαβὼν μὴ ἀπέδωκεν ὀρθῶς καὶ
δικαίως; ἢ πῶς οὐ φανερόν ἐστιν ὑμῖν τὸ τούτου

---

a We learn from § 33 that the contract entailed a penalty
of five thousand drachmae in case a return cargo was not
shipped, but of course payment could not have been exacted
in Bosporus. The speaker seems to identify the overpayment of one thousand three hundred and twenty drachmae
with this penalty ; but the " overpayment " represents
almost exactly the amount of the money Lampis had loaned
to Phormio, plus the thirty per cent interest. It is, of course,
possible that the penalty of five thousand drachmae was to

254

in paying the principal, though they sailed with you and kept pressing you for payment; yet to this man who was not present, you not only returned both principal and interest, but also paid the penalties arising from the agreement [a] though you were under no necessity of doing so? And you had no fear of 27 those men, to whom their agreements gave the right of exacting payment in Bosporus, but declare that you had regard for the claims of my partner, though you wronged him at the outset by not putting on board the goods according to your agreement in setting out from Athens? And now that you have come back to the port where the loan was made, you do not hesitate to defraud the lender, though you claim to have done more than justice required in Bosporus, where you were not likely to be punished? All other 28 men who borrow for the outward and homeward voyage, when they are about to set sail from their several ports, take care to have many witnesses present, and call upon them to attest that the lender's risk begins from that moment [b]; but you rely upon the single testimony of the very man who is your partner in the fraud. You did not bring as a witness my slave who was in Bosporus or my partner, nor did you deliver to them the letters which we gave into your charge, and in which were written instructions that they should keep close watch on you in whatever you might do! Why, men of Athens, what is there 29 which a man of this stamp is not capable of doing, who, after receiving letters, did not deliver them in due and proper course? Or how can you fail to see

be paid if Phormio neither shipped the goods nor paid Lampis, and the lesser sum if payment was made to Lampis without the shipment of a return cargo.

[b] That is, from the moment of sailing.

κακούργημα ἐξ αὐτῶν ὧν ἔπραττεν; καίτοι, ὦ γῆ
καὶ θεοί, προσῆκέ γε τοσοῦτο χρυσίον ἀποδιδόντα,
καὶ πλέον τοῦ δανείσματος, περιβόητον ποιεῖν ἐν
τῷ ἐμπορίῳ, καὶ παρακαλεῖν πάντας ἀνθρώπους,
πρῶτον δὲ τὸν παῖδα τὸν τούτου καὶ τὸν κοινωνόν·
30 ἴστε γὰρ δήπου πάντες, ὅτι δανείζονται μὲν μετ᾽
ὀλίγων μαρτύρων, ὅταν δ᾽ ἀποδιδῶσι, πολλοὺς
παρίστανται μάρτυρας, ἵν᾽ ἐπιεικεῖς δοκῶσιν εἶναι
[916] περὶ τὰ συμβόλαια. σοὶ δ᾽ ἀποδιδόντι τό τε δάνειον
καὶ τοὺς τόκους ἀμφοτέρους, ἑτερόπλῳ τῷ ἀργυρίῳ
κεχρημένῳ, καὶ προστιθέντι ἑτέρας τρεισκαίδεκα
μνᾶς, πῶς οὐχὶ πολλοὺς ἦν παραληπτέον μάρτυρας;
καὶ εἰ τοῦτ᾽ ἔπραξας, οὐδ᾽ ἂν εἷς σοῦ μᾶλλον τῶν
31 πλεόντων ἐθαυμάζετο. σὺ δ᾽ ἀντὶ τοῦ πολλοὺς
μάρτυρας τούτων ποιεῖσθαι πάντας ἀνθρώπους
λανθάνειν ἐπειρῶ, ὥσπερ ἀδικῶν τι. καὶ εἰ μὲν
ἐμοὶ τῷ δανείσαντι ἀπεδίδους, οὐδὲν ἂν ἔδει μαρ-
τύρων· τὴν γὰρ συγγραφὴν ἀνελόμενος ἀπήλλαξο
ἂν τοῦ συμβολαίου· νῦν δ᾽ οὐκ ἐμοί, ἀλλ᾽ ἑτέρῳ
ὑπὲρ ἐμοῦ ἀποδιδούς, καὶ οὐκ Ἀθήνησιν, ἀλλ᾽ ἐν
Βοσπόρῳ, καὶ τῆς συγγραφῆς σοι κειμένης Ἀθήνησι καὶ πρὸς ἐμέ, καὶ ᾧ τὸ χρυσίον ἀπεδίδους
ὄντος θνητοῦ καὶ πέλαγος τοσοῦτον μέλλοντος
πλεῖν, μάρτυρα οὐδέν᾽ ἐποίησω, οὔτε δοῦλον οὔτ᾽
32 ἐλεύθερον. ἡ γὰρ συγγραφή με, φησί, τῷ ναυκλήρῳ ἐκέλευεν ἀποδοῦναι τὸ χρυσίον. μάρτυρας

***

[a] This is best explained by assuming that the contract gave

that his own acts prove his guilt ? Surely (O Earth
and the Gods) when he was paying back so large a
sum, and more than the amount of his loan, it was
fitting that he should make it a much talked of event
on the exchange and to invite all men to be present ;
but especially the servant and partner of Chrysippus.
For you all know, I fancy, that men borrow with few 30
witnesses, but, when they pay, they take care to have
many witnesses present, that they may win a reputation for honesty in business dealings. But in your
case, when you were paying back both the debt and
the interest on both voyages, though you had used
the money for the outward voyage only, and were
adding thirteen minae besides, should you not have
caused many witnesses to be present ? Had you done
so, there is not a single merchant who would have
been held in higher esteem than you. But, as it was, 31
instead of securing many witnesses to these acts you
did everything you could that none should know, as
though you were committing some crime ! Again,
had you been making payment to me, your creditor,
in person, there would have been no need of witnesses,
for you would have taken back the agreement and
so got rid of the obligation ; whereas in making payment, not to me, but to another on my behalf, and not
at Athens but in Bosporus, when your agreement was
deposited at Athens and with me, and when the man
to whom you paid the money was mortal and about
to undertake a voyage over such a stretch of sea, you
called no one as a witness, whether slave or freeman.
Yes, he says, for the agreement bade me pay the cash 32
to the shipowner.[a] But it did not prevent you from

Phormio the right to pay the money to Lampis in Bosporus,
if he did not ship a return cargo to Athens.

δέ γ' οὐκ ἐκώλυε παραλαβεῖν, οὐδὲ τὰς ἐπιστολὰς
ἀποδοῦναι. καὶ οἵδε μὲν πρὸς σὲ δύο συγγραφὰς
ἐποιήσαντο ὑπὲρ τοῦ συμβολαίου, ὡς ἂν οἱ μάλιστ'
ἀπιστοῦντες· σὺ δὲ μόνος μόνῳ φῂς δοῦναι τῷ
ναυκλήρῳ τὸ χρυσίον, εἰδὼς κατὰ σοῦ κειμένην
Ἀθήνησι συγγραφὴν πρὸς τοῦτον.

33 Λέγει δ' ὡς ἡ συγγραφὴ σωθείσης τῆς νεὼς
αὐτὸν ἀποδοῦναι κελεύει τὰ χρήματα. καὶ γὰρ
ἐνθέσθαι τἀγοράσματα εἰς τὴν ναῦν κελεύει σε,
εἰ δὲ μή, πεντακισχιλίας δραχμὰς ἀποτίνειν. σὺ
δὲ τοῦτο μὲν τῆς συγγραφῆς οὐ λαμβάνεις, παρα-
βεβηκὼς δ' εὐθὺς ἐξ ἀρχῆς καὶ τὰ χρήματα οὐκ
[917] ἐνθέμενος, ἀμφισβητεῖς πρὸς ἓν ῥῆμα τῶν ἐν τῇ
συγγραφῇ, καὶ τοῦτ' ἀνῃρηκὼς αὐτός. ὁπότε γὰρ
ἐν τῷ Βοσπόρῳ φῂς μὴ τὰ χρήματ' ἐνθέσθαι εἰς
τὴν ναῦν, ἀλλὰ τὸ χρυσίον τῷ ναυκλήρῳ ἀποδοῦναι,
τί ἔτι περὶ τῆς νεὼς διαλέγει; οὐ γὰρ μετέσχηκας
34 τοῦ κινδύνου διὰ τὸ μηδὲν ἐνθέσθαι. καὶ τὸ μὲν
πρῶτον, ὦ ἄνδρες Ἀθηναῖοι, ὥρμησεν ἐπὶ ταύτην
τὴν σκῆψιν, ὡς ἐντεθειμένος τὰ χρήματα εἰς τὴν
ναῦν· ἐπειδὴ δὲ τοῦτο ἐκ πολλῶν ἔμελλεν ἐλεγχθήσεσθαι ψευδόμενος, ἔκ τε τῆς ἀπογραφῆς τῆς ἐν
Βοσπόρῳ παρὰ τοῖς ἐλλιμενισταῖς καὶ ὑπὸ τῶν ἐν
τῷ ἐμπορίῳ ἐπιδημούντων κατὰ τὸν αὐτὸν χρόνον,
τηνικαῦτα μεταβαλόμενος συνίσταται μετὰ τοῦ
Λάμπιδος καὶ φησὶν ἐκείνῳ τὸ χρυσίον ἀποδεδω-
35 κέναι, ἐφόδιον μὲν λαβὼν τὸ τὴν συγγραφὴν κε-
λεύειν, οὐκ ἂν ἡγούμενος δ' ἡμᾶς εὐπόρως ἐλέγξαι

_____

ᵃ The reference is not wholly clear. It may be that others

summoning witnesses, or from delivering the letters !
The parties here present [a] drew up two agreements
with you in the matter of the loan, showing that they
greatly distrusted you, but you assert that without
a single witness you paid the gold to the shipowner,
although you well know that an agreement against
yourself was deposited at Athens with my colleague
here !

He says that the agreement bids him pay back the 33
money, "when the ship reaches port in safety." Yes,
and it bids you also to put on board the ship the goods
purchased, or else to pay a fine of five thousand
drachmae. You ignore this clause in the agreement,
but after having from the first violated its provisions
by failing to put the goods on board, you raise a dispute about a single phrase in it, though you have by
your own act rendered it null and void. For when
you state that you did not put the goods on board
in Bosporus, but paid the cash to the shipowner, why
do you still go on talking about the ship ? For you
have had no share in the risk, since you put nothing
on board. At first, men of Athens, he seized upon 34
this excuse, pretending that he had shipped the
goods ; but when he saw that the falsity of this claim
was likely to be exposed in many ways,—by the entry
filed with the harbour-masters in Bosporus, and by
the testimony of those who were staying in the port
at the same time—then he changes his tack, enters
into a conspiracy with Lampis, and declares that he
has paid him the money in cash, finding a support for 35
his plea in the fact that the agreement so ordered,
and thinking that we should not find it easy to get

than Chrysippus and his partner had contributed to the sum
lent to Phormio.

DEMOSTHENES

ὅσα μόνοι πρὸς αὑτοὺς αὐτοὶ πράξειαν. καὶ ὁ
Λάμπις, ὅσα μὲν εἶπε πρὸς ἐμὲ πρὶν ὑπὸ τούτου
διαφθαρῆναι, οὐκ ἐντὸς ὢν αὐτοῦ φησιν εἰπεῖν·
ἐπειδὴ δὲ τὸ χρυσίον τοὐμὸν ἐμερίσατο, τότ' ἐντὸς
εἶναί φησιν αὐτοῦ καὶ πάντ' ἀκριβῶς μνημονεύειν.

36 Εἰ μὲν οὖν, ὦ ἄνδρες δικασταί, ἐμοῦ μόνου κατ-
εφρόνει Λάμπις, οὐδὲν ἂν ἦν θαυμαστόν· νῦν δὲ
πολλῷ δεινότερα τούτου πέπρακται αὐτῷ πρὸς
πάντας ὑμᾶς. κήρυγμα γὰρ ποιησαμένου Παιρι-
σάδου ἐν Βοσπόρῳ, ἐάν τις βούληται Ἀθήναζε εἰς
τὸ Ἀττικὸν ἐμπόριον σιτηγεῖν, ἀτελῆ τὸν σῖτον
ἐξάγειν, ἐπιδημῶν ἐν τῷ Βοσπόρῳ ὁ Λάμπις ἔλαβε
τὴν ἐξαγωγὴν τοῦ σίτου καὶ τὴν ἀτέλειαν ἐπὶ τῷ
τῆς πόλεως ὀνόματι, γεμίσας δὲ ναῦν μεγάλην
[918] σίτου ἐκόμισεν εἰς Ἄκανθον κἀκεῖ διέθετο ὁ κοι-
37 νωνήσας τούτῳ ἀπὸ τῶν ἡμετέρων. καὶ ταῦτ'
ἔπραξεν, ὦ ἄνδρες δικασταί, οἰκῶν μὲν Ἀθήνησιν,
οὔσης δ' αὐτῷ γυναικὸς ἐνθάδε καὶ παίδων, τῶν δὲ
νόμων τὰ ἔσχατα ἐπιτίμια προτεθηκότων, εἴ τις
οἰκῶν Ἀθήνησιν ἄλλοσέ ποι σιτηγήσειεν ἢ εἰς τὸ
Ἀττικὸν ἐμπόριον, ἔτι δ' ἐν τοιούτῳ καιρῷ, ἐν ᾧ
ὑμῶν οἱ μὲν ἐν τῷ ἄστει οἰκοῦντες διεμετροῦντο
τὰ ἄλφιτα ἐν τῷ ᾠδείῳ, οἱ δ' ἐν τῷ Πειραιεῖ ἐν
τῷ νεωρίῳ ἐλάμβανον κατ' ὀβολὸν τοὺς ἄρτους καὶ

ᵃ Either the speaker was with Chrysippus at the time
Lampis made this statement, or else Chrysippus is now again
the speaker.
ᵇ A town in Chalcidicê.
ᶜ We learn from Aristophanes, *Vespae*, 1109, that the
Odeum, built by Pericles as a music school, near the great
theatre, was sometimes used as a law-court, and Pollux, viii.
33, states that suits concerning grain were decided there.

at the truth regarding all that they did by themselves alone. And Lampis declares that all that he said to me [a] before he was corrupted by this Phormio was spoken when he was out of his head; but as soon as he got a share of my money, he declares that he is in his right mind and remembers everything perfectly!

Now, men of the jury, if it were toward myself only 36 that Lampis were showing contempt, it would be nothing to cause surprise; but in reality he has acted far more outrageously than Phormio toward you all. For when Paerisades had published a decree in Bosporus that whoever wished to transport grain to Athens for the Athenian market might export it free of duty, Lampis, who was at the time in Bosporus, obtained permission to export grain and the exemption from duty in the name of the state; and having loaded a large vessel with grain, carried it to Acanthus [b] and there disposed of it,—he, who had made himself the partner of Phormio here with our money. And he did this, men of the jury, 37 though he was resident at Athens, and had a wife and children here, and although the laws have prescribed the severest penalties if anyone resident at Athens should transport grain to any other place than to the Athenian market; besides, he did this at a critical time, when those of you who dwelt in the city were having their barley-meal measured out to them in the Odeum, [c] and those who dwelt in Peiraeus were receiving their loaves at an obol each in the dockyard and in the long-porch, [d] having

Compare Oration LIX. § 52. It is easy, therefore, to assume that distribution of grain may have been made there.

[d] The long-porch was a warehouse for grain in the Peiraeus.

ἐπὶ τῆς μακρᾶς στοᾶς τὰ ἄλφιτα, καθ᾽ ἡμίεκτον
μετρούμενοι καὶ καταπατούμενοι.

Καὶ ὅτι ἀληθῆ λέγω, λαβέ μοι τήν τε μαρτυρίαν
καὶ τὸν νόμον.

ΜΑΡΤΥΡΙΑ. ΝΟΜΟΣ

38 Φορμίων τοίνυν τούτῳ χρώμενος κοινωνῷ καὶ
μάρτυρι οἴεται δεῖν ἀποστερῆσαι τὰ χρήμαθ᾽ ἡμᾶς,
οἵ γε σιτηγοῦντες διατετελέκαμεν εἰς τὸ ὑμέτερον
ἐμπόριον, καὶ τριῶν ἤδη καιρῶν κατειληφότων τὴν
πόλιν, ἐν οἷς ὑμεῖς τοὺς χρησίμους τῷ δήμῳ ἐξητά-
ζετε, οὐδενὸς τούτων ἀπολελείμμεθα, ἀλλ᾽ ὅτε μὲν
εἰς Θήβας Ἀλέξανδρος παρῄει, ἐπεδώκαμεν ὑμῖν
39 τάλαντον ἀργυρίου· ὅτε δ᾽ ὁ σῖτος ἐπετιμήθη τὸ
πρότερον καὶ ἐγένετο ἑκκαίδεκα δραχμῶν, εἰσ-
αγαγόντες πλείους ἢ μυρίους μεδίμνους πυρῶν δι-
εμετρήσαμεν ὑμῖν τῆς καθεστηκυίας τιμῆς, πέντε
δραχμῶν τὸν μέδιμνον, καὶ ταῦτα πάντες ἴστε ἐν
τῷ πομπείῳ διαμετρούμενοι· πέρυσι δ᾽ εἰς τὴν
σιτωνίαν τὴν ὑπὲρ τοῦ δήμου τάλαντον ὑμῖν ἐπεδώκαμεν ἐγώ τε καὶ ὁ ἀδελφός.

Καί μοι ἀνάγνωθι τούτων τὰς μαρτυρίας.

ΜΑΡΤΥΡΙΑΙ

40 Ἀλλὰ μὴν εἴ γε δεῖ καὶ τούτοις τεκμαίρεσθαι,
[919] οὐκ εἰκὸς ἦν ἐπιδιδόναι μὲν ἡμᾶς τοσαῦτα χρήματα,
ἵνα παρ᾽ ὑμῖν εὐδοξῶμεν, συκοφαντεῖν δὲ Φορμίωνα, ἵνα καὶ τὴν ὑπάρχουσαν ἐπιείκειαν ἀπο-

---

ᵃ Literally a half-sixth (*i.e.* one-twelfth) of a medimnus, a
measure containing about twelve gallons.
ᵇ In 335 B.C.

262

their meal measured out to them a gallon *a* at a time, and being nearly trampled to death.

In proof that my words are true, take, please, the deposition and the law.

The Deposition. The Law

Phormio, then, with the help of this fellow as his 38 accomplice and witness, thinks proper to rob *us* of our money—*us*, who have continually brought grain to your market, and who in three crises which have come upon the state, during which you put to the test those who were of service to the people, have not once been found wanting. Nay, when Alexander entered Thebes,*b* we made you a free gift of a talent in cash ; and when grain earlier advanced in price 39 and reached sixteen drachmae, we imported more than ten thousand medimni of wheat, and measured it out to you at the normal price of five drachmae a medimnus, and you all know that you had this measured out to you in the Pompeium.*c* And last year my brother and I made a free gift of a talent to buy grain for the people.

Read, please, the depositions which establish these facts.

The Depositions

Surely, if any inference may be based upon these 40 facts, it is not likely that we should freely give such large sums in order to win a good name among you, and then should bring a false accusation against Phormio in order to throw away even the reputation for honourable dealing which we had won. It is

---

c This was a hall near the Dipylon, in which the dresses and other properties used in the Panathenaic procession (πομπή) were kept.

βάλωμεν. δικαίως ἂν οὖν βοηθήσαιτε ἡμῖν, ὦ
ἄνδρες δικασταί. ἐπέδειξα γὰρ ὑμῖν οὔτ' ἐξ ἀρχῆς
τὰ φορτία ἐνθέμενον τοῦτον εἰς τὴν ναῦν ἁπάντων
ὧν ἐδανείσατο Ἀθήνηθεν, τῶν τ' ἐν τῷ Βοσπόρῳ
πραθέντων τοὺς τὰ ἑτερόπλοα δανείσαντας μόλις
41 διαλύσαντα, ἔτι δ' οὔτ' εὐποροῦντα οὔθ' οὕτως ὄντ'
ἀβέλτερον, ὥστ' ἀντὶ δισχιλίων καὶ ἑξακοσίων
δραχμῶν τριάκοντα μνᾶς καὶ ἐννέα ἀποδοῦναι, πρός
τε τούτοις, ὅτε ἀποδοῦναί φησι τὸ χρυσίον Λάμπιδι,
οὔτε τὸν παῖδα παραλαβόντα τὸν ἐμὸν οὔτε τὸν
κοινωνὸν ἐπιδημοῦντα ἐν Βοσπόρῳ. ἐμοὶ δὲ
Λάμπις αὐτὸς μαρτυρῶν φαίνεται ὡς οὐκ ἀπείληφε
42 τὸ χρυσίον, πρὶν ὑπὸ τούτου διαφθαρῆναι. καίτοι
εἰ καθ' ἓν ἕκαστον οὕτως ἐδείκνυε Φορμίων, οὐκ
οἶδ' ὅπως ἂν ἄλλως ἄμεινον ἀπελογήσατο. ὑπὲρ
δὲ τοῦ τὴν δίκην εἰσαγώγιμον εἶναι ὁ νόμος αὐτὸς
διαμαρτύρεται, κελεύων τὰς δίκας εἶναι τὰς ἐμπορικὰς τῶν συμβολαίων τῶν Ἀθήνησι καὶ εἰς τὸ
Ἀθηναίων ἐμπόριον, καὶ οὐ μόνον τῶν Ἀθήνησιν,
ἀλλὰ καὶ ὅσ' ἂν γένηται ἕνεκα τοῦ πλοῦ τοῦ Ἀθήναζε.

Λαβὲ δή μοι τοὺς νόμους.

NOMOI

43 Ὡς μὲν τοίνυν γέγονέ μοι τὸ συμβόλαιον πρὸς
Φορμίων' Ἀθήνησιν, οὐδ' αὐτοὶ ἔξαρνοί εἰσι, παρα-

ᵃ The speaker is about to return to the argument that the
special plea was inadmissible. He says, in effect, I have
shown that Phormio is guilty. If he had been able to prove
his case as clearly (*i.e.* in the suit as instituted) it would
have been his best defence. He could not do so, and therefore had recourse to a special plea, arguing that my suit
264

right, therefore, that you should come to our aid, men of the jury. I have shown you that Phormio in the first place did not put on board the vessel goods to the value of all the loans which he had secured at Athens, and that with the proceeds from the goods sold in Bosporus he with difficulty satisfied his creditors who had lent money for the outward voyage ; further, that he was not well off, and not so **41** foolish as to pay thirty-nine minae instead of twenty-six hundred drachmae ; and besides all this, that when, as he says, he paid the money to Lampis he summoned neither my slave nor my partner, who was at the time in Bosporus, as a witness. Again, Lampis himself is shown to have testified to me, before he was corrupted by Phormio, that he had not received the money. Yet,[a] if Phormio were thus to **42** prove his case point by point, I do not see what better defence he could have made. But that the action is admissible the law itself solemnly declares, when it maintains that mercantile actions are those for contracts made at Athens or for the Athenian market, and not only those made at Athens, but all that are made for the purpose of a voyage to Athens.

Please take the laws.

THE LAWS

That the contract has been entered into between **43** Phormio and myself at Athens even our opponents themselves do not deny, but they enter a special plea

could not be brought into court. This, however, is inadmissible, and his course in entering it proves that he had no defence.

γράφονται δὲ ὡς οὐκ εἰσαγώγιμον τὴν δίκην οὖσαν.
[920] ἀλλ' εἰς ποῖον δικαστήριον εἰσέλθωμεν, ἄνδρες δικασταί, εἰ μὴ πρὸς ὑμᾶς, οὗπερ τὸ συμβόλαιον ἐποιησάμεθα; δεινὸν γὰρ ἂν εἴη, εἰ μὲν ἕνεκα τοῦ πλοῦ
τοῦ 'Αθήναζε ἠδικούμην, εἶναι ἄν μοι παρ' ὑμῖν
τὸ δίκαιον λαβεῖν παρὰ Φορμίωνος, ἐπειδὴ δὲ τὸ
συμβόλαιον ἐν τῷ ὑμετέρῳ ἐμπορίῳ γέγονε, μὴ
44 φάσκειν παρ' ὑμῖν τούτους ὑφέξειν τὴν δίκην. καὶ
ὅτε μὲν Θεοδότῳ τὴν δίαιταν ἐπετρέψαμεν, ὡμο-
λόγησαν εἶναι καθ' αὑτῶν ἐμοὶ τὴν δίκην εἰσ-
αγώγιμον· νυνὶ δὲ τοὐναντίον λέγουσιν ὧν πρότερον
αὐτοὶ συγκεχωρήκασιν, ὡς δέον παρὰ μὲν τῷ
Θεοδότῳ τῷ ἰσοτελεῖ ὑποσχεῖν αὐτοὺς δίκην ἄνευ
παραγραφῆς, ἐπειδὴ δὲ εἰς τὸ 'Αθηναίων δικαστήριον εἰσερχόμεθα, μηκέτ' εἰσαγώγιμον τὴν δίκην
45 εἶναι. ἐνθυμοῦμαι δ' ἔγωγε, τί ἄν ποτε εἰς τὴν
παραγραφὴν ἔγραψεν, εἰ ὁ Θεόδοτος ἀπέγνω τῆς
δίκης, ὅπου νῦν γνόντος τοῦ Θεοδότου ἀπιέναι ἡμᾶς
εἰς τὸ δικαστήριον, οὔ φησι τὴν δίκην εἶναι εἰσαγώγιμον παρ' ὑμῖν, πρὸς οὓς ἐκεῖνος ἔγνω ἀπιέναι.
πάθοιμι μέντἂν δεινότατα, εἰ οἱ μὲν νόμοι τῶν
'Αθήνησι συμβολαίων κελεύουσι τὰς δίκας εἶναι
πρὸς τοὺς θεσμοθέτας, ὑμεῖς δ' ἀπογνοίητε τῆς
δίκης ὀμωμοκότες κατὰ τοὺς νόμους ψηφιεῖσθαι.
46 Τοῦ μὲν οὖν δανεῖσαι ἡμᾶς τὰ χρήματα αἵ τε
συνθῆκαι καὶ αὐτὸς οὗτός ἐστι μάρτυς· τοῦ δ' ἀποδεδωκέναι οὐδείς ἐστι μάρτυς ἔξω τοῦ Λάμπιδος

alleging that the action is not admissible. But to what tribunal shall we come, men of the jury, if not to you, since it was here in Athens that we made our contract? It would be hard indeed that, if a wrong had been done me in connexion with a voyage to Athens, I should be able to get satisfaction from Phormio in your court, but, when the contract has been made in your market, these men should say that they will not be tried before you. When we referred the case to Theodotus for 44 arbitration, they admitted that my action against them was admissible; but now they say what is the direct opposite of what they have themselves before admitted; as if, forsooth, it were proper that they should be tried before Theodotus, the privileged alien, without a special plea, but, when we enter the Athenian court, the action should no longer be admissible! I for my part am trying to conceive what 45 in the world he would have written in the special plea, if Theodotus had dismissed the suit, when now, after Theodotus has decreed that we should go into court, he declares that the action is not one that can be brought before you, to whom Theodotus bade us go.[a] Surely I should suffer most cruel treatment if, when the laws declare that suits growing out of contracts made at Athens shall be brought before the Thesmothetae, you, who have sworn to decide according to the laws, should dismiss the suit.

That we lent the money is attested by the agree- 46 ment, and by Phormio himself; that it has been repaid is attested by no one except Lampis, who

---

[a] If, under the present circumstances, Phormio's insolence is so great, who can say what it would have been, had the arbitrator decided in his favour?

DEMOSTHENES

τοῦ συναδικοῦντος. καὶ οὗτος μὲν εἰς ἐκεῖνον μόνον
ἀναφέρει τὴν ἀπόδοσιν, ἐγὼ δ' εἴς τε τὸν Λάμπιν
αὐτὸν καὶ τοὺς ἀκούσαντας αὐτοῦ ὅτε οὐκ ἔφη
ἀπειληφέναι τὸ χρυσίον. τούτῳ μὲν οὖν τοὺς
ἐμοὺς μάρτυρας ἔξεστι κρίνειν, εἰ μή φησι τἀληθῆ
μαρτυρεῖν αὐτούς· ἐγὼ δ' οὐκ ἔχω τί χρήσωμαι
[921] τοῖς τούτου μάρτυσιν, οἳ φασιν εἰδέναι τὸν Λάμπιν
μαρτυροῦντα ἀπειληφέναι τὸ χρυσίον. εἰ μὲν γὰρ
ἡ μαρτυρία ἡ τοῦ Λάμπιδος κατεβάλλετο ἐνταῦθ',
ἴσως ἂν ἔφασαν οὗτοι δίκαιον εἶναι ἐπισκήπτεσθαί
μ' ἐκείνῳ· νῦν δ' οὔτε τὴν μαρτυρίαν ταύτην ἔχω,
οὑτοσί τε οἴεται δεῖν ἀθῷος εἶναι οὐδὲν ἐνέχυρον
47 καταλιπὼν ὧν πείθει ὑμᾶς ψηφίσασθαι. πῶς δ'
οὐκ ἂν εἴη ἄτοπον, εἰ αὐτοῦ Φορμίωνος ὁμολογοῦντος δανείσασθαι, φάσκοντος δ' ἀποδεδωκέναι,
τὸ μὲν ὁμολογούμενον ὑπ' αὐτοῦ τούτου ἄκυρον
ποιήσαιτε, τὸ δ' ἀμφισβητούμενον κύριον ψηφίσαισθε; καὶ ὁ μὲν Λάμπις, ᾧ οὗτος σκήπτεται
μάρτυρι, μαρτυρεῖ ἔξαρνος γενόμενος τὸ ἐξ ἀρχῆς
ὡς οὐκ ἀπείληφε τὸ χρυσίον· ὑμεῖς δὲ γνοίητε ὡς
ἀπείληφ' ἐκεῖνος, ᾧ οὐκ εἰσὶ μάρτυρες τοῦ πράγ-
48 ματος; καὶ ὅσα μὲν εἶπε μετὰ τῆς ἀληθείας, μὴ
χρήσαισθε τεκμηρίῳ, ἃ δ' ἐψεύσατο ὕστερον, ἐπειδὴ
διεφθάρη, πιστότερα ταῦθ' ὑπολάβοιτε εἶναι; καὶ

---

a When the arbitrator determined that the case before him
should be tried in court, he sealed in two jars, or boxes (ἐχῖνοι),
268

is an accomplice in the crime. Phormio claims to prove the payment on the testimony of Lampis alone, but I adduce Lampis and those who heard him declare that he had not received the money. Further, Phormio is in a position to bring my witnesses to trial, if he maintains that their testimony is false, but I have no means of dealing with his witnesses, who say they know that Lampis testified that he had received the money. If Lampis's own deposition had been put into court,[a] these men would perhaps have said that I ought to prosecute him for giving false testimony ; but, as it is, I have not this deposition, and Phormio thinks he should get off unscathed, since he has left no valid security for the verdict which he urges you to pronounce.[b] Would it 47 not indeed be absurd if, when Phormio admits that he borrowed, but alleges that he has made payment, you should make of none effect that which he himself admits and by your vote give effect to what is under dispute ? And if, when Lampis, on whose testimony my opponent relies, after at first denying that he had received the money, now testifies to the contrary, you should determine that he has received it, although there are no witnesses to support the fact ? And if you refuse to admit as proofs all that he 48 truthfully stated, and should count more worthy of belief the lies which he told after he had been cor-

___

[a] ll documents bearing upon the case. One of these was assigned to either party in the suit, and only such depositions, citations of laws, or challenges, as were contained in them, might be introduced at the trial.

[b] Phormio relies upon the testimony of Lampis. Under the circumstances it is impossible for me to sue Lampis for perjury, in which case Phormio might be prosecuted for collusion. He therefore hopes to get off scot-free.

269

μήν, ὦ ἄνδρες Ἀθηναῖοι, πολὺ δικαιότερόν ἐστι
τοῖς ἐξ ἀρχῆς ῥηθεῖσι τεκμαίρεσθαι μᾶλλον ἢ τοῖς
ὕστερον τεκταινομένοις. τὰ μὲν γὰρ οὐκ ἐκ παρα-
σκευῆς, ἀλλ' ἐκ τῆς ἀληθείας ἔλεγε, τὰ δ' ὕστερον
ψευδόμενος πρὸς τὸ συμφέρον αὑτῷ.

49 Ἀναμνήσθητε δ', ὦ ἄνδρες Ἀθηναῖοι, ὅτι οὐδ'
αὐτὸς ὁ Λάμπις ἔξαρνος ἐγένετο ὡς οὐκ εἴη εἰρηκὼς
ὅτι οὐκ ἀπείληφε τὸ χρυσίον, ἀλλ' εἰπεῖν μὲν
ὡμολόγει, οὐ μέντοι ἐντός γ' ὢν αὑτοῦ εἰπεῖν.
οὐκ οὖν ἄτοπον, εἰ τῆς ἐκείνου μαρτυρίας τὸ μὲν
[922] πρὸς τοῦ ἀποστεροῦντος πιστῶς ἀκούσεσθε, τὸ δ'
ὑπὲρ τῶν ἀποστερουμένων ἄπιστον ἔσται παρ' ὑμῖν;
50 μηδαμῶς, ὦ ἄνδρες δικασταί. ὑμεῖς γάρ ἐστε
οἱ αὐτοὶ οἱ τὸν ἐπιδεδανεισμένον ἐκ τοῦ ἐμπορίου
πολλὰ χρήματα καὶ τοῖς δανεισταῖς οὐ παρασχόντα
τὰς ὑποθήκας θανάτῳ ζημιώσαντες εἰσαγγελθέντα
ἐν τῷ δήμῳ, καὶ ταῦτα πολίτην ὑμέτερον ὄντα καὶ
51 πατρὸς ἐστρατηγηκότος. ἡγεῖσθε γὰρ τοὺς τοιούτους οὐ μόνον τοὺς ἐντυγχάνοντας ἀδικεῖν, ἀλλὰ καὶ
κοινῇ βλάπτειν τὸ ἐμπόριον ὑμῶν, εἰκότως. αἱ γὰρ
εὐπορίαι τοῖς ἐργαζομένοις οὐκ ἀπὸ τῶν δανειζο-
μένων, ἀλλ' ἀπὸ τῶν δανειζόντων εἰσί, καὶ οὔτε
ναῦν οὔτε ναύκληρον οὔτ' ἐπιβάτην ἔστ' ἀναχθῆναι,
52 τὸ τῶν δανειζόντων μέρος ἂν ἀφαιρεθῇ. ἐν μὲν
οὖν τοῖς νόμοις πολλαὶ καὶ καλαὶ βοήθειαί εἰσιν
αὐτοῖς· ὑμᾶς δὲ δεῖ συνεπανορθοῦντας φαίνεσθαι καὶ
μὴ συγχωροῦντας τοῖς πονηροῖς, ἵν' ὑμῖν ὡς
πλείστη ὠφέλεια παρὰ τὸ ἐμπόριον ᾖ. ἔσται δ',

rupted ? Verily, men of Athens, it is far more
just to draw conclusions from statements made in
the first instance than from those subsequently
fabricated ; for the former he made truthfully, and
not with ulterior purpose, while the later ones are lies
designed to further his interests.

Remember, men of Athens, that even Lampis him- 49
self never denied saying that he had not received
the money ; he admitted that he so stated, but
declared he was not in his right mind at the time.
But would it not be absurd for you to accept as
worthy of credit that part of his testimony which
favours the defrauding party, and to discredit that
which favours the party defrauded ? Nay, men of 50
the jury, I beg you, do not do this. You are the
same persons who punished with death, when he had
been impeached before the assembly, a man who
obtained large additional loans on your exchange,
and did not deliver to his creditors their securities,
though he was a citizen and the son of a man who
had been general. For you hold that such people 51
not only wrong those who do business with them,
but also do a public injury to your mart ; and you
are right in holding this view. For the resources
required by those who engage in trade come not
from those who borrow, but from those who lend ;
and neither ship nor shipowner nor passenger can
put to sea, if you take away the part contributed by
those who lend. In the laws there are many excellent 52
provisions for their protection. It is your duty to
show that you aid the laws in righting abuses, and
that you make no concession to wrongdoers, in
order that you may derive the greatest possible
benefit from your market. You will do so, if you

DEMOSTHENES

ἐὰν φυλάττητε τοὺς τὰ ἑαυτῶν προϊεμένους, κα
μὴ ἐπιτρέπητε ἀδικεῖσθαι ὑπὸ τῶν τοιούτω
θηρίων.

Ἐγὼ μὲν οὖν ὅσαπερ οἷός τ᾽ ἦν εἴρηκα· καλ
δὲ καὶ ἄλλον τινὰ τῶν φίλων, ἐὰν κελεύητε.

protect those who risk their money, and do not allow them to be defrauded by monsters such as these.

I have said all that it was in my power to say. But I am ready to call another of my friends, if you so bid.

AGAINST LACRITUS

INTRODUCTION

THE present speech is, like the preceding one, an answer to one delivered by the opposing party in support of the special plea in bar of action which he had entered; and, also as in the preceding case, it deals more largely with the facts of the suit itself than with the grounds for holding the special plea to be inadmissible.

Androcles, an Athenian, and Nausicrates, of Carystus in Euboea, had lent thirty minae to Artemo and Apollodorus, both of Phaselis in Bithynia. The terms on which the loan was made were that the borrowers should sail from Athens to Mendê or Scionê (towns in the peninsula of Pallenê in Chalcidicê) and there purchase and put on board the ship a cargo of three thousand jars of Mendaean wine, which they were to transport to the Pontus. Then, after disposing of the wine and shipping a return cargo, they were to sail back to Athens, and from the proceeds of the double voyage were to discharge the debt with interest. (The agreement is given in full in §§ 11-15 of the oration, although the genuineness of all such inserted documents is open to question.)

The speaker, Androcles, charges that the borrowers violated the terms of the agreement in that they shipped less than the prescribed quantity of wine; that they secured additional loans upon the security already pledged to himself and his partner; and that they failed to ship an adequate return cargo. Finally, when payment was demanded of them, they falsely asserted that the vessel had been wrecked.

Suit is therefore brought against Lacritus, the brother of Androcles, the latter himself having died in the interim. It is claimed that he, being the inheritor of his brother's estate, should also meet that brother's obligations; and it is further claimed that Lacritus had, at least verbally, guaranteed the performance of the agreement.

Lacritus enters a special plea on the ground that no contract had been made between Androcles and himself; and further declares that, having relinquished his claim to his brother's property, he cannot be held liable for his debts.

Lacritus was a pupil of Isocrates, and § 41 of the speech shows that the speaker sought to make capital out of the general unpopularity of the sophists as a class; for in the popular mind a teacher of rhetoric would be regarded as belonging to that class.

Consult further Schaefer, iii.² pp. 286 ff., and Blass, iii. pp. 562 ff.

XXXV

ΠΡΟΣ ΤΗΝ ΛΑΚΡΙΤΟΥ ΠΑΡΑΓΡΑΦΗΝ

Οὐδὲν καινὸν διαπράττονται οἱ Φασηλῖται, ὦ
ἄνδρες δικασταί, ἀλλ' ἅπερ εἰώθασιν. οὗτοι γὰρ
δεινότατοι μέν εἰσι δανείσασθαι χρήματ' ἐν τῷ
ἐμπορίῳ, ἐπειδὰν δὲ λάβωσι καὶ συγγραφὴν συγ-
γράψωνται ναυτικήν, εὐθὺς ἐπελάθοντο καὶ τῶν
συγγραφῶν καὶ τῶν νόμων καὶ ὅτι δεῖ ἀποδοῦναι
2 αὐτοὺς ἃ ἔλαβον, καὶ οἴονται, ἐὰν ἀποδῶσιν, ὥσπερ
[924] τῶν ἰδίων τι τῶν ἑαυτῶν ἀπολωλεκέναι, ἀλλ' ἀντὶ
τοῦ ἀποδοῦναι σοφίσματα εὑρίσκουσι καὶ παραγραφὰς καὶ προφάσεις, καὶ εἰσὶ πονηρότατοι ἀνθρώπων καὶ ἀδικώτατοι. τεκμήριον δὲ τούτου·
πολλῶν γὰρ ἀφικνουμένων εἰς τὸ ὑμέτερον ἐμπόριον
καὶ Ἑλλήνων καὶ βαρβάρων, πλείους δίκαι εἰσὶν
ἑκάστοτε αὐτῶν τῶν Φασηλιτῶν ἢ τῶν ἄλλων
3 ἁπάντων. οὗτοι μὲν οὖν τοιοῦτοί εἰσιν· ἐγὼ δ', ὦ
ἄνδρες δικασταί, χρήματα δανείσας Ἀρτέμωνι τῷ
τούτου ἀδελφῷ κατὰ τοὺς ἐμπορικοὺς νόμους, εἰς
τὸν Πόντον καὶ πάλιν Ἀθήναζε, τελευτήσαντος
ἐκείνου πρὶν ἀποδοῦναί μοι τὰ χρήματα, Λακρίτῳ
τουτῳὶ εἴληχα τὴν δίκην ταύτην κατὰ τοὺς αὐτοὺς

---

[a] Phaselis was a town in Bithynia, on the southern coast of
Asia Minor.

[b] The courts for the settlement of maritime cases sat from

278

XXXV

ANDROCLES AGAINST LACRITUS IN REPLY TO THE LATTER'S SPECIAL PLEA

THE Phaselites,[a] men of the jury, are up to no new tricks ; they are merely doing what it is their wont to do. For they are the cleverest people at borrowing money on your exchange ; but, as soon as they get it and have drawn up a maritime contract, they straightway forget the contract and the laws, and that they are under obligation to pay back what they have received. They consider that, if they pay 2 their debts, it is like having lost something of their own private property, and, instead of paying, they invent sophisms, and special pleas, and pretexts ; and are the most unprincipled and dishonest of men. Here is a proof of this. Out of the hosts of people, both Greeks and barbarians, who frequent your exchange, the Phaselites alone have more lawsuits, whenever the courts sit,[b] than all others put together. That is the sort of people they are. But I, men of the 3 jury, lent money to Artemo, this fellow's brother, in accordance with the commercial laws for a voyage to Pontus and back. As he died before having repaid me the money I have brought this suit against Lacritus here in accordance with the same laws

September to April, the period when the sea was closed to navigation. See Oration XXXIII. § 23.

νόμους τούτους, καθ᾽ οὕσπερ τὸ συμβόλαιον ἐποιη-
4 σάμην, ἀδελφῷ ὄντι τούτῳ ἐκείνου καὶ ἔχοντι
ἅπαντα τὰ Ἀρτέμωνος, καὶ ὅσ᾽ ἐνθάδε κατέλιπε
καὶ ὅσα ἦν αὐτῷ ἐν τῇ Φασήλιδι, καὶ κληρονόμῳ
ὄντι τῶν ἐκείνου ἁπάντων, καὶ οὐκ ἂν ἔχοντος
τούτου δεῖξαι νόμον, ὅστις αὐτῷ δίδωσιν ἐξουσίαν
ἔχειν μὲν τὰ τοῦ ἀδελφοῦ καὶ διῳκηκέναι ὅπως
ἐδόκει αὐτῷ, μὴ ἀποδιδόναι δὲ τἀλλότρια χρήματα,
ἀλλὰ λέγειν νῦν ὅτι οὐκ ἔστι κληρονόμος, ἀλλ᾽
5 ἀφίσταται τῶν ἐκείνου. ἡ μὲν τουτουὶ Λακρίτου
πονηρία τοιαύτη ἐστίν· ἐγὼ δ᾽ ὑμῶν δέομαι, ὦ
ἄνδρες δικασταί, εὐνοϊκῶς ἀκοῦσαί μου περὶ τοῦ
πράγματος τουτουί· κἂν ἐλέγξω αὐτὸν ἀδικοῦντα
ἡμᾶς τε τοὺς δανείσαντας καὶ ὑμᾶς οὐδὲν ἧττον,
βοηθεῖτε ἡμῖν τὰ δίκαια.

6 Ἐγὼ γάρ, ὦ ἄνδρες δικασταί, αὐτὸς μὲν οὐδ᾽
ὁπωστιοῦν ἐγνώριζον τοὺς ἀνθρώπους τούτους·
[925] Θρασυμήδης δ᾽ ὁ Διοφάντου υἱός, ἐκείνου τοῦ
Σφηττίου, καὶ Μελάνωπος ὁ ἀδελφὸς αὐτοῦ ἐπι-
τήδειοί μοί εἰσι, καὶ χρώμεθ᾽ ἀλλήλοις ὡς οἷόν
τε μάλιστα. οὗτοι προσῆλθόν μοι μετὰ Λακρίτου
τουτουί, ὁπόθεν δήποτε ἐγνωρισμένοι τούτῳ (οὐ
7 γὰρ οἶδα), καὶ ἐδέοντό μου δανεῖσαι χρήματ᾽ εἰς
τὸν Πόντον Ἀρτέμωνι τῷ τούτου ἀδελφῷ καὶ
Ἀπολλοδώρῳ, ὅπως ἂν ἐνεργοὶ ὦσιν, οὐδὲν εἰδώς,
ὦ ἄνδρες δικασταί, οὐδ᾽ ὁ Θρασυμήδης τὴν τούτων
πονηρίαν, ἀλλ᾽ οἰόμενος εἶναι ἐπιεικεῖς ἀνθρώπους
καὶ οἱοίπερ προσεποιοῦντο καὶ ἔφασαν εἶναι, καὶ
ἡγούμενος ποιήσειν αὐτοὺς πάντα ὅσαπερ ὑπ-
8 ισχνοῦντο καὶ ἀνεδέχετο Λάκριτος οὑτοσί. πλεῖστον δ᾽ ἄρ᾽ ἦν ἐψευσμένος, καὶ οὐδὲν ᾔδει οἵοις
θηρίοις ἐπλησίαζε τοῖς ἀνθρώποις τούτοις. κἀγὼ
280

under which I made the contract, since he is the 4
brother of Artemo and has possession of all his
property, both all that he left here and all that he
had at Phaselis, and is the heir to his whole estate ;
and since he can show no law which gives him the
right to hold his brother's property and to have administered it as he pleased, and yet to refuse to pay
back money which belongs to others and to say
now that he is not the heir, but has nothing to do
with the dead man's affairs. Such is the rascality of 5
this fellow, Lacritus; but I beg of you, men of the
jury, to give me a favourable hearing in regard to this
matter and, if I prove to you that he has wronged
us, who lent the money, and you as well, to render
us the aid that is our due.

I myself, men of the jury, had not the slightest 6
acquaintance with these men ; but Thrasymedes the
son of Diophantus, that well-known Sphettian,[a] and
Melanopus, his brother, are friends of mine, and we
are on the most intimate terms possible. These
men came up to me with Lacritus here, whose
acquaintance they had made in some way or other—
how, I do not know,—and asked me to lend money 7
to Artemo, this man's brother, and to Apollodorus for a voyage to Pontus, that they might be
engaged in a trading enterprise. Thrasymedes like
myself knew nothing of the rascality of these people,
but supposed them to be honourable men and such
as they pretended and declared themselves to be ;
and that they would do all that they promised and
that this fellow Lacritus undertook that they should
do. He was utterly deceived, and had no idea what 8
monsters these men were with whom he was associat-

---

[a] Sphettus was a deme of the tribe Acamantis.

DEMOSTHENES

πεισθεὶς ὑπὸ τοῦ Θρασυμήδους καὶ τοῦ ἀδελφοῦ
αὐτοῦ, καὶ Λακρίτου τουτουὶ ἀναδεχομένου μοι
πάντ' ἔσεσθαι τὰ δίκαια παρὰ τῶν ἀδελφῶν τῶν
αὐτοῦ, ἐδάνεισα μετὰ ξένου τινὸς ἡμετέρου Καρυ-
9 στίου τριάκοντα μνᾶς ἀργυρίου. βούλομαι οὖν, ὦ
ἄνδρες δικασταί, τῆς συγγραφῆς ἀκοῦσαι ὑμᾶς
πρῶτον, καθ' ἣν ἐδανείσαμεν τὰ χρήματα, καὶ
τῶν μαρτύρων τῶν παραγενομένων τῷ δανείσματι·
ἔπειτα περὶ τῶν ἄλλων ἐπιδείξομεν, οἷα ἐτοιχω-
ρύχησαν οὗτοι περὶ τὸ δάνειον.
Λέγε τὴν συγγραφήν, εἶτα τὰς μαρτυρίας.

ΣΥΓΓΡΑΦΗ

10 Ἐδάνεισαν Ἀνδροκλῆς Σφήττιος καὶ Ναυσικράτης
Καρύστιος Ἀρτέμωνι καὶ Ἀπολλοδώρῳ Φασηλίταις
[926] δραχμὰς ἀργυρίου τρισχιλίας Ἀθήνηθεν εἰς Μένδην
ἢ Σκιώνην, καὶ ἐντεῦθεν εἰς Βόσπορον, ἐὰν δὲ βούλωνται, τῆς ἐπ' ἀριστερὰ μέχρι Βορυσθένους, καὶ
πάλιν Ἀθήναζε, ἐπὶ διακοσίαις εἴκοσι πέντε τὰς χιλίας,
ἐὰν δὲ μετ' Ἀρκτοῦρον ἐκπλεύσωσιν ἐκ τοῦ Πόντου
ἐφ' Ἱερόν, ἐπὶ τριακοσίαις τὰς χιλίας, ἐπὶ οἴνου
κεραμίοις Μενδαίοις τρισχιλίοις, ὃς πλεύσεται ἐκ
Μένδης ἢ Σκιώνης ἐν τῇ εἰκοσόρῳ, ἣν Ὑβλήσιος
11 ναυκληρεῖ. ὑποτιθέασι δὲ ταῦτα, οὐκ ὀφείλοντες ἐπὶ
τούτοις ἄλλῳ οὐδενὶ οὐδὲν ἀργύριον, οὐδ' ἐπιδανείσονται. καὶ ἀπάξουσι τὰ χρήματα τὰ ἐκ τοῦ Πόντου
ἀντιφορτισθέντα Ἀθήναζε πάλιν ἐν τῷ αὐτῷ πλοίῳ
ἅπαντα. σωθέντων δὲ τῶν χρημάτων Ἀθήναζε, ἀποδώσουσιν οἱ δανεισάμενοι τοῖς δανείσασι τὸ γιγνόμενον

---

* Carystus was a town in Euboea.
ᵇ Towns in the peninsula of Pallenê, in Chalcidicê.
Weather conditions would determine which port should be
entered.

ing. I allowed myself to be persuaded by Thrasymedes and his brother, and upon the assurance given
me by this Lacritus, that his brothers would do everything that was right, I, with the help of a Carystian,[a]
who was a friend of mine, lent thirty minae in silver.
I wish you first, men of the jury, to hear the agree- 9
ment in accordance with which we lent the money,
and the witnesses who were present when the loan
was made ; after that I shall take up the remaining
features of the case, and show you how like burglars
they acted in the matter of this loan.

Read the agreement, and then the depositions.

THE AGREEMENT

Androcles of Sphettus and Nausicrates of Carystus lent to 10
Artemo and Apollodorus, both of Phaselis, three thousand
drachmae in silver for a voyage from Athens to Mendê or
Scionê,[b] and thence to Bosporus—or if they so choose, for
a voyage to the left parts of the Pontus as far as the Bory-
sthenes,[c] and thence back to Athens, on interest at the rate of
two hundred and twenty-five drachmae on the thousand ; but,
if they should sail out from Pontus to Hieron[d] after the
rising of Arcturus,[e] at three hundred on the thousand, on
the security of three thousand jars of wine of Mendê, which
shall be conveyed from Mendê or Scionê in the twenty-oared
ship of which Hyblesius is owner. They give these goods as 11
security, owing no money upon them to any other person,
nor will they make any additional loan upon this security ;
and they agree to bring back to Athens in the same vessel
all the goods put on board in Pontus as a return cargo ; and,
if the goods are brought safe to Athens, the borrowers are to
pay to the lenders the money due in accordance with the

---

[c] The modern Dnieper.
[d] This was a place, called Hieron from a temple of Zeus,
at the entrance to the Thracian Bosporus on the Asiatic side.
[e] About the middle of September. This was considered
a perilous season for navigation ; hence the higher rate of
interest.

ἀργύριον κατὰ τὴν συγγραφὴν ἡμερῶν εἴκοσιν, ἀφ' ἧς
ἂν ἔλθωσιν Ἀθήναζε, ἐντελὲς πλὴν ἐκβολῆς, ἧς ἂν οἱ
σύμπλοι ψηφισάμενοι κοινῇ ἐκβάλωνται, καὶ ἄν τι
πολεμίοις ἀποτείσωσιν· τῶν δ' ἄλλων ἁπάντων ἐντελές.
καὶ παρέξουσι τοῖς δανείσασι τὴν ὑποθήκην ἀνέπαφον
κρατεῖν, ἕως ἂν ἀποδῶσι τὸ γιγνόμενον ἀργύριον κατὰ
12 τὴν συγγραφήν. ἐὰν δὲ μὴ ἀποδῶσιν ἐν τῷ συγκειμένῳ
χρόνῳ, τὰ ὑποκείμενα τοῖς δανείσασιν ἐξέστω ὑποθεῖναι
καὶ ἀποδόσθαι τῆς ὑπαρχούσης τιμῆς· καὶ ἐάν τι
ἐλλείπῃ τοῦ ἀργυρίου, ὃ[1] δεῖ γενέσθαι τοῖς δανείσασι
κατὰ τὴν συγγραφήν, παρὰ Ἀρτέμωνος καὶ Ἀπολλοδώρου ἔστω ἡ πρᾶξις τοῖς δανείσασι καὶ ἐκ τῶν τούτων
ἁπάντων, καὶ ἐγγείων καὶ ναυτικῶν, πανταχοῦ ὅπου ἂν
[927] ὦσι, καθάπερ δίκην ὠφληκότων καὶ ὑπερημέρων ὄντων,
13 καὶ ἑνὶ ἑκατέρῳ τῶν δανεισάντων καὶ ἀμφοτέροις. ἐὰν
δὲ μὴ εἰσβάλωσι, μείναντες ἐπὶ κυνὶ ἡμέρας δέκα ἐν
Ἑλλησπόντῳ, ἐξελόμενοι ὅπου ἂν μὴ σῦλαι ὦσιν Ἀθηναίοις, καὶ ἐντεῦθεν καταπλεύσαντες Ἀθήναζε τοὺς τόκους
ἀποδόντων τοὺς πέρυσι γραφέντας εἰς τὴν συγγραφήν.
ἐὰν δέ τι ἡ ναῦς πάθῃ ἀνήκεστον ἐν ᾗ ἂν πλέῃ τὰ
χρήματα, σωτηρία δ' ἔσται τῶν ὑποκειμένων, τὰ περιγενόμενα κοινὰ ἔστω τοῖς δανείσασιν. κυριώτερον δὲ
περὶ τούτων ἄλλο μηδὲν εἶναι τῆς συγγραφῆς.

Μάρτυρες Φορμίων Πειραιεύς, Κηφισόδοτος Βοιώτιος,
Ἡλιόδωρος Πιθεύς.

14 Λέγε δὴ καὶ τὰς μαρτυρίας.

MAPTYPIA

Ἀρχενομίδης Ἀρχεδάμαντος Ἀναγυράσιος μαρτυρεῖ
συνθήκας παρ' ἑαυτῷ καταθέσθαι Ἀνδροκλέα Σφήττιον,

¹ ὃ] οὗ Blass.

ᵃ The ten days following the rising of Sirius—July 25
to August 5—were, it was thought, apt to be stormy.
ᵇ In such ports Athenian ships would be safe.

agreement within twenty days after they shall have arrived at Athens, without deduction save for such jettison as the passengers shall have made by common agreement, or for money paid to enemies; but without deduction for any other loss. And they shall deliver to the lenders in their entirety the goods offered as security to be under their absolute control until such time as they shall themselves have paid the money due in accordance with the agreement. And, if they 12 shall not pay it within the time agreed upon, it shall be lawful for the lenders to pledge the goods or even to sell them for such price as they can get; and if the proceeds fall short of the sum which the lenders should receive in accordance with the agreement, it shall be lawful for the lenders, whether severally or jointly, to collect the amount by proceeding against Artemo and Apollodorus, and against all their property whether on land or sea, wheresoever it may be, precisely as if judgement had been rendered against them and they had defaulted in payment. And, if they do not 13 enter Pontus, but remain in the Hellespont ten days after the rising of the dog-star,[a] and disembark their goods at a port where the Athenians have no right of reprisals,[b] and from thence complete their voyage to Athens, let them pay the interest written into the contract the year before.[c] And if the vessel in which the goods shall be conveyed suffers aught beyond repair, but the security is saved, let whatever is saved be the joint property of the lenders. And in regard to these matters nothing shall have greater effect than the agreement.[d]

Witnesses: Phormio of Peiraeus, Cephisodotus of Boeotia, Heliodorus of Pitthus.[e]

Now read the depositions.   14

The Deposition

Archenomides, son of Archedamas, of Anagyrus, deposes that Androcles of Sphettus, Nausicrates of Carystus, and

---

[c] If the return voyage is delayed until the legal year has expired (at the summer solstice) the rate of interest is to remain unchanged.

[d] That is, the terms of the contract shall be absolute; compare § 39.

[e] Pitthus (Pithus) was a deme of the tribe Cecropis.

Ναυσικράτην Καρύστιον, Ἀρτέμωνα, Ἀπολλόδωρον Φασηλίτας, καὶ εἶναι παρ' ἑαυτῷ ἔτι κειμένην τὴν συγγραφήν.

Λέγε δὴ καὶ τὴν τῶν παραγενομένων μαρτυρίαν.

ΜΑΡΤΥΡΙΑ

Θεόδοτος ἰσοτελής, Χαρῖνος Ἐπιχάρους Λευκονοεύς, Φορμίων Κτησιφῶντος Πειραιεύς, Κηφισόδοτος Βοιώτιος, Ἡλιόδωρος Πιθεὺς μαρτυροῦσι παρεῖναι, ὅτ' ἐδάνεισεν Ἀνδροκλῆς Ἀπολλοδώρῳ καὶ Ἀρτέμωνι ἀργυρίου τρισχιλίας δραχμάς, καὶ εἰδέναι τὴν συγγραφὴν καταθεμένους παρὰ Ἀρχενομίδῃ Ἀναγυρασίῳ.

15 Κατὰ τὴν συγγραφὴν ταύτην, ὦ ἄνδρες δικασταί, ἐδάνεισα τὰ χρήματα Ἀρτέμωνι τῷ τούτου ἀδελφῷ, [928] κελεύοντος τούτου καὶ ἀναδεχομένου ἅπαντ' ἔσεσθαί μοι τὰ δίκαια κατὰ τὴν συγγραφήν, καθ' ἣν ἐδάνεισα τούτου αὐτοῦ γράφοντος καὶ συσσημηναμένου, ἐπειδὴ ἐγράφη. οἱ μὲν γὰρ ἀδελφοὶ οἱ τούτου ἔτι νεώτεροι ἦσαν, μειράκια κομιδῇ, οὑτοσὶ δὲ Λάκριτος Φασηλίτης, μέγα πρᾶγμα, Ἰσοκράτους 16 μαθητής· οὗτος ἦν ὁ πάντα διοικῶν, καὶ ἑαυτῷ με τὸν νοῦν προσέχειν ἐκέλευεν· αὐτὸς γὰρ ἔφη ποιήσειν μοι τὰ δίκαια ἅπαντα καὶ ἐπιδημήσειν Ἀθήνησι, τὸν δ' ἀδελφὸν τὸν αὑτοῦ Ἀρτέμωνα πλεύσεσθαι ἐπὶ τοῖς χρήμασι. καὶ τότε μέν, ὦ ἄνδρες δικασταί, ὅτ' ἐβούλετο τὰ χρήματα λαβεῖν παρ' ἡμῶν, καὶ ἀδελφὸς ἔφη εἶναι καὶ κοινωνὸς τοῦ Ἀρτέμωνος, καὶ λόγους θαυμασίως ὡς πιθανοὺς 17 ἔλεγεν· ἐπειδὴ δὲ τάχιστα ἐγκρατεῖς ἐγένοντο τοῦ ἀργυρίου, τοῦτο μὲν διενείμαντο καὶ ἐχρῶντο ὅ τι ἐδόκει τούτοις, κατὰ δὲ τὴν συγγραφὴν τὴν ναυ-

Artemo and Apollodorus, both of Phaselis, deposited articles of agreement with him, and that the agreement is still in custody in his hands.

Read also the deposition of those who were present.

THE DEPOSITION

Theodotus, privileged alien, Charinus, son of Epichares, of Leuconium, Phormio, son of Ctephisophon, of Peiraeus, Cephisodotus of Boeotia and Heliodorus of Pitthus depose that they were present when Androcles lent to Artemo three thousand drachmae in silver, and that they know they deposited the agreement with Archenomides of Anagyrus.

In accordance with this agreement, men of the 15 jury, I lent the money to Artemo, this man's brother, at the request of Lacritus, and upon his engaging that I should receive everything that was my due in accordance with the agreement under which the loan was made. Lacritus himself drew up the agreement and joined in sealing it after it was written ; for his brothers were still youngish, in fact mere boys, but he was Lacritus, of Phaselis, a personage of note, a pupil of Isocrates.[a] It was he who managed 16 the whole matter, and he bade me look to him ; for he declared that he would himself do everything that was right for me, and that he would stay in Athens, while his brother Artemo would sail in charge of the goods. At that time, men of the jury, when he wanted to get the money from us, he declared that he was both the brother and the partner of Artemo, and spoke with wondrous persuasiveness ; but, as 17 soon as they got possession of the money, they divided it, and used it as they pleased ; while as for the maritime agreement on the terms of which they

---

[a] The noted orator, essayist, and teacher of rhetoric.

τικήν, καθ' ἣν ἔλαβον τὰ χρήματα, οὔτε μέγα οὔτε
μικρὸν ἔπραττον, ὡς αὐτὸ τὸ ἔργον ἐδήλωσεν.
οὑτοσὶ δὲ Λάκριτος ἁπάντων ἦν τούτων ὁ ἐξηγητής.
καθ' ἕκαστον δὲ τῶν γεγραμμένων ἐν τῇ συγγραφῇ
ἐπιδείξω τούτους οὐδ' ὁτιοῦν πεποιηκότας ὑγιές.

18 Πρῶτον μὲν γὰρ γέγραπται ὅτι ἐπ' οἴνου
κεραμίοις τρισχιλίοις ἐδανείσαντο παρ' ἡμῶν τὰς
τριάκοντα μνᾶς, ὡς ὑπαρχούσης αὐτοῖς ὑποθήκης
ἑτέρων τριάκοντα μνῶν, ὥστ' εἰς τάλαντον ἀργυρίου τὴν τιμὴν εἶναι τοῦ οἴνου καθισταμένην, σὺν
τοῖς ἀναλώμασιν, οἷς ἔδει ἀναλίσκεσθαι εἰς τὴν
[929] κατασκευὴν τὴν περὶ τὸν οἶνον· τὰ δὲ τρισχίλια
κεράμια ἄγεσθαι ταῦτα εἰς τὸν Πόντον ἐν τῇ
19 εἰκοσόρῳ, ἣν Ὑβλήσιος ἐναυκλήρει. γέγραπται
μὲν ταῦτα ἐν τῇ συγγραφῇ, ὦ ἄνδρες δικασταί,
ἧς ὑμεῖς ἀκηκόατε· οὗτοι δ' ἀντὶ τῶν τρισχιλίων
κεραμίων οὐδὲ πεντακόσια κεράμια εἰς τὸ πλοῖον
ἐνέθεντο, ἀλλ' ἀντὶ τοῦ ἠγοράσθαι αὐτοῖς τὸν οἶνον,
ὅσον προσῆκε, τοῖς χρήμασιν ἐχρῶντο ὅ τι ἐδόκει
τούτοις, τὰ δὲ κεράμια τὰ τρισχίλια οὐδ' ἐμέλλησαν
οὐδὲ διενοήθησαν ἐνθέσθαι εἰς τὸ πλοῖον κατὰ τὴν
συγγραφήν.

Ὅτι δ' ἀληθῆ ταῦτα λέγω, λαβὲ τὴν μαρτυρίαν
τῶν συμπλεόντων ἐν τῷ αὐτῷ πλοίῳ τούτοις.

ΜΑΡΤΥΡΙΑ

20 Ἐρασικλῆς μαρτυρεῖ κυβερνᾶν τὴν ναῦν ἣν
Ὑβλήσιος ἐναυκλήρει, καὶ εἰδέναι Ἀπολλόδωρον ἀγόμενον ἐν τῷ πλοίῳ οἴνου Μενδαίου κεράμια τετρακόσια

---

[a] The κεράμιον held about six gallons.
[b] Perhaps a bit of carelessness on the part of the writer

secured the money, in no matter great or small did they carry out its provisions, as the facts themselves make clear. And in all these things this fellow Lacritus was the prime mover. I shall take up the clauses of the contract one by one, and shall show that in no single instance have these men done what was right.

In the first place it stands written that they 18 borrowed from us thirty minae on three thousand jars [a] of wine, giving out that they possessed security for thirty minae more, so that the price of the wine would amount to a talent of money, including the expenses to be incurred in the stowage of the wine; and that these three thousand jars were to be conveyed to Pontus in the twenty-oared ship, of which Hyblesius was owner. These provisions, men of the 19 jury, stand written in the agreement which you have heard. But instead of three thousand jars, these men did not put even five hundred on board the boat; and instead of having bought the quantity of wine which they should have, they used the money in whatever way they pleased; as for those three thousand jars which the agreement called for, they never meant nor intended to put them on board.

To prove that these statements of mine are true, take the deposition of those who sailed with them in the same ship.

THE DEPOSITION

Erasicles deposes that he was pilot of the ship of which 20 Hyblesius was owner, and that to his knowledge Apollodorus [b] was conveying in the ship four hundred and fifty

of this spurious deposition. In § 16 we are told that it was Artemo who was to sail with the cargo.

πεντήκοντα, καὶ οὐ πλείω· ἄλλο δὲ μηδὲν ἀγώγιμον
ἄγεσθαι ἐν τῷ πλοίῳ Ἀπολλόδωρον εἰς τὸν Πόντον.

Ἱππίας Ἀθηνίππου Ἁλικαρνασσεὺς μαρτυρεῖ συμπλεῖν ἐν τῇ Ὑβλησίου νηὶ διοπεύων τὴν ναῦν, καὶ
εἰδέναι Ἀπολλόδωρον τὸν Φασηλίτην ἀγόμενον ἐν τῷ
πλοίῳ ἐκ Μένδης εἰς τὸν Πόντον οἴνου Μενδαίου κεράμια
τετρακόσια πεντήκοντα, ἄλλο δὲ μηδὲν φορτίον.

Πρὸς τούσδ' ἐξεμαρτύρησεν Ἀρχιάδης Μνησωνίδου
Ἀχαρνεύς· Σώστρατος Φιλίππου Ἱστιαιόθεν, Εὐμάριχος
Εὐβοίου Ἱστιαιόθεν, Φιλτιάδης Κτησίου Ξυπεταιῶν,
Διονύσιος Δημοκρατίδου Χολλείδης.

21 Περὶ μὲν οὖν τοῦ πλήθους τοῦ οἴνου, ὅσον ἔδει
αὐτοὺς ἐνθέσθαι εἰς τὸ πλοῖον, ταῦτα διεπράξαντο,
[930] καὶ ἤρξαντο εὐθὺς ἐντεῦθεν ἀπὸ τοῦ πρώτου γε-
γραμμένου παραβαίνειν καὶ μὴ ποιεῖν τὰ γεγραμμένα. μετὰ δὲ ταῦτ' ἔστιν ἐν τῇ συγγραφῇ, ὅτι
ὑποτιθέασι ταῦτ' ἐλεύθερα καὶ οὐδενὶ οὐδὲν ὀφείλοντες, καὶ ὅτι οὐδ' ἐπιδανείσονται ἐπὶ τούτοις παρ'
22 οὐδενός. ταῦτα διαρρήδην γέγραπται, ὦ ἄνδρες
δικασταί. οὗτοι δὲ τί ἐποίησαν; ἀμελήσαντες τῶν
γεγραμμένων ἐν τῇ συγγραφῇ δανείζονται παρά
τινος νεανίσκου, ἐξαπατήσαντες ὡς οὐδενὶ οὐδὲν
ὀφείλοντες· καὶ ἡμᾶς τε παρεκρούσαντο καὶ ἔλαθον
δανεισάμενοι ἐπὶ τοῖς ἡμετέροις, ἐκεῖνόν τε τὸν
νεανίσκον τὸν δανείσαντα ἐξηπάτησαν ὡς ἐπ' ἐλευ-
θέροις τοῖς χρήμασι δανειζόμενοι· τοιαῦτα τούτων
ἐστὶ τὰ κακουργήματα. ταῦτα δὲ πάντ' ἐστὶ τὰ
σοφίσματα Λακρίτου τουτουί.

---

[a] Affidavits, taken down in writing in the presence of
witnesses appointed for the purpose, and verified by them
under oath, were accepted as evidence when the individuals
could not be present in person.

jars of Mendaean wine, and no more ; and that Apollodorus conveyed no other cargo in the ship to Pontus.

Hippias, son of Athenippus, of Halicarnassus, deposes that he too sailed in the ship of Hyblesius as supercargo of the vessel and that to his knowledge Apollodorus of Phaselis was conveying in the ship from Mendê to Pontus four hundred and fifty jars of Mendaean wine, and no other cargo.

In addition to these, written affidavits [a] were submitted by Archiades, son of Mnesonidas, of Acharnae, Sostratus, son of Philip, of Histiaea, Eumarichus, son of Euboeus, of Histiaea, Philtiades, son of Ctesias, of Xypetê, and Dionysius, son of Democratides, of Cholleidae.[b]

In regard, then, to the quantity of wine which it **21** was their duty to put on board the ship that was what they contrived to do ; and from this point they began from its very first clause to violate the agreement and to fail to perform what it required. The next clause that stands written in the agreement states that they pledge these goods free from all encumbrances ; that they owe nothing to anyone upon them ; and that they will not secure further loans upon them from anyone. This is expressly stated, **22** men of the jury. But what have these men done ? Disregarding the terms of the agreement they borrow money from a certain youth, whom they deceived by stating that they owed nothing to anybody. Thus they cheated us, and without our knowledge borrowed money upon our security, and they also deceived that young man who lent them the money by alleging that the goods upon which they borrowed from him were unencumbered. Such are the rascalities of these men, and they are all clever devisings of this man Lacritus.

[b] Acharnae was a deme of the tribe Oeneïs, Xypetê a deme of the tribe Cecropis, and Cholleidae a deme of the tribe Leontis.

"Ότι δ' ἀληθῆ λέγω καὶ ἐπεδανείσαντο χρήματα
παρὰ τὴν συγγραφήν, μαρτυρίαν ἀναγνώσεται ὑμῖν
23 αὐτοῦ τοῦ ἐπιδανείσαντος. λέγε τὴν μαρτυρίαν.

ΜΑΡΤΥΡΙΑ

"Ἄρατος Ἁλικαρνασσεὺς μαρτυρεῖ δανεῖσαι Ἀπολλοδώρῳ ἕνδεκα μνᾶς ἀργυρίου ἐπὶ τῇ ἐμπορίᾳ, ἣν ἦγεν
ἐν τῇ Ὑβλησίου νηὶ εἰς τὸν Πόντον, καὶ τοῖς ἐκεῖθεν
ἀνταγορασθεῖσι, καὶ μὴ εἰδέναι αὐτὸν δεδανεισμένον
παρὰ Ἀνδροκλέους ἀργύριον· οὐ γὰρ ἂν δανεῖσαι αὐτὸς
Ἀπολλοδώρῳ τὸ ἀργύριον.

24 Αἱ μὲν πανουργίαι τοιαῦται τῶν ἀνθρώπων τούτων εἰσίν. γέγραπται δὲ μετὰ ταῦτα ἐν τῇ συγγραφῇ, ὦ ἄνδρες δικασταί, ἐπειδὰν ἀποδῶνται ἐν
[931] τῷ Πόντῳ ἃ ἦγον, πάλιν ἀνταγοράζειν χρήματα καὶ
ἀντιφορτίζεσθαι καὶ ἀπάγειν Ἀθήναζε τὰ ἀντιφορτισθέντα, καὶ ἐπειδὰν ἀφίκωνται Ἀθήναζε, ἀποδοῦναι εἴκοσιν ἡμερῶν τὸ ἀργύριον ἡμῖν δόκιμον·
ἕως δ' ἂν ἀποδῶσι, κρατεῖν τῶν χρημάτων ἡμᾶς,
καὶ ἀνέπαφα παρέχειν τούτους, ἕως ἂν ἀπολάβωμεν.
25 γέγραπται μὲν ταῦτα οὑτωσὶ ἀκριβῶς ἐν τῇ συγ-
γραφῇ· οὗτοι δ', ὦ ἄνδρες δικασταί, ἐνταῦθα καὶ
ἐπεδείξαντο μάλιστα τὴν ὕβριν καὶ τὴν ἀναίδειαν
τὴν ἑαυτῶν, καὶ ὅτι οὐδὲ μικρὸν προσεῖχον τοῖς
γράμμασι τοῖς γεγραμμένοις ἐν τῇ συγγραφῇ, ἀλλ'
ἡγοῦντο εἶναι τὴν συγγραφὴν ἄλλως ὕθλον καὶ
φλυαρίαν. οὔτε γὰρ ἀντηγόρασαν οὐδὲν ἐν τῷ
Πόντῳ οὔτε ἀντεφορτίσαντο ὥστε ἄγειν Ἀθήναζε·
ἡμεῖς τε οἱ δανείσαντες τὰ χρήματα ἡκόντων αὐτῶν

---

^a Certified, that is, as to weight and fineness. Tampering
with gold and silver coins seems not to be a merely modern
device.

To prove that I am speaking the truth and that they did borrow additional sums contrary to the agreement, the clerk shall read you the deposition of the man himself who made the additional loan. Read the deposition. **23**

THE DEPOSITION

Aratus of Halicarnassus deposes that he lent to Apollodorus eleven minae in silver on the merchandise which he was conveying in the ship of Hyblesius to Pontus, and on the goods purchased there as a return cargo ; and that he was unaware that the defendant had borrowed money from Androcles ; for otherwise he would not himself have lent the money to Apollodorus.

Such are the rascalities of these men. But after **24** this it stands written in the agreement, men of the jury, that when they should have sold in Pontus the goods which they brought thither, they should purchase with the proceeds other goods as a return cargo, and should bring this return cargo back to Athens ; and that when they should have reached Athens, they should within twenty days repay us in certified coin[a] ; and that pending the payment we should have control of the goods, and that they should deliver them to us in their entirety until we should get back our money. These terms stand **25** written thus precisely in the agreement. But these people, men of the jury, have here shown most strikingly their own insolence and shamelessness, and that they paid not the slightest heed to the terms written in the agreement ; but regarded the agreement as mere trash and nonsense. For they neither purchased any other goods in Pontus nor took on board any return cargo to be conveyed to Athens ; and we who had lent the money, when

τούτων ἐκ τοῦ Πόντου οὐκ εἴχομεν ὅτου ἐπιλαβοί-
μεθα οὐδ' ὅτου κρατοῖμεν, ἕως κομισαίμεθα τὰ
ἡμέτερ' αὐτῶν· οὐδ' ὁτιοῦν γὰρ εἰσήγαγον εἰς τὸν
26 λιμένα τὸν ὑμέτερον οὗτοι. ἀλλὰ πεπόνθαμεν
καινότατον, ὦ ἄνδρες δικασταί· ἐν γὰρ τῇ πόλει τῇ
ἡμετέρᾳ αὐτῶν, οὐδὲν ἀδικοῦντες οὐδὲ δίκην ὠφλη-
κότες οὐδεμίαν τούτοις, σεσυλήμεθα τὰ ἡμέτερ'
αὐτῶν ὑπὸ Φασηλιτῶν, ὥσπερ δεδομένων συλῶν
Φασηλίταις κατ' Ἀθηναίων. ἐπειδὰν γὰρ μὴ
θέλωσιν ἀποδοῦναι ἃ ἔλαβον, τί ἄν τις ἄλλο ὄνομ'
ἔχοι θέσθαι τοῖς τοιούτοις,[1] ἢ ὅτι ἀφαιροῦνται βίᾳ
τὰ ἀλλότρια; ἐγὼ μὲν οὐδ' ἀκήκοα πώποτε
πρᾶγμα μιαρώτερον, ἢ ὃ οὗτοι διαπεπραγμένοι εἰσὶ
[932] περὶ ἡμᾶς, καὶ ταῦθ' ὁμολογοῦντες λαβεῖν παρ'
27 ἡμῶν τὰ χρήματα. ὅσα μὲν γὰρ ἀμφισβητήσιμά
ἐστι τῶν συμβολαίων, κρίσεως δεῖται, ὦ ἄνδρες
δικασταί· τὰ δὲ παρ' ἀμφοτέρων ὁμολογηθέντα τῶν
συντιθεμένων, καὶ περὶ ὧν συγγραφαὶ κεῖνται ναυ-
τικαί, τέλος ἔχειν ἅπαντες νομίζουσι, καὶ χρῆσθαι
προσήκει τοῖς γεγραμμένοις. ὅτι δὲ κατὰ τὴν
συγγραφὴν οὐδ' ὁτιοῦν πεποιήκασιν, ἀλλ' εὐθὺς ἀπ'
ἀρχῆς ἀρξάμενοι ἐκακοτέχνουν καὶ ἐπεβούλευον
μηδὲν ὑγιὲς ποιεῖν, ὑπό τε τῶν μαρτύρων καὶ αὐτοὶ
ὑφ' ἑαυτῶν ἐλέγχονται οὑτωσὶ καταφανῶς.
28 Ὁ δὲ πάντων δεινότατον διεπράξατο Λάκριτος
οὑτοσί, δεῖ ὑμᾶς ἀκοῦσαι· οὗτος γὰρ ἦν ὁ πάντα
ταῦτα διοικῶν. ἐπειδὴ γὰρ ἀφίκοντο δεῦρο, εἰς μὲν
τὸ ὑμέτερον ἐμπόριον οὐ καταπλέουσιν, εἰς φωρῶν

---

[1] τοῖς τοιούτοις] τῷ τοιούτῳ Blass.

[a] On the right of reprisal, cf. § 13 above, and see Smith,
Dictionary of Antiquities, art. " Sylae."

these men themselves returned from Pontus, had nothing which we could lay hold of or keep in possession until we should recover our money; for these men brought nothing whatsoever into your harbour. Nay, we have suffered the most unheard-of treatment, men of the jury. In our own city, without 26 ourselves having committed any wrong, or having had judgement rendered against us in their favour, we have been robbed of our own possessions by these men who are Phaselites, just as if rights of reprisal had been given to Phaselites against Athenians.[a] For when they refuse to pay back what they received, what other name can one give to such people, than that they take by force the goods of others? For my own part, I have never heard of a more abominable act than that which these men have committed in relation to us, and that, too, while admitting that they received the money from us. For whereas all 27 clauses in contracts which are open to dispute require a judicial decision, men of the jury, those on the contrary which are admitted by both the contracting parties, and concerning which there exist maritime agreements, are held by all men to be final; and the parties are bound to abide by what is written. That these men, however, have fulfilled not a single one of the provisions of the agreement, but that from the very first they meditated fraud and purposed dishonest action has been thus clearly proven against them by the depositions of witnesses and by themselves.

You must now hear the most outrageous thing 28 which this fellow Lacritus has done; for it was he who managed the whole affair. When they arrived here they did not put into your port, but came to

δὲ λιμένα ὁρμίζονται, ὅς ἐστιν ἔξω τῶν σημείων
τοῦ ὑμετέρου ἐμπορίου, καὶ ἔστιν ὅμοιον εἰς φωρῶν
λιμένα ὁρμίσασθαι, ὥσπερ ἂν εἴ τις εἰς Αἴγιναν ἢ
εἰς Μέγαρα ὁρμίσαιτο· ἔξεστι γὰρ ἀποπλεῖν ἐκ τοῦ
λιμένος τούτου ὅποι ἄν τις βούληται καὶ ὁπηνίκ' ἂν
29 δοκῇ αὐτῷ. καὶ τὸ μὲν πλοῖον ὥρμει ἐνταῦθα
πλείους ἢ πέντε καὶ εἴκοσιν ἡμέρας, οὗτοι δὲ περι-
επάτουν ἐν τῷ δείγματι τῷ ὑμετέρῳ, καὶ ἡμεῖς
προσιόντες διελεγόμεθα, καὶ ἐκελεύομεν τούτους
ἐπιμελεῖσθαι ὅπως ἂν ὡς τάχιστ' ἀπολάβωμεν
τὰ χρήματα. οὗτοι δ' ὡμολόγουν τε καὶ ἔλεγον
ὅτι αὐτὰ ταῦτα περαίνοιεν. καὶ ἡμεῖς τούτοις τε
προσῇμεν, καὶ ἅμ' ἐπεσκοποῦμεν εἴ τι ἐξαιροῦνταί
30 ποθεν ἐκ πλοίου ἢ πεντηκοστεύονται. ἐπειδὴ δ'
ἡμέραι τε ἦσαν συχναὶ ἐπιδημοῦσι τούτοις, ἡμεῖς
τ' οὐδ' ὁτιοῦν ηὑρίσκομεν οὔτ' ἐξῃρημένον οὔτε
[933] πεπεντηκοστευμένον ἐπὶ τῷ ὀνόματι τῷ τούτων,
ἐνταῦθ' ἤδη μᾶλλον προσεκείμεθα ἀπαιτοῦντες.
καὶ ἐπειδὴ ἠνωχλοῦμεν αὐτοῖς, ἀποκρίνεται Λάκριτος οὑτοσί, ἀδελφὸς ὁ Ἀρτέμωνος, ὅτι οὐκ ἂν
οἷοί τ' εἴησαν ἀποδοῦναι, ἀλλ' ἀπόλωλεν ἅπαντα τὰ
χρήματα· καὶ ἔφη Λάκριτος δίκαιόν τι ἔχειν λέγειν
31 περὶ τούτων. καὶ ἡμεῖς, ὦ ἄνδρες δικασταί,
ἠγανακτοῦμεν ἐπὶ τοῖς λεγομένοις, πλέον δ' οὐδὲν
ἦν ἀγανακτοῦσιν ἡμῖν· τούτοις γὰρ οὐδ' ὁτιοῦν
ἔμελεν. οὐδὲν δ' ἧττον ἠρωτῶμεν αὐτούς, ὅντινα
τρόπον ἀπολωλότ' εἴη τὰ χρήματα. Λάκριτος δ'
οὑτοσὶ ναυαγῆσαι ἔφη τὸ πλοῖον παραπλέον ἐκ

---

[a] Some small inlet, which cannot be identified with certainty, used by thieves and smugglers. See Judeich, *Topo-
graphie von Athen*, p. 450.

[b] A place in the market where samples of goods could be
displayed. Compare Oration L. § 24.

anchor in Thieves' Harbour,[a] which is outside of the signs marking your port ; and to anchor in Thieves' Harbour is the same as if one were to anchor in Aegina or Megara ; for anyone can sail forth from that harbour to whatever point he wishes and at any moment he pleases. Well, their vessel lay at anchor 29 there for more than twenty-five days, and these men walked about in your sample-market.[b] We on our part talked to them and bade them see to it that we received our money back as soon as possible ; and they agreed, and said they were trying to arrange that very thing. While we thus approached them, we at the same time kept an eye on them to see whether they disembarked anything from the ship, or paid any harbour-dues.[c] But when they had been in 30 town a good many days, and we found that nothing had been disembarked from the ship, nor had any harbour-dues been paid in their name, we began from then on to press them more and more with our demands. And when we made ourselves burdensome to them, this fellow Lacritus, the brother of Artemo, answered that they would be unable to pay us, for all their goods were lost ; and Lacritus declared he could make out a good case in the matter.[d] We, men 31 of the jury, were indignant at these words, but we gained nothing by our indignation, for these men cared not a fig for it. Nevertheless we asked them in what way the goods had been lost. This man, Lacritus, said that the ship had been wrecked while

[c] The books of the harbour-masters would show whether the tax of 2 per cent had been collected, and thus whether any goods had been landed.

[d] A sharp thrust at the sophist, ever ready " to make the worse the better reason."

297

Παντικαπαίου εἰς Θεοδοσίαν, ναυαγήσαντος δὲ τοῦ
πλοίου ἀπολωλέναι τὰ χρήματα τοῖς ἀδελφοῖς τοῖς
ἑαυτοῦ, ἃ ἔτυχεν ἐν τῷ πλοίῳ ἐνόντα· ἐνεῖναι δὲ
τάριχός τε καὶ οἶνον Κῷον καὶ ἄλλ' ἄττα, καὶ
ταῦτα ἔφασαν πάντα ἀντιφορτισθέντα μέλλειν ἀπ-
32 άγειν Ἀθήναζε, εἰ μὴ ἀπώλετο ἐν τῷ πλοίῳ. καὶ ἃ
μὲν ἔλεγε, ταῦτ' ἦν· ἄξιον δ' ἀκοῦσαι τὴν βδελυρίαν
τῶν ἀνθρώπων τούτων καὶ τὴν ψευδολογίαν. πρός
τε γὰρ τὸ πλοῖον τὸ ναυαγῆσαν οὐδὲν ἦν αὐτοῖς
συμβόλαιον, ἀλλ' ἦν ἕτερος ὁ δεδανεικὼς Ἀθήνηθεν
ἐπὶ τῷ ναύλῳ τῷ εἰς τὸν Πόντον καὶ ἐπ' αὐτῷ
τῷ πλοίῳ (Ἀντίπατρος ὄνομα ἦν τῷ δεδανεικότι,
Κιτιεὺς τὸ γένος)· τό τ' οἰνάριον τὸ Κῷον ὀγδοήκοντα στάμνοι ἐξεστηκότος οἴνου, καὶ τὸ τάριχος
ἀνθρώπῳ τινὶ γεωργῷ παρεκομίζετο ἐν τῷ πλοίῳ
ἐκ Παντικαπαίου εἰς Θεοδοσίαν, τοῖς ἐργάταις τοῖς
περὶ τὴν γεωργίαν χρῆσθαι. τί οὖν ταύτας τὰς
προφάσεις λέγουσιν; οὐδὲν γὰρ προσήκει.

33
[934] Καί μοι λαβὲ τὴν μαρτυρίαν, πρῶτον μὲν τὴν
Ἀπολλωνίδου ὅτι Ἀντίπατρος ἦν ὁ δανείσας ἐπὶ
τῷ πλοίῳ, τούτοις δ' οὐδ' ὁτιοῦν προσήκει τῆς
ναυαγίας, ἔπειτα τὴν Ἐρασικλέους καὶ τὴν Ἱππίου,
ὅτι ὀγδοήκοντα μόνον κεράμια παρήγετο ἐν τῷ
πλοίῳ.

---

[a] Panticapaeum is the modern Kertsch, and Theodosia the
modern Kaffa in the Crimea.
[b] The speaker's contention is that even if the ship was
wrecked, that fact does not release Lacritus from his obliga-
298

sailing along the coast from Panticapaeum to Theodosia,[a] and that in the wreck of the vessel the goods
of his brothers which were at the time on board were
lost ; there was on board salt fish, Coan wine, and
sundry other things ; this, they said, had been put on
board as a return cargo, and they had intended to
bring it to Athens, had it not been lost in the ship.
That is what he said ; but it is worth your while to 32
learn the abominable wickedness of these men, and
their mendacity. Concerning the vessel which was
wrecked they had no contract,[b] but it was another
man who had lent from Athens upon the freight to
Pontus, and on the vessel itself. (Antipater was the
lender's name ; he was a Citian[c] by birth.) The
Coan wine (eighty jars of wine that had turned sour)
and the salt fish were being transported in the vessel
for a certain farmer from Panticapaeum to Theodosia
for the use of the labourers on his farm. Why, then,
do they keep alleging these excuses ? It is in no
wise fitting.

Now please take the depositions ; first that of 33
Apollonides, showing that it was Antipater who lent
money upon the vessel, and that these men were in
no wise affected by the shipwreck ; and then that of
Erasicles and that of Hippias, showing that only
eighty jars were being transported in the vessel.

tion ; for the loan made by Androcles was secured not by
the ship, which appears to have been mortgaged to Antipater,
but upon the cargo of Mendaean wine and the return cargo
which was to have been brought from Pontus. The wares
lost (by jettison when the ship was damaged) were not, the
speaker holds, the return cargo. That the ship was not
actually lost seems a necessary inference from § 28, where it
is stated that she returned to Athens.

  [c] Citium is a port in Cyprus.

ΜΑΡΤΥΡΙΑΙ

Ἀπολλωνίδης Ἁλικαρνασσεὺς μαρτυρεῖ εἰδέναι δανείσαντα Ἀντίπατρον, Κιτιέα τὸ γένος, χρήματα Ὑβλησίῳ
εἰς τὸν Πόντον ἐπὶ τῇ νηὶ ἣν Ὑβλήσιος ἐναυκλήρει,
καὶ τῷ ναύλῳ τῷ εἰς τὸν Πόντον· κοινωνεῖν δὲ καὶ
αὐτὸς τῆς νεὼς Ὑβλησίῳ, καὶ συμπλεῖν ἑαυτοῦ οἰκέτας
ἐν τῇ νηί, καὶ ὅτε διεφθάρη ἡ ναῦς, παρεῖναι τοὺς
οἰκέτας τοὺς ἑαυτοῦ καὶ ἀπαγγέλλειν ἑαυτῷ, καὶ ὅτι
ἡ ναῦς κενὴ διεφθάρη παραπλέουσα εἰς Θεοδοσίαν ἐκ
Παντικαπαίου.

34   Ἐρασικλῆς μαρτυρεῖ συμπλεῖν Ὑβλησίῳ κυβερνῶν
τὴν ναῦν τὴν εἰς τὸν Πόντον, καὶ ὅτε παρέπλει ἡ ναῦς
εἰς Θεοδοσίαν ἐκ Παντικαπαίου, εἰδέναι κενὴν τὴν ναῦν
παραπλέουσαν, καὶ Ἀπολλοδώρου αὐτοῦ τοῦ φεύγοντος
νυνὶ τὴν δίκην μὴ εἶναι οἶνον ἐν τῷ πλοίῳ, ἀλλὰ
παράγεσθαι τῶν ἐκ Θεοδοσίας τινὶ οἴνου Κῷα κεράμια
περὶ ὀγδοήκοντα.

Ἱππίας Ἀθηνίππου Ἁλικαρνασσεὺς μαρτυρεῖ συμπλεῖν Ὑβλησίῳ διοπεύων τὴν ναῦν, καὶ ὅτε παρέπλει
ἡ ναῦς εἰς Θεοδοσίαν ἐκ Παντικαπαίου, ἐνθέσθαι
Ἀπολλόδωρον εἰς τὴν ναῦν ἐρίων ἀγγεῖον ἐν ᾧ δύο
καὶ ταρίχους κεράμια ἕνδεκα ἢ δώδεκα καὶ δέρματ'
αἴγεια, δύο δέσμας ἢ τρεῖς, ἄλλο δ' οὐδέν.

Πρὸς τούσδ' ἐξεμαρτύρησεν Εὐφίλητος Δαμοτίμου
Ἀφιδναῖος, Ἱππίας Τιμοξένου Θυμαιτάδης, Σώστρατος
[935] Φιλίππου Ἱστιαιόθεν, Ἀρχενομίδης Στράτωνος Θριάσιος,
Φιλτάδης[1] Κτησικλέους Ξυπεταιῶν.

35   Ἡ μὲν ἀναίδεια τοιαύτη τῶν ἀνθρώπων τούτων
ἐστίν. ὑμεῖς δ', ὦ ἄνδρες δικασταί, ἐνθυμεῖσθε

---

[1] So Kirchner : φιλτιάδης.

[a] No full cargo, that is ; merely the salt fish and the Coan
wine mentioned above.

THE DEPOSITIONS

Apollonides of Halicarnassus deposes that to his knowledge Antipater, a Citian by birth, lent money to Hyblesius for a voyage to Pontus on the ship of which Hyblesius was in command, and on the freight to Pontus, and that he was himself part-owner of the ship with Hyblesius; that slaves of his own were passengers on the ship; and that, when the ship was wrecked, his servants were present and reported the fact to him, and also the further fact that the ship, having no cargo,[a] was wrecked while sailing along the coast to Theodosia from Panticapaeum.

Erasicles deposes that he sailed with Hyblesius as pilot of **34** the ship to Pontus, and when the ship was sailing along the coast to Theodosia from Panticapaeum he knows that the ship had no cargo; and that Apollodorus, the very man who is now defendant in this suit,[b] had no wine on board the vessel, but that about eighty jars of Coan wine were being conveyed for a certain man of Theodosia.

Hippias, son of Athenippus, of Halicarnassus, deposes that he sailed with Hyblesius as supercargo of the ship, and that when the ship was sailing along the coast to Theodosia from Panticapaeum, Apollodorus put on board the ship one or two hampers of wool, eleven or twelve jars of salt fish, and goat-skins—two or three bundles—and nothing else.

In addition to these, written affidavits[c] were submitted by Euphiletus, son of Damotimus, of Aphidnae, Hippias, son of Timoxenus, of Thymaetadae, Sostratus, son of Philip, of Histiaea, Archenomides, son of Strato, of Thria, and Philtades, son of Ctesicles, of Xypetê.[d]

Such is the shamelessness of these men. Now, men **35** of the jury, take thought in your own minds, whether

---

[b] If this clause is not an interpolation, we must assume that Apollodorus was being sued as co-defendant with Lacritus. But this whole inserted document may well be spurious.

[c] See note a above, p. 290.

[d] Aphidnae was a deme of the tribe Acantis; Thymaetadae, a deme of the tribe Hippothontis; Thria, a deme of the tribe Oeneïs; and Xypetê, a deme of the tribe Cecropis.

πρὸς ὑμᾶς αὐτούς, εἴ τινας πώποτ' ἴστε ἢ ἠκούσατε
οἶνον Ἀθήναζε ἐκ τοῦ Πόντου κατ' ἐμπορίαν εἰσ-
αγαγόντας, ἄλλως τε καὶ Κῷον. πᾶν γὰρ δήπου
τοὐναντίον εἰς τὸν Πόντον ὁ οἶνος εἰσάγεται ἐκ τῶν
τόπων τῶν περὶ ἡμᾶς, ἐκ Πεπαρήθου καὶ Κῶ καὶ
Θάσιος καὶ Μενδαῖος καὶ ἐξ ἄλλων πόλεων παντο-
δαπός· ἐκ δὲ τοῦ Πόντου ἕτερά ἐστιν ἃ εἰσάγεται
δεῦρο.

36
[936] Κατεχόμενοι δ' ὑφ' ἡμῶν καὶ ἐλεγχόμενοι
εἴ τι περιγένοιτο τῶν χρημάτων ἐν τῷ Πόντῳ,
ἀπεκρίνατο Λάκριτος οὑτοσί, ὅτι ἑκατὸν στατῆρες
Κυζικηνοὶ περιγένοιντο, καὶ τοῦτο τὸ χρυσίον δεδανεικὼς εἴη ἀδελφὸς αὐτοῦ ἐν τῷ Πόντῳ ναυκλήρῳ,
τινὶ Φασηλίτῃ, πολίτῃ καὶ ἐπιτηδείῳ ἑαυτοῦ, καὶ
οὐ δύναιτο κομίσασθαι, ἀλλὰ σχεδόν τι ἀπολωλὸς
37 εἴη καὶ τοῦτο. ταῦτ' ἐστὶν ἃ ἔλεγε Λάκριτος
οὑτοσί. ἡ δὲ συγγραφὴ οὐ ταῦτα λέγει, ὦ ἄνδρες
δικασταί, ἀλλ' ἀντιφορτισαμένους ἀπάγειν κελεύει
Ἀθήναζε, οὐ δανείζειν τούτους ὅτῳ ἂν βούλωνται
ἐν τῷ Πόντῳ τὰ ἡμέτερα ἄνευ ἡμῶν, ἀλλ' Ἀθήναζε
παρέχειν ἀνέπαφα ἡμῖν, ἕως ἂν ἡμεῖς ἀπολάβωμεν
τὰ χρήματα ὅσ' ἐδανείσαμεν.

Καί μοι ἀναγίγνωσκε τὴν συγγραφὴν πάλιν.

ΣΥΓΓΡΑΦΗ

38
[937] Πότερον, ὦ ἄνδρες δικασταί, δανείζειν κελεύει
τούτους ἡ συγγραφὴ τὰ ἡμέτερα, καὶ ταῦτ' ἀνθρώπῳ ὃν ἡμεῖς οὔτε γιγνώσκομεν οὔθ' ἑοράκαμεν
πώποτε, ἢ ἀντιφορτισαμένους κομίσαι Ἀθήναζε
39 καὶ φανερὰ ποιῆσαι ἡμῖν καὶ ἀνέπαφα παρέχειν; ἡ
μὲν γὰρ συγγραφὴ οὐδὲν κυριώτερον ἐᾷ εἶναι τῶν

302

you ever knew or heard of any people importing wine by way of trade from Pontus to Athens, and especially Coan wine. The very opposite is, of course, the case. Wine is carried to Pontus from places around us, from Peparethos, and Cos, and Thasos [a] and Mendê, and from all sorts of other places ; whereas the things imported here from Pontus are quite different.

When we refused to let them off, and questioned 36 them as to whether any of the goods were saved in Pontus, the defendant, Lacritus, answered that one hundred Cyzicene staters [b] were saved ; and that his brother had lent this sum in gold in Pontus to a certain shipowner of Phaselis, a fellow-countryman and friend of his ; and that he was unable to get it back, so that this also was as good as lost. This is 37 what was said by this fellow, Lacritus ; but the agreement, men of the jury, does not say this. It bids these men to take on board a return cargo, and bring it back to Athens ; not to lend our property without our consent to whomsoever in Pontus they pleased, but to deliver it in its entirety to us at Athens, until we should recover all the money which we had lent.

Now, please read the agreement again.

The Agreement is read again

Does the agreement, men of the jury, bid these 38 men lend our money, and that to a man whom we do not know, and have never seen ? or does it bid them put on board their ship a return cargo and convey it to Athens, and there display it to us, and deliver it to us in its entirety ? The agreement does 39 not permit anything to have greater effect than the

[a] Peparethos, now Skopelos ; Cos and Thasos retain their ancient names.
[b] See note a on Oration XXXIV. p. 252.

ἐγγεγραμμένων, οὐδὲ προσφέρειν οὔτε νόμον οὔτε
ψήφισμα οὔτ' ἄλλ' οὐδ' ὁτιοῦν πρὸς τὴν συγγραφήν·
τούτοις δ' εὐθὺς ἐξ ἀρχῆς οὐδὲν ἐμέλησε τῆς συγγραφῆς ταύτης, ἀλλὰ τοῖς χρήμασιν ἐχρῶντο τοῖς
ἡμετέροις ὥσπερ ἰδίοις οὖσιν αὐτῶν· οὕτως εἰσὶν
οὗτοι κακοῦργοι σοφισταὶ καὶ ἄδικοι ἄνθρωποι.
40 ἐγὼ δέ, μὰ τὸν Δία τὸν ἄνακτα καὶ τοὺς θεοὺς
ἅπαντας, οὐδεπώποτ' ἐφθόνησα οὐδ' ἐπετίμησα, ὦ
ἄνδρες δικασταί, εἴ τις βούλεται σοφιστὴς εἶναι καὶ
Ἰσοκράτει ἀργύριον ἀναλίσκειν· μαινοίμην γὰρ ἄν,
εἴ τί μοι τούτων ἐπιμελὲς εἴη. οὐ μέντοι μὰ Δία
οἶμαί γε δεῖν ἀνθρώπους καταφρονοῦντας καὶ οἰο-
μένους δεινοὺς εἶναι ἐφίεσθαι τῶν ἀλλοτρίων, οὐδ'
ἀφαιρεῖσθαι, τῷ λόγῳ πιστεύοντας· πονηροῦ γὰρ
41 ταῦτά γ' ἐστι σοφιστοῦ καὶ οἰμωξομένου. Λάκριτος
[938] δ' οὑτοσί, ὦ ἄνδρες δικασταί, οὐ τῷ δικαίῳ πιστεύων εἰσελήλυθε ταύτην τὴν δίκην, ἀλλ' ἀκριβῶς
εἰδὼς τὰ πεπραγμέν' ἑαυτοῖς περὶ τὸ δάνεισμα
τοῦτο, καὶ ἡγούμενος δεινὸς εἶναι καὶ ῥᾳδίως
λόγους ποριεῖσθαι περὶ ἀδίκων πραγμάτων, οἴεται
παράξειν ὑμᾶς ὅποι ἂν βούληται. ταῦτα γὰρ ἐπ-
αγγέλλεται καὶ δεινὸς εἶναι, καὶ ἀργύριον αἰτεῖ καὶ
μαθητὰς συλλέγει περὶ αὐτῶν τούτων ἐπαγγελλό-
42 μενος παιδεύειν. καὶ πρῶτον μὲν τοὺς ἀδελφοὺς
τοὺς αὐτοῦ ἐπαίδευσε τὴν παιδείαν ταύτην, ἣν
ὑμεῖς αἰσθάνεσθε πονηρὰν καὶ ἄδικον, ὦ ἄνδρες
δικασταί, δανείζεσθαι ἐν τῷ ἐμπορίῳ ναυτικὰ χρήματα καὶ ταῦτ' ἀποστερεῖν καὶ μὴ ἀποδιδόναι. πῶς
ἂν γένοιντο πονηρότεροι ἄνθρωποι ἢ τοῦ παιδεύον-

---

a The close parallel between this passage and the portrayal

terms contained in it, nor that anyone should bring
forward any law or decree or anything else whatever
to contravene its provisions ; yet these men from the
very outset paid no heed to this agreement, but made
use of our money as if it had been their very own ;
so rascally are they as sophists and dishonest as men.
For my own part, I swear by Zeus the king and by 40
all the gods, I never made it a matter of reproach
to anyone, men of the jury, nor blamed him, if he
chose to be a sophist and to pay money to Isocrates ;
I should be mad if I concerned myself about anything
of that sort. But, by Zeus, I do not think it right that
men, because they look down on people and think
themselves clever, should covet the property of others
and seek to defraud them, trusting in their power of
speech. That is the part of a rascally sophist, who
should be made to suffer for it. This fellow Lacritus, 41
men of the jury, has not come into court relying on
the justice of his case, but realizing perfectly what he
and his brothers have done in the matter of this
loan ; and because he considers that he is clever
and will easily provide arguments to defend evil
practices,[a] he thinks he will lead you astray just as
he pleases. For it is precisely in these matters that
he professes himself to be clever, and he asks money,
and collects pupils, promising to instruct them in
these very things. In the first place, he instructed 42
his own brothers in this art, which you, men of the
jury, see to be evil and unjust—the art of borrowing
on your exchange money for a maritime adventure,
and then defrauding the lenders, and refusing to
pay them. How could there be men baser than

of the " school " of Socrates in the *Clouds* of Aristophanes
will hardly escape the reader.

τος τὰ τοιαῦτα ἢ αὐτῶν τῶν παιδευομένων; ἐπεὶ
δ' οὖν δεινός ἐστι καὶ πιστεύει τῷ λέγειν καὶ ταῖς
43 χιλίαις δραχμαῖς, αἷς δέδωκε τῷ διδασκάλῳ, κελεύ-
σατε αὐτὸν διδάξαι ὑμᾶς, ἢ ὡς τὰ χρήματ' οὐκ
ἔλαβον παρ' ἡμῶν, ἢ ὡς λαβόντες ἀποδεδώκασιν, ἢ
ὅτι τὰς ναυτικὰς συγγραφὰς οὐ δεῖ κυρίας εἶναι, ἢ
ὡς δεῖ ἄλλο τι χρήσασθαι τοῖς χρήμασιν ἢ ἐφ' οἷς
ἔλαβον κατὰ τὴν συγγραφήν. τούτων ὅ τι βούλεται
πεισάτω ὑμᾶς. καὶ ἔγωγε καὶ αὐτὸς συγχωρῶ
σοφώτατον εἶναι τοῦτον, ἐὰν ὑμᾶς πείσῃ τοὺς περὶ
τῶν συμβολαίων τῶν ἐμπορικῶν δικάζοντας. ἀλλ'
εὖ οἶδ' ὅτι οὐδὲν ἂν τούτων οἷός τ' εἴη οὗτος οὔτε
διδάξαι οὔτε πεῖσαι.

44 Χωρὶς δὲ τούτων, φέρε πρὸς τῶν θεῶν, ὦ ἄνδρες
[939] δικασταί, εἰ τοὐναντίον συνεβεβήκει, μὴ ὁ τούτου
ἀδελφὸς ὁ τετελευτηκὼς ἐμοὶ ὤφειλε χρήματα, ἀλλ'
ἐγώ τῷ τούτου,[1] τάλαντον ἢ ὀγδοήκοντα μνᾶς ἢ
πλέον ἢ ἔλαττον, ἆρ' ἂν οἴεσθε Λάκριτον τουτονί,
ὦ ἄνδρες δικασταί, τοὺς αὐτοὺς λόγους λέγειν,
οἷσπερ νυνὶ καταχρῆται, ἢ φάσκειν ἂν αὐτὸν οὐκ
εἶναι κληρονόμον ἢ ἀφίστασθαι τῶν τοῦ ἀδελφοῦ,
καὶ οὐκ ἂν πάνυ πικρῶς εἰσπράττειν με, ὥσπερ καὶ
παρὰ τῶν ἄλλων εἰσπέπρακται, εἴ τίς τι ἐκείνῳ τῷ
τετελευτηκότι ὤφειλεν ἢ ἐν Φασήλιδι ἢ ἄλλοθί που;
45 καὶ εἴγε τις ἡμῶν φεύγων δίκην ὑπὸ τούτου παραγραφὴν ἐτόλμησε παραγράφεσθαι, μὴ εἰσαγώγιμον
εἶναι τὴν δίκην, εὖ οἶδ' ὅτι ἠγανάκτει ἂν οὗτος καὶ
ἐσχετλίαζε πρὸς ὑμᾶς, δεινὰ φάσκων πάσχειν καὶ
παρανομεῖσθαι, εἰ μή τις αὐτῷ τὴν δίκην ψηφιεῖται

----

[1] τούτου] τούτων Blass.

the one who teaches such an art, or than those who learn of him? Since, then, he is so clever, and trusts in his power of speaking and in the one thousand drachmae which he has paid to his teacher, bid him show you, either that they did not borrow 43 the money from us, or that, having borrowed it, they have paid it back; or that agreements for overseas trade ought not to be binding; or that it is right for people to use money for some other purpose than that for which they received it under agreement. Let him prove to you whatever one of these propositions he chooses. If he can so prove it to you who sit to decide cases of mercantile contracts, I certainly concede that he is the cleverest of men. But I know well that he would not be able to prove it to you or induce you to believe any one of them.

But apart from all this, suppose, by heaven, men 44 of the jury, that the case were reversed,—that it was not this man's dead brother who owed me the money, but that I owed *his* brother a talent, or eighty minae, or more or less; do you fancy that this fellow, Lacritus, would employ the same language that he now so lavishly uses? or would say that he is not the heir and has nothing to do with his brother's affairs? or that he would not exact payment from me mercilessly, as he has from the others who owed anything to the deceased, whether in Phaselis or anywhere else? And, if any one of us, being defendant 45 in a suit brought by him, had dared to enter a special plea declaring that the action was not one that could be brought into court, I know well that he would have waxed indignant, and would have protested to you, declaring that he was suffering treatment that was outrageous and contrary to law, if anyone voted

εἰσαγώγιμον εἶναι, ἐμπορικὴν οὖσαν. ἔπειτα, ὦ
Λάκριτε, σοὶ μὲν τοῦτο δίκαιον δοκεῖ εἶναι, ἐμοὶ
δὲ διὰ τί οὐκ ἔσται; οὐχ ἅπασιν ἡμῖν οἱ αὐτοὶ
νόμοι γεγραμμένοι εἰσὶ καὶ τὸ αὐτὸ δίκαιον περὶ
46 τῶν ἐμπορικῶν δικῶν; ἀλλ' οὕτω βδελυρός τίς
ἐστι καὶ ὑπερβάλλων ἅπαντας ἀνθρώπους τῷ
πονηρὸς εἶναι, ὥστ' ἐπιχειρεῖ πείθειν ὑμᾶς ψηφίσασθαι μὴ εἰσαγώγιμον εἶναι τὴν ἐμπορικὴν δίκην
ταύτην, δικαζόντων ὑμῶν νυνὶ τὰς ἐμπορικὰς δίκας.

Ἀλλὰ τί κελεύεις, ὦ Λάκριτε; μὴ ἱκανὸν εἶναι
ἡμᾶς ἀποστερεῖσθαι ἃ ἐδανείσαμεν χρήματα ὑμῖν,
ἀλλὰ καὶ εἰς τὸ δεσμωτήριον παραδοθῆναι ὑφ'
ὑμῶν προσοφλόντας τὰ ἐπιτίμια, ἐὰν μὴ ἐκτίνωμεν;
47 καὶ πῶς οὐκ ἂν δεινὸν εἴη καὶ σχέτλιον καὶ αἰσχρὸν
[940] ὑμῖν, ὦ ἄνδρες δικασταί, εἰ οἱ δανείσαντες ἐν
τῷ ἐμπορίῳ τῷ ὑμετέρῳ χρήματα ναυτικὰ καὶ
ἀποστερούμενοι ὑπὸ τῶν δανεισαμένων καὶ ἀπο-
στερούντων ἀπάγοιντο εἰς τὸ δεσμωτήριον; ταῦτ'
ἐστίν, ὦ Λάκριτε, ἃ τουτουσὶ πείθεις; ἀλλὰ ποῦ
χρὴ λαβεῖν δίκην, ὦ ἄνδρες δικασταί, περὶ τῶν
ἐμπορικῶν συμβολαίων; παρὰ ποίᾳ ἀρχῇ ἢ ἐν τίνι
χρόνῳ; παρὰ τοῖς ἕνδεκα; ἀλλὰ τοιχωρύχους καὶ
κλέπτας καὶ τοὺς ἄλλους κακούργους τοὺς ἐπὶ
θανάτῳ οὗτοι εἰσάγουσιν. ἀλλὰ παρὰ τῷ ἄρχοντι;
48 οὐκοῦν ἐπικλήρων καὶ ὀρφανῶν καὶ τῶν τοκέων τῷ
ἄρχοντι προστέτακται ἐπιμελεῖσθαι. ἀλλὰ νὴ Δία
παρὰ τῷ βασιλεῖ; ἀλλ' οὐκ ἐσμὲν γυμνασίαρχοι,

---

[a] A board of police commissioners, having jurisdiction in
the case of capital crimes, and charged with the custody of
those convicted.

[b] The archon (ἐπώνυμος) had the duty of passing judgement

that his action, being a mercantile one, was not one that could be brought. Then, Lacritus, if you consider this just for yourself, why should it not be just for me? Do not the same laws stand written for us all? and have we not all the same rights in regard to mercantile suits? But he is a man 46 so vile, so surpassing all human kind in baseness, that he seeks to induce you to vote that this mercantile action cannot be brought when you are now sitting to judge mercantile suits.

What is it you would have, Lacritus? Is it not enough that we should be robbed of the money we lent you but should we also be given over to prison by you, if we do not pay the costs adjudged against us? Would it not be outrageous, and cruel, and shameful, 47 for you, men of the jury, if those who have lent money in your port for an adventure overseas, and have been defrauded of it, should be led off to prison by those who borrowed and are seeking to evade payment? Is it this, Lacritus, that you would have these gentlemen sanction? But, men of the jury, where are we to obtain justice in the matter of commercial contracts? before what magistrates, or at what time? Before the Eleven *a*? But they bring into court burglars and thieves and other evil-doers who are charged with capital crimes. Before the Archon *b*? But it is for heiresses, and orphans, and parents that 48 the Archon is appointed to care. Then before the King-archon *c*? But we are not gymnesiarchs, nor

upon complaints of parents, orphans, and unmarried girls who had inherited property. See Aristotle, *Constitution of Athens*, 56. 6-7.

c The functions of the King-archon were largely religious, and the gymnesiarchs, or superintendents of the festal games, were under his control. See Aristotle, *ibid.* 57.

οὐδὲ ἀσεβείας οὐδένα γραφόμεθα. ἀλλ' ὁ πολέμ-
αρχος εἰσάξει. ἀποστασίου γε καὶ ἀπροστασίου.
οὐκοῦν ὑπόλοιπόν ἐστιν οἱ στρατηγοί. ἀλλὰ τοὺς
τριηράρχους καθιστάσιν, ἐμπορικὴν δὲ δίκην οὐ-
49 δεμίαν εἰσάγουσιν. ἐγὼ δ' εἰμὶ ἔμπορος, καὶ σὺ
ἀδελφὸς καὶ κληρονόμος ἑνὸς τῶν ἐμπόρων τοῦ
λαβόντος παρ' ἡμῶν τὰ ἐμπορικὰ χρήματα. ποῖ
οὖν δεῖ ταύτην εἰσελθεῖν τὴν δίκην; δίδαξον, ὦ
Λάκριτε, μόνον δίκαιόν τι λέγων καὶ κατὰ τοὺς
νόμους. ἀλλ' οὐκ ἔστιν οὕτω δεινὸς ἄνθρωπος
οὐδείς, ὅστις ἂν περὶ τοιούτων πραγμάτων ἔχοι τι
δίκαιον εἰπεῖν.

50 Οὐ τοίνυν ταῦτα μόνον, ὦ ἄνδρες δικασταί, δεινὰ
ἐγὼ πάσχω ὑπὸ Λακρίτου τουτουί, ἀλλὰ καὶ χωρὶς
τοῦ ἀποστερεῖσθαι τὰ χρήματα εἰς τοὺς ἐσχάτους
ἂν κινδύνους ἀφικόμην τὸ τούτου μέρος, εἰ μή μοι
[941] ἡ συγγραφὴ ἐβοήθει ἡ πρὸς τούτους, καὶ ἐμαρτύρει
ὅτι εἰς τὸν Πόντον ἔδωκα τὰ χρήματα καὶ πάλιν
Ἀθήναζε. ἴστε γάρ, ὦ ἄνδρες δικασταί, τὸν νόμον
ὡς χαλεπός ἐστιν, ἐάν τις Ἀθηναίων ἄλλοσέ ποι
σιτηγήσῃ ἢ Ἀθήναζε, ἢ χρήματα δανείσῃ εἰς ἄλλο
τι ἐμπόριον ἢ τὸ Ἀθηναίων, οἷαι ζημίαι περὶ
τούτων εἰσίν, ὡς μεγάλαι καὶ δειναί.

51 Μᾶλλον δ' αὐτὸν ἀνάγνωθι αὐτοῖς τὸν νόμον, ἵν'
ἀκριβέστερον μάθωσιν.

ΝΟΜΟΣ

Ἀργύριον δὲ μὴ ἐξεῖναι ἐκδοῦναι Ἀθηναίων καὶ τῶν
μετοίκων τῶν Ἀθήνησι μετοικούντων μηδενί, μηδὲ ὧν

---

a The third archon, originally minister of war, presided
over the court in which cases regarding the rights of aliens
were settled. See Aristotle, *Constitution of Athens*, 58.

are we indicting anyone for impiety. Or will the
Polemarch ^a bring us into court ? Yes, for disregard
of a patron, or for having no patron.^b Well then,
the Generals ^c are left. But they appoint the trierarchs ; they bring no mercantile suits into court. I, 49
however, am a merchant, and you are the brother
and heir of a merchant, who got from me money
for a mercantile venture. Before whom, then, should
this suit be entered ? Tell me, Lacritus ; only say
what is just and according to law. But there lives
no man clever enough to be able to say anything that
is just in connexion with a case like yours.

It is not in these matters only, men of the jury, 50
that I have suffered outrageous wrongs at the hands
of this man Lacritus ; for, besides being defrauded
of my money, I should have been brought into the
gravest danger, so far as his power went, if the agreement made with these men had not come to my aid
by bearing witness that I lent the money for a voyage
to Pontus and back to Athens. For you know, men
of the jury, how severe the law is, if any Athenian
transports corn to any other port than the port of
Athens, or lends money for use in any market save
that of Athens; you know what penalties there are in
such cases, and how severe and to be dreaded they are.

However, read them the law itself, that they may 51
have more exact information.

The Law

It shall be unlawful for any Athenian or any alien residing
at Athens or for any person over whom they have control,

^b A resident alien was required to be enrolled under some
citizen as patron.
^c Ten Generals were appointed annually, one of whom had
judicial functions connected with the appointment of
trierarchs. See Aristotle, *Constitution of Athens*, 61. 1.

οὗτοι κύριοί εἰσιν, εἰς ναῦν ἥτις ἂν μὴ μέλλῃ ἄξειν
σῖτον Ἀθήναζε, καὶ τἄλλα τὰ γεγραμμένα περὶ ἑκάστου
αὐτῶν. ἐὰν δέ τις ἐκδῷ παρὰ ταῦτ᾽, εἶναι τὴν φάσιν
καὶ τὴν ἀπογραφὴν τοῦ ἀργυρίου πρὸς τοὺς ἐπιμελητάς,
καθάπερ τῆς νεὼς καὶ τοῦ σίτου εἴρηται, κατὰ ταὐτά.
καὶ δίκη αὐτῷ μὴ ἔστω περὶ τοῦ ἀργυρίου, οὗ ἂν ἐκδῷ
ἄλλοσέ ποι ἢ Ἀθήναζε· μηδὲ ἀρχὴ εἰσαγέτω περὶ
τούτου μηδεμία.

52   Ὁ μὲν νόμος, ὦ ἄνδρες δικασταί, οὕτω χαλεπός
ἐστιν· οὗτοι δ᾽ οἱ μιαρώτατοι ἀνθρώπων ἁπάντων,
γεγραμμένον διαρρήδην ἐν τῇ συγγραφῇ Ἀθήναζε
πάλιν ἥκειν τὰ χρήματα, εἰς Χίον ἐπέτρεψαν κατ-
αχθῆναι ἃ ἐδανείσαντο Ἀθήνηθεν παρ᾽ ἡμῶν. δα-
νειζομένου γὰρ ἐν τῷ Πόντῳ τοῦ ναυκλήρου τοῦ
Φασηλίτου ἕτερα χρήματα παρά τινος Χίου ἀνθρώπου, οὐ φάσκοντος δὲ τοῦ Χίου δανείσειν, ἐὰν μὴ
ὑποθήκην λάβῃ ἅπανθ᾽ ὅσ᾽ ἦν περὶ τὸν ναύκληρον,
καὶ ἐπιτρέπωσι ταῦτα οἱ πρότερον δεδανεικότες,
[942]   ἐπέτρεψαν ταῦτα ὑποθήκην γενέσθαι τῷ Χίῳ τὰ
53   ἡμέτερα καὶ κύριον ἐκεῖνον γενέσθαι ἁπάντων, καὶ
οὕτως ἀπέπλεον ἐκ τοῦ Πόντου μετὰ τοῦ Φαση-
λίτου ναυκλήρου καὶ μετὰ τοῦ Χίου τοῦ δεδανει-
κότος, καὶ ὁρμίζονται ἐν φωρῶν λιμένι, εἰς δὲ τὸ
ὑμέτερον ἐμπόριον οὐχ ὡρμίσαντο. καὶ νυνί, ὦ
ἄνδρες δικασταί, τὰ Ἀθήνηθεν δανεισθέντα χρήματα
εἰς τὸν Πόντον καὶ πάλιν ἐκ τοῦ Πόντου Ἀθήναζε
54   εἰς Χίον κατηγμένα ἐστὶν ὑπὸ τούτων. ὅπερ οὖν
ἐν ἀρχῇ ὑπεθέμην τοῦ λόγου, ὅτι καὶ ὑμεῖς ἀδικεῖσθε οὐδὲν ἧττον τῶν δόντων ἡμῶν τὰ χρήματα.
σκοπεῖτε δ᾽, ὦ ἄνδρες δικασταί, πῶς οὐκ ἀδικεῖσθε,

to lend money on any vessel which is not going to bring to Athens grain or the other articles specifically mentioned.[a] And if any man lends out money contrary to this decree, information and an account of the money shall be laid before the harbour-masters in the same manner as is provided in regard to the ship and the grain. And he shall have no right to bring action for the money which he has lent for a voyage to any other place than to Athens, and no magistrate shall bring any such suit to trial.

The law, men of the jury, is thus severe. But these 52 men, the most abominable of humankind, although it stands expressly written in the agreement that the money should come back to Athens, allowed what they borrowed from us at Athens to be conveyed to Chios. For when the Phaselite shipowner wanted to borrow other money in Pontus from a certain Chian, and the Chian declared he would not lend it unless he should receive as security all the goods which the shipowner had on board or in his keeping, and unless those who had made the former loan should consent to this, these men nevertheless permitted these goods of ours to become security for the Chian, and put them all into his control. On 53 these terms they sailed back from Pontus with the Phaselite shipowner and the Chian who had made the loan, and put into Thieves' Harbour, without anchoring in your port. And now, men of the jury, money which was lent for a voyage from Athens to Pontus and back again from Pontus to Athens has been brought to Chios by these men. It is, therefore, just 54 as I assumed at the beginning of my speech—you are wronged no less than we who lent the money. Consider, men of the jury, how the wrong touches

---

[a] The reader does not quote the law in full, but abridges it, and adds this clause as a sort of " et cetera."

ἐπειδάν τις τῶν νόμων τῶν ὑμετέρων κρείττων
ἐγχειρῇ εἶναι, καὶ τὰς συγγραφὰς τὰς ναυτικὰς
ἀκύρους ποιῇ καὶ καταλύῃ, καὶ τὰ χρήματα τὰ
παρ' ἡμῶν εἰς Χίον ᾖ διαπεσταλκώς, πῶς οὐκ
ἀδικεῖ ὁ τοιοῦτος ἄνθρωπος καὶ ὑμᾶς;

55 Ἐμοὶ μὲν οὖν ἐστιν, ὦ ἄνδρες δικασταί, πρὸς
τούτους ὁ λόγος· τούτοις γὰρ ἔδωκα τὰ χρήματα.
τούτοις δ' ἔσται πρὸς τὸν ναύκληρον ἐκεῖνον τὸν
Φασηλίτην, τὸν πολίτην τὸν αὐτῶν, ᾧ φασὶ δανεῖσαι τὰ χρήματα ἄνευ ἡμῶν παρὰ τὴν συγγραφήν·
οὐδὲ γὰρ ἡμεῖς ἴσμεν τίνα ἐστὶ τὰ πεπραγμένα
τούτοις πρὸς τὸν ἑαυτῶν πολίτην, ἀλλ' αὐτοὶ οὗτοι
56 ἴσασιν. ταῦτα ἡγούμεθα δίκαια εἶναι, καὶ ὑμῶν
δεόμεθα, ὦ ἄνδρες δικασταί, βοηθεῖν ἡμῖν τοῖς
ἀδικουμένοις, καὶ κολάζειν τοὺς κακοτεχνοῦντας
καὶ σοφιζομένους, ὥσπερ οὗτοι σοφίζονται. καὶ
ἐὰν ταῦτα ποιῆτε, ὑμῖν τε αὐτοῖς τὰ συμφέροντα
ἔσεσθε ἐψηφισμένοι, καὶ περιαιρήσεσθε τῶν πονη-
[943] ρῶν ἀνθρώπων τὰς πανουργίας ἁπάσας, ἃς ἔνιοι
πανουργοῦσι περὶ τὰ συμβόλαια τὰ ναυτικά.

you also. When a man seeks to set himself above your laws, and makes of no effect nautical agreements, but does away with them, and has sent away to Chios money lent here on our exchange, is it not clear that such a man wrongs you as well as us ?

My words, men of the jury, are addressed to these 55 people only, for it was to them that I lent the money. It will remain for them to deal with that Phaselite shipowner, their own countryman, to whom they say they lent the money unknown to us and contrary to the agreement. For we do not know what transactions were entered into by them with their countryman ; but they know themselves. This we hold to be a just 56 course ; and we beg you, men of the jury, to come to the aid of us who are being wronged, and to punish those who devise evil and resort to sophistries, as these men do. If you do this, you will be found to have decided in accordance with your own interests, and will rid yourselves of all the rascalities of unprincipled men, which certain ones of them are employing in regard to maritime contracts.

FOR PHORMIO

INTRODUCTION

THE Phormio for whom this speech was written—
quite a different person from the Phormio of Oration
XXXIV.—had been a slave in the employ of Pasio,
the banker, who was one of the notable figures in the
business world of Athens in the early part of the
fourth century B.C. Pasio had himself been originally
a slave, but had been given his freedom by his em-
ployer, and had later on been granted the rights of
citizenship because of his services to the state.

Phormio had long managed Pasio's business, a bank
in Peiraeus and a shield-factory, and had in turn been
rewarded by receiving his freedom. At the time of
Pasio's death, Phormio was operating both establishments on lease from Pasio.

Pasio left behind him at his death a widow,
Archippê, and two sons, the elder, Apollodorus,
twenty-four years old, and the young Pasicles, a
minor of ten. By his will Pasio directed that Phormio
should marry the widow and become one of the
guardians of the minor son. The estate was to remain undivided, and Phormio was to continue as
lessee of his bank and factory, until Pasicles should
come of age ; but we learn from the present speech,
§ 8, that, owing to the large drafts made by Apollodorus upon the property held in common, the
guardians determined to protect the interests of his

319

minor brother by making a distribution of the property. This was accordingly done, Phormio retaining the bank and the shield-factory, on which he paid the rental as lessee.

When Pasicles came of age, a final settlement was made. Phormio's lease was terminated, and he received a discharge from all liabilities. Apollodorus took charge of the factory and Pasicles of the bank.

At the death of Archippê, Apollodorus put in a claim for three thousand drachmae for property, alleged to be in Phormio's possession, and the matter was referred to private arbitrators. These decided in favour of the claimant, and Phormio paid the amount, receiving from Apollodorus a second release from all demands.

Nevertheless, some eighteen or twenty years after Pasio's death Apollodorus instituted the action with which the present speech is concerned. He brought suit against Phormio for twenty talents, alleging that banking stock left by Pasio had been fraudulently appropriated by Phormio. The latter denied the charge, and entered a special plea in bar of action. The plea is based upon the fact that Apollodorus had given him a release from all claims, and on the further fact that the statute of limitations forbade the bringing of the suit after the lapse of so many years. As in other similar cases, however, the speaker devotes more time to the discussion of the main issue than to arguments supporting the special plea.

This oration, universally accepted as a genuine work of Demosthenes, is also universally recognized as a masterpiece of forensic art. We learn from the speech of Apollodorus against Stephanus (Oration XLV.) that the court not only upheld the plea, but would not listen to him when he attempted to reply. He did not receive even a fifth part of the votes cast,[a] and was therefore condemned to pay the ἐπωβολία, or one-sixth of the amount claimed.

The interesting question of the relation of this oration to those of Apollodorus against Stephanus (whom he charged with giving false witness in the present trial), and the ethical problems involved, if those orations also come from Demosthenes, will be discussed in the introduction to Oration XLV.

This speech is discussed in Schaefer, iii.[2] pp. 164 ff., and in Blass, iii. pp. 461 ff., who accepts Clinton's dating, 350/49, cf. §§ 26, 19 and 38. Pasio died in 370/69.

[a] See note a on p. 50.

XXXVI

ΠΑΡΑΓΡΑΦΗ ΥΠΕΡ ΦΟΡΜΙΩΝΟΣ

Τὴν μὲν ἀπειρίαν τοῦ λέγειν, καὶ ὡς ἀδυνάτως ἔχει Φορμίων, αὐτοὶ πάντες ὁρᾶτ᾽, ὦ ἄνδρες Ἀθηναῖοι· ἀνάγκη δ᾽ ἐστὶ τοῖς ἐπιτηδείοις ἡμῖν, ἃ σύνισμεν πολλάκις τούτου διεξιόντος ἀκηκοότες, λέγειν καὶ διδάσκειν ὑμᾶς, ἵν᾽ εἰδότες καὶ μεμαθηκότες ὀρθῶς τὰ δίκαια παρ᾽ ἡμῶν, ἂν ᾖ δίκαια καὶ 2 εὔορκα, ταῦτα ψηφίσησθε. τὴν μὲν οὖν παραγραφὴν ἐποιησάμεθα τῆς δίκης, οὐχ ἵν᾽ ἐκκρούοντες χρόνους ἐμποιῶμεν, ἀλλ᾽ ἵνα τῶν πραγμάτων, ἐὰν ἐπιδείξῃ μηδ᾽ ὁτιοῦν ἀδικοῦνθ᾽ ἑαυτὸν οὑτοσί, ἀπαλλαγή τις αὐτῷ γένηται παρ᾽ ὑμῖν κυρία. ὅσα γὰρ παρὰ τοῖς ἄλλοις ἐστὶν ἀνθρώποις ἰσχυρὰ καὶ [945] βέβαια, ἄνευ τοῦ παρ᾽ ὑμῖν ἀγωνίσασθαι, ταῦτα πάντα πεποιηκὼς Φορμίων οὑτοσί, καὶ πολλὰ μὲν 3 εὖ πεποιηκὼς Ἀπολλόδωρον τουτονί, πάντα δ᾽, ὅσων κύριος τῶν τούτου κατελείφθη, διαλύσας καὶ παραδοὺς δικαίως, καὶ πάντων ἀφεθεὶς μετὰ ταῦτα

---

[a] This is not merely the conventional plea of inexperience (compare XXXIV. 1); Phormio was by now an old man, and further, since he was a manumitted slave, he can have had no training which would equip him for the task, and furthermore, he was, of course, of barbarian birth. His friends, therefore, came to his aid, and one of them speaks in his behalf.

322

XXXVI

A FRIEND, PLEADING FOR PHORMIO,
A SPECIAL PLEA

PHORMIO's inexperience in speaking,[a] and his utter helplessness, you all see for yourselves, men of Athens. It is necessary for us, his friends, to state and set forth for you the facts, which we know full well from having heard him often relate them; in order that, when you have duly learned from us and have come to know the rights of the case, you may give a verdict that is both just and in harmony with your oaths. We have put in a special plea in bar of action, 2 not that we may evade the issue and waste time, but that, if the defendant[b] shows that he has committed no wrong whatsoever, he may win in your court an acquittal which will be final. For all that in the minds of other people brings about a firm and lasting settlement without engaging in a trial before you —all this Phormio here has done; he has done many 3 kindnesses to this man Apollodorus; he has duly paid and delivered up to the plaintiff everything belonging to him of which he had been left in control, and has since received a discharge from all further claims;

---

[b] The terms " plaintiff " and " defendant," as used in the translation of this oration, apply to the suit brought against Phormio.

τῶν ἐγκλημάτων, ὅμως, ὡς ὁρᾶτ᾽, ἐπειδὴ φέρειν
τοῦτον οὐχ οἷός τ᾽ ἐστί, δίκην ταλάντων εἴκοσιν
λαχὼν αὐτῷ ταύτην συκοφαντεῖ. ἐξ ἀρχῆς οὖν
ἅπαντα τὰ πραχθέντα τούτῳ πρὸς Πασίωνα καὶ
Ἀπολλόδωρον ὡς ἂν δύνωμαι διὰ βραχυτάτων
εἰπεῖν πειράσομαι, ἐξ ὧν εὖ οἶδ᾽ ὅτι ἥ τε τούτου
συκοφαντία φανερὰ γενήσεται, καὶ ὡς οὐκ εἰσαγώγιμος ἡ δίκη γνώσεσθ᾽ ἅμα ταῦτ᾽ ἀκούσαντες.

4 Πρῶτον μὲν οὖν ὑμῖν ἀναγνώσεται τὰς συνθήκας,
καθ᾽ ἃς ἐμίσθωσε Πασίων τὴν τράπεζαν τουτωὶ
καὶ τὸ ἀσπιδοπηγεῖον. καί μοι λαβὲ τὰς συνθήκας
καὶ τὴν πρόκλησιν καὶ τὰς μαρτυρίας ταυτασί.

ΣΥΝΘΗΚΑΙ. ΠΡΟΚΛΗΣΙΣ. ΜΑΡΤΥΡΙΑΙ

Αἱ μὲν οὖν συνθῆκαι, καθ᾽ ἃς ἐμίσθωσεν ὁ Πασίων τουτωὶ τὴν τράπεζαν καὶ τὸ ἀσπιδοπηγεῖον
ἤδη καθ᾽ ἑαυτὸν ὄντι, αὗταί εἰσιν, ὦ ἄνδρες Ἀθη-
ναῖοι· δεῖ δ᾽ ὑμᾶς ἀκοῦσαι καὶ μαθεῖν, ἐκ τίνος
τρόπου προσώφειλε τὰ ἕνδεκα τάλανθ᾽ ὁ Πασίων
5 ἐπὶ τὴν τράπεζαν. οὐ γὰρ δι᾽ ἀπορίαν ταῦτ᾽
ὤφειλεν, ἀλλὰ διὰ φιλεργίαν. ἡ μὲν γὰρ ἔγγειος
ἦν οὐσία Πασίωνι μάλιστα ταλάντων εἴκοσιν, ἀργύριον δὲ πρὸς ταύτῃ δεδανεισμένον ἴδιον πλέον
ἢ πεντήκοντα τάλαντα. ἐν τούτοις ἀπὸ τῶν παρα-
[946] καταθηκῶν τῶν τῆς τραπέζης ἕνδεκα τάλαντ᾽
6 ἐνεργὰ ἦν. μισθούμενος οὖν ὅδε τὴν ἐργασίαν

---

[a] We learn from Oration XLV. §§ 25-31 that the challenge
to Apollodorus demanded that he have the original lease
unsealed if he questioned the copy submitted.

[b] He had been given his freedom by Pasio.

[c] The word naturally denotes industry, but the clause might
possibly be rendered " because he did not wish capital to lie
idle "; so Dareste. In Oration XLV. § 33, Apollodorus

nevertheless, as you see, because Phormio can no longer submit to his demands, Apollodorus has instituted this vexatious and baseless suit for twenty talents. From the beginning, therefore, I shall try to set forth for you as briefly as possible all the transactions Phormio has had with Pasio and Apollodorus. From these, I am sure, the malicious conduct of the plaintiff will become clear to you, and at the same time, having heard this recital, you will determine that the action is not maintainable.

First the clerk shall read to you the articles of 4 agreement, in accordance with which Pasio leased to the defendant the bank and the shield-factory. Take, please, the articles of agreement, the challenge,[a] and these depositions.

THE ARTICLES OF AGREEMENT. THE CHALLENGE. THE DEPOSITIONS

These, men of Athens, are the articles of agreement in accordance with which Pasio leased the bank and the shield-factory to the defendant, after the latter had now become his own master.[b] But you must hear and understand how it was that Pasio came to owe the eleven talents to the bank. He owed that 5 amount, not because of poverty, but because of his thrift.[c] For the real property of Pasio was about twenty talents, but in addition to this he had more than fifty talents in money of his own [d] lent out at interest. Among these were eleven talents of the bank's deposits, profitably invested. When, therefore, 6 my client leased the business of the bank and took

implies that the debt was due to mismanagement on the part of Phormio.

[d] As eleven talents of this money belonged to the bank, this phrase is open to question.

αὐτὴν τῆς τραπέζης καὶ τὰς παρακαταθήκας λαμβάνων, ὁρῶν ὅτι, μήπω τῆς πολιτείας αὐτῷ παρ'
ὑμῖν οὔσης, οὐχ οἷός τ' ἔσοιτ' εἰσπράττειν ὅσα
Πασίων ἐπὶ γῇ καὶ συνοικίαις δεδανεικὼς ἦν, εἵλετο
μᾶλλον αὐτὸν τὸν Πασίωνα χρήστην ἔχειν τούτων
τῶν χρημάτων, ἢ τοὺς ἄλλους χρήστας, οἷς προ-
ειμένος ἦν. καὶ οὕτω διὰ ταῦτ' ἐγράφη προσοφείλων ὁ Πασίων ἔνδεκα τάλαντα, ὥσπερ καὶ
μεμαρτύρηται ὑμῖν.

7 Ὃν μὲν τοίνυν τρόπον ἡ μίσθωσις ἐγένετο, μεμαρτύρηται ὑμῖν ὑπ' αὐτοῦ τοῦ ἐπικαθημένου·
ἐπιγενομένης δ' ἀρρωστίας τῷ Πασίωνι μετὰ
ταῦτα, σκέψασθ' ἃ διέθετο. λαβὲ τῆς διαθήκης τὸ
ἀντίγραφον καὶ τὴν πρόκλησιν ταυτηνὶ καὶ τὰς
μαρτυρίας ταυτασί, παρ' οἷς αἱ διαθῆκαι κεῖνται.

ΔΙΑΘΗΚΗ. ΠΡΟΚΛΗΣΙΣ. ΜΑΡΤΥΡΙΑΙ

8 Ἐπειδὴ τοίνυν ὁ Πασίων ἐτετελευτήκει ταῦτα
διαθέμενος, Φορμίων οὑτοσὶ τὴν μὲν γυναῖκα λαμβάνει κατὰ τὴν διαθήκην, τὸν δὲ παῖδ' ἐπετρόπευεν.
ἁρπάζοντος δὲ τούτου καὶ πόλλ' ἀπὸ κοινῶν τῶν
χρημάτων ἀναλίσκειν οἰομένου δεῖν, λογιζόμενοι
πρὸς ἑαυτοὺς οἱ ἐπίτροποι, ὅτι, εἰ δεήσει κατὰ τὰς
διαθήκας, ὅσ' ἂν οὗτος ἐκ κοινῶν τῶν χρημάτων
ἀναλώσῃ, τούτοις ἐξελόντας ἀντιμοιρεὶ τὰ λοιπὰ
[947] νέμειν, οὐδ' ὁτιοῦν ἔσται περιόν, νείμασθαι τὰ ὄνθ'
9 ὑπὲρ τοῦ παιδὸς ἔγνωσαν. καὶ νέμονται τὴν ἄλλην

---

[a] That is, of Pasicles, who was a minor. That the guardian
should marry the widow was a common provision (so in the
case of Demosthenes' own mother; see Oration XXVII. § 7).

over the deposits, realizing that, if he had not yet obtained the right of citizenship with you, he would be unable to recover the moneys which Pasio had lent on the security of land and lodging-houses, he chose to have Pasio himself as debtor for these sums, rather than the others to whom he had lent them. It was for this reason that Pasio was set down as owing eleven talents, as has been stated to you in the depositions.

In what manner the lease was made, you know **7** from the deposition of the manager of the bank himself. After this, Pasio became ill ; and observe how he disposed of his estate. Take the copy of the will, and this challenge, and these depositions made by those in whose custody the will is deposited.

THE WILL. THE CHALLENGE. THE DEPOSITIONS

When Pasio had died, after making this will, **8** Phormio, the defendant, took his widow to wife in accordance with the terms of the will and undertook the guardianship of his son.[a] Inasmuch, however, as the plaintiff was rapacious, and seemed to think it right that he should spend large sums out of the fund which was as yet undivided, the guardians, calculating in their own minds that, if it should be necessary under the terms of the will to deduct from the undivided fund, share for share, an equivalent of what the plaintiff spent, and then distribute the remainder, there would be nothing left to distribute, determined in the interest of the boy to divide the property. And they did distribute all the estate **9**

In Oration XLV. Apollodorus denies that he had been challenged to produce the will, or that such a will had been left by his father.

οὐσίαν πλὴν ὧν ἐμεμίσθωθ' οὑτοσί· τούτων δὲ τῆς
προσόδου τὴν ἡμίσειαν τούτῳ ἀπεδίδοσαν. ἄχρι
μὲν οὖν τούτου τοῦ χρόνου πῶς ἔνεστ' ἐγκαλεῖν
αὐτῷ μισθώσεως; οὐ γὰρ νῦν, ἀλλὰ τότ' εὐθὺς
ἔδει χαλεπαίνοντα φαίνεσθαι. καὶ μὴν οὐδὲ τὰς
ἐπιγιγνομένας μισθώσεις ὡς οὐκ ἀπείληφεν ἔστ'
10 εἰπεῖν αὐτῷ. οὐ γὰρ ἄν ποτ', ἐπειδὴ δοκιμα-
σθέντος Πασικλέους ἀπηλλάττετο τῆς μισθώσεως
ὅδε, ἀφῆκατ' ἂν αὐτὸν ἁπάντων τῶν ἐγκλημάτων,
ἀλλὰ τότ' ἂν παραχρῆμ' ἀπῃτεῖτ', εἴ τι προσ-
ώφειλεν ὑμῖν.

Ὡς τοίνυν ταῦτ' ἀληθῆ λέγω, καὶ ἐνείμαθ' οὗτος
πρὸς τὸν ἀδελφὸν παῖδ' ὄντα, καὶ ἀφῆκαν τῆς
μισθώσεως καὶ τῶν ἄλλων ἁπάντων ἐγκλημάτων,
λαβὲ ταυτηνὶ τὴν μαρτυρίαν.

ΜΑΡΤΥΡΙΑ

11 Εὐθὺς τοίνυν, ὦ ἄνδρες Ἀθηναῖοι, ὡς ἀφεῖσαν
τουτονὶ τῆς μισθώσεως, νέμονται τὴν τράπεζαν καὶ
τὸ ἀσπιδοπηγεῖον, καὶ λαβὼν αἵρεσιν Ἀπολλόδωρος, αἱρεῖται τὸ ἀσπιδοπηγεῖον ἀντὶ τῆς τραπέζης. καίτοι εἰ ἦν ἰδία τις ἀφορμὴ τουτῳὶ πρὸς
τῇ τραπέζῃ, τί δή ποτ' ἂν εἵλετο τοῦτο μᾶλλον
ἢ κείνην; οὔτε γὰρ ἡ πρόσοδος ἦν πλείων, ἀλλ'
ἐλάττων (τὸ μὲν γὰρ τάλαντον, ἡ δ' ἑκατὸν μνᾶς
ἔφερεν), οὔτε τὸ κτῆμ' ἥδιον, εἰ προσῆν χρήματα
τῇ τραπέζῃ ἴδια. ἀλλ' οὐ προσῆν. διόπερ σω-

---

[a] Addressed to the two brothers, Apollodorus and Pasicles.
[b] By right of seniority.

except the property on which the defendant had taken a lease; and of the revenue accruing from this they duly paid one-half to the plaintiff. Up to that time, then, how is it possible for him to make complaint regarding the lease? For it is not now that he should show his indignation; he should at once have done so then. Moreover, he cannot say that he has not received the rents which became due subsequently. For in that case, when Pasicles came of age and 10 Phormio relinquished the lease, you [a] would never have freed him from all claims, but would then instantly have demanded payment, if he had owed you anything.

To prove that I speak the truth in this and that the plaintiff did divide the property with his brother, who was still a minor, and that they released Phormio from his liability under the lease and from all other charges, take this deposition.

THE DEPOSITION

As soon, then, as they had released the defendant 11 from the lease, men of Athens, they at once divided between them the bank and the shield-factory, and Apollodorus, having the choice,[b] chose the shield-factory in preference to the bank. Yet, if the plaintiff had any private capital in the bank, why in the world should he have chosen the factory by preference? The income was not greater; nay, it was less (the factory produced a talent, and the bank, one hundred minae); nor was the property more agreeable,[c] assuming that he had private capital in the bank. But he had no such capital. So the plaintiff was wise

---

[c] That is, the conduct of a manufacturing business entailed more labour and trouble than the management of a bank.

[948] φρονῶν εἵλετο τἀσπιδοπηγεῖον· τὸ μὲν γὰρ κτῆμ'
ἀκίνδυνόν ἐστιν, ἡ δ' ἐργασία προσόδους ἔχουσ'
ἐπικινδύνους ἀπὸ χρημάτων ἀλλοτρίων.

12 Πολλὰ δ' ἄν τις ἔχοι λέγειν κἀπιδεικνύναι σημεῖα
τοῦ τοῦτον συκοφαντεῖν ἐγκαλοῦντ' ἀφορμήν. ἀλλ'
οἶμαι μέγιστον μέν ἐστιν ἁπάντων τεκμήριον τοῦ
μηδεμίαν λαβεῖν ἀφορμὴν εἰς ταῦτα τουτονί, τὸ ἐν
τῇ μισθώσει γεγράφθαι προσοφείλοντα τὸν Πασίων'
ἐπὶ τὴν τράπεζαν, οὐ δεδωκότ' ἀφορμὴν τουτῳί,
δεύτερον δὲ τὸ τοῦτον ἐν τῇ νομῇ μηδὲν ἐγκαλοῦντα
φαίνεσθαι, τρίτον δ', ὅτι μισθῶν ἑτέροις ὕστερον
ταὐτὰ ταῦτα τοῦ ἴσου ἀργυρίου, οὐ φανήσεται
13 προσμεμισθωκὼς ἰδίαν ἀφορμήν. καίτοι εἰ, ἣν ὁ
πατὴρ παρέσχε, ὑπὸ τοῦδ' ἀπεστερεῖτο, αὐτὸν νῦν
προσῆκεν ἐκείνοις[1] ἄλλοθεν πορίσαντα δεδωκέναι.

'Ως τοίνυν ταῦτ' ἀληθῆ λέγω, καὶ ἐμίσθωσεν
ὕστερον Ξένωνι καὶ Εὐφραίῳ καὶ Εὔφρονι καὶ
Καλλιστράτῳ, καὶ οὐδὲ τούτοις παρέδωκ' ἰδίαν
ἀφορμήν, ἀλλὰ τὰς παρακαταθήκας καὶ τὴν ἀπὸ
τούτων ἐργασίαν αὐτὴν ἐμισθώσαντο, λαβέ μοι τὴν
τούτων μαρτυρίαν, καὶ ὡς τὸ ἀσπιδοπηγεῖον
εἵλετο.

ΜΑΡΤΥΡΙΑ

14 Μεμαρτύρηται μὲν τοίνυν ὑμῖν, ὦ ἄνδρες 'Αθη-
ναῖοι, ὅτι καὶ τούτοις ἐμίσθωσαν καὶ οὐ παρέδωκαν

---

[1] ἐκείνοις omitted by Blass.

---

a If it were true that Apollodorus had been defrauded by
Phormio of capital which Pasio had invested in the bank,
then, when the bank was let to new lessees on the same
terms as before, Apollodorus would have had to make up
the missing capital from some other source.

in choosing the factory. For that is a property which involves no risk, while the bank is a business yielding a hazardous revenue from money which belongs to others.

Many proofs might one advance and set forth to 12 show that the plaintiff's claim to a sum of banking capital is malicious and baseless. But the strongest proof of all that Phormio received no capital is, I think, this : that Pasio is set down in the lease as debtor to the bank, not as having given banking capital to the defendant. The second proof is that the plaintiff is shown to have made no demands at the time of the distribution of the property. The third is that when he subsequently leased the same business to others for the same sum, he will be shown not to have leased any private capital of his own along with it. And yet, 13 if he had been defrauded by the defendant of capital which his father left, he would himself on that assumption have had to provide it from some other source and given it to the new lessees.[a]

To prove that I speak the truth in this, and that Apollodorus subsequently leased the bank to Xeno and Euphraeus, and Euphro, and Callistratus, and that he delivered no private capital to them either, but that they leased only the deposits and the right to the profits accruing from them, take, please, the deposition which proves these matters, and proves also that he chose the shield-factory.

THE DEPOSITION

Evidence has been submitted to you, men of 14 Athens, that they[b] granted a lease to these men also,

[b] The plural denotes the two brothers, Apollodorus and Pasicles.

ἰδίαν ἀφορμὴν οὐδεμίαν, καὶ ἐλευθέρους τ' ἀφεῖσαν
ὡς μεγάλ' εὖ πεπονθότες, καὶ οὐκ ἐδικάζοντ' οὔτ'
ἐκείνοις τότ' οὔτε τούτῳ. ὃν μὲν τοίνυν χρόνον ἡ
μήτηρ ἔζη, ἡ πάντ' ἀκριβῶς ταῦτ'[1] εἰδυῖα, οὐδὲν
ἔγκλημα πώποτ' ἐποιήσατο πρὸς τουτονὶ Φορμίων'
[949] Ἀπολλόδωρος· ὡς δ' ἐτελεύτησεν ἐκείνη, τρισχιλίας
ἐγκαλέσας ἀργυρίου δραχμὰς πρὸς αἷς ἔδωκεν
ἐκείνη δισχιλίαις τοῖς τούτου παιδίοις, καὶ χιτω-
15 νίσκον τινὰ καὶ θεράπαιναν, ἐσυκοφάντει. καὶ οὐδ'
ἐνταῦθα τούτων οὐδὲν ὧν νῦν ἐγκαλεῖ λέγων φανήσεται. ἐπιτρέψας δὲ τῷ τε τῆς ἑαυτοῦ γυναικὸς
πατρὶ καὶ τῷ συγκηδεστῇ τῷ αὐτοῦ καὶ Λυσίνῳ
καὶ Ἀνδρομένει, πεισάντων τούτων Φορμίωνα τουτονὶ δοῦναι δωρεὰν τὰς τρισχιλίας καὶ τὸ προσόν,
καὶ φίλον μᾶλλον ἔχειν τοῦτον ἢ διὰ ταῦτ' ἐχθρὸν
εἶναι, λαβὼν τὸ σύμπαν πεντακισχιλίας, καὶ πάντων
ἀφεὶς τῶν ἐγκλημάτων τὸ δεύτερον εἰς τὸ ἱερὸν τῆς
16 Ἀθηνᾶς ἐλθών, πάλιν, ὡς ὁρᾶτε, δικάζεται, πάσας
αἰτίας συμπλάσας καὶ ἐγκλήματ' ἐκ παντὸς τοῦ
χρόνου τοῦ πρὸ τούτου (τοῦτο γάρ ἐστι μέγιστον
ἁπάντων), ἃ οὐδεπώποτ' ᾐτιάσατο.

Ὡς τοίνυν ταῦτ' ἀληθῆ λέγω, λαβέ μοι τὴν γνῶσιν
τὴν γενομένην ἐν ἀκροπόλει, καὶ τὴν μαρτυρίαν
τῶν παραγενομένων, ὅτ' ἠφίει τῶν ἐγκλημάτων

---

[1] ταῦτ' omitted by Blass.

---

[a] These men would appear to have been slaves originally,
and, like Phormio himself, were rewarded with emancipation.
The alternative rendering, "freed them from all claims,"
seems less probable.

and gave over to them no private banking-capital; and that they gave them their freedom,[a] as if having received great benefits from them; and at that time they went to law neither with them nor with Phormio. Indeed, as long as his mother was living, who had an accurate knowledge of all these matters, Apollodorus never made any complaint against Phormio, the defendant; but after her death he brought a malicious and baseless suit claiming three thousand drachmae in money, in addition to two thousand drachmae which she had given to Phormio's children,[b] and a bit of underwear and a serving-girl. Yet even here he will be shown to have said nothing 15 of the claims which he now makes. He referred the matter for arbitration to the father of his own wife, and the husband of his wife's sister, and to Lysinus and Andromenes,[c] and they induced Phormio to make him a present of the three thousand drachmae and the additional items, and thus to have him as a friend rather than as an enemy because of this. So the plaintiff received in all five thousand drachmae, and going to the temple of Athena,[d] gave Phormio for the second time a release from all demands. Yet, 16 as you see, he is suing him again, having trumped up all sorts of accusations, and gathered from all past time charges (and this is the most outrageous thing of all) which he had never made before.

To prove that I am speaking the truth in this, take, please, the award that was made in the Acropolis, and the deposition of those who were present, when

[b] Children, that is, whom she had borne to Phormio.
[c] The two first named represented Apollodorus; the latter two, Phormio.
[d] Presumably, the Parthenon; see § 16 ἐν τῇ ἀκροπόλει and cf. Andoc. i. 42 and Isocr. Trapez. 20.

DEMOSTHENES

ἁπάντων Ἀπολλόδωρος, λαμβάνων τοῦτο τὸ
ἀργύριον.

17 Ἀκούετε τῆς γνώσεως, ὦ ἄνδρες δικασταί, ἣν
ἔγνω Δεινίας, οὗ τὴν θυγατέρ᾽ οὗτος ἔχει, καὶ
Νικίας ὁ τὴν ἀδελφὴν τῆς τούτου γυναικὸς ἔχων.
ταῦτα τοίνυν λαβὼν καὶ ἀφεὶς ἁπάντων τῶν ἐγκλημάτων, ὥσπερ ἢ πάντων τεθνεώτων τούτων ἢ τῆς
ἀληθείας οὐ γενησομένης φανερᾶς, δίκην τοσούτων
ταλάντων λαχὼν τολμᾷ δικάζεσθαι.

18 Τὰ μὲν οὖν πεπραγμένα καὶ γεγενημένα Φορμίωνι πρὸς Ἀπολλόδωρον, ἐξ ἀρχῆς ἅπαντ᾽ ἀκη-
[950] κόατ᾽, ὦ ἄνδρες Ἀθηναῖοι. οἶμαι δ᾽ Ἀπολλόδωρον
τουτονί, οὐδὲν ἔχοντα δίκαιον εἰπεῖν περὶ ὧν ἐγκαλεῖ, ἅπερ παρὰ τῷ διαιτητῇ λέγειν ἐτόλμα, ταῦτ᾽
ἐρεῖν, ὡς τὰ γράμμαθ᾽ ἡ μήτηρ ἠφάνικεν πεισθεῖσ᾽
ὑπὸ τούτου, καὶ τούτων ἀπολωλότων οὐκ ἔχει τίνα
19 χρὴ τρόπον ταῦτ᾽ ἐξελέγχειν ἀκριβῶς. περὶ δὴ
τούτων καὶ ταύτης τῆς αἰτίας σκέψασθ᾽ ἡλίκ᾽ ἂν
τις ἔχοι τεκμήρι᾽ εἰπεῖν ὅτι ψεύδεται. πρῶτον μὲν
γάρ, ὦ ἄνδρες Ἀθηναῖοι, τίς ἐνείματ᾽ ἂν τὰ πατρῷα
μὴ λαβὼν γράμματα, ἐξ ὧν ἔμελλεν εἴσεσθαι τὴν
καταλειφθεῖσαν οὐσίαν; οὐδὲ εἷς δήπου. καίτοι
δυοῖν δέοντ᾽ εἴκοσιν ἔτη ἐστὶν ἐξ ὅτου ἐνείμω, καὶ
οὐκ ἂν ἔχοις ἐπιδεῖξαι, ὡς ἐνεκάλεσας πώποθ᾽ ὑπὲρ
20 τῶν γραμμάτων. δεύτερον δέ, τίς οὐκ ἄν, ἡνίκα
Πασικλῆς ἀνὴρ γεγονὼς ἐκομίζετο τὸν λόγον τῆς
ἐπιτροπῆς, εἰ δι᾽ αὐτοῦ τὰ γράμματ᾽ ὤκνει τὴν

334

Apollodorus, on receiving this money, gave a release from all claims.

THE AWARD. THE DEPOSITION

You hear the award, men of the jury, which was 17 rendered by Deinias, whose daughter the plaintiff has married, and Nicias, who is husband to her sister. However, even though he has received this money, and has given a release from all claims, he has the audacity to bring suit for so many talents, just as if all these people were dead, or as if the truth would not be brought to light.

All the dealings, then, and transactions which 18 Phormio has had with Apollodorus you have heard, men of Athens, from the beginning. But I fancy that Apollodorus, the plaintiff, being unable to advance any just grounds in support of his claim, will repeat what he had the audacity to say before the arbitrator, that his mother made away with the papers at Phormio's instigation, and that, owing to the loss of these, he has no way of proving his claim strictly. But in regard 19 to these statements and this accusation, observe what convincing proofs one could advance to show that he is lying. In the first place, men of Athens, what man would have accepted a distribution of his inheritance, if he had not papers from which he could determine the amount of estate left him? No man, assuredly. Yet it is eighteen years, Apollodorus, since you accepted the distribution, and you cannot show that you at any time made any complaint about the papers. In the second place, when Pasicles had come 20 of age, and was receiving the report of his guardians' administration, what man, even though he shrank from accusing his mother with his own lips of having

μητέρ' αἰτιᾶσθαι διεφθαρκέναι, τούτῳ ταῦτ' ἐδήλωσεν, ὅπως διὰ τούτου ταῦτ' ἠλέγχθη; τρίτον δ',
ἐκ ποίων γραμμάτων τὰς δίκας ἐλάγχανες; οὗτος
γὰρ πολλοῖς τῶν πολιτῶν δίκας λαγχάνων πολλὰ
χρήματ' εἰσπέπρακται, γράφων εἰς τὰ ἐγκλήματα
" ἔβλαψέ μ' ὁ δεῖν' οὐκ ἀποδιδοὺς ἐμοὶ τὸ ἀργύριον,
ὃ κατέλιπεν ὁ πατὴρ ὀφείλοντ' αὐτὸν ἐν τοῖς γράμ-
21 μασιν." καίτοι εἰ ἠφάνιστο τὰ γράμματα, ἐκ
ποίων γραμμάτων τὰς δίκας ἐλάγχανεν;

Ἀλλὰ μὴν ὅτι ταῦτ' ἀληθῆ λέγω, τὴν μὲν νομὴν
ἀκηκόαθ', ἣν ἐνείματο, καὶ μεμαρτύρηται ὑμῖν· τῶν
δὲ λήξεων τούτων ἀναγνώσεται ὑμῖν τὰς μαρτυρίας.
λαβὲ τὰς μαρτυρίας μοι.

ΜΑΡΤΥΡΙΑΙ

[951] Οὐκοῦν ἐν ταύταις ταῖς λήξεσιν ὡμολόγηκεν
ἀπειληφέναι τὰ τοῦ πατρὸς γράμματα· οὐ γὰρ δὴ
συκοφαντεῖν γε, οὐδ' ὧν οὐκ ὤφειλον οὗτοι δικάζεσθαι φήσειεν ἄν.

22 Νομίζω τοίνυν, ὦ ἄνδρες Ἀθηναῖοι, μεγάλων καὶ
πολλῶν ὄντων ἐξ ὧν ἔστιν ἰδεῖν οὐκ ἀδικοῦντα
Φορμίωνα τουτονί, μέγιστον ἁπάντων εἶναι, ὅτ
Πασικλῆς, ἀδελφὸς ὢν Ἀπολλοδώρου τουτουί,
οὔτε δίκην εἴληχεν οὔτ' ἄλλ' οὐδὲν ὧν οὗτος ἐγκαλεῖ. καίτοι οὐ δήπου τὸν μὲν παῖδ' ὑπὸ τοῦ
πατρὸς καταλειφθέντα, καὶ οὗ τῶν ὄντων κύριος
ἦν, ἐπίτροπος καταλελειμμένος, οὐκ ἂν ἠδίκει, σὲ
336

destroyed the papers, would have failed to reveal
the fact to his brother, so that through him it might
have been thoroughly investigated ?   In the third
place, what were the papers upon which you based
the action which you brought ?   For the plaintiff has
brought suits against many citizens, and has recovered large sums of money, charging in his complaints, " So and so has injured me by not paying
back to me the money which my father's papers show
he owed the latter at his death."   But, if the papers 21
had been made away with, on the basis of what
papers did he commence his suits ?

In proof that I am speaking the truth in this, you
have heard the distribution which he accepted, and
the evidence in proof of it has been presented to you.
The clerk will now read you the depositions having to
do with these actions.   Please take the depositions.

THE DEPOSITIONS

In these complaints, then, he has admitted that he
had received his father's papers ; for he surely would
not say that he was bringing baseless charges, or
that he was suing these men for what they did not
owe.

There are many strong proofs from which one can 22
see that the defendant Phormio is not in the wrong ;
but the strongest of all, in my opinion, is this : that
Pasicles, though he is the brother of Apollodorus, the
plaintiff, has neither entered suit nor made any of
the charges which the plaintiff makes.   But surely
the defendant would not have abstained from wronging one who had been left a minor by his father, and
over whose property he had control, since he had
been left as his guardian, yet would have wronged

δέ, ὃς ἀνὴρ κατελείφθης τέτταρα καὶ εἴκοσιν ἔτη
γεγονώς, καὶ ὑπὲρ σαυτοῦ ῥᾳδίως ἂν τὰ δίκαι'
ἐλάμβανες εὐθύς, εἴ τι ἠδικοῦ. οὐκ ἔστι ταῦτα.

Ὡς τοίνυν ταῦτ' ἀληθῆ λέγω καὶ ὁ Πασικλῆς
οὐδὲν ἐγκαλεῖ, λαβέ μοι τὴν τούτου μαρτυρίαν.

ΜΑΡΤΥΡΙΑ

23 Ἃ τοίνυν ἤδη περὶ αὐτοῦ τοῦ μὴ εἰσαγώγιμον
εἶναι τὴν δίκην δεῖ σκοπεῖν ὑμᾶς, ταῦτ' ἀνα-
μνήσθητ' ἐκ τῶν εἰρημένων. ἡμεῖς γάρ, ὦ ἄνδρες
Ἀθηναῖοι, γεγενημένου μὲν διαλογισμοῦ καὶ ἀφέσεως τῆς τραπέζης καὶ τοῦ ἀσπιδοπηγείου τῆς
μισθώσεως, γεγενημένης δὲ διαίτης καὶ πάλιν
πάντων ἀφέσεως, οὐκ ἐώντων τῶν νόμων δίκας
24 ὧν ἂν ἀφῇ τις ἅπαξ λαγχάνειν, συκοφαντοῦντος
τούτου καὶ παρὰ τοὺς νόμους δικαζομένου, παρ-
εγραψάμεθ' ἐκ τῶν νόμων μὴ εἶναι τὴν δίκην εἰσαγώγιμον. ἵν' οὖν εἰδῆθ' ὑπὲρ οὗ τὴν ψῆφον οἴσετε,
τὸν νόμον θ' ὑμῖν τοῦτον ἀναγνώσεται καὶ τὰς
[952] μαρτυρίας ἐφεξῆς τῶν παρόντων, ὅτ' ἠφίει τῆς
μισθώσεως καὶ τῶν ἄλλων ἁπάντων ἐγκλημάτων
Ἀπολλόδωρος.

Λαβέ μοι τὰς μαρτυρίας ταυτασὶ καὶ τὸν νόμον.

ΜΑΡΤΥΡΙΑΙ. ΝΟΜΟΣ

25 Ἀκούετε τοῦ νόμου λέγοντος, ὦ ἄνδρες Ἀθηναῖοι, τά τ' ἄλλ' ὧν μὴ εἶναι δίκας, καὶ ὅσα

you, who at your father's death were left a man of four and twenty, and who on your own behalf would easily and immediately have obtained justice, if any wrong had been done you. That is impossible.

To prove that I am speaking the truth in this, and that Pasicles makes no complaint, take, please, the deposition regarding the matter.

THE DEPOSITION

The points which you should now consider in regard 23 to my plea that the action is not admissible, I beg you to recall from what has already been said. We, men of Athens, inasmuch as an accounting had been made and a discharge given from the lease of the bank and of the shield-factory ; inasmuch as there had been an arbitrator's award and again a discharge from all claims ; inasmuch also as the laws do not allow suits to be brought in cases where a discharge has once been given ; and inasmuch as the plaintiff 24 makes a baseless and malicious claim, and brings suit contrary to the laws ; we have put in a special plea as allowed by the laws that his suit is not admissible. In order, then, that you may understand the matter regarding which you are going to vote, he shall read you this law and the depositions in sequence of those who were present when Apollodorus discharged Phormio from the lease and from all other claims.

Take these depositions, please, and the law.

THE DEPOSITIONS. THE LAW

You hear the law, men of Athens, stating other 25 cases in which suit may not be brought, and in particular those in which anyone has given a release or

DEMOSTHENES

τις ἀφῆκεν ἢ ἀπήλλαξεν. εἰκότως· εἰ γάρ ἐστι
δίκαιον, ὧν ἂν ἅπαξ γένηται δίκη, μηκέτ' ἐξεῖναι
δικάζεσθαι, πολὺ τῶν ἀφεθέντων δικαιότερον μὴ
εἶναι δίκας. ὁ μὲν γὰρ ἐν ὑμῖν ἡττηθείς, τάχ'
ἂν εἴποι τοῦθ' ὡς ἐξηπατήθηθ' ὑμεῖς· ὁ δ' αὑτοῦ
φανερῶς καταγνοὺς καὶ ἀφεὶς καὶ ἀπαλλάξας, τίν'
ἂν αὑτὸν αἰτίαν αἰτιασάμενος τῶν αὐτῶν πάλιν
εἰκότως δικάζοιτο; οὐδεμίαν δήπου. διόπερ τοῦτο
πρῶτον ἔγραψεν ὁ τὸν νόμον θεὶς ὧν μὴ εἶναι δίκας,
ὅσα τις ἀφῆκεν ἢ ἀπήλλαξεν. ἃ τωδὶ γέγον'
ἀμφότερα· καὶ γὰρ ἀφῆκεν καὶ ἀπήλλαξεν. ὡς δ'
ἀληθῆ λέγω, μεμαρτύρηται ὑμῖν, ὦ ἄνδρες Ἀθηναῖοι.

26 Λαβὲ δή μοι καὶ τὸν τῆς προθεσμίας νόμον.

ΝΟΜΟΣ

Ὁ μὲν τοίνυν νόμος, ὦ ἄνδρες Ἀθηναῖοι, σαφῶς
οὑτωσὶ τὸν χρόνον ὥρισεν· Ἀπολλόδωρος δ' οὑτοσί, παρεληλυθότων ἐτῶν πλέον ἢ εἴκοσι, τὴν
ἑαυτοῦ συκοφαντίαν ἀξιοῖ περὶ πλείονος ὑμᾶς ποιήσασθαι τῶν νόμων, καθ' οὓς ὀμωμοκότες δικάζετε.
καίτοι πᾶσι μὲν τοῖς νόμοις προσέχειν εἰκός ἐσθ'
ὑμᾶς, οὐχ ἥκιστα δὲ τούτῳ, ὦ ἄνδρες Ἀθηναῖοι.
27 δοκεῖ γάρ μοι καὶ ὁ Σόλων οὐδενὸς ἄλλου ἕνεκα
θεῖναι αὐτόν, ἢ τοῦ μὴ συκοφαντεῖσθαι ὑμᾶς. τοῖς

---

[a] The two verbs ἀφιέναι and ἀπαλλάττειν seem at times to
be virtual synonyms, used freely with the redundancy of
legal usage. In some cases, however, ἀφιέναι refers clearly to
the creditor's act, and ἀπαλλάττειν to the effect on the debtor.
Parallel passages are Orations XXXVII. §§ 1 and 19 ; and
XXXVIII. § 1.

[b] It was the custom at Athens to emphasize the sanctity

340

discharge.[a] And with good reason. For if it is just that suit may not be brought again for cases which have once been tried, it is far more just that suit be not allowed for claims in which a discharge has been given. For a man who has lost his suit in your court might perhaps say that you had been deceived; but when a man has plainly decided against himself, by giving a release and discharge, what complaint can he bring against himself that will give him the right to bring suit again regarding the same matters? None whatever, of course. Therefore the man who framed this law placed first among cases in which suit may not be brought all those in which a man has given a release or discharge. Both of these have been given by the plaintiff; for he has released and discharged the defendant. That I am speaking the truth, men of Athens, has been proved to you by the evidence presented.

Take now, please, the statute of limitations. 26

THE LAW

The law, men of Athens, has thus clearly defined the time. But this man Apollodorus, when more than twenty years have gone by, demands that you pay more heed to his malicious charges than to the laws in accordance with which you have sworn to give judgement. You should have regard to all the laws, but to this one, men of Athens, above all others. For, in my judgement, Solon[b] framed it for 27 no other purpose than to prevent your having to be subjected to malicious and baseless actions. For in

of a given law by attributing its enactment to the great lawgiver, Solon. So, in Sparta, laws were conventionally assumed to have been enacted by Lycurgus.

μὲν γὰρ ἀδικουμένοις τὰ πέντ' ἔτη ἱκανὸν ἡγήσατ'
[953] εἶναι εἰσπράξασθαι· κατὰ δὲ τῶν ψευδομένων τὸν
χρόνον ἐνόμισε σαφέστατον ἔλεγχον ἔσεσθαι. καὶ
ἅμ' ἐπειδὴ ἀδύνατον ἔγνω ὂν τούς τε συμβάλλοντας
καὶ τοὺς μάρτυρας ἀεὶ ζῆν, τὸν νόμον ἀντὶ τούτων
ἔθηκεν, ὅπως μάρτυς εἴη τοῦ δικαίου τοῖς ἐρήμοις.
28 Θαυμάζω τοίνυν ἔγωγ', ὦ ἄνδρες δικασταί,
τί ποτ' ἐστὶν ἃ πρὸς ταῦτ' ἐπιχειρήσει λέγειν
Ἀπολλόδωρος οὑτοσί. οὐ γὰρ ἐκεῖνό γ' ὑπείληφεν,
ὡς ὑμεῖς, μηδὲν ὁρῶντες εἰς χρήματα τοῦτον ἠδικημένον, ὀργιεῖσθ' ὅτι τὴν μητέρ' ἔγημεν αὐτοῦ
Φορμίων. οὐ γὰρ ἀγνοεῖ τοῦτο, οὐδ' αὐτὸν λέληθεν, οὐδ' ὑμῶν πολλούς, ὅτι Σωκράτης ὁ τραπε-
ζίτης ἐκεῖνος, παρὰ τῶν κυρίων ἀπαλλαγεὶς ὥσπερ
ὁ τούτου πατήρ, ἔδωκεν Σατύρῳ τὴν ἑαυτοῦ γυ-
29 ναῖκα, ἑαυτοῦ ποτὲ γενομένῳ. ἕτερος Σωκλῆς
τραπεζιτεύσας ἔδωκε τὴν ἑαυτοῦ γυναῖκα Τιμο-
δήμῳ τῷ νῦν ἔτ' ὄντι καὶ ζῶντι, γενομένῳ ποθ'
αὑτοῦ. καὶ οὐ μόνον ἐνθάδε τοῦτο ποιοῦσιν οἱ περὶ
τὰς ἐργασίας ὄντες ταύτας, ὦ ἄνδρες Ἀθηναῖοι,
ἀλλ' ἐν Αἰγίνῃ ἔδωκε Στρυμόδωρος Ἑρμαίῳ τῷ
ἑαυτοῦ οἰκέτῃ τὴν γυναῖκα, καὶ τελευτησάσης
ἐκείνης ἔδωκε πάλιν τὴν θυγατέρα τὴν ἑαυτοῦ.
30 καὶ πολλοὺς ἂν ἔχοι τις εἰπεῖν τοιούτους. εἰκότως·
ὑμῖν μὲν γάρ, ὦ ἄνδρες Ἀθηναῖοι, τοῖς γένει
πολίταις, οὐδὲ ἓν πλῆθος χρημάτων ἀντὶ τοῦ γένους
καλόν ἐστιν ἑλέσθαι· τοῖς δὲ τοῦτο μὲν δωρειὰν ἢ
παρ' ὑμῶν ἢ παρ' ἄλλων τινῶν λαβούσῃ, τῇ τύχῃ

---

a It is probable that the word " gave " refers to provisions
in the will of Strymodorus. We must then assume that the
wife died after the will was made, but before the death of
Strymodorus. So Sandys.

the case of those who were wronged, he thought that a period of five years was enough to enable them to recover what was their due ; while the lapse of time would best serve to convict those who advanced false claims. At the same time, since he realized that neither the contracting parties nor the witnesses would live for ever, he put the law in their place, that it might be a witness of truth for those who had no other defence.

I, for my part, am wondering, men of the jury, 28 what in the world the plaintiff, Apollodorus, will try to say in reply to these arguments. For he can hardly have made this assumption that you, although seeing that he has suffered no wrong financially, will be indignant because Phormio has married his mother. For he is not unaware of this—it is no secret to him or to many of you—that Socrates, the well-known banker, having been set free by his masters just as the plaintiff's father had been, gave his wife in marriage to Satyrus who had been his slave. Another, 29 Socles, who had been in the banking business, gave his wife in marriage to Timodemus, who is still in being and alive, who had been his slave. And it is not here only, men of Athens, that those engaged in this line of business so act ; but in Aegina Strymodorus gave his wife in marriage to Hermaeus, his own slave, and again, after her death, gave him his own daughter.[a] And one could mention many other such cases ; and 30 no wonder. For although to you, men of Athens, who are citizens by birth, it would be a disgrace to esteem any conceivable amount of wealth above your honourable descent, yet those who obtain citizenship as a gift either from you or from others, and who in

δ' ἐξ ἀρχῆς ἀπὸ τοῦ χρηματίσασθαι καὶ ἑτέρων
πλείω κτήσασθαι καὶ αὐτῶν τούτων ἀξιωθεῖσι,
ταῦτ' ἐστὶ φυλακτέα. διόπερ Πασίων ὁ πατὴρ ὁ
[954] σὸς οὐ πρῶτος οὐδὲ μόνος, οὐδ' αὐτὸν ὑβρίζων
οὐδ' ὑμᾶς τοὺς υἱεῖς, ἀλλὰ μόνην ὁρῶν σωτηρίαν
τοῖς ἑαυτοῦ πράγμασιν, εἰ τοῦτον ἀνάγκη ποιήσειεν
οἰκεῖον ὑμῖν, ἔδωκε τὴν ἑαυτοῦ γυναῖκα, μητέρα δ'
31 ὑμετέραν τούτῳ. πρὸς μὲν οὖν τὰ συμφέροντ' ἐὰν
ἐξετάζῃς, καλῶς βεβουλευμένον αὐτὸν εὑρήσεις· εἰ
δὲ πρὸς γένους δόξαν ἀναίνει Φορμίωνα κηδεστήν,
ὅρα μὴ γελοῖον ᾖ σὲ ταῦτα λέγειν. εἰ γάρ τις
ἔροιτό σε, ποῖόν τιν' ἡγεῖ τὸν πατέρα τὸν σεαυτοῦ
εἶναι, χρηστὸν εὖ οἶδ' ὅτι φήσειας ἄν. πότερ' οὖν
οἴει μᾶλλον ἐοικέναι τὸν τρόπον καὶ πάντα τὸν βίον
Πασίωνι σαυτὸν ἢ τουτονί; ἐγὼ μὲν εὖ οἶδ' ὅτι[1]
τοῦτον. εἶθ' ὅς ἐστιν ὁμοιότερος σοῦ τῷ σῷ πατρί,
τοῦτον, εἰ τὴν μητέρα τὴν σὴν ἔγημ', ἀναίνει;
32 ἀλλὰ μὴν ὅτι δόντος γε κἀπισκήψαντος τοῦ σοῦ
πατρὸς ταῦτ' ἐπράχθη, οὐ μόνον ἐκ τῆς διαθήκης
ἔστιν ἰδεῖν, ὦ ἄνδρες Ἀθηναῖοι, ἀλλὰ καὶ σὺ
μάρτυς αὐτὸς γέγονας. ὅτε γὰρ τὰ μητρῷα πρὸς
μέρος ἠξίους νέμεσθαι, ὄντων παίδων ἐκ τῆς
γυναικὸς Φορμίωνι τουτῳί, τόθ' ὡμολόγεις κυρίως
δόντος τοῦ πατρὸς τοῦ σοῦ κατὰ τοὺς νόμους αὐτὴν
γεγαμῆσθαι. εἰ γὰρ αὐτὴν εἶχε λαβὼν ἀδίκως ὅδε
μηδενὸς δόντος, οὐκ ἦσαν οἱ παῖδες κληρονόμοι,

---

[1] εὖ οἶδ' ὅτι] γὰρ εὖ οἶδ' ὅτι Blass.

the first instance, thanks to this good fortune, were counted worthy of the same privileges, because of their success in money-making, and their possession of more wealth than others, must hold fast to these advantages. So your father Pasio—and he was neither the first nor the last to do this—without bringing disgrace upon himself or upon you, his sons, but seeing that the only protection for his business was that he should bind the defendant to you by a family tie, for this reason gave to him in marriage his own wife, your mother. If, then, you examine his conduct 31 in the light of practical utility you will find that he determined wisely ; but if from family pride you scorn Phormio as stepfather, see if it be not absurd for you to speak thus. For, if one were to ask you what sort of a man you deem your father to have been, I am sure that you would say, " an honourable man." Now, then, which of you two do you think more resembles Pasio in character and in manner of life, yourself or Phormio ? I know well that you think Phormio does. Then do you scorn this man who is more like your father than you are yourself, just because he has married your mother ? But that 32 this arrangement was made by your father's grant and solemn injunction may not only be seen from the will, men of Athens, but you yourself, Apollodorus, are a witness to the fact. For when you claimed the right to distribute your mother's estate share by share—and she had left children by the defendant, Phormio—you then acknowledged that your father had given her with full right, and that she had been married in accordance with the laws. For if Phormio had taken her to wife wrongfully, and no one had given her—then the children were not heirs, and if

τοῖς δὲ μὴ κληρονόμοις οὐκ ἦν μετουσία τῶν
ὄντων.

Ἀλλὰ μὴν ὅτι ταῦτ' ἀληθῆ λέγω, μεμαρτύρηται
τὸ τέταρτον μέρος λαβεῖν καὶ ἀφεῖναι τῶν ἐγκλημάτων ἁπάντων.

33 Κατ' οὐδὲν τοίνυν, ὦ ἄνδρες Ἀθηναῖοι, δίκαιον
οὐδὲν ἔχων εἰπεῖν, ἀναιδεστάτους λόγους ἐτόλμα
[955] λέγειν πρὸς τῷ διαιτητῇ, περὶ ὧν προακηκοέναι
βέλτιόν ἐσθ' ὑμᾶς, ἕνα μὲν τὸ παράπαν μὴ γενέσθαι
διαθήκην, ἀλλ' εἶναι τοῦτο πλάσμα καὶ σκευώρημ'
ὅλον, ἕτερον δ' εἵνεκα τούτου πάντα ταῦτα συγχωρεῖν τὸν πρὸ τοῦ χρόνον καὶ οὐχὶ δικάζεσθαι,
ὅτι μίσθωσιν ἤθελεν αὐτῷ φέρειν Φορμίων πολλὴν
καὶ ὑπισχνεῖτ' οἴσειν· ἐπειδὴ δ' οὐ ποιεῖ ταῦτα, τη-
34 νικαῦτα, φησί, δικάζομαι. ὅτι δὴ ταῦτ' ἀμφότερ',
ἂν λέγῃ, ψεύσεται καὶ τοῖς ὑφ' ἑαυτοῦ πεπραγ-
μένοις ἐναντί' ἐρεῖ, σκοπεῖτ' ἐκ τωνδί. ὅταν μὲν
τοίνυν τὴν διαθήκην ἀρνῆται, ἐκ τίνος τρόπου
πρεσβεῖα λαβὼν τὴν συνοικίαν κατὰ τὴν διαθήκην
ἔχει, τοῦτ' ἐρωτᾶτ' αὐτόν. οὐ γὰρ ἐκεῖνό γ' ἐρεῖ,
ὡς ὅσα μὲν πλεονεκτεῖν τόνδ' ἔγραψ' ὁ πατὴρ,
35 κύρι' ἐστὶ τῆς διαθήκης, τὰ δ' ἄλλ' ἄκυρα. ὅταν δ'
ὑπὸ τῶν τοῦδ' ὑποσχέσεων ὑπάγεσθαι φῇ, μέμνησθ'
ὅτι μάρτυρας ὑμῖν παρεσχήμεθα, οἳ χρόνον πολὺν
τοῦδ' ἀπηλλαγμένου μισθωταὶ τούτοις ἐγίγνοντο
τῆς τραπέζης καὶ τοῦ ἀσπιδοπηγείου. καίτοι τόθ',
ὁπηνίκ' ἐμίσθωσεν ἐκείνοις, τῷδ' ἐγκαλεῖν παρα-

---

[a] Illegitimate children could not inherit; and the fact
that Apollodorus recognized the children of Phormio and
Archippê as heirs, proves that he admitted the legality of
the marriage.

[b] There were four children: Apollodorus and Pasicles,
and the two born of Phormio and Archippê.

they were not heirs they had no right of sharing in the property.[a]

To prove that I am speaking the truth in this evidence has been submitted showing that he received a fourth share[b] and gave a release from all claims.

Having, then, on no single point, men of Athens, 33 any just claim to advance, he had the audacity to make before the arbitrator the most shameless assertions which it is best that you should hear in advance: first that no will was made at all, but that this is a fiction and forgery from beginning to end; and, secondly, that the reason why he had made all these concessions up to now, and had abstained from going to law, was because Phormio was willing to pay him a large rent, and promised that he would do so. But since he does not do this, now, he says, I go to law. But that both of these statements, if he makes 34 them, will be false and inconsistent with his own conduct, pray observe from the following considerations. When he denies the will, ask him this, how it came that he received the lodging-house under the will as being the elder.[c] He surely will not claim that all the clauses which his father wrote in the will in his favour are valid, and the others invalid. And 35 when he says that he was misled by the defendant's promises, remember that we have brought before you as witnesses those who for a long time, after Phormio had given it up, became lessees under the two brothers of the bank and the shield-factory. And yet it was when he granted the lease to these men, that he should at once have made his charges

[c] A right not often recognized in Attic law. Compare Oration XXXIX. § 29.

χρῆμ' ἐχρῆν, εἴπερ ἀληθῆ ἦν ὑπὲρ ὧν τότ' ἀφεὶς
νῦν τούτῳ δικάζεται.

Ὡς τοίνυν ἀληθῆ λέγω, καὶ πρεσβεῖά τε τὴν
συνοικίαν ἔλαβεν κατὰ τὴν διαθήκην, καὶ τῷδ' οὐχ
ὅπως ἐγκαλεῖν ᾤετο δεῖν, ἀλλ' ἐπῄνει, λαβὲ τὴν
μαρτυρίαν.

ΜΑΡΤΥΡΙΑ

36 Ἵνα τοίνυν εἰδῆτ', ὦ ἄνδρες Ἀθηναῖοι, ὅσα
χρήματ' ἔχων ἐκ τῶν μισθώσεων καὶ ἐκ τῶν χρεῶν
ὡς ἀπορῶν καὶ πάντ' ἀπολωλεκὼς ὀδυρεῖται,
[956] βραχέ' ἡμῶν ἀκούσατε. οὗτος γὰρ ἐκ μὲν τῶν
χρεῶν ὁμοῦ τάλαντ' εἴκοσιν εἰσπέπρακται ἐκ τῶν
γραμμάτων ὧν ὁ πατὴρ κατέλιπεν, καὶ τούτων ἔχει
πλέον ἢ τὰ ἡμίσεα· πολλῶν γὰρ τὰ μέρη τὸν
37 ἀδελφὸν ἀποστερεῖ. ἐκ δὲ τῶν μισθώσεων, ὀκτὼ
μὲν ἐτῶν ἃ Φορμίων εἶχε τὴν τράπεζαν, ὀγδοήκοντα μνᾶς τοῦ ἐνιαυτοῦ ἑκάστου, τὸ ἥμισυ τῆς
ὅλης μισθώσεως· καὶ ταῦτ' ἐστὶν δέκα τάλαντα
καὶ τετταράκοντα μναῖ· δέκα δὲ τῶν μετὰ ταῦτα,
ὧν ἐμίσθωσαν Ξένωνι καὶ Εὐφραίῳ καὶ Εὔφρονι
καὶ Καλλιστράτῳ, τάλαντον τοῦ ἐνιαυτοῦ ἑκάστου.
38 χωρὶς δὲ τούτων, ἐτῶν ἴσως εἴκοσι τῆς ἐξ ἀρχῆς
νεμηθείσης οὐσίας, ἧς αὐτὸς ἐπεμελεῖτο, τὰς προσόδους, πλέον ἢ μνᾶς τριάκοντα. ἐὰν δ' ἅπαντα
συνθῆτε, ὅσ' ἐνείματο, ὅσ' εἰσεπράξατο, ὅσ' εἴληφε
μίσθωσιν, πλέον ἢ τετταράκοντα τάλαντ' εἰληφὼς

---

^a The debts, that is, due to his father.

^b The rent of the factory was a talent a year, and that of
the bank a talent and forty minae, making a total of one
hundred and sixty minae annually, or eighty minae apiece
for each of the two brothers, or ten talents and forty minae
for the eight-year period.

^c The rents under the new lease remained the same as

348

against the defendant if there were any truth in the claims, for which he then gave a release, but for which he now brings suit against him.

To prove that I am speaking the truth that he took the lodging-house under the terms of the will as being the elder, and that he not only thought it right to make no claims against the defendant, but on the contrary praised his conduct, take the deposition.

THE DEPOSITION

That you may know, men of Athens, what large **36** sums he has received from the rents and from the debts[a]—he, who will presently wail as though he were destitute and had lost everything—hear a brief account from me. This man has collected twenty talents in all owing to debts he has recovered from the papers which his father left, and of these sums more than half he keeps in his possession ; for in many instances he is defrauding his brother of his share. From **37** the lessee, for the eight years during which Phormio had the bank, he received eighty minae a year, half of the whole rent. These items make ten talents and forty minae.[b] For ten years after that, during which they subsequently leased the bank to Xeno and Euphraeus and Euphro and Callistratus, he received a talent every year.[c] Besides this he has had for about **38** twenty years the income of the property originally divided, of which he himself had charge, more than thirty minae. If you add all these sums together,— what he got from the distribution, what he recovered from the debts, and what he has collected as rent, it will be plain that he has received more than forty before, but Apollodorus received only that from the shield-factory, or a talent annually.

φανήσεται, χωρὶς ὧν οὗτος εὖ πεποίηκε, καὶ τῶν
μητρῴων, καὶ ὧν ἀπὸ τῆς τραπέζης ἔχων οὐκ
ἀποδίδωσι πένθ᾽ ἡμιταλάντων καὶ ἑξακοσίων δραχ-
39 μῶν. ἀλλὰ νὴ Δία ταῦθ᾽ ἡ πόλις εἴληφε, καὶ δεινὰ
πέπονθας πολλὰ καταλελῃτουργηκώς. ἀλλ᾽ ἃ μὲν
ἐκ κοινῶν ἐλῃτούργεις τῶν χρημάτων, σὺ καὶ
ἀδελφὸς ἀνηλώσατε· ἃ δ᾽ ὕστερον, οὐκ ἔστιν ἄξια,
μὴ ὅτι δυοῖν ταλάντοιν προσόδου, ἀλλ᾽ οὐδ᾽ εἴκοσι
μνῶν. μηδὲν οὖν τὴν πόλιν αἰτιῶ, μηδ᾽ ἃ σὺ τῶν
ὄντων αἰσχρῶς καὶ κακῶς ἀνήλωκας, ὡς ἡ πόλις
εἴληφε, λέγε.

40 Ἵνα δ᾽ εἰδῆτ᾽, ὦ ἄνδρες Ἀθηναῖοι, τό τε πλῆθος
τῶν χρημάτων ὧν εἴληφε, καὶ τὰς λῃτουργίας ἃς
λελῃτούργηκεν, ἀναγνώσεται ὑμῖν καθ᾽ ἓν ἕκαστον.
[957] Λαβέ μοι τὸ βιβλίον τουτὶ καὶ τὴν πρόκλησιν
ταυτηνὶ καὶ τὰς μαρτυρίας ταυτασί.

BIBΛION. ΠΡΟΚΛΗΣΙΣ. ΜΑΡΤΥΡΙΑΙ

41 Τοσαῦτα μὲν τοίνυν χρήματ᾽ εἰληφώς, καὶ χρέα
πολλῶν ταλάντων ἔχων, ὧν τὰ μὲν παρ᾽ ἑκόντων,
τὰ δ᾽ ἐκ τῶν δικῶν εἰσπράττει, ἃ τῆς μισθώσεως
ἔξω τῆς τραπέζης καὶ τῆς ἄλλης οὐσίας, ἣν κατέλιπε Πασίων, ὠφείλετ᾽ ἐκείνῳ καὶ νῦν παρειλή-
φασιν οὗτοι, καὶ τοσαῦτ᾽ ἀνηλωκὼς ὅσ᾽ ὑμεῖς
ἠκούσατε, οὐδὲ πολλοστὸν μέρος τῶν προσόδων,
μὴ ὅτι τῶν ἀρχαίων, εἰς τὰς λῃτουργίας, ὅμως
ἀλαζονεύσεται καὶ τριηραρχίας ἐρεῖ καὶ χορηγίας.
42 ἐγὼ δ᾽, ὡς μὲν οὐκ ἀληθῆ ταῦτ᾽ ἐρεῖ, ἐπέδειξα,

---

a As a matter of fact Apollodorus had served as trierarch
with distinction, and had been most liberal in his expenditures. See Oration L. §§ 11 ff., and Oration XLV. § 78.

talents, to say nothing of the present Phormio made him, and his inheritance from his mother, and what he has had from the bank and does not pay back— two and one-half talents and six hundred drachmae. Ah, but, you will tell us, the state has received these 39 sums, and you have been outrageously treated, having used up your fortune in public services ! No ; what you expended in public service out of the undivided funds, you and your brother expended jointly ; and what you gave after that does not amount to the interest, I will not say on two talents, but even on twenty minae. Do not, then, accuse the state, nor say that the state has received that portion of your patrimony which you have shamefully and wickedly squandered.

That you may know, men of Athens, the amount 40 of property which he has received, and the public services which he has assumed, the clerk shall read to you the items one by one.

Please take this list and this challenge and these depositions.

THE LIST. THE CHALLENGE. THE DEPOSITIONS

All these moneys he has received ; he has debts 41 due him to the value of many talents, which he is collecting, some by voluntary payments, some by bringing action. These debts were owing to Pasio— quite apart from the rent of the bank and the other property which he left ;—and these the two brothers have recovered. He has expended upon public services merely what you have heard, the smallest fraction of his income, not to say of his capital ; and yet he will assume a bragging air, and will talk about his expenditures for trierarchal and choregic services.[a] I have shown you that these assertions of his will be 42

351

οἶμαι μέντοι, κἂν εἰ ταῦτα πάντ' ἀληθῆ λέγοι,
κάλλιον εἶναι καὶ δικαιότερον τόνδ' ἀπὸ τῶν αὑτοῦ
λητουργεῖν ὑμῖν, ἢ τούτῳ δόντας τὰ τοῦδε, μικρὰ
τῶν πάντων αὐτοὺς μετασχόντας, τόνδε μὲν ἐν ταῖς
ἐσχάταις ἐνδείαις ὁρᾶν, τοῦτον δ' ὑβρίζοντα καὶ εἰς
ἅπερ εἴωθεν ἀναλίσκοντα.

43 Ἀλλὰ μὴν περὶ τῆς γ' εὐπορίας, ὡς ἐκ τῶν
τοῦ πατρὸς τοῦ σοῦ κέκτηται, καὶ ὧν ἐρωτήσειν
ἔφησθα, πόθεν τὰ ὄντα κέκτηται Φορμίων, μόνῳ
τῶν ὄντων ἀνθρώπων σοὶ τοῦτον οὐκ ἔνεστ' εἰπεῖν
τὸν λόγον. οὐδὲ γὰρ Πασίων ὁ σὸς πατὴρ ἐκτήσαθ'
εὑρὼν οὐδὲ τοῦ πατρὸς αὐτῷ παραδόντος, ἀλλ' ἢ
παρὰ τοῖς αὑτοῦ κυρίοις Ἀντισθένει καὶ Ἀρχεστράτῳ τραπεζιτεύουσι πεῖραν δούς, ὅτι χρηστός
44 ἐστι καὶ δίκαιος, ἐπιστεύθη. ἔστι δ' ἐν ἐμπορίῳ
καὶ χρήμασιν ἐργαζομένοις ἀνθρώποις φίλεργον
δόξαι καὶ χρηστὸν εἶναι τὸν αὐτὸν θαυμαστὸν
ἡλίκον. οὔτ' οὖν ἐκείνῳ τοῦθ' οἱ κύριοι παρέδωκαν, ἀλλ' αὐτὸς ἔφυ χρηστός, οὔτε τῷδ' ὁ
[958] σὸς πατήρ· σὲ γὰρ ἂν πρότερον τοῦδε χρηστὸν
ἐποίησεν, εἰ ἦν ἐπ' ἐκείνῳ. εἰ δὲ τοῦτ' ἀγνοεῖς,
ὅτι πίστις ἀφορμὴ τῶν πασῶν ἐστι μεγίστη πρὸς
χρηματισμόν, πᾶν ἂν ἀγνοήσειας. χωρὶς δὲ τούτων πολλὰ καὶ τῷ σῷ πατρὶ καὶ σοὶ καὶ ὅλως
τοῖς ὑμετέροις πράγμασι Φορμίων γέγονεν χρήσιμος. ἀλλ' οἶμαι τῆς σῆς ἀπληστίας καὶ τοῦ σοῦ
45 τρόπου τίς ἂν δύναιτ' ἐφικέσθαι; καὶ δῆτα θαυ-

---

[a] Contrast with this passage the statements of Apollodorus himself regarding his manner of life in Oration XLV.
§ 77.

[b] The order of the words suggests a slight contrast between
δόξαι and εἶναι.

false ; however, even if they should all prove to be true, I think it more honourable and more just that he should continue to render public service from his own funds, than that you should give him the defendant's property, and while receiving yourselves but a small portion of the whole, should see the defendant reduced to extreme poverty, and the plaintiff in wanton insolence and spending his money in the manner that has been his wont.[a]

With regard now to Phormio's wealth and his 43 having got it from your father's estate, and the questions you said you were going to ask as to how Phormio acquired his fortune, you have the least right of any man in the world to speak thus. For Pasio, your father, did not acquire his fortune, any more than Phormio did, by good luck or by inheritance from his father, but he gave proof to the bankers, Antisthenes and Archestratus, who were his masters, that he was a good man and an honest, and so won their confidence. It is remarkable what a striking 44 thing it is in the eyes of people who are active in commercial life and in banking, when the same man is accounted industrious and is honest.[b] Well ; this quality was not imparted to Pasio by his masters ; he was himself honest by nature ; nor did your father impart it to Phormio. It was yourself, rather than Phormio, whom he would have made honest, if he had had the power. If you do not know that for money-making the best capital of all is trustworthiness, you do not know anything at all. But, apart from all this, Phormio has in many ways shown himself useful to your father and to you, and in general to your affairs. But your insatiate greed and your character, I take it, no one could adequately express.

μάζω πῶς οὐ λογίζῃ πρὸς σεαυτόν, ὅτι ἔστιν
Ἀρχεστράτῳ, τῷ ποτὲ τὸν σὸν πατέρα κτησαμένῳ,
υἱὸς ἐνθάδ’, Ἀντίμαχος, πράττων οὐ κατ’ ἀξίαν,
ὃς οὐ δικάζεταί σοι, οὐδὲ δεινά φησι πάσχειν, εἰ
σὺ μὲν χλανίδα φορεῖς, καὶ τὴν μὲν λέλυσαι, τὴν
δ’ ἐκδέδωκας ἑταίραν, καὶ ταῦτα γυναῖκ’ ἔχων
ποιεῖς, καὶ τρεῖς παῖδας ἀκολούθους περιάγει, καὶ
ζῇς ἀσελγῶς ὥστε καὶ τοὺς ἀπαντῶντας αἰσθάνε-
46 σθαι, αὐτὸς δ’ ἐκεῖνος πολλῶν ἐνδεής ἐστιν. οὐδὲ
τὸν Φορμίων’ ἐκεῖνος οὐχ ὁρᾷ. καίτοι εἰ κατὰ
τοῦτ’ οἴει σοι προσήκειν τῶν τούτου, ὅτι τοῦ
πατρός ποτ’ ἐγένετο τοῦ σοῦ, ἐκείνῳ προσήκει
μᾶλλον ἢ σοί· ὁ γὰρ αὖ σὸς πατὴρ ἐκείνων ἐγένετο,
ὥστε καὶ σὺ καὶ οὗτος ἐκείνου γίγνεσθ’ ἐκ τοῦδε
τοῦ λόγου. σὺ δ’ εἰς τοῦθ’ ἥκεις ἀγνωμοσύνης,
ὥσθ’ ἃ προσῆκέ σοι τοὺς λέγοντας ἐχθροὺς νομί-
47 ζειν, ταῦτ’ αὐτὸς ποιεῖς ἀνάγκην εἶναι λέγειν, καὶ
ὑβρίζεις μὲν σαυτὸν καὶ τοὺς γονέας τεθνεῶτας,
προπηλακίζεις δὲ τὴν πόλιν, καὶ ἃ τῆς τούτων
φιλανθρωπίας ἀπολαύσας εὕρεθ’ ὁ σὸς πατὴρ καὶ
μετὰ ταῦτα Φορμίων οὑτοσί, ταῦτ’ ἀντὶ τοῦ κοσ-
[959] μεῖν καὶ περιστέλλειν, ἵνα καὶ τοῖς δοῦσιν ὡς
εὐσχημονέστατ’ ἐφαίνετο καὶ τοῖς λαβοῦσιν ὑμῖν,
ἄγεις εἰς μέσον, δεικνύεις, ἐλέγχεις, μόνον οὐκ
48 ὀνειδίζεις οἷον ὄντα σ’ ἐποίησαντ’ Ἀθηναῖον. εἶτ’
εἰς τοῦθ’ ἥκεις μανίας (τί γὰρ ἄλλο τις εἴπῃ;) ὥστ’
οὐκ αἰσθάνει, ὅτι καὶ νῦν ἡμεῖς μὲν ἀξιοῦντες,

ᵃ That is, of course, the right of citizenship.

I am surprised that you do not of yourself make this 45
reflection, that Archestratus, to whom your father
formerly belonged, has a son here, Antimachus, who
fares not at all as he deserves, and who does not go
to law with you and say that he is outrageously
treated, because you wear a soft mantle, and have
redeemed one mistress, and have given another in
marriage (all this, while you have a wife of your
own), and take three attendant slaves about with
you, and live so licentiously that even those who
meet you on the street perceive it, while he himself is in great destitution. Nor does he fail to 46
see Phormio's condition. And yet if on this ground
you think you have a claim on Phormio's property,
because he once belonged to your father, Antimachus has a stronger claim than you have. For
your father in his turn belonged to those men, so
that both you and Phormio by this argument belong
to Antimachus. But you are so lost to all proper
feeling, that you yourself compel people to say
things which you ought to hate anyone for saying.
You disgrace yourself and your dead parents, and 47
you cast reproach upon the state, and instead of
adorning and cherishing this good fortune [a] which
your father, and afterward Phormio have come to
enjoy through the kindness of these men, so that
it might have appeared as the highest of honours for
those who gave it and for you who obtained it, you
drag it into public view, you point the finger of scorn
at it, you criticize it ; you all but taunt the Athenians
for admitting to citizenship a person like yourself.
Indeed you have come to such a pitch of insanity— 48
what other name can one find for it ?—as not to see
that at this moment *we*, who claim that, since Phormio

ἐπειδήπερ ἀπηλλάγη Φορμίων, μηδέν' ὑπόλογον
εἶναι, εἴ ποτε τοῦ σοῦ πατρὸς ἐγένετο, ὑπὲρ σοῦ
λέγομεν, σὺ δὲ μηδέποτ' ἐξ ἴσου σοι γενέσθαι τοῦτον ἀξιῶν, κατὰ σαυτοῦ λέγεις· ἃ γὰρ ἂν σὺ δίκαια
σαυτῷ κατὰ τούτου τάξῃς, ταὐτὰ ταῦθ' ἥξει κατὰ
σοῦ παρὰ τῶν τὸν σὸν πατέρ' ἐξ ἀρχῆς κτησα-
μένων.

Ἀλλὰ μὴν ὅτι κἀκεῖνος ἦν τινῶν, εἶτ' ἀπηλλάγη τὸν αὐτὸν τρόπον, ὅνπερ οὗτος ἀφ' ὑμῶν,
λαβέ μοι ταυτασὶ τὰς μαρτυρίας, ὡς ἐγένετο
Πασίων Ἀρχεστράτου.

see Phormio's condition. . . . .

ΜΑΡΤΥΡΙΑΙ

49   Εἶτα τὸν σώσαντα μὲν ἐξ ἀρχῆς τὰ πράγματα
καὶ πολλὰ χρήσιμον αὐτὸν παρασχόντα τῷ πατρὶ
τῷ τούτου, τοσαῦτα δ' αὐτὸν τοῦτον ἀγάθ' εἰργασμένον, ὅσ' ὑμεῖς ἀκηκόατε, τοῦτον οἴεται δεῖν ἑλὼν
τηλικαύτην δίκην ἀδίκως ἐκβαλεῖν. οὐ γὰρ ἄλλο
γ' ἔχοις οὐδὲν ἂν ποιῆσαι. εἰς μὲν γὰρ τὰ ὄντ' εἰ
βλέποις ἀκριβῶς, ταῦθ' εὑρήσεις ὧν ἔστιν, ἐάν, ὃ
50 μὴ γένοιτ', ἐξαπατηθῶσιν οὗτοι. ὁρᾷς τὸν Ἀριστό-
λοχον τὸν Χαριδήμου· ποτ' εἶχεν ἀγρόν, εἶτά γε
νῦν πολλοί· πολλοῖς γὰρ ἐκεῖνος ὀφείλων αὐτὸν
ἐκτήσατο. καὶ τὸν Σώσινομον καὶ τὸν Τιμόδημον
καὶ τοὺς ἄλλους τραπεζίτας, οἳ, ἐπειδὴ διαλύειν
ἐδέησεν οἷς ὤφειλον, ἐξέστησαν ἁπάντων τῶν
[960] ὄντων. σὺ δ' οὐδὲν οἴει δεῖν σκοπεῖν οὐδ' ὧν ὁ

---

[a] The property of Phormio consisted chiefly in the money
of the depositors which he had invested in divers ways. If
heavy damages were assessed against him, the depositors
would at once demand their money, and such a run on the
bank would be ruinous.

has received his freedom, it should not be remembered against him that he once belonged to your father, are speaking in your interest ; while *you*, in insisting that he should never be on a footing of equality with yourself, are speaking against yourself ; for the same rule, which you lay down as just for yourself against Phormio, will be advanced against you by those who at the first were the masters of your father.

To prove that Pasio also was somebody's slave, and that he afterwards won his freedom in the same manner in which Phormio won his from you, take, please, these depositions, which show that Pasio belonged to Archestratus.

The Depositions

The man, then, who at the first saved the family 49 fortune, and rendered himself useful in many ways to this man's father, the man who has conferred upon Apollodorus himself all the benefits of which you have heard, he it is against whom the plaintiff seeks a judgement with such heavy damages, and thinks proper to cast out in ruin contrary to all right. For that, Apollodorus, is all that you could possibly accomplish. For, if you look closely at the property, you will see to whom it belongs, in case—which heaven forbid !— these jurymen are misled by you.[a] Do you see 50 Aristolochus, son of Charidemus ? Once he possessed some land ; now many people own it ; for he acquired it while he was in debt to many. And Sosinomus and Timodemus and the other bankers, who, when they had to settle with their creditors, had to give up all their property. But you think it unnecessary to have regard even for the precautions

πατὴρ σοῦ πολλῷ βελτίων ὢν καὶ ἄμεινον φρονῶν
51 πρὸς ἅπαντ᾽ ἐβουλεύσατο· ὅς, ὦ Ζεῦ καὶ θεοί,
τοσούτῳ τοῦτον ἡγεῖτο σοῦ πλείονος ἄξιον εἶναι καὶ
σοὶ καὶ ἑαυτῷ καὶ τοῖς ὑμετέροις πράγμασιν, ὥστ᾽
ἀνδρὸς ὄντος σοῦ τοῦτον, οὐ σὲ τῶν ἡμίσεων κατέλιπεν ἐπίτροπον καὶ τὴν γυναῖκ᾽ ἔδωκε καὶ ζῶν
αὐτὸν ἐτίμα, δικαίως, ὦ ἄνδρες Ἀθηναῖοι· οἱ μὲν
γὰρ ἄλλοι τραπεζῖται μίσθωσιν οὐ φέροντες, ἀλλ᾽
αὐτοὶ αὐτοῖς ἐργαζόμενοι, πάντες ἀπώλοντο, οὗτος
δὲ μίσθωσιν φέρων δύο τάλαντα καὶ τετταράκοντα
52 μνᾶς ὑμῖν ἔσωσε τὴν τράπεζαν. ὧν ἐκεῖνος μὲν
χάριν εἶχεν, σὺ δ᾽ οὐδένα ποιεῖ λόγον, ἀλλ᾽ ἐναντία
τῇ διαθήκῃ καὶ ταῖς ἀπ᾽ ἐκείνης ἀραῖς, γραφείσαις
ὑπὸ τοῦ σοῦ πατρός, ἐλαύνεις, διώκεις, συκοφαντεῖς. ὦ βέλτιστ᾽, εἰ οἷόν τε σὲ τοῦτ᾽ εἰπεῖν, οὐ
παύσει, καὶ γνώσει τοῦθ᾽ ὅτι πολλῶν χρημάτων
τὸ χρηστὸν εἶναι λυσιτελέστερόν ἐστι; σοὶ γοῦν,
εἴπερ ἀληθῆ λέγεις, χρήματα μὲν τοσαῦτ᾽ εἰληφότι
πάντ᾽ ἀπόλωλεν, ὡς φής· εἰ δ᾽ ἦσθ᾽ ἐπιεικής, οὐκ
ἂν ποτ᾽ αὔτ᾽ ἀνήλωσας.
53 Ἀλλ᾽ ἔγωγε μὰ τὸν Δία καὶ θεοὺς πανταχῇ
σκοπῶν οὐδὲν ὁρῶ, δι᾽ ὅ τι ἂν σοὶ πεισθέντες τουδὶ
καταψηφίσαιντο. τί γάρ; ὅτι πλησίον ὄντων τῶν
ἀδικημάτων ἐγκαλεῖς; ἀλλ᾽ ἔτεσιν καὶ χρόνοις
ὕστερον αἰτιᾷ. ἀλλ᾽ ὅτι τοῦτον ἀπράγμων ἦσθα
τὸν χρόνον; καὶ τίς οὐκ οἶδ᾽ ὅσα πράγματα πράττων οὐ πέπαυσαι, οὐ μόνον δίκας ἰδίας διώκων οὐκ

which your father, a far better man than you and a
wiser, took to meet all contingencies. He—O Zeus 51
and the gods—esteemed Phormio to be so much more
valuable than you both to yourself and to him and to
your business, that, although you were a man grown,
it was to Phormio, not to you, that he left the control
of the leases, and gave him his wife in marriage and
honoured him as long as he lived. And justly too,
men of Athens. For other bankers, who had no rent
to pay, but carried on their business on their own
account, have all come to ruin ; while Phormio, who
paid a rent of two talents and forty minae, saved the
bank for you. For this Pasio was grateful to him, 52
but you make no account of it. Nay, in defiance of
the will and the imprecations written in it by your
father, you harass him, you prosecute him, you
calumniate him. My good sir—if you can be addressed by this term—will you not desist, and know
this—that to be honest profits more than great
wealth ? In your own case, at any rate, although,
if your words are true, you received all this money,
it has all been lost, as you say. But, if you had
been a man of character, you would not have squandered it.

For my own part, by Zeus and the gods, though 53
I look at the matter from every side, I can see no
reason why the jury should be induced by you to
give a verdict against the defendant. Why should
they ? Because you make your charges so soon after
the offence ? But you make them years and ages
later. Ah, but you avoided the trouble of lawsuits
all this time ? But who does not know of all the cases
in which you have been engaged without ceasing,
not only prosecuting private suits of no less import-

ἐλάττους ταυτησί, ἀλλὰ καὶ δημοσίᾳ συκοφαντῶν
καὶ κρίνων τινάς; οὐχὶ Τιμομάχου κατηγόρεις;
οὐ Καλλίππου τοῦ νῦν ὄντος ἐν Σικελίᾳ; οὐ πάλιν
[961] Μένωνος; οὐκ Αὐτοκλέους; οὐ Τιμοθέου; οὐκ
54 ἄλλων πολλῶν; καίτοι πῶς ἔχει λόγον σὲ Ἀπολλόδωρον ὄντα, πρότερον τῶν κοινῶν, ὧν μέρος
ἠδικοῦ, δίκην ἀξιοῦν λαμβάνειν, ἢ τῶν ἰδίων ὧν νῦν
ἐγκαλεῖς, ἄλλως τε καὶ τηλικούτων ὄντων, ὡς σὺ
φῄς; τί ποτ' οὖν ἐκείνων κατηγορῶν τόνδ' εἴας;
οὐκ ἠδικοῦ, ἀλλ' οἶμαι συκοφαντεῖς νῦν. ἡγοῦμαι
τοίνυν, ὦ ἄνδρες Ἀθηναῖοι, πάντων μάλιστ' εἰς τὸ
πρᾶγμ' εἶναι τούτων μάρτυρας παρασχέσθαι· τὸν
γὰρ συκοφαντοῦντ' ἀεὶ τί χρὴ νομίζειν νῦν ποιεῖν;
55 καὶ νὴ Δί' ἔγωγ', ὦ ἄνδρες Ἀθηναῖοι, νομίζω,
πάνθ' ὅσα τοῦ τρόπου τοῦ Φορμίωνός ἐστι σημεῖα
καὶ τῆς τούτου δικαιοσύνης καὶ φιλανθρωπίας, καὶ
ταῦτ' εἰς τὸ πρᾶγμ' εἶναι πρὸς ὑμᾶς εἰπεῖν. ὁ μὲν
γὰρ περὶ πάντ' ἄδικος τάχ' ἄν, εἰ τύχοι, καὶ τοῦτον
ἠδίκει· ὁ δὲ μηδένα μηδὲν ἠδικηκώς, πολλοὺς δ'
εὖ πεποιηκὼς ἑκών, ἐκ τίνος εἰκότως ἂν τρόπου
τοῦτον μόνον ἠδίκει τῶν πάντων;

Τούτων τοίνυν τῶν μαρτυριῶν ἀκούσαντες γνώσεσθε τὸν ἑκατέρου τρόπον.

---

a Timomachus, Meno, and Autocles (see Oration L.) were
successive commanders of the Athenian fleet in Thracian
waters, where Apollodorus served as trierarch. Callippus
is all but certainly to be identified with the trierarch of that
name, who at the bidding of Timomachus, and after Apollo-

ance than the present one, but maliciously trumping up public charges, and bringing men to trial? Did you not accuse Timomachus? Did you not accuse Callippus, who is now in Sicily? Or, again, Meno? or Autocles? or Timotheus? or hosts of others? [a] But 54 is it reasonable to believe that you, who are Apollodorus, would deem it your duty to seek satisfaction for public wrongs, which touched you only in part, sooner than for the private wrongs, concerning which you now bring charges, especially when they were as grave as you now claim? Why, then, did you accuse those men, and leave Phormio alone? You were suffering no wrong, but methinks the charges which you are now bringing are baseless and malicious. I think, then, men of Athens, that nothing could be 55 more to the purpose than to bring forward witnesses to these facts. For if one is continually making baseless charges, what can one expect him to do now? In truth, men of Athens, I think that whatever serves as an index of Phormio's character, and of his uprightness and his generosity, I may rightly bring before you as something quite to the purpose. For one who is dishonest in all matters might perhaps have wronged the plaintiff among others; but a man who has never wronged anybody in anything, but, on the contrary, has voluntarily done good to many, how could he reasonably be thought to have wronged Apollodorus alone of all men?

When you have heard these depositions, you will know the character of either.

dorus's own refusal to do so, had transported the exile Callistratus from Macedonia to Thasos. Timotheus was the well-known Athenian general, against whom Apollodorus brought also a private suit to recover funds (Oration XLIX.).

DEMOSTHENES

56 Ἴθι δὴ λαβὲ τὰς πρὸς Ἀπολλόδωρον τῆς πονηρίας.

Ἆρ' οὖν ὅμοιος οὑτοσί; σκοπεῖτε. λέγε.

Ἀνάγνωθι δὴ καὶ ὅσα δημοσίᾳ χρήσιμος τῇ
πόλει γέγον' οὑτοσί.

57 Τοσαῦτα τοίνυν, ὦ ἄνδρες Ἀθηναῖοι, Φορμίων
χρήσιμος τῇ πόλει γεγονὼς καὶ πολλοῖς ὑμῶν, καὶ
οὐδέν' οὔτ' ἰδίᾳ οὔτε δημοσίᾳ κακὸν οὐδὲν εἰργα-
σμένος, οὐδ' ἀδικῶν Ἀπολλόδωρον τουτονί, δεῖται
[962] καὶ ἱκετεύει καὶ ἀξιοῖ σωθῆναι, καὶ ἡμεῖς συν-
δεόμεθ' οἱ ἐπιτήδειοι ταῦθ' ὑμῶν. ἐκεῖνο δ' ὑμᾶς
ἀκοῦσαι δεῖ. τοσαῦτα γάρ, ὦ ἄνδρες Ἀθηναῖοι,
χρήμαθ' ὑμῖν ἀνεγνώσθη προσηυπορηκώς, ὅσ' οὔθ'
οὗτος οὔτ' ἄλλος οὐδεὶς κέκτηται. πίστις μέντοι
Φορμίωνι παρὰ τοῖς εἰδόσι καὶ τοσούτων καὶ
πολλῷ πλειόνων χρημάτων, δι' ἧς καὶ αὐτὸς ἑαυτῷ
58 καὶ ὑμῖν χρήσιμός ἐστιν. ἃ μὴ προῆσθε, μηδ'
ἐπιτρέψητ' ἀνατρέψαι τῷ μιαρῷ τούτῳ ἀνθρώπῳ,
μηδὲ ποιήσητ' αἰσχρὸν παράδειγμα, ὡς τὰ τῶν
ἐργαζομένων καὶ μετρίως ἐθελόντων ζῆν τοῖς
βδελυροῖς καὶ συκοφάνταις ὑπάρχει παρ' ὑμῶν

---

[a] I follow Sandys in the interpretation of this passage.

Now read those which bear upon the baseness of 56 Apollodorus.

THE DEPOSITIONS

Is this fellow of like stamp ? Consider. Read on.

THE DEPOSITIONS

Now read all the services which Phormio has rendered to the state.

THE DEPOSITIONS

Phormio, then, men of Athens, who has in so many 57 ways proved himself of service to the state and to many of you, and has never done harm to anyone either in public or in private, and who is guilty of no wrong toward this man Apollodorus, begs and implores and claims your protection, and we, his friends, join in the same plea to you. Of another fact, too, you should be informed. Depositions have been read to you, men of Athens, showing that the defendant has supplied you with funds in excess of the whole amount that he or anybody else possesses ; but Phormio has credit with those who know him for so great an amount and for far larger sums, and through this he is of service both to himself and to you.[a] Do not throw this away, 58 nor suffer this abominable fellow to destroy it ; do not establish a shameful precedent, that it is permitted by you that rascals and sycophants should take the property of those who are active in business and who lead well-ordered lives   Far greater advantage

λαβεῖν· πολὺ γὰρ χρησιμώτερ' ὑμῖν παρὰ τῷδ' ὄνθ'
ὑπάρχει. ὁρᾶτε γὰρ αὐτοὶ καὶ ἀκούετε τῶν μαρ-
59 τύρων, οἷον ἑαυτὸν τοῖς δεηθεῖσιν παρέχει. καὶ
τούτων οὐδὲν εἵνεκα τοῦ λυσιτελοῦντος εἰς χρήματα
πεποίηκεν, ἀλλὰ φιλανθρωπίᾳ καὶ τρόπου ἐπι-
εικείᾳ. οὔκουν ἄξιον, ὦ ἄνδρες Ἀθηναῖοι, τὸν
τοιοῦτον ἄνδρα προέσθαι τούτῳ, οὐδὲ τηνικαῦτ'
ἐλεεῖν ὅτ' οὐδὲν ἔσται τουτῳὶ πλέον, ἀλλὰ νῦν ὅτε
κύριοι καθέστατε σῶσαι· οὐ γὰρ ἔγωγ' ὁρῶ καιρόν,
60 ἐν ᾧ τινι μᾶλλον ἂν βοηθήσειέ τις αὐτῷ. τὰ μὲν
οὖν πόλλ' ὧν Ἀπολλόδωρος ἐρεῖ, νομίζετ' εἶναι
λόγον καὶ συκοφαντίας, κελεύετε δ' αὐτὸν ὑμῖν
ἐπιδεῖξαι, ἢ ὡς οὐ διέθετο ταῦθ' ὁ πατήρ, ἢ ὡς ἔστι
τις ἄλλη μίσθωσις πλὴν ἧς ἡμεῖς δείκνυμεν, ἢ ὡς
οὐκ ἀφῆκεν αὐτὸν διαλογισάμενος τῶν ἐγκλημάτων
ἁπάντων, ἃ ἔγνω θ' ὁ κηδεστὴς ὁ τούτου καὶ οὗτος
αὐτὸς συνεχώρησεν, ἢ ὡς διδόασιν οἱ νόμοι δικάζεσθαι τῶν οὕτω πραχθέντων, ἢ τῶν τοιούτων τι
61 δεικνύναι. ἐὰν δ' ἀπορῶν αἰτίας καὶ βλασφημίας
[963] λέγῃ καὶ κακολογῇ, μὴ προσέχετε τὸν νοῦν, μηδ'
ὑμᾶς ἡ τούτου κραυγὴ καὶ ἀναίδει' ἐξαπατήσῃ,
ἀλλὰ φυλάττετε καὶ μέμνησθ' ὅσ' ἡμῶν ἀκηκόατε.
κἂν ταῦτα ποιῆτε, αὐτοί τ' εὐορκήσετε καὶ τουτονὶ
δικαίως σώσετε, ἄξιον ὄντα νὴ τὸν Δία καὶ θεοὺς
ἅπαντας.
62 Ἀνάγνωθι λαβὼν αὐτοῖς τὸν νόμον καὶ τὰς μαρτυρίας τασί.

accrues to you from this wealth while it remains in the possession of the defendant. For you see for yourselves, and you hear from the witnesses, what a friend he shows himself to be to those in need. And 59 not one of these acts has he done with a view to pecuniary advantage, but from generosity and kindliness of disposition. So it is not right, men of Athens, that you should give up such a man to be the prey of Apollodorus. Do not show Phormio pity at a time when it will be of no profit to him, but now when it is in your power to save him ; for I see no time in which one could more fittingly come to his aid than now. Most of what Apollodorus will say you must regard 60 as mere talk and baseless calumny. Bid him demonstrate to you, either that his father did not make this will, or that there is another lease than the one which we produce ; or that he himself after going over the reckoning did not give Phormio a release from all the claims regarding which his father-in-law made the award with the plaintiff's own concurrence ; or that the laws permit one to bring action regarding matters thus decided. Or bid him try to show anything of that sort. But if, for want of proofs, he goes on 61 uttering charges and calumnies and abuse, do not heed him, nor let his noisy talk and shamelessness lead you astray. Nay, keep in mind, and remember all that you have heard. If you do this you will be faithful to your oaths, and will save the defendant, as justice bids. By Zeus and all the gods he deserves it.

Take, and read them the law and these deposi-62 tions.

DEMOSTHENES

ΝΟΜΟΣ. ΜΑΡΤΥΡΙΑΙ

Οὐκ οἶδ' ὅ τι δεῖ πλείω λέγειν. οἶμαι γὰρ ὑμᾶς
οὐδὲν ἀγνοεῖν τῶν εἰρημένων. ἐξέρα τὸ ὕδωρ.

ᵃ The speaker concludes without having exhausted the
time allowed him ; there is, therefore, water left in the water-
clock. This he effectively bids the attendant to pour out.

The Law. The Depositions

I do not know what reason there is why I should say more; for I believe that nothing that I have said has escaped you. Pour out the water.[a]

Oration XXXVIII. closes with these same words. In Oration LIV., while depositions are being read, the attendant is bidden to check the flow of the water.

AGAINST PANTAENETUS

INTRODUCTION

THIS somewhat difficult speech deals with a complicated situation growing out of successive transfers of a mining property in the district of Maroneia, in Attica. A certain Telemachus had originally purchased[a] the property from the state, and Pantaenetus bought it from him. Since, however, he lacked capital—whether to pay the purchase price or to carry on the work does not appear—he borrowed money from Mnesicles and others. After this transaction had been completed, and the title to the property had consequently passed to Mnesicles, Pantaenetus, finding himself unable to pay what was due when Mnesicles called for his money, was again forced to seek financial help, this time from Nicobulus and Evergus. These men agreed to purchase the mine from Mnesicles, and to lease it to Pantaenetus, receiving their interest in the form of rent from the profits of the mine. Pantaenetus, on his part, was by the terms of the lease given the right to buy back the mine within a given time.

After this matter had been arranged, Nicobulus went away on a trip to Pontus, and in his absence, Pantaenetus having failed to pay the stipulated rent, Evergus took possession of the property—the mine,

[a] The "purchase" amounted to a perpetual lease, the title remaining vested in the state.

the slaves, and the accumulated silver ore. Whether he was within his rights in taking this action or whether he exceeded them is not made wholly clear (the word $\pi\lambda\eta\mu\mu\epsilon\lambda\tilde{\omega}\nu$ [a] is applied to his act in § 26) ; but Pantaenetus subsequently brought suit against him and recovered the large sum of two talents as damages.

When Nicobulus returned to Athens, he found that Evergus had taken over the mine. However, some new creditors of Pantaenetus had presented themselves advancing claims against the property ; and Evergus and Nicobulus were glad to arrange a settlement whereby they became vendors of the mine to these claimants and themselves received the money which they had advanced. Nicobulus wisely exacted from Pantaenetus a release and discharge from all claims.

After Pantaenetus had won his suit against Evergus, he brought a similar suit against Nicobulus, alleging that the latter had abetted Evergus in the violent acts by which he had taken possession of the property. Nicobulus entered a special plea that the action was not admissible primarily because of the release and discharge given him by Pantaenetus, but also because the action for damages was one which could not properly be brought before a court sitting to decide mining cases.

It was in support of this plea in bar of action that the present speech was delivered. It is of high interest on account of the light which it throws on the question of the control and operation of the silver

---

[a] This word is borrowed from the field of music, but it came to be freely used to gloss over " mistakes " in the realm of morals.

mines in the region of Laurium.   Regarding these, the
English reader can find much information in Boeckh's
" Dissertation on the Silver Mines of Laurion," in
his *Public Economy of Athens*, pp. 615 ff. (Ed. 2,
translated by Lewis), and in the standard manuals
on Greek antiquities.   The Introduction prefixed to
Kennedy's translation of this oration in his *Demosthenes*, vol. iv. pp. 219-224 (Bohn), is most helpful.

The oration is discussed in Schaefer, iii.² pp. 200 ff.,
and in Blass, iii. pp. 477 ff.

XXXVII

ΠΑΡΑΓΡΑΦΗ ΠΡΟΣ ΠΑΝΤΑΙΝΕΤΟΝ

Δεδωκότων, ὦ ἄνδρες δικασταί, τῶν νόμων
παραγράψασθαι, περὶ ὧν ἄν τις ἀφεὶς καὶ ἀπαλλάξας δικάζηται, γεγενημένων ἀμφοτέρων μοι
πρὸς Πανταίνετον τουτονί, παρεγραψάμην, ὡς ἠκού-
σατ᾽ ἀρτίως, μὴ εἰσαγώγιμον εἶναι τὴν δίκην, οὐκ
οἰόμενος δεῖν ἀφεῖσθαι τοῦ δικαίου τούτου, οὐδ᾽,
ἐπειδὰν ἐξελέγξω πρὸς ἅπασι τοῖς ἄλλοις καὶ ἀφει-
κότα τοῦτον ἐμαυτὸν καὶ ἀπηλλαγμένον, ἐγγενέσθαι
τούτῳ μὴ φάσκειν ἀληθῆ με λέγειν, καὶ ποιεῖσθαι
τεκμήριον, ὡς, εἴπερ ἐπράχθη τι τοιοῦτον, παρεγραψάμην ἂν αὐτόν, ἀλλ᾽ ἐπὶ ταύτης τῆς σκήψεως
εἰσελθὼν ἀμφότερ᾽ ὑμῖν ἐπιδεῖξαι, καὶ ὡς οὐδὲν
ἠδίκηκα τοῦτον, καὶ ὡς παρὰ τὸν νόμον μοι δικά-
2 ζεται. εἰ μὲν οὖν ἐπεπόνθει τι τούτων Πανταίνετος
ὧν νῦν ἐγκαλεῖ, κατ᾽ ἐκείνους ἂν τοὺς χρόνους
εὐθὺς ἐφαίνετό μοι δικαζόμενος, ἐν οἷς τὸ συμβόλαιον ἡμῖν πρὸς ἀλλήλους ἐγένετο, οὐσῶν μὲν
ἐμμήνων τούτων τῶν δικῶν, ἐπιδημούντων δ᾽ ἡμῶν
ἀμφοτέρων, ἁπάντων δ᾽ ἀνθρώπων εἰωθότων παρ᾽

ᵃ That is, within a month from the time of filing the suit ;
" the object being that the mine-proprietor might not be
too long detained from his business." (Boeckh, quoted by
Sandys.)

XXXVII

NICOBULUS AGAINST PANTAENETUS, A SPECIAL PLEA

INASMUCH as the laws, men of the jury, have granted that a special plea be entered in cases where a man, after having given a release and discharge, nevertheless brings suit, and as both of these have been given me by Pantaenetus here, I have pleaded, as you have just now heard, that his suit is not admissible. I did not think that I should forgo this right, or that, after I had proved among other things that the plaintiff had released me, and that I had got rid of him, it should be open to him to declare that I was uttering a falsehood and to try to employ the argument that, if any such release had been granted me, I should have put in a special plea to bar his suit. No, I determined to come before you relying on this plea and to prove both points—that I have never done the plaintiff any wrong, and that he is suing me contrary to law. If Pantaenetus had suffered any of the wrongs 2 with which he now charges me, he would be found to have brought suit against me at the time when the contract between us was made, for these actions must be decided within the month,[a] and both Evergus and I were in town; since all men are wont to be most indig-

αὐτὰ τἀδικήματα μᾶλλον ἢ χρόνων ἐγγεγενημένων
[967] ἀγανακτεῖν. ἐπειδὴ δ' οὐδὲν ἠδικημένος, ὡς καὶ
ὑμεῖς οἶδ' ὅτι φήσετε, ἐπειδὰν τὰ πεπραγμέν'
ἀκούσητε, τῷ κατορθῶσαι τὴν πρὸς Εὔεργον δίκην
ἐπηρμένος συκοφαντεῖ, ὑπόλοιπόν ἐστι παρ' ὑμῖν,
ὦ ἄνδρες δικασταί, ἐπιδείξανθ' ὡς οὐδ' ὁτιοῦν
ἀδικῶ, καὶ μάρτυρας ὧν ἂν λέγω παρασχόμενον,
3 πειράσασθαι σῴζειν ἐμαυτόν. δεήσομαι δὲ καὶ
δίκαια καὶ μέτρι' ὑμῶν ἁπάντων, ἀκοῦσαί τέ μου
περὶ ὧν παρεγραψάμην εὐνοϊκῶς, καὶ προσέχειν
ὅλῳ τῷ πράγματι τὸν νοῦν· πολλῶν γὰρ δικῶν ἐν
τῇ πόλει γεγενημένων, οὐδένα πω δίκην οὔτ' ἀν-
αιδεστέραν οὔτε συκοφαντικωτέραν οἶμαι φανήσε-
σθαι δεδικασμένον ἧς νῦν οὑτοσὶ λαχὼν εἰσελθεῖν
τετόλμηκεν. ἐξ ἀρχῆς δ', ὡς ἂν οἷός τ' ὦ διὰ
βραχυτάτων, ἅπαντα τὰ πραχθέντα διηγήσομαι
πρὸς ὑμᾶς.
4 Ἐδανείσαμεν πέντε καὶ ἑκατὸν μνᾶς ἐγὼ καὶ
Εὔεργος, ὦ ἄνδρες δικασταί, Πανταινέτῳ τουτῳί,
ἐπ' ἐργαστηρίῳ τ' ἐν τοῖς ἔργοις ἐν Μαρωνείᾳ καὶ
τριάκοντ' ἀνδραπόδοις. ἦν δὲ τοῦ δανείσματος
τετταράκοντα μὲν καὶ πέντε μναῖ ἐμαί, τάλαντον δ'
Εὐέργου. συνέβαινε δὲ τοῦτον ὀφείλειν Μνησικλεῖ
μὲν Κολλυτεῖ τάλαντον, Φιλέᾳ δ' Ἐλευσινίῳ καὶ
5 Πλείστορι πέντε καὶ τετταράκοντα μνᾶς. πρατὴρ
μὲν δὴ τοῦ ἐργαστηρίου καὶ τῶν ἀνδραπόδων ὁ
Μνησικλῆς ἡμῖν γίγνεται· καὶ γὰρ ἐώνητ' ἐκεῖνος

---

a Evergus and Nicobulus, as stated in the Introduction,
had leased the mining property to Pantaenetus. As the
lessee failed to pay the interest, Evergus, in the absence of
Nicobulus, who had gone abroad, took possession of the
property and even seized some silver which a slave of
Pantaenetus was bringing to his master that he might make

nant at the very time of their wrongs, and not after a period has intervened. Since, however, the plaintiff, though he has suffered no wrong, as I know well you will yourselves agree when you have heard the facts, elated by the success of his suit against Evergus,[a] brings a malicious and baseless action, there is no other course left me, men of the jury, than to prove in your court that I am guilty of no wrong whatever, to produce witnesses in support of what I say, and to endeavour to save myself. I shall make a reasonable 3 and fair request of you all, that you hear with goodwill what I have to say regarding my special plea, and that you give your attention to every aspect of the case. For, while hosts of cases have been tried in Athens, I think it will be shown that no man has ever brought before you one so marked by shamelessness and malice as this, which this fellow has had the audacity to bring into your court. I shall with all possible brevity set before you all the facts of the case.

Evergus and I, men of the jury, lent to this man 4 Pantaenetus one hundred and five minae on the security of a mining property in Maroneia[b] and of thirty slaves. Of this loan forty-five minae belonged to me, and a talent to Evergus. It happened that the plaintiff also owed a talent to Mnesicles of Collytus[c] and forty-five minae to Phileas of Eleusis and Pleistor. The vendor 5 to us of the mining property and the slaves was Mnesicles, for he had purchased them for the plaintiff

a payment due to the state. Because of this Pantaenetus became a debtor to the state and was required to pay double the amount due. He then sued Evergus, and won a verdict of two talents damages.

[b] Maroneia was a small district in the mining area of Laurium in Attica.

[c] Collytus was a deme of the tribe Aegeïs.

αὐτὰ τούτῳ παρὰ Τηλεμάχου τοῦ πρότερον κε-
κτημένου· μισθοῦται δ' οὗτος παρ' ἡμῶν τοῦ
γιγνομένου τόκου τῷ ἀργυρίῳ, πέντε καὶ ἑκατὸν
δραχμῶν τοῦ μηνὸς ἑκάστου. καὶ τιθέμεθα συνθήκας, ἐν αἷς ἥ τε μίσθωσις ἦν γεγραμμένη καὶ
6 λύσις τούτῳ παρ' ἡμῶν ἔν τινι ῥητῷ χρόνῳ. πρα-
[968] χθέντων δὲ τούτων ἐλαφηβολιῶνος μηνὸς ἐπὶ
Θεοφίλου ἄρχοντος, ἐγὼ μὲν ἐκπλέων εἰς τὸν
Πόντον εὐθὺς ᾠχόμην, οὗτος δ' ἐνθάδ' ἦν καὶ
Εὔεργος. τὰ μὲν δὴ πραχθέντα τούτοις πρὸς
αὐτούς, ἕως ἀπεδήμουν ἐγώ, οὐκ ἂν ἔχοιμ' εἰπεῖν.
οὔτε γὰρ ταὐτὰ λέγουσιν οὔτ' ἀεὶ ταῦθ' οὗτός γε,
ἀλλὰ τοτὲ μὲν ἐκπεσεῖν ὑπ' ἐκείνου βίᾳ παρὰ τὰς
συνθήκας ἐκ τῆς μισθώσεως, τοτὲ δ' αὐτὸν αἴτιον
αὑτῷ πρὸς τὸ δημόσιον γενέσθαι τῆς ἐγγραφῆς,
7 τοτὲ δ' ἄλλ' ὅ τι ἂν βούληται. ἐκεῖνος δ' ἁπλῶς
οὔτε τοὺς τόκους ἀπολαμβάνων οὔτε τῶν ἄλλων
τῶν ἐν ταῖς συνθήκαις ποιοῦντος οὐδὲν τούτου,
ἐλθὼν παρ' ἑκόντος τούτου λαβὼν ἔχειν τὰ ἑαυτοῦ·
μετὰ ταῦτα δ' ἀπελθόντα τοῦτον ἥκειν τοὺς ἀμ-
φισβητήσοντας ἄγοντα, αὐτὸς δ' οὐχ ὑπεξελθεῖν
ἐκείνοις, τοῦτον δ' οὐχὶ κωλύειν ἔχειν ὅσ' ἐμι-
σθώσατο, εἰ ποιοίη τὰ συγκείμενα. τούτων μὲν
8 δὴ τοιούτους ἀκούω λόγους. ἐκεῖνο δ' οἶδ' ὅτι, εἰ
μὲν οὗτος ἀληθῆ λέγει καὶ δεινὰ πέπονθεν, ὥσπερ
φήσ', ὑπὸ τοῦ Εὐέργου, ἔχει δίκην ἧς ἐτιμήσατ'

---

[a] That is, in March 347 b.c.
[b] See note a, p. 376, and the Introduction.

from Telemachus, the former owner; and the plaintiff leased them from us at a rent equal to the interest accruing on the money, a hundred and five drachmae a month. We drew up an agreement in which the terms of the lease were stated, and the right was given the plaintiff of redeeming these things from us within a given time. When these transactions had 6 been completed in the month of Elaphebolion in the archonship of Theophilus,[a] I at once sailed away for Pontus, but the plaintiff and Evergus remained here. What transactions they had with one another while I was away, I cannot state, for they do not tell the same story, nor is the plaintiff always consistent with himself; sometimes he says that he was forcibly ousted from his leasehold by Evergus in violation of the agreement; sometimes that Evergus was the cause of his being inscribed as a debtor to the state;[b] sometimes anything else that he chooses to say. But 7 Evergus tells a plain and consistent story, that since he was not receiving his interest, and the plaintiff was not performing any of the other things stipulated in the agreement, he went and took from the plaintiff, with the latter's consent, what was his own, and kept it; that after this the plaintiff went away, but came back bringing men to make claim to the property; that he on his own part did not give way in their favour, but made no objection to the plaintiff's holding that for which he had given a lease, provided he should observe the terms of the agreement. From these men, then, I hear stories of this sort. This, 8 however, I know well, that, if the plaintiff speaks the truth, and has been outrageously treated, as he says, by Evergus, he has had satisfaction to the amount at which he himself assessed his damages; for he came

αὐτός· εἷλε γὰρ εἰσελθὼν αὐτὸν ὡς ὑμᾶς, καὶ οὐ
δήπου τῶν αὐτῶν παρὰ τοῦ τε πεποιηκότος δίκαιός
ἐστι δίκην λαβεῖν, καὶ παρ' ἐμοῦ τοῦ μηδ' ἐπι-
δημοῦντος· εἰ δ' ὁ Εὔεργος ἀληθῆ λέγει, σεσυκο-
φάντηται μὲν ὡς ἔοικεν ἐκεῖνος, ἐγὼ δ' οὐδ' οὕτως
τῶν αὐτῶν φεύγοιμ' ἂν δίκην εἰκότως.

Ὡς οὖν ταῦτα πρῶτον ἀληθῆ λέγω, τούτων τοὺς
μάρτυρας ὑμῖν παρέξομαι.

ΜΑΡΤΥΡΕΣ

9 Ὅτι μὲν τοίνυν καὶ πρατὴρ ἦν ἡμῖν τῶν κτημά-
[969] των ὅσπερ ἐξ ἀρχῆς αὐτὸς ἐώνητο, καὶ κατὰ τὰς
συνθήκας οὗτος ἐμισθώσαθ' ἡμέτερον ὂν τὸ ἐργαστήριον καὶ τἀνδράποδα, καὶ οὔτε παρῆν ἐγὼ τοῖς
μετὰ ταῦτα πρὸς Εὔεργον τούτῳ πραχθεῖσιν οὔτ'
ἐπεδήμουν ὅλως, ἔλαχέν τε τὴν δίκην ἐκείνῳ καὶ
οὐδὲν πώποθ' ἡμῖν ἐνεκάλει, ἀκούετε τῶν μαρτύ-
10 ρων, ὦ ἄνδρες δικασταί. ἐπειδὴ τοίνυν ἀφικόμην
σχεδόν τι πάντ' ἀπολωλεκὼς ὅσ' ἔχων ἐξέπλευσα,
ἀκούσας καὶ καταλαβὼν τοῦτον μὲν ἀφεστηκότα,
τὸν δ' Εὔεργον ἔχοντα καὶ κρατοῦνθ' ὧν ἐωνήμεθα,
θαυμαστῶς ὡς ἐλυπήθην, ὁρῶν τὸ πρᾶγμά μοι
περιεστηκὸς εἰς ἄτοπον· ἢ γὰρ κοινωνεῖν ἔδει τῆς
ἐργασίας καὶ τῶν ἐπιμελειῶν τῷ Εὐέργῳ, ἢ χρήστην ἀντὶ τούτου τὸν Εὔεργον ἔχειν, καὶ πρὸς
ἐκεῖνον πάλιν μίσθωσιν γράφειν καὶ συμβόλαιον

into your court and won his suit against him ; and surely he has no right to obtain damages for the same wrongs both from the one who committed them and from me, who was not even in Athens. But, if it is Evergus who speaks the truth, he has been made the object, it appears, of a baseless and malicious charge ; but even so there is no ground for my being sued on the same charge.

To prove, in the first place, that I am speaking the truth in this, I shall bring before you the witnesses to establish these facts.

THE WITNESSES

That, therefore, the man who sold us the property **9** was the man who had been the original purchaser ; that under the agreement the plaintiff rented the mining establishment and the slaves, recognizing them as belonging to us ; that I was not present at the transactions which subsequently took place between the plaintiff and Evergus, and indeed was not even in Athens ; that he brought suit against Evergus, and never made any charge against me,—all this, men of the jury, you hear from the witnesses. Well, then, when I came back, having lost practically **10** everything I had when I sailed, I heard, and found it was true, that the plaintiff had given up the property and that Evergus was in possession and control of what we had purchased. I was distressed beyond words, seeing that the matter had got into an awkward predicament ; for it was now necessary for me either to enter into partnership with Evergus for the working and management of the property, or have him for a debtor instead of Pantaenetus, and draw up a new lease and enter into a contract with him ; and I liked

11 ποιεῖσθαι· τούτων δ᾽ οὐδέτερον προηρούμην. ἀηδῶς
δ᾽ ἔχων οἷς λέγω τούτοις, ἰδὼν τὸν Μνησικλέα τὸν
πρατῆρα τούτων ἡμῖν γεγενημένον, προσελθὼν
ἐμεμφόμην αὐτῷ, λέγων οἷον ἄνθρωπον προὔξέ-
νησέ μοι, καὶ τοὺς ἀμφισβητοῦντας καὶ τί ταῦτ᾽
ἐστὶν ἠρώτων. ἀκούσας δ᾽ ἐκεῖνος, τῶν μὲν ἀμφι-
σβητούντων κατεγέλα, συνελθεῖν δ᾽ ἔφη τούτους βούλεσθαι πρὸς ἡμᾶς, καὶ συνάξειν αὐτὸς ἡμᾶς, καὶ
παραινέσειν τούτῳ πάντα ποιεῖν τὰ δίκαι᾽ ἐμοί, καὶ
12 οἴεσθαι πείσειν. ὡς δὲ συνήλθομεν, τὰ μὲν πολλὰ
τί δεῖ λέγειν; ἧκον δ᾽ οἱ δεδανεικέναι φάσκοντες
τούτῳ, ἐπὶ τῷ ἐργαστηρίῳ καὶ τοῖς ἀνδραπόδοις ἃ
ἡμεῖς ἐπριάμεθα παρὰ Μνησικλέους, καὶ οὐδὲν ἦν
ἁπλοῦν οὐδ᾽ ὑγιὲς τούτων. πάντα δ᾽ ἐξελεγχόμενοι
ψευδῆ λέγοντες, καὶ τοῦ Μνησικλέους βεβαιοῦντος
[970] ἡμῖν, προκαλοῦνται πρόκλησιν ἡμᾶς ὡς οὐ δεξο-
μένους, ἢ κομίσασθαι τὰ χρήματα πάντα παρ᾽
αὐτῶν καὶ ἀπελθεῖν, ἢ διαλῦσαι σφᾶς ὑπὲρ ὧν
ἐνεκάλουν, αἰτιώμενοι πολλῷ πλείονος ἄξι᾽ ἔχειν
13 ὧν ἐδεδώκειμεν χρημάτων. ἀκούσας δ᾽ ἐγώ, παρα-
χρῆμ᾽, οὐδὲ βουλευσάμενος, κομίσασθαι συνεχώ-
ρησα, καὶ τὸν Εὔεργον ἔπεισα. ἐπειδὴ δ᾽ ἔδει τὰ
χρήμαθ᾽ ἡμᾶς ἀπολαμβάνειν καὶ τὸ πρᾶγμ᾽ εἰς
τοῦτο προῆκτο, οὐκ ἔφασαν μετὰ ταῦτα δώσειν
οἱ τότ᾽ ἐκεῖν᾽ ἐπαγγειλάμενοι, εἰ μὴ πρατῆρες
γιγνοίμεθ᾽ ἡμεῖς τῶν κτημάτων αὐτοῖς, νοῦν
ἔχοντες, ὦ ἄνδρες Ἀθηναῖοι, κατ᾽ αὐτό γε

neither of these alternatives. Being vexed at the 11
matters of which I am telling you, and happening to
see Mnesicles, who had sold us the property, I came
up to him, and reproached him, telling what sort of a
man he had recommended to me, and I questioned
him regarding the claimants, asking what this was all
about. On hearing this, he laughed at the claimants,
but stated that they wished to have a conference with
us. He declared that he would bring us together,
and that he would urge the plaintiff to do all that was
right in my regard, and he thought he would persuade
him to do so. When we had our meeting—what need 12
is there to tell you all the details ?—the men came
who claimed to have made loans to the plaintiff on
the security of the mining property and the slaves,
which we bought from Mnesicles ; and there was
nothing straightforward or honest about them. Then,
when they were convicted of falsehood in all their
statements and Mnesicles confirmed our having
bought the property, they offered us a challenge,
assuming that we should not accept it, either to take
all our money from them and withdraw, or to settle
with them by paying their claims ; for the security
which we held was, they claimed, worth far more
than the sums we had lent. When I heard this, on 13
the spur of the moment and without even taking
thought, I agreed to take my money, and I persuaded
Evergus to adopt the same course. But when the
time came for us to receive our money, the matter
having been brought to this conclusion, the people
who had previously made the offer declared then that
they would not pay us unless we became vendors to
them of the property, and in this point anyway, men
of Athens, they were prudent ; for they saw in what

τοῦτο· ἑώρων γὰρ ἡμᾶς οἳ ἐσυκοφαντούμεθα ὑπὸ τούτου.

Ὡς οὖν καὶ ταῦτ' ἀληθῆ λέγω, λαβέ μοι καὶ ταύτας τὰς μαρτυρίας.

ΜΑΡΤΥΡΙΑΙ

14 Ἐπειδὴ τοίνυν τὸ πρᾶγμ' ἐνταῦθ' εἰστήκει, καὶ τὰ μὲν χρήματ' οὐ προῖενθ' οὓς ἐπήγαγεν οὗτος, ἡμεῖς δ' εἰκότως ἐφαινόμεθ' ὧν ἐωνήμεθα κρατεῖν, ἱκέτευεν ἐδεῖτ' ἠντιβόλει πρατῆρας ἡμᾶς γίγνεσθαι. ἀξιοῦντος δὲ τούτου καὶ πολλὰ δεηθέντος ἐμοῦ, καὶ 15 τί οὐ ποιήσαντος; καὶ τοῦθ' ὑπέμεινα. ὁρῶν δ' αὐτόν, ὦ ἄνδρες Ἀθηναῖοι, κακοήθη, καὶ τὸ μὲν ἐξ ἀρχῆς τοῦ Μνησικλέους κατηγοροῦντα πρὸς ἡμᾶς, πάλιν δ' ᾧ φίλος ἦν τὰ μάλιστα, τῷ Εὐέργῳ, τούτῳ προσκεκρουκότα, καὶ τὸ μὲν πρῶτον ὡς ἐγὼ κατέπλευσα, ἄσμενον φάσκονθ' ἑορακέναι με, ἐπειδὴ δ' ἔδει τὰ δίκαια ποιεῖν, ἐμοὶ πάλιν δυσκολαίνοντα, καὶ ἅπασιν μέχρι τοῦ προλαβεῖν καὶ τυχεῖν ὧν ἂν δέηται φίλον ὄντα, μετὰ ταῦτα δ' 16 ἐχθρὸν καὶ διάφορον γιγνόμενον, ἠξίουν ἀπαλλατ-
[971] τόμενος καὶ πρατὴρ ὑπὲρ τούτου γιγνόμενος, πάντων ἀφεθεὶς τῶν ἐγκλημάτων καὶ ἀπαλλαγείς, οὕτω διαλύεσθαι. τούτων δὲ συγχωρηθέντων, οὗτος μὲν ἀφῆκεν ἁπάντων ἐμέ, ἐγὼ δὲ πρατήρ, ὥσπερ ἐδεῖθ' οὗτος, τῶν κτημάτων ἐγιγνόμην, καθάπερ αὐτὸς ἐπριάμην παρὰ Μνησικλέους. κομισάμενος δὲ τἀμαυτοῦ, καὶ τοῦτον οὐδ' ὁτιοῦν

baseless and malicious charges we were involved by this fellow.

To prove that I am speaking the truth in this, take, please, these depositions also.

THE DEPOSITIONS

When the matter stood thus, and the people whom 14 the plaintiff had introduced to us would not give up the money, and it was clear that we were rightfully in possession of what we had purchased, he begged, and implored, and besought us to sell the property. As he made this demand and begged me most earnestly—there is nothing he did not do—I gave way in this matter also. I saw, however, men of 15 Athens, that he was a man of evil disposition, that at the outset he had made charges to us against Mnesicles, and then had quarrelled with Evergus, with whom he was on terms of closest friendship; that at the first, when I returned from my voyage, he pretended that he was glad to see me, but when the time came for him to do what was right, he became surly with me; that he was a friend to all men until he got some advantage and attained what he wanted, and thereafter became their foe and was at variance with them; I therefore thought it best, if 16 I withdrew and assumed the position of vendor in this man's interest, that I should obtain a full release and discharge from all claims, and thus make a final settlement with him. This was agreed to, and he gave me a release in full, while I, as he begged me to do, assumed the position of vendor of the property, exactly as I had myself bought it from Mnesicles. Having, then, recovered my money, and having done the plaintiff no wrong whatsoever, I imagined, by

ἀδικῶν, μὰ τοὺς θεούς, οὐδ᾽ ἂν εἴ τι γένοιτ᾽, ᾠήθην
ἂν δίκην μοι λαχεῖν ποτὲ τούτου.

17 Τὰ μὲν δὴ γεγενημένα, καὶ περὶ ὧν οἴσετε τὴν
ψῆφον, καὶ δι᾽ ἃ τὴν δίκην συκοφαντούμενος παρεγραψάμην μὴ εἰσαγώγιμον εἶναι, ταῦτ᾽ ἐστίν, ὦ
ἄνδρες δικασταί. παρασχόμενος δὲ μάρτυρας, οἳ
παρῆσαν ἡνίκ᾽ ἀφιέμην ὑπὸ τούτου καὶ ἀπηλλατ-
τόμην, ὡς οὐκ εἰσαγώγιμος ἐκ τῶν νόμων ἐστὶν ἡ
δίκη, μετὰ ταῦτ᾽ ἐπιδείξω.

Καί μοι λέγε ταύτην τὴν μαρτυρίαν.

Λέγε δή μοι καὶ τὴν τῶν ἐωνημένων μαρτυρίαν,
ἵν᾽ εἰδῆθ᾽ ὅτι τούτου κελεύοντος αὐτ᾽ ἀπεδόμην οἷς
οὗτος ἐκέλευσεν.

18 Οὐ τοίνυν μόνον ἡμῖν εἰσιν οὗτοι μάρτυρες, ὡς
ἀφείμεθα καὶ νῦν συκοφαντούμεθα, ἀλλὰ καὶ Πανταίνετος αὐτός. ὅτε γὰρ λαγχάνων Εὐέργῳ τὴν
δίκην εἴασεν ἐμέ, τότ᾽ ἐμαρτύρει οὗτος πρὸς ἔμ᾽
αὐτῷ μηδὲν ἔγκλημ᾽ ὑπόλοιπον εἶναι· οὐ γὰρ ἂν
δήπου, τῶν αὐτῶν ἀδικημάτων παρόντοιν ἀμφοῖν
ὁμοίως ἐγκαλῶν, τὸν μὲν εἴασεν τῷ δ᾽ ἐδικάζετο.
ἀλλὰ μὴν ὅτι γ᾽ οὐκ ἐῶσιν οἱ νόμοι περὶ τῶν οὕτω
πραχθέντων πάλιν λαγχάνειν, οἶμαι μὲν ὑμᾶς καὶ
[972] μηδὲν εἰπόντος ἐμοῦ γιγνώσκειν.

Ὅμως δὲ λέγ᾽ αὐτοῖς καὶ τὸν νόμον τουτονί.

386

the gods, that, no matter what should happen, he would never bring a suit against me.

These, men of the jury, are the facts regarding 17 which you are to cast your votes, these are the grounds upon which I have entered the special plea that this baseless and malicious suit is not maintainable. I shall bring forward witnesses who were present when I was given a release and discharge by the plaintiff, and shall then proceed to prove that under the law the suit is not maintainable.

Please read this deposition.

The Deposition

Now, please, read the deposition of the purchasers, that you may be assured that I sold the property at the bidding of the plaintiff and to the persons to whom he bade me sell it.

The Deposition

Not only have I these witnesses to prove that I 18 have been released and am now the object of a baseless and malicious charge, but Pantaenetus himself is a witness also. For when, in bringing suit against Evergus, he left me out of the question, he himself bore witness that he had no further claim against me. For surely, assuming that he had the same charge to bring against both for the same wrongdoing, he would not, when both were at hand, have passed over the one and brought suit against the other. However, that the laws do not allow a fresh suit to be brought regarding matters that have been thus settled you know, I presume, even without my telling you.

Nevertheless, read them this law also.

ΝΟΜΟΣ

19 Ἀκούετ᾽, ὦ ἄνδρες Ἀθηναῖοι, τοῦ νόμου λέγοντος ἄντικρυς, ὧν ἂν ἀφῇ καὶ ἀπαλλάξῃ τις,
μηκέτι τὰς δίκας εἶναι. καὶ μὴν ὅτι γ᾽ ἀμφότερ᾽
ἐστὶ πεπραγμένα ταῦτα τούτῳ πρὸς ἡμᾶς, ἠκούσατε τῶν μαρτύρων. ἁπάντων μὲν τοίνυν τῶν ἐν
τοῖς νόμοις ἀπειρημένων οὐ προσήκει δικάζεσθαι,
ἥκιστα δὲ τούτων. ἃ μὲν γὰρ τὸ δημόσιον πέπρα-
κεν, ἔχοι τις ἂν εἰπεῖν ὡς ἀδίκως οὐ προσήκοντα
20 πέπρακεν· καὶ περὶ ὧν ἔγνω τὸ δικαστήριον, ἔστιν
εἰπεῖν ὡς ἐξαπατηθὲν τοῦτ᾽ ἐποίησε, καὶ περὶ τῶν
ἄλλων τῶν ἐν τῷ νόμῳ καθ᾽ ἕκαστου γένοιτ᾽ ἄν τις
εἰκότως λόγος. ἃ δ᾽ αὐτὸς ἐπείσθη καὶ ἀφῆκεν,
οὐκ ἔνι δήπουθεν εἰπεῖν οὐδ᾽ ἑαυτὸν αἰτιάσασθαι, ὡς
οὐ δικαίως ταῦτ᾽ ἐποίησεν. οἱ μὲν οὖν παρὰ τῶν
ἄλλων τι τούτων δικαζόμενοι, τοῖς ὑφ᾽ ἑτέρων
δικαίοις ὡρισμένοις οὐκ ἐμμένουσιν, ὁ δ᾽ ὧν ἂν
ἀφῇ πάλιν λαγχάνων τοῖς ὑφ᾽ ἑαυτοῦ. διὸ πάντων
μάλιστ᾽ ἄξιον τούτοις χαλεπαίνειν.

21 Οὐκοῦν ὡς μὲν ἀφῆκέ με πάντων, ὅτ᾽ ἐγιγνόμην
τῶν ἀνδραπόδων πρατήρ, ἐπέδειξα· ὅτι δ᾽ οὐκ
ἐῶσιν οἱ νόμοι τούτων εἶναι δίκας, ἀκηκόατ᾽ ἀρτίως
ἀναγιγνωσκομένου τοῦ νόμου. ἵνα δ᾽, ὦ ἄνδρες
Ἀθηναῖοι, μή τις οἴηται τοῖς περὶ τῶν πραγμάτων
αὐτῶν δικαίοις ἁλισκόμενόν μ᾽ ἐπὶ τοῦτ᾽ ἀποχωρεῖν,
καὶ καθ᾽ ἕκαστον ὧν ἐγκαλεῖ βούλομαι δεῖξαι αὐτὸν
ψευδόμενον.

388

The Law

You hear the law, men of Athens, expressly stating 19 that in cases where anyone has given a release and discharge, there shall be no further action. And that both these have been effected between the plaintiff and myself, you have heard from the witnesses. One should not, of course, bring suit in any case when the law forbids it, but least of all ought one in a case like this. For in regard to sales made by the state, one might claim that it had made the sale unjustly, or had sold what was not its own ; and in regard to 20 court decisions it might be claimed that the decision had been rendered through error ; and in all other cases where the law forbids action exception might plausibly be taken to each one. But when anyone has himself yielded to argument and given a release, he cannot in the very nature of the case charge himself with having acted unjustly. Those who bring suit in defiance of any other of these provisions fail to abide by what others have determined to be just ; but he who again brings suit in matters regarding which he has given a release fails to abide by his own decision. Therefore, against all such your anger should be particularly severe.

Well then, that he released me from all claims, 21 when I sold the slaves to him, I have proved to you ; and that the laws do not allow suits to be brought in such cases you have heard from the law which has just been read. However, that no one of you, men of Athens, may suppose that it is because I am at a disadvantage regarding the rights of the matters at issue that I have recourse to this special plea, I propose to show you that in every one of his charges against me his statements are false.

DEMOSTHENES

22 Λέγε δ' αὐτὸ τὸ ἔγκλημ', ὅ μοι δικάζεται.

[973]   ΕΓΚΛΗΜΑ

Ἔβλαψέ με Νικόβουλος ἐπιβουλεύσας ἐμοὶ καὶ τῇ
οὐσίᾳ τῇ ἐμῇ, ἀφελέσθαι κελεύσας Ἀντιγένην τὸν
ἑαυτοῦ οἰκέτην τὸ ἀργύριον τοῦ ἐμοῦ οἰκέτου, ὃ ἔφερε
καταβολὴν τῇ πόλει τοῦ μετάλλου, ὃ ἐγὼ ἐπριάμην
ἐνενήκοντα μνῶν, καὶ αἴτιος ἐμοὶ γενόμενος ἐγγραφῆναι
τὸ διπλοῦν τῷ δημοσίῳ.

23 Ἐπίσχες. ταυτὶ πάνθ', ἃ νῦν ἐγκέκληκεν ἐμοί,
πρότερον τὸν Εὔεργον αἰτιασάμενος τὴν δίκην εἷλεν.
μεμαρτύρηται μὲν δὴ καὶ ἐν ἀρχῇ μοι τοῦ λόγου
πρὸς ὑμᾶς, ὡς ἀπεδήμουν, ὅτε τούτοις αἱ πρὸς
ἀλλήλους ἐγίγνοντο διαφοραί· οὐ μὴν ἀλλὰ καὶ ἐκ
τοῦ ἐγκλήματος τούτου δῆλόν ἐστιν. οὐδαμοῦ γὰρ
ὡς ἐγώ τι πεποίηκα τούτων ἔγραψεν, ἀλλ' ὑπο-
γράψας ἐπιβουλεῦσαί μ' αὐτῷ καὶ τῇ οὐσίᾳ, προστάξαι φησὶ τῷ παιδὶ ταῦτα ποιεῖν, ψευδόμενος·
πῶς γὰρ ἐγὼ προσέταξ' ἄν, ὃς ὅτ' ἐξέπλεον τῶν
γενησομένων ἐνταῦθ' οὐδ' ὁτιοῦν δήπουθεν ᾔδειν;
24 εἶτα καὶ πόση μωρία, λέγονθ' ὡς ἐπεβούλευον
ἀτιμῶσαι καὶ τὰ ἔσχατα πρᾶξαι, οἰκέτῃ με ταῦτα
προστάξαι γεγραφέναι, ἃ οὐδὲ πολίτης πολίτην
δύναιτ' ἂν ποιῆσαι; τί οὖν ἐστι τοῦτο; οὐκ ἔχων
οἶμαι κατ' οὐδὲν διὰ τὴν ἀποδημίαν εἰς ἐμὲ τούτων
ἀνενεγκεῖν τι, συκοφαντεῖν δὲ βουλόμενος, ὡς προσέταξ' ἐνέγραψεν· οὐδὲ γὰρ λόγος ἦν, εἰ μὴ τοῦτ'
ἐποίησεν.

ᵃ Presumably the amount due to the state for the purchase
of the mine, though the sum differs from the amount secured
by the mortgage.
390

Read the complaint itself, which he brings against 22 me.

The Complaint

Nicobulus has harmed me by laying a plot against me and against my property, having ordered Antigenes, his slave, to take away from my slave the silver which he was bringing to be paid to the state for the mining property which I bought for ninety minae,[a] and having also caused me to be inscribed as debtor to the treasury for double that amount.

Stop reading. All these charges which he has 23 now lodged against me he previously made against Evergus, and won his suit. Now evidence has been brought before you in the opening of my speech that I was not in the country when these men quarrelled with one another; but the fact is clear from the complaint itself. For he nowhere stated that I have done any of these things, but, suggesting that I laid a plot against him and against his property, he declares that I ordered my slave to commit these acts; and in this he lies. For how could I have given this order, seeing that at the time I set sail I could by no possibility have had knowledge of what was going to happen here? And then how absurd when he says that I plotted 24 to disenfranchise him and bring him to utter ruin, to have written in the charge that I ordered a slave to do this,—a thing which even a citizen could not do to another citizen.[b] What, then, is the meaning of this? I suppose that, being unable to refer to me the doing of any of these acts, but wishing to go on with his malicious suit, he wrote in the complaint that I had given the order. There was no sense in his charge, if he had not done this.

[b] That is, disenfranchisement could come only by act of the state itself.

Λέγε τἀκόλουθον.

25   Καὶ ἐπειδὴ ὦφλον ἐγὼ τῷ δημοσίῳ, καταστήσας
Ἀντιγένην τὸν ἑαυτοῦ οἰκέτην εἰς τὸ ἐργαστήριον τὸ
ἐμὸν τὸ ἐπὶ Θρασύλλῳ κύριον τῶν ἐμῶν, ἀπαγορεύοντος
ἐμοῦ.

[974] Ἐπίσχες. πάλιν ταυτὶ πάνθ᾽ ὑπ᾽ αὐτοῦ τοῦ πράγματος ἐξελεγχθήσεται ψευδόμενος. γέγραφεν γὰρ
καταστῆσαι μὲν ἐμέ, ἀπαγορεύειν δ᾽ αὐτός. ταῦτα
δ᾽ οὐχ οἷόν τε τὸν μὴ παρόντα. οὔτε γὰρ[1] καθ-
ίστην ἐγώ, ὅ γ᾽ ὢν ἐν τῷ Πόντῳ, οὔτ᾽ ἀπηγόρευεν
26   οὗτος τῷ μὴ παρόντι· πῶς γάρ; πῶς οὖν εἰς
ἀνάγκην ἦλθε ταῦθ᾽ οὕτω γράψαι; ὁ Εὔεργος
τότ᾽ οἶμαι πλημμελῶν ὧν δέδωκε δίκην, συνήθως
ἔχων ἐμοὶ καὶ γνώριμος ὤν, κατέστησέ τιν᾽ οἰκέτην
οἴκοθεν λαβὼν παρ᾽ ἐμοῦ φυλάττειν ὡς αὐτόν. εἰ
μὲν οὖν ἔγραψε τἀληθές, γέλως ἂν ἦν· τί γάρ, εἰ
κατέστησεν Εὔεργος, ἐγώ σ᾽ ἀδικῶ; φεύγων δὲ
τοῦτο τοιαῦτ᾽ ἠνάγκασται γράφειν, ἵν᾽ ᾖ πρὸς ἔμ᾽
αὐτῷ τὸ ἔγκλημα.

Λέγε τοὐφεξῆς.

Κἄπειτα πείσας τοὺς οἰκέτας τοὺς ἐμοὺς καθέζεσθαι
εἰς τὸν κεγχρεῶνα ἐπὶ βλάβῃ τῇ ἐμῇ.

27   Τουτὶ παντελῶς ἤδη καὶ ἀναιδές ἐστιν· οὐ γὰρ
μόνον ἐκ τοῦ προκαλεῖσθαι τούτους παραδοῦναι,

---

[1] γὰρ γὰρ ἂν Blass.

---

[a] A site in Maroneia, so called from a monument of
Thrasyllus which stood there.
[b] A euphemism for the violence and lawlessness with which
Evergus had been charged by Pantaenetus.

Read what follows.

THE COMPLAINT

And after I had become a debtor to the state, having **25** stationed his slave Antigenes in my mining property at Thrasyllus,[a] in full control of my works, although I forbade him . . .

Stop reading. In all this he will again be convicted of falsehood by the facts themselves ; for he has written in the complaint that I stationed the slave and that he forbade me. But this was impossible in the case of one who was not in the country. Neither did I station anyone, seeing that I was in Pontus, nor did he forbid a man who was not in Athens. How could **26** he ? What was it, then, that forced him to make this statement ? I fancy that Evergus, at the time he made the mistakes[b] for which he has paid the penalty, being on friendly terms with me and well known, took the slave from my house and stationed him at his own works to keep guard. If, then, he had written the truth, it would have been ridiculous. For, if Evergus stationed the slave there, wherein do I wrong you ? It was to avoid this absurdity that he was compelled to write as he did, that his charge might be directed against me.

Read what follows.

THE COMPLAINT

And then having persuaded my slaves to sit in the foundry[c] to my prejudice.

This is out-and-out impudence. Not only from my **27** challenging him to give up these slaves for torture

[c] The precise meaning of κεγχρεών cannot be determined. It seems to have denoted either the pit into which the silver was run when melted, or the furnace in which it was refined.

τοῦτον δὲ μὴ θέλειν, ἀλλὰ καὶ ἐκ πάντων δῆλόν
ἐστι ψεῦδος ὄν. τίνος γὰρ εἵνεκ᾽ ἔπειθον; ἵνα νὴ
Δί᾽ αὐτοὺς κτήσωμαι. ἀλλ᾽ αἱρέσεώς μοι δοθείσης
ἢ ἔχειν ἢ κομίσασθαι τὰ ἐμαυτοῦ, εἱλόμην κομίσασθαι, καὶ ταῦτα μεμαρτύρηται.

Λέγε δὴ τὴν πρόκλησιν ὅμως.

28 Ταύτην τοίνυν οὐχὶ δεξάμενος τὴν πρόκλησιν,
ἀλλὰ φυγών, σκέψασθ᾽ οἷον εὐθέως μετὰ ταῦτ᾽
ἐγκαλεῖ.

Λέγε τοὐχόμενον.

Καὶ κατεργασάμενος τὴν ἀργυρῖτιν, ἣν οἱ ἐμοὶ οἰκέται
ἠργάσαντο, καὶ ἔχων τὸ ἀργύριον τὸ ἐκ ταύτης τῆς
ἀργυρίτιδος.

[975] Πάλιν ταῦτα πῶς ἔνεστ᾽ ἐμοὶ πεπρᾶχθαι τῷ μὴ
παρόντι, καὶ περὶ ὧν Εὐέργου κατεδικάσω;

Λέγε δ᾽ αὐτοῖς τὸ ἐφεξῆς.

29 Καὶ ἀποδόμενος τὸ ἐργαστήριον τὸ ἐμὸν καὶ τοὺς
οἰκέτας παρὰ τὰς συνθήκας, ἃς ἔθετο πρός με.

Ἐπίσχες. τουτὶ πολὺ πάνθ᾽ ὑπερβέβληκε τἆλλα.
πρῶτον μὲν γὰρ παρὰ τὰς συνθήκας φησίν, ἃς ἔθετο
πρός με. αὗται δ᾽ εἰσὶ τίνες; ἐμισθώσαμεν τῶν
τόκων τῶν γιγνομένων τούτῳ τὰ ἡμέτερ᾽ ἡμεῖς, καὶ
ἄλλ᾽ οὐδέν· πρατὴρ μὲν γὰρ ὁ Μνησικλῆς ἡμῖν
30 ἐγεγόνει τούτου παρόντος καὶ κελεύοντος. μετὰ
ταῦτα τὸν αὐτὸν τρόπον ἡμεῖς ἑτέροις ἀπεδόμεθα,

and from his refusing to do so, but from every circumstance of the case its falsehood is manifest. Why, pray, should I have induced them to do this? That, forsooth, I might get possession of them. But when the option was given me either to keep the property or to recover my money, I chose to recover my money; and of this you have heard the evidence.

Nevertheless, read the challenge.

THE CHALLENGE

Although he did not accept the challenge, but declined it, see what a charge he makes immediately thereafter. 28

Read what comes next.

THE COMPLAINT

And having reduced the silver-ore which my slaves had dug, and keeping the silver smelted from that ore.

Again, how could this have been done by me when I was not here?—things, too, for which you won a judgement against Evergus?

Read the further charges.

THE COMPLAINT

And having sold my mining property and the slaves, contrary to the agreement which he had made with me. 29

Stop reading. This far outdoes all the rest. For in the first place he says, "contrary to the agreement which he had made with me." What agreement is this? We leased our own property to this man, at a rent equal to the interest on the loan; that was all. It was Mnesicles who sold it to us, in the presence of the plaintiff and at his request. Afterwards in the same way we sold the property to others on the same 30

ἐφ' οἷσπερ αὐτοὶ ἐπριάμεθα,[1] οὐ μόνον κελεύοντος
ἔτι τούτου, ἀλλὰ καὶ ἱκετεύοντος· οὐδεὶς γὰρ
ἤθελεν δέχεσθαι τοῦτον πρατῆρα. τί οὖν αἱ τῆς
μισθώσεως ἐνταῦθα συνθῆκαι; τί τοῦτ', ὦ φαυ-
λότατ' ἀνθρώπων, ἐνέγραψας;

Ἀλλὰ μὴν ὅτι σοῦ κελεύοντος καὶ ἐφ' οἷσπερ ἐω-
νήμεθ' αὐτοὶ πάλιν ἀπεδόμεθα, λέγε τὴν μαρτυρίαν.

ΜΑΡΤΥΡΙΑ

31 Μαρτυρεῖς τοίνυν καὶ σύ· ἃ γὰρ ἡμεῖς πέντε καὶ
ἑκατὸν μνῶν ἐωνήμεθα, ταῦθ' ὕστερον τριῶν ταλάντων καὶ δισχιλίων καὶ ἑξακοσίων ἀπέδου σύ· καίτοι
τίς ἂν καθάπαξ πρατῆρά σ' ἔχων σοὶ δραχμὴν
ἔδωκε μίαν;

Ἀλλὰ μὴν ὅτι ταῦτ' ἀληθῆ λέγω, κάλει μοι
τούτων τοὺς μάρτυρας.

ΜΑΡΤΥΡΕΣ

32 Ἔχων μὲν τοίνυν ἣν ἐπείσθη τῶν αὑτοῦ τιμήν,
δεηθεὶς δ' ἐμοῦ τὸ γενέσθαι πρατῆρα καθ' ὃ συν-
[976] έβαλον ἀργύριον, αὐτὸς δυοῖν ταλάντοιν προσδικά-
ζεται. καὶ τὰ λοιπὰ τῶν ἐγκλημάτων ἔτ' ἐστὶ
δεινότερα.

Λέγε δή μοι τὸ λοιπὸν τοῦ ἐγκλήματος.

ΕΓΚΛΗΜΑ

33 Ἐνταυθὶ πόλλ' ἄττα καὶ δεινά μοι ἅμ' ἐγκαλεῖ·
καὶ γὰρ αἴκειαν καὶ ὕβριν καὶ βιαίων καὶ πρὸς
ἐπικλήρους ἀδικήματα. τούτων δ' εἰσὶν ἑκάστου

---

[1] ἐφ' . . . ἐπριάμεθα omitted by Blass.

[a] The title was not vested in Pantaenetus, but in the other
claimants to whom it had been transferred at his request.

[b] See § 45 ; and compare the oration against Meidias
(XXI.) § 79.

terms upon which we had ourselves bought it, and the plaintiff not only urged but actually implored us to do so ; for no one was willing to accept him as the vendor. What, then, does the agreement to lease it have to do with the matter ? Why, most worthless of men, did you insert that clause ?

However, to prove that we resold the property at your request, and on the same terms as those upon which we ourselves bought it, read the deposition.

The Deposition

You are yourself also a witness to this ; for what we **31** purchased for one hundred and five minae, this you afterward sold for three talents and twenty-six hundred drachmae. And yet who, if he had you[a] as one to complete a final sale, would have given a single drachma ?

To prove that I speak the truth in this, call, please, the witnesses who establish the facts.

The Witnesses

He has, then, received the sum which he agreed to **32** take for his property,—he even begged me that I should assume the position of vendor for the sum which I had advanced—yet this same man sues me for two talents more. And the rest of the charges are even more outrageous.

Read, please, the remainder of the complaint.

The Complaint

Here he brings against me in one mass a host of **33** dreadful charges ; for he accuses me of assault and battery, outrage, and of violent wrongs even against heiresses.[b] But for each of these wrongdoings actions

χωρὶς αἱ δίκαι, καὶ οὔτε πρὸς ἀρχὴν τὴν αὐτὴν
οὔθ᾽ ὑπὲρ τιμημάτων τῶν αὐτῶν, ἀλλ᾽ ἡ μὲν αἴκεια
καὶ τὰ τῶν βιαίων πρὸς τοὺς τετταράκοντα, αἱ δὲ
τῆς ὕβρεως πρὸς τοὺς θεσμοθέτας, ὅσα δ᾽ εἰς ἐπικλήρους, πρὸς τὸν ἄρχοντα. οἱ δὲ νόμοι καὶ τούτων
διδόασι τὰς παραγραφὰς ἀντιλαγχάνειν, περὶ ὧν
οὐκ εἰσὶν εἰσαγωγεῖς.

Λέγ᾽ αὐτοῖς τουτονὶ τὸν νόμον.

ΝΟΜΟΣ

34 Τοῦτο τοίνυν ἐμοῦ παραγεγραμμένου πρὸς τῇ
ἄλλῃ παραγραφῇ, καὶ οὐκ ὄντων εἰσαγωγέων τῶν
θεσμοθετῶν ὑπὲρ ὧν λαγχάνει Πανταίνετος, ἐξαλή-
λιπται καὶ οὐ πρόσεστι τῇ παραγραφῇ. τὸ δ᾽ ὅπως
ὑμεῖς σκοπεῖτε· ἐμοὶ μὲν γάρ, ἕως ἂν ἔχω τὸν
νόμον αὐτὸν δεικνύναι, οὐδ᾽ ὁτιοῦν διαφέρει· οὐ
γὰρ τὸ γιγνώσκειν καὶ συνιέναι τὰ δίκαι᾽ ὑμῶν
ἐξαλεῖψαι δυνήσεται.

35 Λαβὲ δὴ καὶ τὸν μεταλλικὸν νόμον· καὶ γὰρ ἐκ
τούτου δείξειν οἴομαι, οὔτ᾽ οὖσαν εἰσαγώγιμον τὴν
δίκην, χάριτός τ᾽ ἂν μᾶλλον ἄξιος ἢ τοῦ συκοφαντεῖσθαι.

Λέγε.

ΝΟΜΟΣ

Οὗτος σαφῶς ὁ νόμος διείρηκεν, ὧν εἶναι δίκας
προσήκει μεταλλικάς. οὐκοῦν ὁ μὲν νόμος, ἄν τις
[977] ἐξείλλῃ τινὰ τῆς ἐργασίας, ὑπόδικον ποιεῖ· ἐγὼ δ᾽
οὐχ ὅπως αὐτὸς ἐξείλλω τοῦτον, ἀλλ᾽ ὧν ἄλλος

---

^a " The Forty " were circuit judges.
^b That is, the chief archon.

are separate ; they do not come before the same magistrates and they are not for the recovery of the same penalties. Assault and battery and crimes of violence come before the Forty [a] ; cases of outrage before the Thesmothetae ; and all crimes against heiresses before the Archon.[b] And the laws grant the filing of pleas to bar action also in case of charges brought before magistrates who have not due competency.

Read them this law.

THE LAW

Although I had entered this exception in bar of 34 action in addition to the other, and although the Thesmothetae have not competency in the matters concerning which Pantaenetus is bringing his suit, it has been erased, and is not found in the plea as written. How this has come about it is for you to consider.[c] To me, so long as I am able to produce the law itself, it makes not the slightest difference ; for he will not be able to erase from your minds your power to know and understand the right.

Take also the mining law. For I think I can show 35 you from this, too, that the action is not maintainable, and that I deserve thanks rather than to be made the object of a baseless and malicious charge.

Read.

THE LAW

This law has clearly defined in what cases mining actions may properly be brought. Observe—the law makes a man liable if he eject another from his workings ; but I, far from ejecting the plaintiff, gave over

[c] He hints that the omission of the exception filed by him was not an accident.

ἀπεστέρει, τούτων ἐγκρατῆ κατέστησα καὶ παρέδωκα, καὶ πρατὴρ τούτου δεηθέντος ἐγενόμην.
36 ναί, φησίν· ἀλλὰ κἂν ἄλλα ἀδικῇ τις περὶ τὰ
μέταλλα, καὶ τούτων εἰσὶ δίκαι. ὀρθῶς γ', ὦ
Πανταίνετε· ἀλλὰ ταῦτα τί ἐστιν; ἂν τύφῃ τις, ἂν
ὅπλ' ἐπιφέρῃ, ἂν ἐπικατατέμνῃ τῶν μέτρων ἐντός.
ταῦτ' ἐστὶ τἄλλα, ὧν οὐδὲν δήπου πέπρακται πρὸς
ὑμᾶς ἐμοί, πλὴν εἰ τοὺς κομιζομένους ἃ προεῖντό
σοι, μεθ' ὅπλων ἥκειν νομίζεις. εἰ δὲ ταῦθ' ἡγεῖ,
πρὸς ἅπαντας τοὺς προϊεμένους τὰ ἑαυτῶν εἰσι
37 σοι δίκαι μεταλλικαί. ἀλλ' οὐ δίκαιον. φέρε γάρ,
ὅστις ἂν μέταλλον παρὰ τῆς πόλεως πρίηται, τοὺς
κοινοὺς παρελθὼν νόμους, καθ' οὓς καὶ διδόναι καὶ
λαμβάνειν πᾶσι προσήκει δίκας, ἐν ταῖς μεταλ-
λικαῖς δικάσεται, ἐὰν δανείσηται παρά τού τι; ἂν
κακῶς ἀκούσῃ; ἂν πληγὰς λάβῃ; ἂν κλοπὴν
ἐγκαλῇ; ἂν προεισφορὰν μὴ κομίζηται; ἂν ὅλως
38 ἄλλο τι; ἐγὼ μὲν οὐκ οἴομαι, ἀλλὰ τὰς μεταλλικὰς
εἶναι δίκας τοῖς κοινωνοῦσι μετάλλου καὶ τοῖς
συντρήσασιν εἰς τὰ τῶν πλησίον καὶ ὅλως τοῖς
ἐργαζομένοις τὰ μέταλλα καὶ τῶν ἐν τῷ νόμῳ τι
ποιοῦσι, τῷ δὲ δανείσαντι Πανταινέτῳ, καὶ ταῦτ'
ἀπειληφότι γλίσχρως καὶ μόλις παρὰ τούτου, οὐκ
εἶναι δίκην μεταλλικὴν πρὸς φευκτέον, οὐδ' ἐγγύς.
39 'Ως μὲν οὖν οὔτ' ἠδίκηκα τοῦτον οὐδὲν οὔτ'
εἰσαγώγιμος ἐκ τῶν νόμων ἐστὶν ἡ δίκη, ταῦτ' ἂν

to him and put him in possession of that of which another was seeking to deprive him ; and I became the vendor of it at his request. Yes, says he, but if **36** one commit other wrongs concerning mines, for these, too, actions may be brought. Certainly, Pantaenetus; but what are these ? If one smokes out another, if one makes an armed attack, if one makes cuttings which encroach upon another's workings. These are the other cases ; but I, of course, have done nothing of this sort to you, unless you hold that people who seek to recover what they had risked in a loan to you are making an armed attack. If you hold that view, you have mining suits against all those who risk their own money. But there is no justice in that. For **37** consider—if a man purchases a mine from the state, shall he disregard the general laws in accordance with which all men are bound to render and obtain justice, and bring suit in a mining court, if he borrows from another ?—if he be evil spoken of ?—if he be beaten ?—if he charge one with theft ?—if he fail to recover money advanced for another's tax ?—if, in short, he has any other ground for action ? I think not. Mining suits, in my judgement, are to be brought **38** against those sharing in the business of mining and those who have bored through into another's property, and, in short, against those engaged in mining who do any of the things mentioned in the law. But a man who has lent money to Pantaenetus, and by persistently sticking to him has with difficulty got it back, is not also to be made defendant in a mining suit ; I should say not !

That I have, therefore, done no wrong to the de- **39** fendant and that the suit is not admissible under the laws one may easily determine from a considera-

τις σκοπῶν ῥᾳδίως γνοίη. οὐδὲν τοίνυν δίκαιον
ἔχων οὐδὲ καθ' ἓν λέγειν ὑπὲρ ὧν ἐγκαλεῖ, ἀλλὰ
[978] καὶ ψευδῆ γεγραφὼς εἰς τὸ ἔγκλημα καὶ περὶ ὧν
ἀφῆκε δικαζόμενος, τοῦ ἐξελθόντος, ὦ ἄνδρες Ἀθηναῖοι, μηνός, ἐπειδὴ ἔμελλον εἰσιέναι τὴν δίκην, ἤδη
τῶν δικαστηρίων ἐπικεκληρωμένων, προσελθὼν καὶ
περιστήσας τοὺς μεθ' αὑτοῦ, τὸ ἐργαστήριον τῶν
40 συνεστώτων, πρᾶγμα ποιεῖ πάνδεινον· ἀναγιγνώ-
σκει μοι πρόκλησιν μακράν, ἀξιῶν, ὅν φησιν οἰκέτην ταῦτα συνειδέναι, βασανίζεσθαι, κἂν μὲν ᾖ
ταῦτ' ἀληθῆ, τὴν δίκην ἀτίμητον ὀφλεῖν αὐτῷ, ἐὰν
δὲ ψευδῆ, τὸν βασανιστὴν Μνησικλέα ἐπιγνώμον'
εἶναι τῆς τιμῆς τοῦ παιδός. λαβὼν δ' ἐγγυητὰς
τούτων παρ' ἐμοῦ, καὶ σημηναμένου τὴν πρόκλησιν
41 ἐμοῦ, οὐχ ὡς δίκαιον ὄν· ποῦ γάρ ἐστι δίκαιον, ἐν
οἰκέτου σώματι καὶ ψυχῇ, ἢ δύ' ὠφληκέναι τάλαντα, ἢ μηδὲν τὸν συκοφαντοῦντα ζημιοῦσθαι;
ἀλλ' ἐγὼ πολλῷ τῷ δικαίῳ περιεῖναι βουλόμενος
συνεχώρουν. καὶ μετὰ ταῦτα προσκαλεῖται μέν με
τὴν δίκην πάλιν, ἐπειδὴ θᾶττον ἀνείλετο τὰς παρα-
καταβολάς· οὕτως εὐθὺς ἦν δῆλος οὐδ' οἷς αὐτὸς
42 ὡρίσατ' ἐμμένων δικαίοις. ἐπειδὴ δ' ἥκομεν πρὸς
τὸν βασανιστήν, ἀντὶ τοῦ τὴν πρόκλησιν ἀνοίξας
δεῖξαι τὰ γεγραμμένα καὶ κατὰ ταῦτα πράττειν ὅ
τι δόξαι (διὰ γὰρ τὸν θόρυβον τότε καὶ τὸ μέλλειν

---

a There is much obscurity here. The acceptance of the
challenge by Nicobulus should have put an end to the
action. The plaintiff had then the right to take back the

tion of these points. So, as he had not a single valid argument to advance in support of his charges, but had even incorporated false statements in his complaint, and was bringing suit regarding claims for which he had given a release, last month, men of Athens, when I was on the point of entering the court, and the court-rooms had already been allotted to the jurymen, he came up to me and surrounded me with his minions (that gang of his fellow-conspirators), and did a most outrageous thing. He read me a long 40 challenge, demanding that a slave who, he claimed, was acquainted with the facts, should be put to the torture; and that, if the facts as alleged by him were true, I should have to pay him the damages charged without adjustment by the jury; but if they were false, Mnesicles, the torturer, should determine the value of the slave. When he had received sureties to this agreement from me and I had sealed the challenge (not that I thought it fair; for how could it be fair 41 that it should depend upon the body and life of a slave, whether I should be condemned to pay two talents, or the bringer of this malicious suit get off scot-free? But I, wishing to prevail by a preponderance of fair play, made this concession)—after this he again summoned me in the suit, as soon as he had taken back his deposits; [a] so clear did he make it at once that he would not abide by the conditions which he had himself laid down. But when we had come 42 before the torturer, instead of opening the challenge, showing its contents, and proceeding in accordance with its terms to do what seemed right (for on account of the turmoil at that time and the fact that

sum deposited (as court-fees πρυτανεῖα?) when the suit was brought.

καλεῖσθαι τὴν δίκην τοιοῦτον ἦν· προκαλοῦμαί
σε ταυτί· δέχομαι· φέρε τὸν δακτύλιον· λαβέ· τίς
δ' ἐγγυητής; οὑτοσί· οὐδὲν οὔτ' ἀντίγραφον, οὔτ'
ἀλλ' οὐδὲν ἐποιησάμην τοιοῦτον) ἀντὶ δὴ τοῦ ταῦθ'
[979] οὕτως ὥσπερ λέγω πράττειν, ἑτέραν ἧκεν ἔχων
πρόκλησιν, ἀξιῶν αὐτὸς βασανίζειν τὸν ἄνθρωπον,
καὶ ἐπιλαβόμενος εἷλκε, καὶ ἐνέλειπεν οὐδὲν ἀσελ-
43 γείας. καὶ ἔγωγ' ἐνεθυμήθην, ὦ ἄνδρες δικασταί,
ἡλίκον ἐστὶ πλεονέκτημα τὸ καταπεπλάσθαι τὸν
βίον. ἐγὼ γὰρ ἐμαυτῷ ταῦτα πάσχειν ἐδόκουν
καταφρονούμενος τῷ ἁπλῶς καὶ ὡς πέφυκα ζῆν,
καὶ δίκην διδόναι παμμεγέθη ταῦτ' ἀνεχόμενος.

Ὅτι δ' οὖν ἠναγκαζόμην, παρ' ἃ ἡγούμην δίκαι'
εἶναι, ἀντιπροκαλεῖσθαι, καὶ τὸν οἰκέτην παρεδίδουν,
καὶ ὅτι ταῦτ' ἀληθῆ λέγω, λέγε τὴν πρόκλησιν.

ΠΡΟΚΛΗΣΙΣ

44 Φυγὼν μὲν τοίνυν ταῦτα, φυγὼν δ' ἃ τὸ πρῶτον
αὐτὸς προὐκαλέσατο, ἔγωγ', ὅ τι ποτ' ἐρεῖ πρὸς
ὑμᾶς, θαυμάζω. ἵνα δ' εἰδῆθ' ὑφ' οὗ φησὶ καὶ τὰ
δεινὰ πεπονθέναι, θεάσασθε. οὗτός ἐστιν ὁ Πανταίνετον ἐκβαλών, οὗτός ἐσθ' ὁ κρείττων τῶν
φίλων τῶν Πανταινέτου καὶ τῶν νόμων. οὐ γὰρ
ἔγωγ' ἐπεδήμουν, οὐδ' αὐτὸς ἐγκαλεῖ.

45 Βούλομαι δ' ὑμῖν καὶ δι' ὧν τοὺς πρότερον δικαστὰς ἐξαπατήσας εἷλε τὸν Εὔεργον εἰπεῖν, ἵν' εἰδῆθ'

ᵃ His own desire to live simply and naturally had caused
him to be imposed upon, and to be despised as one lacking in
spirit. The passage is variously interpreted, and the text is
uncertain. The mss. have καταπεπλῆχθαι, which yields no
satisfactory sense, unless with Wolf we insert the negative
μή. The meaning in that case would be that a life of ruthless
self-assertion is a "great gain."

the case was about to be called, it was like this : I
offer you this challenge.—I accept it.—Let me have
your ring.—Take it.—Who is your surety ?—This
man here.—and I had taken no copy or anything else
of that sort) ; instead of acting in the way of which I
speak, he had brought with him a different challenge,
insisting that he should himself torture the man, and
he laid hold of him, dragged him this way and that,
and went beyond all bounds in blackguardly action.
On my part, men of the jury, I was led to reflect what 43
gain there is in a life moulded to serve one's ends.[a]
For it seemed to me that I was suffering this treatment because I was despised as one who lived a
simple and natural life, and that I was paying a heavy
penalty in having to submit to this.

However, to prove that I was compelled to give a
counter-challenge contrary to what I thought was
right, that I offered to give up the slave, and that I
am speaking the truth in this, read the challenge.

THE CHALLENGE

Since he refused this, and refused the challenge 44
which he himself gave at the first, I wonder what in
the world he will have to say to you. But that you
may know who it is at whose hands he claims to have
suffered these indignities—behold him ![b] This is the
man who dispossessed Pantaenetus ; this is the man
who was stronger than the friends of Pantaenetus,
and stronger than the laws. For I myself was not in
Athens ; even he does not make that charge.

I wish to tell you also the means by which he misled 45
the former jury, and convicted Evergus, that you

[b] Here the speaker effectively brings before the jury the
slave, Antigenes—a feeble, old man.

ὅτι καὶ νῦν οὐδὲν οὔτ' ἀναιδείας οὔτε τοῦ ψεύδεσθαι παραλείψει. πρὸς δὲ τούτοις καὶ περὶ ὧν ἐμοὶ
δικάζεται νυνί, τὰς αὐτὰς οὔσας ἀπολογίας εὑρή-
σετε· ὅσπερ ἔλεγχος ἀκριβέστατός ἐστιν ὑπὲρ τοῦ
τότ' ἐκεῖνον σεσυκοφαντῆσθαι. οὗτος γὰρ ᾐτιάσατ'
ἐκεῖνον πρὸς ἅπασι τοῖς ἄλλοις, ἐλθόντ' εἰς ἀγρὸν
ὡς αὑτόν, ἐπὶ τὰς ἐπικλήρους εἰσελθεῖν καὶ τὴν
μητέρα τὴν αὑτοῦ, καὶ τοὺς νόμους ἧκεν ἔχων τοὺς
46
[980]
τῶν ἐπικλήρων πρὸς τὸ δικαστήριον. καὶ πρὸς μὲν
τὸν ἄρχοντα, ὃν τῶν τοιούτων οἱ νόμοι κελεύουσιν
ἐπιμελεῖσθαι, καὶ παρ' ᾧ τῷ μὲν ἠδικηκότι κίνδυνος περὶ τοῦ τί χρὴ παθεῖν ἢ ἀποτεῖσαι, τῷ δ'
ἐπεξιόντι μετ' οὐδεμιᾶς ζημίας ἡ βοήθεια, οὐδέπω
καὶ τήμερον ἐξήτασται, οὐδ' εἰσήγγειλεν οὔτ' ἔμ'
οὔτε τὸν Εὔεργον ὡς ἀδικοῦντας, ἐν δὲ τῷ δικαστηρίῳ ταῦτα κατηγόρει καὶ δυοῖν ταλάντοιν εἷλε
47 δίκην. ἦν γάρ, οἶμαι, κατὰ μὲν τοὺς νόμους προ-
ειδότα τὴν αἰτίαν, ἐφ' ᾗ κρίνεται, ῥᾴδιον τἀληθῆ
καὶ τὰ δίκαι' ἐπιδείξαντ' ἀποφεύγειν, ἐν δὲ μεταλ-
λικῇ δίκῃ, περὶ ὧν οὐδ' ἂν ἤλπισεν αὐτοῦ
κατηγορηθήσεσθαι, χαλεπὸν παραχρῆμ' ἔχειν ἀπολύσασθαι τὴν διαβολήν· ἡ δ' ὀργὴ παρὰ τῶν
ἐξηπατημένων ὑπὸ τούτου δικαστῶν, ἐφ' ᾧ τὴν
48 ψῆφον εἶχον πράγματι, τοῦτο κατεψηφίσατο. καίτοι τὸν ἐκείνους ἐξηπατηκότα τοὺς δικαστάς, ἆρ'
ὀκνήσειν ὑμᾶς ἐξαπατᾶν οἴεσθε; ἢ πεπιστευκότα

---

* Possibly, " the charges against me."
b Whereas in court the plaintiff ran the risk of having to
pay the heavy penalty of the ἐπωβολία, if he failed to make
good his case. See note a, p. 50.
c Due to the alleged intrusion into the women's apartments.

may realize that in this trial also there will be no limit to his impudence and that he will shrink from no falsehoods. More than this; in regard to his present suit against me, you will find my means of defence [a] are the same as those of Evergus, which is the most convincing proof that Evergus has been the victim of a malicious and baseless charge. For in addition to all the other accusations the plaintiff charged that Evergus came to his home in the country, and made his way into the apartments of his daughters, who were heiresses, and of his mother; and he brought with him into court the laws concerning heiresses. And yet up to this day he has never **46** had the case examined before the Archon, whom the law appoints to have charge of such matters, and before whom the wrongdoer runs the risk of having punishment or fine adjudged against him, while by the prosecutor redress is sought without risk; [b] nor has he impeached either me or Evergus as wrongdoers, but he made these charges in the court-room, and secured a verdict for two talents. For, I take it, **47** it would have been an easy matter for Evergus, if he had known in advance (as under the laws he should have known) the charge on which he was being tried, to set forth the truth of the matter and the justice of his cause, and so win acquittal; but in a mining suit regarding matters concerning which he could never have imagined that he would be accused, it was hard to find, off hand, means to free himself from the false charges; and the indignation [c] of the jurymen, who were misled by the plaintiff, found him guilty in the matter upon which they sat in judgement. And yet **48** do you think that the man who deceived those jurymen will hesitate to try to deceive you?—or that he

407

εἰσιέναι τοῖς πράγμασιν, ἀλλ' οὐ τοῖς λόγοις καὶ
τοῖς συνεστῶσι μεθ' αὑτοῦ μάρτυσι, τῷ τ' ἀ-
καθάρτῳ καὶ μιαρῷ Προκλεῖ, τῷ μεγάλῳ τούτῳ, καὶ
Στρατοκλεῖ τῷ πιθανωτάτῳ πάντων ἀνθρώπων καὶ
πονηροτάτῳ, καὶ τῷ μηδὲν ὑποστελλόμενον μηδ'
49 αἰσχυνόμενον κλαήσειν καὶ ὀδυρεῖσθαι; καίτοι τοσούτου δεῖς ἐλέου τινὸς ἄξιος εἶναι, ὥστε μισηθείης
ἂν δικαιότατ' ἀνθρώπων ἐξ ὧν πεπραγμάτευσαι·
ὅς γ' ὀφείλων μνᾶς ἑκατὸν καὶ πέντε καὶ οὐχ οἷός
τ' ὢν διαλῦσαι, τοὺς ταῦτα συνευπορήσαντας καὶ
γενομένους αἰτίους σοι τοῦ τὰ δίκαια ποιῆσαι τοῖς
[981] συμβαλοῦσιν ἐξ ἀρχῆς, χωρὶς ὧν περὶ αὐτὰ τὰ
συμβόλαι' ἠδίκεις, καὶ πρὸς ἀτιμῶσαι ζητεῖς. καὶ
τοὺς μὲν ἄλλους τοὺς δανειζομένους ἴδοι τις ἂν
ἐξισταμένους τῶν ὄντων· σοὶ δ' ὁ συμβεβληκὼς
τοῦτο πέπονθε, καὶ δανείσας τάλαντον, δι' ὤφληκε
50 συκοφαντηθείς. ἐγὼ δὲ τετταράκοντα μνᾶς δανείσας, δυοῖν ταλάντοιν ταυτηνὶ φεύγω δίκην. καὶ
ἐφ' οἷς δανείσασθαι μὲν οὐδεπώποτ' ἠδυνήθης
ἑκατὸν μνῶν πλέον, πέπρακας δὲ καθάπαξ τριῶν
ταλάντων καὶ δισχιλίων, εἰς ταῦτα τέτταρ' ὡς
ἔοικεν ἠδίκησαι τάλαντα. ὑπὸ τοῦ ταῦτα; ὑπὸ τοῦ
οἰκέτου νὴ Δία τοὐμοῦ. τίς δ' ἂν οἰκέτῃ παρα-
χωρήσειε πολίτης τῶν αὑτοῦ; ἢ τίς ἂν φήσειεν,
ὧν δίκην λαχὼν ἥρηκεν οὗτος Εὔεργον, τούτων καὶ
51 τὸν ἐμὸν παῖδ' ὑπεύθυνον εἶναι προσήκειν; χωρὶς
δὲ τούτων αὐτὸς αὑτὸν οὗτος ἀφῆκε τῶν τοιούτων

---

[a] That is, in round numbers. In § 31 the sum is given as
three talents, twenty-six hundred drachmae.

comes into court with his confidence fixed upon the facts, and not rather upon assertions and upon the witnesses who are in league with him (that foul blackguard Procles, the tall fellow there, and Stratocles, the smoothest-tongued of men and the basest), and in his readiness to weep and wail without disguise or shame? But *you* are so far from deserving pity, 49 that more than any man in the world you should rightly be detested for the deeds you have wrought —*you* who, owing one hundred and five minae and not being able to satisfy your creditors, and then finding men who helped you to raise the money and enabled you to do what was right by those who originally made the loan, are seeking, quite apart from the wrongs you committed against them in regard to the loan itself, also to deprive them of their civic rights. In the case of other men one may see borrowers having to give up their property, but in your case it is the lender who has come to this plight, and, having lent a talent, has been forced to pay two talents as the victim of a baseless charge; and I, who lent forty minae, am defendant 50 in this suit for two talents. Again, on property on which you were never able to borrow more than one hundred minae, and which you sold outright for three talents and two thousand drachmae,[a] you have, as it seems, sustained damages to the amount of four talents! From whom? From my slave, you will say. But what citizen would let himself be ousted from his own property by a slave? Or who would say that it is right that my slave be held responsible for acts, for which the plaintiff has brought action against Evergus and obtained a verdict? Besides all this, the plaintiff has himself given him a 51

αἰτιῶν ἁπασῶν. οὐ γὰρ νῦν ἔδει λέγειν, οὐδ' εἰς
τὴν πρόκλησιν γράφειν ἐν ᾗ βασανίζειν ἐξῄτει,
ἀλλὰ λαχόντ' ἐκείνῳ τὴν δίκην τὸν κύριον διώκειν
ἐμέ. νῦν δ' εἴληχεν μὲν ἐμοί, κατηγορεῖ δ' ἐκείνου.
ταῦτα δ' οὐκ ἐῶσιν οἱ νόμοι· τίς γὰρ πώποτε τῷ
δεσπότῃ λαχών, τοῦ δούλου τὰ πράγμαθ', ὥσπερ
κυρίου, κατηγόρησεν;

52 Ἐπειδὰν τοίνυν τις αὐτὸν ἔρηται " καὶ τί δίκαιον
ἕξεις λέγειν πρὸς Νικόβουλον; " μισοῦσι, φησίν,
Ἀθηναῖοι τοὺς δανείζοντας· Νικόβουλος δ' ἐπί-
φθονός ἐστι, καὶ ταχέως βαδίζει, καὶ μέγα φθέγγ-
εται, καὶ βακτηρίαν φορεῖ· ταῦτα δ' ἐστὶν ἅπαντα,
φησίν, πρὸς ἐμοῦ. καὶ ταῦτ' οὐκ αἰσχύνεται λέγων,
οὐδὲ τοὺς ἀκούοντας οἴεται μανθάνειν, ὅτι συκο-
φαντοῦντός ἐστι λογισμὸς οὗτος, οὐκ ἀδικουμένου.

53 ἐγὼ δ' ἀδικεῖν μὲν οὐδένα τῶν δανειζόντων οἴομαι,
[982] μισεῖσθαι μέντοι τινὰς εἰκότως ἂν ὑφ' ὑμῶν, οἳ
τέχνην τὸ πρᾶγμα πεποιημένοι, μήτε συγγνώμης
μήτ' ἄλλου τινός εἰσιν ἀλλ' ἢ τοῦ πλείονος. διὰ
γὰρ τὸ καὶ δεδανεῖσθαι πολλάκις, μὴ μόνον αὐτὸς
τούτῳ δανεῖσαι, οὐδ' ἐγὼ τούτους ἀγνοῶ, οὐδὲ
φιλῶ, οὐ μέντοι γ' ἀποστερῶ μὰ Δί' οὐδὲ συκο-

54 φαντῶ. ὅστις δ' εἴργασται μὲν ὥσπερ ἐγὼ
πλέων καὶ κινδυνεύων, εὐπορήσας δὲ μικρῶν ἐδά-
νεισε ταῦτα, καὶ χαρίσασθαι βουλόμενος καὶ μὴ
λαθεῖν διαρρυὲν αὐτὸν τἀργύριον, τί τις ἂν τοῦτον
εἰς ἐκείνους τιθείη; εἰ μὴ τοῦτο λέγεις, ὡς ὃς ἂν
σοὶ δανείσῃ, τοῦτον δημοσίᾳ μισεῖσθαι προσήκει.

ᵃ Compare Oration XLV. § 77.

410

release from all charges of this kind. He ought not to be stating these charges now, nor to have inserted them in the challenge in which he demanded the slave for torture, but to have instituted suit against him, and to have prosecuted me as his owner. As it is, he has instituted suit against me, but accuses him. This the laws do not permit. For whoever instituted suit against the master, and charged the facts against his slave—as though the slave had any authority of his own?

When anyone asks him, "What valid charges will 52 you be able to make against Nicobulus?" he says, "The Athenians hate money-lenders; Nicobulus is an odious fellow; he walks fast,[a] he talks loud, and he carries a cane; and (he says) all these things count in my favour." He is not ashamed to talk in this way, and also fancies that his hearers do not understand that this is the reasoning, not of one who has suffered wrong, but of a malicious pettifogger. I, for my 53 part, do not regard a money-lender as a wrongdoer, although certain of the class may justly be detested by you, seeing that they make a trade of it, and have no thought of pity or of anything else, except gain. Since I have myself often borrowed money, and not merely lent it to the plaintiff, I know these people well; and I do not like them, either; but, by Zeus, I do not defraud them, nor bring malicious charges against them. But if a man has done business as I 54 have, going to sea on perilous journeys, and from his small profits has made these loans, wishing not only to confer favours, but to prevent his money from slipping through his fingers without his knowing it, why should one set him down in that class?—unless you mean this, that anyone who lends money to you ought to be detested by the public.

Λέγε δή μοι τὰς μαρτυρίας, τίς ἐγὼ πρὸς τοὺς
συμβάλλοντας ἀνθρώπους καὶ πρὸς τοὺς δεομένους
εἰμί.

ΜΑΡΤΥΡΙΑΙ

55 Τοιοῦτος, ὦ Πανταίνετ', ἐγώ, ὁ ταχὺ βαδίζων,
καὶ τοιοῦτος σύ, ὁ ἀτρέμας. ἀλλὰ μὴν περὶ τοὐμοῦ
γε βαδίσματος ἢ τῆς διαλέκτου, τἀληθῆ πάντ' ἐρῶ
πρὸς ὑμᾶς, ὦ ἄνδρες δικασταί, μετὰ παρρησίας.
ἐγὼ γὰρ οὐχὶ λέληθ' ἐμαυτὸν οὐδ' ἀγνοῶ, οὐ τῶν
εὖ πεφυκότων κατὰ ταῦτ' ὢν ἀνθρώπων, οὐδὲ τῶν
λυσιτελούντων ἑαυτοῖς. εἰ γὰρ ἐν οἷς μηδὲν ὠφε-
λοῦμαι ποιῶν, λυπῶ τινάς, πῶς οὐκ ἀτυχῶ κατὰ
56 τοῦτο τὸ μέρος; ἀλλὰ τί χρὴ παθεῖν; ἂν τῷ δεῖνι
δανείσω, διὰ ταῦτα δίκην προσοφλεῖν; μηδαμῶς.
κακίαν γάρ μοι καὶ πονηρίαν οὔθ' οὗτος προσοῦσαν
οὐδεμίαν δείξει, οὔθ' ὑμῶν τοσούτων ὄντων οὐδὲ
εἷς σύνοιδεν. τἄλλα δὲ ταῦθ' ἕκαστος ἡμῶν, ὅπως
[983] ἔτυχεν, πέφυκεν οἶμαι. καὶ φύσει μάχεσθαι μὲν
ἔχοντ' οὐκ εὔπορόν ἐστιν (οὐ γὰρ ἂν ἀλλήλων
διεφέρομεν οὐδέν), γνῶναι δ' ἰδόνθ' ἕτερον κἀπι-
57 πλῆξαι ῥᾴδιον. ἀλλὰ τί τούτων ἐμοὶ πρὸς σέ,
Πανταίνετε; πολλὰ καὶ δεινὰ πέπονθας; οὐκοῦν
εἴληφας δίκην. οὐ παρ' ἐμοῦ γε; οὐδὲ γὰρ
ἠδικήθης οὐδὲν ὑπ' ἐμοῦ. οὐ γὰρ ἄν ποτ' ἀφῆκας,
οὐδ', ὅτ' Εὐέργῳ προηροῦ λαγχάνειν, εἴασας ἐμέ,
οὐδὲ πρατὴρ' ἠξίωσας ὑποστῆναι τόν γε δεινά σε

412

Read me, please, the depositions, to show what manner of man I am to those who lend money, and to those who need my help.

THE DEPOSITIONS

Such am I, Pantaenetus, the fast walker, and such **55** are you, who walk slowly. However, regarding my gait and my manner of speech, I will tell you the whole truth, men of the jury, with all frankness. I am perfectly aware—I am not blind to the fact— that I am not one of those favoured by nature in these respects, nor of those who are an advantage to themselves. For if in matters in which I reap no profit, I annoy others, surely I am to this extent unfortunate. But what is to come of it ? If I lend money to so- **56** and-so, am I for this reason also to lose my suit ? Surely not. The plaintiff cannot point out any baseness or villainy attaching to me, nor does a single one among you, many as you are, know any such thing against me. As to these other qualities, each one of us, I take it, is as nature happened to make him ; and to fight against nature, when one has these characteristics, is no easy task (for otherwise we should not differ from one another) ; though to recognize them in looking on another and to criticize them is easy. But which one of these qualities has any **57** bearing on my dispute with you, Pantaenetus ? You have suffered many grievous wrongs ? Well, you have had satisfaction. Not from me ? No ; for you were not wronged in any way by me. Otherwise you would never have given me the release, nor, when you were making up your mind to bring suit against Evergus, would you have passed me by ; nor would you have demanded that one who had done you many grievous wrongs should undertake to be vendor

413

καὶ πόλλ' εἰργασμένον. εἶτα καὶ πῶς ἂν ὁ μὴ
58 παρὼν μηδ' ἐπιδημῶν ἐγώ τί σ' ἠδίκησα; εἰ
τοίνυν ὡς οἷόν τε μέγιστ' ἠδικῆσθαι δοίη τις αὐτῷ
καὶ ἐρεῖν ἅπαντ' ἀληθῆ περὶ τούτων νυνί, ἐκεῖνό γ'
οἶμαι πάντας ἂν ὑμᾶς ὁμολογῆσαι, ὅτι πολλὰ
συμβέβηκεν ἠδικῆσθαί τισιν ἤδη μείζω τῶν εἰς
χρήματα γιγνομένων ἀδικημάτων· καὶ γὰρ ἀκού-
σιοι φόνοι καὶ ὕβρεις εἰς ἃ μὴ δεῖ καὶ πολλὰ
τοιαῦτα γίγνεται. ἀλλ' ὅμως ἁπάντων τούτων
ὅρος καὶ λύσις τοῖς παθοῦσι τέτακται τὸ πεισθέντας
59 ἀφεῖναι. καὶ τοῦθ' οὕτω τὸ δίκαιον ἐν πᾶσιν
ἰσχύει, ὥστ', ἐὰν ἑλών τις ἀκουσίου φόνου καὶ
σαφῶς ἐπιδείξας μὴ καθαρόν, μετὰ ταῦτ' αἰδέσηται
καὶ ἀφῇ, οὐκέτ' ἐκβαλεῖν κύριος τὸν αὐτόν ἐστιν.
οὐδέ γ', ἂν ὁ παθὼν αὐτὸς ἀφῇ τοῦ φόνου, πρὶν
τελευτῆσαι, τὸν δράσαντα, οὐδενὶ τῶν λοιπῶν
συγγενῶν ἔξεστ' ἐπεξιέναι, ἀλλ' οὓς ἐκπίπτειν καὶ
φεύγειν, ἂν ἁλίσκωνται, καὶ τεθνάναι τάττουσιν οἱ
νόμοι, τούτους ἐὰν ἀφεθῶσιν ἅπαξ,[1] ἁπάντων ἐκλύει
60 τῶν δεινῶν τοῦτο τὸ ῥῆμα. εἶθ' ὑπὲρ μὲν ψυχῆς
καὶ τῶν μεγίστων οὕτως ἰσχύει καὶ μένει τἀφεῖναι,
ὑπὲρ δὲ χρημάτων καὶ ἐλαττόνων ἐγκλημάτων
ἄκυρον ἔσται; μηδαμῶς. οὐ γὰρ εἰ μὴ τῶν
[984] δικαίων ἐγὼ παρ' ὑμῖν τεύξομαι, τοῦτ' ἔστιν δεινότατον, ἀλλ' εἰ πρᾶγμα δίκαιον ὡρισμένον ἐκ
παντὸς τοῦ χρόνου νυνὶ καταλύσετε ἐφ' ἡμῶν.[2]

---

[1] ἀφεθῶσιν ἅπαξ,] ἀφεθῶσιν, ἅπαξ Blass.
[2] ἐφ' ἡμῶν omitted by Blass.

---

[a] The following passage is repeated almost verbatim in
the next oration, §§ 21 and 22.

[b] Homicide, even if accidental, entailed pollution, which
required expiation.

414

of the property. Besides, how could I have wronged you, when I was not present or even in the country? Well then, suppose[a] one should grant that Pantae- 58 netus has suffered the greatest possible wrongs, and that everything which he will now allege about these matters is true, this, at least, I presume, you would all admit: that it has happened to others ere now to have suffered many wrongs more serious than pecuniary wrongs. For involuntary homicides, outrages on what is sacred, and many other such crimes are committed; yet in all these cases the fact that they have yielded to persuasion and given a release is appointed for the parties wronged as a limit and settlement of the dispute. And this just principle 59 is so binding among all men, that if anyone having convicted another of involuntary homicide, and clearly shown him to be polluted,[b] subsequently takes pity on him and releases him, he has no longer the right to have the same person driven into exile. Again, if the victim himself before his death releases the murderer from bloodguiltiness, it is not lawful for any of the remaining kinsmen to prosecute; but those whom the laws sentence to banishment and exile and death, upon conviction, if they are once released, are by that word freed from all evil consequences. If, then, when life and all that 60 is most precious are at stake, a release has this power and validity, shall it be without effect when money is at stake, or claims of lesser importance? Surely not. For the thing most to be feared is, not that I should fail to obtain justice in your court, but that you should now in our day do away with a just practice, established from the beginning of time.

AGAINST NAUSIMACHUS

INTRODUCTION

NAUSIMACHUS and Xenopeithes were sons of a rich merchant and banker, named Nausicrates. At his death they became the wards of Aristaechmus, against whom, on attaining their majority, they brought suit for damages in the amount of eighty talents, charging him with breach of trust in the conduct of the guardianship. The suit was compromised, and upon paying the claimants three talents Aristaechmus received a release in full. Shortly after this he died.

Years afterwards—fourteen years after the release had been given and twenty-two years after the conclusion of the guardianship—Nausimachus and Xenopeithes separately brought suit against each of his four children (making eight actions in all), claiming damages in the sum of four talents, or thirty minae in each suit. The claimant in the present action maintained that Aristaechmus, after the release given him, had collected a debt of one hundred staters due to Nausicrates from an individual in Bosporus. This amounted to two thousand eight hundred drachmae (see Oration XXXIV. § 23), or, in round numbers with some allowance for interest, about thirty minae.

The defendant for whom this speech was written interposed a special plea in bar of action, based upon the full release given to Aristaechmus, and upon the statute of limitations, which precluded wards,

418

after the lapse of five years, from bringing suit to establish claims growing out of matters connected with guardianship, He makes also the oft-repeated charge that the suit was baseless and malicious.

See further Schaefer, iii.² pp. 207 ff., and Blass, iii. pp. 482 ff.

XXXVIII

ΠΑΡΑΓΡΑΦΗ ΠΡΟΣ ΝΑΥΣΙΜΑΧΟΝ
ΚΑΙ ΞΕΝΟΠΕΙΘΗΝ

Δεδωκότων, ὦ ἄνδρες δικασταί, τῶν νόμων παραγράψασθαι, περὶ ὧν ἄν τις ἀφεὶς καὶ ἀπαλλάξας
πάλιν δικάζηται, γεγενημένων ἀμφοτέρων τῷ πατρὶ
[985] πρὸς Ναυσίμαχον καὶ Ξενοπείθην τοὺς εἰληχότας
ἡμῖν, παρεγραψάμεθ᾽, ὥσπερ ἠκούσατ᾽ ἀρτίως, μὴ
2 εἰσαγώγιμον εἶναι τὴν δίκην. δεήσομαι δὲ καὶ
δίκαια καὶ μέτρι᾽ ὑμῶν ἁπάντων, πρῶτον μὲν
εὐνοϊκῶς ἀκοῦσαί μου λέγοντος, εἶτ᾽, ἐὰν ἀδικεῖσθαι δοκῶ καὶ μὴ προσήκοντος ἐγκλήματος φεύγειν
δίκην, βοηθῆσαί μοι τὰ δίκαια. ὃ μὲν γὰρ ὑμεῖς
ἐπὶ τῇ δίκῃ τίμημ᾽ ἀκηκόατε, τριάκοντ᾽ εἰσὶ μναῖ,
ὧν δὲ φεύγομεν χρημάτων, τέτταρα τάλαντα. ὄντες
γὰρ δύο τέτταρας εἰλήχασι δίκας ἡμῖν, τῶν αὐτῶν
χρημάτων πάσας, τρισχιλίων ἑκάστην, βλάβης· καὶ
νυνὶ πρὸς τριάκοντα μνῶν ἐπίγραμμα, ὑπὲρ το-
3 σούτων χρημάτων εἰς ἀγῶνα καθέσταμεν. τὴν μὲν

---

[a] The opening sentences of this speech repeat almost
verbatim those of the preceding oration.
[b] From this it is plain that each of the two claimants
brought suit against each of the four sons of Aristaechmus.
420

XXXVIII

ONE OF THE SONS OF ARISTAECH-MUS AGAINST NAUSIMACHUS AND XENOPEITHES, A SPECIAL PLEA

INASMUCH as the laws, men of the jury, have granted that a special plea may be entered in cases where a man, after giving a release and discharge,[a] nevertheless brings suit, and as both of these have been given to our father by Nausimachus and Xenopeithes who have commenced suit against us, we have pleaded, as you have just now heard, that their suit is not admissible. I shall make of you all a just 2 and reasonable request: first, that you listen to my words with goodwill, and, secondly, that if you think that I am being wronged and made defendant in a suit which has no valid basis, you render me the succour which is my due. The damages claimed in the action are, as you have heard, thirty minae; but the sum for which we are really being sued is four talents. For there are two of them, and they have entered four suits against us, all for a like amount, each for three thousand drachmae damages;[b] and now on a complaint for thirty minae we are brought to trial for so large a sum. The malicious actions of 3

This makes eight suits for thirty minae each, so that the total amount is four talents.

οὖν συκοφαντίαν τὴν τούτων, καὶ μεθ' ὅσης ἐπι-
βουλῆς ἐληλύθασιν ἐφ' ἡμᾶς, ἐξ αὐτῶν τῶν πεπραγμένων εἴσεσθε. ἀναγνώσεται δὲ πρῶτον μὲν ὑμῖν
τὰς μαρτυρίας, ὡς ἀφεῖσαν τὸν πατέρ' ἡμῶν ὧν
ἐνεκάλεσαν εἰς τὴν ἐπιτροπήν· κατὰ γὰρ τοῦτο καὶ
παρεγραψάμεθα, μὴ εἰσαγώγιμον εἶναι τὴν δίκην.
   Καί μοι λέγε ταυτασὶ τὰς μαρτυρίας.

ΜΑΡΤΥΡΙΑΙ

4 "Οτι μὲν τοίνυν, ὦ ἄνδρες δικασταί, καὶ δίκας
ἔλαχον τῆς ἐπιτροπῆς καὶ ἀφεῖσαν ταύτας καὶ τὰ
συγχωρηθέντα χρήματ' ἔχουσιν, ἀκούετε τῶν μαρτυριῶν. ὅτι δ' οὐκ ἐῶσιν οἱ νόμοι περὶ τῶν οὕτω
πραχθέντων αὖθις δικάζεσθαι, νομίζω μὲν ἅπαντας
ὑμᾶς εἰδέναι, κἂν μηδὲν εἴπω περὶ αὐτῶν ἐγώ,
βούλομαι δ' ὅμως καὶ τὸν νόμον ὑμῖν αὐτὸν ἀνα-
γνῶναι.
   Λέγε τὸν νόμον.

ΝΟΜΟΣ

5 'Ακούετ', ὦ ἄνδρες δικασταί, τοῦ νόμου σαφῶς
λέγοντος ἕκασθ', ὧν μὴ εἶναι δίκας· ὧν ἔν ἐστιν,
ὁμοίως τοῖς ἄλλοις κύριον, περὶ ὧν ἄν τις ἀφῇ καὶ
ἀπαλλάξῃ, μὴ δικάζεσθαι. οὕτω τοίνυν καὶ μετὰ
πολλῶν μαρτύρων τῆς ἀφέσεως γεγονυίας, καὶ
φανερῶς ἀπολύοντος ἡμᾶς τοῦ νόμου, εἰς τοῦτ'
6 ἐληλύθασιν ἀναισχυντίας οὗτοι καὶ τόλμης, ὥστε
τεττάρων μὲν καὶ δέκ' ἐτῶν γεγενημένων ἀφ' οὗ
τὸν πατέρ' ἡμῶν ἀφεῖσαν, εἴκοσιν δὲ καὶ δυοῖν ἀφ'

these men, and the guile with which they have proceeded against us, you will come to know from the facts themselves. But first the clerk shall read to you the depositions which show that they released our father from the charges which they made in the matter of his guardianship; for it is on this ground that we entered our plea that the action is not maintainable.

Please read these depositions.

THE DEPOSITIONS

That they entered suit, men of the jury, regarding **4** the guardianship; that they dropped those actions; and that they have in their possession the sums of money agreed upon, you hear from the witnesses. That the laws do not allow suit to be entered afresh regarding matters which have been thus settled, I presume you know, even if I say nothing about the matter; nevertheless I want to read you the law itself.

Read the law.

THE LAW

You hear the law, men of the jury, expressly stat- **5** ing the several cases in which there shall be no actions. One of them (and it is as binding as any of the others) is that suit may not be brought in matters for which anyone has given a release and discharge. Yet, although the release was thus given in the presence of numerous witnesses, and although the law manifestly absolves us, these men have come to such a pitch of shamelessness and audacity, that, when **6** fourteen years have elapsed from the time when they gave my father a release, and twenty-two years after

οὗ τυγχάνουσιν γεγραμμένοι,[1] τετελευτηκότος δὲ
καὶ τοῦ πατρὸς τοῦ ἡμετέρου, πρὸς ὃν αὐτοῖς
ἐγένονθ᾽ αἱ ἀπαλλαγαί, καὶ τῶν ἐπιτρόπων, οἳ μετὰ
τὸν κείνου θάνατον τῶν ἡμετέρων ἐγένοντο κύριοι,
καὶ τῆς ἑαυτῶν μητρός, ἥτις ἅπαντα ταῦτ᾽ ᾔδει,
καὶ διαιτητῶν καὶ μαρτύρων καὶ πάντων ὡς εἰπεῖν,
τὴν ἡμετέραν ἀπειρίαν καὶ τὴν ἐξ ἀνάγκης ἄγνοιαν
τῶν πεπραγμένων ἕρμαιον νομίσαντες ἑαυτῶν, τὰς
δίκας ἡμῖν ἔλαχον ταυτασί, καὶ λόγον οὔτε δίκαιον
7 οὔτ᾽ ἐπιεικῆ τολμῶσι λέγειν. φασὶ γὰρ οὐκ ἀποδόσθαι τὰ πατρῷ᾽ ὧν ἐκομίζοντο χρημάτων, οὐδ᾽
ἀποστῆναι τῶν ὄντων, ἀλλ᾽ ὅσ᾽ αὐτοῖς κατελείφθη
χρέα καὶ σκεύη καὶ ὅλως χρήματα, ταῦθ᾽ ἑαυτῶν
γίγνεσθαι. ἐγὼ δ᾽ οἶδ᾽ ἀκούων ὅτι τὴν οὐσίαν
Ξενοπείθης καὶ Ναυσικράτης ἅπασαν χρέα κατ-
έλιπον, καὶ φανερὰν ἐκέκτηντο μικράν τινα·
εἰσπραχθέντων δὲ τῶν χρεῶν καί τινων σκευῶν
πραθέντων, ἔτι δ᾽ ἀνδραπόδων, καὶ τὰ χωρία καὶ
τὰς συνοικίας ἐπρίανθ᾽ οἱ ἐπίτροποι, ἃ παρέλαβον
8 οὗτοι. εἰ μὲν οὖν μηδὲν ἠμφεσβητήθη περὶ τούτων
πρότερον, μηδ᾽ ὡς οὐ καλῶς διῳκημένων εἰς δίκην
[987] ἦλθεν, ἄλλος ἂν ἦν λόγος· ἐπειδὴ δ᾽ ὅλην τὴν ἐπι-
τροπὴν ἐγκαλέσαντες οὗτοι καὶ δίκας λαχόντες
χρήματ᾽ ἐπράξαντο, πάντα ταῦτ᾽ ἀφεῖται τότε.

---

[1] γεγραμμένοι] ἐγγεγραμμένοι Blass.

[a] This passage offers difficulties. The best established
text can be rendered only as above ; but the question at
once arises : why the long lapse of time between the filing
of the suit and the settlement? Again, the use of γεγραμμένοι
of a civil suit is surprising, although this difficulty might be
met by assuming (with Kennedy) that a public prosecution
is meant ; but even so the eight-year period remains un-
explained.

they had first indicted him,[a] when my father was now
dead, with whom the settlement had been made,
and also the guardians who after his death had charge
of our property, when their own mother, too, was
dead, who was well-informed regarding all these
matters, and the arbitrators, the witnesses, and almost everybody else, if I may so say, counting our
inexperience and necessary ignorance a boon to
themselves, they have instituted these suits against
us, and have the audacity to make statements which
are neither just nor reasonable. They declare that 7
they did not sell their father's estate for the money
which they received, nor did they give up the property, but that all that was left them—credits, furniture, and even money—still belongs to them. I, for
my part, know by hearsay that Xenopeithes and
Nausicrates [b] left their entire property in outstanding
debts, and possessed very little tangible property ;
and that when the debts had been collected and some
furniture and slaves had been sold, their guardians
purchased the farms and lodging-houses, which our
opponents received from them. If there had been 8
no dispute about these matters before, and no suit
had been entered charging maladministration of the
property, it would have been another story ; but
since these men brought suit against our father in the
matter of his general conduct as guardian and recovered damages, all these matters were at that time

If with ᴍꜱ. A we read ἐγγεγραμμένοι, and render, " after
they had been enrolled as citizens," we still have to ask
why they should have waited eight years after attaining
their majority before seeking an accounting from their
guardians.

[b] The former was the uncle, the latter the father of the
plaintiff.

οὔτε γὰρ οὗτοι τοὐνόματος δήπου τοῦ τῆς ἐπιτροπῆς τὰς δίκας ἐδίωκον, ἀλλὰ τῶν χρημάτων,
οὔτ' ἐκεῖνοι τοὔνομα τοῦτ' ἐωνοῦνθ' ὧν ἀπέτεισαν
χρημάτων, ἀλλὰ τἀγκλήματα.

9 Ὅτι μὲν οὖν ὧν πρὸ τῶν ἀπαλλαγῶν εἰσέπραξε
χρεῶν ὁ πατήρ, ἢ ὅλως ἔλαβεν χρημάτων ἐκ τῆς
ἐπιτροπῆς, οὐδενός εἰσι δίκαι τούτοις καθ' ἡμῶν
ἀπηλλαγμένοις, ἐξ αὐτῶν τῶν νόμων καὶ τῆς ἀφέσεως ἱκανῶς πάντας ἡγοῦμαι ὑμᾶς μεμαθηκέναι.
ὅτι δ' ὕστερον οὐκ ἔνι τὴν κομιδὴν γεγενῆσθαι τούτων τῶν χρημάτων (τοῦτο γὰρ πλάττουσιν οὗτοι
10 καὶ παράγουσι), τοῦτο βούλομαι δεῖξαι. τὸν μὲν γὰρ
πατέρ' οὐδ' ἂν αἰτιάσαιντο λαβεῖν· τέτταρσι γὰρ ἢ
τρισὶ μησὶν ὕστερον ἢ διελύσατο πρὸς τούτους
ἐτελεύτησεν. ὡς δ' οὐδὲ Δημάρετον τὸν κατα-
λειφθένθ' ἡμῶν ἐπίτροπον λαβεῖν οἷόν τε (καὶ γὰρ
τοῦτον ἔγραψαν εἰς τὸ ἔγκλημα), καὶ τοῦτ' ἐπι-
11 δείξω. μέγιστοι μὲν οὖν ἡμῖν εἰσιν οὗτοι μάρτυρες·
οὐδαμοῦ γὰρ φανήσονται δίκην εἰληχότες ζῶντι τῷ
Δημαρέτῳ· οὐ μὴν ἀλλὰ καὶ τὸ πρᾶγμ' ἄν τις αὐτὸ
σκοπῶν καὶ θεωρῶν ἴδοι, οὐ μόνον οὐχὶ λαβόντα,
ἀλλ' οὐδ' ἐνὸν αὐτῷ λαβεῖν. ἦν μὲν γὰρ τὸ χρέως
ἐν Βοσπόρῳ, ἀφίκετο δ' οὐδεπώποτ' εἰς τὸν τόπον
τοῦτον ὁ Δημάρετος· πῶς οὖν εἰσέπραξεν; ἔπεμψε
12 νὴ Δί', εἴποι τις ἄν, τὸν κομιούμενον. σκοπεῖτε δὴ
[988] τοῦθ' οὑτωσί. ὤφειλεν Ἑρμῶναξ στατῆρας ἑκατὸν
παρὰ Ναυσικράτους λαβὼν τούτοις. τούτων Ἀρίστ-

---

[a] The Athenian stater was a gold coin worth twenty
drachmae.

released. For our opponents, I take it, did not bring suit for the mere name " mal-administration in guardianship," but for the money; nor did the guardians buy off this name with the money which they paid, but they bought off the claims.

That, therefore, these men have no right of action 9 against us for the debts which our father collected before the settlement, or, in general, for moneys which he received by virtue of his guardianship, seeing that they have given a release for their claims, I think you have all adequately learned from the laws themselves and from the release. Moreover, that it is impossible that the collection of these funds should have been made subsequently (this is the story they are making up to lead you astray), I wish to prove. As for my father, they cannot charge that he 10 received them; for he died three or four months after the settlement was made with them; and that Demaretus, whom our father left as our guardian, could not have received them either (for they have written his name also in their complaint), this, too, I shall show. These men are themselves our strongest 11 witnesses; for they will be shown never to have brought suit against Demaretus in his lifetime; but, more than that, anyone who examines and studies the case itself will see, not only that he did not receive the money, but that it was impossible that he should have received it. For the debt was in Bosporus, a place which Demaretus never visited; how, then, could he have collected it? Ah, but, they will say, he sent someone to get the money. But 12 look at the matter in this way. Hermonax owed these men one hundred staters,^{a} which he had received from Nausicrates. Aristaechmus was for

αἰχμος ἐπίτροπος καὶ κηδεμὼν ἐγένεθ' ἑκκαίδεκ'
ἔτη. οὐκοῦν ἅ γε τούτων ἀνδρῶν γεγονότων δι'
ἑαυτοῦ διέλυε χρήμαθ' ὁ Ἑρμῶναξ, οὐκ ἀπέδωκεν
ὅτ' ἦσαν παῖδες· οὐ γὰρ δίς γε ταὐτὰ κατετίθει.
ἔστιν οὖν οὕτω τις ἀνθρώπων ἄτοπος, ὥσθ' ἃ τοὺς
κυρίους διεκρούσατο μὴ καταθεῖναι τοσοῦτον χρόνον, ταῦτα τῷ μὴ κυρίῳ πέμψαντι γράμμαθ' ἑκὼν
ἀποδοῦναι; ἐγὼ μὲν οὐκ οἶμαι.

13 Ἀλλὰ μὴν ὡς ἀληθῆ λέγω, καὶ ὁ μὲν πατὴρ
ἐτελεύτησεν εὐθέως μετὰ τὰς διαλύσεις, τῷ Δη-
μαρέτῳ δ' οὐδεπώποθ' οὗτοι τῶν χρημάτων τούτων
δίκην ἔλαχον, οὐδ' ὅλως ἐξέπλευσεν ἐκεῖνος οὐδ'
ἀπεδήμησεν ἐκεῖσε, λαβὲ τὰς μαρτυρίας.

14 Ὅτι μὲν τοίνυν οὔθ' ὁ πατὴρ μετὰ τὴν ἄφεσιν τὰ
χρήματ' εἰσέπραξεν, οὔτ' ἂν ἔδωκεν ἑκὼν οὐδείς,
εἴ τιν' ἔπεμψεν ὁ Δημάρετος, οὔτ' ἀνέπλευσεν αὐτὸς
οὐδ' ἀφίκετ' ἐκεῖσε, δῆλον ἐκ τῶν χρόνων καὶ τῶν
μαρτυριῶν ὑμῖν γέγονεν. βούλομαι τοίνυν καὶ
ὅλως ψευδομένους αὐτοὺς ὅλον τὸ πρᾶγμ' ἐπιδεῖξαι.
οὗτοι γὰρ γεγράφασιν εἰς ὃ νῦν ἔγκλημα διώκουσιν,
ὀφείλειν ἡμᾶς τὸ ἀργύριον κομισαμένου τοῦ πατρός,
καὶ παραδόντος αὐτοῖς τὸ χρέως ἐν τῷ λόγῳ τῆς
ἐπιτροπῆς ὀφειλόμενον.

Καί μοι λέγ' αὐτὸ τὸ ἔγκλημα λαβών.

15 Ἀκούετε γεγραμμένον ἐν τῷ ἐγκλήματι " παραδόντος ἐμοὶ τοῦ Ἀρισταίχμου τὸ χρέως ἐν τῷ λόγῳ

sixteen years the guardian and caretaker of these men. Therefore, the money which Hermonax paid in his own person after these men had come of age, he had not paid when they were minors ; for he certainly did not pay the same debt twice. Now is there any man so silly as voluntarily to pay money to one not entitled to it, who demanded it by letter, when he had for so long a time evaded payment to the rightful owners ? For my part, I think there is not.

However, to prove that I am speaking the truth, 13 —that our father died immediately after the settlement, that these men never brought suit against Demaretus for this money, and that he absolutely never went to sea, nor visited Bosporus, take the depositions.

The Depositions

Well then, that our father did not collect the money 14 after the release ; that no one would voluntarily have paid the money, if Demaretus had sent someone to get it ; and that he himself neither put out to sea nor visited Bosporus, has been made clear to you from the dates and the depositions. I wish, then, to show you that their whole statement too of the case is absolute falsehood. They have written in the complaint which they are now prosecuting, that we owe the money, inasmuch as our father received it in payment, and passed it over to them as a debt due and payable in his account of his guardianship.

Take, and read me, please, the complaint itself.

The Complaint

You hear it stated in the complaint, " inasmuch as 15 Aristaechmus passed the debt over to me in his

[989] τῆς ἐπιτροπῆς.'' ὅτε τοίνυν ἐλάγχανον τῷ πατρὶ
τῆς ἐπιτροπῆς, τἀναντί᾽ ἐγράψαντο τούτων· ὡς γὰρ
οὐκ ἀποδόντι λόγον τότ᾽ ἐγκαλοῦντες φαίνονται.
Λέγ᾽ αὐτὸ τὸ ἔγκλημα, ὃ τότ᾽ ἔλαχον τῷ πατρί.

ΕΓΚΛΗΜΑ

16 Ἐν ποίῳ δὴ λόγῳ νῦν ἐγκαλεῖθ᾽ ὡς παρέδωκεν,
ὦ Ξενοπείθη καὶ Ναυσίμαχε; τότε μὲν γὰρ ὡς
οὐκ ἀποδόντι δίκας ἐλαγχάνετε καὶ χρήματ᾽ ἐπράτ-
τεσθε. εἰ δ᾽ ἐπ᾽ ἀμφότερ᾽ ἔσται συκοφαντεῖν ὑμῖν,
καὶ τοτὲ μὲν τοῦ μὴ παραδοῦναι χρήματ᾽ ἐπράξασθε, τοτὲ δ᾽ ὡς παραδόντος διώκετε, οὐδὲν
κωλύει καὶ τρίτον τι σκοπεῖν μετὰ ταῦτα, ὅτου
πάλιν δικάσεσθε. οἱ νόμοι δ᾽ οὐ ταῦτα λέγουσιν,
ἀλλ᾽ ἅπαξ περὶ τῶν αὐτῶν πρὸς τὸν αὐτὸν εἶναι
τὰς δίκας.

17 Ἵνα τοίνυν εἰδῆτ᾽, ὦ ἄνδρες δικασταί, ὅτι οὐ
μόνον οὐκ ἀδικοῦνται νῦν, ἀλλὰ καὶ παρὰ πάντας
ἡμῖν δικάζονται τοὺς νόμους, βούλομαι καὶ τοῦτον
ὑμῖν τὸν νόμον εἰπεῖν, ὃς διαρρήδην λέγει, ἐὰν πέντ᾽
ἔτη παρέλθῃ καὶ μὴ δικάσωνται, μηκέτ᾽ εἶναι τοῖς
ὀρφανοῖς δίκην περὶ τῶν ἐκ τῆς ἐπιτροπῆς ἐγκλημάτων.

Καὶ ὑμῖν ἀναγνώσεται τὸν νόμον.

ΝΟΜΟΣ

18 Ἀκούετ᾽, ὦ ἄνδρες δικασταί, τοῦ νόμου λέγοντος
ἄντικρυς, ἐὰν μὴ πέντ᾽ ἐτῶν δικάσωνται, μηκέτ᾽

account of his guardianship." But, when they brought suit against my father in the matter of his guardianship, they wrote the very opposite of this ; for they plainly charged him with not rendering an account.

Read, please, the complaint itself, which they then brought against my father.

THE COMPLAINT

In what account, pray, Xenopeithes and Nausi- 16 machus, do you now charge that he passed the debt over to you ? For at one time you brought suit and demanded money on the ground that he rendered no account. But if it is to be permitted you to bring your malicious charge on both grounds, and at one time you collected money because he did not hand something over to you, and at another are suing him on the ground that he did hand it over, there is nothing to prevent your looking for some third ground after this, so as to commence proceedings afresh. But that is not what the laws state : they declare that suit may be brought once only against the same person for the same acts.

Now, men of the jury, that you may know that 17 they not only have suffered no wrong in the present case, but that they are bringing suit in defiance of all your laws, I wish to cite to you this statute also, which expressly states that, if five years have elapsed and they have brought no suit, it is no longer permitted to orphans to bring suit regarding claims connected with guardianship.

The clerk will read you this law.

THE LAW

You hear the law, men of the jury, flatly stating 18 that if they do not bring suit within five years, they

εἶναι δίκην. οὐκοῦν ἐλάχομεν, φαῖεν ἄν. καὶ διελύσασθέ γε, ὥστ' οὐκ εἰσὶν αὖθις ὑμῖν δίκαι. ἢ δεινόν γ' ἂν εἴη, εἰ τῶν μὲν ἐξ ἀρχῆς ἀδικημάτων οὐ δίδωσιν ἔξω πέντ' ἐτῶν τὰς δίκας τοῖς ὀρφανοῖς ὁ νόμος κατὰ τῶν οὐκ ἀφειμένων ἐπιτρόπων, πρὸς δὲ τοὺς ἐξ ἐκείνων ἡμᾶς, περὶ ὧν αὐτοὺς ἀφήκατε, [990] εἰκοστῷ νῦν ἔτει δίκην τελέσαισθ' ὑμεῖς.

19 Ἀκούω τοίνυν αὐτοὺς τὰ μὲν περὶ τῶν πραγμάτων αὐτῶν καὶ τῶν νόμων δίκαια φεύξεσθαι, παρεσκευάσθαι δὲ λέγειν, ὡς πολλὰ χρήματ' αὐτοῖς κατελείφθη καὶ ταῦτ' ἀπεστερήθησαν, καὶ τεκμηρίῳ χρήσεσθαι τούτου τῷ μεγέθει τῶν δικῶν ἃς ἐξ ἀρχῆς ἔλαχον, καὶ τὴν ὀρφανίαν ὀδυρεῖσθαι, καὶ τὸν τῆς ἐπιτροπῆς λόγον διεξιέναι· καὶ ταῦτ' εἶναι καὶ τοιαῦθ' οἷς πεπιστεύκασι καὶ δι' ὧν ὑμᾶς 20 ἐξαπατήσειν οἴονται. ἐγὼ δὲ τὸ μὲν τῶν δικῶν μέγεθος τῶν τότε ληχθεισῶν, μεῖζον ἡγοῦμαι τεκμήριον ἡμῖν εἶναι ὡς ἐσυκοφαντεῖθ' ὁ πατήρ, ἢ τούτοις ὡς πόλλ' ἀπεστεροῦντο. ὀγδοήκοντα μὲν γὰρ τάλαντ' ἔχων ἐλέγχειν, οὐδὲ εἷς ἂν τρία λαβὼν ἀπηλλάγη· τοσούτων δὲ χρημάτων φεύγων ἐπιτροπῆς, οὐδεὶς ἔστιν ὅστις οὐκ ἂν ἔδωκε τρία τάλαντα, τὸν κίνδυνον ὠνούμενος καὶ τὰ φύσει τότε τούτοις πλεονεκτήμαθ' ὑπάρχοντα. καὶ γὰρ ὀρφανοὶ καὶ νέοι καὶ ὁποῖοί τινές εἰσιν ἀγνῶτες ἦσαν· ταῦτα δὲ πάντες φασὶν μεγάλων δικαίων ἰσχύειν πλέον παρ' ὑμῖν.

have no longer the right to sue. But we did bring suit, they may say. Yes, and you made a settlement, too ; so you have no right to bring a fresh suit. Else it would be an outrageous thing, if for original wrong-doings the law does not allow suit to be brought by orphans after five years against guardians who have not been released, but now in the twentieth year you are to maintain an action against us, the children of your guardians, for matters concerning which you did give them a release.

But I hear that they are going to shun arguments 19 based upon the facts of the case and upon the laws, and are prepared to assert that a large estate was left them and that they were defrauded of it ; and that they will advance as a proof of this the large sum asked as damages in their original suit, and they will wail over their orphanhood, and will go through the guardianship accounts. These and such-like points are the ones upon which they have fixed their trust, and by which they hope to beguile you. For my own 20 part, I think that the large sum asked as damages in the suits then brought is a stronger proof for us, that our father was the victim of a malicious action, than for them, that they were being defrauded of a large estate. For if he could prove his claims for eighty talents, no man in the world would have accepted three talents in settlement ; whereas anyone, being defendant in a guardianship suit involving such large sums, would have paid three talents to buy off the risk and the advantages with which at that time nature supplied these men. They were orphans and young, and you were ignorant of their real characters; and everyone says that in your courts these things have more weight than strong arguments.

21 Ὅτι τοίνυν οὐδ' ἀνάσχοισθ' ἂν αὐτῶν εἰκότως
οὐδὲν περὶ τῆς ἐπιτροπῆς, καὶ τοῦτ' οἴομαι δείξειν.
εἰ γὰρ ὡς οἷόν τε μέγιστ' ἠδικῆσθαι δοίη τις αὐτοῖς
καὶ ἐρεῖν ἅπαντ' ἀληθῆ περὶ τούτων νυνί, ἐκεῖνό
γ' οἶμαι πάντας ἂν ὑμᾶς ὁμολογῆσαι, ὅτι πολλὰ
συμβέβηκεν ἠδικῆσθαί τισιν ἤδη μείζω τῶν εἰς
χρήματα γιγνομένων ἀδικημάτων· καὶ γὰρ ἀκού-
σιοι φόνοι καὶ ὕβρεις εἰς ἃ μὴ δεῖ καὶ πολλὰ τοιαῦτα
[991] γίγνεται. ἀλλ' ὅμως ἁπάντων τούτων ὅρος καὶ
λύσις τοῖς παθοῦσι τέτακται τὸ πεισθέντας ἀφεῖναι.
22 καὶ τοῦθ' οὕτω τὸ δίκαιον ἐν πᾶσιν ἰσχύει, ὥστ'
ἐὰν ἑλών τις ἀκουσίου φόνου καὶ σοφῶς ἐπιδείξας
μὴ καθαρόν, μετὰ ταῦτ' αἰδέσηται καὶ ἀφῇ, οὐκέτ'
ἐκβαλεῖν κύριος τὸν αὐτόν ἐστιν. εἶθ' ὑπὲρ μὲν
ψυχῆς καὶ τῶν μεγίστων οὕτως ἰσχύει καὶ μένει
τἀφεῖναι, ὑπὲρ δὲ χρημάτων καὶ ἐλαττόνων ἐγκλημάτων ἄκυρον ἔσται; μηδαμῶς. οὐ γὰρ εἰ μὴ
τῶν δικαίων ἐγὼ παρ' ὑμῖν τεύξομαι, τοῦτ' ἔστιν
δεινότατον, ἀλλ' εἰ πρᾶγμα δίκαιον ὡρισμένον ἐκ
παντὸς τοῦ χρόνου νυνὶ καταλυθήσεται.[1]
23 Οὐκ ἐμίσθωσαν ἡμῶν τὸν οἶκον, ἴσως ἐροῦσιν.
οὐ γὰρ ἐβούλεθ' ὁ θεῖος ὑμῶν Ξενοπείθης, ἀλλὰ
φήναντος Νικίδου τοὺς δικαστὰς ἔπεισεν ἐᾶσαι
διοικεῖν αὐτόν· καὶ ταῦτ' ἴσασι πάντες. πολλὰ
διήρπασαν ἡμῶν ἐκεῖνοι. οὐκοῦν ἦν ἐπείσθητέ γε,
τούτων δίκην παρ' αὐτῶν ἔχετε, καὶ οὐ δήπουθεν

---

[1] καταλυθήσεται] καταλύσετε Blass (as in XXXVII. § 60).

[a] The following passage is repeated almost verbatim from the preceding oration, §§ 58 ff.
[b] If a guardian did not fufil the duties imposed by his position, any citizen might charge him before the archon with breach of trust.

Moreover, I think I can also prove that you might **21** with good reason refuse to hear a word from them in regard to the guardianship. ^a For suppose one should grant that they have suffered the greatest possible wrongs, and that everything which they will now allege about these matters is true, this, at least, I presume you would all admit : that it has happened to others ere now to have suffered many wrongs more serious than pecuniary wrongs. For involuntary homicides, outrages on what is sacred, and many other such crimes are committed; yet in all these cases the fact they have yielded to persuasion and given a release is appointed for the parties wronged as a limit and settlement of the dispute. And this just principle **22** is so binding among all men, that, if one, having convicted another of involuntary homicide, and clearly shown him to be polluted, subsequently takes pity upon him, and releases him, he has no longer the right to have the same person driven into exile. If, then, when life and all that is most precious are at stake, a release has this power and validity, shall it be without effect, when money is at stake, or claims of lesser importance ? Surely not. For the thing most to be feared is, not that I should fail to obtain justice in your court, but that a just practice, established from the beginning of time, should now be done away with.

" They did not let our property," they will perhaps **23** say. No ; for your uncle Xenopeithes did not want it let, but, after Nicidas had denounced him for this,^b induced the jurors to allow him to administer it ; and this everybody knows. " They robbed us of huge sums." Well, for this you have received from them the damages upon which you agreed ; and, I take it,

24 πάλιν δεῖ λαβεῖν ὑμᾶς παρ' ἐμοῦ. ἵνα δὲ μηδ'
οἴησθ' εἶναί τι ταῦτα, ἔστι μὲν οὐκ ἴσον (πῶς γάρ;)
πρὸς τοὺς πράξαντας διαλυσαμένους τῶν οὐκ εἰδότων κατηγορεῖν, ὅμως δ', ὦ Ξενοπείθη καὶ Ναυσίμαχε, εἰ μεγάλ' ὑμῖν καὶ θαυμάστ' εἶναι τὰ
δίκαια ταῦθ' ὑπολαμβάνετε, ἀποδόντες τὰ τρία
τάλαντα περαίνετε. ὧν δὲ τοῦ μὴ κατηγορῆσαι
τοσαῦτα χρήματ' ἐπράξασθε, πρὶν ἂν ταῦτ' ἀπο-
δῶτε, σιωπᾶν ἐστὲ δίκαιοι, καὶ μὴ κατηγορεῖν καὶ
ἔχειν· ἔσχατον γὰρ ἤδη πραγμάτων τοῦτό γε.

25 Τάχα τοίνυν καὶ τριηραρχίας ἐροῦσι, καὶ τὰ ὄνθ'
[992] ὡς ἀνηλώκασιν εἰς ὑμᾶς. ἐγὼ δ' ὅτι μὲν ψεύσονται,
καὶ πόλλ' ἀπολωλεκότες τῶν ὄντων αὐτοῖς, μικρὰ
τῆς πόλεως μετειληφυίας, οὐ δικαίαν οὐδὲ γιγνο-
μένην χάριν ἀξιώσουσιν κομίζεσθαι παρ' ὑμῶν,
ἐάσω. ἀξιῶ δὲ καὶ αὐτός, ὦ ἄνδρες δικασταί,
εἶναι τοῖς λητουργοῦσιν ὑμῖν ἅπασι χάριν τιν'
ὑπάρχουσαν παρ' ὑμῶν. τίσιν δὲ μεγίστην; τοῖς
ὃ μὲν χρήσιμον τῇ πόλει τοῦ πράγματός ἐστι
ποιοῦσιν, ὃ δ' αἰσχρὸν ἅπαντες ἂν εἶναι φήσαιεν καὶ
26 ὄνειδος μὴ κατασκευάζουσιν. οἱ μὲν τοίνυν μετὰ
τοῦ λητουργεῖν τὰ σφέτερ' αὐτῶν διεφθαρκότες,
τὴν βλασφημίαν ἀντὶ τῆς χρείας τῇ πόλει κατα-
λείπουσιν· οὐδεὶς γὰρ αὐτὸς αὑτοῦ κατηγόρησε
πώποτε, ἀλλ' ὡς ἡ πόλις τὰ ὄντ' ἀφῄρηται λέγει.
οἱ δ' ὅσα μὲν προστάττεθ' ὑμεῖς ποιοῦντες προθύμως, τῇ περὶ τἄλλα δὲ σωφροσύνῃ τὰ ὄντα σώ-

you are not entitled to recover it again from me. But, 24
that you may not think there is anything in all this—
it is of course not fair (how could it be ?) after having
come to a settlement with the guilty parties, to accuse
persons who know nothing about the case—none the
less, Xenopeithes and Nausimachus, if you have the
idea that your claims are so marvellously valid, pay
back three talents, and go on with your suit. After
having exacted so large a sum for not pressing your
charges, you are bound to keep silent until you
have paid this back—not to make the charges and
keep the money ; that is the very extreme of unfair
dealing.

Now it is likely that they will talk about their 25
trierarchies, and say that they have expended their
property upon you. That their statements will be
false ; that they have squandered much of their
property upon themselves, while the state has received but a small share ; and that they will deem
it right to reap from you a gratitude that is not
deserved nor due—all this I shall pass over. I myself,
men of the jury, deem it right that somewhat of
gratitude should be accorded by you to all who bear
the public burdens. But to whom should you accord
most gratitude ? To those who, while in their actions
doing what is of service to the state, do not bring to
pass what all would call a shame and a reproach. But 26
those who while performing public services have
squandered their own property, bring the state into
disrepute instead of rendering her service. For no
man ever yet blamed himself ; on the contrary, he
declares that the state has taken away his property.
But those who with ready hearts perform all the
duties you lay upon them, and who by the soberness

ζοντες, οὐ μόνον κατὰ τοῦτ᾽ ἐκείνων πλεονεκτοῖεν
ἂν εἰκότως, ὅτι καὶ γεγόνασι χρήσιμοι καὶ ἔσονται,
ἀλλ᾽ ὅτι καὶ χωρὶς ὀνείδους ταῦτα παρ᾽ αὐτῶν
ὑμῖν γίγνεται. ἡμεῖς μὲν τοίνυν εἰς ὑμᾶς τοιοῦτοι
φανούμεθ᾽ ὄντες· τούτους δ᾽ ἐάσω, μή με φῶσιν
κακῶς αὐτοὺς λέγειν.

27 Οὐ τοίνυν θαυμάσαιμ᾽ ἄν, εἰ καὶ δακρύειν καὶ
ἐλεινοὺς ἑαυτοὺς πειρῷντο ποιεῖν. ἐγὼ δ᾽ ἀξιῶ
πρὸς ταῦθ᾽ ὑπολαμβάνειν ἅπαντας ὑμᾶς, ὅτι τῶν
αἰσχρῶν ἐστι, μᾶλλον δ᾽ οὐδὲ δικαίων, τὰ μὲν
ὄντα κατεσθίοντας καὶ παροινοῦντας μετ᾽ Ἀριστο-
κράτους καὶ Διογνήτου καὶ τοιούτων ἑτέρων
αἰσχρῶς καὶ κακῶς ἀνηλωκέναι, τὰ δ᾽ ἀλλότρι᾽
ὥστε λαβεῖν, δακρύειν νυνὶ καὶ κλάειν. ἐπ᾽ ἐκείνοις
[993] ἐκλάετ᾽ ἄν, οἷς ἐποιεῖτε, δικαίως. νῦν δ᾽ οὐ δεῖ
δακρύειν, ἀλλ᾽ ὡς οὐκ ἀφήκατε δεικνύναι, ἢ ὡς
εἰσὶν ὧν ἀφήκατ᾽ αὖθις ὑμῖν δίκαι, ἢ ὡς εἰκοστῷ
λαγχάνειν ἔτει δίκαιόν ἐστι, τοῦ νόμου πέντ᾽ ἔτη
τὴν προθεσμίαν δεδωκότος· ταῦτα γάρ ἐσθ᾽ ὑπὲρ ὧν
28 οὗτοι δικάζουσιν. ἐὰν δὲ μὴ δύνωνται ταῦθ᾽, ὡς
οὐ δυνήσονται, ἡμεῖς ὑμῶν ἁπάντων, ὦ ἄνδρες
δικασταί, δεόμεθα μὴ ἡμᾶς προέσθαι τούτοις, μηδὲ
τετάρτην οὐσίαν ἔτι δοῦναι τρεῖς ἑτέρας κακῶς
διῳκηκόσιν, ἣν παρ᾽ ἑκόντων ἔλαβον τῶν ἐπιτρόπων, ἣν ὑπὲρ τῶν δικῶν εἰσεπράξαντο, ἣν
πρῴην ἀφείλοντ᾽ Αἰσίου δίκην ἑλόντες, ἀλλ᾽ ἡμᾶς
τὰ ἡμέτερ᾽, ὥσπερ ἐστὶ δίκαιον, ἐὰν ἔχειν· ἃ καὶ
ὑμῖν ἐστιν ἐπ᾽ ὠφελείᾳ μείζονι παρ᾽ ἡμῖν ὄντ᾽ ἢ

438

of their lives in other matters preserve their property, rightly have the better of the others in this respect, that they both have been and will be of service, and also because this service accrues to you from them without reproach. We shall be found to be men of this type in our relations to you; as for them, I shall pass them by, that they may not charge that I am speaking evil of them.

I should not be surprised if they try to shed tears 27 and make themselves seem worthy of pity. But I deem that, in view of this, you should all remember that it is the part of shameless men, or rather of men with no sense of right, after having squandered their fortune in gluttony and wine-bibbing along with Aristocrates and Diognetus and others of that stamp in shameful and evil fashion, to weep and wail now in the hope of getting what belongs to others. You would have good cause to weep over your former doings. Yet it is not now a time to weep, but to prove that you did not give a release, or that action may be had afresh for the matters released, or that it is legal to bring an action after the lapse of twenty years, when the law has fixed five years as the limit. These are the questions which these gentlemen are to decide. If they are unable to prove these things, as they 28 will be unable, we beg of you all, men of the jury, not to deliver us up as prey to these men, nor to give yet a fourth fortune to those who have mismanaged three others—that which they received from their guardians without compulsion, that which they exacted by compromising their suits, and that which the other day they took from Aesius by a judgement—but to allow us, as is right, to retain what is our own. It is of greater service to you in our hands than in theirs.

παρὰ τούτοις, καὶ δικαιότερον δήπου τὰ ἡμέτερα
ἡμᾶς ἐστιν ἔχειν ἢ τούτους.

Οὐκ οἶδ᾽ ὅ τι δεῖ πλείω λέγειν· οἶμαι γὰρ ὑμᾶς
οὐδὲν ἀγνοεῖν τῶν εἰρημένων. ἐξέρα τὸ ὕδωρ.

---

^a The speaker closes with a brief paragraph which occurs
also at the end of Oration XXXVI.

And surely it is more just that we should have what is our own than that they should have it.

I do not know what reason there is why I should say more [a]; for I believe that nothing that I have said has escaped you. Pour out the water.

AGAINST BOEOTUS

I

INTRODUCTION

In approaching this oration the reader should bear in mind the fact that in ancient Athens a man had no other name than his given name. This, in connexion with the name of his father and that of his deme, was a clear and definite designation ; but if two individuals, having the same father and the same deme, had also the same given name, infinite confusion was bound to result, as this speech makes abundantly clear.

In the present instance a certain Mantitheus, son of Mantias, of Thoricus, brings suit against his half-brother, Boeotus, to prevent him from calling himself Mantitheus.

Mantias, an Athenian citizen, had legally married a daughter of Polyaratus, and had by her a son to whom he gave the name Mantitheus. This son was formally recognized by the father at the festival held on the tenth day after his birth ; was duly entered in the lists of the clan ; and upon reaching the age of eighteen was regularly inscribed by Mantias on the register of the deme under the name of Mantitheus (see § 29 of this speech). Further, while the father was still living, and at his wish, Mantitheus had in due and legal form married an Athenian girl (Oration XL § 12). The speaker's right to the name Mantitheus would therefore seem to be clear and indisputable.

Mantias, however, had at some time (precisely when, is not made wholly clear) formed a connexion with another woman of Athenian birth, named Plangon. To her two sons were born, and, as they grew up, they claimed that Mantias was their father. Mantias himself is represented in this and in the following speech as being unconvinced of the fact, and as unwilling to recognize the youths as his sons. At the last, when a suit was threatened to compel him to recognize them, he took the following course. For political reasons he did not wish the suit to come to trial, so he made an arrangement with Plangon whereby he was to place in the hands of a third party a sum of money for her, and then challenge her to declare under oath that he was the father of her sons. She, on her part, agreed that she would refuse the oath, and after that all matters between them would be at an end. These steps were duly taken, but Plangon, in violation of the agreement, accepted the oath and swore that Mantias was the father of both her sons. After this, no other course being open to him, Mantias acknowledged the boys as his, and had them entered on the lists of the clan, giving the elder the name Boeotus and the younger the name Pamphilus. The plaintiff in this suit declared that he had himself already been entered under the name of Mantitheus, a name borne by his paternal grandfather, whose name was regularly given to the eldest son in a family.

Mantias died before the sons of Plangon were entered on the register of the deme, and Boeotus proceeded to have himself entered under the name of Mantitheus, claiming, it would seem, to be older than his half-brother, and so entitled to bear the

grandfather's name. He also alleged that Mantia
had given him the name Boeotus as an insult (for th
Boeotians were looked down upon by the Athenians
although it was in fact the name of his maternal uncle

Against this alleged usurpation of the name whic
was properly his own the plaintiff protests vigorousl
emphasizing the confusion which had resulted, an
which was bound to result, if he and his half-broth
were to have identical names. He had, after h
father's death, acknowledged the two sons of Plango
as co-heirs with himself of his father's estate, and ha
divided the property with them ; but he brings su
to have Boeotus estopped from calling himse
Mantitheus.

If we accept the statements of the speaker at the
face value (always a rash procedure in the case of on
pleading in an Athenian court), Mantitheus woul
appear to have a clear case. Yet it is all but certai
that judgement was given against him. In Oratio
XL. § 18 (a speech again delivered by this sam
Mantitheus against the same defendant in a suit t
recover his mother's marriage-portion) we are tol
that, when the arbitrator had given a decision agains
him, Boeotus allowed the matter to go by defaul
claiming that the case did not concern him, as hi
name was Mantitheus, not Boeotus, a course whic
he would hardly have dared to take, if the court i
the present suit had decided that he had no right t
the name. Again, in the same passage, the plainti
declares that, under the circumstances, he was force
to bring suit against the defendant under the nam
of Mantitheus. Proof that is virtually conclusive i
also afforded by the fact that in an inscription whic
dates from the year after Mantias' death, the tw

446

Mantitheuses are mentioned together with Pamphilus, as heirs of Mantias (see Schaefer, iii.² p. 220) ; and Dionysius of Halicarnassus, in his treatment of the orator Deinarchus, cites the second of the two orations as Πρὸς Μαντίθεον περὶ προικός, whereas he cites the former as Πρὸς Βοιωτὸν ὑπὲρ τοῦ ὀνόματος.

Various views have been held : that Plangon was the legal wife of Mantias (a very dubious conclusion, although it receives some support from the claim made in Oration XL. that she brought Mantias a dowry) ; or that Mantias married her after the adoption of her sons (but this seems disproved by the language of Oration XL. § 9) ; and finally, and most probably, that Boeotus was really the elder of the two. In that case, as he had been entered on the register of the deme (however irregularly) under the name of Mantitheus, the court may have held that he was entitled to bear it.

This speech is discussed in Schaefer, iii.² pp. 214 ff., and in Blass, iii. pp. 473 ff., who dates it c. 348. See also Kirchner, *Prosopographia Attika*, under " Mantitheus 9675." The inscription mentioned on p. 446 is *I.G.* ii². 1622, lines 435-443.

XXXIX

ΠΡΟΣ ΒΟΙΩΤΟΝ ΠΕΡΙ ΤΟΥ ΟΝΟΜΑΤΟΣ

A

Οὐδεμιᾷ φιλοπραγμοσύνῃ μὰ τοὺς θεούς, ὦ ἄνδρες δικασταί, τὴν δίκην ταύτην ἔλαχον Βοιωτῷ,
[995] οὐδ' ἠγνόουν ὅτι πολλοῖς ἄτοπον δόξει τὸ δίκην ἐμὲ
λαγχάνειν, εἴ τις ἐμοὶ ταῦτ' ὄνομ' οἴεται δεῖν ἔχειν·
ἀλλ' ἀναγκαῖον ἦν ἐκ τῶν συμβησομένων, εἰ μὴ
2 τοῦτο διορθώσομαι, ἐν ὑμῖν κριθῆναι. εἰ μὲν οὖν
ἑτέρου τινὸς οὗτος ἔφη πατρὸς εἶναι καὶ μὴ τοὐμοῦ,
περίεργος ἂν εἰκότως ἐδόκουν εἶναι φροντίζων ὅ τι
βούλεται καλεῖν αὐτὸς ἑαυτόν. νῦν δὲ λαχὼν δίκην
τῷ πατρὶ τὠμῷ καὶ μεθ' ἑαυτοῦ κατασκευάσας
ἐργαστήριον συκοφαντῶν, Μνησικλέα θ', ὃν ἴσως
γιγνώσκετε πάντες, καὶ Μενεκλέα τὸν τὴν Νίνον
ἑλόντ' ἐκεῖνον, καὶ τοιούτους τινάς, ἐδικάζεθ' υἱὸς
εἶναι φάσκων ἐκ τῆς Παμφίλου θυγατρὸς καὶ δεινὰ
3 πάσχειν καὶ τῆς πατρίδος ἀποστερεῖσθαι. ὁ πατὴρ
δὲ (πᾶσα γὰρ εἰρήσεται ἡ ἀλήθει', ὦ ἄνδρες δικασταί) ἅμα μὲν φοβούμενος εἰς δικαστήριον εἰσιέναι,

---

[*] This strong phrase occurs also in Oration XL. § 9.
[b] Ninus was a priestess who was put to death, as the
scholiast on Demosthenes XIX. § 281 tells us, for supplying
love-potions to young men. The case seems to have been
a notorious one, and reflected little credit on Menecles.

448

MANTITHEUS AGAINST BOEOTUS IN REGARD TO THE NAME

I

It was not from any love of litigation, I protest by the gods, men of the jury, that I brought this suit against Boeotus, nor was I unaware that it will seem strange to many people that I should bring suit because somebody thought right to have the same name as myself; but it was necessary to have the matter decided in your court, in view of the consequences that must result if I do not get this matter righted. If the defendant declared himself the son of another 2 father and not of my own, I should naturally have seemed meddlesome in caring by what name he chose to call himself; but, as it is, he brought suit against my father, and having got up a gang of blackmailers *a* to support him—Mnesicles, whom you all probably know, and that Menecles who secured the conviction of Ninus,*b* and others of the same sort—he went into court, alleging that he was my father's son by the daughter of Pamphilus, and that he was being outrageously treated, and robbed of his civic rights. My 3 father (for the whole truth shall be told you, men of the jury) feared to come into court lest someone, on

μή τις οἵ ὑπὸ πολιτευομένου ἑτέρωθί που λε-
λυπημένος ἐνταῦθ᾽ ἀπαντήσειεν αὐτῷ, ἅμα δ᾽
ἐξαπατηθεὶς ὑπὸ τῆς τουτουὶ μητρός, ὀμοσάσης
αὐτῆς ἦ μήν, ἐὰν ὅρκον αὐτῇ διδῷ περὶ τούτων, μὴ
ὀμεῖσθαι, τούτων δὲ πραχθέντων οὐδὲν ἔσεσθαι ἔτ᾽
αὐτοῖς, καὶ μεσεγγυησαμένης ἀργύριον, ἐπὶ τούτοις
4 δίδωσι τὸν ὅρκον. ἡ δὲ δεξαμένη, οὐ μόνον τοῦτον,
ἀλλὰ καὶ τὸν ἀδελφὸν τὸν ἕτερον πρὸς τούτῳ
κατωμόσατ᾽ ἐκ τοῦ πατρὸς εἶναι τοὐμοῦ. ὡς δὲ
τοῦτ᾽ ἐποίησεν, εἰσάγειν εἰς τοὺς φράτερας ἦν
ἀνάγκη τούτους καὶ λόγος οὐδεὶς ὑπελείπετο.
εἰσήγαγ᾽, ἐποιήσατο, ἵνα τἀμ μέσῳ συντέμω,
ἐγγράφει τοῖς Ἀπατουρίοις τουτονὶ μὲν Βοιωτὸν
5 εἰς τοὺς φράτερας, τὸν δ᾽ ἕτερον Πάμφιλον, Μαντί-
[996] θεος δ᾽ ἐνεγεγράμμην ἐγώ. συμβάσης δὲ τῷ πατρὶ
τῆς τελευτῆς πρὶν τὰς εἰς τοὺς δημότας ἐγγραφὰς
γενέσθαι, ἐλθὼν εἰς τοὺς δημότας οὗτος ἀντὶ
Βοιωτοῦ Μαντίθεον ἐνέγραψεν ἑαυτόν. τοῦτο δ᾽
ὅσα βλάπτει ποιῶν πρῶτον μὲν ἐμέ, εἶτα καὶ
ὑμᾶς, ἐγὼ διδάξω, ἐπειδὰν ὧν λέγω παράσχωμαι
μάρτυρας.

ΜΑΡΤΥΡΕΣ

6 Ὃν μὲν τοίνυν τρόπον ἡμᾶς ἐνέγραψ᾽ ὁ πατήρ,
ἀκούετε τῶν μαρτυριῶν· ὅτι δ᾽ οὐκ οἰομένου τούτου

---

[a] This money was evidently to be paid to her for fulfilling
her promise to refuse the oath.
[b] Admission to the clan was necessary, if full family rights
were to be secured.
[c] The Apaturia was a family festival occurring in the
month Pyanepsion (October-November), and was the time

the ground of having elsewhere received some injury from him in his public life, should confront him here ; and at the same time he was deceived by this man's mother. For she had sworn that if he should tender her an oath in this matter, she would refuse it, and that, when this had been done, all relations between them would be at an end ; and she had also had money deposited in the hands of a third party on her behalf [a] ;—on these conditions, then, my father tendered her the oath. But she accepted it, 4 and swore that not only the defendant, but his brother too, her other son, was my father's child. When she had done this it was necessary to enter them among the clansmen,[b] and there was no excuse left. My father did enter them ; he adopted them as his children ; and (to cut short the intervening matters) he enrolled the defendant at the Apaturia [c] as Boeotus on the list of the clansmen, and the other as Pamphilus. But I had already been enrolled as Mantitheus. My father's 5 death happened before the entries were made on the register of the demesmen,[d] but the defendant went and enrolled himself on the register as Mantitheus, instead of Boeotus. How great a wrong he did in this—to me, in the first place, but also to you—I shall show, as soon as I have brought forward witnesses to prove my assertions.

The Witnesses

You have heard from the witnesses the manner in 6 which our father enrolled us ; I shall now show to

when children were regularly registered in the lists of clan-members.

[d] Enrolment on the register of the deme marked the beginning of a young man's political life. It took place when he reached the age of eighteen.

δεῖν ἐμμένειν, δικαίως καὶ ἀναγκαίως ἔλαχον τὴν
δίκην, τοῦτ' ἤδη δείξω. ἐγὼ γὰρ οὐχ οὕτω δήπου
σκαιός εἰμ' ἄνθρωπος οὐδ' ἀλόγιστος, ὥστε τῶν
μὲν πατρῴων, ἃ πάντ' ἐμὰ ἐγίγνετο, ἐπειδήπερ
ἐποιήσατο τούτους ὁ πατήρ, συγκεχωρηκέναι τὸ
τρίτον νείμασθαι μέρος καὶ στέργειν ἐπὶ τούτῳ,
περὶ δ' ὀνόματος ζυγομαχεῖν, εἰ μὴ τὸ μὲν ἡμᾶς
μεταθέσθαι μεγάλην ἀτιμίαν ἔφερεν καὶ ἀνανδρίαν,
τὸ δὲ τοῦτον ἔχειν ταῦτ' ὄνομ' ἡμῖν διὰ πόλλ'
ἀδύνατον ἦν.

7 Πρῶτον μὲν γάρ, εἰ δεῖ τὰ κοινὰ τῶν ἰδίων εἰπεῖν
πρότερον, τίν' ἡ πόλις ἡμῖν ἐπιτάξει τρόπον, ἄν τι
δέῃ ποιεῖν; οἴσουσι νὴ Δί' οἱ φυλέται τὸν αὐτὸν
τρόπον ὅνπερ καὶ τοὺς ἄλλους. οὐκοῦν Μαντίθεον
Μαντίου Θορίκιον οἴσουσιν, ἐὰν χορηγὸν ἢ γυμνα-
σίαρχον ἢ ἑστιάτορ' ἢ ἄν τι τῶν ἄλλων φέρωσιν.
τῷ δῆλον οὖν ἔσται πότερον σὲ φέρουσιν ἢ 'μέ;
8 σὺ μὲν γὰρ φήσεις ἐμέ, ἐγὼ δὲ σέ. καὶ δὴ καλεῖ
μετὰ τοῦθ' ὁ ἄρχων ἢ πρὸς ὅντιν' ἂν ᾖ. οὐχ ὑπ-
ακούομεν, οὐ λῃτουργοῦμεν. πότερος ταῖς ἐκ τῶν
[997] νόμων ἔσται ζημίαις ἔνοχος; τίνα δ' οἱ στρατηγοὶ

---

[a] Literally, "to strive with one under the same yoke."
Such metaphors were very common in Greek antiquity,
when horses as well as oxen were driven under the yoke.

[b] The appointment of citizens to undertake the various
"liturgies" (such as, e.g., the trierarchy) was made from tax-
groups chosen by the several tribes.

[c] Thoricus was a deme of the tribe Acamantis.

[d] The choregus had for his duties the equipment and
training of a chorus for the dramatic contests at one of the
great festivals. For this purpose the tribe chose one of its
richest members.

[e] The gymnasiarch was appointed by the tribe to maintain
a team to represent it in the torch-races, which formed a
feature of certain Athenian festivals.

you that, as the defendant did not choose to abide
by this enrolment, it was both just and necessary for
me to bring suit. For I am surely not so stupid nor
unreasonable a person as to have agreed to take only
a third of my father's estate (though the whole of
it was coming to me), seeing that my father had
adopted these men, and to be content with that, and
then to engage in a quarrel with my kin *a* about a
name, were it not that for me to change mine would
bring great dishonour and a reputation for cowardice,
while for my opponent to have the same name as
myself was on many accounts impossible.

To begin with (assuming that it is best to mention **7**
public matters before private), in what way will the
state give its command to us, if any duty is to be
performed ? The members of the tribe will, of course,*b*
nominate us in the same way as they nominate other
people. Well then ; they will bring forward the
name of Mantitheus, son of Mantias, of Thoricus,*c*
if they are nominating one for choregus *d* or gymnasiarch *e* or feaster of the tribe *f* or for any other
office. By what, then, will it be made clear whether
they are nominating you or me ? You will say it is I ;
I shall say it is you.*g* Well, suppose that after this **8**
the Archon summons us, or any other magistrate,
before whom the case is called. We do not obey the
summons ; we do not undertake the service. Which
of us is liable to the penalties provided by law ? And
in what manner will the generals enter our names,

f This third form of public service entailed the duty of
giving the annual dinner (in the Prytaneum (?)) to the
members of the tribe.

g That is, each of them would seek to shift the burden of
the required service, so that the other would have to bear it.

τρόπον ἐγγράψουσιν, ἂν εἰς συμμορίαν ἐγγράφωσιν,
ἢ ἂν τριήραρχον καθιστῶσιν; ἢ ἂν στρατεία τις
ᾖ, τῷ δῆλον ἔσται πότερός ἐσθ' ὁ κατειλεγμένος;
9 τί δ', ἂν ἄλλη τις ἀρχὴ καθιστῇ λῃτουργεῖν, οἷον
ἄρχων, βασιλεύς, ἀθλοθέται, τί σημεῖον ἔσται πότερον καθιστᾶσιν; προσπαραγράψουσι νὴ Δία τὸν
ἐκ Πλαγγόνος, ἂν σὲ γράφωσιν, ἂν δ' ἐμέ, τῆς ἐμῆς
μητρὸς τοὔνομα. καὶ τίς ἤκουσε πώποτε, ἢ κατὰ
ποῖον νόμον προσπαραγράφοιτ' ἂν τοῦτο τὸ γράμμα
ἢ ἄλλο τι πλὴν ὁ πατὴρ καὶ ὁ δῆμος; ὧν ὄντων
10 ἀμφοῖν τῶν αὐτῶν πολλὴ ταραχὴ συμβαίνει. φέρ',
εἰ δὲ κριτὴς καλοῖτο Μαντίθεος Μαντίου Θορίκιος,
τί ἂν ποιοῖμεν; ἢ βαδίζοιμεν ἂν ἄμφω; τῷ γὰρ
ἔσται δῆλον πότερον σὲ κέκληκεν ἢ 'μέ; πρὸς
Διός, ἂν δ' ἀρχὴν ἡντινοῦν ἡ πόλις κληροῖ, οἷον
βουλῆς, θεσμοθέτου, τῶν ἄλλων, τῷ δῆλος ἡμῶν ὁ
λαχὼν ἔσται; πλὴν εἰ σημεῖον, ὥσπερ ἂν ἄλλῳ
τινί, τῷ χαλκίῳ προσέσται· καὶ οὐδὲ τοῦθ' ὁπο-
τέρου ἐστὶν οἱ πολλοὶ γνώσονται. οὐκοῦν ὁ μὲν
αὑτόν, ἐγὼ δ' ἐμαυτὸν φήσω τὸν εἰληχότ' εἶναι.
11 λοιπὸν εἰς τὸ δικαστήριον ἡμᾶς εἰσιέναι. οὐκοῦν
ἐφ' ἑκάστῳ τούτων δικαστήριον ἡμῖν ἡ πόλις
καθιεῖ, καὶ τοῦ μὲν κοινοῦ καὶ ἴσου, τοῦ τὸν λαχόντ'
ἄρχειν, ἀποστερησόμεθα, ἀλλήλους δὲ πλυνοῦμεν,

---

[a] The word κριτής does not signify a judge in a court of
law, but apparently a judge in some festival contest.
[b] In Athens the members of the senate (βουλή) of five
hundred—fifty from each of the ten tribes—were chosen by
lot.
[c] The six minor archons bore this name; see note a on p. 202.
[d] Every candidate had an identification tablet inscribed
with his full name (that is, his given name, the name of his

if they are listing names for a tax-company? or if they are appointing a trierarch? Or, if there be a military expedition, how will it be made clear which of us is on the muster-roll? Or again, if any other 9 magistrate, the Archon, the King-Archon, the Stewards of the Games, makes an appointment for some public service, what sign will there be to indicate which one of us they are appointing? Are they in heaven's name to add the designation "son of Plangon," if they are entering your name, or add the name of my mother if they are entering mine? But who ever heard of such a thing? or by what law could this special designation be appended, or anything else, except the name of the father and the deme? And seeing that both of these are the same great confusion must result. Again, suppose Mantitheus, son 10 of Mantias, of Thoricus should be summoned as judge,[a] what should we do? Should we go, both of us? For how is it to be clear whether he has summoned you or me? Or, by Zeus, suppose the state is appointing to any office by lot, for example that of Senator,[b] that of Thesmothet,[c] or any of the rest; how will it be clear which one of us has been appointed?—unless some mark shall be attached to the tablet,[d] as there might be to anything else; and even then people will not know to which of us two it belongs. Well then, he will say that he has been appointed, and I shall say that I have. The only 11 course left is for us to go into court. So the city will order a court to be set up for each of the cases; and we shall be cheated of the fair and equal right, that the one chosen by lot shall hold office. Then we shall

father, and the name of his deme), and this was placed in the urn for drawing.

καὶ ὁ τῷ λόγῳ κρατήσας ἄρξει. καὶ πότερ᾽ ἂν
βελτίους εἴημεν τῶν ὑπαρχουσῶν δυσκολιῶν ἀπαλ-
λαττόμενοι, ἢ καινὰς ἔχθρας καὶ βλασφημίας ποιού-
μενοι; ἃς πᾶσ᾽ ἀνάγκη συμβαίνειν, ὅταν ἀρχῆς ἢ
12 τινος ἄλλου πρὸς ἡμᾶς αὐτοὺς ἀμφισβητῶμεν. τί
[998] δ᾽, ἂν ἄρα (δεῖ γὰρ ἅπαντα ἡμᾶς ἐξετάσαι) ἅτερος
ἡμῶν πείσας τὸν ἕτερον, ἂν λάχῃ, παραδοῦναι αὐτῷ
τὴν ἀρχήν, οὕτω κληρῶται, τὸ δυοῖν πινακίοιν τὸν
ἕνα κληροῦσθαι τί ἄλλ᾽ ἐστίν; εἶτ᾽ ἐφ᾽ ᾧ θάνατον
ζημίαν ὁ νόμος λέγει, τοῦθ᾽ ἡμῖν ἀδεῶς ἐξέσται
πράττειν; πάνυ γε· οὐ γὰρ ἂν αὐτὸ ποιήσαιμεν.
οἶδα κἀγώ, τὸ γοῦν κατ᾽ ἐμέ· ἀλλ᾽ οὐδ᾽ αἰτίαν
τοιαύτης ζημίας ἐνίους ἔχειν καλόν, ἐξὸν μή.

13 Εἶεν. ἀλλὰ ταῦτα μὲν ἡ πόλις βλάπτεται· ἐγὼ δ᾽
ἰδίᾳ τί; θεάσασθ᾽ ἡλίκα, καὶ σκοπεῖτ᾽ ἄν τι δοκῶ
λέγειν· πολὺ γὰρ χαλεπώτερα ταῦθ᾽ ὧν ἀκηκόατ᾽
ἐστίν. ὁρᾶτε μὲν γὰρ ἅπαντες αὐτὸν χρώμενον,
ἕως μὲν ἔζη, Μενεκλεῖ καὶ τοῖς περὶ κεῖνον ἀνθρώποις, νῦν δ᾽ ἑτέροις ἐκείνου βελτίοσιν οὐδέν, καὶ
τὰ τοιαῦτ᾽ ἐζηλωκότα καὶ δεινὸν δοκεῖν εἶναι
14 βουλόμενον· καὶ νὴ Δί᾽ ἴσως ἔστιν. ἂν οὖν προϊόντος τοῦ χρόνου τῶν αὐτῶν τι ποιεῖν τούτοις
ἐπιχειρῇ (ἔστι δὲ ταῦτα γραφαί, φάσεις, ἐνδείξεις,
ἀπαγωγαί), εἶτ᾽ ἐπὶ τούτων τινὶ (πολλὰ γὰρ τἀν-

ᵃ Possibly, " an eloquent speaker."

berate each other, and he who shall prevail by his words will hold office. And in which case should we be better off—by trying to rid ourselves of our existing resentments, or by arousing fresh animosities and recriminations? For these must of necessity result, when we wrangle with one another about an office or anything else. But suppose again (for we must 12 examine every phase of the matter), one or the other of us persuades the other, in case he is chosen, to yield the office to him, and so obtains the appointment? What is this but one man drawing lots with two tablets? Shall it, then, be permitted us to do with impunity a thing for which the law appoints the penalty of death? "Why, certainly, for we should not do it," you may say. I know that, at least so far as I am concerned; but it is not right that some persons should even be liable to this penalty, when they need not be.

Very well; but in these cases it is the state that is 13 injured: what harm does it do me individually? Observe in what serious ways I am harmed, and consider if there be anything in what I say. Indeed the wrong done to me is far more grievous than what you have heard. You all know, for instance, that he was intimate with Menecles during his lifetime, and with his crowd, and that he now associates with others no better than Menecles, and that he has cherished the same ambitions, and desires to be thought a clever fellow [a]; and, by Zeus, I dare say he is. Now, if, as time goes on, he undertakes to 14 set on foot any of the same practices as these men (these are indictments, presentments for contraband, informations, arrests) and on the basis of one of these he is condemned to pay a fine to the state (for there

θρώπινα, καὶ τοὺς πάνυ δεινοὺς ἑκάστοθ᾽, ὅταν
πλεονάζωσ᾽, ἐπίστασθ᾽ ὑμεῖς κοσμίους ποιεῖν) ὄφλῃ
τῷ δημοσίῳ, τί μᾶλλον οὗτος ἐγγεγραμμένος ἔσται
ἐμοῦ· ὅτι νὴ Δί᾽ εἴσονται πάντες πότερός ποτ᾽
15 ὦφλεν. καλῶς. ἂν δ᾽, ὃ τυχὸν γένοιτ᾽ ἄν, χρόνος
διέλθῃ καὶ μὴ ἐκτεισθῇ τὸ ὄφλημα, τί μᾶλλον οἱ
τούτου παῖδες ἔσονται τῶν ἐμῶν ἐγγεγραμμένοι,
ὅταν τοὔνομα χὠ πατὴρ καὶ ἡ φυλὴ καὶ πάντ᾽ ᾖ
ταὐτά; τί δ᾽, εἴ τις δίκην ἐξούλης αὐτῷ λαχών,
[999] μηδὲν ἐμοὶ φαίη πρὸς αὑτὸν εἶναι, κυρίαν δὲ ποιη-
σάμενος ἐγγράψαι, τί μᾶλλον ἂν εἴη τοῦτον ἢ ἔμ᾽
16 ἐγγεγραφώς· τί δ᾽, εἴ τινας εἰσφορὰς μὴ θείη; τί
δ᾽, εἴ τις ἄλλη περὶ τοὔνομα γίγνοιτ᾽ ἢ λῆξις δίκης
ἢ δόξ᾽ ὅλως ἀηδής; τίς εἴσεται τῶν πολλῶν
πότερός ποθ᾽ οὗτός ἐστι, δυοῖν Μαντιθέοιν ταὐτοῦ
πατρὸς ὄντοιν; φέρ᾽, εἰ δὲ δίκην ἀστρατείας
φεύγοι, χορεύοι δ᾽ ὅταν στρατεύεσθαι δέῃ; καὶ γὰρ
νῦν, ὅτ᾽ εἰς Ταμύνας παρῆλθον οἱ ἄλλοι, ἐνθάδε
τοὺς χοᾶς ἄγων ἀπελείφθη καὶ τοῖς Διονυσίοις
καταμείνας ἐχόρευεν, ὡς ἅπαντες ἑωρᾶθ᾽ οἱ ἐπι-
17 δημοῦντες. ἀπελθόντων δ᾽ ἐξ Εὐβοίας τῶν στρα-
τιωτῶν, λιποταξίου προσεκλήθη, κἀγὼ ταξιαρχῶν
τῆς φυλῆς, ἠναγκαζόμην κατὰ τοὐνόματος τοῦ
ἐμαυτοῦ πατρόθεν δέχεσθαι τὴν λῆξιν· καὶ εἰ

---

^a A town in Euboea.
^b This name was given to the second day of the festival
Anthesteria, held in February-March.
^c Service in the chorus at the Dionysiac festival would
entitle the individual to exemption from military service for
the time being—an easy way out for the " slacker."
^d The taxiarchs were military officers, each in command
of his tribe's contingent of hoplites.

are many vicissitudes in mortal affairs, and you know well how to keep in due bounds even the most clever people on any occasion when they overreach themselves), why will his name be entered on the record any more than mine? "Because," it may be said, "everybody will know which of us two was fined." Very good; but suppose (what might very well 15 happen) that time passes and the debt is not paid; why is there any greater likelihood that the defendant's children will be entered on the list of state debtors any more than my own, when the name of the father and the tribe, and all else are identical? Suppose, now, somebody should bring a suit for ejectment against him, and should state that he had nothing to do with me, but, having had the writ registered, should enter the name, why will the name he has entered be that of my opponent any more than my own? What if he fails to pay any of the property- 16 taxes? What if the name be involved in the filing of any other suit, or, in general, in any unpleasant scandal? Who, among people at large, will know which of the two it is, when there are two Mantitheuses having the same father? Suppose, again, that he should be prosecuted for evasion of military service, and should be serving as chorister when he ought to be abroad with the army—as, a while ago, when the rest went over to Tamynae,[a] he was left behind here keeping the feast of Pitchers,[b] and remained here and served in the chorus at the Dionysia,[c] as all of you who were at home saw; then, after the 17 soldiers had come back from Euboea, he was summoned on a charge of desertion, and I, as taxiarch of our tribe,[d] was compelled to receive the summons, since it was against my name, that of my father being

μισθὸς ἐπορίσθη τοῖς δικαστηρίοις, εἰσῆγον ἂν
δῆλον ὅτι. ταῦτα δ' εἰ μὴ σεσημασμένων ἤδη
συνέβη τῶν ἐχίνων, κἂν μάρτυρας ὑμῖν παρεσχόμην.

18 εἶεν. εἰ δὲ ξενίας προσκληθείη; πολλοῖς δὲ
προσκρούει, καὶ ὃν ἠναγκάσθη τρόπον ποιήσασθαι
ὁ πατὴρ αὐτόν, οὐ λέληθεν. ὑμεῖς δ', ὅτε μὲν
τοῦτον οὐκ ἐποιεῖθ' ὁ πατήρ, τὴν μητέρ' ἀληθῆ
λέγειν ἡγεῖσθ' αὐτοῦ· ἐπειδὰν δ' οὕτω γεγονὼς
οὗτος ὀχληρὸς ᾖ, πάλιν ὑμῖν ποτε δόξει κεῖνος
ἀληθῆ λέγειν. τί δ', εἰ ψευδομαρτυριῶν ἁλώσεσθαι
προσδοκῶν ἐφ' οἷς ἐρανίζει τούτοις τοῖς περὶ αὑτόν,
ἐρήμην ἐάσειε τελεσθῆναι τὴν δίκην; ἆρά γε
μικρὰν ἡγεῖσθε βλάβην, ὦ ἄνδρες Ἀθηναῖοι, ἐν
κοινωνίᾳ τὸν ἅπαντα βίον τῆς τούτου δόξης καὶ
τῶν ἔργων εἶναι;

19 Ὅτι τοίνυν οὐδ' ἃ διεξελήλυθ' ὑμῖν μάτην φο-
[1000] βοῦμαι, θεωρήσατε. οὗτος γὰρ ἤδη καὶ γραφάς
τινας, ὦ ἄνδρες Ἀθηναῖοι, πέφευγεν, ἐφ' αἷς οὐδὲν
αἴτιος ὢν ἐγὼ συνδιαβάλλομαι, καὶ τῆς ἀρχῆς
ἠμφεσβήτει, ἣν ὑμεῖς ἔμ' ἐχειροτονήσατε, καὶ
πολλὰ καὶ δυσχερῆ διὰ τοὔνομα συμβέβηκεν ἡμῖν,
ὧν, ἵν' εἰδῆθ', ἑκάστων μάρτυρας ὑμῖν παρέξομαι.

ΜΑΡΤΥΡΕΣ

20 Ὁρᾶτ', ὦ ἄνδρες Ἀθηναῖοι, τὰ συμβαίνοντα, καὶ
τὴν ἀηδίαν τὴν ἐκ τοῦ πράγματος. εἰ τοίνυν μηδὲν

---

[a] Evidently shortage of funds might prevent the courts
from sitting; and the Euboean campaign had depleted
the treasury.

[b] The ἐχῖνοι were receptacles in which documents, etc.,
pertaining to the case were put under seal, to be opened only
when the case was called. See note a on Oration XXXIV.
p. 268.

added ; and if pay had been available for the juries,[a]
I should certainly have had to bring the case into
court. If this had not occurred after the boxes [b]
had already been sealed, I should have brought you
witnesses to prove it. Well then ; suppose he were 18
summoned on the charge of being an alien. And he
does make himself obnoxious to many, and the way
in which my father was compelled to adopt him is
no secret. You, on your part, while my father was
refusing to acknowledge him, believed that his mother
was telling the truth ; but when, with his parentage
thus established, he makes himself odious, you will
some day on the contrary conclude that my father's
story was true. Again, what if my opponent, in the
expectation of being convicted of perjury for the
services[c] which he freely grants his associates, should
allow the suit to go by default ? Do you think it
would be a slight injury that I should be my whole
life long a sharer of his reputation and his doings ?

Pray observe that my fear regarding the things I 19
have set forth to you is not a vain one. He has
already, men of Athens, been defendant in certain
suits, in which, although I have been wholly innocent,
odium has attached to my name as well as his ; and
he has laid claim to the office to which you had elected
me ; and many unpleasant things have happened to
me because of the name ; regarding each one of
which I will produce witnesses to inform you fully.

THE WITNESSES

You see, men of Athens, what keeps happening 20
and the annoyance resulting from the matter. But

[c] The " service " at which the speaker hints is presumably
the bearing of false testimony.

ἀηδὲς ἦν ἐκ τούτων, μηδ' ὅλως ἀδύνατον ταὐτὸν
ἔχειν ὄνομ' ἡμῖν συνέβαινεν, οὐ δήπου τοῦτον μὲν
δίκαιον τὸ μέρος τῶν ἐμῶν χρημάτων ἔχειν κατὰ
τὴν ποίησιν, ἣν ὁ πατὴρ αὐτὸν ἀναγκασθεὶς ἐποιήσατο, ἐμὲ δ' ἀφαιρεθῆναι τοὔνομα, ὃ βουλόμενος
καὶ οὐδ' ὑφ' ἑνὸς βιασθεὶς ἔθετο. οὐκ ἔγωγ'
ἡγοῦμαι.

Ἵνα τοίνυν εἰδῆτε, ὅτι οὐ μόνον εἰς τοὺς
φράτερας οὕτως, ὡς μεμαρτύρηται, ὁ πατὴρ τὴν
ἐγγραφὴν ἐποιήσατο, ἀλλὰ καὶ τὴν δεκάτην ἐμοὶ
ποιῶν τοὔνομα τοῦτ' ἔθετο, λαβέ μοι καὶ ταύτην
τὴν μαρτυρίαν.

21 Ἀκούετ', ἄνδρες Ἀθηναῖοι, ὅτι ἐγὼ μέν εἰμ' ἐπὶ
τοὐνόματος τούτου πάντα τὸν χρόνον, τοῦτον δὲ
Βοιωτὸν εἰς τοὺς φράτερας, ἡνίκ' ἠναγκάσθη,
ἐνέγραψ' ὁ πατήρ. ἡδέως τοίνυν ἐροίμην ἂν αὐτὸν
ἐναντίον ὑμῶν· εἰ μὴ ἐτελεύτησ' ὁ πατήρ, τί ἂν
ποτ' ἐποίεις πρὸς τοῖς δημόταις; οὐκ ἂν εἴας
σαυτὸν ἐγγράφειν Βοιωτόν; ἀλλ' ἄτοπον δίκην μὲν
λαγχάνειν τούτου, κωλύειν δὲ πάλιν. καὶ μὴν εἴ
γ' εἴας αὐτόν, ἐνέγραψεν ἄν σ' εἰς τοὺς δημότας,
[1001] ὅπερ εἰς τοὺς φράτερας. οὐκοῦν δεινόν, ὦ γῆ καὶ
θεοί, φάσκειν μὲν ἐκεῖνον ἑαυτοῦ πατέρ' εἶναι,
τολμᾶν δ' ἄκυρα ποιεῖν ἃ κεῖνος ἔπραξε ζῶν.

22 Ἐτόλμα τοίνυν πρὸς τῷ διαιτητῇ πρᾶγμ' ἀναιδέ-

---

a The child was formally named at a ceremony held on
the tenth day after birth, and attended by members of the
family and close friends.

even if there were no annoying results, and if it were not absolutely impossible for us both to have the same name, it surely is not fair for him to have his share of my property by virtue of the adoption which my father made under compulsion, and for me to be robbed of the name which that father gave me of his own free will and under constraint from no one. I, certainly, think it is not.

Now, to show you that my father not only made the entry in the list of the clansmen in the manner which has been testified to you, but that he gave me this name when he kept the tenth day after my birth,[a] please take this deposition.

THE DEPOSITION

You hear then, men of Athens, that I have always 21 been in possession of the name Mantitheus; but that my father, when he was compelled to enter him, entered the defendant in the list of clansmen as Boeotus. I should be glad, then, to ask him in your presence, " If my father had not died, what would you have done in the presence of your demesman? Would you not have allowed yourself to be registered as Boeotus?" But it would have been absurd to bring suit to force this and then afterwards to seek to prevent it. And yet, if you had allowed him, my father would have enrolled you in the register of demesmen by the same name as he did in that of the clansmen. Then, O Earth and the Gods, it is monstrous for him to claim that Mantias is his father, and yet to have the audacity to try to make of none effect what Mantias did in his lifetime.

He had the effrontery, moreover, to make before 22 the arbitrator the most audacious assertions, that

στατον λέγειν, ὡς ὁ πατὴρ αὐτοῦ δεκάτην ἐποίησεν
ὥσπερ ἐμοῦ καὶ τοὔνομα τοῦτ' ἔθετ' αὐτῷ, καὶ
μάρτυράς τινας παρείχετο, οἷς ἐκεῖνος οὐδεπώποτ'
ὤφθη χρώμενος. ἐγὼ δ' οὐδέν' ὑμῶν ἀγνοεῖν
οἴομαι, ὅτι οὔτ' ἂν ἐποίησεν δεκάτην οὐδεὶς παιδίου
μὴ νομίζων αὐτοῦ δικαίως εἶναι, οὔτε ποιήσας καὶ
στέρξας, ὡς ἂν υἱόν τις στέρξαι, πάλιν ἔξαρνος
23 ἐτόλμησε γενέσθαι. οὐδὲ γὰρ εἴ τι τῇ μητρὶ πρὸς
ὀργὴν ἦλθε τῇ τούτων, τούτους ἂν ἐμίσει, νομίζων
αὐτοῦ εἶναι· πολὺ γὰρ μᾶλλον εἰώθασιν, ὧν ἂν
ἑαυτοῖς διενεχθῶσιν ἀνὴρ καὶ γυνή, διὰ τοὺς παῖδας
καταλλάττεσθαι ἢ δι' ἂν ἀδικηθῶσιν ὑφ' αὑτῶν,
τοὺς κοινοὺς παῖδας πρὸς μισεῖν. οὐ τοίνυν ἐκ
τούτων ἔστ' ἰδεῖν μόνον, ὅτι ψεύσεται, ταῦτ' ἐὰν
λέγῃ, ἀλλὰ πρὶν ἡμέτερος φάσκειν συγγενὴς εἶναι,
εἰς Ἱπποθωντίδ' ἐφοίτα φυλὴν εἰς παῖδας χορεύσων.
24 καίτοι τίς ἂν ὑμῶν οἴεται τὴν μητέρα πέμψαι τοῦτον
εἰς ταύτην τὴν φυλήν, δεινὰ μέν, ὥς φησ', ὑπὸ τοῦ
πατρὸς πεπονθυῖαν, δεκάτην δ' εἰδυῖαν πεποιηκότ'
ἐκεῖνον καὶ πάλιν ἔξαρνον ὄντα; ἐγὼ μὲν οὐδέν'
ἂν οἶμαι. εἰς γὰρ τὴν Ἀκαμαντίδ' ὁμοίως ἐξῆν
σοι φοιτᾶν, καὶ ἐφαίνετ' ἂν οὖσ' ἀκόλουθος ἡ φυλὴ
τῇ θέσει τοὐνόματος.

Ὡς τοίνυν ταῦτ' ἀληθῆ λέγω, τούτων μάρτυρας
ὑμῖν τοὺς συμφοιτῶντας καὶ τοὺς εἰδότας παρέξομαι.

---

[a] This passage is repeated with slight changes in the
following oration § 29.

[b] That is, to the tribe to which his mother belonged, not
to that of Mantias, which was the Acamantis. The speaker
would have this indicate that the mother was conscious that
the boy was not the son of Mantias.

my father kept the tenth day after birth for him, just as for me, and gave him the name Mantitheus ; and he brought forward as witnesses persons with whom my father was never known to be intimate. But I think that not one of you is unaware that no man would have kept the tenth day for a child which he did not believe was rightly his own ; nor, if he had kept the day and shown the affection one would feel for a son, would afterward have dared to deny him. For even if he might have got into some quarrel 23 with the mother of these children, he would not have hated them, if he believed them to be his own. *For man and wife are much more apt, in cases where they are at variance with one another, to become reconciled for the sake of their children, than, on the ground of the injuries which they have done one to the other, to hate their common children also. However, it is not from these facts alone that you may see that he will be lying, if he makes these statements ; but, before he claimed to be a kinsman of ours, he used to go to the tribe Hippothontis to dance in the chorus of boys.* And yet, who among you imagines 24 that his mother would have sent him to this tribe, if, as she alleges, she had been cruelly treated by my father, and knew that he had kept the tenth day, and afterward denied it ? Not one, I am sure. For it would have been just as much your right to go to school to the tribe Acamantis, and then the tribe would have been in manifest agreement with the giving of the name.

To prove that I am speaking the truth in this, I shall bring before you as witnesses those who went to school with him, and know the facts.

DEMOSTHENES

MAPTYPEΣ

25 Οὕτω τοίνυν φανερῶς παρὰ τὸν τῆς αὑτοῦ μητρὸς
ὅρκον καὶ τὴν τοῦ δόντος ἐκείνη τὸν ὅρκον εὐήθειαν,
πατρὸς τετυχηκὼς καὶ ἀνθ᾽ Ἱπποθωντίδος ἐν
Ἀκαμαντίδι φυλῇ γεγονώς, οὐκ ἀγαπᾷ Βοιωτὸς
οὑτοσί, ἀλλὰ καὶ δίκας ἐμοὶ δύ᾽ ἢ τρεῖς εἴληχεν
ἀργυρίου πρὸς αἷς καὶ πρότερόν μ᾽ ἐσυκοφάντει.
καίτοι πάντας οἶμαι τοῦθ᾽ ὑμᾶς εἰδέναι, τίς ἦν
26 χρηματιστὴς ὁ πατήρ. ἐγὼ δ᾽ ἐάσω ταῦτα. ἀλλ᾽
εἰ δίκαι᾽ ὀμώμοκεν ἡ μήτηρ ἡ τούτων, ἐπ᾽ αὐτο-
φώρῳ συκοφάντην ἐπιδεικνύει τοῦτον ταῖς δίκαις
ταύταις. εἰ γὰρ οὕτω δαπανηρὸς ἦν, ὥστε γάμῳ
γεγαμηκὼς τὴν ἐμὴν μητέρα, ἑτέραν εἶχε γυναῖκα,
ἧς ὑμεῖς ἐστέ, καὶ δύ᾽ οἰκίας ᾤκει, πῶς ἂν ἀργύριον
τοιοῦτος ὢν κατέλιπεν;

27 Οὐκ ἀγνοῶ τοίνυν, ὦ ἄνδρες Ἀθηναῖοι, ὅτι
Βοιωτὸς οὑτοσὶ δίκαιον μὲν οὐδὲν ἕξει λέγειν, ἥξει
δ᾽ ἐπὶ ταῦθ᾽ ἅπερ ἀεὶ λέγει, ὡς ἐπηρέαζ᾽ ὁ πατὴρ
αὐτῷ πειθόμενος ὑπ᾽ ἐμοῦ, ἀξιοῖ δ᾽ αὐτὸς ὡς δὴ
πρεσβύτερος ὢν τοὔνομ᾽ ἔχειν τὸ τοῦ πρὸς πατρὸς
πάππου. πρὸς δὴ ταῦτ᾽ ἀκοῦσαι βέλτιον ὑμᾶς
βραχέα. ἐγὼ γὰρ οἶδα τοῦτον, ὅτ᾽ οὔπω συγγενὴς
ἦν ἐμοί, ὁρῶν ὥσπερ ἂν ἄλλον τιν᾽ οὑτωσί, νεώ-
τερον ὄντ᾽ ἐμοῦ καὶ συχνῷ, ὅσ᾽ ἐξ ὄψεως, οὐ μὴν
28 ἰσχυρίζομαι τούτῳ· καὶ γὰρ εὔηθες. ἀλλ᾽ εἴ τις

466

THE WITNESSES

Nevertheless, although it is so plain that by his 25 mother's oath and the simplicity of him who tendered the oath to her, he has obtained a father and established his birth in the tribe Acamantis, instead of Hippothontis, the defendant Boeotus is not content with this, but has actually entered two or three suits against me for money, in addition to the malicious and baseless actions which he brought against me before. And yet I think you all know what sort of a man of business my father was.[a] I will say nothing 26 about this ; but if the mother of these men has sworn truly, it absolutely proves that the fellow is acting as a malicious pettifogger in these suits. For if my father was so extravagant that, after having married my mother in lawful wedlock, he kept another woman, whose children you are, and maintained two establishments, how pray, if he were a man of this sort, could he have left any money ?

I am well aware, men of Athens, that the defendant, 27 Boeotus, will have no valid argument to advance, but will have recourse to the statements he is always making, that my father was induced by me to treat him with despite ; and he claims the right, alleging that he is older than I, to bear the name of his paternal grandfather. As to this, it is better for you to listen to a few statements. I remember seeing him, before he became a relative of mine, casually, as one might see anyone else, and thought him younger than I, and to judge by appearances, much younger ; but I will not insist upon this, for it would be silly to do so. However, suppose one should ask 28

[a] He was so poor a man of business that after his death his heirs had to pay off indebtedness incurred by him.

ἔροιτο Βοιωτὸν τουτονί, ὅτ' ἐν Ἱπποθωντίδι φυλῇ
χορεύειν ἠξίους, οὔπω τοῦ πατρὸς εἶναι φάσκων
υἱὸς τοῦ ἐμοῦ, τί σαυτὸν ἔχειν δικαίως ἂν θείης
ὄνομα; εἰ γὰρ Μαντίθεον, οὐκ ἂν διὰ τοῦτό γε
φαίης ὅτι πρεσβύτερος εἶ ἐμοῦ. ὃς γὰρ οὐδὲ τῆς
[1003] φυλῆς τότε σοι προσήκειν ἡγοῦ τῆς ἐμῆς, πῶς ἂν
29 τοῦ γε πάππου τοὐμοῦ ἠμφεσβήτεις; ἔτι δ', ὦ
ἄνδρες Ἀθηναῖοι, τὸν μὲν τῶν ἐτῶν χρόνον οὐδεὶς
οἶδεν ὑμῶν (ἐγὼ μὲν γὰρ ἐμοὶ πλείον', οὗτος δ'
ἑαυτῷ φήσει), τὸν δὲ τοῦ δικαίου λόγον πάντες
ἐπίστασθε. ἔστι δ' οὗτος τίς; ἀφ' οὗ παῖδας
ἐποιήσατο τούτους ὁ πατήρ, ἀπὸ τούτου καὶ νομίζεσθαι. πρότερον τοίνυν ἔμ' εἰς τοὺς δημότας ἐνέγραψε Μαντίθεον, πρὶν εἰσαγαγεῖν τοῦτον εἰς τοὺς
φράτερας. ὥστ' οὐ τῷ χρόνῳ μόνον, ἀλλὰ καὶ τῷ
δικαίῳ πρεσβεῖον ἔχοιμ' ἂν ἐγὼ τοὔνομα τοῦτ'
30 εἰκότως. εἶεν. εἰ δέ τίς σ' ἔροιτ' " εἰπέ μοι
Βοιωτέ, πόθεν νῦν Ἀκαμαντίδος φυλῆς γέγονας καὶ
τῶν δήμων Θορίκιος καὶ υἱὸς Μαντίου, καὶ τὸ
μέρος τῶν ὑπ' ἐκείνου καταλειφθέντων ἔχεις; "
οὐδὲν ἂν ἄλλ' ἔχοις εἰπεῖν, πλὴν ὅτι κἀμὲ ζῶν
ἐποιήσατο Μαντίας. τί τεκμήριον, εἴ τις ἔροιτ', ἢ
μαρτύριόν ἐστί σοι τούτου; εἰς τοὺς φράτεράς μ'
εἰσήγαγε, φήσειας ἄν. τί οὖν σ' ἐνέγραψ' ὄνομ', εἴ
τις ἔροιτο, Βοιωτὸν ἂν εἴποις· τοῦτο γὰρ εἰσήχθης.
31 οὐκοῦν δεινόν, εἰ τῆς μὲν πόλεως καὶ τῶν ὑπ'
ἐκείνου καταλειφθέντων διὰ τοὔνομα τοῦτο μέτεστι
468

this Boeotus the following questions : " When you thought it right to join the chorus in the tribe Hippothontis before you claimed to be the son of my father, what name would you have set down as rightly belonging to you ? For if you should say, Mantitheus, you could not do so on the plea that you are older than I; for since at that time you did not suppose you had any connexion even with my tribe, how could you claim to be related to my grandfather ? Besides, 29 men of Athens, not one of you knows the number of the years, for I shall say that I am the elder, and he will say that he is, but you all understand the just way of reckoning. And what is this ? That these men should be considered children of my father from the date when he adopted them. Well then, he entered me on the register of the demesmen as Mantitheus, before he introduced this man to the clansmen. Therefore not by virtue of time only, but also by virtue of justice I have the right to bear this name as a mark of seniority. Very well. Now, sup- 30 pose one should ask you this question ? " Tell me, Boeotus, how is it that you have now become a member of the tribe Acamantis, and of the deme Thoricus, and a son of Mantias, and have your share in the property left by him ? " You could give no other answer than, " Mantias while living acknowledged me, too, as his son." If one should ask you what proof you had of this or what evidence, you would say, " He introduced me to the clansmen." But if one asked under what name he enrolled you, you would say, " Boeotus," for that is the name by which you were introduced. It is, then, an outrage 31 that whereas thanks to that name you have a share in the right of citizenship and in the estate left by

σοι, τοῦτο δ' ἀξιοῖς ἀφεὶς ἕτερον μεταθέσθαι σαυτῷ.
φέρ', εἴ σ' ὁ πατὴρ ἀξιώσειεν ἀναστάς, ἢ μένειν
ἐφ' οὗ σ' αὐτὸς ἐποιήσατ' ὀνόματος, ἢ πατέρ'
ἄλλον σαυτοῦ φάσκειν εἶναι, ἆρ' οὐκ ἂν μέτρι'
ἀξιοῦν δοκοίη; ταὐτὰ τοίνυν ταῦτ' ἐγώ σ' ἀξιῶ,
ἢ πατρὸς ἄλλου σαυτὸν παραγράφειν, ἢ τοὔνομ'
32 ἔχειν ὃ 'κεῖνος ἔδωκέ σοι. νὴ Δί', ἀλλ' ὕβρει καὶ
[1004] ἐπηρείᾳ τινὶ τοῦτ' ἐτέθη σοι. ἀλλὰ πολλάκις μέν,
ὅτ' οὐκ ἐποιεῖθ' ὁ πατὴρ τούτους, ἔλεγον οὗτοι ὡς
οὐδὲν χείρους εἰσὶν οἱ τῆς μητρὸς τῆς τούτου συγγενεῖς τῶν τοῦ πατρὸς τοὐμοῦ. ἔστιν δ' ὁ Βοιωτὸς
ἀδελφοῦ τῆς τούτου μητρὸς ὄνομα. ἐπειδὴ δ'
εἰσάγειν ὁ πατὴρ τούτους ἠναγκάζετο, ἐμοῦ προεισ-
ηγμένου Μαντιθέου, οὕτω τοῦτον εἰσάγει Βοιωτόν,
τὸν ἀδελφὸν δ' αὐτοῦ Πάμφιλον. ἐπεὶ σὺ δεῖξον,
ὅστις Ἀθηναίων ταῦτ' ὄνομα αὐτοῦ παισὶν ἔθετο
δυοῖν κἂν δείξῃς, ἐγὼ συγχωρήσω δι' ἐπήρειάν σοι
33 τοῦτο τοὔνομα θέσθαι τὸν πατέρα. καίτοι εἴ γε
τοιοῦτος ἦσθα, ὥστε ποιήσασθαι μὲν σαυτὸν ἀναγ-
κάσαι, ἐξ ὅτου δ' ἀρέσεις ἐκείνῳ τρόπου μὴ σκοπεῖν, οὐκ ἦσθ' οἷον δεῖ τὸν προσήκοντ' εἶναι περὶ
τοὺς γονέας, οὐκ ὢν δ' οὐκ ἐπηρεάζου δικαίως ἄν,
ἀλλ' ἀπωλώλεις. ἢ δεινόν γ' ἂν εἴη, εἰ κατὰ μὲν
τῶν ὑπὸ τοῦ πατρὸς αὐτοῦ νομιζομένων παίδων οἱ
περὶ τῶν γονέων ἰσχύσουσι νόμοι, κατὰ τῶν δ'
αὐτοὺς εἰσβιαζομένων ἄκοντας ποιεῖσθαι, ἄκυροι
γενήσονται.
34 Ἀλλ', ὦ χαλεπώτατε Βοιωτέ, μάλιστα μὲν ὧν
πράττεις πάντων παῦσαι, εἰ δ' ἄρα μὴ βούλει,

---

[a] The word chosen is the one properly used of aliens who
seek to arrogate to themselves the rights of citizenship.

my father, you should see fit to fling it aside and take
another name. Come ; suppose my father were to
rise from the grave and demand of you either to abide
by the name under which he adopted you, or to declare yourself the son of some other father, would his
demand not be thought a reasonable one? Well then,
I make this same demand of you, either to add to your
name that of another father, or to keep the name
which Mantias gave you. Ah, you may say, but that 32
name was given you by way of derision or insult. No ;
very often, during the time when my father refused to
acknowledge them, these men used to say that the
kinsfolk of the defendant's mother were quite as good
as those of my father. Boeotus is the name of his
mother's brother ; and when my father was compelled to bring them into the clan, when I had already
been introduced as Mantitheus, he introduced the
defendant as Boeotus, and his brother as Pamphilus.
For I challenge you to show me any Athenian who
ever gave the same name to two of his sons. If you
can, I will grant that my father gave you this name
by way of insult. And yet, if your character was such 33
that you could force him to adopt you, but not study
how you might please him, you were not what a true
son ought to be toward his parents ; and, if you were
not, you would have deserved, not only to be treated
with indignity, but even to be put to death. It would
indeed be an outrageous thing, if the laws concerning
parents are to be binding upon children whom the
father recognizes as his own, but are to be of no effect
against those who have forced themselves in [a] and
compelled an unwilling adoption.

You unconscionable Boeotus, do, pray, give up 34
your present ways ; but, if indeed you are unwilling

ἐκεῖνό γε πρὸς Διὸς πιθοῦ· παῦσαι μὲν σαυτῷ
παρέχων πράγματα, παῦσαι δ' ἐμὲ συκοφαντῶν,
ἀγάπα δ' ὅτι σοι πόλις, οὐσία, πατὴρ γέγονεν.
οὐδεὶς ἀπελαύνει σ' ἀπὸ τούτων, οὔκουν ἔγωγε.
ἀλλ' ἂν μέν, ὥσπερ εἶναι φῂς ἀδελφός, καὶ τὰ ἔργ'
ἀδελφοῦ ποιῇς, δόξεις εἶναι συγγενής, ἂν δ' ἐπι-
βουλεύῃς, δικάζῃ, φθονῇς, βλασφημῇς, δόξεις εἰς
ἀλλότρι' ἐμπεσὼν ὡς οὐ προσήκουσιν οὕτω χρῆ-
35
[1005] σθαι. ἐπεὶ ἔγωγ' οὐδ' εἰ τὰ μάλισθ' ὁ πατὴρ ὄντα
σ' ἑαυτοῦ μὴ ἐποιεῖτ' ἀδικῶ. οὐ γὰρ ἐμοὶ προσῆκεν
εἰδέναι, τίνες εἰσὶν υἱεῖς ἐκείνου, ἀλλ' ἐκείνῳ δεῖξαι,
τίν' ἐμοὶ νομιστέον ἔστ' ἀδελφόν. ὃν μὲν τοίνυν
οὐκ ἐποιεῖτό σε χρόνον, οὐδ' ἐγὼ προσήκονθ'
ἡγούμην, ἐπειδὴ δ' ἐποιήσατο, κἀγὼ νομίζω. τί
τούτου σημεῖον; τῶν πατρῴων ἔχεις τὸ μέρος
μετὰ τὴν τοῦ πατρὸς τελευτήν· ἱερῶν, ὁσίων
μετέχεις· ἀπάγει σ' οὐδεὶς ἀπὸ τούτων. τί βούλει;
ἂν δὲ φῇ δεινὰ πάσχειν καὶ κλάῃ καὶ ὀδύρηται καὶ
κατηγορῇ μου, ἃ μὲν ἂν λέγῃ, μὴ πιστεύετε (οὐ
γὰρ δίκαιον μὴ περὶ τούτων ὄντος τοῦ λόγου νυνί),
ἐκεῖνο δ' ὑπολαμβάνετε, ὅτι οὐδὲν ἔστ' αὐτῷ ἧττον
δίκην λαμβάνειν Βοιωτῷ κληθέντι. τί οὖν φιλο-
36 νικεῖς; μηδαμῶς· μὴ ἔχ' οὕτω πρὸς ἡμᾶς ἐθελ-
έχθρως· οὐδὲ γὰρ ἐγὼ πρὸς σέ, ἐπεὶ καὶ νῦν, ἵνα

to, do, in Heaven's name, accept advice in this at
least; cease to make trouble for yourself, and cease
bringing malicious and baseless charges against me;
and be content that you have gained citizenship, an
estate, a father. No one is trying to dispossess you
of these things; certainly not I. Nay, if, as you
claim to be a brother, you also act as a brother,
people will believe that you are of our blood; but if
you go on plotting against me, suing me, evincing
malice toward me, slandering me, you will be thought
to have intruded yourself into what belonged to others,
and then to be treating it as though it were not rightly
yours. I certainly am doing you no wrong, even if it 35
were never so true that my father refused to recognize
you, though you were really his son. It was not my
part to know who were his sons, but it was his to show
me whom I must regard as a brother. Therefore,
during the time in which he refused to recognize you,
I also counted you as no relative; but ever since he
adopted you, I too regard you as a kinsman. What
is the proof of this? You possess your portion of my
father's estate after his death; you share in the
religious rites, and civic privileges. No one seeks to
exclude you from these. What is it that you would
have? But if he says that he is being outrageously
treated, if he weeps and wails, and makes charges
against me, do not believe what he says. It is not
right that you should, since our argument is not now
about these matters. But take this attitude—that he
can just as well get satisfaction under the name of
Boeotus. Why are you, then, so fond of wrangling?
Desist, I beg you; do not be so ready to cherish 36
enmity against me. I am not so minded toward you.
For even now—lest the fact escape your notice—I

μηδὲ τοῦτο λάθῃ σε, ὑπὲρ σοῦ λέγω μᾶλλον, ἀξιῶν
μὴ ταὐτὸν ἔχειν ὄνομ' ἡμᾶς. εἰ γὰρ μηδὲν ἄλλο
ἀνάγκη τὸν ἀκούσαντ' ἐρέσθαι πότερος, δύ' ἂν ὦσι
Μαντίθεοι Μαντίου. οὐκοῦν, ὃν ἠναγκάσθη ποιήσασθαι, σὲ ἂν λέγῃ, ἐρεῖ. τί οὖν ἐπιθυμεῖς τούτων;

Ἀνάγνωθι δέ μοι λαβὼν δύο ταυτασὶ μαρτυρίας,
ὡς ἐμοὶ Μαντίθεον καὶ τούτῳ Βοιωτὸν ὁ πατὴρ
ὄνομ' ἔθετο.

37 Λοιπὸν ἡγοῦμαι τοῦθ' ὑμῖν ἐπιδεῖξαι, ὦ ἄνδρες
Ἀθηναῖοι, ὡς οὐ μόνον εὐορκήσετε, ἂν ἀγὼ λέγω
ψηφίσησθε, ἀλλὰ καὶ ὡς οὗτος αὐτὸς αὑτοῦ κατ-
[1006] έγνω Βοιωτὸν ἀλλ' οὐ Μαντίθεον ὄνομα δικαίως
ἂν ἔχειν. λαχόντος γὰρ ἐμοῦ τὴν δίκην ταύτην
Βοιωτῷ Μαντίου Θορικίῳ, ἐξ ἀρχῆς τ' ἠντεδίκει
καὶ ὑπώμνυθ' ὡς ὢν Βοιωτός, καὶ τὸ τελευταῖον,
ἐπεὶ οὐκέτ' ἐνῆν αὐτῷ διακρούσασθαι, ἐρήμην
ἐάσας καταδιαιτῆσαι, σκέψασθε πρὸς θεῶν τί
38 ἐποίησεν· ἀντιλαγχάνει μοι τὴν μὴ οὖσαν Βοιωτὸν
αὐτὸν προσαγορεύσας. καίτοι ἐξ ἀρχῆς τ' ἔδει ἐὰν
αὐτὸν τελέσασθαι τὴν δίκην κατὰ Βοιωτοῦ, εἴπερ
μηδὲν προσῆκεν αὐτῷ τοὐνόματος, ὕστερόν τε μὴ
αὐτὸν φαίνεσθαι ἐπὶ τῷ ὀνόματι τούτῳ ἀντιλαγχά-
νοντα τὴν μὴ οὖσαν. ὃς οὖν αὐτὸς αὑτοῦ κατέγνω
δικαίως ἂν εἶναι Βοιωτός, τί ὑμᾶς ἀξιώσει τοὺς
ὀμωμοκότας ψηφίζεσθαι;
474

am speaking rather in your interest than in my own, in insisting that we should not have the same name. If there were no other reason, at least anyone hearing it must ask which of us is meant if there are two Mantitheuses, sons of Mantias. Then he will say, " The one whom he was compelled to adopt," if he means you. How can you desire this ?

Now take, please, and read these two depositions, proving that my father gave me the name Mantitheus, and him the name Boeotus.

THE DEPOSITIONS

It remains, I think, to show you, men of Athens, 37 that not only will you be fulfilling your oaths, if you give the verdict for which I ask, but also that the defendant has given judgement against himself, that he should rightly bear the name of Boeotus, and not Mantitheus. For when I had entered this suit against Boeotus, son of Mantias, of Thoricus, at the first he accepted service of the suit, and put in an oath for delay, as being Boeotus ; but finally, when there was no longer room for evasion, he allowed the arbitrators to give judgement against him by default, and then, in Heaven's name, see what he did—he got this 38 judgement for non-appearance set aside, entitling himself Boeotus. And yet he ought in the first place to have allowed me to get my suit finished as against Boeotus, if that name did not, in fact, pertain to him at all, and not subsequently be found getting the judgement for non-appearance set aside under this name. When a man has thus given judgement against himself that he is properly Boeotus, what verdict can he demand that you sworn jurors shall give ?

DEMOSTHENES

Ὡς δὲ ταῦτ' ἀληθῆ λέγω, λαβέ μοι τὴν ἀντίληξιν καὶ τὸ ἔγκλημα τουτί.

39 Εἰ μὲν τοίνυν οὗτος ἔχει δεῖξαι νόμον, ὃς ποιεῖ κυρίους εἶναι τοὺς παῖδας τοῦ ἑαυτῶν ὀνόματος, ἃ λέγει νῦν οὗτος ὀρθῶς ἂν ψηφίζοισθε. εἰ δ' ὁ μὲν νόμος, ὃν πάντες ἐπίστασθ' ὁμοίως ἐμοί, τοὺς γονέας ποιεῖ κυρίους οὐ μόνον θέσθαι τοὔνομ' ἐξ ἀρχῆς, ἀλλὰ κἂν πάλιν ἐξαλεῖψαι βούλωνται κἀποκηρῦξαι, ἐπέδειξα δ' ἐγὼ τὸν πατέρ', ὃς κύριος ἦν ἐκ τοῦ νόμου, τούτῳ μὲν Βοιωτόν, ἐμοὶ δὲ Μαντίθεον θέμενον, πῶς ὑμῖν ἔστιν ἄλλο τι πλὴν ἁγὼ
40 λέγω ψηφίσασθαι; ἀλλὰ μὴν ὧν γ' ἂν μὴ ὦσι νόμοι, γνώμῃ τῇ δικαιοτάτῃ δικάσειν ὀμωμόκατε, ὥστ' εἰ μηδεὶς ἦν περὶ τούτων κείμενος νόμος, κἂν
[1007] οὕτω δικαίως πρὸς ἐμοῦ τὴν ψῆφον ἔθεσθε. τίς γάρ ἐστιν ὑμῶν ὅστις ταῦτ' ὄνομα αὐτοῦ παισὶ τέθειται δυοῖν; τίς δ', ᾧ μήπω παῖδές εἰσί, θή-
41 σεται; οὐδεὶς δήπου. οὐκοῦν ὃ δίκαιον τῇ γνώμῃ τοῖς ὑμετέροις αὐτῶν παισὶν ὑπειλήφατε, τοῦτο καὶ περὶ ἡμῶν εὐσεβὲς γνῶναι. ὥστε καὶ κατὰ τὴν δικαιοτάτην γνώμην καὶ κατὰ τοὺς νόμους καὶ κατὰ τοὺς ὅρκους καὶ κατὰ τὴν τούτου προσομολογίαν, ἐγὼ μὲν μέτρι' ὑμῶν, ὦ ἄνδρες Ἀθηναῖοι, δέομαι καὶ δίκαι' ἀξιῶ, οὗτος δ' οὐ μόνον οὐ μέτρια, ἀλλ' οὐδ' εἰωθότα γίγνεσθαι.

To prove that I am speaking the truth in this, take the decision setting aside the judgement for non-appearance and this complaint.

THE DECISION. THE COMPLAINT

If, now, my opponent can point out a law which gives 39 children the right to choose their own names, you would rightly give the verdict for which he asks. But if the law, which you all know as well as I, gives parents the right not only to give the name in the first place, but also to cancel it and renounce it by public declaration, if they please ; and if I have shown that my father, who had this authority under the law, gave to the defendant the name Boeotus, and to me the name Mantitheus, how can you render any other verdict than that for which I ask ? Nay, more, 40 in cases which are not covered by the laws, you have sworn that you will decide as in your judgement is most just, so that even if there were no law concerning these matters, you would have been bound to cast your votes in my favour. For who is there among you who has given the same name to two of his children ? Who, that is as yet childless, will do so ? No one, assuredly. Well then, what in your minds you have 41 decided to be right for your own children, it is your sacred duty to decide also in our case. Therefore on the basis of what you deem most just, on the basis of the laws, your oaths, and the admissions this man has made, my request of you, men of Athens, is reasonable, and my claims just ; while my opponent asks what is not only unreasonable, but contrary to established usage.

AGAINST BOEOTUS
II

INTRODUCTION

This speech was delivered by the same Mantitheus in a second suit against Boeotus (to whom after his apparent victory in the preceding suit we should properly give the name Mantitheus) to recover the marriage-portion of his mother. He states that, after striving for eleven years to reach a settlement, he has found it necessary to bring the case into court.

It appears that after his father's death he had recognized his two half-brothers as entitled each to a one-third share in his father's estate, but had claimed for himself a talent over and above his own share, as due to him from his mother's dowry. The older Mantitheus (Boeotus) met this action by a counter-claim that a like sum was due to him from his mother, Plangon. (It is stated in § 20 of this speech that she had brought Mantias a portion of more than one hundred minae.) At the first an arrangement was made whereby the estate of Mantias was divided between the three, the family house and the slaves alone being reserved pending the settlement of the conflicting claims.

Much bitterness, however, continued to exist between the two Mantitheuses, and the wrangling went on for years. The plaintiff in this suit claims that, although he had accepted " Boeotus " and Pamphilus as his father's sons, and had shared the estate with them, their licentious manner of life made it impossible for him and his daughter—a young woman of marriageable age—to live with them, so that he had been virtually ousted from his home. He even states that they might go so far as to seek to take his life by poison (§ 57).

The case came before the arbitrator, Solon, but, owing—the speaker claims—to the evasions and delays of the defendant, it was prolonged, and Solon died before an award was made. Both parties then reopened their suits each against the other, and when at last judgement was given against Boeotus he ignored it, claiming—perhaps with good reason—that his name was Mantitheus. Accordingly in the eleventh year suit was again brought against him under that name. He again met this with a counterclaim, not in this instance for his mother's portion, but for some other property which is not specified (§ 17).

The writer of this speech is familiar with the preceding one, and repeats some of its arguments, but his work bears the marks of a different hand, so that this oration, while undoubtedly a genuine piece of Greek forensic oratory, seems not to be by Demosthenes.

See further Schaefer, iii.² pp. 220 ff., and Blass, iii. pp. 509 ff.

XL

ΠΡΟΣ ΒΟΙΩΤΟΝ ΠΕΡΙ ΠΡΟΙΚΟΣ ΜΗΤΡΩΙΑΣ

Β

Πάντων ἐστὶν ἀνιαρότατον, ὦ ἄνδρες δικασταί, ὅταν τις ὀνόματι μὲν ἀδελφὸς προσαγορευθῇ τινων, τῷ δ' ἔργῳ ἐχθροὺς ἔχῃ τούτους, καὶ ἀναγκάζηται πολλὰ καὶ δεινὰ παθὼν ὑπ' αὐτῶν εἰσιέναι εἰς
2 δικαστήριον, ὃ νῦν ἐμοὶ συμβέβηκεν. οὐ γὰρ μόνον ἀτύχημά μοι ἐξ ἀρχῆς ἐγένετο, διότι Πλαγγὼν ἡ τούτων μήτηρ ἐξαπατήσασα τὸν πατέρα μου καὶ ἐπιορκήσασα φανερῶς, ἠνάγκασεν αὐτὸν ὑπομεῖναι τούτους ποιήσασθαι, καὶ διὰ τοῦτο τὰ δύο μέρη τῶν πατρῴων ἀπεστερήθην· ἀλλὰ πρὸς τούτοις ἐξελήλαμαι μὲν ἐκ τῆς πατρῴας οἰκίας ὑπὸ τούτων, ἐν ᾗ καὶ ἐγενόμην καὶ ἐτράφην, καὶ εἰς ἣν οὐχ ὁ
3 πατὴρ αὐτοὺς ἀλλ' ἐγὼ τελευτήσαντος ἐκείνου
[1009] παρεδεξάμην, ἀποστεροῦμαι δὲ τὴν προῖκα τῆς ἐμαυτοῦ μητρός, περὶ ἧς νυνὶ δικάζομαι, αὐτὸς μὲν τούτοις δίκας ὑπὲρ ὧν ἐνεκάλουν μοι πάντων δεδωκώς, πλὴν εἴ τινα νῦν ἕνεκα τῆς δίκης ταύτης ἀντειλήχασί μοι συκοφαντοῦντες, ὡς καὶ ὑμῖν ἔσται

482

XL

MANTITHEUS AGAINST BOEOTUS REGARDING HIS MOTHER'S MARRIAGE-PORTION

II

NOTHING is more painful, men of the jury, than when a man is addressed by name as " brother " of certain persons, whom in fact he regards as enemies, and when he is compelled, on account of the many cruel wrongs which he has suffered at their hands, to come into court; as is my case now. For instance, I have 2 not only had the misfortune in the beginning that Plangon, the mother of these men, by deceit and manifest perjury, compelled my father to bring himself to acknowledge them, and that consequently I was robbed of two-thirds of my inheritance ; but, in addition to this, I have been driven by these men out of the house of my fathers, in which I was born and brought up, and into which they were admitted, not by my father, but by myself after his death ; and I 3 am being robbed of my mother's dowry, for which I am now bringing suit, although I have myself given them satisfaction in all the matters in which they made claims upon me, except some trifling cross-demands which they have maliciously brought against me on account of this action, as will be perfectly

καταφανές, παρὰ δὲ τούτοιν ἐν ἕνδεκα ἔτεσιν οὐ
δυνάμενος τυχεῖν τῶν μετρίων, ἀλλὰ νῦν εἰς ὑμᾶς
4 βοηθοὺς καταπεφευγώς. δέομαι οὖν ἁπάντων ὑμῶν,
ὦ ἄνδρες δικασταί, μετ᾽ εὐνοίας τέ μου ἀκοῦσαι
οὕτως ὅπως ἂν δύνωμαι λέγοντος, κἂν ὑμῖν δεινὰ
δοκῶ πεπονθέναι, συγγνώμην ἔχειν μοι ζητοῦντι
κομίσασθαι τἀμαυτοῦ, ἄλλως τε καὶ εἰς θυγατρὸς
ἔκδοσιν· συνέβη γάρ μοι δεηθέντος τοῦ πατρὸς
ὀκτωκαιδεκέτη γῆμαι, καὶ διὰ τοῦτο εἶναί μοι
5 θυγατέρα ἤδη ἐπίγαμον. ὥστ᾽ ἐμοὶ μὲν δικαίως
ἂν ἀδικουμένῳ διὰ πολλὰ βοηθήσαιτε, τούτοις δ᾽
εἰκότως ἂν ὀργίζοισθε· οἵτινες, ὦ γῆ καὶ θεοί, ἐξὸν
αὐτοῖς τὰ δίκαια ποιήσασι μὴ εἰσίεναι εἰς δικαστήριον, οὐκ αἰσχύνονται μὲν ἀναμιμνήσκοντες
ὑμᾶς, εἴ τι ἢ ὁ πατὴρ ἡμῶν μὴ ὀρθῶς διεπράξατο,
ἢ οὗτοι εἰς ἐκεῖνον ἥμαρτον, ἀναγκάζουσι δ᾽ ἐμὲ
δικάζεσθαι αὐτοῖς. ἵνα δ᾽ ἀκριβῶς εἰδῆτε, ὡς οὐκ
ἐγὼ τούτου αἴτιός εἰμι ἀλλ᾽ οὗτοι, ἐξ ἀρχῆς ὑμῖν,
ὡς ἂν ἐν βραχυτάτοις δύνωμαι, διηγήσομαι τὰ
πραχθέντα.
6 Ἡ γὰρ μήτηρ ἡ ἐμή, ὦ ἄνδρες δικασται, θυγάτηρ
μὲν ἦν Πολυαράτου Χολαργέως, ἀδελφὴ δὲ Μενεξένου καὶ Βαθύλλου καὶ Περιάνδρου. ἐκδόντος
δ᾽ αὐτὴν τοῦ πατρὸς Κλεομέδοντι τῷ Κλέωνος
[1010] υἱεῖ, καὶ προῖκα τάλαντον ἐπιδόντος, τὸ μὲν πρῶτον
τούτῳ συνῴκει· γενομένων δ᾽ αὐτῇ τριῶν μὲν
θυγατέρων, υἱοῦ δ᾽ ἑνὸς Κλέωνος, καὶ μετὰ ταῦτα
τοῦ ἀνδρὸς αὐτῇ τελευτήσαντος, ἀπολιποῦσα τὸν
7 οἶκον καὶ κομισαμένη τὴν προῖκα, πάλιν ἐκδόντων

ᵃ Cholargus was a deme of the tribe Acamantis.

clear to you also ; yet in the course of eleven years I have been unable to obtain from them a reasonable settlement, and so at length I have had recourse to you for help. I beg you all, men of the jury, to listen 4 to me with goodwill, while I speak as best I can ; and if I seem to you to have suffered cruel wrongs, to pardon me for seeking to recover what is my own, especially as it is for a marriage-portion for my daughter. For it so happened that I married at my father's request when I was only eighteen, and that I have a daughter who is already of marriageable age. It is, therefore, just on many accounts that you should 5 aid me who am being wronged, and fitting that you should feel indignation against the men, who—O Earth and the Gods—when they need not have come into court at all had they done what is fair, are not ashamed to remind you of any improper acts of my father, or of wrongs which they committed against him, but even force me to go to law with them. To make you understand clearly that it is they, not I, who are to blame for this, I will set forth to you the facts of the case from the beginning with the utmost possible brevity.

My mother, men of the jury, was the daughter of 6 Polyaratus, of Cholargus,[a] and sister of Menexenus, and Bathyllus and Periander. Her father gave her in marriage to Cleomedon, son of Cleon,[b] adding a talent as her marriage-portion ; and at the first she dwelt with him as his wife, and bore him three daughters and one son, Cleon. After this her husband died, and she left his family, receiving back her marriage-portion. Her brothers, Menexenus and 7

---

[b] The famous demagogue, known to us from Thucydides and Aristophanes.

αὐτὴν τῶν ἀδελφῶν Μενεξένου καὶ Βαθύλλου (ὁ
γὰρ Περίανδρος ἔτι παῖς ἦν) καὶ τὸ τάλαντον ἐπι-
δόντων, συνῴκησε τῷ ἐμῷ πατρί. καὶ γίγνομαι
αὐτοῖς ἐγώ τε καὶ ἄλλος ἀδελφὸς νεώτερος ἐμοῦ,
ὃς ἔτι παῖς ὢν ἐτελεύτησεν.

Ὡς δ' ἀληθῆ λέγω, περὶ τούτων ὑμῖν πρῶτον
τοὺς μάρτυρας παρέξομαι.

ΜΑΡΤΥΡΕΣ

8 Τὴν μὲν τοίνυν μητέρα τὴν ἐμὴν οὕτως ὁ πατήρ
μου γήμας εἶχε γυναῖκα ἐν τῇ οἰκίᾳ τῇ ἑαυτοῦ, ἐμέ
τε ἐπαίδευε καὶ ἠγάπα, ὥσπερ καὶ ὑμεῖς ἅπαντες
τοὺς ὑμετέρους παῖδας ἀγαπᾶτε. τῇ δὲ τούτων
μητρὶ Πλαγγόνι ἐπλησίαζεν ὅντινα δή ποτ' οὖν
9 τρόπον· οὐ γὰρ ἐμὸν τοῦτο λέγειν ἐστί. καὶ οὕτως
οὐ πάντα γε ἦν ὑπὸ τῆς ἐπιθυμίας κεκρατημένος,
ὥστ' οὐδὲ τῆς μητρὸς τῆς ἐμῆς ἀποθανούσης
ἠξίωσεν αὐτὴν εἰς τὴν οἰκίαν παρ' ἑαυτὸν εἰσδέξασθαι, οὐδὲ τούτους, ὡς υἱεῖς εἰσιν αὐτοῦ, πεισθῆναι·
ἀλλὰ τὸν μὲν ἄλλον χρόνον οὗτοι διῆγον οὐκ ὄντες
τοὐμοῦ πατρός, ὡς καὶ ὑμῶν οἱ πολλοὶ ἴσασιν,
ἐπειδὴ δ' οὗτος αὐξηθεὶς καὶ μεθ' αὑτοῦ παρα-
σκευασάμενος ἐργαστήριον συκοφαντῶν, ὧν ἡγεμὼν
ἦν Μνησικλῆς καὶ Μενεκλῆς ἐκεῖνος ὁ τὴν Νῖνον
ἑλών, μεθ' ὧν οὗτος ἐδικάζετό μου τῷ πατρὶ
10 φάσκων υἱὸς εἶναι ἐκείνου, συνόδων γιγνομένων
πολλῶν ὑπὲρ τούτων, καὶ τοῦ πατρὸς οὐκ ἂν
[1011] φάσκοντος πεισθῆναι, ὡς οὗτοι γεγόνασιν ἐξ αὐτοῦ,
τελευτῶσα ἡ Πλαγγών, ὦ ἄνδρες δικασταί (πάντα
γὰρ εἰρήσεται τἀληθῆ πρὸς ὑμᾶς), μετὰ τοῦ Μενεκλέους ἐνεδρεύσασα τὸν πατέρα μου καὶ ἐξαπατή-

Bathyllus (for Periander was still a boy) then gave
her again in marriage with the talent for her dowry,
and she dwelt with my father as his wife. There were
born to them myself and another brother, younger
than I, who died while still a child.

To prove that I am speaking the truth, I will first
bring forward witnesses to establish these facts.

THE WITNESSES

My father, then, having thus married my mother, 8
maintained her as his wife in his own house ; and he
brought me up and showed me a father's affection
such as you also all show to your children. But
with Plangon, the mother of these men, he formed a
connexion of some sort or other (it is not for me to
say what it was) ; however, he was not so wholly the 9
slave of his passion as to deem it right even after my
mother's death to receive the woman into his own
house, or to admit that the defendants were his
children. No, for all the rest of the time they lived as
not being sons of my father, as most of you know ;
but after Boeotus had grown up and had associated
with himself a gang of blackmailers,[a] whose leaders
were Mnesicles and that Menecles who secured
the conviction of Ninus, in connexion with these
men he brought suit against my father, claiming
that he was his son. Many meetings took place 10
about these matters, and my father declared that
he would never be convinced that these men were
his children, and finally Plangon, men of the jury
(for the whole truth shall be told you), having in
conjunction with Menecles laid a snare for my father,

---

[a] On this whole passage compare the preceding oration,
§ 2.

σασα ὅρκῳ, ὃς μέγιστος δοκεῖ καὶ δεινότατος παρὰ
πᾶσιν ἀνθρώποις εἶναι, ὡμολόγησε τριάκοντα
μνᾶς λαβοῦσα τούτους μὲν τοῖς αὑτῆς ἀδελφοῖς
εἰσποιήσειν υἱεῖς, αὐτὴ δ᾽, ἂν πρὸς τῷ διαιτητῇ
προκαλῆται αὐτὴν ὁ πατήρ μου ὀμόσαι ἦ μὴν
τοὺς παῖδας ἐξ αὐτοῦ γεγονέναι, οὐ δέξεσθαι τὴν
πρόκλησιν· τούτων γὰρ γενομένων οὔτε τούτους
ἀποστερήσεσθαι τῆς πόλεως, τῷ τε πατρί μου
οὐκέτι δυνήσεσθαι αὐτοὺς πράγματα παρέχειν, τῆς
11 μητρὸς αὐτῶν οὐ δεξαμένης τὸν ὅρκον. συγχωρηθέντων δὲ τούτων—τί ἂν ὑμῖν μακρολογοίην;—ὡς
γὰρ πρὸς τὸν διαιτητὴν ἀπήντησε, παραβᾶσα πάντα
τὰ ὡμολογημένα ἡ Πλαγγών, δέχεταί τε τὴν
πρόκλησιν καὶ ὄμνυσιν ἐν τῷ Δελφινίῳ ἄλλον ὅρκον
ἐναντίον τῷ προτέρῳ, ὡς καὶ ὑμῶν οἱ πολλοὶ
ἴσασι· περιβόητος γὰρ ἡ πρᾶξις ἐγένετο. καὶ
οὕτως ὁ πατήρ μου διὰ τὴν ἑαυτοῦ πρόκλησιν
ἀναγκασθεὶς ἐμμεῖναι τῇ διαίτῃ, ἐπὶ μὲν τοῖς
γεγενημένοις ἠγανάκτει καὶ βαρέως ἔφερε, καὶ εἰς
τὴν οἰκίαν οὐδ᾽ ὣς εἰσδέξασθαι τούτους ἠξίωσεν,
εἰς δὲ τοὺς φράτερας ἠναγκάσθη εἰσαγαγεῖν. καὶ
τοῦτον μὲν ἐνέγραψε Βοιωτόν, τὸν δ᾽ ἕτερον Πάμ-
12 φιλον. ἐμὲ δ᾽ εὐθὺς ἔπειθε περὶ ὀκτωκαίδεκ᾽ ἔτη
γεγενημένον τὴν Εὐφήμου γῆμαι θυγατέρα, βουλόμενος παῖδας ἐξ ἐμοῦ γενομένους ἐπιδεῖν. ἐγὼ δ᾽,
[1012] ὦ ἄνδρες δικασταί, νομίζων δεῖν καὶ πρότερον καὶ
ἐπειδὴ οὗτοι ἐλύπουν αὐτὸν δικαζόμενοι καὶ πράγ-

---

^a A quotation from *Iliad*, xv. 37 f.
^b These would be ensured to them by the fact of their
being enrolled in the clan register ; but if they were enrolled
as sons of the brothers of Plangon, they could no longer
" make trouble " for Mantias by claiming to be sons of his.

and deceived him by an oath that among all mankind is held to be the greatest and most awful,[a] agreed that, if she were paid thirty minae, she would get her brothers to adopt these men, and that, on her own part, if my father should challenge her before the arbitrator to swear that the children were in very truth his sons, she would decline the challenge. For if this were done, she said, the defendants would not be deprived of their civic rights,[b] but they would no longer be able to make trouble for my father, seeing that their mother had refused the oath. When these 11 terms had been accepted—for why should I make my story a long one?—he went to meet her before the arbitrator, and Plangon, contrary to all that she had agreed to do, accepted the challenge, and swore in the Delphinium[c] an oath which was the very opposite of her former one, as most of you know well; for the transaction became a notorious one. Thus, my father was compelled on account of his own challenge to abide by the arbitrator's award, but he was indignant at what had been done, and took the matter heavily to heart, and did not even so consent to admit these men into his house; but he was compelled to introduce them to the clansmen. The defendant he enrolled as Boeotus, and the other as Pamphilus. As for me, he forthwith persuaded me, 12 for I was about eighteen years of age, to marry the daughter of Euphemus, wishing to live to see children born to me. I, men of the jury, as before, so especially then, when these men were beginning to annoy him with lawsuits and were proving troublesome, thought

[c] The temple of Apollo Delphinius, situated somewhere near the ancient entrance to the Acropolis.

ματα παρέχοντες, ἐμὲ τοὐναντίον εὐφραίνειν ἅπαντα
ποιοῦνθ' ὅσ' ἐκείνῳ χαριεῖσθαι μέλλοιμι, ἐπείσθην
13 αὐτῷ. γήμαντος δέ μου τὸν τρόπον τοῦτον,
ἐκεῖνος μὲν τὸ θυγάτριόν μοι ἐπιδὼν γενόμενον, οὐ
πολλοῖς ἔτεσιν ὕστερον ἀρρωστήσας ἐτελεύτησεν·
ἐγὼ δ', ὦ ἄνδρες δικασταί, ζῶντος μὲν τοῦ πατρὸς
οὐδὲν ᾤμην δεῖν ἐναντιοῦσθαι αὐτῷ, τελευτήσαντος
δ' ἐκείνου εἰσεδεξάμην τε τούτους εἰς τὴν οἰκίαν
καὶ τῶν ὄντων ἁπάντων μετέδωκα, οὐχ ὡς ἀδελφοῖς οὖσιν (οὐδὲ γὰρ ὑμῶν τοὺς πολλοὺς λελήθασιν
ὃν τρόπον οὗτοι γεγόνασιν), νομίζων δ' ἀναγκαῖον
εἶναί μοι, ἐπειδὴ ὁ πατὴρ ἐξηπατήθη, πείθεσθαι
14 τοῖς νόμοις τοῖς ὑμετέροις. καὶ οὕτως ὑπ' ἐμοῦ
εἰς τὴν οἰκίαν εἰσδεχθέντες, ὡς ἐνεμόμεθα τὰ
πατρῷα, ἀξιοῦντος ἐμοῦ ἀπολαβεῖν τὴν τῆς μητρὸς
προῖκα ἀντενεκάλουν καὶ οὗτοι, καὶ ἔφασαν ὀφείλε-
σθαι καὶ τῇ αὑτῶν μητρὶ τὴν ἴσην προῖκα. συμ-
βουλευσάντων δ' ἡμῖν τῶν παρόντων, τὰ μὲν ἄλλα
πάντα ἐνειμάμεθα, τὴν δ' οἰκίαν καὶ τοὺς παῖδας
τοὺς διακόνους τοῦ πατρὸς ἐξαιρέτους ἐποιησάμεθα,
15 ἵν' ἐκ μὲν τῆς οἰκίας, ὁποτέροις ἂν ἡμῶν φαίνηται
ὀφειλομένη ἡ προίξ, οὗτοι αὐτὴν κομίσωνται, ἐκ
δὲ τῶν παίδων κοινῶν ὄντων, ἐάν τι οὗτοι τῶν
πατρῴων ἐπιζητῶσι, πυνθάνωνται, καὶ βασανίζοντες αὐτοὺς καὶ ἄλλῳ ὅτῳ ἂν τρόπῳ βούλωνται
ζητοῦντες.

Ὅτι δὲ καὶ ταῦτ' ἀληθῆ λέγω, ἐκ τούτων τῶν
μαρτυριῶν εἴσεσθε.

ᵃ Below (§ 20, end) the amount is set at more than 100
minae, not a talent merely.

that I, on the contrary, ought to strive to gladden
him by doing everything whereby I could give him
pleasure, and so obeyed him. When I had married 13
in this way, and he had lived to see my little daughter
born, not many years later he fell sick and died.
Then, although during my father's lifetime, men of
the jury, I had thought it my duty to oppose him in
nothing, yet after his death I received these men
into the house, and gave them a share of all the
property, not as being really my brothers (for most
of you are well aware of the manner in which they
became such), but thinking that, as my father had
been beguiled, it was my duty to obey your laws.
And when they had thus been received by me into 14
the house, we proceeded to divide the inheritance ;
and upon my demanding that my mother's marriage-
portion be repaid to me, these men put in a counter-
claim, and alleged that a portion of like amount was
owing to their mother.[a] On the advice of friends
who were present we divided all the rest of the
property but kept apart the house and the domestic
servants of my father, in order that whichever party 15
of us might establish his claim to the dowry should
recover it from the value of the house ; and from
the slaves, who were common property, the defendants, should they wish to search out[b] any of my
father's effects, might make inquiry by torturing
them, or by prosecuting their search in any other
way they might please.

That I am speaking the truth in this also you will
know from these depositions.

[b] The precise meaning of this phrase is open to question.
It may imply a claim that some property had been omitted
from the inventory or in some way concealed.

DEMOSTHENES

16 Μετὰ ταῦτα τοίνυν οὗτοί τ' ἐμοὶ δίκας ἔλαχον
ὑπὲρ ὧν ἐνεκάλουν κἀγὼ τούτοις ὑπὲρ τῆς προικός.
καὶ τὸ μὲν πρῶτον παραγραψάμενοι Σόλωνα
Ἐρχιέα διαιτητὴν τούτῳ ἐπετρέψαμεν δικάσαι περὶ
ὧν ἐνεκαλοῦμεν ἀλλήλοις· ὡς δ' οὐκ ἀπήντων οὗτοι,
ἀλλ' ἐφυγοδίκουν καὶ χρόνος διετρίβετο συχνός, τῷ
μὲν Σόλωνι συνέβη τελευτῆσαι τὸν βίον, οὗτοι δὲ
πάλιν ἐξ ὑπαρχῆς λαγχάνουσί μοι τὰς δίκας, καὶ
ἐγὼ τούτῳ, προσκαλεσάμενος αὐτὸν καὶ ἐπιγραψά-
μενος ἐπὶ τὸ ἔγκλημα Βοιωτόν· τοῦτο γὰρ αὐτῷ ὁ
17 πατὴρ ἔθετο τοὔνομα. περὶ μὲν οὖν ὧν οὗτοί μοι
ἐδικάζοντο, παρόντος τούτου καὶ ἀντιδικοῦντος καὶ
οὐκ ἔχοντος ἐπιδεῖξαι οὐδὲν ὧν ἐνεκάλουν, ἀπεδιήτησέ μου ὁ διαιτητής· καὶ οὗτος συνειδὼς αὑτῷ
ἀδίκως ἐγκαλοῦντι οὔτε ἐφῆκεν εἰς τὸ δικαστήριον,
οὔτε νῦν περὶ ἐκείνων εἴληχέ μοι δίκην οὐδεμίαν,
ἀλλὰ περὶ ἄλλων τινῶν, λύσειν τοῖς ἐγκλήμασι τούτοις τὴν δίκην ταύτην οἰόμενος. ἣν δ' ἐγὼ τοῦτον
ἐδίωκον τότε περὶ τῆς προικός, ἐπιδημοῦντος τούτου ἐνθάδε καὶ οὐκ ἀπαντήσαντος πρὸς τὸν δι-
18 αιτητήν, ἐρήμην κατεδιήτησεν αὐτοῦ. οὗτος δ', ὦ
ἄνδρες δικασταί, οὔτε ἠντεδίκει τότε παρὼν οὔτ'
ἔφη με καταδιαιτήσασθαι τὴν δίκην αὐτοῦ· οὐ γὰρ
εἶναι Βοιωτὸν αὐτῷ ὄνομα, ἀλλὰ Μαντίθεον, καὶ
οὕτως ὀνόματι ἀμφισβητῶν ἔργῳ τὴν προῖκά με
τῆς μητρὸς ἀποστερεῖ. ἀπορῶν δ' ἐγὼ τί ἄν τις

---

[a] Erchia was a deme of the tribe Aegeïs.
[b] Boeotus evidently hoped that making claims on his own
behalf he could offset the claim of Mantitheus for the dowry
of his mother.

492

THE DEPOSITIONS

After this these men brought action against me to **16** establish their claims, and I sued them for the marriage-portion. At the first we had Solon, of Erchia,[a] registered as arbitrator, and submitted to him for decision the claims we advanced against each other. These men, however, did not appear, but avoided the hearing; and thus considerable time was wasted, and it came about that Solon died. These men then instituted their suit against me afresh, and I my suit against the defendant, summoning him under the name of Boeotus, and inscribing that name on the complaint; for that was the name my father gave him. In the suit which these men brought against **17** me, Boeotus appeared and fought the case, but, since he was unable to establish any of their claims, the arbitrator decided in my favour; and Boeotus, conscious that he was making charges without any just basis, did not appeal to a jury, and has not now entered any suit against me in regard to these matters, but in regard to some others, thinking to break down this suit of mine by these counter-charges.[b] In the suit which at that time I was carrying on against Boeotus in regard to the marriage-portion, since he was here in Athens and did not appear before the arbitrator, the latter gave judgement against him by default. And Boeotus, men of **18** the jury, though he was here at the time would not contest the suit, but declared that I had not received the arbitrator's verdict against *him*, for his name was not Boeotus, but Mantitheus; and thus, by quibbling about a name, he is in fact depriving me of my mother's portion. As I was at a loss to know how

493

χρήσαιτο τῷ πράγματι, οὕτω πάλιν τὴν αὐτὴν
δίκην λαχὼν αὐτῷ Μαντιθέῳ ἐνδεκάτῳ ἔτει νῦν εἰς
ὑμᾶς καταπέφευγα.

[1014] Ὡς δὲ καὶ ταῦτ᾽ ἀληθῆ λέγω, ἀναγνώσεται τὰς
περὶ τούτων μαρτυρίας.

ΜΑΡΤΥΡΙΑΙ

19 Ὅτι μὲν τοίνυν, ὦ ἄνδρες δικασταί, ἥ τε μήτηρ
μου τάλαντον ἐπενεγκαμένη προῖκα, ἐκδοθεῖσα ὑπὸ
τῶν ἀδελφῶν τῶν αὐτῆς, ὥσπερ οἱ νόμοι κελεύουσι,
συνῴκησε τῷ πατρί, καὶ ὃν τρόπον ἐγὼ τούτους
εἰσεδεξάμην εἰς τὴν οἰκίαν τοῦ πατρὸς τελευτήσαντος, καὶ ὅτι ἀπέφυγον αὐτοὺς τὰς δίκας ἅς μοι
ἐνεκάλουν, ταῦτα μὲν πάντα καὶ μεμαρτύρηται ὑμῖν
καὶ ἐπιδέδεικται.

Ἴθι δὴ λαβὲ καὶ τὸν περὶ τῆς προικὸς νόμον
τουτονί.

ΝΟΜΟΣ

20 Οὕτω τοίνυν τοῦ νόμου ἔχοντος, οἶμαι τουτονὶ
Βοιωτὸν ἢ Μαντίθεον, ἢ ὅ τι ποτ᾽ ἄλλο χαίρει
προσαγορευόμενος, δικαίαν μὲν ἀπολογίαν καὶ
ἀληθινὴν οὐδεμίαν ἕξειν εἰπεῖν, ἐπιχειρήσειν δὲ τῇ
τόλμῃ καὶ τῇ θρασύτητι τῇ ἑαυτοῦ πιστεύοντα
περιιστάναι τὰς αὑτῶν συμφορὰς εἰς ἐμέ, ἅπερ
καὶ ἰδίᾳ ποιεῖν εἴωθε, λέγων ὡς δημευθείσης τῆς
Παμφίλου οὐσίας, ὃς ἦν πατὴρ τῆς Πλαγγόνος, τὰ
περιγενόμενα χρήματα ὁ πατὴρ ὁ ἐμὸς ἔλαβεν ἐκ
τοῦ βουλευτηρίου, καὶ οὕτως ἀποφαίνειν πειρώμενος τὴν μὲν αὑτοῦ μητέρα ἐπενεγκαμένην προῖκα

---

[a] The Bouleuterion, the meeting-place of the Council of
500, has been identified with a building found on the east

494

one should deal with a matter like this, I instituted the same suit afresh against him as Mantitheus, and now in the eleventh year I have come to you for help.

To prove that I am speaking the truth in this also, the clerk will read the depositions dealing with these matters.

THE DEPOSITIONS

That my mother, therefore, men of the jury, bring- 19 ing a talent as her dowry, and given in marriage by her brothers, as the laws command, lived with my father as his wife ; the manner, too, in which I received these men into the house after my father's death ; and the fact that I obtained a verdict in the suits which they brought against me ;—all this has been established for you by proofs and by testimony.

Come now, take also this law concerning the marriage-portion.

THE LAW

Such being the law, I fancy that this man—call him 20 Boeotus or Mantitheus, or any other name by which he likes to be addressed—will have no valid or genuine defence to offer, but, relying upon his own audaciousness and effrontery, will endeavour to attach to me the misfortunes of his own family, as he is wont to do also in private life ; and will allege that when the property of Pamphilus, who was the father of Plangon, was confiscated, my father took from out the council-chamber [a] the surplus proceeds [b] ; and he will thus try to show that his own mother brought a dowry of

slope of the " Theseum " hill, overlooking the Agora. See Vanderpool, *Hesperia*, iv. pp. 470 ff.

[b] The amount, that is, over and above the debt to the treasury.

πλεῖν ἢ ἑκατὸν μνᾶς, τὴν δ' ἐμὴν ἄπροικον φάσκων
21 συνοικῆσαι. ταῦτα διέξεισιν, ὦ ἄνδρες δικασταί,
οὔτε μαρτυρίαν οὐδεμίαν ἐμβεβλημένος ὑπὲρ τούτων, οὔτ' ἀγνοῶν ὡς οὐδὲν ὑγιὲς λέγει, ἀλλ' ἀκριβῶς εἰδώς, ὅτι ὁμολογῶν μὲν ἀδικεῖν ἐν ὑμῖν οὐδείς
[1015] πω ἀπέφυγε, ψευδόμενος δὲ καὶ παραγωγὰς λέγων
ἤδη τις δίκην οὐκ ἔδωκεν. ἵν' οὖν μὴ ἐξαπατηθῆτε
ὑπ' αὐτοῦ, βέλτιον εἶναί μοι δοκεῖ βραχέα καὶ περὶ
22 τούτου πρὸς ὑμᾶς εἰπεῖν. ἐὰν γὰρ λέγῃ ὡς ἡ μὲν
ἐμὴ μήτηρ οὐκ ἐπηνέγκατο προῖκα, ἡ δὲ τούτων
ἐπηνέγκατο, ἐνθυμεῖσθ' ὅτι περιφανῶς ψεύδεται.
πρῶτον μὲν γὰρ Πάμφιλος ὁ πατὴρ τῆς τούτου
μητρὸς πέντε τάλαντα τῷ δημοσίῳ ὀφείλων ἐτελεύτησε, καὶ τοσούτου ἐδέησε περιγενέσθαι τι τοῖς
ἐκείνου παισὶ τῆς οὐσίας ἀπογραφείσης καὶ δημευθείσης, ὥστ' οὐδὲ τὸ ὄφλημα πᾶν ὑπὲρ αὐτοῦ
ἐκτέτεισται, ἀλλ' ἔτι καὶ νῦν ὁ Πάμφιλος ὀφείλων
τῷ δημοσίῳ ἐγγέγραπται. πῶς οὖν οἷόν τε τὸν
ἐμὸν πατέρα χρήματα λαβεῖν ἐκ τῆς Παμφίλου
οὐσίας, ἢ οὐδ' αὐτὸ τὸ ὄφλημα τῇ πόλει ἱκανὴ
23 ἐγένετο ἐκτεῖσαι; ἔπειτ', ὦ ἄνδρες δικασταί,
ἐνθυμεῖσθ' ὅτι, εἰ τὰ μάλιστα περιεγένετο τὰ
χρήματα ταῦτα, ὥσπερ οὗτοί φασιν, οὐκ ἂν ὁ ἐμὸς
πατὴρ αὐτὰ ἔλαβεν, ἀλλ' οἱ τοῦ Παμφίλου υἱεῖς
Βοιωτὸς καὶ Ἡδύλος καὶ Εὐθύδημος, οἳ οὐκ ἂν
δήπου ἐπὶ μὲν τῷ τἀλλότρια λαμβάνειν ὁτιανοῦν
ἐποίουν, ὡς καὶ ὑμεῖς ἅπαντες ἴστε, τὰ δ' αὑτῶν
τὸν ἐμὸν πατέρα περιεῖδον κομισάμενον.

more than one hundred minae, while my mother (he
will claim) brought my father no portion whatever.
These things he will state at length to you, men of 21
the jury, although he has not put a single deposition
in the box to substantiate them, and knows very well
that there is not a word of truth in what he says ;
for he is fully conscious that in your court no man
who confessed his guilt was ever acquitted, whereas
by lying and advancing arguments to lead you astray
many a man ere now has avoided paying the penalty
for his deeds. In order, then, that you may not be
deceived by him, I think it is better to speak to you
briefly about this matter also. For if he shall say 22
that my mother did not bring with her a marriage-
portion, while their mother did, bear in mind that
he is manifestly lying. To begin with, Pamphilus,
the father of this man's mother, died owing five
talents to the public treasury, and so far from there
being any surplus proceeds for his children after his
property had been scheduled and confiscated, even
his indebtedness has not been paid in full, but to
this day Pamphilus stands inscribed as a debtor to
the treasury. How, then, can it be that my father
received money from the estate of Pamphilus, which
proved inadequate to pay in full even the debt due to
the city ? Furthermore, men of the jury, bear this 23
in mind, that were it never so true that this surplus
money did accrue as these men pretend, it was not
my father who would have received it, but the sons of
Pamphilus, Boeotus and Hedylus and Euthydemus ;
and, I fancy, they are not men who would go to all
lengths to get hold of the property of others, as you all
know, and yet at the same time quietly have allowed
my father to take possession of what was theirs.

24 Ὅτι μὲν τοίνυν ἥ γε τούτων μήτηρ οὐκ ἐπηνέγκατο
προῖκα, ἀλλ' οὗτοι τοῦτο ψεύδονται, ἱκανῶς ὑμᾶς
μεμαθηκέναι νομίζω· ὅτι δ' ἡ ἐμὴ μήτηρ ἐπηνέγκατο,
ῥᾳδίως ἐγὼ δείξω. πρῶτον μὲν γὰρ Πολυαράτου
θυγάτηρ ἦν, ὃς καὶ ὑφ' ὑμῶν ἐτιμᾶτο καὶ πολλὴν
οὐσίαν ἐκέκτητο· ἔπειτα μεμαρτύρηται ὑμῖν, ὡς καὶ
[1016] ἡ ἀδελφὴ αὐτῆς τοσαύτην προῖκα ἐπενεγκαμένη
25 Ἐρυξιμάχῳ συνῴκησε, τῷ Χαβρίου κηδεστῇ. πρὸς
δὲ τούτοις φαίνεταί μου ἡ μήτηρ τὸ πρῶτον ἐκδοθεῖσα Κλεομέδοντι, οὗ φασι τὸν πατέρα Κλέωνα
τῶν ὑμετέρων προγόνων στρατηγοῦντα, Λακεδαι-
μονίων πολλοὺς ἐν Πύλῳ ζῶντας λαβόντα, μάλιστα
πάντων ἐν τῇ πόλει εὐδοκιμῆσαι· ὥστ' οὔτε τὸν
ἐκείνου προσῆκεν υἱὸν ἄπροικον αὐτὴν γῆμαι, οὔτε
Μενέξενον καὶ Βάθυλλον εἰκός ἐστιν, αὐτούς τε
οὐσίαν πολλὴν κεκτημένους καὶ Κλεομέδοντος
τελευτήσαντος κομισαμένους τὴν προῖκα, ἀποστερῆσαι τὴν ἀδελφὴν τὴν ἑαυτῶν, ἀλλὰ προσθέντας
αὐτοὺς ἐκδοῦναι τῷ ἡμετέρῳ πατρί, καθάπερ καὶ
αὐτοὶ πρὸς ὑμᾶς καὶ οἱ ἄλλοι μεμαρτυρήκασιν.
26 χωρὶς δὲ τούτων ἐνθυμήθητε, διὰ τί ἄν ποτε ὁ
πατήρ, εἴπερ ἡ μὲν ἐμὴ μήτηρ μὴ ἦν ἐγγυητὴ μηδ'
ἠνέγκατο προῖκα, ἡ δὲ τούτων ἠνέγκατο, τοὺς μὲν
οὐκ ἔφη αὑτοῦ υἱεῖς εἶναι, ἐμὲ δὲ καὶ ἐποιεῖτο καὶ
ἐπαίδευεν; ὅτι νὴ Δί', ὡς οὗτοι φήσουσιν, ἐμοὶ
χαριζόμενος καὶ τῇ ἐμῇ μητρὶ τούτους ἠτίμαζεν.

---

a The famous Athenian general, whose victories over the
Lacedaemonians made him one of the most notable figures in
Athenian military history during the first half of the fourth
century B.C.

b A striking instance of the Greek preference for the
spoken rather than the written word.

That the mother of these men did not bring with 24
her a marriage-portion, but that they are lying in
regard to this, I think has been proved to you quite
adequately ; but that my mother did bring one, I
shall easily show. In the first place, she was the
daughter of Polyaratus, who was both honoured by
you citizens, and had acquired a large estate.
Secondly, it has been proved to you by witnesses
that her sister brought a dowry of the like amount
when she married Eryximachus, the brother-in-law
of Chabrias.[a] Besides all this, my mother is shown 25
to have been first given in marriage to Cleomedon,
whose father Cleon, we are told,[b] commanded troops
among whom were your ancestors, and captured alive
a large number of Lacedemonians in Pylos,[c] and won
greater renown than any other man in the state ; so it
was not fitting that the son of that famous man should
wed my mother without a dowry, nor is it likely that
Menexenus and Bathyllus, who had large fortunes
themselves, and who, after Cleomedon's death, received back the dowry, defrauded their own sister ;
rather, they would themselves have added to her
portion, when they gave her in marriage to my
father, as they themselves and the others have testified before you. And besides this, just consider why 26
in the world, if my mother had not been a lawfully
espoused wife, and had brought no dowry, while the
mother of these men did, should my father have
denied that they were his sons, and have acknowledged me, and brought me up ? Because, forsooth,
as these men will claim, he dishonoured them in order
to show favour to me and my mother ! But my mother 27

[c] This was in 425 B.C. The account is given in Thucydides,
iv. 3 ff.

27 ἀλλ' ἐκείνη μὲν ἔτι παῖδα μικρὸν ἐμὲ καταλιποῦσα
αὐτὴ τὸν βίον ἐτελεύτησεν, ἡ δὲ τούτων μήτηρ
Πλαγγὼν καὶ πρότερον καὶ μετὰ ταῦτα εὐπρεπὴς
τὴν ὄψιν οὖσα ἐπλησίαζεν αὐτῷ· ὥστε πολὺ μᾶλλον
εἰκὸς ἦν αὐτὸν διὰ τὴν ζῶσαν γυναῖκα, ἧς ἐρῶν
ἐτύγχανε, τὸν τῆς τεθνεώσης υἱὸν ἀτιμάζειν, ἢ δι'
ἐμὲ καὶ τὴν τετελευτηκυῖαν τοὺς ἐκ τῆς ζώσης καὶ
28 πλησιαζούσης αὐτῷ παῖδας μὴ ποιεῖσθαι. καίτοι
οὗτός γ' εἰς τοῦτο τόλμης ἥκει, ὥστε φησὶ τὸν
[1017] πατέρα μου δεκάτην ὑπὲρ αὐτοῦ ἑστιᾶσαι. καὶ
περὶ τούτου μόνον Τιμοκράτους καὶ Προμάχου
ἐμβέβληται μαρτυρίας, οἳ οὔτε γένει προσήκουσί
μου τῷ πατρὶ οὐδέν, οὔτε φίλοι ἦσαν ἐκείνῳ. οὕτω
δὲ φανερῶς τὰ ψευδῆ μεμαρτυρήκασιν, ὥστε ὃν
πάντων ὑμῶν εἰδότων οὗτος δίκην λαχὼν ἄκοντα
ἠνάγκασε ποιήσασθαι αὐτόν, τοῦτον οὗτοι, ὥσπερ
κλητῆρες, δύο μόνοι ὄντες μαρτυροῦσι δεκάτην ὑπὲρ
29 τούτου ἑστιᾶσαι. οἷς τίς ἂν ὑμῶν πιστεύσειεν;
καὶ μὴν οὐδ' ἐκείνό γε εἰπεῖν αὐτῷ ἐνδέχεται,
ὡς μικρὸν μὲν ὄντα ἐποιεῖτο αὐτὸν ὁ πατήρ, μείζω
δὲ γενόμενον τῇ μητρὶ ὀργισθείς τι τῇ τούτων
ἠτίμαζε· πολὺ γὰρ δήπου μᾶλλον εἰώθασιν, ὧν
ἂν αὐτοῖς διενεχθῶσι γυνὴ καὶ ἀνήρ, διαλλάττε-
σθαι διὰ τοὺς παῖδας ἢ διὰ τὰς πρὸς ἑαυτοὺς ὀργὰς
τοὺς κοινοὺς παῖδας πρὸς μισεῖν. ὥστ' ἐὰν μὲν
ἐπιχειρῇ ταῦτα λέγειν, μὴ ἐπιτρέπετε ἀναισχυντεῖν

---

* See the Introduction to the preceding oration, p. 444.
ᵇ Perhaps to be identified with the Timocrates against
whom Demosthenes delivered Oration XXIV.

died, leaving me still a little boy, whereas the mother of these men, Plangon, who was a handsome woman, maintained her connexion with him both before and after that ; so that it was much more likely that for the sake of the living woman, with whom he was in love all this time, he would dishonour the son of her who was dead, than that for my sake and my dead mother's he would refuse to acknowledge the children of her who was living and maintaining her connexion with him. My opponent, however, has come to such 28 a pitch of audacity as to declare that my father made a feast for him on the tenth day.[a] And in regard to this he has put in depositions of Timocrates [b] and Promachus alone, who are in no way related to my father, and were not friends of his. The testimony they have borne is so patently false, that, whereas you all know that Boeotus by instituting proceedings forced my father against his will to acknowledge him these men, like witnesses to a summons—and only two of them—depose that he made a feast for this fellow on the tenth day ! Is there anyone of you 29 who can believe that ? And assuredly it is not open to him to say this, either—that when he was a little child my father acknowledged him, but that when he was grown he scorned him because of some quarrel with the mother of these men ; [c] for surely man and wife are much more apt, in cases where they are at variance with one another, to become reconciled for the sake of their children than, because of their enmity toward each other, to hate their common children as well. If, therefore, he attempts to say this, do not permit him to brazen it out. And should he go on to talk 30

[c] Compare the parallel passage in the preceding oration, § 23.

30 ἂν δὲ λέγῃ περὶ τῶν δικῶν ἃς ἀπεδιήτησέ μου ὁ
διαιτητής, καὶ φάσκῃ ὑπ᾽ ἐμοῦ ἀπαράσκευος
ληφθῆναι, πρῶτον μὲν μέμνησθε ὅτι οὐκ ὀλίγος
χρόνος ἐγένετο, ἐν ᾧ ἔδει παρασκευάσασθαι αὐτόν,
ἀλλ᾽ ἔτη πολλά, ἔπειθ᾽ ὅτι οὗτος ἦν ὁ διώκων,
ὥστε πολὺ μᾶλλον ἦν εἰκός[1] ἐμὲ ὑπὸ τούτου
31 ἀπαράσκευον ληφθῆναι, ἢ τοῦτον ὑπ᾽ ἐμοῦ. ἔτι
δὲ πάντες ὑμῖν οἱ πρὸς τῷ διαιτητῇ παρόντες
μεμαρτυρήκασιν, ὡς οὗτος παρών, ὅτε ἀπεδιήτησέ
μου ὁ διαιτητής, οὔτε ἐφῆκεν εἰς τὸ δικαστήριον
ἐνέμεινέ τε τῇ διαίτῃ. καίτοι ἄτοπον δοκεῖ μοι
εἶναι, εἰ οἱ μὲν ἄλλοι, ὅταν οἴωνται ἀδικεῖσθαι, καὶ
τὰς πάνυ μικρὰς δίκας εἰς ὑμᾶς ἐφιᾶσιν, οὗτος δέ
μοι περὶ προικὸς δίκην ταλάντου λαχών, ταύτης,
ὡς αὐτός φησιν, ἀδίκως ἀποδιαιτηθείσης ἐνέμεινεν.
32 νὴ Δί᾽, ἀπράγμων γὰρ ἴσως ἐστὶν ἄνθρωπος καὶ οὐ
[1018] φιλόδικος. ἐβουλόμην μεντἄν, ὦ ἄνδρες δικασταί,
τοιοῦτον αὐτὸν εἶναι. νυνὶ δ᾽ ὑμεῖς μὲν οὕτως ἐστὲ
κοινοὶ καὶ φιλάνθρωποι, ὥστ᾽ οὐδὲ τοὺς τῶν τριάκοντα υἱεῖς φυγαδεῦσαι ἐκ τῆς πόλεως ἠξιώσατε·
οὗτος δ᾽ ἐμοὶ μετὰ Μενεκλέους τοῦ πάντων τούτων
ἀρχιτέκτονος ἐπιβουλεύσας, καὶ ἐξ ἀντιλογίας καὶ
λοιδορίας πληγὰς συναψάμενος, ἐπιτεμὼν τὴν
κεφαλὴν αὐτοῦ τραύματος εἰς Ἄρειον πάγον με
προσεκαλέσατο, ὡς φυγαδεύσων ἐκ τῆς πόλεως.
33 καὶ εἰ μὴ Εὐθύδικος ὁ ἰατρός, πρὸς ὃν οὗτοι τὸ

---

[1] πολὺ . . . εἰκός] πολὺ ἦν ἂν μᾶλλον εἰκὸς Blass.

about the actions brought by them, which the arbitrator decided in my favour, and claim that he was caught by me unprepared, remember, first, that it was not a short time that he had in which to prepare himself, but a great many years, and secondly, that it was he who brought the suit, so that it was much more likely that I should be taken unprepared by him than he by me. And further, all those who were present 31 before the arbitrator have given testimony that Boeotus was present when the arbitrator gave his decision in my favour and that he did not appeal to the court, but acquiesced in the decision. And yet it seems to me a strange thing that, whereas other men, who consider that they are being wronged,[a] bring before you on appeal cases even of the slightest import, this fellow, who had brought suit against me to recover a talent as the marriage-portion, and had this suit decided against him by the arbitrator, unjustly, as he claims, should acquiesce in the decision. Ah, but it may be said that he is a man who loves 32 peace and hates litigation. I could indeed wish, men of the jury, that he were a man of that type. But here is the truth : you are so generous and so kind toward your fellow-men that you did not deem it right to banish from the city even the sons of the Thirty Tyrants[b] ; but Boeotus, plotting against me with Menecles, who is the prime mover in all these schemes, having managed to get up a quarrel that from disputes and revilings should come to blows, cut his own head, and summoned me before the Areopagus on a charge of murderous assault, with the intention of driving me into exile from the city. And if Euthydicus, the physician,—to whom these 33

---

[a] That is, by the arbitrator's award.   [b] In 403 B.C.

πρῶτον ἦλθον δεόμενοι ἐπιτεμεῖν τὴν κεφαλὴν
αὐτοῦ, πρὸς τὴν ἐξ Ἀρείου πάγου βουλὴν εἶπε τὴν
ἀλήθειαν πᾶσαν, τοιαύτην ἂν δίκην οὗτος εἰλήφει
παρ' ἐμοῦ οὐδὲν ἀδικοῦντος, ἣν ὑμεῖς οὐδὲ κατὰ
τῶν τὰ μέγιστ' ἀδικούντων ὑμᾶς ἐπιχειρήσαιτ' ἂν
ποιήσασθαι.

Ἵνα δὲ μὴ δοκῶ διαβάλλειν αὐτόν, ἀνάγνωθί
μοι τὰς μαρτυρίας.

ΜΑΡΤΥΡΙΑΙ

34 Τοῦτον μὲν τοίνυν οὕτω μέγαν καὶ φοβερὸν
ἀγῶνά μοι οὐχ ὡς εὐήθης ὤν, ἀλλ' ὡς ἐπίβουλος
καὶ κακοῦργος κατεσκεύασεν. μετὰ δὲ ταῦτα ἀντὶ
τοῦ ὀνόματος οὗ ἔθετο αὐτῷ ὁ πατὴρ Βοιωτόν,
ὥσπερ καὶ πρὸς ὑμᾶς μεμαρτύρηται, ἐπειδὴ ἐκεῖνος
ἐτελεύτησε, Μαντίθεον ἑαυτὸν ἐγγράψας εἰς τοὺς
δημότας, καὶ τοῦ αὐτοῦ ἐμοὶ καὶ πατρὸς καὶ δήμου
προσαγορευόμενος, οὐ μόνον τὴν δίκην ταύτην,
περὶ ἧς νυνὶ δικάζομαι, ἀνάδικον ἐποίησεν, ἀλλὰ
καὶ χειροτονησάντων ὑμῶν ἐμὲ ταξίαρχον, ἧκεν
αὐτὸς ἐπὶ τὸ δικαστήριον δοκιμασθησόμενος, δίκην
[1019] τε ἐξούλης ὠφληκώς, ταύτην οὐκ αὐτὸς ὠφληκέναι
35 φησίν, ἀλλ' ἐμέ. ὡς δ' ἐν κεφαλαίῳ εἰπεῖν, κακά
μοι παρέχων ἠνάγκασέ με λαχεῖν αὐτῷ δίκην περὶ
τοῦ ὀνόματος, οὐχ ἵνα χρήματα παρ' αὐτοῦ λάβω,
ὦ ἄνδρες δικασταί, ἀλλ' ἵν', ἐὰν ὑμῖν δοκῶ δεινὰ
πάσχειν καὶ βλάπτεσθαι μεγάλα, οὗτος καλῆται
Βοιωτός, ὥσπερ ὁ πατὴρ αὐτῷ ἔθετο.

ᵃ By claiming that his name was Mantitheus, not Boeotus,
he made of no effect the judgement rendered against him
under the latter name.

men had gone in the first instance, asking him to
make a cut on the head of Boeotus—had not told to
the court of the Areopagus the whole truth, this man
would have taken such vengeance upon me, who
was guilty of no wrong toward him, as you would
not try to inflict on those who were guilty of the
greatest wrongs toward you.

That I may not be thought to be slandering him,
read, please, the depositions.

The Depositions

This great and formidable contest, then, he got up 34
against me, not as a simple-minded fellow, but as
a conspirator and a villain.   But after this, instead of
the name, Boeotus, which my father had given him,
as has been proved to you by witnesses, after my
father's death he had his name inscribed on the list
of the demesmen as Mantitheus, and being further
addressed by the name of the same father and the
same deme as I myself, he not only forced a retrial
of the case in which I am now suing him,[a] but when
you had elected me taxiarch, he came in person to
the court to pass the probationary test[b] ; and when
judgement had been given against him in an ejectment suit, he declared that it was not against him
but against me that the judgement had been given.
And to sum up the matter for you, he gave me so 35
much trouble that he compelled me to bring suit
against him regarding the name, not in order to get
money from him, men of the jury, but that, if it
should appear to you that I am being outrageously
treated and am suffering grievous wrongs, he may go
on being called Boeotus, as my father named him.

[b] Every Athenian elected to public office had to pass a
scrutiny (δοκιμασία) and prove his full citizenship.

"Ότι τοίνυν ἀληθῆ καὶ ταῦτα λέγω, λαβέ μοι καὶ τὰς περὶ τούτων μαρτυρίας.

36 Πρὸς τούτοις τοίνυν καὶ ὅτι ἐγὼ στρατευόμενος καὶ μετὰ Ἀμεινίου ξενολογήσας, ἄλλοθέν τε χρήματα εὐπορήσας, καὶ ἐκ Μυτιλήνης παρὰ τοῦ ὑμετέρου προξένου Ἀπολλωνίδου καὶ παρὰ τῶν φίλων τῆς πόλεως λαβὼν τριακοσίους στατῆρας Φωκαιᾶς, ἀνήλωσα εἰς τοὺς στρατιώτας, ἵνα πρᾶξίς τις πραχθείη καὶ ὑμῖν καὶ ἐκείνοις συμφέρουσα, 37 περὶ τούτων μοι δικάζεται ὡς πατρικὸν κεκομισμένῳ χρέως παρὰ τῆς πόλεως τῆς Μυτιληναίων, Καμμῦ τῷ τυραννοῦντι Μυτιλήνης ὑπηρετῶν, ὃς καὶ ὑμῖν κοινῇ καὶ ἐμοὶ ἰδίᾳ ἐχθρός ἐστιν.

"Ότι δ' ὁ πατὴρ ἡμῶν, ἣν ἐψηφίσαντο αὐτῷ δωρειὰν οἱ Μυτιληναῖοι, εὐθὺς αὐτὸς ἐκομίσατο, καὶ ὡς οὐδὲν ὠφείλετο αὐτῷ χρέως ἐν Μυτιλήνῃ, τῶν ὑμετέρων φίλων παρέξομαι μαρτυρίαν.

38 "Εχων τοίνυν, ὦ ἄνδρες δικασταί, καὶ ἄλλα πολλὰ καὶ δεινὰ λέγειν, ἃ οὗτος καὶ εἰς ἐμὲ καὶ εἰς ὑμῶν ἐνίους ἡμάρτηκεν, ἀναγκάζομαι διὰ τὸ ὀλίγον εἶναί 1020] μοι τὸ ὕδωρ παραλιπεῖν. νομίζω δὲ καὶ ἐκ τούτων

---

[a] Apparently an otherwise unknown commander of mercenary troops, under whom Mantitheus served as taxiarch.

[b] A state representative in a foreign land, somewhat analogous to our consul.

[c] The stater of Phocaea (a city on the coast of Ionia) was

To prove that I am speaking the truth in this also, take, please, the depositions bearing on these matters.

THE DEPOSITIONS

In addition to all this, on the charge that, when I 36 was on military service and had collected mercenaries with Ameinias [a] (seeing that I was well-provided with funds from other sources, and had collected from Mytilene from your proxenus [b] Apollonides and the friends of our city three hundred Phocaic staters,[c] and had spent that sum upon these troops, in order that a matter might be prosecuted which was of advantage to you and to them alike)—for this he 37 brings suit against me, alleging that I had collected a debt due to my father from the city of the Mytileneans. In this he was seeking to serve Cammys,[d] tyrant of Mytilene, who is an enemy of Athens and a private enemy of mine.

But to prove that my father at the time received in person the reward which the people of Mytilene voted him, and that no debt was owing to him in Mytilene, I will produce a deposition of your friends.

THE DEPOSITION

I could mention many other outrageous acts of 38 which Boeotus has been guilty, men of the jury, both against myself and against you ; but I am compelled to pass them by as but little water is left me in the clepsydra.[e] I think, however, that, even as it is, you

a gold coin somewhat heavier than the stater of Cyzicus (Oration XXXIV. § 23).

[d] A tyrant of Mytilene, otherwise unknown.

[e] The water-clock.

ὑμῖν ἱκανῶς ἐπιδεδεῖχθαι, ὡς οὐ τοῦ αὐτοῦ
ἀνθρώπου ἐστίν, ἀγῶνα μέν μοι περὶ φυγῆς κατα-
σκευάζειν καὶ δίκας οὐδὲν προσηκούσας δικάζεσθαι,
πρὸς δὲ τὸν διαιτητὴν ἀπαντᾶν ἀπαράσκευον. ὥστε
περὶ μὲν τούτων ἂν ἐπιχειρῇ λέγειν, οὐκ οἶμαι ὑμᾶς
39 ἀποδέξεσθαι. ἂν δὲ λέγῃ ὡς ἀξιοῦντος αὐτοῦ
ἐπιτρέψαι Κόνωνι τῷ Τιμοθέου περὶ ἁπάντων, ἐγὼ
οὐκ ἐβουλόμην ἐπιτρέπειν, ἐνθυμεῖσθε ὡς[1] ἐξαπατᾶν
ὑμᾶς ἐπιχειρήσει. ἐγὼ γὰρ περὶ μὲν ὧν αἱ δίκαι
οὔπω τέλος εἶχον, ἕτοιμος ἦν ἐπιτρέπειν καὶ Κόνωνι καὶ ἄλλῳ διαιτητῇ ἴσῳ, ὅτῳ οὗτος βούλοιτο·
περὶ δὲ ὧν τρὶς πρὸς τὸν διαιτητὴν ἀπαντήσαντος
τούτου καὶ ἀντιδικοῦντος, ὁ μὲν διαιτητὴς ἀπέγνω
μου, οὗτος δὲ τοῖς γνωσθεῖσιν ἐνέμεινεν, ὡς καὶ
ὑμῖν μεμαρτύρηται, οὐκ ᾤμην δίκαιον εἶναι ταῦτα
40 πάλιν ἀνάδικα γίγνεσθαι· τί γὰρ ἂν ἦν πέρας ἡμῖν
τοῦ διαλυθῆναι, εἰ τὰ κατὰ τοὺς νόμους διαιτηθέντα
λύσας, ἑτέρῳ διαιτητῇ ἐπέτρεψα περὶ τῶν αὐτῶν
ἐγκλημάτων; ἄλλως τε καὶ ἀκριβῶς εἰδὼς ὅτι, εἰ
καὶ πρὸς τοὺς ἄλλους μὴ ἐπιεικές ἐστι ταῖς διαίταις
ἰσχυρίζεσθαι, πρός γε τοῦτον ἁπάντων δικαιότατον
41 ἦν οὕτως προσφέρεσθαι. φέρε γάρ, εἴ τις αὐτὸν
ξενίας γράψαιτο, λέγων ὡς διομνύμενος ὁ πατὴρ
οὐκ ἔφη τοῦτον υἱὸν αὐτοῦ εἶναι, ἔσθ' ὅτῳ ἂν ἄλλῳ
ἰσχυρίζοιτο πρὸς ταῦτα, ἢ διότι τῆς μητρὸς αὐτῶν
ὀμοσάσης καὶ τοῦ διαιτητοῦ γνό⸱τος ἠναγκάσθη ὁ
42 πατὴρ ἡμῶν ἐμμεῖναι τῇ διαίτῃ; οὐκοῦν δεινόν, εἰ

---

[1] ὡς: ᾗ Blass.

[a] The grandson of the famous Athenian general of this
name.

have been shown conclusively that the same man who
got up against me a suit involving the risk of banishment, and sued me on charges which concerned me
not at all, is not one who would have come before the
arbitrator unprepared ; so that if he tries to say
anything about this, I imagine that you will not
tolerate it. If, however, he declares that he offered **39**
to turn over all matters at issue between us to
Conon,[a] son of Timotheus, for arbitration, and that I
refused to submit them, be sure that he will be trying
to mislead you. I, for my part, was ready to submit
all matters upon which a decision had not yet been
rendered, either to Conon or to any other impartial
arbitrator whom Boeotus might choose ; but matters
regarding which the arbitrator had given a decision
in my favour, after Boeotus had thrice appeared before
him and contested the case,—a decision in which
Boeotus acquiesced, as witnesses have testified to
you,—these matters, I thought, could not justly be
reopened. For to what final settlement could we ever **40**
have come, if I had made invalid a decision given
by an arbitrator in accordance with the laws, and had
referred the same charge to the decision of another
arbitrator ?—especially as I knew full well that, even
though in relation to other men it is not proper to
insist overmuch on the decisions of arbitrators, yet
it is peculiarly fair to deal thus with Boeotus. For **41**
come, suppose someone should indict him for the
usurpation of the rights of citizenship, declaring that
my father denied on oath that this man was his son ;
could he rely on anything else to meet this charge
than that, because of their mother's oath and the
decision of the arbitrators, my father was forced to
abide by the award ? It would, then, be an out- **42**

DEMOSTHENES

οὗτος αὐτὸς κατὰ γνῶσιν διαιτητοῦ ὑμέτερος πολίτης γεγενημένος καὶ πρὸς ἐμὲ τὴν οὐσίαν νειμά-
[1021] μενος καὶ τυχὼν τῶν μετρίων ἁπάντων, ἃς ἐγὼ
δίκας τοῦτον ἀπέφυγον παρόντα καὶ ἀντιδικοῦντα
καὶ τοῖς γνωσθεῖσιν ἐμμένοντα, ταύτας ἀναδίκους
ἀξιῶν γίγνεσθαι δίκαιόν τι δοκοίη λέγειν ὑμῖν,
ὥσπερ, ὅταν μὲν τούτῳ συμφέρῃ, δέον εἶναι κυρίας
τὰς διαίτας, ὅταν δὲ μὴ συμφέρῃ, προσῆκον τὴν
τούτου γνώμην κυριωτέραν γενέσθαι τῶν κατὰ τοὺς
43 ὑμετέρους νόμους γνωσθέντων. ὃς οὕτως ἐπί-
βουλός ἐστιν, ὥστε καὶ τὴν δίαιταν ταύτην ἐπιτρέπειν με προὐκαλεῖτο, οὐχ ὅπως ἀπαλλαγῇ πρός με,
ἀλλ' ἵν', ὥσπερ καὶ πρότερον ἕνδεκα ἔτη διήγαγε
κακουργῶν, οὕτως καὶ νῦν τὰ ἀποδιαιτηθέντα μου
λύσας ἐξ ἀρχῆς με συκοφαντῇ καὶ τὴν δίκην ταύτην
44 ἐκκρούῃ. τεκμήριον δὲ τούτου μέγιστον· οὔτε γὰρ
τὴν πρόκλησιν ἐδέχετο, ἣν ἐγὼ κατὰ τοὺς νόμους
προὐκαλούμην αὐτόν, πρότερόν τε Ξενίππῳ, ὃν
οὗτος προὐβάλετο διαιτητήν, ἐπιτρέψαντός μου
περὶ τῆς τοῦ ὀνόματος δίκης, ἀπηγόρευεν αὐτῷ μὴ
διαιτᾶν.

Ὅτι δὲ καὶ ταῦτ' ἀληθῆ λέγω, ἐκ τῆς μαρτυρίας
καὶ τῆς προκλήσεως εἴσεσθε.

ΜΑΡΤΥΡΙΑ. ΠΡΟΚΛΗΣΙΣ

45 Ταύτην τοίνυν τὴν πρόκλησιν οὐ δεξάμενος, ἀλλ'
ἐνεδρεύων με καὶ τὴν δίκην ὅτι πλεῖστον χρόνον
ἐκκρούειν βουλόμενος, κατηγορήσει, ὡς ἐγὼ πυνθά-
νομαι, οὐ μόνον ἐμοῦ, ἀλλὰ καὶ τοῦ πατρός, λέγων
ὡς ἐκεῖνος ἐμοὶ χαριζόμενος πολλὰ τοῦτον ἠδίκησεν.

rageous thing, if this man, after having become a
citizen of your city through an arbitrator's decision,
and having secured a share of my inheritance, and
obtained all that was fair, should be thought by you
to have any justice in his claim, when he demanded
the reopening of the suits in which I won my acquittal,
when he was present and argued against it, and
acquiesced in the verdict ; just as though, when it is
to his interest, awards ought to be valid, but, when
it is not to his interest, his opinion should have more
weight than decisions rendered in accordance with
your laws. He is such a crafty schemer that his 43
purpose even in this proposal of arbitration was not
made that he might be rid of his disputes with me,
but that, as he had for eleven years previously
carried on his knavery, so now, by rendering invalid
the decisions given in my favour by the arbitrator,
he might afresh institute his malicious proceedings
against me, and elude the present suit. Here is a 44
convincing proof of this. He would not accept the
challenge which I gave him according to the laws ;
and when I had previously referred the suit about
the name to Xenippus, whom he had proposed as
arbitrator, he forbade him to render any decision.

That I am speaking the truth on these matters
also you will learn from the deposition and the
challenge.

The Deposition. The Challenge

This challenge, then, he did not accept, wishing 45
rather to lay a snare for me and to delay the suit as
long as he possibly could ; and now, as I learn, he will
accuse not only me, but my father as well, alleging
that my father wronged him in many ways in order to

ὑμεῖς δ', ὦ ἄνδρες δικασταί, μάλιστα μέν, ὥσπερ
αὐτοὶ οὐκ ἂν ἀξιώσαιτε κακῶς ἀκούειν ὑπὸ τῶν
ὑμετέρων παίδων, οὕτω μηδὲ τούτῳ ἐπιτρέπετε
46 περὶ τοῦ πατρὸς βλασφημεῖν· καὶ γὰρ ἂν εἴη δεινόν,
[1022] εἰ αὐτοὶ μὲν πρὸς τοὺς ἐπὶ τῆς ὀλιγαρχίας πολλοὺς
τῶν πολιτῶν ἀκρίτους ἀποκτείναντας διαλλαγέντες
ἐμμένετε ταῖς ὁμολογίαις, ὥσπερ χρὴ τοὺς καλοὺς
κἀγαθοὺς ἄνδρας, τούτῳ δὲ πρὸς τὸν πατέρα ζῶντα
καὶ διαλυθέντι καὶ πολλὰ παρὰ τὸ δίκαιον πλεον-
εκτήσαντι, νῦν μνησικακεῖν ἐπιτρέψαιτε καὶ κακῶς
47 ἐκεῖνον λέγειν. μηδαμῶς, ὦ ἄνδρες δικασταί, ἀλλὰ
μάλιστα μὲν κωλύετ' αὐτὸν ταῦτα ποιεῖν, ἂν δ'
ἄρα βιάζηται ὑμᾶς καὶ λοιδορῆται, ἐνθυμεῖσθ' ὅτι
αὐτὸς ἑαυτοῦ καταμαρτυρεῖ μὴ ἐξ ἐκείνου γεγενῆσθαι. οἱ μὲν γὰρ φύσει παῖδες ὄντες, κἂν
πρὸς ζῶντας διενεχθῶσι τοὺς πατέρας, ἀλλ' οὖν
τελευτήσαντάς γε αὐτοὺς ἐπαινοῦσιν· οἱ δὲ
νομιζόμενοι μὲν υἱεῖς, μὴ ὄντες δὲ γένει ἐξ ἐκείνων,
ῥᾳδίως μὲν αὐτοῖς διαφέρονται ζῶσιν, οὐδὲν δὲ
48 φροντίζουσι περὶ τεθνεώτων βλασφημοῦντες. χωρὶς
δὲ τούτων ἐνθυμεῖσθε ὡς ἄτοπόν ἐστιν, εἰ οὗτος
τὸν πατέρα ὡς ἁμαρτόντα εἰς αὐτὸν λοιδορήσει, διὰ
τὰ ἐκείνου ἁμαρτήματα ὑμέτερος πολίτης γεγενημένος. κἀγὼ μὲν διὰ τὴν τούτων μητέρα τὰ δύο
μέρη τῆς οὐσίας ἀφαιρεθείς, ὅμως ὑμᾶς αἰσχύνομαι
49 λέγειν περὶ ἐκείνης τι φλαῦρον· οὗτος δ', ὃν

ᵃ The allusion is to the amnesty declared after the expul-
sion of the Thirty Tyrants. For this "gentleness" of the
democracy see Aristotle, *Constitution of Athens*, 22. 4.
512

show favour to me. But I beg you, men of the jury, as
you would yourselves deem it an unseemly thing to be
evil spoken of by your own children, not to allow this
man either to speak evil of his father. For it would **46**
indeed be an outrageous thing when you yourselves,
after having come to terms with those who in the
time of the oligarchy put to death without trial
numbers of your countrymen, abide by your com-
pact with them,[a] as men of honour should do, that
you should allow this man, who was reconciled with
my father while he lived, and won many advantages
to which he had no right, now to renew the quarrel
and to speak evil of that father when he is no more.
Do not suffer this, men of the jury. If it be possible, **47**
prevent him from acting in this way ; but if he persists in defying you and in speaking evil of my father,
remember that he is bearing witness against himself
that he is no son of his. For those who are true-born
children, even though they may quarrel with their
fathers while they are alive, yet speak well of them
when they are dead ; whereas those who are
accounted sons, but are not in truth children of their
supposed fathers, quarrel with them without scruple
while they are alive, and think nothing of slandering
them when they are dead. And, besides, think how **48**
absurd it is that this fellow should abuse my father
for his failings toward him, when it was thanks to
this father's failings [b] that he became a citizen of
your state. I, on my part, have, thanks to the mother
of these men, been deprived of two-thirds of my
property, but for all that I have too much respect
for you to speak disparagingly of her. But Boeotus **49**

---

[b] " There is a play on the double sense of ἁμαρτάνειν, which
is often used as a euphemism for the frailties of love."—Paley.

ἠνάγκασεν αὐτῷ πατέρα γενέσθαι, τοῦτον οὐκ
αἰσχύνεται ψέγων ἐναντίον ὑμῶν, ἀλλ' εἰς τοῦτ'
ἀμαθίας ἥκει, ὥστε τῶν νόμων ἀπαγορευόντων
μηδὲ τοὺς τῶν ἄλλων πατέρας κακῶς λέγειν τεθνεῶτας, οὗτος, οὗ φησιν υἱὸς εἶναι, τοῦτον λοι-
[1023] δορήσει, ᾧ προσῆκε καὶ εἴ τις ἄλλος ἐβλασφήμει
περὶ αὐτοῦ ἀγανακτεῖν.

50 Οἶμαι δ' αὐτόν, ὦ ἄνδρες δικασταί, ἐπειδὰν τῶν
ἄλλων ἀπορῇ, κακῶς τέ με ἐπιχειρήσειν λέγειν καὶ
διαβάλλειν πειράσεσθαι, διεξιόνθ' ὡς ἐγὼ μὲν καὶ
ἐτράφην καὶ ἐπαιδεύθην καὶ ἔγημα ἐν τῇ τοῦ πατρὸς
οἰκίᾳ, αὐτὸς δ' οὐδενὸς τούτων μετέσχεν. ὑμεῖς δ'
ἐνθυμεῖσθ' ὅτι ἐμὲ μὲν ἡ μήτηρ παῖδα καταλιποῦσα
ἐτελεύτησεν, ὥστε μοι ἱκανὸν ἦν ἀπὸ τοῦ τόκου τῆς
51 προικὸς καὶ τρέφεσθαι καὶ παιδεύεσθαι· ἡ δὲ τούτων
μήτηρ Πλαγγών, τρέφουσα μεθ' αὑτῆς τούτους καὶ
θεραπαίνας συχνὰς καὶ αὐτὴ[1] πολυτελῶς ζῶσα, καὶ
εἰς ταῦτα τὸν πατέρα τὸν ἐμὸν χορηγὸν ἑαυτῇ ὑπὸ
τῆς ἐπιθυμίας ἔχουσα καὶ πολλὰ δαπανᾶν ἀναγκά-
ζουσα, οὐκ ἴσα δήπου τῆς ἐκείνου οὐσίας ἐμοὶ
ἀνήλωκεν, ὥστε πολὺ μᾶλλον προσῆκεν ἐμὲ τούτοις
52 ἐγκαλεῖν, ἢ αὐτὸν ἐγκλήματ' ἔχειν ὑπὸ τούτων. ὃς
πρὸς τοῖς ἄλλοις εἴκοσι μὲν μνᾶς δανεισάμενος μετὰ
τοῦ πατρὸς παρὰ Βλεπαίου τοῦ τραπεζίτου εἰς
ὠνήν τινα μετάλλων, ἐπειδὴ ὁ πατὴρ ἐτελεύτησε,
τὰ μὲν μέταλλα πρὸς τούτους ἐνειμάμην, τὸ δάνειον
δ' αὐτὸς εἰσεπράχθην, ἑτέρας δὲ χιλίας εἰς τὴν τοῦ
πατρὸς ταφὴν παρὰ Λυσιστράτου Θορικίου δανεισάμενος, ἰδίᾳ ἐκτέτεικα.

Ὡς δ' ἀληθῆ καὶ ταῦτα λέγω, ἐκ τούτων τῶν
μαρτυριῶν εἴσεσθε.

---

[1] αὐτὴ omitted by Blass.

feels no shame in disparaging before you the man whom he compelled to become his father, and has even come to such a pitch of vulgarity that, although the laws forbid speaking ill even of other men's fathers after they are dead, he will slander the man whose son he claims to be; whereas it would be proper for him to show resentment if anyone else spoke evil of him.

I fancy, men of the jury, that, when he is at a loss 50 for anything else to say, he will undertake to speak evil of me, and will try to bring me into disrepute, rehearsing at length how I was reared and educated and married in my father's house, while he had no share in any of these advantages. But I bid you bear in mind that my mother died leaving me a child, so that the interest of her marriage-portion was sufficient to rear and educate me; whereas Plangon, the 51 mother of these men, maintained them and a host of female servants in her own house, and herself lived lavishly, having my father ready, because of his passion for her, to supply the funds for all this, and forcing him to heavy expenditures. She therefore spent far more of his property than I did, so that I might with far better reason bring charges against them than they against me. For, besides all the 52 rest, in connexion with my father I borrowed twenty minae from Blepaeus the banker, for the purchase of some mining properties, and after my father's death I shared the mines with these men, but had to pay the loan myself. I also borrowed another thousand drachmae from Lysistratus of Thoricus for my father's funeral, and have personally paid the debt.

That I am speaking the truth on these matters also you will learn from these depositions.

53 Τοσαῦτα τοίνυν ἐμοῦ ἐλαττουμένου φανερῶς,
οὗτος νῦν σχετλιάζων καὶ δεινοπαθῶν καὶ τὴν
[1024] προῖκά με τῆς μητρὸς ἀποστερήσει; ἀλλ᾽ ὑμεῖς,
ὦ ἄνδρες δικασταί, πρὸς Διὸς καὶ θεῶν μὴ κατα-
πλαγῆτε ὑπὸ τῆς κραυγῆς τῆς τούτου· πολὺς γάρ,
πολὺς καὶ τολμηρός ἐστιν ἄνθρωπος, καὶ οὕτως
κακοῦργος, ὥστε περὶ ὧν ἂν μὴ ἔχῃ μάρτυρας
παρασχέσθαι, ταῦτα φήσει ὑμᾶς εἰδέναι, ὦ ἄνδρες
δικασταί, ὃ πάντες ποιοῦσιν οἱ μηδὲν ὑγιὲς λέ-
54 γοντες. ὑμεῖς οὖν ἐάν τι τοιοῦτον τεχνάζῃ, μὴ
ἐπιτρέπετε αὐτῷ, ἀλλ᾽ ἐξελέγχετε, καὶ ὅ τι ἂν μὴ
ἕκαστος ὑμῶν εἰδῇ, μηδὲ τὸν πλησίον δοκιμαζέτω
εἰδέναι, ἀλλ᾽ ἀξιούτω τοῦτον ἀποδεικνύναι σαφῶς
ὑπὲρ ὧν ἂν λέγῃ, καὶ μὴ ὑμᾶς φάσκοντα εἰδέναι,
περὶ ὧν αὐτὸς οὐδὲν ἕξει εἰπεῖν δίκαιον, ἀποδιδρά-
σκειν τὴν ἀλήθειαν, ἐπεὶ καὶ ἐγώ, ὦ ἄνδρες δικασταί, πάντων ὑμῶν εἰδότων ὃν τρόπον ἀναγκασθεὶς
ὁ πατήρ μου ἐποιήσατο τούτους, οὐδὲν ἧττον
δικάζομαι νῦν αὐτοῖς καὶ μάρτυρας ὑποδίκους
55 παρέσχημαι. καίτοι οὐκ ἴσος γ᾽ ἡμῖν ἐστιν ὁ
κίνδυνος, ἀλλ᾽ ἐμοὶ μέν, ἐὰν ὑμεῖς νυνὶ ὑπὸ τούτων
ἐξαπατηθῆτε, οὐκ ἐξέσται ἔτι δικάσασθαι περὶ τῆς
προικός· τούτοις δ᾽, εἰ φασὶν ἀδίκως ἀποδιαιτῆσαί
μου τὸν διαιτητὴν τὰς δίκας, καὶ τότ᾽ ἐξῆν εἰς ὑμᾶς
ἐφεῖναι καὶ νῦν ἐκγενήσεται πάλιν, ἐὰν βούλωνται,
56 παρ᾽ ἐμοῦ λαβεῖν ἐν ὑμῖν τὸ δίκαιον. καὶ ἐγὼ μέν,
ἐάν, ὃ μὴ γένοιτο, ὑμεῖς με ἐγκαταλίπητε, οὐχ ἕξω

ᵃ Liable, that is, to prosecution for perjury, if their testimony be proved false.

When I am thus so clearly at a disadvantage in 53
so many respects, shall this man now by making a
great to-do and outcry about his wrongs, rob me also
of my mother's marriage-portion ? But do not, men
of the jury, I beg you by Zeus and the Gods, do not
be overwhelmed by the noise he makes. He is a
violent fellow, violent and ready to go to all lengths ;
and he is so unscrupulous that, if he has no witnesses
to prove a fact, he will say that it is well known to
you, men of the jury,—a trick to which all those have
recourse who have no just argument to advance. If 54
he shall try any such trick, do not tolerate it ; expose
him. What anyone of you does not know, let him
deem that his neighbour does not know either. Let
him demand that Boeotus prove clearly whatever
statements he may make, and not shirk the truth by
declaring that you know things about which he will
have no just argument to advance ; since I, on my
part, men of the jury, although you all know the
way in which my father was compelled to adopt these
men, am none the less suing them at law, and have
brought forward witnesses responsible for their testimony.[a] And yet the risk is not the same for both of 55
us. On my part, if you are now led astray by these
men, it will not be open to me to bring suit again
for the marriage-portion ; but they, if they claim
that the arbitrator was wrong in giving his decision
in my favour, as at that time they had the right to
appeal to your court, so now again will be permitted,
if they so wish, to recover their rights from me in
your court. I, if you leave me in the lurch, which I 56
pray may not happen, shall have no means of giving

πόθεν προῖκα ἐπιδῶ τῇ θυγατρί, ἧς τῇ μὲν φύσει
πατήρ εἰμι, τὴν δ' ἡλικίαν αὐτῆς εἰ ἴδοιτε, οὐκ ἂν
θυγατέρα μου ἀλλ' ἀδελφὴν εἶναι αὐτὴν νομίσαιτε·
οὗτοι δέ, ἐὰν ὑμεῖς μοι βοηθήσητε, οὐδὲν ἐκ τῶν
[1025] ἰδίων ἀποτείσουσιν, ἀλλ' ἐκ τῆς οἰκίας τὰ ἐμὰ ἐμοὶ
ἀποδώσουσιν, ἣν ἐξειλόμεθα μὲν κοινῇ πάντες εἰς
τὴν ἔκτεισιν τῆς προικός, οἰκοῦντες δ' αὐτὴν οὗτοι
57 μόνοι διατελοῦσιν. οὔτε γὰρ ἁρμόττει μοι θυγατέρα ἐπίγαμον ἔχοντι οἰκεῖν μετὰ τοιούτων,[1] οἳ οὐ
μόνον αὐτοὶ ἀσελγῶς ζῶσιν, ἀλλὰ καὶ ὁμοίους
αὑτοῖς ἑτέρους πολλοὺς εἰς τὴν οἰκίαν εἰσάγουσιν,
οὔτε μὰ τὸν Δί' ἀσφαλὲς εἶναί μοι νομίζω συζῆν
τούτοις ἐν τῷ αὐτῷ· ὅπου γὰρ οὕτω φανερῶς
μοι ἐπιβουλεύσαντες εἰς Ἄρειον πάγον ἀγῶνα
κατεσκεύασαν, τίνος οὗτοι ἢ φαρμακείας ἂν ἢ
58 κακουργίας τοιαύτης ὑμῖν ἀποσχέσθαι δοκοῦσιν; οἳ
γε πρὸς τοῖς ἄλλοις (ἀρτίως γὰρ καὶ τοῦτο ἀν-
εμνήσθην) εἰς τοσαύτην ὑπερβολὴν τόλμης ἥκουσιν,
ὥστε καὶ Κρίτωνος μαρτυρίαν ἐνεβάλοντο, ὡς
ἐώνηται τὸ τρίτον παρ' ἐμοῦ μέρος τῆς οἰκίας· ἥν,
ὅτι ψευδής ἐστι, ῥᾳδίως εἴσεσθε. πρῶτον μὲν γὰρ
οὐχ οὕτω μετρίως ζῇ Κρίτων, ὥστε παρ' ἑτέρου
οἰκίαν ὠνεῖσθαι, ἀλλ' οὕτω πολυτελῶς καὶ ἀσώτως,
ὥστε πρὸς τοῖς ἑαυτοῦ καὶ τὰ τῶν ἄλλων ἀνα-
λίσκειν· ἔπειτ' οὐ μαρτυρεῖ τούτῳ νῦν, ἀλλ' ἐμοὶ
ἀντιδικεῖ· τίς γὰρ ὑμῶν οὐκ οἶδεν, ὅτι μάρτυρες
μέν εἰσιν οὗτοι, οἷς μὴ μέτεστι τοῦ πράγματος, περὶ
οὗ ἡ δίκη ἐστίν, ἀντίδικοι δ' οἱ κοινωνοῦντες τῶν
πραγμάτων, ὑπὲρ ὧν ἂν δικάζηταί τις αὐτοῖς; ὃ

---

[1] τοιούτων] τούτων Blass.

a dowry to my daughter, whose own father I am, although, if you see her size, you would deem she was not my daughter but my sister ; [a] but these men, if you come to my aid, will pay nothing out of their own property, but will restore to me what is my own from the house which by common agreement we reserved for the settlement of the marriage-portion, but in which these men have been living by themselves. For it is not fitting that I, having a daughter 57 of marriageable age, should dwell with men of their sort, who are not only themselves living licentious lives, but who also bring into the house a host of others of like stamp with themselves ; nay, by Zeus, I do not deem it safe to live in the same house with them myself. When they have thus openly laid a plot, and got up a charge against me before the Areopagus, do you suppose there is any poisoning or any other such villainy from which they would abstain ? Besides all the rest (for this has occurred 58 to me just now), they have come to such a pitch of audacity as to have put in a deposition of Crito, alleging that he has purchased from me my one-third share in the house. Now that this is false you will easily perceive ; for in the first place Crito does not live so economically as to be able to purchase a house from someone else, but so extravagantly and licentiously that he spends the property of others as well as his own. Again, he is not now this man's witness, but rather my adversary. For who among you is ignorant that witnesses are those who have no interest in the matter at issue in the suit ; while adversaries are those who are involved in the matters in regard to which one goes to law with them ? The latter is

---

[a] See above, § 12.

59 Κρίτωνι συμβέβηκεν. ἔτι δὲ τοσούτων ὑμῶν ὄντων, ὦ ἄνδρες δικασταί, καὶ τῶν ἄλλων Ἀθηναίων πολλῶν, ἄλλος μὲν οὐδεὶς αὐτῷ παραγενέσθαι μεμαρτύρηκε, Τιμοκράτης δὲ μόνος, ὥσπερ ἀπὸ [1026] μηχανῆς, μαρτυρεῖ μὲν δεκάτην ἑστιᾶσαι τούτῳ τὸν ἐμὸν πατέρα, ἡλικιώτης ὢν τοῦ νυνὶ φεύγοντος τὴν δίκην, φησὶ δὲ πάνθ᾽ ἁπλῶς εἰδέναι ἃ δὴ τούτοις συμφέρει, μαρτυρεῖ δὲ νυνὶ μόνος Κρίτωνι παρεῖναι, ὅτε παρ᾽ ἐμοῦ τὴν οἰκίαν ἐωνεῖτο. ὃ τίς ἂν ὑμῶν πιστεύσειεν; ἄλλως τε καὶ ὅτι οὐ περὶ τῆς οἰκίας, πότερα ἐώνηται Κρίτων αὐτὴν ἢ μή, νυνὶ δικάζομαι, ἀλλὰ περὶ προικός, ἣν ἐνεγκαμένης τῆς μητρὸς οἱ νόμοι κελεύουσιν ἐμὲ κομίζεσθαι.

60 ὥστε καθάπερ ὑμῖν ἐγὼ καὶ ἐκ μαρτυριῶν πολλῶν καὶ ἐκ τεκμηρίων ἐπέδειξα, ἐπενεγκαμένην μὲν τὴν μητέρα μου τάλαντον προῖκα, οὐ κομισάμενον δὲ τοῦτ᾽ ἐμὲ ἐκ τῆς πατρῴας οὐσίας, ἐξαίρετον δ᾽ ἡμῖν γενομένην τὴν οἰκίαν εἰς ταῦτα, οὕτω κελεύετε καὶ τοῦτον ἐπιδεικνύναι ὑμῖν, ἢ ὡς οὐκ ἀληθῆ λέγω, ἢ ὡς οὐ προσήκει μοι κομίσασθαι τὴν προῖκα· περὶ

61 τούτων γὰρ ὑμεῖς νυνὶ τὴν ψῆφον οἴσετε. ἐὰν δὲ μὴ ἔχων περὶ ὧν φεύγει τὴν δίκην μήτε μάρτυρας ἀξιόχρεως παρασχέσθαι μήτ᾽ ἄλλο πιστὸν μηδέν, ἑτέρους παρεμβάλλῃ λόγους κακουργῶν, καὶ βοᾷ καὶ σχετλιάζῃ μηδὲν πρὸς τὸ πρᾶγμα, πρὸς Διὸς καὶ θεῶν μὴ ἐπιτρέπετε αὐτῷ, ἀλλὰ βοηθεῖτέ μοι

---

* The *deus ex machina* of the tragic stage.

the case with Crito. And furthermore, out of all **59**
your number, men of the jury, out of all the host of
the rest of the Athenians, not a single other person
has testified that he was present at this sale ; Timocrates alone, like a god from the machine,[a] testified
that my father gave a feast to Boeotus on the tenth
day (and Timocrates is of the same age as the present
defendant !). Timocrates declares that he has per-
fect knowledge of all that is for the advantage of
these men ; and now on his own sole authority he
testifies that he was present with Crito when he
bought the house from me. Who among you will
believe this ? Not one, of course ; especially since
I am not now suing about the house to determine
whether Crito bought it or not, but about the
marriage-portion which, seeing that my mother
brought it with her, the laws declare that I should
recover. Therefore, as I have proved to you by an **60**
abundance of testimony and of circumstantial evidence that my mother did bring a talent as her
dowry ; that I have not recovered it from my father's
estate ; and that the house was set apart by us to
secure its payment ; so do you demand of Boeotus
that he prove to you, either that I am not speaking
the truth, or that it is not right that I should recover
the marriage-portion ; for these are the questions
regarding which you are now going to cast your
votes. But if, having no trustworthy witnesses, nor **61**
any other proofs regarding the matters upon which
he is being sued, he shall try unscrupulously to introduce irrelevant arguments, and if he indulges in out-
cries and protestations which have nothing to do with
the matter, I adjure you by Zeus and the Gods, do
not tolerate it ; nay, render me the help that is my

τὰ δίκαια, ἐξ ἁπάντων τῶν εἰρημένων ἐνθυμούμενοι,
ὅτι πολὺ δικαιότερόν ἐστι τὴν τῆς ἐμῆς μητρὸς
προῖκα τῇ ἐμῇ θυγατρὶ εἰς ἔκδοσιν ὑμᾶς ψηφίσασθαι, ἢ Πλαγγόνα καὶ τούτους πρὸς τοῖς ἄλλοις καὶ
τὴν οἰκίαν τὴν εἰς τὴν προῖκα ἐξαίρετον γενομένην
ἀφελέσθαι ἡμᾶς παρὰ πάντα τὰ δίκαια.

due, remembering in the light of all that I have urged that it is far more just that you should by your verdict give my mother's portion to my daughter for her dowry, than that Plangon and these men, in addition to all the rest that they have done, should, in utter defiance of justice, rob me also of my house, which was set apart to secure the payment of the marriage-portion.

THE LOEB CLASSICAL LIBRARY

VOLUMES ALREADY PUBLISHED

LATIN AUTHORS

1

THE LOEB CLASSICAL LIBRARY

CICERO: DE REPUBLICA, DE LEGIBUS, SOMNIUM SCIPIONIS. Clinton W. Keyes.

CICERO: DE SENECTUTE, DE AMICITIA, DE DIVINATIONE. W. A. Falconer.

CICERO: IN CATILINAM, PRO MURENA, PRO SULLA, PRO FLACCO. Louis E. Lord.

CICERO: LETTERS TO ATTICUS. E. O. Winstedt. 3 Vols.

CICERO: LETTERS TO HIS FRIENDS. W. Glynn Williams. 3 Vols.

CICERO: PHILIPPICS. W. C. A. Ker.

CICERO: PRO ARCHIA, POST REDITUM, DE DOMO, DE HARUSPICUM RESPONSIS, PRO PLANCIO. N. H. Watts.

CICERO: PRO CAECINA, PRO LEGE MANILIA, PRO CLUENTIO, PRO RABIRIO. H. Grose Hodge.

CICERO: PRO CAELIO, DE PROVINCIIS CONSULARIBUS, PRO BALBO. R. Gardner.

CICERO: PRO MILONE, IN PISONEM, PRO SCAURO, PRO FONTEIO, PRO RABIRIO POSTUMO, PRO MARCELLO, PRO LIGARIO, PRO REGE DEIOTARO. N. H. Watts.

CICERO: PRO QUINCTIO, PRO ROSCIO AMERINO, PRO ROSCIO COMOEDO, CONTRA RULLUM. J. H. Freese.

CICERO: PRO SESTIO, IN VATINIUM. R. Gardner.

[CICERO]: RHETORICA AD HERENNIUM. H. Caplan.

CICERO: TUSCULAN DISPUTATIONS. J. E. King.

CICERO: VERRINE ORATIONS. L. H. G. Greenwood. 2 Vols.

CLAUDIAN. M. Platnauer. 2 Vols.

COLUMELLA: DE RE RUSTICA, DE ARBORIBUS. H. B. Ash, E. S. Forster, E. Heffner. 3 Vols.

CURTIUS, Q.: HISTORY OF ALEXANDER. J. C. Rolfe. 2 Vols.

FLORUS. E. S. Forster; and CORNELIUS NEPOS. J. C. Rolfe.

FRONTINUS: STRATAGEMS AND AQUEDUCTS. C. E. Bennett and M. B. McElwain.

FRONTO: CORRESPONDENCE. C. R. Haines. 2 Vols.

GELLIUS. J. C. Rolfe. 3 Vols.

HORACE: ODES AND EPODES. C. E. Bennett.

HORACE: SATIRES, EPISTLES, ARS POETICA. H. R. Fairclough.

JEROME: SELECT LETTERS. F. A. Wright.

JUVENAL AND PERSIUS. G. G. Ramsay.

LIVY. B. O. Foster, F. G. Moore, Evan T. Sage, A. C. Schlesinger and R. M. Geer (General Index). 14 Vols.

LUCAN. J. D. Duff.

THE LOEB CLASSICAL LIBRARY

TERTULLIAN: APOLOGIA AND DE SPECTACULIS. **T. R.** Glover; MINUCIUS FELIX. G. H. Rendall.
VALERIUS FLACCUS. J. H. Mozley.
VARRO: DE LINGUA LATINA. R. G. Kent. 2 Vols.
VELLEIUS PATERCULUS AND RES GESTAE DIVI AUGUSTI. F. W. Shipley.
VIRGIL. H. R. Fairclough. 2 Vols.
VITRUVIUS: DE ARCHITECTURA. F. Granger. 2 Vols.

GREEK AUTHORS

ACHILLES TATIUS. S. Gaselee.
AELIAN: ON THE NATURE OF ANIMALS. A. F. Scholfield. 3 Vols.
AENEAS TACTICUS, ASCLEPIODOTUS AND ONASANDER. The Illinois Greek Club.
AESCHINES. C. D. Adams.
AESCHYLUS. H. Weir Smyth. 2 Vols.
ALCIPHRON, AELIAN AND PHILOSTRATUS: LETTERS. A. R. Benner and F. H. Fobes.
APOLLODORUS. Sir James G. Frazer. 2 Vols.
APOLLONIUS RHODIUS. R. C. Seaton.
THE APOSTOLIC FATHERS. Kirsopp Lake. 2 Vols.
APPIAN'S ROMAN HISTORY. Horace White. 4 Vols.
ARATUS. *Cf.* CALLIMACHUS.
ARISTOPHANES. Benjamin Bickley Rogers. 3 Vols. Verse trans.
ARISTOTLE: ART OF RHETORIC. J. H. Freese.
ARISTOTLE: ATHENIAN CONSTITUTION, EUDEMIAN ETHICS, VIRTUES AND VICES. H. Rackham.
ARISTOTLE: THE CATEGORIES. ON INTERPRETATION. H. P. Cooke; PRIOR ANALYTICS. H. Tredennick.
ARISTOTLE: GENERATION OF ANIMALS. A. L. Peck.
ARISTOTLE: HISTORIA ANIMALIUM. A. L. Peck. 3 Vols. Vol. I.
ARISTOTLE: METAPHYSICS. H. Tredennick. 2 Vols.
ARISTOTLE: METEOROLOGICA. H. D. P. Lee.
ARISTOTLE: MINOR WORKS. W. S. Hett. " On Colours," " On Things Heard," " Physiognomics," " On Plants," " On Marvellous Things Heard," " Mechanical Problems," " On Indivisible Lines," " Situations and Names of Winds," " On Melissus, Xenophanes, and Gorgias."

THE LOEB CLASSICAL LIBRARY

ARISTOTLE: NICOMACHEAN ETHICS. H. Rackham.
ARISTOTLE: OECONOMICA AND MAGNA MORALIA. G. C.
  Armstrong. (With Metaphysics, Vol. II.)
ARISTOTLE: ON THE HEAVENS. W. K. C. Guthrie.
ARISTOTLE: ON THE SOUL, PARVA NATURALIA, ON BREATH.
  W. S. Hett.
ARISTOTLE: PARTS OF ANIMALS. A. L. Peck; MOTION AND
  PROGRESSION OF ANIMALS. E. S. Forster.
ARISTOTLE: PHYSICS. Rev. P. Wicksteed and F. M. Corn-
  ford. 2 Vols.
ARISTOTLE: POETICS; LONGINUS ON THE SUBLIME. W.
  Hamilton Fyfe; DEMETRIUS ON STYLE. W. Rhys Roberts.
ARISTOTLE: POLITICS. H. Rackham.
ARISTOTLE: POSTERIOR ANALYTICS. H. Tredennick; TOPICS.
  E. S. Forster.
ARISTOTLE: PROBLEMS. W. S. Hett. 2 Vols.
ARISTOTLE: RHETORICA AD ALEXANDRUM. H. Rackham.
  (With Problems, Vol. II.)
ARISTOTLE: SOPHISTICAL REFUTATIONS. COMING-TO-BE AND
  PASSING-AWAY. E. S. Forster; ON THE COSMOS. D. J. Fur-
  ley.
ARRIAN: HISTORY OF ALEXANDER AND INDICA. Rev. E.
  Iliffe Robson. 2 Vols.
ATHENAEUS: DEIPNOSOPHISTAE. C. B. Gulick. 7 Vols.
BABRIUS AND PHAEDRUS (Latin). B. E. Perry.
ST. BASIL: LETTERS. R. J. Deferrari. 4 Vols.
CALLIMACHUS: FRAGMENTS. C. A. Trypanis.
CALLIMACHUS: HYMNS AND EPIGRAMS, AND LYCOPHRON.
  A. W. Mair; ARATUS. G. R. Mair.
CLEMENT OF ALEXANDRIA. Rev. G. W. Butterworth.
COLLUTHUS. *Cf.* OPPIAN.
DAPHNIS AND CHLOE. *Cf.* LONGUS.
DEMOSTHENES I: OLYNTHIACS, PHILIPPICS AND MINOR
  ORATIONS: I-XVII AND XX. J. H. Vince.
DEMOSTHENES II: DE CORONA AND DE FALSA LEGATIONE.
  C. A. Vince and J. H. Vince.
DEMOSTHENES III: MEIDIAS, ANDROTION, ARISTOCRATES,
  TIMOCRATES, ARISTOGEITON. J. H. Vince.
DEMOSTHENES IV-VI: PRIVATE ORATIONS AND IN NEAERAM.
  A. T. Murray.
DEMOSTHENES VII: FUNERAL SPEECH, EROTIC ESSAY,
  EXORDIA AND LETTERS. N. W. and N. J. DeWitt.

THE LOEB CLASSICAL LIBRARY

DIO CASSIUS : ROMAN HISTORY. E. Cary. 9 Vols.

DIO CHRYSOSTOM. 5 Vols. Vols. I and II. J. W. Cohoon. Vol. III. J. W. Cohoon and H. Lamar Crosby. Vols. IV and V. H. Lamar Crosby.

DIODORUS SICULUS. 12 Vols. Vols. I-VI. C. H. Oldfather. Vol. VII. C. L. Sherman. Vol. VIII. C. B. Welles. Vols. IX and X. Russel M. Geer. Vol. XI. F. R. Walton.

DIOGENES LAERTIUS. R. D. Hicks. 2 Vols.

DIONYSIUS OF HALICARNASSUS : ROMAN ANTIQUITIES. Spelman's translation revised by E. Cary. 7 Vols.

EPICTETUS. W. A. Oldfather. 2 Vols.

EURIPIDES. A. S. Way. 4 Vols. Verse trans.

EUSEBIUS : ECCLESIASTICAL HISTORY. Kirsopp Lake and J. E. L. Oulton. 2 Vols.

GALEN : ON THE NATURAL FACULTIES. A. J. Brock.

THE GREEK ANTHOLOGY. W. R. Paton. 5 Vols.

THE GREEK BUCOLIC POETS (THEOCRITUS, BION, MOSCHUS). J. M. Edmonds.

GREEK ELEGY AND IAMBUS WITH THE ANACREONTEA. J. M. Edmonds. 2 Vols.

GREEK MATHEMATICAL WORKS. Ivor Thomas. 2 Vols.

HERODES. *Cf.* THEOPHRASTUS : CHARACTERS.

HERODOTUS. A. D. Godley. 4 Vols.

HESIOD AND THE HOMERIC HYMNS. H. G. Evelyn White.

HIPPOCRATES AND THE FRAGMENTS OF HERACLEITUS. W. H. S. Jones and E. T. Withington. 4 Vols.

HOMER : ILIAD. A. T. Murray. 2 Vols.

HOMER : ODYSSEY. A. T. Murray. 2 Vols.

ISAEUS. E. S. Forster.

ISOCRATES. George Norlin and LaRue Van Hook. 3 Vols.

ST. JOHN DAMASCENE : BARLAAM AND IOASAPH. Rev. G. R. Woodward and Harold Mattingly.

JOSEPHUS. 9 Vols. Vols. I-IV. H. St. J. Thackeray. Vol. V. H. St. J. Thackeray and Ralph Marcus. Vols. VI and VII. Ralph Marcus. Vol. VIII. Ralph Marcus and Allen Wikgren. Vol. IX. L. H. Feldman.

JULIAN. Wilmer Cave Wright. 3 Vols.

LONGUS : DAPHNIS AND CHLOE. Thornley's translation revised by J. M. Edmonds ; and PARTHENIUS. S. Gaselee.

LUCIAN. 8 Vols. Vols. I-V. A. M. Harmon. Vol. VI. K. Kilburn.

THE LOEB CLASSICAL LIBRARY

Lycophron. *Cf.* Callimachus.

Lyra Graeca. J. M. Edmonds. 3 Vols.

Lysias. W. R. M. Lamb.

Manetho. W. G. Waddell; Ptolemy: Tetrabiblos. F. E. Robbins.

Marcus Aurelius. C. R. Haines.

Menander. F. G. Allinson.

Minor Attic Orators. 2 Vols. K. J. Maidment and J. O. Burtt.

Nonnos: Dionysiaca. W. H. D. Rouse. 3 Vols.

Oppian, Colluthus, Tryphiodorus. A. W. Mair.

Papyri. Non-Literary Selections. A. S. Hunt and C. C. Edgar. 2 Vols. Literary Selections (Poetry). D. L. Page.

Parthenius. *Cf.* Longus.

Pausanias: Description of Greece. W. H. S. Jones. 5 Vols. and Companion Vol. arranged by R. E. Wycherley.

Philo. 10 Vols. Vols. I-V. F. H. Colson and Rev. G. H. Whitaker. Vols. VI-X. F. H. Colson. General Index. Rev. J. W. Earp.

Two Supplementary Vols. Translation only from an Armenian Text. Ralph Marcus.

Philostratus: The Life of Apollonius of Tyana. F. C. Conybeare. 2 Vols.

Philostratus: Imagines; Callistratus: Descriptions. A. Fairbanks.

Philostratus and Eunapius: Lives of the Sophists. Wilmer Cave Wright.

Pindar. Sir J. E. Sandys.

Plato: Charmides, Alcibiades, Hipparchus, The Lovers, Theages, Minos and Epinomis. W. R. M. Lamb.

Plato: Cratylus, Parmenides, Greater Hippias, Lesser Hippias. H. N. Fowler.

Plato: Euthyphro, Apology, Crito, Phaedo, Phaedrus. H. N. Fowler.

Plato: Laches, Protagoras, Meno, Euthydemus. W. R. M. Lamb.

Plato: Laws. Rev. R. G. Bury. 2 Vols.

Plato: Lysis, Symposium, Gorgias. W. R. M. Lamb.

Plato: Republic. Paul Shorey. 2 Vols.

Plato: Statesman, Philebus. H. N. Fowler; Ion. W. R. M. Lamb.

THE LOEB CLASSICAL LIBRARY

PLATO : THEAETETUS AND SOPHIST. H. N. Fowler.
PLATO : TIMAEUS, CRITIAS, CLITOPHO, MENEXENUS, EPISTULAE. Rev. R. G. Bury.
PLUTARCH : MORALIA. 15 Vols. Vols. I–V. F. C. Babbitt. Vol. VI. W. C. Helmbold. Vol. VII. P. H. De Lacy and B. Einarson. Vol. IX. E. L. Minar, Jr., F. H. Sandbach, W. C. Helmbold. Vol. X. H. N. Fowler. Vol. XI. L. Pearson, F. H. Sandbach. Vol. XII. H. Cherniss, W. C. Helmbold.
PLUTARCH : THE PARALLEL LIVES. B. Perrin. 11 Vols.
POLYBIUS. W. R. Paton. 6 Vols.
PROCOPIUS : HISTORY OF THE WARS. H. B. Dewing. 7 Vols.
PTOLEMY : TETRABIBLOS. Cf. MANETHO.
QUINTUS SMYRNAEUS. A. S. Way. Verse trans.
SEXTUS EMPIRICUS. Rev. R. G. Bury. 4 Vols.
SOPHOCLES. F. Storr. 2 Vols. Verse trans.
STRABO : GEOGRAPHY. Horace L. Jones. 8 Vols.
THEOPHRASTUS : CHARACTERS. J. M. Edmonds ; HERODES, etc. A. D. Knox.
THEOPHRASTUS : ENQUIRY INTO PLANTS. Sir Arthur Hort. 2 Vols.
THUCYDIDES. C. F. Smith. 4 Vols.
TRYPHIODORUS. Cf. OPPIAN.
XENOPHON : CYROPAEDIA. Walter Miller. 2 Vols.
XENOPHON : HELLENICA, ANABASIS, APOLOGY, AND SYMPOSIUM. C. L. Brownson and O. J. Todd. 3 Vols.
XENOPHON : MEMORABILIA AND OECONOMICUS. E. C. Marchant.
XENOPHON : SCRIPTA MINORA. E. C. Marchant.

VOLUMES IN PREPARATION

GREEK AUTHORS

PLOTINUS. A. H. Armstrong.

DESCRIPTIVE PROSPECTUS ON APPLICATION

LONDON   CAMBRIDGE, MASS.
WILLIAM HEINEMANN LTD   HARVARD UNIV. PRESS